Alternative Risk Strategies

Alternative Risk Strategies

Edited by Morton Lane

RISK
BOOKS

Published by Risk Books, a division of the Risk Waters Group.

Haymarket House
28–29 Haymarket
London SW1Y 4RX
Tel: +44 (0)20 7484 9700
Fax: +44 (0)20 7484 9758
E-mail: books@riskwaters.com
Sites: www.riskbooks.com
        www.riskpublications.com

Every effort has been made to secure the permission of individual copyright
holders for inclusion.

© Risk Waters Group Ltd 2002   © Reprinted 2003

ISBN 1 899 332 63 4

British Library Cataloguing in Publication Data
A catalogue record for this book is available from the British Library

Risk Books Commissioning Editor: Sarah Jenkins
Desk Editor: Kathryn Roberts

Typeset by Mark Heslington, Scarborough, North Yorkshire

Printed and bound in Great Britain by Selwood Printing Ltd, West Sussex

To Phyllis Lane – my mother

Contents

Authors

Peter Allen joined Ernst & Young in 2001 to lead the development of the firm's alternative risk transfer (ART) consultancy. Before joining Ernst & Young he was head of ART at Lloyd's and program director of *lloyds.com*. Peter has worked in the London insurance market since 1982. He has been a director of a firm of Lloyd's brokers and deputy underwriter of a Lloyd's syndicate. He was educated at Cambridge and has an MBA from the City University Business School.

Derek Bain joined Axa in Dublin as chief actuary at the start of 2002. He has over 13 years experience in the general insurance field, the majority of which was spent in the retail market. Prior to this he worked at Ernst & Young where he primarily worked with personal lines clients, and was directly involved in the actuarial reserve analysis of several major UK insurers. He has also worked for Guardian/PMDA group, which is Ireland's largest motor insurer, where he was responsible for all forms of actuarial analysis including compilation and presentation of group reserves. Derek is a graduate of Trinity College, Dublin, a fellow of the Institute of Actuaries and a fellow of the Royal Statistical Society.

Peter Blum is a research associate in the financial analysis and risk modelling group of Converium Reinsurance Ltd and a PhD student in financial and insurance mathematics at the ETH (Swiss Federal Institute of Technology, Zurich). Both Peter's academic and industrial activities are centred around the financial valuation of reinsurance and econometric issues in insurance, reinsurance and investment, with particular emphasis on the method of dynamic financial analysis (DFA). Prior to joining Converium, Peter was a programmer, software quality engineer and project leader in the electronics industry for several years. Peter holds a diploma (MA) in mathematics from ETH and a federal certificate of capacity (BSc) in software engineering.

Kenneth J. Bock is head of the planned Munich American Capital Markets group that combines the capital markets platforms of Munich Re and American Re. He joined American Re Financial Products in May 1999 as managing director of American Re Securities Corporation (ARSC). In August 2000 he was named president of the AmRe Capital Markets Group, which included ARSC, AmRe's derivatives trading company, American Re Capital Markets, Inc, and the Entertainment/Media Finance Group. Prior to joining American Re Kenneth served as regional head of Structured Finance at Paribas. He was vice president with UBS Securities' Financial Institutions Group. Prior to UBS, he spent eleven years with Morgan Stanley in several capacities within the Fixed Income and Investment Banking Divisions. Kenneth received his MBA from New York University's Stern School and his BS in economics from New York University's College of Business and Public Administration.

Mike Brosnan is a partner in Ernst & Young's Transaction Support Services Practice, specialising in the insurance industry. He has extensive experience providing transaction and advisory services to clients in the insurance and reinsurance industries. Mike, a graduate of Boston College, has over 21 years of experience with Ernst & Young covering a wide variety of services. In addition to audit responsibilities for certain large Securities and Exchange Commission (SEC) registrants, Mike provides advisory services to insurance companies and financial institutions. He has assisted third party intermediaries in the design and development of reinsurance products. He has also developed statutory and Generally Accepted Accounting Principles (GAAP) accounting models to support complex capital markets products and reinsurance transactions. Mike has frequently presented industry developments and related technical matters to financial institutions and is also a frequent speaker on insurance transactions and accounting and reporting matters.

Christoph Bürer has held various positions in the area of alternative risk transfer (ART) at the Zurich Financial Services Group at their locations in Zurich, London and Luxembourg. As the head of the captive division within the Centre of Excellence ART of Zurich Continental Europe Corporate, he is currently responsible for Zurich's captive consulting, captive management and fronting activities on the Continent. Christoph holds a Masters degree in law from the University of Zurich, Switzerland.

Omar J. Chaudhary is an analyst in the Risk Markets Group at Goldman Sachs. He has focused primarily on life insurance securitisation and played a key role in the structuring, modelling and placement of the Prudential Holdings, LLC transaction in 2001. He has also executed catastrophe securitisation transactions and placed strategic insurance to manage merger risk. He joined the Summer Analyst Program in 1999 followed by the Financial Analyst Program in 2000. He received a BS in Finance and Economics from Boston College in 2000.

Christopher L. Culp is managing director of CP Risk Management LLLC and adjunct associate professor of finance at the Graduate School of Business of the University of Chicago. He consults on corporate financial strategy, alternative risk management methods, and capital allocation for non-financial corporates, electric utilities, banks, (re-)insurance firms, and insurance brokers. He teaches graduate-level courses on derivatives, alternative risk transfer (ART) products, and risk management. Christopher is the author of two books, *The ART of Risk Management: Alternative Risk Transfer, Capital Structure, and Convergences Between Insurance and Capital Markets*, and *The Risk Management Process*, and also co-edited *Corporate Hedging in Theory and Practice* with Merton Miller.

J. David Cummins is the Harry J. Loman professor at the Wharton School of the University of Pennsylvania and senior fellow at the Wharton Financial Institutions Center. His fields of specialisation include financial risk management and financial intermediation. David has published more than sixty refereed journal articles and several books, including *Changes in the Life Insurance Industry: Efficiency, Technology, and Risk Management* (co-editor) and *Deregulating Property-Liability Insurance: Restoring Competition and Increasing Market Efficiency* (editor). David has also served as consultant to numerous business and governmental organisations, including the Federal Reserve Bank of New York. He holds MA and PhD degrees from the University of Pennsylvania.

Nigel Davies has worked in the Financial Services Authority (FSA) (and its predecessor bodies) for six years. He is currently manager of the Insurance Firms Division, and is responsible for the regulation of London market companies. He represents the FSA on a number of international bodies; the International Association of Insurance Supervisors (IAIS) committees on reinsurance and alternative risk transfer. He is co-author of the IAIS issues paper on reinsurance. He is also involved in European Uuion (EU) issues and, in Brussels, sits on the working groups currently considering reinsurance supervision. In 2001, he represented the UK in the Council of Ministers for the adoption of directives on the first stage of the solvency margin review process for life and non-life business. He is a chartered accountant, and prior to becoming a regulator, worked at Marsh & McLennan and Ernst & Young.

John DeCaro is a vice president of Cochran, Caronia & Co, where he is responsible for the sales, trading and research of risk-linked securities (RLS). John was previously an associate director and head trader at Aon Capital Markets (ACM). He was instrumental in developing ACM's expertise in the sales, syndication, portfolio management and trading of RLS through his market making and institutional sales coverage responsibilities. Prior to joining Aon Capital Markets in 1997, John was a member of Aon's Financial Risk Management group. He previously worked as a quantitative analyst for Morningstar, Inc. John is a chartered financial analyst. He received a BS in finance from the University of South Carolina, and an MS in financial markets and trading from the Illinois Institute of Technology.

Alexandra Dias is currently a PhD student within the mathematics department at ETH (Swiss Federal Institute of Technology, Zurich). Her research is focused on the modelling of dependence in risk management. (Stipend from the Foundation for Science and Technology, Lisbon, Portugal.)

Neil Doherty is the Ronald A. Rosenfeld professor and professor of insurance and risk management at the Wharton School. A principal area of interest is in corporate risk management focusing on the financial strategies for managing risks that traditionally have been insurable. He has written three books on this area: *Corporate Risk Management: A Financial Exposition*, 1985; *The Financial Theory of Insurance Pricing* with S. D'Arcy, 1987; and *Integrated Risk Management*, 2000; as well as several recent papers. The second of his three major areas of interest is the economics of risk and information, and he has written several papers on this area. A third area of interest, on which he ahs also written, is in the failure of insurance markets and how they might be re-designed. He qualified as a fellow of the Chartered Insurance Institute and received his PhD from Cranfield School of Management in 1979.

Bryon Ehrhart is president of Aon Re Services and leads a team of actuarial and financial professionals that is dedicated to the analysis of risks borne by insurance companies and large corporations. Bryon and the group he leads developed the catastrophe equity puts (CatEPuts) product. Bryon has significant experience working with property and casualty insurance, life insurance and large corporate clients. Bryon has authored statutory language dealing with catastrophe pools or products that has become law in four states. He has provided testimony to state legislators on catastrophe pools and their operations. He has made presentations to the National Association of Insurance Commissioners (NAIC) Emerging Accounting Issues Work Group on catastrophe reinsurance alternatives, and has authored sections of the NAIC's Accounting Practices and Procedures Manual. Bryon is a frequent speaker on issues dealing with the structuring of catastrophe reinsurance programs. He is a graduate of Illinois State University with a BS in accounting, a Certified Public Accountant and a member of the American Institute of Certified Public Accountants.

Paul Embrechts is professor of mathematics at the ETH (Swiss Federal Institute of Technology, Zurich) specialising in actuarial mathematics and mathematical finance. Previous academic positions include the Universities of Leuven, Limburg and London (Imperial College), and visiting appointments at the University of Strasbourg, ESSEC Business School in Paris and the Scuola Normale in Pisa. Paul consults for a number of leading financial institutions and insurance companies, and is a member of the Board of Directors of Bank Julius Baer and appointed actuary for Swiss Re. He is a fellow of the Institute of Mathematical Statistics, honorary fellow of the Institute of Actuaries, editor of the *Actuarial Studies in Non-life Insurance (ASTIN) Bulletin*, on the Advisory Board of *Finance and Stochastics* and associate editor of numerous scientific journals. He is a member of the Board of the Swiss Association of Actuaries and belongs to various national and international research and academic advisory committees. Together with C. Klueppelberg and T. Mikosch, he is a co-author of the influential book *Modelling of Extremal Events for Insurance and Finance*.

Mark Gibbas is a senior research scientist and meteorologist at Applied Insurance Research Inc (AIR). He has worked extensively in many areas in meteorology including remote sensing, numerical weather and climate prediction, algorithm development, forecast system design and time-series analysis. Mark is responsible for AIR's long-range weather/climate forecasting and associated products for insurance, reinsurance, and weather derivative interests. Prior to joining AIR, he led the team at Litton-TASC responsible for developing long-range forecasting systems to service energy interests. Additionally, Mark has conducted research for the World Meteorological Organization as part of the Ibero-American Climate Project, where he assessed the meteorological and climatological capabilities of numerous Latin American countries. He earned his BS at Plymouth State College, graduating *summa cum laude* with a major in meteorology and minors in mathematics and computer science.

David Govrin is a vice president of Goldman Sachs and a senior member of the firm's Risk Markets Group. He has been with Goldman Sachs since January 1997. Prior to joining Goldman Sachs, he was a senior vice president at Guy Carpenter & Co where he worked from 1989 to 1997. Before 1989, David worked in fixed income operations for Dean Witter for three years, and Horizon Bank as a credit analyst for one year. He received his Bachelor of Science in Business Administration in 1985 from the University of Denver and a Masters in business from New York University in 1991.

Daniel Grieger joined Swiss Re in 1999 and is currently working as a structured credit specialist in Swiss Re's Credit Solutions & Asset Re unit in Zurich. Prior to this, he worked for two years for Commerzbank in retail banking. He holds a degree in finance and business administration from the University of St Gallen, and is currently working on a credit risk related doctorate thesis at the Swiss Banking Institute at the University of Zurich. Daniel has published several insurance- and credit related articles in Swiss and international newspapers and magazines.

David Heike is a vice president at Lehman Brothers covering asset-backed securities (ABS), including credit cards, rate reduction bonds, autos, and cat bonds. He was ranked for ABS/Other Strategy in Institutional Investor's 2001 All-America Fixed Income Research survey. He has also done modelling work on the valuation of mortgage collateralised bond obligations (CBOs), the determinants of mortgage returns, and the interaction of excess returns across fixed income markets. His research has been published in the *Journal of Fixed Income* and *Global Reinsurance*. Prior to working at Lehman Brothers, David worked as a finance professor at the Ivey Business School in Canada. David has a PhD in finance from the University of Michigan.

Derrell Hendrix has been involved in international financial markets for over 20 years. He spent 18 years at Citibank, in various international locations, where he held senior positions in relationship management, derivatives and securities trading as well as derivatives structuring. He left Citibank to join the Bank of Boston in 1995, where he assumed responsibility for derivatives trading, sales and structuring functions. Derrell left the Bank of Boston in 1996 to collaborate with Hannover Re in the foundation of The RISConsulting Group and in the conclusion of the K2 swap transaction. As the president and chief executive officer of RISConsulting, Derrell has been instrumental in attracting and providing solutions for complex risk-related problems for a number of world-class clients and partners, such as Hannover Re, Rolls-Royce and BAE SYSTEMS. Derrell received a BA (*magna cum laude*) from Amherst College and an MA from the Fletcher School of Law and Diplomacy. He is also a member of the board of directors of Converium.

Neil Hohmann joined RISC in September 2000 and is managing consultant, holding primary responsibility for the coordination of the company's modelling and risk integration activities. Neil has also coordinated the modelling of alternative risk transactions including cat securitisation, synthetic collateralised loan obligations (CLOs), and life reinsurance. Neil is a former director of research at Swiss Re, North American Division, and associate of Swiss Re Capital Partners. He is also founder and former president of Midway Consulting. As an economist at the Economic Research Service of the US Department of Agriculture, he had articles published in the areas of climate change risks and energy economics. He has been published in leading economics journals, including the *American Economics Review* and the *Quarterly Journal of Economics*. Neil graduated *magna cum laude* from Yale University with an undergraduate degree in economics, and holds Master's and PhD degrees in economics from the University of Chicago. He was also a pre-doctoral fellow of the American Bar Association.

Stephen Hough joined BAE SYSTEMS Capital as its commercial director in December 2001. The company was established to provide innovative financing solutions to support the Group's business. He completed a similar programme for Saab AB for its regional aircraft portfolio in 2000. In 1997 Stephen became a member of the team looking into the transfer of the financial risks in the portfolio of regional aircraft, and he helped complete the Financial Risk Insurance Programme in 1998. In 1990, he established a sales credit function so that the financial exposures the company had accepted on its regional aircraft portfolio could be understood, and also so that ways of managing this exposure could be examined. This led to his involvement in defining the provisions the company took in 1992 against this portfolio. After a commercial apprenticeship with Hawker Siddeley Aviation, (which subsequently became part of British Aerospace, now BAE SYSTEMS), he became responsible for negotiating sales contracts and associated sales finance agreements for the regional turboprop aircraft. Stephen graduated in management sciences from the University of Manchester Institute of Science and Technology in 1970.

Tony Jones is the partner who leads Ernst & Young's Property/Casualty Actuarial Group. He is a fellow of the Institute of Actuaries with 20 years experience as an actuary working in general insurance. He has extensive experience of commercial lines insurance and reinsurance, including ART covering pricing, reinsurance, loss reserving and capital allocation. Amongst his many past assignments he assumed, on a secondment basis, overall responsibility for managing Lloyd's based Equitas Reserving Project.

Andrew Kaiser is a managing director and head of the Risk Markets Group at Goldman Sachs. The Risk Markets Group is responsible for meeting the insurance/operational risks of the firm's corporate, insurance and reinsurance clients through traditional insurance markets intermediation, or through innovative capital markets applications. Andrew joined Goldman Sachs in 1986 in the mortgage securities department. In 1989, he joined the investment banking division where he assumed responsibility for the firm's activities with large financial institutions. Andrew attended Brown University and received a BA degree from Stanford University in 1983.

Jacqueline M. Keating is a consulting actuary with the New York office of Milliman USA. She joined the firm in 1982. She consults for financial institutions on a variety of matters including asset-liability risk management, mutual company conversions, mergers and acquisitions, securitisations, regulatory cashflow testing and rehabilitations. Jacqueline has worked on a number of mutual company conversions, both demutualisations and conversions to mutual insurance holding companies. For these conversion projects, Jacqueline was involved in the policyholder dividend protection aspects of the conversions, including the funding of closed blocks. She has served on Milliman's Life Steering Committee (a steering committee for Milliman's life insurance consultants since 1997), and coordinated Milliman's research activities for most of that period. Jacqueline is a fellow of the Society of Actuaries (FSA), and a Member of the American Academy of Actuaries (MAAA).

Mahmoud Khater is senior vice president and chief technology officer of EQECAT Inc, a division of ABS Consulting. Mahmoud holds a BS and MS in Civil Engineering form Cairo University, and a PhD from Cornell University in Structural Engineering with emphasis on probabilistic risk assessment. He is the chief architect behind the technology in EQECAT's risk assessment models. As chief technology officer Mahmoud is responsible for the science, engineering and stochastic algorithms involved in EQECAT's products and services. In addition, he manages EQECAT's Consulting Group.

John Kiernan is a managing director in the Insurance Products Group at Lehman Brothers responsible for structuring and distribution of risk linked securities. John has been employed at Lehman since July, 1998. John holds a BA in applied maths/economics from Brown University (1986).

Rodney Kreps is a managing director of Guy Carpenter, a fellow of the Casualty Actuarial Society and a member of the American Academy of Actuaries. In the past he has been chair of the Committee on the Theory of Risk of the Casualty Actuarial Society (CAS). He has worked as an academic for fifteen years, acquiring tenure as an associate professor of physics. After working in construction for seven years, Rodney moved to Fireman's Fund where he worked in workers' compensation, reserving, database design, and reinsurance. He moved to Sedgwick Re (now Guy Carpenter) in 1989, and has actively pursued theoretical and practical reinsurance models, contract designs, and financial modelling. He has written papers for the refereed journal proceedings of the CAS and has spoken frequently at CAS and other events. Rodney holds a BS from Stanford and a doctorate from Princeton in theoretical physics.

Shiv Kumar is a vice president in the Risk Markets Group at Goldman Sachs where he has led or co-led execution of several transactions involving securitisation of catastrophe, life or weather risk. Before joining the Risk Markets Group in New York, Shiv worked as the risk management officer for Arrow Re in Bermuda. Prior to that, Shiv led the Services and Analytics Group at Applied Insurance Research, a consulting firm specialising in catastrophe risk. He received a PhD from Stanford University, an MS from Rensselaer Polytechnic Institute and a BTech from the Indian Institute of Technology.

Dennis E. Kuzak is a senior vice president of EQECAT, Inc in their Oakland, California home office. His responsibilities include catastrophic risk management consulting to insurance and financial industry clients and Global 500 corporations, as well as capital market transactions involving cat bonds and swaps. Prior to joining EQECAT, he held financial management positions in a multinational manufacturing company and was an investment manager for a US$25 billion mortgage lending institution. He has a BS in civil engineering from Purdue University, an MS in structural engineering from the Massachusetts Institute of Technology, and an MBA in finance from the Stanford Graduate School of Business.

David Lalonde is senior vice president at AIR, Inc responsible for the Services and Analytics group, providing catastrophe loss analysis services (CLAS) and risk transfer services (RTS). He is extensively involved in the securitisation of insurance risk, portfolio optimisation, ratemaking, dynamic risk evaluation and analysis models and the development of CATRADER. Prior to joining AIR, he was a director of Coopers & Lybrand where he directed a team of actuaries who provided a wide variety of consulting services to insurance companies and self-insured organisations to help them assess and manage their risk. Prior to that, David was chief actuary at the Insurance Corporation of British Columbia, where he reported to the company's Board of Directors on a wide range of strategic and operational issues. David is a fellow of the Casualty Actuarial Society, a fellow of the Canadian Institute of Actuaries, and a member of the American Academy of Actuaries. David earned his BMath (Honours) in actuarial science with statistics from the University of Waterloo. He is chair of the CAS Advisory Committee on securitisation/risk financing and a member of the Insurance Securitisation Task Force.

Morton Lane is the president of Lane Financial, LLC, a broker-dealer engaged in consulting and transaction activity at the intersection of the reinsurance and capital markets. He is also a director of Select Re, Bermuda. Previously, Morton has been senior managing director of the Capital Markets Division at Gerling Global Financial Products (GGFP), president of Discount Corp of New York Futures, senior managing director and head of commodities of Bear Stearns & Co, president of Lind-Waldock, investment officer for The World Bank, and lecturer at the London Graduate School of Business Studies. Morton is a prominent speaker on insurance and securitisation and has written numerous articles on this subject. In 2001, he was awarded the Charles A. Hachemeister Prize for his article on "Pricing Risk Transfer Transactions" published in the *Actuarial Studies in Non-life Insurance (ASTIN) Bulletin*. He has co-authored two books, *The Treasury Bond Basis* and *Eurodollar Futures*. He has also designed and taught courses at the University of Chicago Graduate School of Business. Morton earned his B Soc Sc from Birmingham University, and his PhD in mathematics, business administration and computer science from the University of Texas.

S. Ming Lee is senior vice president of Applied Insurance Research (AIR), Inc, and directs AIR's risk assessment and risk transfer-related activities for the weather and corporate risk management markets. He also directs the firm's practice in risk transfer services involving capital market transactions, and was directly involved in such securitisation deals as George Town Re, Residential Re (1997 – 2001), Mosaic Re (I and II), Domestic Inc, Juno Re, NeHi Inc, and Trinom, Inc. Before joining AIR, Ming held a variety of senior executive level positions in the computer software industry. Ming holds a BS in electrical engineering from the Massachusetts Institute of Technology and an MBA from Stanford Graduate School of Business.

John A. Major is senior vice president of Guy Carpenter & Company, Inc, the world's leading reinsurance intermediary. His responsibilities include the development of new risk transfer products, and research and development for applications in asset modelling, catastrophe modelling, and portfolio management. Prior to joining Guy Carpenter, John was principal of his own research consulting firm, assistant director of research at the Travelers Insurance Company, and teaching fellow at Harvard University. He received a BS in mathematics from Worcester Polytechnic Institute and an MA in mathematics from Harvard University. He is an associate of the Society of Actuaries, member of the American Academy of Actuaries, and is on the board of contributors of *Financing Risk & Reinsurance*.

Enda McDonnell is president and chief executive officer of Access Reinsurance Inc, the world's most innovative reinsurance intermediary. Enda has been in the reinsurance industry for 12 years. He began his reinsurance career in 1990 with Guy Carpenter & Co in New York. In 1997, he joined EW Blanch Company, where he established and managed a trading group producing industry loss warrantees (ILWs), weather and retrocessional business. He then joined Willis Re in New York where he also set up and managed a retrocessional team. Enda was educated in Ireland where he was born and raised. He received his Bachelor of Commerce degree and Masters in business studies degree from University College Dublin. He currently holds the Chartered Property Casualty Underwriters (CPCU) and Access Re (ARe) designations. In addition to Enda's achievements in the reinsurance industry, he is also a keen fundraiser for the National Childhood Cancer Foundation. He organises the annual "St Baldrick's Day" in which reinsurance professionals have their heads shaved to raise money for the charity. Since its inception in 2000, approximately US$1 million has been raised for the charity.

Matthew McKenna is an analyst at Cochran, Caronia & Co, an investment banking boutique in Chicago. He is responsible for providing research and quantitative analyses to support investment banking services to clients in a variety of insurance related sectors nationwide. Matthew received his Bachelors in business administration in finance with high honours from the University of Notre Dame.

Michael J. Millette joined Goldman Sachs & Co in 1994 and is a vice president in the Risk Markets Group. He leads the firm's life insurance practice for structured reinsurance and securitisation, and has managed life transactions exceeding US$7 billion. He also oversees the pricing and distribution of catastrophe- and other risk-linked bonds. Prior to joining the Risk Markets Group, Michael spent several years in the Fixed Income Division of Goldman Sachs, in which he led the Insurance Industry Resource Group. He has been published in numerous industry publications including *Best's Review* and the *Record of the Society of Actuaries*. Prior to joining Goldman Sachs, Michael worked in the Investment Division of John Hancock and in the Corporate Finance group for insurers at Citibank. He is a Chartered Financial Analyst and a member of the New York Society of Securities Analysts. He has a BA (honours) in history from Cornell and a Masters in finance from Boston College.

David Mocklow is a managing director of Cochran, Caronia & Co, an investment banking firm focused on the insurance industry. He is primarily responsible for the structuring and execution of risk-linked securities, and for providing investment banking services to insurance industry clients nationwide. David was previously a director at Aon Capital Markets and head of Global Sales and Trading. He is experienced in the structuring and sales of structured products, including risk-linked securities and risk swaps. Prior to joining Aon Corporation in 1997, he was an assistant vice president at ACE Ltd, where he helped launch the financial lines underwriting department. David was an underwriter in both the financial lines and Directors and Officer's (D&O) underwriting departments for more than four years. Prior to ACE, he spent seven years as an officer at the Bank of Bermuda Ltd. David is a chartered financial analyst and earned a BA from the University of Western Ontario in Canada.

David K. A. Mordecai is managing director of structured products for Clinton Group, a hedge fund with over US$8 billion of assets under management. Previously, David was vice president of financial engineering and principal finance at AIG structured products, Inc. As a member of both AIG Global Investment Group and of AIG Risk Finance Division's executive committee, he specialised in the development of structured portfolio transactions for financial institutions, including, pension and investment firms, commercial and investment banks, commodity trading advisors (CTAs) and hedge funds. Prior to working for AIG, he was a director at Fitch IBCA, Inc and also previously worked for NatWest, Bankers Trust and WestLB. He has an MBA in finance from the New York University Graduate School of Business, and is currently a research fellow for a PhD at the University of Chicago Graduate School of Business. His research focuses on the statistical analysis of hedge fund leverage and performance. David serves on the advisory board of the International Association of Financial Engineers (IAFE), and is a member of the steering committee for the IAFE global working group on hedge fund risk disclosure. In addition, he is a participant in the insurance project of the National Bureau of Economic Research (NBER), and Editor-in-Chief of the *Journal of Risk Finance*.

Clive O'Connell is a law graduate from University College London, and a solicitor. He is a partner in the Reinsurance and International Risk team at Barlow Lyde & Gilbert. He has twenty years experience in dealing with reinsurance disputes in a variety of jurisdictions including the USA, England, Continental Europe and the Far East. He has advised extensively upon numerous reinsurance transactions and connected regulatory issues, including the creation of new products in the sphere of alternative risk transfer as well as traditional reinsurance. He is a contributing author to *Reinsurance Practice and the Law*, has written chapters for two of the Chartered Insurance Institute (CII) course books, and frequently writes in the reinsurance trade press including a regular column in *The Review*.

Richard D. Phillips is an associate professor and a research associate in the Center for Risk Management and Insurance Research at Georgia State University, and is also a senior fellow at the Wharton Financial Institutions Center. Richard held a previous appointment as a visiting scholar at the Federal Reserve Bank of Atlanta. Richard's research interests lie at the intersection of finance theory and insurance economics. He has published papers in academic and policy journals including such journals as the

Journal of Risk and Insurance, the *Journal of Financial Services Research*, the *Journal of Law and Economics*, the *Journal of Insurance Regulation*, and the *North American Actuarial Journal*. Richard is a member of the American Finance Association, the American Risk and Insurance Association, the Risk Theory Society, and the Financial Management Association. Richard's PhD and MS degrees are in managerial science and applied economics from the Wharton School at the University of Pennsylvania. He graduated, with honours, from the University of Minnesota earning a BS in mathematics.

Uwe E. Remy joined Swiss Re in 1994 and is director and European head of structured credit in Swiss Re's Credit Solutions & Asset Re unit in Zurich. Uwe is currently responsible for the underwriting of Swiss Re's structured credit products, including credit derivatives. Prior to this he worked for several years for Gerling Speziale Kreditversicherungs AG and Winterthur Re where he had several roles such as underwriting and claims management. Uwe holds a university degree in maths from the University of Cologne in Germany. His publications include several insurance- and credit related articles in Swiss and international newspapers and magazines. He is also is a frequent speaker and panellist on credit related conferences.

Bill Riker is currently president and chief operating officer of Renaissance Re Holding, a Bermuda based reinsurance company. He has over 17 years of reinsurance industry experience including; former vice president of Applied Insurance Research, Inc (providers of CATMAP) and former senior vice president in charge of treaty and facultative operations for American Royal Re. He has significant experience designing, selling, consulting on and using catastrophe models. He is a chartered property casualty underwriter and has a BA in economics and BSE in mechanical engineering from Duke University.

David Rule joined the Bank of England in 1990 and has worked in banking supervision, domestic financial markets and financial stability analysis. He is currently head of the Bank's Gilt-Edged and Money Markets Division. He has recently published articles on credit derivatives and on risk transfers between banks, insurance companies and capital markets in the Bank's Financial Stability Review. He has a degree in modern history from Balliol College Oxford and further degrees in politics from the University of Toronto and economics from Queens' College, Cambridge.

Steven I. Schreiber is a consulting actuary with the New York office of Milliman USA. He joined the firm in 1986, spent 3 years in Milliman's Tokyo office, and rejoined the New York office in the summer of 1998.

Since returning from Japan, Steven has been project manager for several demutualisation projects and has been involved in mergers and acquisitions, corporate restructurings, securitisations, and Generally Accepted Accounting Principles (GAAP) conversions. Steven also has continued working on projects in Japan and other international markets. Steven has served on Milliman's Life Steering Committee (a steering committee for Milliman's life insurance consultants) since 1998 and is the editor of the Milliman Global Insurance newsletter. Steven is a fellow of the Society of Actuaries (FSA), and a Member of the American Academy of Actuaries (MAAA).

Manfred W. Seitz is a member of the Munich Re Executive Management and head of the Alternative Risk Solutions Division. He has been active in the area of alternative risk transfer (ART) from the very beginning and was a frequent speaker or conference-chairman at many ART conferences around the world. In 2000, he organised and supervised Munich Re's issuance of the PRIME Capital cat bonds, the largest reinsurance securitisation so far. Prior to assuming responsibility for ART and Retrocession in 1991, Manfred was head of the US department in Munich Re's North America Division, and also head of the Client Audit Department as from 1987. Before this assignment, he spent nine years in the US as vice president of Munich Management Corporation/Munich Re United States Branch, in charge of large international clients and as deputy to the president. Manfred started his reinsurance career as a trainee at Munich Re in 1972, and completed insurance studies at the Professional School for Insurance in Munich in 1975. In addition to his primary functions at Munich Re, he serves as chairman and director at several specialty and ART reinsurance companies.

Samit Shah joined the Property & Casualty actuarial practice of Ernst & Young in September 1999. During his time at Ernst & Young Samit has gained extensive experience of the London market, in particular assisting Lloyd's managing agents with their reserving and forecasting processes. He is also involved in the introduction of new actuarial solutions for the insurance industry including those related to customer relationship management. Before joining Ernst & Young he graduated from the London School of Economics with a first class honours degree in mathematics and economics.

Michael Steel is the head of Benfield ReMetrics, coordinating the activities of all of the groups within ReMetrics and is also head of the ReMetrics broking team. He has been involved in insurance and reinsurance since 1989, and prior to joining Greig Fester in 1996, worked at INSTRAT. Michael has completed many alternative risk transfer (ART) transactions including the US$500 million nuclear placement in 1994 (at the time the largest syndicated ART transaction), and the loss portfolio transfer (LPT)/ sale for CGNU's Lloyds' operations at the end of 2000 (a £2.3 billion limit – at the time, the largest commercial reinsurance transaction). Michael is registered with the Securities and Futures Authority (SFA) registered and has also spoken at a number of conferences on dynamic financial analysis (DFA) modelling and non-traditional reinsurance transactions. He gained his BSc (Hons) in statistics and mathematics at Brunel University.

Yuichi Takeda , is a Chartered Financial Analyst (CFA), and is head of the Integrated Solutions Group at Tokio Marine Management, Inc, a New York based subsidiary of the Tokio Marine and Fire Insurance Co, Ltd. He is currently responsible for managing risk financing projects, including risk securitisations, catastrophe risk swaps and dynamic financial analysis. Yuichi has been with the Tokio Marine group for 18 years, having had various positions in corporate strategic planning, financial planning, asset-liability management and alternative risk transfer (ART) products. His recent activities also include speaking at various conferences on ART, and supporting a project on financing and managing extreme risks at the Wharton School of the University of Pennsylvania.

Joan Lamm-Tennant is the senior vice president and practice leader for General Cologne Re Capital Consultants (GRCC) – a consulting arm of General Cologne Re who advise insurance companies on risk and capital management strategies. Prior to establishing GRCC, Joan was the Thomas G. Labrecque chair in business and professor of finance at Villanova University. Her publications appear in such journals as the *Journal of Business, Journal of Banking and Finance* and *Journal of Risk and Insurance*. During these years, she also consulted with numerous insurance companies, actuarial firms, accounting firms, and consulting firms on risk and capital management. She currently serves on the board of directors for Selective Insurance Company, Charter Oak State College and Connecticut State Academic Awards. Prior to completing her doctorate, she worked in finance and systems at United States Automobile Association. Joan received a BBA in accounting and a MBA in finance from St Mary's University. She also received a PhD in finance, investments and insurance from the University of Texas at Austin.

Oscar Tymon began his career in the London Insurance market in 1977 with the specialist North American broker R K Carvill & Company. After 10 years in a variety of broking and management roles, Oscar accepted an underwriting position with the Terra Nova Insurance Company. After 5 years underwriting specialist North American reinsurance clients, Oscar joined the Centre Group in 1992. For the last 9 years, Oscar has been developing Centre's business in Europe and has managed a broad range of transactions. These include long term coverages for UK mortgage indemnity, asset residual value programmes, structured finance and other structured insurance and reinsurance transactions. Oscar currently has a broad range of responsibilities, including the London and Paris branches of Centre's Dublin based insurer, as well as European business development.

Shaun Wang is an assistant vice president and research director at SCOR Reinsurance Company, where his current responsibilities include enterprise risk management and capital allocation. Before joining SCOR, he was a faculty member of actuarial science at the University of Waterloo, Canada. He has published over 30 articles on the subjects of risk measurement, correlation modelling, and the pricing of risk. He is a fellow of the Casualty Actuarial Society and a member of the American Academy of Actuaries.

Paul Wöhrmann is a member of the executive management of Zurich Financial Services' business unit Zurich Continental Europe Corporate. As the head of the Centre of Excellence for alternative risk transfer (ART), he has responsibility for Zurich's ART business in Continental Europe. Previously he headed the Swiss-based ART operation. Prior responsibilities included insurance and reinsurance arrangements with a special emphasis on ART. He is the author of various publications dealing with ART instruments, and is a frequent chairman and speaker at ART conferences. Paul earned a PhD in economics from the University of Fribourg, Switzerland.

Gordon Woo is a catastrophe consultant, specialising in mathematical aspects of insurance risk modelling. For the past year, he has been consulting for Risk Management Solutions, developing new catastrophe models and undertaking cat bond risk analysis. Prior to this, he was a principal risk consultant at EQECAT. Gordon is the author of the book, *The Mathematics of Natural Catastrophes*. Based on this work, he has delivered a course on catastrophe modelling in the centre for financial mathematics at King's College, London. He holds degrees in mathematics, theoretical physics and computer science from Cambridge University, he was a Kennedy Scholar at Massachusetts Institute of Technology (MIT), and a fellow of Harvard University.

Gabriele Zeindler is a managing director at Swiss Re. This involves being a deal team leader and structurer/underwriter for alternative asset reinsurance transactions at Swiss Re's financial services business group, (Credit & Asset Re), where she has worked since its formation in 1999. Prior to 1999, she worked for Swiss Re's international business department, starting in 1994 as a professional indemnity insurance underwriter, and moving in

1996 into the area of structuring alternative risk transfer solutions for Swiss Re's Atrium Corporation, followed by Swiss Re New Markets. During this time, she developed her expertise and reputation in the area of highly innovative transactions for insurance companies and corporate institutions. Gabriele holds a law degree from the University of Zurich and is regarded as an industry specialist in the area of alternative asset re transactions. She has published several articles, and is a regular presenter at various industry conferences, both in the area of insurance and investment banking.

Introduction

OBJECTIVE

My objective for this book was to bring together the best practitioners and best thinkers in the world of alternative risk transfer and securitisation.

I believe that I have succeeded.

I feel honoured to have been asked to edit such an important book and I have been gratified by the high rate of acceptances to my invitations to contribute to the book. The high acceptance rate is, I believe, testimony to the fact that such a book is long overdue. A tremendous amount of creative and experimental energy has been expended in the last ten to fifteen years; much has only partially seen the public light of day. Private transactions are, by and large, not the subject of great publicity or scrutiny. Nevertheless important things have been going on in the hinterland between finance and (re)insurance.[1] A general exposure and review of those developments can be of enormous benefit to both new and existing participants in this arena. New participants are exposed to the scope of possibility. Existing participants can compare notes on parallel developments. Everyone can benefit from a review of the intellectual challenges. I hope that this text delivers such benefits.

TITLE

Book titles are by definition guides to contents. They are also sometimes difficult to pin down. Alternative risk strategies strikes a balance between alternative risk transfer (ART) and risk management strategies. The term 'alternative' in ART has been used almost exclusively in the context of insurance, to denote insurances that are non-traditional. (Although the term is arguably out of date since much ART is now mainstream in insurance-land.) 'Alternative' in the world of investments also means non-traditional. (Again, however, the increasing investment in such 'alternatives' as hedge funds by traditional fund managers make the term a bit out of date.) In any event, 'alternative' in this books' context refers to both senses of the word, to both asset and liability managers' interpretations. The term 'risk' ought to be clear enough. The subject of the book is how 'risk' is transferred, how it is priced, how it should be evaluated and what may or may not be usefully transferred. Finally 'strategies' is chosen rather deliberately to convey the idea that at this point in time, many of the ideas contained herein do require strategic thinking. The concepts presented are still being developed, are not widespread, certainly not yet 'tradable', and so tactical considerations are premature.

STANDARDS

The contributors to the book have been asked to provide submissions that are informational, instructional, introspective, insightful and, where possible, inspired. Since that directive has largely been achieved, the contributors thereby form a rather distinct in-group. I have also asked that the contributions be 'fresh' and not unduly promotional. I am grateful that all of the contributors have adhered to that spirit. In many of the pieces you will find a discussion of other possible ideas or competing strategies. This book is not the bible of 'alternative risk' prescriptions. It is a record of various approaches that have emerged over the past decade and the questions that will drive developments in the next.

SCOPE

This is a big book. It covers a lot of ground. Perhaps it covers too much. However a lot has been done that belongs under the same general umbrella. All of the contributions involve the intersection of insurance and finance. All the contributions involve transactions that have one party ceding risk and another party assuming it, in exchange for considerations. Sometimes this transfer takes place within insurance markets, sometimes between insurance markets and capital markets. What is remarkable is that no coherent theoretical framework guides these transactions. None are satisfactorily covered by the capital asset pricing model (CAPM) or any of its intellectual competitors. Indeed a trawl through the indices of business or finance textbooks at the major business schools rarely reveals a reference to insurance. The transactions in the book fall into the void of 'incomplete markets', shorthand, I would venture, for 'we don't have a theory'. One important reason for this state of affairs is that such markets are not transparent. They are opaque. The last decade of development has begun to change that. This book, among other things, seeks to add to the transparency by exposing new instruments, new practices and sometimes, even, transaction prices.

The complete scope of the book is described in the organisation section. Large as it is, there are still areas that are absent from the text, largely because of time and space considerations. Some notable holes are: discussion of the role of rating agencies, monoline financial guarantee companies, the growing weather derivatives markets, post mortems of the now defunct catastrophe derivatives market and the new area of whole business securitisation. They may have to wait until a later edition.

ORGANISATION

The book is organised into six sections plus an introduction and an after-word. Beyond this introductory section, Section One contains a description of the principal vehicles by which risk is transferred. It reviews the forms as much as the substance of transfer. Section Two reviews the pricing of such transfers. In nearly all the transactions herein the assuming company is presented with an independent third party risk analysis that has been generated from some modelling process. Section Three demonstrates the types of modelling available to the risk evaluators. Some approaches have become specialised to certain industries. They are recorded in Section Four.

Many of the transferred risks can be evaluated as stand alone invest-ments. However that is a sub optimal analysis. Because of the complexity and skewed nature of the risk, such investments can only be properly eval-uated in the context of both the cedent's and assumer's portfolio. Section Five groups several contributions on the subject of evaluating risks in a portfolio context.

Finally nothing practical can proceed without legal, accounting and reg-ulatory review. The book concludes with Section Six on these other perspectives on alternative risk transfer.

Of course several other ways of organising the chapters present them-selves, I hope this provides a coherent treatment of some excellent contributions. More detailed descriptions of each section follow.

Section One: product types for transferring, financing, transforming and retaining risk.

We open Section One with a discussion of the pluses and minuses of using alternative risk transfer instruments. The view of the traditional reinsurer is given first, followed by a scientific analysis of basis risk. The listed risk transfer products all contain elements of basis risks. An opening review of this important feature is therefore all the more relevant.

At 120 years of age Munich Re, as one of the largest and most powerful reinsurers, might be expected to reflect a traditional view of reinsurance. Indeed it does. And yet, it has been one of the leaders in the ART and secu-ritisation markets of the last few years. In the opening chapter of this section Manfred Seitz (a member of executive management at Munich Re) and Kenneth Bock (Munich American Capital Markets) reflect on recent developments versus traditional approaches to risk transfer.[2] They endorse the view that there are many benefits, as well as costs to be recognised to each approach. One benefit they assert, and almost everyone acknowl-edges, is that traditional reinsurance contains no basis risk. But, how big a problem is basis risk? Chapter 2 by Richard Phillips of Georgia State University, David Cummins of the Wharton School of the University of Pennsylvania and David Lalonde of Applied Insurance Research (AIR) addresses the question directly. They take certain indexed structures (not unlike the now-defunct Chicago Board of Trade catastrophe derivatives) and quantify basis risk exactly. Not surprisingly, the trade off is quite acceptable for well-designed structures.

Chapter 3 by David Mocklow, John DeCaro (formerly of Aon) and Matthew McKenna (now all at Cochran, Caronia) addresses catastrophe (cat) bonds. These bonds are the poster boys of the ART revolution. Despite the fact that cat bonds have not grown as much as expected, the concept is now enshrined into the psyche. People (often who know very little about insurance) refer to 'cat bonds' as readily as they might corporate bonds. Mocklow, DeCaro and McKenna know the realities more intimately, having participated in the design and promotion of several. They describe the bonds, their history and offer their own theories on the conundrums that still exist about them – particularly pricing.

An instrument that is more used but less known is the industy loss warranty (ILW). Enda McDonnell (formerly of Willis Re, now of Access Re), perhaps the lead broker of these instruments, does us the service of providing a long overdue, in-depth description of these ILWs in Chapter 4. ILWs combined elements of both reinsurance and derivatives and of course basis risk (see above).

On the 'most recent innovative forms' front are 'risk swaps'. Yuichi Takeda of Tokio Marine is a pioneer in the development of risk swaps together with his initial counterparty State Farm Insurance Company. In Chapter 5 Takeda describes the considerable corporate benefits of, and thoughtfully and thoroughly lays out the qualifications that should go into, swapping insurance risks.

Christopher Culp from the University of Chicago, who has made his own considerable contribution to this area with a recent book on the subject, examines contingent capital in Chapter 6.[3] More important, he lays out a clear intellectual framework for viewing the appropriate way to put contingent capital in the more conventional context of corporate finance. His ability to provide a rigorous framework has been honed over years by his association with the late Nobel Laureate Merton Miller. Bryon Ehrhart of Aon complements Culp's discussion with a review of contingent covers as well as contingent capital. Ehrhart was one of the originators of the aptly named CatEPut. The distinction between contingent capital and contingent cover is not always obvious, but it is an important distinction. Contingent capital solutions, if enacted, will affect the firm's capital structure, contingent covers will not. Contingent covers affect the income statement not the balance sheet.

Chapter 8 defines and illustrates 'finite reinsurance'. Oscar Tymon, a legacy member of Centre Re, provides the valuable service of illuminating finite covers. Refreshingly, he also takes us back to the origins of finite reinsurance by Steven Gluckstern and the late Michael Palm, founders of Centre Reinsurance.

If none of the above transfer risk mechanisms, or reinsurance, is available to a risk bearing entity, then they must retain the risk. But that is not the end of the story. In Chapter 9, Paul Wöhrmann and Christoph Bürer of Zurich Financial Services provide an overview of, and detail the benefits of, setting up a captive insurance company. Given the enormous growth of captives in recent years those benefits must be considerable.

Section Two: the price of risk, and its volatility.

Whether insurance risk is transferred in a derivative, cat bond, ILW, risk swap, finite cover or contingently via an option or stand by, a price is associated with that transfer. Even if risk is retained in a captive it has a price or value, as will become evident the moment the captive tries to reinsure itself. Furthermore those prices must compete with the price of traditional reinsurance if they are to be useful to cedents. They must also compete with capital market prices if the risk is taken by traditional investors. But how is the price of reinsurance set? How should the price of cat bonds, etc be determined? Section Two is devoted to these questions.

John Major and Rodney Kreps of Guy Carpenter lift the curtain on the first question by an empirical analysis of industry practice. Their survey shows that many factors figure into the traditional price of reinsurance, above and beyond the explicit risk parameters of the deal. That in itself is revealing, but more important they lay out the framework for contrasting pricing practice with pricing theory. Theirs is one of rare insight into industry methods. Their theoretical pricing work is based on the original work for which Kreps was awarded the Dorweiler prize in 1998.[4]

Shaun Wang looks into pricing even more deeply. One of the drawbacks in Kreps original formulation of pricing is that it does not lead to 'layer independent' pricing. In other words, the combined price of a junior and an adjacent senior layer, under the formula, will not necessarily equal the price of the combined layer. (It is also a drawback of some of my own and other price formulas.) Wang takes up the challenge that implies and pursues the transformation solution proposed by Gary Venter (a double Dorweiler Prize-winner in 1986 and 1999). Indeed he takes that concept further by proposing a two-factor model which links back, under the appropriately defined circumstances, to options theory and the CAPM. It is a very promising approach.

Whatever pricing method is used at a particular point in time, reinsurance prices fluctuate. While not exactly news, the inconvenient fact of price fluctuation is often a surprise to some who think that the insurance has an 'actuarial fair' and therefore stable price. Joan Lamm-Tennant of General Cologne Re takes advantage of the enormous upheavals visited on the insurances markets, post-September 11 2001, to examine how prices fluctuate. Sudden and large changes in reinsurance rates are important signals to capital providers. As she shows, such providers were not looking the other way. Extreme scarcity and extreme prices were avoided by the responsiveness of capital.

Section Three: assessing individual risks by modelling.

Investors who lend money to corporations by buying bonds look to third parties to provide them with independent risk evaluations. Three of them are well known; Standard and Poors, Moody's and Fitch IBCA, the rating agencies. They provide assessments summarised as letter ratings. Each letter rating is associated with some frequency of default, although how the agency arrives at the letter rating is not always clear. One favours frequency of loss, another uses expected loss levels and the third claims to use a blend.

In the opinion of some, cat bonds and other risk transfers offer a higher standard. They present bond purchasers with precise statistics, albeit with appropriate qualifiers. Those statistics are usually derived from elaborate models of the risk under consideration. Actuarial firms have always provided this type of analysis to its insurance clients, but three firms who service the securitisation market have emerged paralleling corporate rating agencies. They are AIR, EQECAT and Risk Management Services (RMS). Each has contributed a chapter to this section.

Dennis Kuzak and Mahmoud Khater from EQECAT present the fundamental building blocks of natural catastrophe modelling. Their presentation is enhanced by the fact that they have participated in many of the deals discussed elsewhere in the book. So have AIR and RMS who also specialise in natural catastrophe modelling. However I have asked them to contribute on different aspects of modelling.

In Chapter 14 Gordon Woo of RMS uses his experience in natural catastrophe modelling to think from first principles about modelling man-made catastrophes, in particular terrorism. He discharges this task quite brilliantly, showing just how robust the modelling process can be.

AIR in the personages of Mark Gibbas and Ming Lee show how the same techniques can be applied to modelling weather. Everybody forecasts it of course, but Gibbas and Lee show that it can be modelled and how weather derivatives can thereby be priced. It is a revelation to some that the simple movement of, or upgrade of, rain guage measurement devices can vastly distort historic databases.

Geo-physical modelling (represented by the previous three approaches) is not the only approach to quantification of risk. Paul Embrechts of The Swiss Federal Institute of Technology pioneered 'extreme value theory' to analyse sparse, but often only, data of say losses, to generate loss distributions and thereby derive probabilities.[3] Here, in Chapter 16, Peter Blum, Alexandra Dias and Paul Embrechts extend the sparse data analysis to the issue of correlation. In a nutshell, Blum, Dias and Embrechts observe there may be considerable differences between the correlation among small loss outcomes and among large loss outcomes. They remind us that arguments about zero or low beta may be at best illusory, and at worst dangerous, if pricing does not comprehend such relationships.

Concluding this modelling section is a description of economic modelling techniques. Award winner Derrell Hendrix and his colleague Neil Hohmann of RISConsulting Company, show how models can be built to assess residual value or aircraft lease return probabilities.

Section Four: industry specific practices and solutions.

The models that are developed and the transfer instruments that are utilised by particular industries often take on specialised forms. This section reviews those forms for particular industries.

Perhaps the area where insurance has made its biggest incursions into the capital markets is credit. Indeed, Swiss Re is one of the largest credit derivatives players in the world. Uwe Remy and Daniel Grieger describe the role that Swiss Re plays and how it serves their risk-taking appetite. Insurers have always taken credit risk. What is new is assuming credit risk on the liability side (underwriting side) of the balance sheet by multiline property and casualty reinsurers.

Life insurance is not new. It was and is at the very foundation of the insurance industry. Until recently however it resisted the full blandishments of ART and securitisation. As Michael Millette, Shiv Kumar and Omar J. Chaudhary (all of Goldman Sachs) together with Jacqueline Keating and Steven Schreiber (from Milliman USA) detail, there have been life insurance securitisations in the past 10 years but most of those have dealt with securitising commission cashflows. Now however, as they describe, we have seen the first deal containing embedded mortality risk. Investors are the beneficiaries of third party actuarial work of Milliman USA. Given Goldman Sachs' record as the leader in the development of cat bonds and other risk-linked securities we can probably expect to see many more such embedded mortality risk deals.

Perhaps no area represents the successful marriage of transferring capital market risk to insurers than the indirect removal of some contingent liabilities from the balance sheets of aviation manufacturers. Stephen Hough of BAE SYSTEMS describes the motivations and execution of the strategy in Chapter 20. Aside from its own undoubted intrinsic merit, this chapter serves to bring together a superb concrete real life illustration of both the theoretical framework provided by Culp in his contribution and the utility of economic modelling provided by Hendrix and Hohmann in theirs.

Another path-breaking development is described by Gabriele Zeindler. Swiss Re wrapped the terminal value of a portfolio of 'private equity' investments. Swiss Re provides downside capital guaranty to investors. The structure has been replicated both by Swiss Re and its competitors. Such deals promise to make an area of the investment universe, previously unavailable to small investors, accessible.

An area where insurance undoubtedly provides a service to the capital markets is the facilitation of mergers and acquisitions. One only has to reflect on the dilemma presented to putative acquirers of the likes of Enron or Anderson (How big is the liability?) to see the utility of insurance solutions. David Govrin and Andrew Kaiser of Goldman Sachs expertly describe general costs and benefits of insurance solutions for significant investment banking transactions. They also deliver some intriguing case studies.

Finally, as a conclusion to Section Four, David K. A. Mordecai of Clinton Group Inc. addresses the unique asset-management liability management services provided by hedge funds to insurers and pension managers. In the insurance world one encounters the question 'what exactly is a hedge fund?' more often than one might expect. Mordecai shows that the considerations and rationales of hedge fund managers are not too different from those of insurers.

Section Five: portfolio considerations

Most risk transfer solutions cannot be evaluated on a stand-alone basis. They must be evaluated in the context of both the cedent's and assumer's portfolio. Many agree with this concept. Many pay lip service to it. Few practice it. There are good reasons. Number one, it is intellectually difficult. Number two, until recently it has been technically impractical. Both reasons are beginning to be addressed.

Neil Doherty of the Wharton School at the University of Pennsylvania lays out the intellectual case. He views the insurance portfolio allocation decision as a special case of risk allocation in the firm generally. In the process, he presents the case that decision making by internal rate of return evaluations pursues a different end from decision making by risk adjusted rate of return (RAROC). In this Chapter (24), and in several important books he has authored, Doherty provides a most coherent intellectual framework for allocation decisions in a risky environment. He also draws attention to a variety of yet to be resolved theoretical questions. Not that Neil is just a theoretician. His insights are informed by the practical consulting he does for, among others, General Re.

Bill Riker on the other hand is distinctly a practitioner, and he has to resolve allocation questions daily. As president of Renaissance Re, undoubtedly the most successful specialist cat writing firm of the Bermuda class of the 1990s, and also alumnus of AIR, he writes with authority about a different aspect of portfolio management. His piece gives practical voice to the message of the earlier Blum, Dias and Embrechts chapter. Portfolio assessment of risk is a necessary, but not a sufficient condition for success. Even with an evaluation method that is portfolio based, his message is that correlation, properly considered, should be ignored at one's peril.

The juxtaposition between Doherty and Riker is deliberate, but neither provides a complete prescription for followers. Michael Steel of Benfield

Group does describe a commercial service that will allow for complicated structures to be evaluated within a portfolio of other complicated structures – his group's ReMetrics model. Most intermediaries these days present some sort of model for this type of evaluation, often referred to as Dynamic Financial Analysis (DFA). Steel has had a hand in the development of a couple of these. Indeed he was present at the foundation of the Guy Carpenter's 'Meta' model, working with Rodney Kreps and Gary Venter of Sedgwick's Instrat unit (now absorbed into Marsh and McLennan). Importantly Steel shows how it can be done and what to consider.

Portfolio evaluation for fixed income investors is generally easier than it is for insurers. Bonds are relatively standardised and their symmetrical marked-to-market returns lend themselves to a convenient algebra of integration. Notwithstanding, cat bonds present investors with both an opportunity and a challenge to their comfortable portfolio integration. David Heike and John Kiernan of Lehman Brothers set out the case in Chapter 27.

The final piece in this section is by Peter Allen, now of Ernst and Young Consulting, formerly of the Lloyds Association. No book about insurance is complete without a tip of the hat to Lloyds, the 350-year-old market. When it comes to resource allocation problems, Lloyds has to make risk transfer prices explicit in a way that many companies need not do internally. (Transfer prices are, after all the obverse of the allocation decision.) Lloyds has a central guaranty fund. The Association's issue is how should they charge the member syndicates for its use? What signals should they send to the members to encourage prudent 'group use' of the fund, by syndicates who are making independent risk taking decisions, and which simultaneously discourages imprudent use? The answer is a risk based capital system that is both innovative and controversial. That system is not the subject here, rather, Allen who helped design the original system, raises the further question how should new products (financial guaranty), be grafted onto the system? We are privileged to glean an insight into the thought process at work in this venerable institution.

Section Six: other perspectives.
Wrapping up the book we conclude with a section referencing what used to be known as the professions; accounting, law and regulation.

In Chapter 29, Michael Brosnan of Ernst and Young (the accounting division this time) discusses accounting issues in ART and finite reinsurance. He provides the excellent service of bringing together all the important pronouncements relating to finite reinsurance in one place. He further provides important examples where appropriate accounting treatments can distort legitimate transactions, as well as occasions where less legitimate transactions can appear to be blessed by creative use of accounting.

Brosnan raises suitable cautions in the latter case and places himself squarely on the conservative side of the rather broad non-bright line.

A similar message comes from Clive O'Connell of Barlow Lyde and Gilbert, subtitling his piece 'some hard lessons learned'. Refreshingly he bases his message about mitigating legal risks on the foundations of insurance. If there is one dimension about insurance that non-insurance people fail to appreciate it is the principle of indemnity. Insurance can replace a loss, it cannot deliver a profit. Some important legal judgments may be avoided by adhering to this and similarly important foundation principles.

Nigel Davies of the Financial Service Authority (FSA) and David Rule of the Bank of England give the regulators and central bankers point of view respectively. FSA is charged with promulgating and enforcing regulation of all UK financial services. The Bank of England has a responsibility for the overall UK financial system. The convergence of capital and insurance markets challenges regulatory frameworks and raises issues for international financial stability more generally. We are fortunate that both contributors have been candid, both about the existing rules and the potential challenges. What is clear is how good regulators strive to achieve the right balance between a light enough regulatory touch to allow, even encourage, innovation, while providing enough of a threat to prevent abuse.

Afterword

I have taken the liberty as editor of the book to contribute an afterword. In it I reflect on the status of the cat bond market and its future direction. Cat bonds represented the greatest potential revolution to reinsurance in many a decade. But candidly these bonds have yet to live up to their promise. I believe there still will be a revolution but maybe other forms or techniques have yet to emerge. I re-review the benefits to insured and reinsured alike and try to produce my own prescription for future developments.

ACKNOWLEDGEMENTS

A secret of this book is that it was produced on a very short time line. In other words it was produced in the heat of what has been the most momentous renewal season in decades. I am all the more grateful for the contributions of so many busy professionals. When I accepted the assignment I relied on the old adage 'If you want to get something done, ask a busy man'. It proved to be truer than even I had expected. Everyone in this book, professional and academic alike produced extremely high quality work under extraordinary circumstances. We are all beneficiaries.

One person, Sarah Jenkins of Risk Books, is more responsible for the books success than any other. She and I played what has become known as the good cop/bad cop routine in encouraging authors to produce their pieces on time. But, as Dennis Kuzak remarked – she is just too nice – even though most people had not met her they actually didn't want to disappoint her, and most people didn't need the bad cop role for which she was obviously miscast.

Other acknowledgements must be accorded Oscar-like to all those who have contributed to my prior knowledge of this fascinating area. Andrew Martin, now of Willis Re, and his colleagues from the pioneering Instrat group were valued partners in a joint venture 'Sedgwick Lane Financial LLC' 1997 to 2000. We worked with superb Sedgwick people like Rodney Kreps, Gary Venter, Sal Zaffino, Scott Goodell, John Mellows and Steve Patterson. We were also fortunate to work with forward-looking cedents like Darren Redhead and Roger Walker of Reliance National. Later on I was invited by Peter Gentile of Gerling Global Financial Products to bring some new thinking to Gerling. The practice I gained by working with Gerhard Neibuhr and Maralyn Fichte was invaluable. I am also grateful to Pat Arbor former chairman, and Richard Sandor former vice chairman, of the Chicago Board of Trade for the chance to head up the catastrophe derivatives initiative back in the mid 1990s.

On the unnamed side, executives from the largest to the smallest reinsurance entities have been extraordinarily generous with their time and access. An industry so welcoming to outsiders is clearly also receptive to new ideas. It is destined for even greater innovations.

None of this personal sequence would have been possible without dedicated colleagues and staff. In particular John Finn and Oleg Movchan were valued co-workers. Dianne Louise was an exceptionally talented, extraordinarily gifted and extremely dedicated executive assistant for many years. Finally my current and long time business partner Roger Beckwith has been invaluable to this project and many others.

My wife Claudia provided constant encouragement and support and my children Megan, David and Rhodri gave daily inspiration. I am grateful to all but take full responsibility for errors, omissions, oversights and the inevitable misjudgements.

Morton Lane
March 2002.

1 Insurance and reinsurance are often used interchangeably in this text. Reinsurance is the insurance of insurance companies. It is generally less regulated than insurance, and therefore has been able to experiment with new solutions more freely. In particular, reinsurance prices are more volatile, thereby motivating greater need for risk transfer.
2 Exact positions, titles and other honourifics of all authors are listed under "Authors" in the previous pages.
3 All relevant books authored by contributors are listed at the end of this introduction in "Further reading".
4 For more information on the Dorweiler Prize see: http://www.casact.org/aboutcas/dorweilr.htm

FURTHER READING

Bernstein, P. L., 1992, *Capital Ideas, The Improbable Origins of Modern Wall Street* (New York: The Free Press).

Bernstein, P. L., 1996, *Against the Gods, The Remarkable Story of Risk* (New York: John Wiley & Sons, Ltd).

Booth, G., ed., 2000, *Modern ART Practice* (London: Reactions Publishing Group).

Briys, E., and F. deVarenne, 2000, *The Fisherman and the Rhinoceros, How International Finance Shapes Everyday Life* (Chichester: John Wiley & Sons, Ltd).

Culp, C. L., 2001, *The Risk Management Process* (New York: John Wiley & Sons, Ltd).

Culp, C. L., 2002, *The ART of Risk Management* (New York: John Wiley & Sons, Ltd).

Doherty, N. A., 2000, *Integrated Risk Management* (New York: McGraw-Hill).

Embrechts, P., ed., 2000, *Extremes and Integrated Risk Management* (London: Risk Books).

Froot, K. A., 1999, *The Financing of Catastrophic Risk* (Chicago: The University of Chicago Press).

Himick, M., ed., 1998, *Securitized Insurance Risk, Strategic Opportunities for Insurers and Investors* (Chicago: Greenlake Publishing Company, Ltd).

Jaeger, L., *Managing Risk in Alternative Investment Strategies* (Prentice Hall), forthcoming.

Kiln, R., and S. Kiln, 1996, *Reinsurance Underwriting*, Second Edition (London: LLP Ltd).

Kunreuther, H. and R. J. Sr. Roth, eds., 1998, *Paying the Price* (Washington: Joseph Henry Press).

Shimpi, P. A., ed., 1999, *Integrating Corporate Risk Management* (New York: Texere).

Strain, R. W., ed., 1980, *Reinsurance* (New York: Strain Publishing Inc).

Woo, G., 1999, *The Mathematics of Natural Catastrophes* (London: Imperial College Press).

Part I

Product types for transferring, financing, transforming and retaining risk

1

Reinsurance Versus Other Risk-Transfer Instruments – The Reinsurer's Perspective

Kenneth J. Bock and Manfred W. Seitz

Munich American Capital Markets and Munich Reinsurance Company[1]

In this chapter we provide an overview of the functions and types of traditional reinsurance before turning to tools for transferring risk between the (re)insurance and the capital markets and looking at the reinsurer's role in these markets. Finally, we will review some current developments and provide an outlook on the future.

INTRODUCTION

The days when insurers and reinsurers operated in safe environments, protected from internal competition by tariffs, regulation and monopolistic structures, are gone or are on the way out due to the emergence of the market economy. Deregulation and liberalisation, shareholder value and economic value added are becoming commonplace concepts, and consequently competitive prices and conditions are set to become the norm. In the short-term this may cause problems for insurers and insurance buyers although, in the long-term, competition benefits buyers and sellers of insurance and reinsurance alike.

Could the function fulfilled by the insurance industry in economic life be performed instead, and possibly better, by others? If the answer is "yes" or "maybe" then reinsurers have to ask themselves how they can improve their services and concepts – or face the consequences.

As reinsurers, the authors are strong advocates of the view that the insurance industry performs the functions of risk assessment, risk management and risk-carrying in a very efficient manner, by applying and continually refining methods and models founded on risk theory and actuarial mathematics. In this respect, it occupies a unique position that cannot be copied by others unless they "mutate" into insurers, with all the regulatory consequences.

The crucial factor, however, is not how insurers see things, but how the markets rate the efficiency of insurance in comparison with the efficiency of competing, substitute products. The financial services industry as a whole is undergoing a process of tremendous change. The ongoing changes within the financial services industry make it imperative to rethink the profile of a sector such as reinsurance and its position in the insurance industry's value chain.

All sectors of the financial services industry are characterised by ongoing attempts to streamline and shorten the value chain. This is designed to save transaction costs and typically results in the break-up of existing client relationships. The once clearly defined value chain reaching from the original client, the insured, via the sales organisation and the product designer to the ultimate risk carrier, is increasingly being restructured. We can see this in:

❑ the shifting functions within the insurance industry between primary insurance and reinsurance;
❑ the role that the Internet and e-business are beginning to play in the financial markets;
❑ the growing demand from very large multinational firms for "integrated financial solutions and risk management", in the face of which the classic distinctions between the various financial services sectors are steadily declining in importance.

Only a few financial institutions worldwide are in a position to act as equal partners to the world's largest firms from trade and industry; they have to be on the same level in terms of global accessibility, capital resources and capacity, professional expertise, and the breadth of the services they offer. At the same time they must provide holistic solutions that are individually tailored to the client's risk or financial situation.

In this client segment the traditional division between insurers, reinsurers and capital market institutions is making less and less sense. Primary insurers – side by side with reinsurers – often act as co-insurers. From a purely economic view, it is no longer important whether a certain product is formally insurance or reinsurance, or whether insurance solutions are combined with banking approaches to create a mixed product, as is happening in the field of securitisation. Figure 1 provides an overview of the main non-traditional solutions.

FUNCTIONS AND TYPES OF TRADITIONAL REINSURANCE

The previous section illustrated the degree to which the (re)insurance industry is in a state of flux and that there is no simple "yes" or "no" to the question of whether capital markets are an alternative to reinsurance. Indeed, the authors would argue that the capital markets are complementary to reinsurance. Before discussing this in greater detail, it is useful to

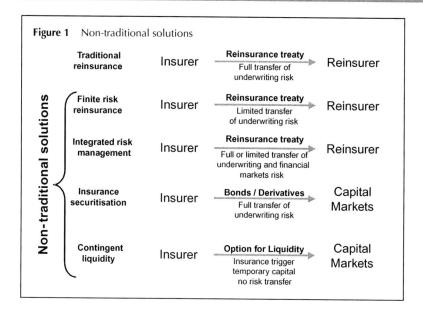

Figure 1   Non-traditional solutions

summarise the main functions and types of traditional reinsurance to provide the reader with a better understanding of how reinsurance performs in the economy today.

Reinsurers provide protection to insurers in the same way that insurers cover policyholders – they provide coverage against unforeseen or extraordinary losses. In a reinsurance contract, one insurance company (the reinsurer, or assuming insurer) charges a premium to indemnify another insurance company (the ceding insurer, or cedent) against all or part of the loss it may sustain under a policy or policies of insurance. For all but the largest insurance companies, reinsurance is almost a prerequisite for offering insurance against hazardous events where there is the potential for catastrophic losses, to limit (as much as possible) annual fluctuations in the losses that insurers must bear themselves.

The general economic functions of reinsurance

One function of reinsurance relates to the world economy, and concerns matters such as the geographical spread of high-value risks or cover for catastrophic events for which no sufficient local capacity is available. It helps to enhance the development of an international network of insurance.

A second general economic function is stabilisation through the settlement of losses and the coverage of the economic value of the insured objects as well as the protection of employment.

Generally, risk aversion is behind the decision of a cedent seeking protection via a reinsurance contract. This is also the driving force for entrepreneurs: insurance and reinsurance protection increases the amount of financial support from banks for further investment, or in many cases is a precondition for companies to obtain such support. Entrepreneurs will be more prepared to take risks if they have insurance and risk-management support or backing for research activities.

Finally, reinsurance contributes significantly to GDP by collecting capital (in the form of insurance or reinsurance premiums) and by efficiently redistributing capital to the economy by investing premiums collected in other financial operations.

Risk assumption factors

In addition to general economic functions, a modern reinsurer has to satisfy the three principal needs of its clients (mainly insurers) in the traditional areas: risk assumption, financing and service.

The risk assumption function of reinsurance consists of three factors:

1. Reduction of the insurer's total liability. The reinsurer takes over part of the risk written by the insurer, leading to reduced total loss potential for the insurer and better balanced portfolios.
2. The reinsurer increases the insurer's underwriting capacity by accepting a (non-proportional) share of the risks and by providing part of the necessary reserves.
3. The reinsurer stabilises underwriting results by balancing the random fluctuations in the business performance of the insurer's net account by supporting or replacing unknown fluctuating loss costs by known (reinsurance) premiums, especially in the case of non-proportional reinsurance and accumulation protection (in reinsurance terms: "risk of random fluctuations").

The financing function

The overall objective of regulatory solvency requirements is generally to protect the interests of insureds in their business relationship with insurers in the sense that the insurers should always be in a position to fulfil their obligations arising from insurance contracts and pay claims when necessary. If a certain part of the gross premium is transferred to a reinsurer, the insurer's solvency margin may be significantly influenced and its capital or the net premium income ratio enhanced through surplus relief reinsurance. In this way, the reinsurer can reduce the immediate need for capital and fulfil regulatory solvency margin requirements; reinsurance performs the function of a capital substitute instrument.

In addition, an insurer may consider spread loss agreements that allow the transfer of losses to the reinsurer and payback of these losses at a later point in time. These will help balance underwriting results in periods of poor business experience until the necessary improvement measures are taken, and thus ensure balance sheet continuity.

Finally, reinsurance treaties can be used for cost financing – for example of product development or acquisition of new business in life insurance.

Functions of reinsurance as a service provider

The range of services offered by a reinsurer includes the provision of information on new developments and products and on the performance of other markets through knowledge transfer to, and training and education of, cedents' staff.

A reinsurer also assists in introducing new classes of business through marketing seminars and product development, and assistance in wording policies and calculating tariffs. This is backed by consulting services and assistance in inspecting risks, probable maximum loss (PML) assessment, premium calculation, loss prevention and claims settlement as well as advice with regard to risk management and structuring insurance portfolios, not to mention efficient reinsurance programmes.

Finally, a reinsurer consults with regard to whole markets, support for mergers and acquisitions, risk distribution and retrocession. Consulting services may also encompass less directly insurance-related areas such as the IT sector and asset management, including asset-liability management.

Major products and types of reinsurance agreements

Reinsurance agreements can be divided into proportional and non-proportional types.

Proportional reinsurance means that, when the risk is written, it is split into a retained share and a ceded share. The insurer cedes a proportional share of liability, premiums and claims. Common treaty types include quota share treaties and surplus treaties (meaning, retention by the insurer up to a certain amount of liability). Thus, according to the treaty type, the contractually defined ratio between cedent and reinsurer may be identical for all risks (quota share agreements) or it may vary from risk to risk (all other proportional reinsurance types). In all cases, however, the premium will be split according to the obligation to pay losses.

By contrast, in a *non-proportional* (or excess of loss, "XL") reinsurance contract the premium is negotiated between the insurer and the reinsurer. In the event of a claim, the reinsurer pays the part of the claim that exceeds the agreed amount and remains within a contractually defined cover limit. The share of the claim to be paid by the reinsurer cannot be calculated until the claim occurs. Unlike in proportional reinsurance, non-proportional reinsurance restricts losses. The contract defines an amount up to which the insurer pays all losses (in insurance terms this is called the "deductible", "net retention", "priority" or "excess point"). Non-proportional treaties are usually classified by the type of loss in relation to priority and limit:

1. single risk loss ("each and every loss, each and every risk");
2. accumulated single losses arising out of one event; or
3. accumulated losses incurred during one year.

In determining a suitable price for a non-proportional cover, the reinsurer considers the loss experience of past years as well as the losses to be expected from that type and composition of risk (exposure rating) on the basis of actuarial calculations. Future developments could move towards broader products covering multiple lines and multiple years if technically feasible and economically viable solutions can be achieved for both clients and the insurance industry. Similarly, the broadening of finite risk and alternative risk transfer (ART) products within the range of traditional insurance products is likely to expand.

RISK TRANSFER BETWEEN THE (RE)INSURANCE AND THE CAPITAL MARKETS

In recent years the financial markets have offered an additional source of capacity and financing to complement traditional (re)insurance products. A fact common to banking and insurance products is that "money" takes on the function of a commodity. Both sectors deal with their clients' financial concerns. Both sectors have expertise in the field of asset management. The sectors differ in their range of services between large commercial clients on the one hand and small businesses and private individuals on the other.

However, there is a great difference between the way banks and insurance companies handle and control risks.

Securitisation

Sometimes it is desirable to transfer insurance covers to the capital markets in the form of a marketable security (bonds or insurance derivatives), rather than to the (re)insurance market. Securitisation enables the unbundling and repackaging of risks and expands the range of tradable risks in the capital markets through issuance of securities or derivatives. The use of insurance securitisation and other risk-transfer techniques as means of covering insurance risks and as tools for additional and alternative capacity can be traced back at least as far as 1996, when the underlying risks were recognised in the capital market as a new asset class.

The differences between a securitisation and a derivative structure are as follows. In a typical securitisation transaction (as shown in Figure 2), the cedent sells (in insurance terms "retrocedes") the risk directly or via a reinsurance company (depending on the regulatory and accounting environment) to a special purpose vehicle (SPV). The SPV enters into a reinsurance contract with the cedent (or into a retrocession contract with the reinsurer) on the one side and simultaneously issues bonds to investors on the other. As the underlying risk in the initial transactions was natural peril catastrophic risk, the term "catastrophe bonds" (or "cat bonds") has been used.

The funds raised through the issuance of securities are available to make payments to the cedent (or in a retrocession contract to the reinsurer) if the predefined loss event occurs. Otherwise it is available to repay investor principal at the maturity of the transaction.

Insurance derivatives

Insurance derivatives enable investors to assume insurance risk via an unfunded capital market instrument in the form of options or swaps. The basis of such a transaction may be a market loss index (such as the PCS Index of the US Property Claim Service) or a parametric trigger. A market loss index reflects the losses incurred in the insurance industry after a natural catastrophe. A parametric trigger links the cover to a natural catastrophe, which must comply with precisely defined and transparent criteria in terms of severity (the Richter scale for earthquakes, or wind velocity for windstorms).

Insurance derivatives can be transacted either via exchanges or in an over-the-counter (OTC) format. The Chicago Board of Trade (CBOT) has for several years traded in standardised options contracts on the basis of market loss indices for nine regions in the US, with coverage periods for natural catastrophes (hurricane, earthquake) of up to one year. Volume is

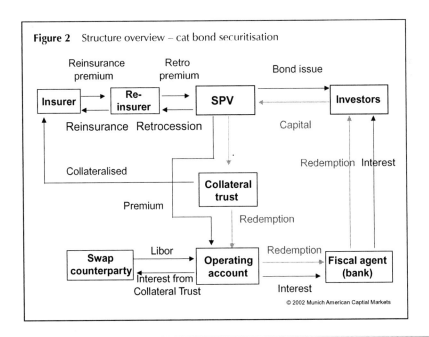

Figure 2   Structure overview – cat bond securitisation

© 2002 Munich American Captial Markets

still relatively low and this market cannot be described as liquid at this stage.

A fundamental advantage of insurance derivatives is that they are much quicker and easier to structure and close than bond issues. The transaction costs are therefore well below those involved in a bond issue. On the other hand, a bond issue can raise – at least theoretically – greater volumes of capital than a derivative. Insurance derivatives also contain counterparty risk that manifests itself when the investors cannot meet the indemnification payment.

Contingent capital structures

For several years now the capital markets have offered contingent capital programmes for debt or equity financing with insurance event triggers. The objective is to secure an insurance company's financial standing in the aftermath of a significant insurance event, when traditional refinancing, if available at all, would be costly.

One form of contingent capital structure is an "equity put arrangement", where the cedent pays an option premium for the right to issue preference shares to investors in the case of a natural catastrophe and a subsequent loss of surplus. A "surplus put arrangement" provides for the right to issue surplus notes. The option can be exercised after the occurrence of a predefined trigger event. The investors purchase the shares or the surplus notes with capital.

The benefits deserved from contingent capital structures should be compared to other financing tools providing liquidity at a certain point in time, such as stand-by liquidity facilities or financial reinsurance products. Although official statistics are not available, these structures have played a limited role in the past due to the lack of pricing transparency and different trigger-event calculation methods.

THE ROLE OF THE REINSURER IN A SUCCESSFUL TRANSACTION

Recently, the market for insurance securitisations has witnessed important changes. It has grown slowly and brought new asset classes in to discussion such as credit, life and residual value risks, which have since gained some acceptance in the markets. Traditionally, the concept of transferring insurance risks to the capital markets has been pursued by investment banks and other capital market participants in order to gain a strategic foothold in a new market. Some investment banks and the capital market units of some major reinsurers and insurance brokers have aggressively built up their position and are actively competing for new business. However, the reinsurance industry in general has been more reluctant to define its role in this new market segment. As a professional risk management specialist, a reinsurer can bring added value to insurance securitisation projects, which can be crucial for the success of a transaction.

The reinsurer's role can be seen as a structurer and facilitator, as a sponsor and, finally, as an investor.

The reinsurer as a structurer and facilitator
The key roles that a reinsurer can play in a successful transaction are as follows.

Structurer and project manager
With their expertise in risk management, reinsurers are a logical choice to assume responsibility as structurers and project managers in a capital markets project.

Fronter and transformer
Acting as fronter and transformer of insurance risks, a reinsurer can provide surplus relief to its client and ensure compliance with regulations. This means the reinsurer enters into a reinsurance agreement with the cedent and retrocedes the risk to the SPV, which covers its contingent liabilities through the issue of bonds. (A bond directly issued by the cedent would not be considered reinsurance and would therefore not help to optimise the solvency ratio or provide capital relief, which is one of the essential features of reinsurance. Furthermore, the premium would not be accounted as a deductible business expense.)

Provision of risk assessment and evaluation
Analysing and assessing risks are the key competencies of a reinsurer. It collects the relevant data and develops models as well as the statistical basis for underwriting the risks. The underwriting comprises the analysis and assessment of a risk or a risk portfolio. Its purpose is to make the risk calculable and thus understandable, even to non-experts.

Provision of risk assumption capacity
One of the reinsurer's main functions is assuming and retaining risks in such a transaction either through additional coverage or the acceptance of the basis or currency risk. A reinsurer can provide additional coverage above or below an insurance securitisation transaction or can assume a substantial part of the securitised risk by way of co–reinsurance.

In the case of the reinsurer assuming the basis risk (as shown in Figure 3), the client cedes a portfolio of risks and is indemnified for actual losses. At the same time the reinsurer transfers the risk into the capital markets in the form of an index or parametric trigger-based transaction. The nature of indexes or parameters is such that this contract might not match the losses of the portfolio of risks ceded to the reinsurer. Sometimes when the sponsor experiences a loss, the contract will not pay as much as the loss, but sometimes it will pay more – hence the reinsurer assumes the basis risk.

Most investors prefer index or parametric trigger-based transactions to indemnity-based ones due the clarity of the trigger definition, which has no relationship to the underlying insurance business. The moral hazard is therefore excluded.

Marketing and investment consultant
If the underlying risk has already been underwritten by a specialist reinsurer, which has itself assumed and retained a portion of the risk, participation by the reinsurer in the active marketing of a transaction can provide an increased level of comfort for investors.

Reinsurers as providers of bridge and back-up cover
A reinsurer may support the cedent by providing bridge cover during the time needed to set up a securitisation. Back-up cover may become necessary if the establishment of a securitisation structure fails or the issue cannot be placed in the capital markets.

Reinstatement
Unlike conventional reinsurance, insurance securitisation does not provide for continued insurance protection after the occurrence of a loss event. As soon as the available funds in the collateral trust have been used up, coverage is exhausted. In conventional reinsurance, at least one reinstatement is common practice. In this situation a reinsurer can provide the necessary extension of coverage of the securitisation in the form of a reinstatement. Such reinstatements may also be transferred to the capital markets by way of a stand-alone option or a swap.

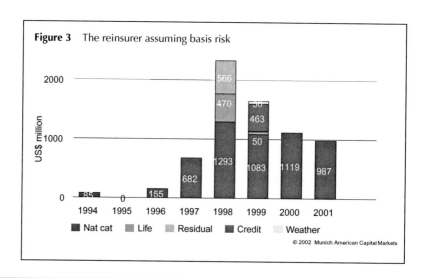

Figure 3 The reinsurer assuming basis risk

© 2002 Munich American Capital Markets

Loss settlement

A reinsurer is both a provider of capacity and a provider of services connected with reinsurance: the risk-management experience, advice and support offered by the reinsurer with respect to loss settlement after an insured event has occurred also constitutes an important factor in the field of insurance securitisation. In addition to structuring, fronting and risk carrying, the responsibility for loss verification and settlement represents an important function of the reinsurer.

Finally, arranging and negotiating a close-out settlement or commutation of any outstanding loss reserves on the scheduled maturity date should be performed by the reinsurer. A close-out or a commutation is a payment to the ceding company in settlement of all future liabilities under the reinsurance and retrocession agreements.

In the case of complete close-outs within a relatively short time after maturity of the bond, investors will know whether they have incurred a loss of their capital and the amount of the loss rather than going into a lengthy run-off of loss reserves. The reinsurer's active involvement in the loss settlement is a viable credibility factor and may be an important way to strengthen investors' confidence and contribute to the successful placement of a bond issue.

The reinsurer as a sponsor

Insurance and reinsurance companies can act as sponsors of securitisations. Capital market deals diversify a reinsurer's source of retrocession capacity. Munich Re, for example, recently placed a total of US$300 million in risk-linked securities, the largest ever such placement, to provide protection against different types of natural catastrophe events: US Hurricane, California Earthquake and European Windstorm.

The bonds provide Munich Re with an additional risk management tool and fixed conditions for the three-year term. There were four reasons motivating Munich Re to enter into such a transaction:

1. It allowed diversification of the sources of retrocessional capacity.
2. The transaction represented an important step for Munich Re to obtain fully collateralised protection against significant low-frequency, high-severity natural perils in regions with particularly high insurance exposures – specifically, the US and Europe.
3. Due to Munich Re's significant exposures, the coverage was large enough to provide meaningful cover.
4. The coverage established a platform for capital markets hedging.

The prospects for a more frequent transfer of insurance market risks to capital markets are still uncertain. Since the first risk-linked securities were issued in 1996, there have been some 50 transactions by 31 different issuers with an average size of about US$100 million. Those deals represented US$7 billion in risk capacity from inception to date and were purchased by approximately 120 capital market investors, 30 of them core investors.[2] Yet while the market has seen steady growth, it is still very small compared to the insurance and reinsurance industry, with the industry's annual gross premiums exceeding US$ 2,000 billion (life and non-life).

By making use of the opportunities to transfer insurance risks to the capital markets, it would appear at least theoretically possible to include risks that are on the borderline of insurability or reinsurability. However, it remains to be seen how the capital markets react if and when they are actually hit by a major loss event. As things stand at present, there are still questions as to whether or to what extent securitisation can establish itself as a lasting solution to supplement conventional insurance and reinsurance cover.

Hurdles such as the time-consuming and costly nature of arranging such deals stand in the way of securitisation's establishment. Thus, a thorough analysis of all arguments for or against pursuing a securitisation should be performed at the very beginning of such projects.

The reinsurer as an investor

One reason for the success of the securitisation of insurance risks, such as catastrophe risks, is that it can open the door for additional investors: (hedge) fund managers, commercial banks and life insurance companies are increasingly interested in adding assets to their portfolio that are less correlated with other asset classes. Insurers and reinsurers have also been active investors in this asset class.

DEVELOPMENTS AND OUTLOOK SINCE 11 SEPTEMBER, 2001

Since the inception of the cat bond market in the mid-1990s, the product has competed with extremely low pricing in the reinsurance industry. Taking this into account together with the high pricing levels in the capital markets, the huge transactions costs and the limited investor base, securitising risk has not made economic sense for most potential issuers. Those that have issued cat bonds have mostly done so either because of the other benefits of securitisation, such as publicity, or as an investment in the future of the market.

The events surrounding 11 September, 2001 have created extra for top industrial and insurance executives who have to deal with risk management, balance sheet management and liquidity management. Due to the expected capacity shortage and increasing price levels it was assumed that reinsurance buyers would accelerate the demand for alternative solutions. Yet, the wave of cat bond issuance that industry professionals were predicting in the weeks following the 11 September attacks has not materialised. Insurance industry analysts were predicting a potentially huge increase in the cost of reinsurance policies, making securities whose payments were linked to natural disasters a more attractive means of shedding risk.

However, property-casualty insurers around the world have been able to raise more than US$20 billion of equity capital since then. The new capital has flooded in faster than insurers originally expected, as investors have sought to take advantage of the potential for the firms to stage a quick turn-around by raising premiums. However, this new capacity has had no small effect on most areas of reinsurance so far. On the contrary, as some players have withdrawn capacity from the market and others have turned to restrictive underwriting practices, a certain insurance capacity drain has been observable. For this reason, cat bonds seem to have lost some of their appeal as an economic tool for transferring insurance risk.

For this reason, cat bonds seem to have lost some of their appeal as an economic tool for transferring insurance risk. Market analysts now estimate about US$2 billion of issuance for 2002, which would be approximately double the size of the previous year's. But even these optimistic figures would not help to give this market the necessary boost that capital market professionals have been long awaiting.

Where will developments go from here?
Overall, it may be said that globalisation, consolidation, the convergence of the financial services industries, and the restructuring of the value chain should lead to more efficient markets. Indeed, (re)insurance markets are increasingly interconnected with other parts of the financial sector.

What is the future of the converging risk markets? What role will reinsurers and capital markets play?

Two key trends should be mentioned:

1. the continued increase in size and exposure of (non-life) risks and in the demand for cover for new types of risk; and
2. the continued boom in life assurance and pension products.

Rising demand for risk covers
Risk will continue to grow in magnitude and exposure. Private individuals, industrial clients and increasingly other institutions, such as municipalities, "risk retention groups" or "affinity groups", have higher exposures, more complex risks and seek solutions well beyond risk transfer. This is a challenge for primary insurers and in particular for reinsurers – but also an opportunity.

As long as the economists tell us that a macroeconomic slowdown in the world economy is only reflecting economic cycles and not the beginning of a structural change, the global market for risk protection is expected to continue growing. According to economic theories, the demand for risk cover is expected to increase at least at the same rate as the overall economy, but some (including the authors) believe it will grow even faster.

For one reason, the history of economic losses from natural disasters shows that catastrophe potentials soar in comparison with growth in the overall economy. Population growth, urbanisation, and building density in areas highly exposed to windstorms, flooding and earthquakes are expected to lead to an increasing interdependency of risks. On top of this, man-made climatic changes contribute towards accelerating the incidence and severity of windstorm and flood catastrophes. Scientific findings show this to be almost inevitable, even if it is not yet statistically proven (Figure 4).

New technologies like microelectronics and genetic engineering, as well as electronic media like the Internet, produce additional demand for risk cover.

But this (risk) market does not stop there: for instance, there is an increasing demand especially among global clients, for insurance as a means of smoothing results, protecting the balance sheet, and ensuring liquidity. These risks on the asset side of the balance sheet are increasingly becoming correlated with those traditionally resulting from the liability side. Just imagine the possible consequences of a major "disaster scenario" for world stock markets and consequently for the balance sheets of corporates.

It is evident that new concepts for the coverage of these risk accumulations are needed. The demand for such concepts will lead to a further expansion of the risk market.

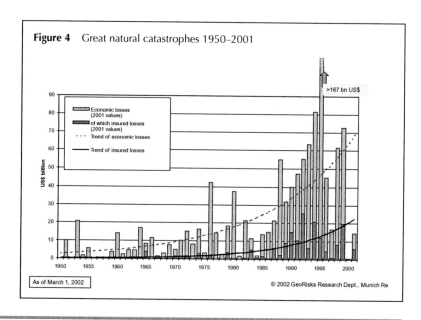

Figure 4 Great natural catastrophes 1950–2001

Old-age products: life assurance and pensions

The demographic picture worldwide is changing. People are living longer and therefore the individual's need to provide for retirement is increasing. Owing to its expected magnitude, the reform of old-age pension systems is destined to become the growth market of the financial services industry in many economies in the next decade. Life, health, and personal accident insurance are likely to grow at a faster rate than the property-casualty classes in the foreseeable future and this is true for most of the developed and developing markets. Today's clients are demanding new, transparent and innovative products focused on living benefits or longevity (the increasing risk of not dying in time). Relevant products include retirement savings, long-term care and disability income protection.

CONCLUSION

Changes in the global financial services business are in their early stages, however certain assumptions can be made. Risk is going to increase and reinsurers are – or should be – in a position to manage risk. It may be inevitable that certain forms of traditional reinsurance may decline but, on the other hand, new business opportunities will emerge. Reinsurers will interact increasingly with other financial institutions as the business and regulatory landscape changes. This evolution of the financial services industry should lead to increased efficiency, a broader business mix and the development of additional competencies stimulated by cross-sector cooperation. In the long run, the end-user clients of financial service providers will benefit.

APPENDIX

The following table provides information showing the major national disasters over the last 20 years and their impact on insured losses as well as economic losses.

Table 1 Natural disasters: US$ billion insurance losses

Rank	Year	Cat event	Area	Ins.losses (US$ billion)	Econ. losses (US$ billion)
27	1983	Hurricane Alicia	US	1.275	3.000
29	1987	Winterstorm	Western Europe	3.100	3.700
6	1989	Hurricane Hugo	Caribbean, US	4.500	9.000
5	1990	Winterstorm Daria	Europe	5.100	6.800
26	1990	Winterstorm Herta	Europe	1.300	1.950
14	1990	Winterstorm Vivian	Europe	2.100	3.250
25	1990	Winterstorm Wiebke	Europe	1.300	2.250
4	1991	Typhoon Mireille	Japan	5.400	10.000
19	1991	Forest fire Oakland fire	US	1.750	2.000
1	1992	Hurricane Andrew	US	17.000	30.000
20	1992	Hurricane Iniki	Hawaii	1.650	3.000
18	1993	Blizzard	US	1.750	5.000
34	1993	Floods	US	1.000	16.000
2	1994	Earthquake	US	15.300	44.000
10	1995	Earthquake	Japan	3.000	100.000
29	1995	Hailstorm	US	1.135	2.000
22	1995	Hurricane Luis	Caribbean	1.500	2.500
15	1995	Hurricane Opal	US	2.100	3.000
21	1996	Hurricane Fran	US	1.600	5.200
28	1998	Ice storm	Canada. US	1.200	2.500
33	1998	Floods	China	1.000	30.000
24	1998	Hailstorm. Tempest	USA	1.350	1.800
7	1998	Hurricane Georges	Caribbean. US	4.000	10.000
30	1999	Hailstorm	Australia	1.100	1.500
23	1999	Tornadoes	US	1.485	2.000
13	1999	Hurricane Floyd	US	2.200	4.500
8	1999	Typhoon Bart	Japan	3.500	5.000
16	1999	Winter storm Anatol	Europe	2.350	2.900
3	1999	Winter storm Lothar	Europe	5.900	11.500
12	1999	Winter storm Martin	Europe	2.500	4.000
32	2000	Typhoon Saomai	Japan	1.050	1.500
31	2000	Floods	UK	1.090	1.500
17	2001	Hailstorm, Tempest	US	1.900	2.500
11	2001	Tropical Storm Allison	US	3.500	6.000

Original figures, not adjusted for inflation. Correct as of March 1, 2002.
© 2002 GeoRisks Research Dept., Munich Re

1 The authors would like to thank Dr Thomas Arnoldt of Munich American Capital Markets, Munich Re/Corporate Planning and Economic Department as well as the Corporate Underwriting/ Property and Geoscience Division for their contributions to this article.
2 Estimation by Munich American Capital Markets.

Managing Risk Using Index-Linked Catastrophic Loss Securities

J. David Cummins, David Lalonde, Richard D. Phillips

The Wharton School, Applied Insurance Research (AIR)
and Georgia State University

Hurricane Andrew in 1992 and the Northridge Earthquake in 1994 resulted in US$30 billion in insured property losses and led insurers to increase significantly their estimates of potential losses from property catastrophes. Insurers who sought to hedge catastrophe (cat) losses following these events quickly learned that reinsurance markets were inadequate to reinsure events in the Andrew–Northridge loss range and would be even less effective in funding anticipated major natural catastrophes (the projected "Big One") in Florida or California, which could cause losses exceeding US$100 billion (Swiss Re, 1997 and Froot, 1998a).[1]

Although substantial new capacity in the form of equity capital flowed into the reinsurance market during the 1990s, it has become clear that reinsurance is not the most efficient way to handle extremely large, infrequent loss events, due to the existence of reinsurance price and availability cycles and other market imperfections (Jaffee and Russell, 1997 and Cummins and Weiss, 2000).[2] Financial innovation in the securities market has the potential to provide better solutions to the cat loss-financing problem – insurance-linked bonds, options and other types of derivatives. The objective of this chapter is to discuss these new financial instruments and demonstrate how insurers and other firms exposed to cat risk can use these securities in their risk management programmes.

The logic behind the securitisation solution is compelling – a US$100 billion loss would amount to about 30% of the equity capital in the US insurance market and about 75% of the equity capital of the international reinsurance market. However, such a loss would be less than 0.5% of the US stock and bond markets and an even smaller percentage of the value of global securities markets. Insurance-linked securities not only provide hedging benefits to insurers but also permit non-insurers such as industrial firms to bypass the insurance market for some types of risk. Securitisation also would help to mitigate the reinsurance underwriting cycle by providing an alternative source of capacity when the reinsurance market experiences its periodic crises. Moreover, it is often argued that catastrophe losses are "zero beta" events, so that cat-loss securities provide a valuable new source of diversification for investors (Litzenberger *et al.*, 1996 and Canter *et al.*, 1997).[3] The development of securitised products covering geographical areas worldwide would enable investors to diversify their holdings of cat risk securities, permitting cat risk to be hedged at much lower risk loadings than in today's reinsurance markets.

The development of the cat risk securities market has been impeded by the lack of a traded underlying asset or commodity, so prices are not observed. In the absence of a traded underlying, cat-risk securities have been structured to pay out on three types of variables:

1. issuer-specific catastrophe loss criteria;
2. insurance-industry catastrophe loss indices; and
3. parametric indices based on the physical characteristics of catastrophic events.

The choice of a triggering variable involves a tradeoff between moral hazard and basis risk (Doherty, 1997). Securities based on insurer-specific (or hedger-specific) losses have low basis risk but expose investors to moral hazard, whereas securities based on industry loss indices or parametric triggers greatly reduce or eliminate moral hazard but expose hedgers to basis risk.[4]

Nearly all of the cat risk securities issued to date that pay out on insurer-specific indices have the same mathematical structure as excess of loss (XOL) reinsurance (Cummins, Lewis and Phillips, 1999) and most such products have been tailored to the needs of the issuer. Although these design features enable the contracts to come close to replicating conventional XOL reinsurance products, they also bring certain limitations. In addition to exposing investors to moral hazard, it is difficult to generate a liquid secondary market in such contracts because they are not standardised. Thus, these contracts expose issuers and investors to liquidity risk, raising the required risk premiums. Contracts tailored specifically to the issuer are also characterised by higher transaction costs than more standardised instruments.

INTRODUCTION

The potential advantages of exchange-traded contracts in reducing liquidity risk and transactions costs mean that this chapter focuses on hedging strategies using index-linked cat risk securities. We propose a hedging strategy aimed at minimising the variance of the insurer's hedged net losses. Such a strategy is consistent with the standard approaches in both the insurance and actuarial literature.[5] The contracts we specify are index linked, so we explicitly analyse their basis risk by conducting three case studies. We use data on the actual county-level exposures of three insurers writing homeowners' insurance in Florida – a national company with a large market share and two regional companies with progressively smaller market shares. We formulate optimal variance hedges for the three case study companies and study the basis risk of the hedges using the hurricane simulation model developed by Applied Insurance Research (AIR), a leading cat modelling firm.[6] The AIR model is used to simulate 10,000 years of hurricane experience in Florida, and the results of the optimal hedges are analysed to measure the degree of basis risk.

Using simulated losses from AIR on the same events for virtually the entire Florida market, we construct industry-wide Florida loss indices to provide triggers for the hedges for the case-study companies. Two types of indices are specified – a state-wide index and four intra-state regional indices. The findings indicate that the large insurer can hedge effectively using either the state-wide or intra-state indices but that the smaller firms must rely on the intra-state indices to achieve acceptable basis risk.[7]

The chapter continues by discussing the most promising cat-loss derivative contracts, the variance hedging strategy, the AIR hurricane model, and the data and empirical techniques used to specify optimal hedges and analyse basis risk.

CATASTROPHIC RISK AND SECURITISATION

In this section we discuss the problem of financing catastrophic loss and explain the role of securitisation in this area. We then provide more details on insurance-linked securities and briefly discuss insurer characteristics hypothesised to be related to hedging efficiency.

The catastrophic loss-financing problem

Both the frequency and the severity of property losses due to natural catastrophes have increased dramatically in recent years. During the period 1970–86, the number of catastrophes averaged about 35 per year. Beginning in 1987, however, the number of catastrophes increased sharply, and from 1990–2001 it exceeded 100 every year (SwissRe, 2002).[8] From 1970–86, insured losses from natural catastrophes exceeded US$5 billion in only one year, and the average catastrophe loss for this period was US$2.6 billion. From 1987–2001, however, insured catastrophe losses exceeded US$8 billion in all but two years, and catastrophe losses averaged US$14.3 billion per year. Since 1986, insurers have paid out US$215 billion in natural catastrophe losses. Although the largest loss, Hurricane Andrew, resulted in only US$18 billion in insured property losses, modelling firms are predicting that losses from a major California Earthquake or Florida Hurricane could exceed US$100 billion. These figures do not include insured losses from man-made catastrophes such as the World Trade Center terrorist attack, which at the time of this writing is expected to cost US$40–70 billion. Financing losses from both natural and man-made catastrophic events is clearly a growing problem affecting both insurance markets and capital markets more generally.

At first glance it might seem that the international insurance and reinsurance markets could easily fund a major property catastrophe. The amount of equity capital in the US property-liability insurance industry is about US$350 billion, and the amount of capital in the international reinsurance market is about US$125 billion. However, most of this capital is committed to backing insurer promises to pay the relatively small, frequent losses covered by the vast majority of insurance and reinsurance policies. Insurance markets are much less efficient in financing large, infrequent events. As a result, the percentage of insured property covered by catastrophe reinsurance is inversely related to the size of the event, and only a small fraction of the property exposure base in hazard-prone US states is covered by catastrophe reinsurance (Swiss Re, 1997 and Froot, 2001). Moreover, reinsurance markets are subject to price and availability cycles, often resulting in price increases and supply restrictions following catastrophic events (Froot, 1998a and Froot and O'Connell, 1999).

Raising additional equity capital in the insurance industry would not be an efficient solution to the cat loss-financing problem because holding capital in an insurer or reinsurer is costly (Jaffee and Russell, 1997). Capital held in insurers is subject to regulatory and agency costs. Tax and accounting rules also penalise insurers for holding capital to cover infrequent (eg, once-in-50-year) events. Informational asymmetries between insurers and capital markets regarding exposure to catastrophic events and the adequacy of loss reserves also increase the cost of holding additional equity. Finally, "excess" capital not currently committed to projects with short or intermediate time horizons is likely to attract corporate raiders (eg, companies with large amounts of cash reserves on their balance sheets may attract hostile takeover bids from investors hoping to use the cash for other purposes).

Securitisation has been developed as a more efficient approach to solving the cat loss-financing problem. Although a US$100 billion catastrophe would amount to about 30% of the equity capital of the US property-liability insurance industry and at least 75% of the equity of the international reinsurance industry, a loss of this magnitude would be less than 0.5% of the value of stocks and bonds traded in US securities markets. Securities markets are also more efficient than insurance markets in reducing information asymmetries and facilitating price discovery. Finally, because natural catastrophes are likely to be zero beta events, cat securities provide a valuable new source of diversification for investors, shifting the efficient investment frontier in a favourable direction (Litzenberger, *et al.*, 1996 and Canter *et al.*, 1997).

Cat options and bonds

To date, the most important cat securities in terms of the amount of risk capital raised have been cat risk bonds. Cat option contracts have also been offered both over-the-counter (OTC) and on the Chicago Board of Trade (CBOT). This section provides the distinguishing features of cat bonds and options and discusses the advantages and disadvantages of each type of contract.

The first catastrophe insurance derivative contracts were introduced by the CBOT, which began listing catastrophic loss futures contracts in 1992. The contracts intended for trading, however, were not the futures themselves but options on the futures. The contracts settled on the basis of an industry-wide loss index compiled by the Insurance Services Office (ISO). The ISO index proved to be unsatisfactory, because it was too highly aggregated and was released infrequently. As a result, the ISO-based contracts were replaced by options that settled on loss indices compiled by Property Claims Services (PCS), an insurance industry statistical agent. Nine indices were available – a national index, five regional indices, and three state indices (for California, Florida and Texas). The indices were based on PCS estimates of catastrophic property losses in the specified geographical areas during quarterly or annual exposure periods.[9] Although the CBOT options are no longer traded due to low trading volume (mainly due to lack of interest in the options by insurers) they represent an important innovation and are likely to provide the model for exchange-traded options that almost certainly will be developed in future years. Over-the-counter options also have been traded, although these usually settle on insurer-specific loss criteria (see Swiss Re, 2001 for further discussion of alternative instruments).

Most cat bonds issued to date have been based on insurer-specific criteria. The structure of a typical cat bond is shown in Figure 1. Capital raised by issuing the bond is invested in safe securities such as Treasury bonds, which are held by a single-purpose reinsurer. This arrangement keeps the transaction off the balance sheet of the issuer and insulates investors from credit risk. The bond issuer holds a call option on the principal in the single-purpose reinsurer with triggering or strike conditions usually expressed in terms of the issuing insurer's losses from a defined catastrophic event. If the defined event occurs, the bond-issuer can withdraw funds from the reinsurer to pay claims, and part or all of the interest and principal payments are forgiven. If the defined catastrophic event does not occur, the investors receive their principal plus interest equal to the risk-free rate plus a risk-premium.

The first successful non-exchange traded capital market product that

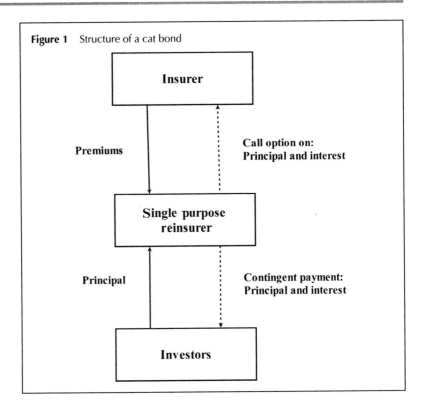

Figure 1 Structure of a cat bond

Insurer

Premiums

Call option on:
Principal and interest

Single purpose
reinsurer

Principal

Contingent payment:
Principal and interest

Investors

insured against catastrophe risk was an US$85 million cat bond issued by Hannover Re in 1994 (Swiss Re, 2001). The first cat bond issued by a non-financial firm, occurring in 1999, covers earthquake losses in the Tokyo region for Oriental Land Company, Ltd., the owner of Tokyo Disneyland. Approximately 60 tranches of cat bonds have been issued since 1993, raising more than US$4 billion in risk capital.

Index-linked cat options and issuer-specific cat bonds can be compared and contrasted in terms of their transaction costs, liquidity, basis risk, and exposure to moral hazard.[10] Cat options are superior to cat bonds in terms of transactions costs. Cat options can be traded inexpensively on an exchange, whereas cat-bond issues are subject to substantially higher transactions costs for legal, investment, auditing and tax advice. Cat options also have the potential to generate a very liquid market due to their standardisation and the anonymity of traders. Although a liquid market in cat bonds can also be envisioned, the bonds issued to date have low market liquidity because they are not standardised and not traded on an exchange.

Index-linked cat options also are superior to issuer-specific cat bonds in terms of exposure to moral hazard. The existence of a cat bond may give an insurer the incentive to relax its underwriting and claims-settlement standards, leading to higher-than-expected losses. Cat options, on the other hand, are relatively free of moral hazard because they settle on industry-wide losses rather than the losses of a specific insurer.[11] The primary advantage of insurer-specific cat bonds over index-linked cat options is that insurer-specific bonds expose the hedger to less basis risk than do the options. The empirical analysis in this chapter is designed to provide information on the degree of basis risk that would be faced by insurers in hedging with index-linked cat-loss securities.

HEDGING STRATEGIES

In this section we present the results of three company-specific case studies based on actual insurers writing homeowners' insurance in Florida. The case studies are designed to illustrate the use of index-linked products in hedging catastrophic risk and to determine the degree of basis risk the insurers would face when hedging with this type of option contract.

We analyse hedges based on a state-wide Florida loss index and four intra-state regional indices. The definitions were provided by Applied Insurance Research based on experience with insurance clients, including analyses conducted in conjunction with the United Services Automobile Insurance (USAA) cat bond issues of 1997–9. The intra-state indices were based on a subdivision of the state into four segments (the Panhandle, Gulf Coast, North Atlantic and South Atlantic). Defining indices on more disaggregated regions such as counties or zip codes would reduce basis risk, but adding more contracts would increase the transactions costs of hedging and potentially reduce market liquidity because the volume of contracts traded in any given region would be smaller than for the more highly aggregated regions. We hypothesised that four regions would be sufficient to enable insurers to hedge effectively without incurring the higher transactions costs and lower liquidity that would result from a finer subdivision of the state.[12]

We consider "buy and hold" hedging strategies covering a single period because this is the standard approach used by insurers when purchasing excess of loss reinsurance contracts and issuing cat bonds.[13] We focus on non-linear hedges where the insurer forms a hedge portfolio comprising a short position in unhedged catastrophe losses and a long position in call option spreads. This approach was adopted because the call option spread is the dominant contractual form in both the cat securities and catastrophe XOL reinsurance markets (see Froot, 1998b and Cummins, Lewis and Phillips, 1999).

Index-hedge effectiveness is measured relative to the performance of "perfect hedges", which pay out on the insurer's own losses. The perfect hedge parallels the results the insurer could attain by purchasing conventional reinsurance contracts or issuing insurer-specific cat bonds, whereas the index hedges are designed to reflect results that could be achieved through trading in index-linked cat options.[14]

Hedge portfolios

The hedging strategies considered here are designed to parallel the structure of XOL reinsurance. The insurer is assumed to form a *hedge portfolio* consisting of a short position in its own unhedged catastrophe losses and a long position in call option spreads on its own losses or on a loss index. Defining insurer j's hedged net loss under loss index i as L_j^i, its net loss under the perfect hedge $(i = P)$ is:

$$L_j^P = L_j - h_j^P [Max(L_j - M_{j'}^P, 0) - Max(L_j - U_{j'}^P, 0)]$$ (1)

where L_j^P is insurer j's hedged loss under the perfect hedge, L_j is insurer j's unhedged loss, h_j^P is the hedge ratio for the perfect hedge, M_j^P is the lower strike price of the call spread, and U_j^P is the upper strike price of the spread.

The perfect hedge is compared to hedges based on loss indices that are not perfectly correlated with the insurer's losses. Insurer j's net loss based on an index consisting of industry-wide, state-level losses is:

$$L_j^S = L_j - h_j^S [Max(L^S - M_{j'}^S, 0) - Max(L^S - U_{j'}^S, 0)]$$ (2)

where L_j^S is insurer j's hedged loss using an industry-wide, state-level loss index, h_j^S is the hedge ratio for the state-level hedge, L^S is $\Sigma_j L_j$, the state-wide losses for the industry, and M_j^S and U_j^S are the lower and upper strike prices for company j's state-level call spread.

Insurer j's hedged loss under the intra-state regional hedge is:

$$L_j^R = \sum_{r=1}^{R} \left[L_{jr} - h_{jr}^R [Max(L_r^R - M_{jr'}^R, 0) - Max(L_r^R - U_{jr'}^R, 0)] \right]$$ (3)

where L_j^R is company j's losses under the intra-state regional hedge, L_{jr} is the unhedged losses of insurer j in region r, h_{jr}^R is hedge ratio for insurer j in region r, L_r^R is industry-wide losses in region r, M_{jr}^R is lower strike price for company j's region r call option spread, U_{jr}^R is upper strike price for company j's region r call spread, and R is the number of regions (R = 4 in our analysis).

Hedging objective

The insurer is assumed to construct the hedge with the objective of minimising a function of L_j^i subject to a cost constraint. Defining the objective function for criterion m as $G_m(L_j^i)$, the optimisation problem using a state-wide hedge, for example, is given as:

Minimise: $G_m(L_j^S)$

$\{h_j^S, M_j^S, U_j^S\}$ (4)

Subject to: $h_j^S[W(L^S, M_j^S) - W(L^S, U_j^S)] \leq C_j$

where C_j is the maximum amount available to insurer j to spend on hedging, $W(L^S, M_j^S)$ and $W(L^S, U_j^S)$ are the prices of call options on industry losses L^S with strike prices M_j^S and U_j^S, respectively.

Thus, the insurer optimises over the hedge ratio and the two strike prices, M_j^S and U_j^S, subject to spending a maximum of C_j on hedging.

The optimisation problem for the perfect hedge is defined similarly. The optimisation problem for the regional hedge is also analogous to Equation (4) except that there are 12 decision variables – four hedge ratios and four sets of lower and upper strike prices. By varying C_j, it is possible to generate an efficient frontier based on each optimisation criterion and loss index.

The hedging strategy we adopt is the minimisation of the variance of the hedged net losses.[15] The variance reduction criterion gives rise to the objective function: $G_1(L_j^i) = \sigma^2[L_j^i(h_j^i, M_j^i, U_j^i)]$, which is the variance of the insurer j's loss net of the payoff on the call option spread using loss index i, where i = P for the perfect hedge, S for the state-wide industry hedge and R for the intra-state regional hedge, where the latter is a function of 12, rather than three, variables.

Hedge efficiency

For each loss index i, we define "hedge effectiveness" as the proportionate reduction in the unhedged value of the criterion function. We denote the hedge effectiveness measure for insurer j based on loss index i as HE_j^i. Under the variance criterion function, for example, the hedge effectiveness of the state-wide index for insurer j is:

$$HE_j^S = 1 - \frac{\sigma^2[L_j^S(h_j^S, M_j^S, U_j^S)]}{\sigma_j^2[L_j]} \qquad (5)$$

Another useful indicator of hedge performance is "hedge efficiency", defined as the hedging effectiveness of the index hedge relative to that of the perfect hedge, ie

$$RHE_j^i = \frac{HE_j^i}{HE_j^P} \qquad (6)$$

where i, being equal to S, is the state-wide hedge and i, being equal to R, is the regional hedge.

Thus, whereas hedge effectiveness provides an absolute measure of hedge performance, hedge efficiency measures hedge performance relative to that of the perfect hedge and thus provides a better measure of the degree of basis risk than hedge effectiveness.

EMPIRICAL METHODOLOGY

This section discusses the catastrophe exposure database used in our modelling exercises as well as the AIR hurricane simulation model. The section concludes with a discussion of the methodology used to solve the optimisation problems to obtain the hedge ratios and strike prices.

The Florida residential property exposure data

The database for the study consists of county-level data, obtained from the Florida Insurance Commissioner, on insured residential property values for 255 of the 264 insurers writing property coverage in Florida in 1998.[16] The insurers in the sample account for 93% of the total insured residential property values in the state. Thus, the results can be interpreted as representative of the entire insurance industry. The exposure data provide the basis for our case studies of three Florida insurers. We also use AIR simulations for the same events over the entire database to construct the state-wide and regional loss indices that provide the triggers for the option hedges.

Catastrophe loss simulations

The simulated catastrophic losses for our sample of insurers are generated using the hurricane model developed by AIR. This section provides a brief description of the model. Further details about the model are provided in Applied Insurance Research (1999).

The hurricane loss estimation methodology employed by AIR is based on well-established scientific theory in meteorology and wind engineering. The simulation models were developed through careful analyses and synthesis of all available historical information and incorporate statistical descriptions of a large number of variables that define both the originating event (eg, a hurricane) and its effect on insured structures. The AIR hurricane model has been used by the insurance industry since 1987 and is well known for its reliability and the credibility of the loss estimates it generates. The AIR model was the first to meet the standards of the Florida Insurance Commission on Hurricane Loss Projection Methodology.

The structure of the simulation model is summarised in Figure 2. The process begins with a Monte Carlo simulation of the number of storms per year for a 10,000-year simulation period, generating more than 18,000 simulated events. The landfall and meteorological characteristics are then simulated for each storm, where the meteorological characteristics include central barometric pressure, radius of maximum winds, forward speed, storm direction, and storm track. Once the model generates the storm characteristics and point of landfall it propagates the simulated storm along a path characterised by the track direction and forward speed. In order to estimate the property losses resulting from the simulated storms, the AIR model generates the complete time profile of wind speeds, or windfield, at each location affected by the storm.

After the model estimates peak wind speeds and the time profile of wind speeds for each location, it generates damage estimates for different types of property exposures by combining data on insured property values and structure characteristics with wind speed information at each location affected by the event. To estimate building damage and the associated losses, the AIR hurricane model uses damageability relationships, or

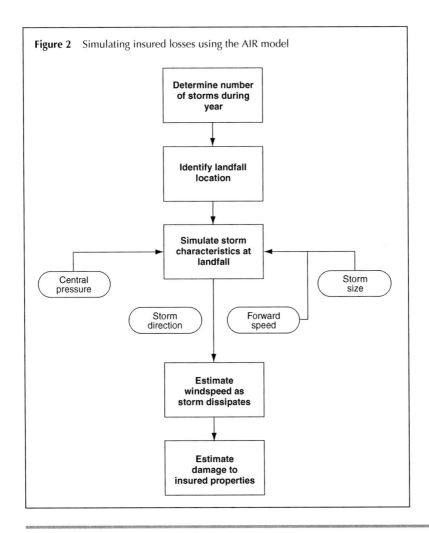

Figure 2   Simulating insured losses using the AIR model

damage functions that have been developed by AIR engineers for a large number of building construction and occupancy classes. In the last component of the catastrophe model, insured losses are calculated by applying the policy conditions to the total damage estimates. Policy conditions include deductibles, coverage limits, coinsurance provisions and a number of other factors.

A fundamental component of the model is AIR's insured property database. AIR has developed databases of estimated numbers, types, and values of properties for residential, commercial, mobile home, and automobile insured values in the US by five-digit postal (zip) codes. These databases have been constructed from a wide range of data sources and reflect the estimated total replacement cost of US property exposures. In the present study, AIR's zip-code level data on insured property values for companies doing business in Florida were used in the simulations and aggregated to the county level using information supplied by the Florida Insurance Department to protect the confidentiality of AIR's databases.

Estimating hedge ratios and strike prices

We adopt a two-stage estimation strategy to solve the optimisation problems defined in Equation (4). In the first stage, we solve the optimisation problems using a "differential evolutionary genetic algorithm" (Goldberg, 1989). Genetic algorithms provide a robust search procedure to solve difficult non-linear or non-smooth optimisation problems (Goldberg, 1989 and Pinter, 1996). The method was adopted because standard optimisation algorithms were not adequate to find global optimums for many of the companies in the Florida sample. Although global optimisation algorithms such as the differential genetic algorithm are superior to conventional methods in extensively exploring the space of possible solutions, they are not necessarily as efficient as conventional methods at finding an optimal solution once the region where the global optimum is located has been identified (Pinter, 1996). Accordingly, the second stage of our estimation methodology was to use the solution results from the genetic algorithm as starting values for a calculus-based optimisation using the Newton–Raphson algorithm.[17]

Constructing the cat-loss indices

As mentioned above, 10,000 years of hurricane experience were simulated for each firm in the Florida sample. The simulations produce the variables L_{jkrt} = hurricane losses for company j, in county k, located in intra-state region r, for simulation year t, where $_j = 1, ..., 255, k = 1, ..., 67, r = 1, ..., 4,$ and $t = 1, ..., 10,000$.

The simulated losses are then used to construct the following loss indices:

$$\text{The "Perfect" Index:} \qquad L_{j..t}^{P} = \sum_{r=1}^{R}\sum_{k=1}^{Kr} L_{jkrt} \qquad\qquad (7)$$

$$\text{The Regional Indicies:} \qquad L_{..rt}^{R} = \sum_{j=1}^{N}\sum_{k=1}^{Kr} L_{jkrt} \qquad\qquad (8)$$

$$\text{The State Index:} \qquad L_{t}^{S} = L_{..t}^{S} = \sum_{r=1}^{R}\sum_{j=1}^{N}\sum_{k=1}^{Kr} L_{jkrt} \qquad\qquad (9)$$

where, N = the number of insurers (255), R = the number of regions (4), Kr = the number of counties in region r and a dot in place of a subscript means that a summation has been taken over that subscript.

Hedge portfolios are formed for each insurer to determine the hedge efficiency of the index hedges.

CASE STUDIES: HEDGING THE RISK OF FLORIDA HURRICANE LOSSES

Three Florida homeowners' insurers were selected for the case studies of index-hedge effectiveness. This section discusses factors expected to be related to hedge effectiveness, describes the characteristics of the companies, and then reports on their ability to hedge catastrophic risk using index-linked contracts.

Factors related to hedge effectiveness

The first factor often mentioned as a determinant of the ability of an insurer to hedge using index-linked products is firm size, either in terms of raw exposures or market share. The hypothesis is that firms with high state-wide market shares need to have exposures in nearly all areas of the state in order to attain a large scale of operations. Such firms are expected to have a significant effect on the industry-wide loss indices and, therefore, relatively low basis risk. A second factor often linked with hedge effectiveness is diversification across the state. The argument is that it is not size *per se* but rather diversification that determines a firm's ability to hedge using index-linked contracts. A more subtle version of this argument is that firms need good state-wide diversification to hedge with state loss indices but only need to have adequate diversification within one or more of the intrastate regions in order to hedge effectively with the regional loss indices. The analysis presented below provides information on the relative importance of size and diversification in determining hedge effectiveness.

The case-study companies

Company A is a large national personal lines insurer that is near the top of the first (largest) size quartile in terms of the total property value exposed to loss in Florida. Company B is a Florida-domiciled insurer near the bottom of the first size quartile. It advertises itself as being "committed to Florida home and business owners". This company is included because it is relatively small for a first-quartile firm but is a firm that targets Florida homeowners' insurance as one of its core lines of business. Company C is a much smaller firm, near the bottom of the second largest size quartile in terms of homeowners' property value exposed to loss in Florida. This company is included to determine whether smaller insurers that have better than average diversification for their size classes are able to hedge effectively using index-linked contracts. Keeping in mind that the firms in the two largest size quartiles account for about 99% of the total exposures in Florida, the firms in the study should provide an indication of the possible hedging effectiveness of firms representing a very high proportion of the total property values exposed to loss in the state.

Summary statistics on the case study companies relative to averages for the four Florida-size quartiles are shown in Table 1. The quartiles are based on the value of property exposed to loss in Florida, with quartile one being the largest and quartile four the smallest. Table 1 also shows the approximate percentages of total state exposures written by each of the case study companies. Company A is in the 5% market-share range, company B is in the 1% range, and company C is much smaller, writing less than 0.1% of total state exposures. Thus, the case-study firms are representative in size of firms in all size ranges except the lowest quartile of insurers.

Columns four and five of Table 1 show that the case study companies are generally more diversified than the average firms in their respective size groups. These two columns show the market share coefficients of variation and Herfindahl indices. Both statistics are based on the distribution of an insurer's percentage exposures by county. The coefficient of variation is the ratio of the standard deviation of the insurer's exposures across the Florida counties divided by the average percentage exposure across counties.

Table 1 Summary statistics: case study companies vs quartile averages

Company	Quartile	State exposures* (%)	County MS CoV	County MS Herfindahl	Expos in ocean-front counties (%)	No. of counties w/expo
Company A	1	5.00	0.363	434	71.4	67
Company B	1	1.00	1.320	895	92.1	65
Company C	2	0.10	1.759	876	43.6	53
Quartile 1		94.7	1.36	836	70.1	58.3
Quartile 2		4.4	2.20	1,262	71.4	44.2
Quartile 3		0.8	3.35	2,399	70.1	29.2
Quartile 4		0.1	5.38	4,479	73.6	12.5

* Approximate percentages

Thus, a low coefficient of variation means that the insurer is highly diversified. The market share Herfindahl index is the sum of the squares of the insurer's county market share percentages. An index of 10,000 would mean that the company had all of its business in one county, and smaller values of the Herfindahl index imply higher levels of diversification. By both measures, companies A, B and C have superior diversification relative to the average insurer in the respective size quartiles (quartile one for companies A and B and quartile two for company C). These companies also have non-zero exposures in a higher proportion of Florida counties than the average firm in their respective size quartiles. The only instance in which a case study company is less diversified than average is for company B, when the measure of diversification is the proportion of business written in ocean-front counties – company B has 92.1% of its exposures in ocean-front counties compared to 70.1% for the average firm in quartile one. Thus, the case study companies are representative of insurers that are likely to be able to hedge more effectively than average rather than representing a random sample of the companies doing business in the state. We comment briefly on how other firms could improve their hedging effectiveness after presenting the results for the case study firms.

Further information on the exposure distribution of the case study companies is provided in Figures 3–5, which show the distribution of company exposures and county market shares of companies A–C, respectively. Company A has a substantial market share in all but a few counties. However, it is clear that its exposures are concentrated in a few counties, many of them with ocean-front exposure. Nevertheless, the fact that company A has significant market penetration throughout the state suggests that it may be able to hedge effectively, even with state-wide hedging instruments. Company B, by contrast, has significant market shares in only about five counties but has at least some of its exposures in nearly every county in the state. Its heaviest concentration of exposures is located along the Gulf Coast, which generally experiences less costly catastrophes than the South Atlantic region. This company has exposure characteristics that may lend themselves to effective hedging using regional contracts. Company C is in a similar position. It has significant market penetration in about six counties and has no exposure in 14 counties. Likewise, its distribution of exposures is not significantly diversified across that state, being heavily concentrated in several central-Florida counties. The prediction based on the market share and exposure maps is that company C probably cannot hedge very effectively with state-wide contracts but may be able to hedge effectively using regional contracts.

Optimal hedges and hedging effectiveness
As discussed above, we solved the variance minimisation problems in Equation (4) for each of the case study companies using options triggered

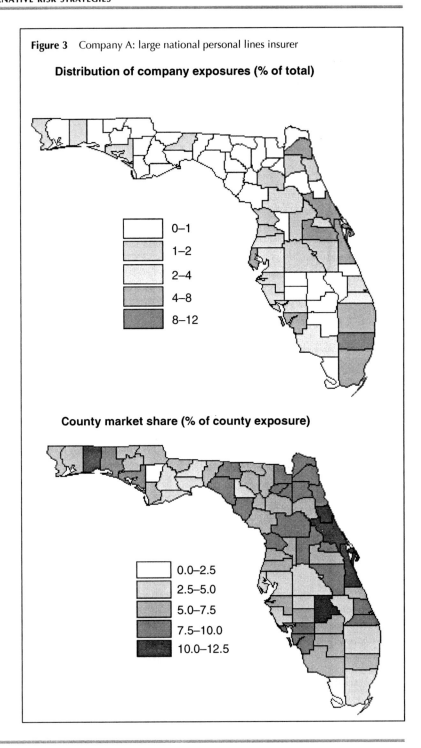

Figure 3 Company A: large national personal lines insurer

Distribution of company exposures (% of total)

Legend:
- 0–1
- 1–2
- 2–4
- 4–8
- 8–12

County market share (% of county exposure)

Legend:
- 0.0–2.5
- 2.5–5.0
- 5.0–7.5
- 7.5–10.0
- 10.0–12.5

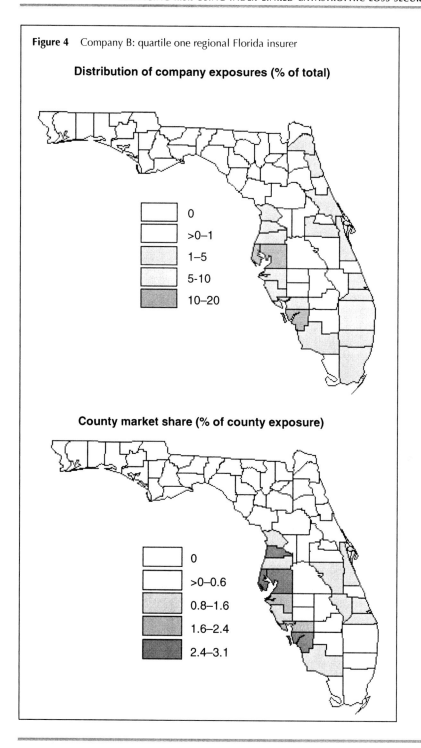

Figure 4 Company B: quartile one regional Florida insurer

Distribution of company exposures (% of total)

0
>0–1
1–5
5-10
10–20

County market share (% of county exposure)

0
>0–0.6
0.8–1.6
1.6–2.4
2.4–3.1

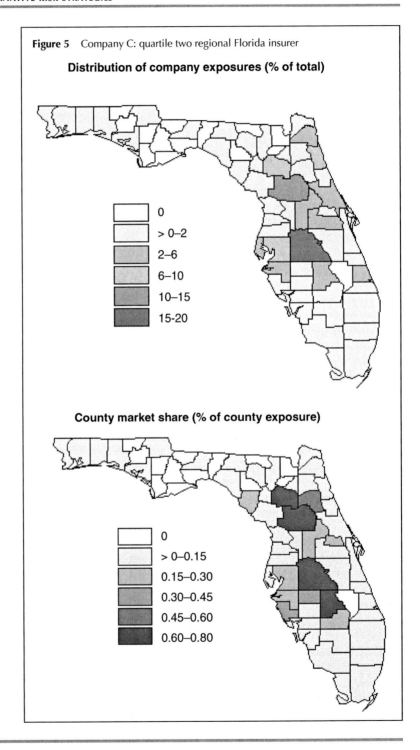

Figure 5 Company C: quartile two regional Florida insurer

Distribution of company exposures (% of total)

0
> 0–2
2–6
6–10
10–15
15-20

County market share (% of county exposure)

0
> 0–0.15
0.15–0.30
0.30–0.45
0.45–0.60
0.60–0.80

by the state-wide and the regional indices (as alternatives). The standard of comparison for the index-linked contracts is the "perfect hedge", which pays out on the insurer's own losses. The perfect hedge parallels the results that the insurer could attain by purchasing conventional reinsurance contracts or issuing insurer-specific cat bonds, whereas the index hedges are designed to reflect results that could be achieved through trading in index-linked cat options.

Prior to discussing hedging effectiveness, it is useful to provide some information on the characteristics of the hedges. Recall that the variance minimisation problems are solved subject to cost constraints, ranging in 5% intervals based on the insurers' expected losses. The problems were initially solved with the assumption that each insurer spends 5% of its expected losses on hedging, and then the cost constraint was relaxed by 5% and the problem solved again, up to a maximum of 50% of expected losses spent on hedging. It is probably unrealistic to assume that an insurer would spend as much as 50% of its expected losses on hedging, but these results were included to show a wide range of potential hedging opportunities.

As an example of hedging strategies, we consider insurer A's optimal hedge positions using the regional contracts at the 20% cost-constraint level. This insurer had *no* hedging expenditures allocated to reducing catastrophe risk in the Florida Panhandle, a result that was consistent for all levels of the cost constraint. This reflects the fact that company A has relatively low exposure to loss in the Panhandle (Figure 3) and also that this region of Florida experiences relatively low losses from hurricanes in comparison with the other three regions. The hedging expenditures were allocated as follows: 15.8% to the North Atlantic region, 21.9% to the Gulf Coast region, and 62.3% to the South Atlantic region. This again is consistent with the insurer's relative exposures across the regions (its highest exposure is in the South Atlantic) as well as the relative hurricane risk in the regions.

Insurer A's lower strike price in the South Atlantic region for the 20% cost constraint was equivalent to an industry-wide loss of US$9.4 billion, indicating that most of its hedging expenditures are directed at hedging large loss events in the region where its property exposure base is highest and where the hurricane risk is also highest. The upper strike price is close to the maximum probable industry loss for the region, indicating that the solution is "virtually full hedging over a large deductible". This outcome is consistent with the economic theory of insurance, which finds that hedging large losses with non-linear contracts has the greatest impact in terms of reducing the firm's risk (Froot, 2001).

Insurer A's hedge ratio in the South Atlantic region is 3.2%. This implies that it would receive 3.2% of the difference between the industry-wide loss in the South Atlantic and the lower strike price for that region, if the South

Atlantic industry loss is above the strike. For example, for an industry-wide loss of US$12 billion, company A would receive about US$88.5 million (recall that the strike price for this contract is US$9.4 billion). The strike prices are generally less and the hedge ratios somewhat larger for company A in the North Atlantic and Gulf Coast regions, reflecting the lower probabilities of large events in these regions. That is, there is a trade-off between the event threshold and event probability such that the marginal reduction in the firm's variance per dollar spent on hedging implies lower strike prices in regions where the chance of extreme events is relatively low.

The striking prices and hedge ratios change in predictable ways as the cost constraints are gradually relaxed. For example, in each region, the lower strike price declines monotonically as the cost constraint increases. The hedge ratio does not vary systematically as the cost constraint declines, but generally fluctuates within a relatively narrow band. For example, in the South Atlantic region, company A's hedge ratio is between 2.9% and 3.3% for nine of the 10 cost constraints (it is 4.4% for the lowest cost constraint). The upper strike price also remains relatively constant as a function of the cost constraint, generally at a level in the neighbourhood of the maximum probable loss in a specific region. Thus, the hedges adhere closely to the economically optimal ideal of "full insurance above a deductible", with the deductible (strike price) being the primary instrument used by the solution algorithm in finding the optimal hedge.

Hedging effectiveness is shown in Figures 6–8, for companies A, B, and C, respectively. The figures show variance reduction frontiers, which plot

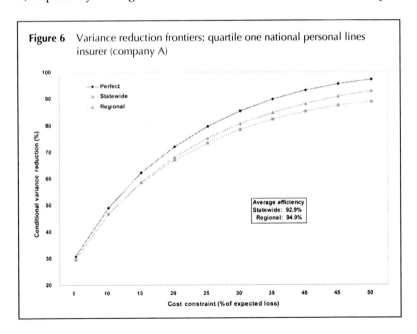

Figure 6   Variance reduction frontiers: quartile one national personal lines insurer (company A)

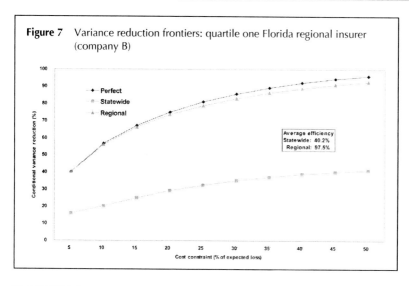

Figure 7 Variance reduction frontiers: quartile one Florida regional insurer (company B)

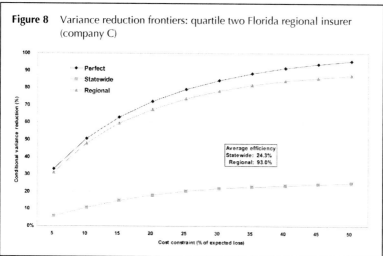

Figure 8 Variance reduction frontiers: quartile two Florida regional insurer (company C)

the percentage reduction in the firms' net loss variance (vertical axis) as a function of the amount spent on hedging (horizontal axis). Three frontiers are shown on each chart, for contracts paying off on the perfect hedge (the firm's own losses), the state-wide loss index, and the regional loss indices. The average efficiencies (the variance reduction with the index hedges ratioed to the variance reduction with the perfect hedges) are more or less constant across cost constraints. Consequently, we show the average efficiency across all 10 cost constraints in a display box on each chart.

Focusing first on company A, we see that there are diminishing marginal returns to hedging – the variance reduction frontiers are increasing and concave in hedge expenditures. It is also clear that company A can hedge effectively using either the state-wide or regional indices. For example, at the 20% cost constraint, insurer A can reduce its variance by 72% using the perfect hedge, 68.2% using the regional hedge, and 67% using the state-wide hedge. The distance between the hedging curves increases with the amounts spent on hedging. At the 35% expenditure level, variance is reduced by 85.4% using the perfect hedge, 80.5% using the regional index contracts, and 78.4% using the state-wide index contracts. The average efficiency statistics show that the state-wide index contracts would reduce company A's variance by 94.9% in comparison with the perfect hedge, and the comparable efficiency statistic for the state-wide hedge in 92.9%.

Whether the reductions in variance based on the index contracts are in some sense "sufficient" to motivate the use of index-linked contracts rather than company-specific contracts is a value judgement in the absence of any additional information on the market value of hedging using alternative objectives. However, although insurers are accustomed to thinking of hedges as "perfect" in the sense of reinsurance, which has low basis risk, the reduction, rather than elimination, of risk is typically the objective in more general hedging contexts. Thus, if transaction costs and pricing were sufficiently attractive in the market for insurance-linked securities, hedging with 95% efficiency might ultimately be viewed as an attractive alternative to hedging with 100% efficiency through more expensive reinsurance contracts, especially keeping in mind that reinsurance is not really perfect due to credit risk, reinsurance cycles and other factors.

Figures 7 and 8 show the variance-reduction frontiers for companies B and C. The figures show that neither of these companies can hedge effectively using state-wide index contracts. Even with 50% of expected losses devoted to hedging, the variance reduction is less than 45% for both firms, in comparison to more than 90% for the perfect hedge contracts. The hedging efficiencies of the state index hedges in comparison with the perfect hedge are only 40.2% and 24.3% for companies B and C, respectively. These results are not surprising given the exposure and market-share mappings for the two firms shown in Figures 4 and 5 and provide an indication that concern about the basis risk of the CBOT option contracts was well founded, at least for some insurers.

State-wide contracts are not a solution to the cat risk problem for companies B and C, but Figures 7 and 8 also show that regional hedging contracts are likely to be viable for these firms. This is particularly noteworthy for company B, where the regional contracts are 97.5% as efficient on average as the perfect hedge contracts. The average efficiency for company C also is quite respectable – 93%. These results are reasonably predictable given the exposure mappings shown in Figures 4 and 5.

The results suggest two important conclusions about smaller firms in Florida:

1. Regional index-linked contracts may be a viable hedging alternative for many smaller firms, suggesting the possibility that a liquid market in regional Florida contracts might be foreseeable.
2. Smaller firms can manage risk more effectively if they pay more attention to their exposure diversification across the state. A significant proportion of the smaller Florida homeowners' insurers are less diversified than insurers B and C and hence could improve their performance and the efficiency of potential hedging solutions by better exposure management, either through underwriting strategies or through pooling arrangements with other small firms.

The results also have implications regarding the relative importance of size and exposure diversification as determinants of hedging effectiveness. The results with company A suggests that size plays a role in enabling firms to hedge effectively using the state-wide contract because it is important to have significant market penetration in all regions of the state in order for the firm's losses to be highly correlated with the industry-wide index. A smaller firm could achieve reasonably high correlation with the state-wide index through careful diversification but such firms are much less important in determining the value of the index and thus will always be at a disadvantage. The results also suggest that diversification within regions is sufficient to hedge effectively with the regional indices – size conveys less of an advantage when the regional contracts are considered.

CONCLUSION

The securities market has responded to the dramatic increase in catastrophe losses since the mid-1980s by developing innovative new derivative securities. The introduction of insurance-linked securities has also been driven by the increasing recognition that conventional insurance and reinsurance markets do not provide efficient mechanisms for financing losses from low-frequency, high-severity events. The two most promising types of cat securities are cat bonds and options. Cat securities can be designed to pay out on three principal type of triggers – company-specific losses, industry-wide aggregate-loss indices and parametric indices relating to a physical measure of the severity of the catastrophe. Most cat bonds issued to date have been based on issuer-specific triggering criteria, whereas the CBOT option contracts and a few bond issues have been based on industry-wide loss triggers.

Index-linked cat-risk securities are superior to issuer-specific contracts because they are more easily standardised, providing the potential for a much more liquid market than is likely to exist for issuer-tailored contracts. Moreover, exchange-traded contracts have lower transaction costs than OTC cat securities and have lower counterparty risk due to the clearance of transactions through the exchange. The principal advantage of issuer-specific contracts over index-linked contracts is that the former have lower basis risk.

In our hedging analysis, we formed portfolios consisting of a short position in the insurer's unhedged losses and a long position in call option spreads on loss indices. Three indices were analysed – a "perfect" index consisting of the insurer's own losses, a state-wide industry loss index, and four intra-state regional industry loss indices obtained by dividing the state into four quadrants. The hedging criterion analysed was the minimisation of the variance of the insurer's hedged net losses. We measured hedging effectiveness by comparing hedges based on the state-wide and intra-state indices with perfect hedges based on each insurer's own losses, and defined hedge efficiency as the ratio of the risk reduction obtained using industry loss index options to the risk reduction obtained using the perfect index.

The principal findings of the study were:

❑ Florida insurers can hedge effectively using contracts based on regional loss indices. As few as four contracts have the potential to generate a liquid market in index-linked cat securities. The results thus suggest that it is not necessary to have contracts based on smaller geographical areas such as zip codes in order for insurers to construct effective hedges.[15]
❑ Hedging through contracts based on state-wide indices is likely to be effective only for relatively large insurers and/or well-diversified smaller insurers in the top two Florida size quartiles. The majority of firms will require sub-state contracts in order to hedge effectively. Nevertheless, the results suggest that a high proportion of the total exposures in Florida could be hedged effectively using index-linked contracts due to the high skewness of the size distribution of Florida insurers.

Three insurers were analysed, with market shares of approximately 5%, 1%, and 0.1% respectively. The firms chosen for the analysis were each relatively well-diversified in comparison to the average insurers in their respective size quadrants. Hence, the results show that even relatively small insurers can hedge effectively using regional contracts, provided that their exposures are reasonably diversified within the Florida regions. An important implication of this findings is that many Florida insurers could reduce their exposure to catastrophic risk and put themselves in a better position to hedge using index-linked derivative contracts if they were to practice better exposure management either through their underwriting decisions or through pooling arrangements with other small insurers.

Overall, our analysis suggests that insurance-linked securities based on exchange-traded, index-linked contracts could be used effectively by insurers in hedging catastrophic risk. This is important given the inefficiency of the global reinsurance market in dealing with this type of loss. In order for a liquid market in index-linked derivatives to develop, however, a number of obstacles would have to be overcome. These include:

❏ Better indices of catastrophe losses need to be developed. The development of index-linked catastrophic loss securities has so far been significantly impeded by the lack of suitable indices. Development and maintenance of cat-loss indices might be an appropriate facilitating role for the federal government, by analogy with the provision of temperature readings by the National Weather Service. This would involve setting up electronic reporting services whereby insurers could rapidly and inexpensively report their catastrophe loss experience to a central source, which would release damage estimates on intra-state regional losses within every major state subject to catastrophe exposures.

❏ A second factor needed for the development of the index-linked market is the education of insurance company management. Managers are accustomed to thinking in terms of reinsurance contracts, which have limited basis risk but are also characterised by low liquidity and exposure to the vagaries of the reinsurance underwriting cycle. A change in institutional thinking of the type that has taken place over the past two decades in terms of corporate finance will be needed to acclimatise insurance company managers to more sophisticated risk management strategies.

❏ The final important factor is the need for development of better pricing models for cat-loss derivatives. The existence of the Black–Scholes model was one of the primary driving forces behind the rapid development of options markets during the 1970s, and models have already been proposed that extend conventional option-pricing models to price other new securities. Pricing cat options is more difficult, however, precisely because these options protect against low-frequency, high-severity events. These event characteristics imply that "jump risk" is more important in pricing cat options than in pricing most other types of derivatives and also that the experience data available to test and calibrate the models are very sparse. The lack of a widely accepted pricing model also may be partly responsible for the high spread premiums characterising most cat risk contracts issued to date. Thus, the development of a pricing model that would solve the cat security-pricing problem would constitute an invaluable contribution to both the academic and practical finance literature.

1 On reinsurance market capacity, see Swiss Re (1997), Cummins and Weiss (2000) and Froot (2001). The "Big One" projection is based on unpublished data from Applied Insurance Research, Boston.

2 Underwriting cycles refer to alternating periods of "hard" and "soft" markets for insurance and reinsurance. During a soft market, prices are relatively low and coverage is readily

available, whereas during a hard market prices are relatively high and coverage supply is restricted (Cummins and Danzon 1997, Cummins and Weiss 2000).

3 Zero beta events are uncorrelated with securities markets. Although it is true historically that the property catastrophes observed in the United States have been "zero beta" from 1949 to the late 1990s, this does not necessarily mean that larger events such as the fabled "Big One" would have no systematic economic impact. Nevertheless, even if cat losses do have positive betas, they are still likely to be valuable for diversification because they securitise economic events that were previously untraded in securities markets.

4 In fact, the perception among insurers that cat index securities are subject to unacceptable levels of basis risk has been identified as the primary obstacle to the more rapid development of the cat-loss securities market (American Academy of Actuaries, 1999).

5 Cummins, Lalonde, and Phillips (2002).

6 The AIR model has been widely used by insurers and reinsurers since 1987 in monitoring their exposure to catastrophic losses and developing underwriting strategies and was the first model to meet the standards of the Florida Insurance Commission on Hurricane Loss Projection Methodology.

7 There have been three previous empirical studies of the basis risk of insurance-linked securities. Harrington and Niehaus (1999) conduct a time-series analysis of the correlation between state-specific loss ratios for a sample of insurers and the PCS cat-loss index and find that PCS derivatives would have provided effective hedges for many homeowners' insurers. Major (1999) conducts a simulation analysis of insurer cat losses based on insurer exposures in Florida and finds that hedging with a state-wide cat index is subject to substantial basis risk. Cummins, Lalonde, and Phillips (2002) analyse hedge efficiency for 255 of the 264 insurers writing homeowners' insurance in Florida and find that most insurers in the top three Florida-size quartiles could hedge effectively using regional loss indices. Unlike the present study, Cummins, Lalonde, and Phillips (2002) does not focus on conducting case studies of specific insurers.

8 These figures are based on the definition of a catastrophe devised by SwissRe. Swiss Re defines losses as catastrophic if they exceed specified dollar valued thresholds that vary by type of catastrophe. For insured property catastrophes other than marine and aviation, Swiss Re defines a catastrophe for 2001 as an event causing at least US$35.1 million in insured property loss (see Swiss Re 2002).

9 The indices were defined as the total accumulated losses divided by US$100 million. For example, a 20/40 Eastern call spread would be in-the-money for a catastrophic loss accumulation in the Eastern region of more than US$2 billion (20 index points). Each index point was worth US$200 on settlement so that one 20/40 call would pay a maximum of US$4,000 (20 points × US$200 per point).

10 Although standardised, exchange-traded cat bonds can certainly be envisioned, this discussion contrasts options with the issuer-specific bonds that have dominated the cat securities market to date.

11 Index-linked options are not totally free of moral hazard problems because large insurers may have the ability to manipulate the index by over-reporting losses to the statistical agent. However, because concentration in insurance markets is relatively low, over-reporting by a large insurer would be significantly diluted at the index level, unlike over-reporting on an insurer-specific instrument; and auditing procedures could be implemented to reduce the probability of successful "cheating".

12 A 1998 attempt to launch zip-code level index contracts (on the Bermuda Commodity Exchange) failed to generate interest among insurers and investors and is currently dormant. Chookaszian and Ward (1998) discuss the proposed indices.

13 Under a buy-and-hold strategy, insurers establish hedges covering fixed periods and are assumed not to close out or modify the hedges prior to the end of the fixed period covered by the hedge.

14 In reality, reinsurance hedges are not really "perfect", so this term is used primarily for convenience. Purchasing reinsurance exposes the buyer to the credit risk of the reinsurer as well as supply and price fluctuations due to the reinsurance underwriting cycle. Moreover, reinsurance contracts usually have cost-sharing provisions to mitigate moral hazard problems and have geographical and other limitations that mean reinsurance collections less than fully indemnify the ceding company.

15 Other strategies, including VAR reduction, have received considerable attention in the literature as hedging criteria (eg, Ahn, *et al.*, 1999). For further discussion of other hedging criteria in the context of index-linked cat risk hedging see Cummins, Lalonde, and Phillips (2002).

16 Data on the nine omitted insurers were not available from the Florida Insurance Commissioner.

17 For further discussion of estimation, see Cummins, Lalonde, and Phillips (2002).

BIBLIOGRAPHY

Ahn, D., J. Boudoukh, M. Richardson, R. and Whitelaw, 1999, "Optimal Risk Management Using Options", *Journal of Finance*, 54, pp. 359–75.

American Academy of Actuaries, 1999, "Evaluating the Effectiveness of Index-Based Insurance Derivatives in Hedging Property/Casualty Insurance Transactions", Report of the Index Securitization Task Force, Washington DC.

Applied Insurance Research, 1999, "AIR Tropical Cyclone Model: United States Region", Technical Document TCUS 9904, AIR, Boston.

Canter, M., J. B. Cole, and R. L. Sandor, 1997, "Insurance Derivatives: A New Asset Class for the Capital Markets and a New Hedging Tool for the Insurance Industry", *Journal of Applied Corporate Finance*, 10(3), pp. 69–83.

Chookaszian, J., and T. Ward, 1998, "Risk Securitization Products on the Rise", *National Underwriter (Property and Casualty/Risk and Benefits Management)*, 102(20), pp. 9, 23.

Cummins, J., and P. Danzon, 1997, "Price Shocks and Capital Flows in Liability Insurance," *Journal of Financial Intermediation*, 6 , pp. 3–38.

Cummins, J. D., D. Lalonde and R. D. Phillips, 2002, *The Basis Risk of Index-Linked CAT Loss Securities*, Working Paper, Wharton Financial Institutions Center, Philadelphia.

Cummins, J. D., C. M. Lewis, and R.D. Phillips, 1999, "Pricing Excess of Loss Reinsurance Against Catastrophic Loss", in: K. A. Froot (ed.) *The Financing of Catastrophe Risk*, (University of Chicago Press).

Cummins, J. D. and M. A. Weiss, 2000, "The Global Market for Reinsurance: Consolidation, Capacity, and Efficiency", Brookings-Wharton Papers on Financial Services.

Doherty, N. A., 1997, "Financial Innovation in the Management of Catastrophe Risk", *Journal of Applied Corporate Finance*, 10, pp. 84–95.

Froot, K. A., 1998a, *The Evolving Market for Catastrophic Event Risk*, (New York: Marsh & McLennan Securities).

Froot, K. A., 1998b, "Mid Ocean Limited – Trading Catastrophe Index Options", Harvard Business School Case 9-278-073, (Boston: Harvard Business School Publishing).

Froot, K. A., 2001, "The Market for Catastrophe Risk: A Clinical Examination", *Journal of Financial Economics*, 60, pp. 529–71.

Froot K. A. and P. J. G. O'Connell, 1999, "The Pricing of U.S. Catastrophe Reinsurance", in: K. Froot (ed.) *The Financing of Catastrophe Risk*, (University of Chicago Press).

Goldberg, D. E., 1989, *Genetic Algorithms in Search, Optimization and Machine Learning*, (Reading: Addison-Wesley).

Harrington, S. E. and G. Niehaus, 1999, "Basis Risk with PCS Catastrophe Insurance Derivative Contracts", *Journal of Risk and Insurance*, 66, pp. 49–82.

Jaffee, D. M. and T. Russell, 1997, "Catastrophe Insurance, Capital Markets, and Uninsurable Risks", *Journal of Risk and Insurance*, 64, pp. 205–30.

Litzenberger, R. H., D. R. Beaglehole, and C. E. Reynolds, 1996, "Assessing Catastrophe Reinsurance-linked Securities as a New Asset Class", *Journal of Portfolio Management*, December, pp. 76–86.

Major, J. A., 1999, "Index Hedge Performance: Insurer Market Penetration and Basis Risk", in: K. A. Froot (ed.) *The Financing of Catastrophe Risk*, (University of Chicago Press).

Pinter, J. D., 1996, *Global Optimization in Action: Continuous and Lipschitz Optimization – Algorithms, Implementations and Applications*, (Norwell MA: Kluwer Academic Publishers).

SwissRe, 1997, "Too Little Reinsurance of Natural Disasters in Many Markets", *Sigma*, 7, pp. 3–22.

Swiss Re, 2001, "Capital Market Innovation in the Insurance Industry", *Sigma*, 3.

Swiss Re, 2002, "Natural Catastrophes and Man-Made Disasters in 2001: Man-Made Losses Take on a New Dimension", *Sigma*, 1.

3

Catastrophe Bonds

David Mocklow, John DeCaro and Matthew McKenna[1]

Cochran, Caronia & Co.

The catastrophe (cat) bond market is generally thought to comprise of only securities exposed to property catastrophes. It was long presumed that property catastrophe risks were the only risks that could be securitised. In fact, there are forms of securitisation that expose investors' principal to other events, like weather risk, mortgage default risk, residual value and credit insurance risks. The vast majority of securities that have been issued since 1997 are indeed property cat bonds but the market today is more commonly referred to as the risk-linked securities (RLS) market.

A number of RLS transactions have taken place: as early as 1992, AIG brought a small RLS deal to market; Hannover Re and Winterthur sponsored securitisations in 1995, and there were a couple of smaller deals such as Reliance's transactions in 1997 and 1998. Transactions in the period before 1997 were somewhat experimental in nature and were generally not replicated. Property catastrophe transactions, which have been issued since 1997, currently form the vast majority of the RLS market. This chapter will focus on the property catastrophe sector of the RLS market and will look at the period from 1997 to today.

The securitisation of insurance can be traced back to 1995 when several investment bankers began to examine the relationship between long-tail casualty risk and the capital required to underwrite this risk. They believed that insurance companies were significantly overcapitalised relative to the risks they were taking. The investment bankers' advice to these companies was to replace equity capital with debt capital. They reasoned that certain types of long-tail risks exhibited lower volatility, which would allow insurance companies to use more leverage and to enhance return on capital for shareholders. Although the insurance companies were intrigued by this analysis, none of them undertook a recapitalisation of its balance sheet because there was minimal shareholder pressure to improve equity returns at the time. Moreover, reinsurance markets were so aggressive that insurance companies were able to protect their capital by buying reinsurance at very cheap prices. Simply put, from a price perspective, securitisation could not compete with the reinsurance marketplace.

Coincidentally, this period was also marked by relatively large increases in short-tail property reinsurance premiums as the direct result of Hurricane Andrew and the Northridge Earthquake. As a result of catastrophic losses caused by the Northridge Earthquake in 1994 and the subsequent withdrawal by insurance companies from the California homeowners market, the much-publicised California Earthquake Authority (CEA) was formed. The creation of the CEA drastically raised the profile of securitisation because the capacity that the CEA demanded for reinsurance protection was considerably greater than the traditional reinsurance market was thought able to provide. The eleventh-hour participation of Berkshire Hathaway in the CEA's reinsurance programme prevented the CEA from attempting the first cat bond as a true predecessor to the property cat RLS market we know today.

It did not originally seem that property catastrophe risks would interest investors. Early market concerns focused on whether investors understood the probability of losses from natural perils and the subsequent potential loss of principal. Notwithstanding a few completed deals, bankers were concerned that investors would be deterred by the perceived binary nature of loss should an event of a large enough magnitude occur. Bankers developed the early versions of cat bonds that form the basis of the products we see at issuance today as a result of early experiments with potential issuers and an active dialogue with investors.

INTRODUCTION

The first section of this chapter will examine the concept of creating a security out of an insured risk. Next, it will examine how the forms of securities have evolved since the first property catastrophe transaction in 1997 and, particularly, how losses from events are determined. The chapter also examines the role that the experts play in securitisation. These experts include the modelling firm, which helps investors understand the risks to which they are exposed when buying bonds, as well as the rating agencies.

INSURANCE AS A SECURITY

In order for an insurance risk to be deemed to be in an investable form, it needs to have a number of the characteristics that are typical of other fixed-income securities. These characteristics include:

1. The "payment" of an amount certain (the principal) by the investor in exchange for a fixed annual return (coupon).

2. A fixed maturity date – at which time the principal is expected to be repaid.
3. A rating to help the investor understand the likelihood that he will receive both timely payment of interest and repayment of principal.

The process by which a securitisation of insurance risk takes place is illustrated in Figure 1. The key to the process is that a special purpose reinsurance vehicle (SPRV) is created with two purposes:

1. Reinsuring the sponsor of the securitisation (the insurer or reinsurer who cedes risk to investors through the securitisation).
2. Issuing securities to investors that provide the capital necessary to pay potential claims under the reinsurance contract.

The SPRV has no other purpose and its initial capital is contributed by a charitable trust. Additional equity or equity-like securities are sold to third party investors to prevent the SPRV from being consolidated on the balance sheet of the sponsor. The sponsor of the transaction is the company that will be the beneficiary of any recoveries from the SPRV when events covered under the bond actually happen.

Investors typically receive a floating-rate coupon of the London Interbank Offered Rate (Libor) plus a spread. The sources of funds for payment of the floating-rate coupon are a portion of the reinsurance premium paid by the sponsor to the SPRV and the return generated by investing the proceeds of the cat bond offering in highly rated investments. Investors in the cat bond are only exposed to losses paid by the SPRV under the terms of its reinsurance contract.

Bankers recognised that other structural features would be required to entice investors to consider cat bond transactions seriously as a new asset class. It was reasoned that if the securities were to eliminate any credit risk

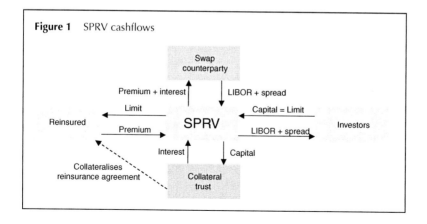

Figure 1 SPRV cashflows

or interest rate risk, then investors would be left solely with the catastrophe risk. This asset class would therefore be appealing to investors because of the significant diversification value that these securities would provide. This was accomplished with two basic structural features. First, the coupon on the bonds consisted of a fixed spread (representing the cost of the protection purchased) plus an amount equivalent to three-month Libor. The Libor component could change at each coupon payment date depending on current three-month Libor levels. Second, the bonds are typically structured with a feature that eliminates credit risk to the sponsor. Investors do not want a situation where the sponsor does not pay the fixed-risk spread to the SPRV. The bonds can be structured in a variety of different ways to eliminate this risk. For example, the sponsor can prepay the entire risk premium to the SPRV or the bonds could be immediately redeemed and principal returned to investors for a failure by the sponsor to pay the fixed spread.

This basic cat bond structure has varied little since 1997.

CHARACTERISTICS OF RISK-LINKED SECURITIES
Loss triggers
Most industry practitioners refer to Residential Re as the first true cat bond because its structure formed the basis for much of the future issuance in the risk-linked securities marketplace. The structure of this transaction helped to demarcate the evolution of the marketplace for securitisations over time.

The four basic types of triggers that are used to determine losses in property catastrophe RLS are:

1. indemnity triggers;
2. parametric triggers;
3. index triggers; and
4. modeled loss triggers.

Indemnity Trigger Deals
Residential Re was structured as a security whereby losses under the reinsurance contract were meant to indemnify USAA (the cedent) for losses that the company suffered as a result of paying claims resulting from a very large hurricane along the East and Gulf coasts of the US. The security had a one-year term and was issued in two separate tranches. One tranche, approximately US$163.8 million, was principal-protected. The second tranche, consisting of approximately US$313 million in securities, was entirely exposed to losses. The structuring of the separate principal-protected tranche was deemed important to the transaction because certain investors provided initial feedback that they did not want their entire investment to be exposed to losses.

Indemnity deals are important for sponsors because these transactions provide the assurance that the sponsor would expect to receive dollar-for-dollar recovery (a full indemnification) for losses. Of the 14 cat bonds issued from 1996 to April 1999, 12 were structured as indemnity deals. From an investor's perspective, however, there were features to these transactions that introduced uncertainty. These features included:

❏ *Data uncertainty.* The possibility that the data used to determine the rating of the bonds might not be sufficient to accurately reflect the actual insurance portfolio that suffers losses.
❏ *Moral hazard.* The potential for human mistakes in the claims-adjusting process, as well as the risk of adverse policy selection. Adverse selection can occur when the sponsor decides to change the underlying business being protected under the terms of the securitisation to a more risky book of business.
❏ *Extension.* The need to extend the maturity of the bonds in order to allow the claims adjusting process to conclude.

The first non-indemnity structured transactions were created to address investor uncertainty with the indemnity securitisation. Figure 2 provides an illustration of the capital structure of Residential Re 2001 as well as some of the terms of the reinsurance contract.

Index Trigger Deals
Index deals were created as the opportunity to buy protection in circumstances where the sponsor felt that the quality of its underlying data would not have supported an indemnity deal. The concept behind the index-based deal is very simple. Its structure is identical to other cat bonds with the exception that losses to principal are not determined by the losses suffered by the sponsor. Instead, an index is used as a proxy for the sponsor's loss experience. For example, Property Claims Services (PCS) creates an insurance industry loss figure from natural catastrophe events. The sponsor estimates the PCS industry loss amount that would equate to its own loss experience from that same event, thereby determining the size of the event the sponsor would need to reinsure. This type of deal allowed sponsors to avoid certain disclosure, but sponsors were left with the basis risk (if the sponsors' losses were better or worse than estimated under the index). Moreover, this structure also left investors with lingering questions about data uncertainty regarding industry exposures as well as extension (meaning the extent to which the industry needed time to calculate losses to report for an index).

SR Earthquake, sponsored by Swiss Re in 1997, was the first index-based deal, apparently creating a trend, as most of the index deals that followed have covered California Earthquake exposures. Figure 3 shows the capital structure of an index-based deal called "Redwood Capital I".

Figure 2 Selected terms and capital structure of Residential Re, 2001

Indicative terms	
Issuer:	Residential Re 2001
Transaction sponsor:	USAA
Initial payment amount:	US$150,000,000
Insurance date:	1 June, 2001
Maturity date:	1 June, 2004
Coupon:	3-month LIBOR plus 4.99%
Coverage type:	Indemnity
Covered perils:	Gulf/East Coast Hurricane
Expected loss:	0.68%
Risk assessment firm:	Applied Insurance Research
Ratings:	BB+ – Standard & Poors Ba2 – Moody's Investors Service
Domicile:	Cayman Islands

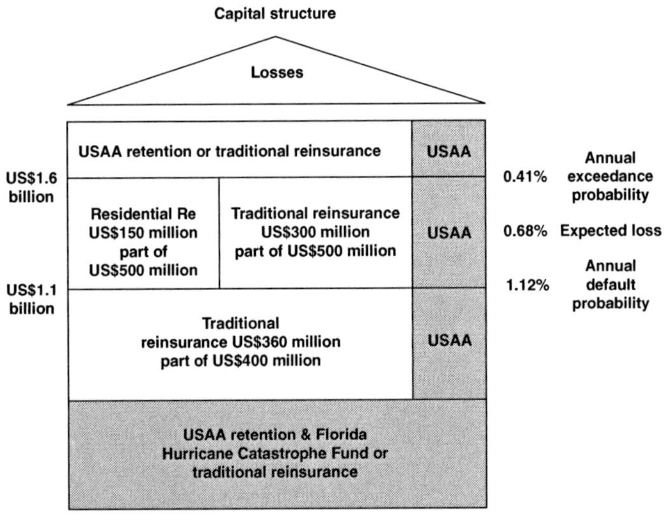

Capital structure

Losses

| USAA retention or traditional reinsurance | USAA | | 0.41% | Annual exceedance probability |

US$1.6 billion

| Residential Re US$150 million part of US$500 million | Traditional reinsurance US$300 million part of US$500 million | USAA | | 0.68% Expected loss |

US$1.1 billion

1.12% Annual default probability

| Traditional reinsurance US$360 million part of US$400 million | USAA |

USAA retention & Florida Hurricane Catastrophe Fund or traditional reinsurance

Parametric Trigger Deals

The cat bond market saw another major development in 1997 with the introduction of the first parametric deal, Parametric Re. The sponsor, Tokio Marine & Fire Insurance Company, decided to eliminate some of the issues associated with indemnity and index-based securitisations with a

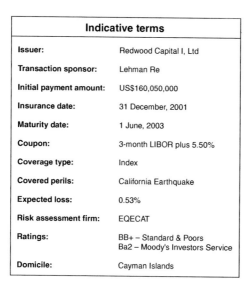

Figure 3   Selected terms and capital structure of Redwood Capital I, Ltd

Indicative terms

Issuer:	Redwood Capital I, Ltd
Transaction sponsor:	Lehman Re
Initial payment amount:	US$160,050,000
Insurance date:	31 December, 2001
Maturity date:	1 June, 2003
Coupon:	3-month LIBOR plus 5.50%
Coverage type:	Index
Covered perils:	California Earthquake
Expected loss:	0.53%
Risk assessment firm:	EQECAT
Ratings:	BB+ – Standard & Poors Ba2 – Moody's Investors Service
Domicile:	Cayman Islands

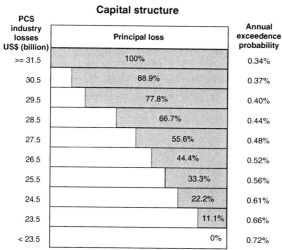

Capital structure

PCS industry losses US$ (billion)	Principal loss	Annual exceedence probability
>= 31.5	100%	0.34%
30.5	88.9%	0.37%
29.5	77.8%	0.40%
28.5	66.7%	0.44%
27.5	55.6%	0.48%
26.5	44.4%	0.52%
25.5	33.3%	0.56%
24.5	22.2%	0.61%
23.5	11.1%	0.66%
< 23.5	0%	0.72%

new type of loss trigger. A parametric transaction is one where losses to investors are simply a function of the magnitude of a catastrophe in a specific, predetermined location. For example, Parametric Re exposed investors to earthquakes of JMA magnitude 7.1 and above in the vicinity of Tokyo. How much Tokio Marine would have to pay its policyholders in the event of this occurrence was absolutely irrelevant – Tokio Marine was assuming this basis risk. In completing this transaction, Tokio Marine removed the moral hazard, data uncertainty, questions about likely damage from a specified event and the need for an extension to calculate losses from investors.

Figure 4 shows the capital structure of a parametric deal called "Atlas Re II".

Modelled Loss Deals
The next major development, in terms of the structuring of loss triggers, took place in 1999. Gerling Global Reinsurance decided to use a modelled loss calculation to determine the recovery from its sponsored transaction, Namazu Re. Modelled loss transactions combined many of the best features of the other traditional structures while providing investors with comfort about the elimination of undesired risks. Losses under this type of security are determined by creating a hypothetical insurance book of business. The sponsor generally elects to use its actual book of business to mitigate basis risk. This notional or hypothetical portfolio is then held in escrow. When an event occurs, the characteristics of that event are then simulated in the model against the portfolio of insurance contracts. The sponsor receives the benefits of a transaction that uses their actual exposures. Investors enjoy a transaction with neither moral hazard or data uncertainty, as well as a structure with no extension required. The reduction or elimination of these uncertainties translates into improvements in ratings, all else being equal. Figure 5 shows the capital structure of modelled loss deal called "Trinom Ltd".

Other structural features
In addition to the type of loss trigger that is used to determine losses to principal, there are other important structural features that serve to differentiate transactions from one another. The major features include:

❏ Term (one-year or multi-year).
❏ Peril (single exposure such as Florida Hurricane only or multi-peril such as Japanese and California Earthquake).
❏ Tranching (multi-tranches covering either different perils or additional events).
❏ Optionality (both traditional and risk-based options).

Term
The first multi-year transaction was Parametric Re in 1997. As a multi-year deal, Parametric Re ensured that investors were exposed to the same amount of event risk each year by making the magnitude of events needed to cause losses the same each year. Pacific Re, a multi-year indemnity deal

Figure 4   Selected terms and capital structure of Atlas Re II

Indicative terms

Issuer:	Atlas Reinsurance
Transaction sponsor:	SCOR
Initial payment amount:	US$50,000,000 Class A US$100,000,000 Class B
Insurance date:	28 December, 2001
Maturity date:	5 January, 2007
Coupon:	3-month LIBOR plus 2.38% – Class A 3-month LIBOR plus 6.75% – Class B
Coverage type:	Parametric
Covered perils:	California Earthquake European Windstorm US Hurricane
Expected loss:	0.05% – Class A 0.90% – Class B
Risk assessment firm:	EQECAT
Ratings: **(S&P/Moody's)**	Class A – A-/A3 Class B – BB+/Ba2
Domicile:	Ireland

Capital structure

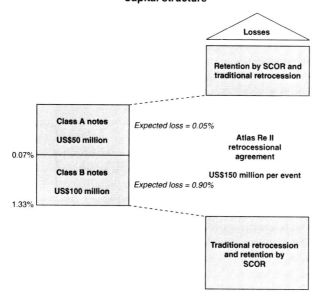

Figure 5 Selected terms and capital structure of Trinom Ltd

Indicative terms	
Issuer:	Trinom Ltd
Transaction sponsor:	Zurich Insurance
Initial payment amount:	US$60,000,000 Class A US$97,000,000 Class B
Insurance date:	15 June, 2001
Maturity date:	18 June, 2004
Coupon:	3-month LIBOR plus 8.00% – Class A 3-month LIBOR plus 4.00% – Class B
Coverage type:	Modelled loss
Covered perils:	California Earthquake European Windstorm US Hurricane
Expected loss:	1.11% – Class A 0.67% – Class B
Risk assessment firm:	Applied Insurance Research
Ratings: **(S&P/Moody's)**	Class A – BB/Ba2 Class B – BB+/Ba1
Domicile:	Bermuda

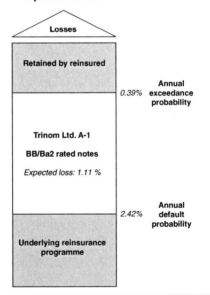

Capital structure

sponsored by Yasuda Fire & Marine in 1998, introduced the same concept of a constant risk profile to indemnity deals for the first time. Investors needed a mechanism that ensured that, each year, the probability of losses under the transaction did not change due to underlying changes in the reinsured book of business. This was accomplished by resetting the dollar attachment point to help ensure that the default probability remained constant from year to year.

Peril

Multi-peril transactions have become popular, especially as the number of deals sponsored by reinsurers has grown. Various transactions have incorporated more than one peril into their structure in a variety of different ways. An early private deal sponsored by Reliance exposed one-fifth of investors' principal to five different perils. Later transactions (such as Halyard Re and Gold Eagle) were entirely exposed to two or more different perils. Finally, we saw transactions, such as Mediterranean Re, where investors' principal was exposed to one peril from a first event and then the remaining principal from a subsequent event involving a separate peril.

Tranching

Some earlier transactions included a principal-protected tranche, but Mosaic Re was the first transaction to introduce the concept of multiple at-risk tranches to the cat bond market. Multiple tranches are a common feature of asset-backed securities (ABS) transactions, but cat bonds had only ever been issued in a single, usually BB-rated tranche, with some also having a principal-protected tranche. Mosaic issued two tranches of securities, each with different rating profiles and coupons. Each of these tranches, however, was exposed to the same perils and did not expose investors to subsequent events. Atlas Re, a transaction sponsored in 1999 by SCOR, was the first transaction where there were multiple tranches that exposed investors to the same perils but either on a first-event or subsequent-event basis. Finally, transactions such as SR Wind (another Swiss Re deal) introduced investors to multi-tranche deals where each tranche covered different perils from the other and then exposed investors to subsequent losses from a second discrete peril.

Optionality

Optionality in cat bonds can be thought of in two ways. There are the traditional debt options, such as puts and calls, and the risk optionality in certain cat bond securities. Risk-based optionality occurs when the cat bond changes form in some way following an event. For example, in Pacific Re, there is a drop-down option at the discretion of the sponsor. In this case, following an event of large enough magnitude (although not one large enough to cause 100% losses to principal) the sponsor has the right to cause the default probability of the bond to increase. In this security, a condition of increasing the default probability is that the issuer must also pay a higher coupon (commonly called a "step-up coupon") for the subsequent event.

Other risk-based options exist. For example, in Trinom Ltd, there is a second-event tranche of securities that can only be put at risk for subsequent events following a large enough first event. Unlike Pacific Re, this security does not expose investors in this tranche to first-event losses.

We will examine how to value these different structural features below, under the heading of "Valuation".

RISK ANALYSIS AND RATING

A key concern for investors is the determination of the level of risk in risk-linked securities. Analysis of historical experience is an inadequate measure of catastrophe exposure due to limited information. Risk assessment through computer simulation provides the best estimate of expected losses from rare catastrophic events. Modelling catastrophic risk provides a relevant measure for all constituents. Computer modelling solves another issue for investors. That is, it provides a uniform, consistent approach to risk assessment so that comparison with other assets is possible. With increased issuance, investors are becoming more comfortable with the value of the loss-probability data provided by independent catastrophe modelling firms.

The key output of the model is the "loss exceedance curve", which describes the amounts of insured losses estimated to result from perils with varying probabilities of occurrence. The loss curve is developed by simulating thousands of hypothetical storms and/or earthquakes in a probabilistic computer model. Each event simulated has a probability of occurrence (an estimate of how frequently the event occurs) and an estimate of the severity of losses caused by the event. The frequency estimate for a simulated event is partly based upon a review of historical records for similar events. The severity of loss caused by that event is based upon damage functions within the model that estimate the damage caused by the physical characteristics of the event on the assets being insured. Once the simulation is complete, the outcomes are ranked to create the loss curve. These probabilistic models and their output files are also used by the rating agencies in the rating process.

There are currently three firms that provide the modelling services for these securities (see Figure 6):

1. Applied Insurance Research (AIR), based in Boston, which was founded in 1987 and pioneered the probabilistic catastrophe modelling technology that is used today.
2. Equecat (EQE), headquartered in Oakland, California, which provided the risk assessment for the very first earthquake securitisation.

3. Risk Management Solutions (RMS), headquartered in Newark, California. RMS was founded at Stanford University in 1988.

These firms have vast amounts of experience and respect in the insurance industry. Their natural hazard risk-modelling software is used by hundreds of insurers, reinsurers, trading companies and other financial institutions worldwide. State governments also use them to set insurance rates.

Although these firms provide services for the same industry using similar models, with each firm owning a model for each peril, the output of those models is often not exactly comparable. Differences are caused by the underlying ideology of the firm modelling the risk. This is a function of the limited amount of data available due to the infrequent nature of such events. Given this fact, the modelling firms base their models on scientific research as well as event observation. Understandably, there is no consensus as each firm gives different weights to differing scientific opinions. (Figure 6 shows the split by modelling the RLS universe.)

When the modelling has been completed, the results are used by the rating agencies to assess the risk of the securities and in order to place a rating on the offering for the market. Rating agencies have long been used as a means of providing independent, third-party insight, analysis and information to the financial community. This service and information is used to help investors determine value in the marketplace.

The rating agencies perform due diligence on the modelling firm, the model used to assess the risk of a catastrophe, and the structure of the bond and SPRV. The agencies typically focus on the reliability of the computer model used to assess the risk of the transaction. This involves several steps.

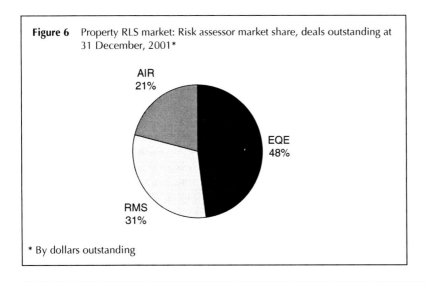

Figure 6   Property RLS market: Risk assessor market share, deals outstanding at 31 December, 2001*

AIR
21%

EQE
48%

RMS
31%

* By dollars outstanding

The integrity and completeness of the historical data is the starting point for any review. This includes questions about the resolution of the data used. In indemnity transactions, the higher the data resolution, the lower the uncertainty. The modelling assumptions, and the research used to support those assumptions, are also questioned and the assumptions are assessed for their effect over time. The loss exceedance curves are stressed and the simulated events are compared with actual historical losses for plausibility. The effects that changes in the model have on the output are reviewed. The agency may employ outside consultants at any time during this process. Ultimately, the goal of the rating agency is to assess the robustness of the model and measure the level of uncertainty. Triggers such as parametric and modelled loss that remove data uncertainty are afforded a greater level of modelled risk for a given rating given the lower level of uncertainty.

The agencies view insurance risk much like default risk on a pool of rated corporate bonds. The probability of attachment and expected loss for the RLS structure is compared to ratings benchmark tables for historical corporate bond default and recovery rates.

Table 1 shows the rating profile of the Atlas Re II Class B Notes.

Table 1   Moody's cumulative default rate table

	Annual probability of any loss		Annual expected loss	
Moody's rating	Corporate bond benchmark (%)	Atlas Re II class B notes	Corporate bond benchmark (%)	Atlas Re II class B notes
Aaa	0.00		0.00	
Aa1	0.00		0.00	
Aa2	0.00		0.00	
Aa3	0.00		0.00	
A1	0.01		0.00	
A2	0.01		0.01	
A3	0.04		0.02	
Baa1	0.09		0.05	
Baa2	0.17		0.09	
Baa3	0.42		0.23	
Ba1	0.87		0.48	
Ba2	1.56	1.33	0.86	0.90
Ba3	2.81		1.55	
B1	4.68		2.57	
B2	7.16		3.94	
B3	11.62		6.39	
Caa	26.00		14.30	

Figure 7 shows the market share of the three major agencies.

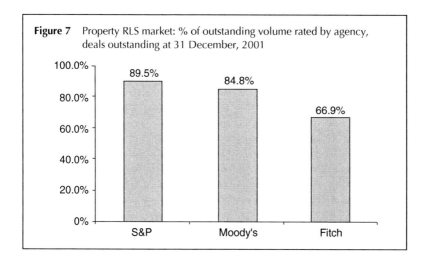

Figure 7 Property RLS market: % of outstanding volume rated by agency, deals outstanding at 31 December, 2001

CURRENT STATE OF THE RLS MARKET
Market size
The net amount of property catastrophe RLS outstanding at 31 December, 2001 totalled US$2.08 billion, of which US$947 million was raised in seven securities issues during 2001. Approximately US$1 billion of new securities were brought to market in both 2000 and 2001. It is anticipated that 2002 will see a growth in issuance due to increases in reinsurance pricing, as a result of the World Trade Center losses.

Sponsor
Of the outstanding property catastrophe RLS, 64% have been sponsored by reinsurance companies. Reinsurers are increasingly turning to the capital markets as a way to hedge their catastrophic exposures (see Figure 8).

Loss trigger
Figure 9 shows the distribution of trigger types in outstanding RLS. It is interesting that only 25% of RLS use an indemnity loss trigger, as virtually 100% of traditional reinsurance is designed to indemnify the reinsured.

Peril
Figure 10 provides a summary of the three major perils to which investors are exposed. Almost 50% of the outstanding RLS expose investors to earthquake risk, either in the US, Japan or Europe.

Region
Figure 11 shows the geographical breakdown of outstanding issuance. The four largest regions are Japan (26%), Europe (22%), California (21%) and Florida (16%).

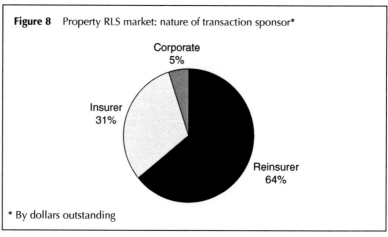

Figure 8   Property RLS market: nature of transaction sponsor*

Corporate
5%

Insurer
31%

Reinsurer
64%

* By dollars outstanding

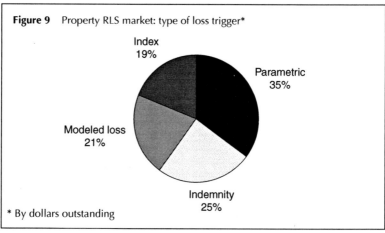

Figure 9   Property RLS market: type of loss trigger*

Index
19%

Parametric
35%

Modeled loss
21%

Indemnity
25%

* By dollars outstanding

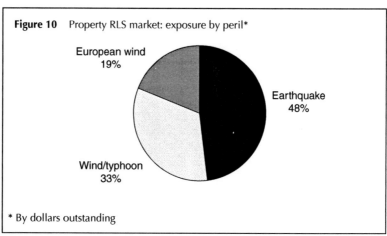

Figure 10   Property RLS market: exposure by peril*

European wind
19%

Earthquake
48%

Wind/typhoon
33%

* By dollars outstanding

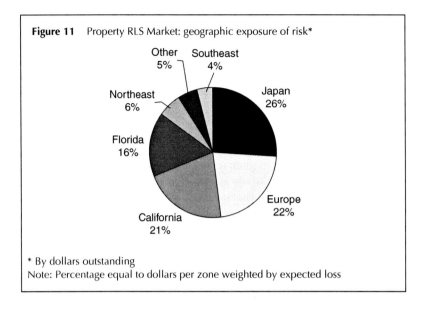

Figure 11   Property RLS Market: geographic exposure of risk*

* By dollars outstanding
Note: Percentage equal to dollars per zone weighted by expected loss

Region and peril
Figure 12 shows the distribution of exposure and peril (such as California Earthquake) across outstanding securities.

Issuance and risk exposure data
Table 2 illustrates the current rated RLS showing, among other things, the sponsor, size of deal, exposures covered and risk assessment, including rating.

VALUATION CONSIDERATIONS FOR RISK-LINKED SECURITIES
Framework
This section is not intended to explicitly identify methods for assessing the relative value of individual RLS issues vs other issues or even different fixed-income sectors. Instead, this section provides a framework to value the structural components of individual securities.

Most market participants price RLS issues using one of three methods:

1. Measuring the multiple of risk premium to expected loss.
2. Comparing the issue's Sharpe Ratio to similar transactions (the Sharpe Ratio is a measure of risk-adjusted return).
3. Comparing RLS pricing vs industry-loss warranty (ILW) pricing from the reinsurance market.

Table 2 Outstanding property catastrophe rated RLS

Issue date	Sponsor	Issuer	Size	Rating S&P/ Moody's	Exposure	Spread at issue	Annual exp. loss[1]	Annual prob attach[1]	Annual prob exhaust[1]	Excess return[2]	Std. dev.[2]	Sharpe Ratio[2]
Dec-01	Lehman Re	Redwood Capital I – Notes	US$160,050	BB+/Ba2	Cal EQ	5.50%	0.53%	0.72%	0.34%	5.05%	6.81%	0.74%
Dec-01	SCOR	Atlas Reinsurance II – Class A	US$50,000	BB+/Ba2	Cal EQ, Eur WS, Jap EQ	2.38%	0.05%	0.07%	0.03%	2.36%	2.08%	1.13%
Dec-01	SCOR	Atlas Reinsurance II – Class B	US$100,000	A-/A3	Cal EQ, Eur WS, Jap EQ	6.75%	0.90%	1.33%	0.53%	5.94%	8.77%	0.68%
Jun-01	Zurich	Trinom Ltd – Class A-1	US$60,000	BB/Ba2	Cal EQ, Eur WS, US HU	8.00%	1.11%	2.42%	0.39%	7.00%	9.26%	0.76%
Jun-01	Zurich	Trinom Ltd – Class A-2	US$97,000	BB+/Ba1	Cal EQ, Eur WS, US HU	4.00%	0.67%	1.01%	0.43%	3.39%	7.65%	0.44%
Jun-01	USAA	Residential Re 2001 – Notes	US$150,000	BB+/Ba2	Gulf HU, E. Coast HU	4.99%	0.68%	1.12%	0.41%	4.38%	7.65%	0.57%
May-01	Swiss Re	SR Wind – Class A-1	US$58,200	BB+/-	Fr WS, FL HU	5.25%	0.68%	1.07%	0.44%	4.64%	7.72%	0.60%
May-01	Swiss Re	SR Wind – Class A-2	US$58,200	BB+/-	Fr WS, FL HU	5.75%	0.76%	1.13%	0.53%	5.07%	8.23%	0.62%
Apr-01	Sorema	Halyard Re (2001) – Notes	US$17,000	BB-[3]	Jap EQ, Jap WS, Fr WS	5.50%	0.22%	0.84%	0.04%	5.36%	3.99%	1.34%
Mar-01	American Re	Gold Eagle 2001 – Notes	US$116,400	BB+/Ba2	Gulf HU, SE HU, NM EQ	5.50%	0.75%	1.18%	0.54%	4.83%	8.21%	0.59%
Feb-01	Swiss Re	Western Capital – Notes	US$97,000	BB+/Ba2	Cal EQ	5.10%	0.55%	0.82%	0.34%	4.62%	6.91%	0.67%
Dec-00	Munich Re	PRIME Capital CalQuake & Eurowind – Notes	US$129,000	BB/Ba3	Cal EQ, Eur WS	7.50%	1.33%	1.69%	1.07%	6.27%	11.07%	0.57%
Dec-00	Munich Re	PRIME Capital Hurricane – Notes	US$159,000	BB+/Baa3	NE HU, FL HU	6.50%	1.27%	1.46%	1.08%	5.32%	10.91%	0.49%
Nov-00	AGF	Mediterranean Re – Class A	US$41,000	BBB+/Baa3	Fr WS, Monaco EQ	2.60%	0.22%	0.28%	0.17%	2.42%	4.50%	0.54%
Nov-00	AGF	Mediterranean Re – Class B	US$88,000	BB+/Ba3	Fr WS, Monaco EQ	5.85%	1.16%	1.41%	0.93%	4.77%	10.34%	0.46%
Jul-00	Vesta	NeHi – Notes	US$41,500	-/Ba3	NE HU, Hawaii HU	4.10%	0.70%	0.87%	0.56%	3.46%	8.03%	0.43%
Mar-00	SCOR	Atlas Reinsurance – Class A	US$70,000	BBB+/-	US EQ, Jap EQ, Eur WS	2.70%	0.11%	0.19%	0.03%	2.63%	2.88%	0.91%
Mar-00	SCOR	Atlas Reinsurance – Class B	US$30,000	BB-/-	US EQ, Jap EQ, Eur WS	3.70%	0.23%	0.29%	0.19%	3.52%	4.65%	0.76%
Mar-00	SCOR	Atlas Reinsurance – Class C	US$100,000	B-/-	US EQ, Jap EQ, Eur WS	14.00%	3.24%	5.47%	1.01%	10.95%	15.47%	0.71%
Nov-99	Gerling	Namazu Re – Notes	US$100,000	BB/-	Jap EQ	4.50%	0.75%	1.00%	0.32%	3.81%	7.75%	0.49%
Jun-99	Gerling	Juno Re – Notes	US$80,000	BB/-	US HU	4.20%	0.45%	0.60%	0.33%	3.81%	6.39%	0.60%
May-99	Oriental Land	Concentric – Notes	US$100,000	BB+/Ba1	Jap EQ	3.10%	0.41%	0.62%	0.21%	2.73%	5.85%	0.47%
Jun-98	Yasuda Fire & Marine	Pacific Re – Notes	US$80,000	-/Ba3	Jap Typn	3.70%	0.88%	0.94%	0.82%	2.87%	9.23%	0.31%
Dec-97	Tokio Marine & Fire	Parametric Re – Notes	US$80,000	-/Ba2	Jap EQ	4.30%	0.70%	1.02%	0.41%	3.66%	7.74%	0.47%

[1] Taken from final offering documents.
[2] Excess Return Standard Deviation and Sharpe Ratio calculated by Cochran, Caronia Securities using spread at issuance, calculated on an actual over 365 basis
[3] Rating by Duff & Phelps

Legend

Cal EQ	=	California Earthquake	Eur WS	=	European Windstorm	E. Coast HU = East Coast US Hurricane
Fr WS	=	French Windstorm	Gulf HU	=	Gulf Coast US Hurricane	Jap EQ = Japanese Earthquake
Monaco EQ	=	Monaco Earthquake	NE HU	=	Northeast Coast US Hurricane	NM EQ = New Madrid Earthquake
US EQ	=	US Earthquake	US HU	=	US Hurricane	

FL HU = Florida Hurricane
Jap Typn = Japanese Typhoon
SE HU = South East Coast US Hurricane

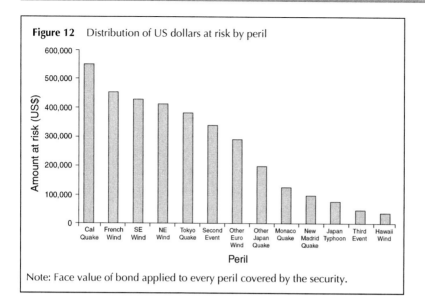

Figure 12 Distribution of US dollars at risk by peril

Note: Face value of bond applied to every peril covered by the security.

Certain RLS issues have unique structural features such as embedded options, multiple risk exposures, and subsequent-event loss triggers. Standard valuation tools, which are based on the expected loss and probabilities of attachment and exhaustion, were not sufficiently robust to accurately compare securities having these features with more plain vanilla structures.

This section identifies security-specific features that affect the required risk premium and provides guidance on how to price such features. We will examine ways to price a multi-peril security compared to a portfolio of single-peril RLS, and will also explore the various embedded options in RLS, such as calls, puts and extensions and options that shift the layer of event risk exposure. Finally, we will briefly introduce the effect of seasonality of event risk on the pricing of RLS.

Pricing multi-peril securities

In order for the capital markets to truly serve as a new source of reinsurance capital, transaction sponsors must be able to issue securities that fulfil a strategic risk transfer need. To date, reinsurance companies that have issued RLS have tended to issue multi-year notes exposed to several different but uncorrelated natural perils, whereas insurance companies have largely issued notes exposed to a single peril.

These issuance patterns largely fit with the capital needs of each type of sponsor. Primary insurance companies are largely exposed to one type of natural peril in a specific geographical area, such as hurricanes in Florida or earthquakes in Tokyo. This results from the aggregation of primary insurance coverage written in a specific geographical area. As such, their reinsurance needs can be met through the reinsurance market, which is used to provide such coverage, or by issuing an RLS exposed to that single peril. Examples of single-peril RLS include Domestic (New Madrid earthquake), Alpha Wind (Florida Hurricane) and Western Capital (California Earthquake).

In contrast, reinsurance companies generally provide protection for insurers and other clients in many different areas, and take in exposure to numerous (uncorrelated) natural perils as they seek to build a diversified portfolio of reinsurance exposure. For example, a reinsurer that writes business in the US is exposed to potential losses arising from earthquakes in California and the New Madrid area and hurricanes along the Gulf and east coasts of the US. Because of their diverse portfolio of risks, reinsurers tend to seek protection from losses caused by any "low frequency, high severity" natural catastrophe to which they are exposed. For this client, it may be more cost efficient to purchase one reinsurance policy covering losses from any of the perils, rather than separate individual policies for each peril. Examples of multi-peril RLS include Atlas Re (Japan and US Earthquake, European Windstorm), Mediterranean Re (French Windstorm, Monaco Earthquake), Prime Capital CalQuake and EuroWind (California Earthquake, European Windstorm), and Trinom (European Windstorm, US Hurricane and Earthquake).

Figure 13 shows the increase in multi-peril issuance since 1997.

A multi-peril RLS, where all the principal can be lost by a single event from any of the covered perils, uses up capacity in multiple risk buckets, so investors expect to receive a capacity charge in the form of a slightly higher risk premium vs the return on a similar portfolio of single-peril securities. Most multi-peril RLS are exposed to some or all of the following risks, which represent peak areas of insured value: California Earthquake, East

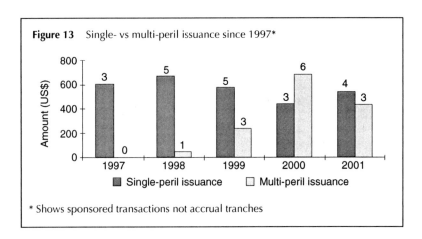

Figure 13   Single- vs multi-peril issuance since 1997*

* Shows sponsored transactions not accrual tranches

Coast Hurricane, European Windstorm and Japanese Earthquake. Investors like to construct their own portfolios with uncorrelated, single-peril RLS, and are usually already exposed to the perils embedded in a multi-peril deal. Multi-peril pricing must therefore increase to attract the marginal investment.

Another factor leading to higher pricing on multi-perils is that investors have increased due diligence to perform in analysing the overlap between current holdings and a multi-peril deal given that there are few, if any, perfect single-peril substitutes for multi-peril issues.

The RLS market has grown to approximately 24 issues, with a total of over US$2 billion of outstanding securities, and there are few perfect substitutes in the market, which makes exact comparisons between securities difficult. Two other factors that make issue comparison difficult are the use of three different modelling firms for risk assessment and the fundamental differences in the underlying business of each transaction sponsor.

The use of different modelling firms for different transactions means that like-with-like comparisons of risk based simply on the loss probabilities are difficult. For example, both Seismic and Western Capital had virtually the same underlying loss trigger (PCS estimates of industry losses from California Earthquakes) and attachment and exhaustion points but used different modelling firms for the risk assessment. In this case it is relatively easy to compare the two securities as they traded virtually on top of each other, but the use of separate modelling firms for the same structure and risk can lead to confusion.

There are generally overlapping exposures between multi- and single-peril issues but, in reality, the location and composition of the underlying risk being securitised can differ. This can introduce basis risk into the comparison of two sets of securities. Take the case of Prime Capital CalQuake and EuroWind. There are no other single-peril bonds that closely represent the exposures in Prime Capital; there are several single-peril California Earthquake securities outstanding, but none of them have the same proportion of risk in northern and southern California as Prime Capital (59% in northern, 41% in southern). Most other securities with California earthquake risk are approximately 40% exposed to northern, 60% exposed to southern. Moreover, only 5% of the European wind exposure in this deal is from France but the only two single-peril European windstorm issues are French wind deals. The use of either Mediterranean B or SR Wind A-1 as a proxy for European Windstorm exposure will also affect the analysis.

There are two methods for comparing the value of a portfolio of single-peril bonds and a multi-peril bond with substantially the same exposures. The first, and easiest, is to compare the expected return and risk premium on an equal monetary amount of a multi-peril asset and a portfolio of single-peril securities. However, the expected loss will differ between the two portfolios given an equal monetary investment in both. This approach is well suited to investors who are solely looking to maximise spread income for a given investment amount subject to purchasing RLS with the same credit rating (and without accounting for the difference in expected loss).

Next, investors can compare the expected return on the two portfolios by equalising the expected loss between portfolios and allowing the monetary amount of each investment to differ. The expected return and risk premium as a percentage of the investment will equal that of the first approach, but the actual monetary returns will differ. To normalise the amount invested, we assume that an investor purchases single-peril notes with cash equity equal to the amount of the multi-peril investment and finances the remainder at Libor plus 100 basis points (bp). This levered return on equity can be more easily compared to the return on equity of the smaller multi-peril investment.

We believe that the use of expected return and expected loss on each alternative is an optimal way to place these investments on equal footing for comparison. Expected return relates the nominal risk premium to the probability of loss in a way that offsets any differences in the layer of risk that is securitised, and factors in the risk of each investment by comparing securities in the same ratings category.

We made the following assumptions in comparing our universe of single- and multi-peril portfolios:

❏ Single-peril securities were selected to closely match the risk profile of the multi-peril security.
❏ Losses to each security were assumed to be binary with an event probability equal to the expected loss in basis points published in transaction offering documents.
❏ Expected losses were assumed to be fungible even if they came from different risk assessors.
❏ Investments were purchased at the initial primary offering.
❏ Expected returns were calculated using the nominal spread at issuance.
❏ Losses were assumed to occur after the receipt of two quarterly coupons.
❏ Each portfolio was capitalised with US$30 million in cash equity.
❏ Leveraged returns assume financing costs of Libor plus 100bp.

We allocated funds in the single-peril portfolio in two different ways. First, we assigned an equal monetary investment to each single peril, regardless of the weight of the peril in the multi-peril asset. In the second alternative, we weighted each single-peril bond in proportion to its percentage of expected loss in the multi-peril asset. There were no significant differences in expected return premium or excess spread between the two outcomes. Table 3 presents the results of the portfolios weighted according to proportion of expected loss by peril.

Table 3 Comparison of single- and multi-peril portfolios of RLS

Implied leverage	Total amount (US$)	No loss probability (%)	ROE (%)	Expected return (%)	Multiple	Return premium (%)	Excess spread (%)	Multiple percentage (%)	Levered ROE (%)	Multi vs levered (%)
	Cal EQ, Eur WS, US HU									
1.64	Trinom A-1 18,300,000	98.89	8.00	6.85	7.21	2.11	2.59	90	8.24	-0.24
	SR A-1, A-2, WC 30,000,000	98.02	5.41	4.74	7.99	–	–	–		
	Cal EQ, Eur WS									
2.17	Prime CalEuro 13,850,000	98.67	7.50	6.12	5.64	1.58	2.33	67	10.04	-2.54
	SR A-1, WC 30,000,000	98.77	5.17	4.54	8.43	–	–	–		
	NE HU, FL HU									
1.85	Prime Hurricane 16,200,000	98.73	6.50	5.19	5.12	1.22	1.83	75	7.80	-1.30
	Res 01, NeHi 30,000,000	98.62	4.67	3.97	6.79	–	–	–		
	Gulf HU, SE HU, New Madrid HU									
1.64	Gold Eagle 2001 18,250,000	99.25	5.50	4.73	7.33	1.18	1.51	84	5.91	-0.41
	Domestic, Juno 30,000,000	99.07	3.99	3.55	8.69	–	–	–		
	US EQ, Jap EQ, Eur WS									
3.00	Atlas C 10,000,000	96.80	14.00	10.57	4.32	6.37	9.05	59	12.85	1.15
	SR A-1, WC, Namazu 30,000,000	98.03	4.95	4.20	7.29	–	–	–		

Legend
Cal EQ = California Earthquake
Jap EQ = Japanese Earthquake
WC = Western Capital

Eur WS = European Windstorm
NE HU = Northeast Coast US Hurricane

FL HU = Florida Hurricane
Res 01 = Residential Re 2001

Gulf HU = Gulf Coast US Hurricane
SR = SR Wind

We looked at five multi-peril deals issued since March, 2000: Atlas Re Class C, Gold Eagle Capital 2001, Prime CalQuake & EuroWind, Prime Hurricane and Trinom Class A-1. The average expected return premium over the portfolio of single-peril BB-rated bonds (excluding Atlas C) was 1.52%, ranging from a low of 1.18% for Gold Eagle 2001 to a high of 2.11% for Trinom A-1. The average excess risk premium on multi-peril securities was 2.07%, ranging from a low of 1.51% for Gold Eagle 2001 to a high of 2.59% for Trinom A-1. The average percentage of the multiple (risk premium divided by expected loss) on the multi-peril bond relative to the single-peril multiple was 79%, ranging from a low of 67% on Prime CalQuake to a high of 90% on Trinom A-1. The average multi-peril RLS in Table 3 has implied leverage of 2.1 times, which means that a US$14.5 million investment in one multi-peril issue has the same expected loss (in actual dollars) as a total investment of US$30 million in a portfolio of single-peril notes.

The need to obtain a credit rating in the BB range means that most multi-peril securities are exposed to losses from individual events that have lower attachment probabilities and expected losses than they would typically have in a BB-rated single-peril RLS. This feature typically results in multi-peril securities having a higher probability of no losses than a portfolio of single-peril notes, while also having a higher probability of a full limit loss compared with the single-peril portfolio.

We note several general rules of thumb. First, BB-rated RLS are generally priced at a discount to the portfolio spread from a levered portfolio of comparable single-peril securities. However, comparing the risk premium to a levered portfolio return will help identify relative value. A quick way to obtain a similar outcome is to compare the multiple of risk premium to expected loss between a multi-peril issue and a comparable portfolio. The higher the relative multiple, the cheaper the multi-peril security (the more attractive it is). We also note that high return premiums and high levels of excess spread are also important indicators of value.

This methodology allows investors who cannot lever their RLS portfolios to estimate a "fair value" for multi-peril securities based on the implied leverage built into each issue and should help these investors make an informed relative-value decision by equalising the expected loss between alternative investments. In addition, investors who can employ leverage will be able to incorporate their own financing costs into this framework and determine what, if any, arbitrage opportunities may exist.

We note that given the basis risk between single- and multi-peril portfolios, combined with the difficulty in financing RLS positions, very little arbitrage activity has occurred to date. However, we also note that most multi-peril securities have been issued at levels that, despite being tighter than those issued on a single-peril portfolio basis, are reasonably close to what would be suggested by a single-peril portfolio. The exceptions, such as Prime CalEuro and Atlas C, tend to have widened in the secondary market (Prime CalEuro) or have traded firm due to the scarcity of each type of risk (Atlas C). Other factors, such as data uncertainty, rating and differences in risk assessment, could also account for the price differential between Atlas C and the single-peril portfolio.

We would note that different categories of RLS investors have diffferent investment parameters. For example, many institutional investors do not have the ability to explicitly lever their RLS portfolios. For these investors, multi-peril RLS offer embedded coverage and higher nominal spread income compared to single-peril issues. In certain instances, investors who can employ leverage could generate higher returns by financing a portion of their investments in single-peril RLS than by purchasing multi-peril RLS.

The end result of this exercise is to establish a mechanism to estimate an appropriate risk premium for multi-peril securities by comparing the issue with a portfolio of single-peril instruments having the same risk exposures, after normalising the expected loss between the two positions. This framework is valid for valuing bonds in both the primary and secondary markets.

Pricing embedded call, put and extension options

When reinsurance prices were softer in 1998 and 1999, issuers wanted to include options in RLS issues giving them the ability to manage the term of their RLS depending on the volatility in the price of comparable reinsurance. Given the turn in the reinsurance market in 2000 after the significant loss year of 1999, no RLS issued since Namazu Re in November 1999 has had an option to alter the term of the security. We are excluding the typical extension options for development periods that are found in most, if not all, RLS. These options typically allow the issuer to extend the maturity, but not the risk period, in exchange for a 30–300bp additional premium so that losses from events that occur near the end of the risk period have sufficient time to develop.

There are two factors that generally suggest that issuers are less likely to include term-management options. First, the terms of RLS issues tend to range from one to five years, naturally mitigating the impact of potential declines in reinsurance prices. Next, the incremental expenses incurred to issue the RLS, combined with the fully collateralised reinsurance protection (and implied cost of collateralisation), add frictional costs that must be recouped before it is economically feasible to replace a securitised cover with reinsurance.

Four RLS issues had term-management options embedded in them: Domestic and Namazu Re had embedded call options, Halyard Re had both call and put options, and Pacific Re has an extension feature. Both Domestic and Namazu Re had effective call premiums at 101% of par (technically 1% additional premiums), but their ability to exercise the option differed. The option in Domestic Re could be exercised only to the extent that the underlying portfolio of risk declined such that the original attachment point had a 0.35% exceedence probability (down from 0.58% at issuance). This protected the sponsor from the obligation to maintain the coverage in the event that the actual exposure declined precipitously.

There were no explicit conditions to the exercise of the Namazu option; investors did not demand additional spread for the call option given the 1% call premium. We would note that a call provision at 101% of par would generally provide investors with sufficient protection given the relatively unlikely use of call options in RLS.

Halyard Re, issued in 1999, had an original term of three years with an annual coupon reset. The expected loss would change each year, based on changes to the covered portfolio of risks. The risk premium would be reset to a market-clearing level each April, at which time both the issuer and investors had the option to participate in the deal for another year. Sorema, the transaction sponsor, wanted to have the option to reset the risk premium at a lower level if reinsurance prices declined. As it turned out, the risk premium rose from 450bp at issuance to 600bp before falling to 550bp for the final risk period. Investors did not explicitly value either of the options and solely treated the notes as having a one-year term.

The extension feature in Pacific Re was different from the examples given above in that the risk period extended upon a triggering typhoon event. Pacific Re covers two risk layers: a first top layer with an annual attachment probability of 0.94%, and a second, lower layer with an annual attachment probability of 5.12%. However, the second layer can only be put at risk if a typhoon occurs and causes losses exceeding a 3.35% annual attachment probability but does not trigger the top layer. Yasuda Fire & Marine, the transaction sponsor, wanted to ensure that it had at least two years of coverage under the second layer. Pacific Re was structured such that if a trigger event occurred within the last two annual risk periods then the term would be extended out for an additional two years of coverage under the lower layer. There was no explicit cost of the extension option in the risk premium at issuance. We note that the effective risk premium for Pacific Re has ranged between 340bp and 425bp since issuance in 1998. Despite the drop-down and extension features, pricing for Pacific Re has reflected its status as the only single-event RLS exposed to Japanese typhoon risk.

Price effect of shifting risk layers
On 31 December, 2001, nine RLS exposed to shifting risk layers or subsequent event triggers accounted for US$584 million, or 28% of the market. Much of the growth in the RLS market since 1999 has come as reinsurers issue securities that complement existing reinsurance programmes. Such

issuers have looked to the capital markets for second- or third-event protection, with US$363 million of subsequent-event securities being issued in 2001 alone.

Our focus on subsequent events or variable risk layers is on risk issued initially in securities form, rather than in option form. Since 1997 only one option to issue RLS upon the occurrence of a triggering event has come to market ("Gemini Re", sponsored by Allianz in late 1998). This is changing as the market matures, but it is probably due to the fact that most institutional investors in the RLS market do not have the ability to explicitly write options – generally, they are allowed only to purchase securities.

It is important to understand the cashflow characteristics of these securities properly when investing in them. Shifts in the risk layers covered by the RLS can cause an actual mark-to-market loss to the securities even in the absence of a catastrophe event causing a permanent loss of principal. Currently, Pacific Re is the only transaction that is exposed to a shifting risk layer on a first-event basis. This section will focus on measuring the effect on the price of a subsequent-event RLS of a shift in the risk layer caused by a triggering event.

Table 4 Outstanding multi-year, multi-event RLS

Size (US$)	Issue	Term	Events	Risks	Aggregate event probability (%)
70.0	Atlas Re A	3	2	Euro Wind, Japan EQ, US EQ	5.47
30.0	Atlas Re B	3	2	Euro Wind, Japan EQ, US EQ	5.47
50.0	Atlas Re II A	3	3	Euro Wind, Japan EQ, US EQ	6.40
100.0	Atlas Re II B	3	2	Euro Wind, Japan EQ, US EQ	6.40
41.0	Mediterranean Re	5	2	French Wind	1.2/1.82
58.2	SR Wind A-1	4	2	Florida PR Wind	1.13
58.2	SR Wind A-2	4	2	French Wind	1.07
97.0	Trinom A-2	3	2	Euro Wind, US EQ, US Wind	8.53

Source: Transaction offering documents

Subsequent-event securities can provide sponsors with protection against catastrophic second or third events. Typically, these securities have higher probability loss layers (once activated) than a bond that only provides first-event coverage. These securities are typically exposed to two or three individual perils and are designed to ensure the availability of fully collateralised, fixed-price reinsurance in case the primary reinsurance market suffers a dislocation from other catastrophic events.

Subsequent-event bonds fall into two broad categories: securities where all covered perils can cause a triggering event and can all be exposed to the next event(s), and securities where one of the perils (in a multi-peril security) exposes the first-event layer and the second-event layer is then exposed to another peril. In addition, these securities can be issued with a fixed-risk premium (81% of the total) or with a step-up risk premium post-trigger (19%). Trinom A-2 is the only pure subsequent-event security to have a step-up coupon after the triggering event has occurred.

Mediterranean Re Class A and both of the SR Wind securities are primarily first-event notes but have a minimal exposure to second-events: 82% of the expected loss in Mediterranean A arises from the first-event Monaco Earthquake exposure, whereas the balance (16% or 4bp of expected loss) is exposed to the second French Windstorm event. Investors have not explicitly priced for the second-event component beyond factoring in the expected loss given that Mediterranean A represents a diversifying risk with an investment-grade rating.

The SR Wind transaction issued in May 2001 has a very unique structure. The A-1 notes are exposed to first-event French Windstorms and subsequent Florida and/or Puerto Rico Hurricanes in excess of the A-2 note attachment. Conversely, the A-2 notes are exposed to Florida and/or Puerto Rico Hurricanes and subsequent French Windstorms in excess of the A-1 note attachment. Interestingly, both bonds have an approximate 1.1% annual probability of attachment, whereas the second-event risk (as measured by the expected loss) in each security is only about 0.01%.

At issuance, investors appear to have priced both tranches as single-peril RLS without factoring in any potential risk from the second-event components. If a French Windstorm occurs and puts the SR Wind A-2 notes at risk to a second French Windstorm (albeit at a 1.1% probability), then the annualised expected loss on the A-2 notes will jump from 0.76% to 1.42% with no commensurate increase in risk premium. The price of the notes should decline to a level reflecting an appropriate risk premium for a 1.42% risk.

For example, if the trigger event occurred in the first year of the four-year term, we note that the A-2 notes would have a stated coupon of three-month Libor plus 575bp and an expected loss of 1.42%. If the required risk premium widened to 700bp (using Prime Hurricane as a valuation proxy with a 6.50% spread for a 1.27% expected loss), the price of the notes would decline by approximately 3.5%.

We would estimate the expected loss due to spread widening to be approximately 4bp, based on a 1.1% probability of a potential 3.5% mark-to-market loss. Although not explicitly referenced in the offering documents, this potential mark-to-market loss can be quantified and does provide value to the transaction sponsor. As such, a prudent investor should be able to identify these exposures and incorporate this risk into the due diligence process.

We can expand upon the process described in the SR Wind example to further illustrate the price effect of a shift to a second-event exposure by looking at the Trinom A-2 issue. Recall that this is the only security where investors receive a step-up in annual coupons as a result of the shift in the risk layer. Trinom A-2 is exposed to the second event over a three-year period across three different perils, each of which has an annual per event occurrence probability between 2.67% and 3.30% (total annual attachment probability on the A-2 notes of 8.53%). The blended, annualised expected loss is 0.67%.

Trinom A-2 paid a base risk premium of 400bp prior to a trigger event and a post-event risk premium of 1600bp. We calculated the blended risk premium by measuring the probability of receiving each of the risk premiums over the transaction term. Assuming that the risk premium increased from 400bp to 1600bp because a trigger event occurred six months after issuance, we calculated the probabilities of receiving the base coupon each year to be 95.7%, 87.6% and 80.1%. The probabilities of receiving the step-up coupon were 100% less the first probabilities. We then multiplied each risk premium by the appropriate probability to get an annual expected premium. We then summed the annual expected risk premium and divided by three to obtain an annualised expected risk premium of 5.46%.

The value of receiving a stepped-up risk premium can be illustrated by examining the principal loss after a trigger event for two scenarios:

1. A fixed-risk premium (5.46%).
2. A step-up risk premium (4% initially and then 16% following the exercise of the option).

We assumed:

❑ The trigger event occurs six months into the term.
❑ The A-2 notes have a duration of 2.2 years.
❑ The appropriate post-trigger market risk premium is 18%
❑ Trinom A-2 is trading at 100% of par pre-exercise.

The first step is to calculate the spread widening, which is 12.54% (18% less 5.46%). We then multiply this by the duration of 2.2 years to give an approximate monetary price decline of 27.588 percentage points. Thus, the new price, post-trigger, for the alternative where investors receive a level risk premium of 5.46% should be 72.412% of par. By comparison, the spread widening under the step-up scenario is only 2% (18% minus 16%). Multiplying the 2% by the 2.2-year duration implies a price decline of 4.4 percentage points, or a new bond price post-trigger of 95.60% of par.

This example is somewhat exaggerated by the relatively long duration and significant spread widening post-event but it illustrates the benefits to investors of receiving a step-up coupon after a triggering event, especially for events with a relatively high probability of occurrence. Investors could also use this framework to perform a sensitivity analysis of the expected principal loss to fixed-spread bonds by creating a matrix of when the trigger event occurs (to estimate the bond duration), estimating post-trigger forward risk premiums (to measure spread widening), and projecting probabilities of each scenario occurring.

Seasonality

At the end of 2001, approximately 74% of the outstanding volume of RLS was exposed to some form of seasonality. The concept of seasonality of event risk refers to the fact that certain types of events, such as hurricanes, typhoons, and windstorms, usually only occur during certain times of the year. This is because the conditions necessary to cause such events are generally present only during June–November (for typhoons and hurricanes) and October–March for extratropical windstorms (in Europe). Conversely, an earthquake is caused by movement along the earth's crusts or inside one of the plates and can occur at anytime throughout the year.

Risk premiums on RLS are paid on a quarterly or semiannual basis and accrue daily. Accordingly, this represents a potential mismatch between the risk premium paid to investors and the actual amount of event risk assumed. We believe that RLS should trade at price levels that match the amount of risk premium remaining in an annual risk period to the amount of event risk left in the annual risk period. Single-peril earthquake bonds, for example, equally match the amount of premium remaining with the amount of remaining risk, as each day that passes burns off an equal amount of risk and risk premium.

A simple example will illustrate the impact of seasonality on pricing for a one-year single-peril hurricane bond (Residential Re 2000). Residential Re represents a key benchmark issue in the RLS market as it indemnifies USAA for losses it suffers from hurricanes making landfall anywhere from Texas to Maine. Residential Re was issued on 1 June and pays an annual risk premium quarterly in arrears on a 1 June–31 May cycle. However, the official US hurricane season begins on 1 June and ends on 30 November (although most of the event risk occurs from August until early October).

Residential Re 2000 paid an annual risk premium of 410bp over Libor. We will assume that the market risk premium for Residential Re 2000 remains constant throughout the year. At the end of June, we estimate that 93% of the event risk remains in the hurricane season but only 92% of the risk premium remains. The appropriate discount margin should be calculated as follows: 93% ÷ 92% × 410bp, or 416bp. This calculation adjusts the discount margin on the securities for the proportion of event risk-to-risk premium remaining on the notes. The fair market value of this bond should be approximately 99.95 at a discount margin of 416bp.

Three months later, at 31 August, we estimate that approximately 56% of the event risk remains but 75% of the risk premium is left. Performing the same calculation, we note that the 410bp market risk premium is now a discount margin of 306bp (56% ÷ 75% × 410bp). The fair market value of the bond should now be approximately 100.73 percent of par. One of the anomalies of this market, however, is that hurricane bonds generally do not begin trading above par until later in September or in early October. We believe that this is due to investor psychological reluctance to buy hurricane bonds at a lower discount margin than at issuance while there is still significant event risk left in the risk period (albeit for a four- to six-week period).

At the official end to hurricane season on 30 November, we would expect the discount margin to tighten to around 100bp due to the lack of event risk remaining but capped by the fact that the credit rating will not be upgraded to investment grade. Accordingly, a 100bp discount margin would lead to an expected price of approximately 101.30 percent of par on the bond. The notes would then trade around Libor plus 100bp (with a declining dollar price) until maturity on 1 June of the following year.

This simple example represents a core framework for valuing RLS at any point during an annual risk period. Given the growth in the RLS market since 1997, there are various combinations of risks (European Wind and California Quake, European Wind only, European Wind and US Wind plus Earthquake, Earthquake and US Wind) that have different patterns of seasonality that impacts the price of these securities. The core principle in understanding how to incorporate different seasonality patterns is to remember to simply match the amount of premium remaining in an annual risk period with the amount of event risk remaining when calculating the discount margin an investor would use for purchasing RLS.

CONCLUSION

Risk-linked securities are often featured as a prominent example of convergence between the insurance and capital markets but they are also often misunderstood. It is the authors' hope that this chapter has provided an insight into how the transactions are structured in order to understand them better and appreciate the value that they can provide issuers. We also hope that we have given some insight into how to value the various different types of transactions in the 144A market. While the components of each deal differ and thus make individual comparisons more challenging, there are some basic tools investors can use to examine the differences between individual securities, whether understanding seasonality or comparing single vs multi-peril RLS.

The chapter closes with some comments about the future for the RLS market. Their role in protecting insurance company capital will become increasingly important as senior managers of insurance companies employ more modern capital management practices. Moreover, the rating agencies are increasingly differentiating the ratings of insurance companies who purchase long-term reinsurance from highly rated counterparties, as takes place in a RLS transaction, vs traditional annual reinsurance purchases from counterparties whose credit profile is not nearly as strong. Finally, RLS will increasingly become accepted as the investor market grows. This will occur as more transactions are brought to market, as liquidity increases, as more dealers support the market and more investors appreciate the diversifying characteristics of the asset.

1   The authors would like to thank Tony Rettino for his invaluable contribution.

BIBLIOGRAPHY

Atlas Reinsurance plc, "US$100,000,000 Floating Rate Notes due April 4, 2003", Final Offering Circular.

Atlas Reinsurance II plc, "US$150,000,000 Floating Rate Notes due January 1, 2005", Final Offering Circular.

Concentric, Ltd., "Floating Rate Notes due May 13, 2004", Final Offering Circular.

DeCaro, J., 2001 "Assessing Relative Value for Multi-Peril Securities", Research Report, 30 May, Aon Capital Markets.

DeCaro, J., 2002, "*Risk-Linked Securities Market – 2001 Review*", Research Report, 4 February, Cochran, Caronia Securities LLC.

Gold Eagle Capital 2001 Limited, "US$116,400,000 Floating Rate Modeled Index Linked Notes due April 2002", Final Offering Circular.

Halyard Re B.V., "Variable Rate Remarketed Reset Notes", Final Offering Circular.

Juno Re, Ltd., "Floating Rate Notes due June 26, 2002", Final Offering Circular.

Mediterranean Re plc, "US$129,000,000 Floating Rate Notes due November 18, 2005", Final Offering Circular.

Namazu Re, Ltd., "US$100,000,000 Floating Rate Notes due December 4, 2004", Final Offering Circular.

NeHi, Inc., "US$41,500,000 Floating Rate Notes due June 9, 2003", Final Offering Circular.

Pacific Re Ltd., "US$80,000,000 Floating Rate Notes due May 31, 2003", Final Offering Circular.

Parametric Re, Ltd., "US$90,000,000 Floating Rate Notes due November 29, 2007", Final Offering Circular.

PRIME Capital CalQuake & Eurowind Ltd., "US$129,000,000 Floating Rate Notes due January 7, 2004", Final Offering Circular.

PRIME Capital Hurricane Ltd., "US$194,000,000 Floating Rate Notes due January 7, 2004", Final Offering Circular.

Redwood Capital I Ltd., "US$160,050,000 Principal At-Risk Variable Rate Notes due January 1, 2003", Final Offering Circular.

Residential Re 2001 Limited, "Variable Rate Notes due June 1, 2004", Final Offering Circular.

SR Wind Ltd., "US$166,400,000 Floating Rate Notes due May 18, 2005", Final Offering Circular.

Trinom Ltd., "US$157,000,000 Floating Rate Notes due June 18, 2004", Final Offering Circular.

Western Capital Limited, "US$97,000,000 Floating Rate Notes due January 7, 2003", Final Offering Circular.

4

Industry Loss Warranties

Enda McDonnell

Access Re

An industry loss warranty (ILW) is a reinsurance contract where the payoff is dependent on two triggers. The first trigger is the insured loss of the buyer, the indemnity, the second trigger is the losses to the underlying insurance industry as a whole, the original insured industry loss. Both triggers have to be hit for the buyer of the ILW to receive a claims payoff. Although the second trigger usually dominates, the first trigger is preserved to ensure that the buyer gets reinsurance accounting treatment. The first trigger distinguishes ILW's from pure derivatives. ILWs are also known as original loss warranties (OLWs) and market loss warranties (MLWs). ILWs are primarily used to protect against property risk, property catastrophe, marine, aviation and satellite losses.

INTRODUCTION

The property catastrophe market is by far the largest ILW market. Nevertheless, the concepts described herein can also be applied to the property per risk, marine, aviation and satellite markets. This chapter provides an historical perspective on how the ILW market has developed, it reviews the key elements of ILWs and the indices used to measure the original insured industry losses. This chapter also provides a list of historical losses, a review of how long it took them to develop in the US, buyer and seller motivations, types of ILWs – which includes examples of current pricing – and finally, it reviews current trends in the ILW market.

Historical perspective

Prior to 1989, there were few large original insured industry losses, (as is later illustrated in Figure 2). The perception at that time was that a US$5 billion original insured industry loss was an unlikely event. A US$10 billion event was considered unthinkable and anyone espousing such a thought would have generally caused some raised eyebrows. Prior to

Hurricane Hugo in September 1989, no single property catastrophe had caused economic damages of more than US$2.3 billion.[1] Nevertheless, reinsurance market participants were aware of the potential of mega catastrophic losses, particularly the occurrence of the 1906 Earthquake in San Francisco,[2] the 1938 storm in New England[3] and Hurricanes Betsy[4] and Camille.[5]

ILWs covering property catastrophe risks originated in London in the late 1980s. The collapse of the market providing coverage for retrocessional (reinsurance of reinsurers) property catastrophe exposures, specifically coverage for retro on retro, ignited the demand for ILWs. In the early 1990s ILW's were perceived to be the only way to obtain full risk transfer coverage for a retrocessional property portfolio. Initially, ILWs were purchased exclusively by clients protecting their assumed reinsurance portfolios. Syndicates at Lloyd's of London were prominent buyers. The first contracts placed covered all property losses on a worldwide basis. The warranty triggers in those contracts were very low by current standards – the highest attachment point for ILW contracts at that time was US$10 billion.[6] Today a number of contracts have attachment points as high as US$50 billion.

The major writers of ILWs in the early 1990s were Berkshire Hathaway and AXA Reassurance. The level of the warranties increased quickly after Typhoon Mireille in Japan in 1991 and Hurricane Andrew in the US in 1992. Warranty levels in the US increased to as high as US$15 billion in the mid 1990s. In the mid to late 1990s, the average attachment points continued to increase with a number of contracts having warranties of up to US$25 billion. By the late 1990s, the attachment points had increased as high as US$50 billion. Despite the loss activity in the early 1990s there has been a significant increase in the number of contracts purchased and in the attachment of those contracts since 1995.

The key elements of an ILW are as follows:
1. Territory: the territory is the geographic area where the loss has to occur to satisfy the warranty trigger. This can range from a single state in the US to a loss being suffered worldwide. (Actually, more than 70% of all ILWs are placed for exposures in the US and its territories and possessions.)
2. Term: this is the duration of the contract. Usually contracts have a term of 12 months, however contracts have been placed stipulating a term as short as a month or as long as up to three years.
3. Perils covered: these can range from all perils to single perils, eg, earthquake. Recently, perils in property ILWs have been limited to natural perils, which include windstorm, tropical storm, hurricane, winter storm, hail, tornado, cyclone, water damage, flood, wind, thunderstorm, snow, ice, freeze, earthquake, tsunami, lightning, wildland fire,

volcanic disturbance/eruption, landslide, subsidence, meteors falling to earth and fire or collapse, following a natural peril.

4. Warranty: this is the currency size (for example, US$) of the original insured industry loss – the trigger.

5. Index: the index is used to determine the size of the loss in property contracts. The most common indices are Property Claims Services (PCS) in the US and either Sigma or the NatCatSERVICE index for losses outside the US.

6. Reporting period: this is the amount of time after a loss occurs that a client has to report a loss to an ILW contract. The majority of property ILWs have a 36-month reporting period, however a minority have a 24-month reporting period. This reporting period normally starts at the date of the loss, however a number of contracts conclude the reporting period 36 months after the expiration of the contract.

7. Limit: this is the amount of protection being purchased. Average size of the limit purchased has increased since 1997 (up to the time of writing) from approximately US$3 million to approximately US$10 million.

8. Retention: this is the amount of retained loss the client keeps before making a recovery under the contract. Usually this is a very low number as the seller is underwriting the industry loss and not the buyers underlying exposures. Retentions are usually set at US$10,000 but may be as high as US$1,000,000.

9. Premium and premium payment dates: the premium for an ILW is usually paid at the inception of the contract. Contracts where the premium is significant may state that the premium is due in a number of instalments. These installments may vary between being due quarterly and semi-annually.

10. Reinstatement: the majority of ILWs have a reinstatement provision. This means that the limit under the contract is reinstated following a loss in return for a reinstatement premium, which is usually equal to the premium paid for the original limit. Bear in mind that the total US dollar recovery under the contract is confined to the original limit plus the number of limits reinstated. Contracts that do not usually have a reinstatement include those where: the territorial scope is limited; the coverage is restricted to a single peril; the warranty is very high or where the buyer of the coverage does not want one. Usually the price for an ILW without a reinstatement is higher than the price with a reinstatement. The amount varies depending on the rate-on-line charged for the contract. (Rate-on-line is the premium paid, divided by the limit of the contract.) Most reinsurers load the up-front price by a factor of 20% to 35% to compensate for the lack of a reinstatement. This rule of thumb emanated in Lloyd's and continues today.

11. General conditions: these general conditions are the same as those usually found in traditional property catastrophe excess of loss contracts

such as access to records, arbitration clause, errors and omissions, nuclear incident exclusion clauses and the intermediary clause.

12. Exclusions: given that the loss payment is primarily based on the original insured industry loss the number of exclusions are limited compared to a traditional property catastrophe excess of loss contract. From a reinsurers viewpoint, the critical issue is what lines of business are included in the loss numbers reported by the Index used.

Indices used

Property Claims Service (PCS), Sigma and Munich Re's NatCat SERVICE are the three indices most widely used in ILWs. A commentary on each follows.

Property Claim Services (PCS)

PCS is a division of the American Insurance Services Group.[7] PCS is responsible for quantifying industry insurance losses for property catastrophe events in the US. It estimates industry-wide anticipated losses to include payments for time element losses, vehicles, inland marine, contents and fixed property lines. In doing so it assigns a number to each catastrophe. For example, it assigned cat number 27 to Hurricane Andrew in 1992 as illustrated in Table 1.

According to PCS they generally combine:

> "two damage-estimating methods to develop the best estimate in the least amount of time. The first method involves surveys of companies, agents, adjusters, public officials and others to develop details on individual company losses and claim volumes and amounts. All information and proprietary data reported to PCS are kept strictly confidential. This data is then compared to market share by line of insurance, along with other trend factors, to develop a total projected loss estimate".[8]

Sigma

Sigma is published approximately eight times a year by Swiss Re's Economic Research and Consulting unit in Zurich, New York and Hong Kong. One of the eight issues is dedicated to review the natural catastrophe and man-made disasters for the previous year.

Sigma publishes a table listing major losses since 1970, a copy of which is shown in Table 2. The reported amount for insured losses from a catastrophe is adjusted annually to compensate for inflation in the US. This is a key difference between PCS and Sigma.

Daily newspaper, direct insurance and reinsurance periodicals, special publications and reports from primary insurers and reinsurers provide the source for the choice of events. Sigma does not claim to be comprehensive, however, given its publishing history since 1970 it is considered in the

Table 1 Top 10 original insured industry losses in the US

Catastrophe #	Event	Year	Period	State	Perils	Estimated Loss (US$)
48	Coordinated terrorist attacks – WTC	2001	September 11	NY, VA and possibly others	Fire and explosion, fire-other	16.596 billion
27	Hurricane Andrew	1992	August 24–26	FL, LA	Wind, tornadoes, flooding	15.5 billion
78	Northridge Earthquake	1994	January 17	CA	Earthquake, fire	12.5 billion
18	Hurricane Hugo	1989	September 17–22	NC, GA, PR, VI, SC, VA	Wind, tornadoes, flooding	4.195 billion
69	Hurricane Georges	1998	September 21–28	PR, VI, FL, AL, MS, LA	Wind, tornadoes, flooding	2.955 billion
44	Tropical Storm Allison	2001	June 5–17	FL, MS, NJ, PA, LA, TX	Flooding, tropical storm and wind	2.5 billion
54	Hurricane Opal	1995	October 4–5	FL, AL, GA, SC, NC, TN	Wind, tornadoes, flooding	2.1 billion
97	Hurricane Floyd	1999	September 14–16	FL, GA, SC, NC, VA, DE, MD, NJ, PA, NY, CT, RI, MA, VT, NH, ME	Wind, tornadoes, flooding	1.96 billion
46	March blizzard	1993	March 11–14	MS, NC, AL, FL, GA, SC, MD, DE, RI, MA, VT, NH, TN, KY, OH, TX, PA, NY, NJ, CT, ME, WV, VA, LA	Wind, hail, tornadoes, snow, ice, freezing	1.75 billion
38	Cat 38	2001	April 6–12	AK, CO, IA, IL, KS, KY, MI, MN, NE, OH, OK, PA, TX, WN	Flooding, hail, snow, ice, freezing	1.9 billion

Source: Property Claims Services

market to be the most acceptable for determining the size of the insured industry loss outside the US.

Swiss Re does not condone the use of Sigma as an index for ILWs. Confidence in Sigma as an index has waned recently resulting from the lack of updates during the year as well as uncertainty regarding the updating of the original insured industry loss numbers that were generally known to be too low for European storm Lothar. Sigma revised their published number for Lothar and some other losses which has mitigated the erosion of confidence.

NatCatSERVICE

Munich Re Group produces its NatCatSERVICE, which identifies and calculates the original insured industry loss for events worldwide. NatCatSERVICE is Munich Re's version of Sigma. Through its affiliation with Reuters, the loss numbers are updated and reported frequently. Consequently, Munich's NatCatSERVICE is becoming more popular as a substitute for Sigma. Some buyers prefer to include both Sigma and NatCatSERVICE as the index.

Historical losses

Table 1 shows the top 10 original insured industry losses in the US. Loss numbers shown do not include losses that result from a catastrophe that involves territories outside the US or its territories and possessions.

Table 2 shows the top 40 original insured losses in the world from 1970 until 2001.

Development of original insured industry losses

How long does it take for the original insured industry loss to fully develop? The answer depends on the peril causing the loss. Historically, wind-related losses develop rather quickly. The largest insured loss from a natural catastrophe in history was Hurricane Andrew at US$15.5 billion in the US in 1992. PCS issued four reports on Andrew with its final report issued 176 days from the date of the loss. (Incidentally, the longest time from the date of loss until the final report for a wind loss in the top 10 insured industry losses was 240 days for Hurricane Hugo.)

The second largest natural catastrophe loss in history, reported at US$12.5 billion, was the Northridge Earthquake in California on January 17, 1994. PCS issued 10 reports on Northridge with the final report issued 602 days from the date of the loss. This is two and a half times longer than Hugo but well within the 24 and 36 month reporting period found in most ILWs.

Table 2   The 40 most costly insurance losses 1970–2001

Insured loss[1]	Date	Event	Country
20,185	8/23/92	Hurricane Andrew	USA, Bahamas
19,000	9/11/01	Terrorist attack in New York and Washington	USA
16,720	1/17/94	Northridge earthquake	USA[2]
7,338	9/27/91	Typhoon Mireille	Japan
6,221	1/25/90	Winterstorm Daria	France, GB, B et al.
6,164	12/25/99	Winterstorm Lothar over Western Europe	France, CH et al.
5,990	9/15/89	Hurricane Hugo	Puerto Rico, USA et al.
4,674	10/15/87	Storm and floods in Europe	Europe
4,323	2/25/90	Winterstorm Vivian	West/central Europe
4,293	9/22/99	Typhoon Bart hits south of country	Japan
3,833	9/20/98	Hurricane Georges	USA, Caribbean
3,150	6/5/01	Tropical storm Allison; rain, floods	USA
2,994	7/6/88	Explosion on platform Piper Alpha	Great Britain
2,872	1/17/95	Great Hanshin earthquake in Kobe	Japan
2,551	12/27/99	Winterstorm Martin over south-west France and Spain	France, Spain, CH
2,508	9/10/99	Hurricane Floyd; heavy downpours, flooding	USA et al.
2,440	10/1/95	Hurricane Opal	USA, Mexico
2,144	3/10/93	Blizzard, tornadoes	USA
2,019	9/11/92	Hurricane Iniki	USA
1,900	4/6/01	Flooding, hail, tornadoes	USA
1,892	10/23/89	Explosion in a petrochemical plant	USA
1,834	9/12/79	Hurricane Frederic	USA
1,806	9/5/96	Hurricane Fran	USA
1,795	9/18/74	Tropical cyclone Fifi	Honduras
1,743	9/3/95	Hurricane Luis in Caribbean	Caribbean
1,665	9/10/88	Hurricane Gilbert	Jamaica et al.
1,594	12/3/99	Winterstorm Anatol	West/northern Europe
1,578	5/3/99	Series of more than 70 tornadoes in the Midwest	USA
1,564	12/17/83	Blizzards, cold wave	USA, Canada et al.
1,560	10/20/91	Forest fires which spread to urban areas, drought	USA
1,546	4/2/74	Tornadoes in 14 states	USA
1,475	4/25/73	Flooding on the Mississippi	USA
1,461	5/15/98	Wind, hail and tornadoes (MN, IA)	USA
1,428	10/17/89	Loma Prieta earthquake	USA
1,413	8/4/70	Hurricane Celia	USA, Cuba
1,386	9/19/98	Typhoon Vicki	Japan, Philippines
1,357	9/21/01	Explosion in fertiliser factory; 4,000 homes destroyed	France
1,337	1/5/98	Cold spell with ice and snow	Canada, USA
1,319	5/5/95	Wind, hail and flooding (TX, NM)	USA
1,300	10/29/91	Hurricane Grace	USA

[1] Excluding liability damage, expressed in US$ millions
[2] Figures for natural catastrophes in the US with permission of Property Claims Service (PCS)
(Source: Swiss Re, sigma)

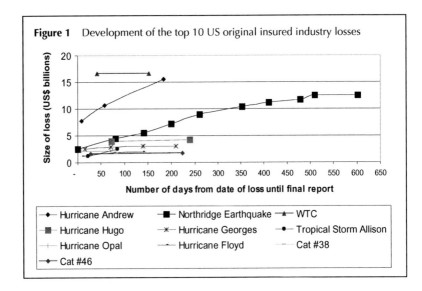

Figure 1   Development of the top 10 US original insured industry losses

Motivations to participate in the ILW market

Motivations for buying these are listed below.

1. Contracts are easy to understand.
2. They are easy to structure.
3. Minimal retention – coverage can drop down to pick up loss excess of retentions as low as US$10,000.
4. Other coverage purchased by the buyer inures to the sole benefit of the buyer.
5. No underwriting information is required as the seller is underwriting the industry loss and not the buyer's portfolio.
6. Pricing may be more competitive than the pricing for traditional coverage. This is owing to the relatively lower level of uncertainty on industry losses compared to the uncertainty that there may be for a specific portfolio.
7. Reinsurers may not give a buyer the credit for changes made to his/her portfolio. A client may feel that the industry loss on which to attach a specific layer may be much higher than the level that a reinsurer considers necessary to attach a layer. Using an ILW focuses the decision on pricing at an agreed attachment point.
8. ILWs provide broad coverage. They may include protection for reinstatement costs, lost profit commissions, no claim bonuses and index-linked securities.
9. Finally, they can fill shortfalls in traditional programmes.

Non-insurance entities have expressed interest in buying and selling ILWs recently. They are able to buy an ILW in two ways. The first is to purchase an ILW with only the original insured industry loss trigger. Removing the ultimate net loss trigger essentially transforms an insurance product into a pure derivative product. The second way is to have an insurance/reinsurance entity, that has significant exposures in the desired territory, purchase the cover for them and then the insurance/reinsurance entity transforms the reinsurance product into a derivative on the other end. A fee, that is negotiated between the transformer and the ultimate buyer, is usually paid to the transformer to perform this service. Selling ILWs by non insurance/reinsurance entities is the reverse of the buying process.

Motivations for selling
1. They are easy to price, underwrite and administer. This is a considerable advantage for a participant looking to enter the reinsurance market.
2. Moral hazard is eliminated from the protected portfolio. The purchaser of the cover cannot select against the reinsurer by significantly increasing their writings because the trigger is the industry loss and not the buyer's own portfolio.
3. The ILW eliminates surprise losses from small events. During every property catastrophe occurrence there is usually one traditional reinsurance programme that gives rise to significantly higher losses than reinsurers predicted. These surprise losses are eliminated when ILWs are sold.
4. They eliminate concerns about poor underwriting information.
5. ILWs build a balanced portfolio by selling coverage in geographic areas where the seller has unsold aggregate.
6. Coverage can be tailored by peril and by territory, thereby allowing the seller to sell unused capacity and maximise returns from a portfolio.
7. The size of loss is usually known within 24 to 36 months from the date of the loss occurrence.

One concern many buyers have with ILWs is the issue of basis risk. Basis risk is the possibility that the outcome is different than expected.[9] In ILW terms, this outcome can be positive or negative. A positive outcome would result in having an original insured industry loss that triggers a recovery and the ultimate net loss to the buyer is lower than expected. This positive outcome may occur because of differences in the geographic distribution of a portfolio compared to the industry, differences in the lines of business written or better selection in the quality of risk in the portfolio compared to the rest of the industry. Accordingly, negative basis risk occurs when these factors go against the buyer of the ILW and the loss on their portfolio is greater than expected while, at the same time, the original insured industry loss does not meet the warranty in the ILW.

There are a number of strategies that help to deal with basis risk. The first is to determine in advance what the likely industry attachment point is for the layer of protection that the buyer wants to protect. This may be done with the help of various catastrophe-modelling tools. Having determined this, the next step is to pick the attachment point or points of the ILWs to buy. Additionally, the amount of limit to purchase at each level should be decided if there is more than one attachment point.

Assume for this example that the likely industry attachment point is US$24 billion and the exhaustion point is US$30 billion. The buyer decides to purchase:

1. a contract that attaches at US$20 billion,
2. another that attaches at US$25 billion, and
3. another that attaches at US$27.5 billion.

The reason to purchase at an attachment point below the predicted level is to minimise any negative basis risk and maximise any positive basis risk. Naturally, the price of the contracts factor into the equation and may determine how much is purchased at each level.

Another strategy is to purchase a pro rata layered ILW that:

1. attaches at US$20 billion and
2. exhausts at US$30 billion with a pro rata payoff in between.

Pro rata/layered ILWs will be discussed later in this chapter.

Types of ILW contracts

Property catastrophe ILWs are structured as occurrence or aggregate contracts. An occurrence contract provides protection against *severe losses* while aggregate contracts protect against *frequency of losses*. Greater than 90% of ILWs are occurrence contracts with the remaining 10% being aggregate contracts. This is because reinsurance buyers have been more concerned with *severity of losses* rather than the *frequency of losses*.

Occurrence contracts
As discussed, occurrence contracts are used to protect a buyer against the severity of losses. In this case, it is usual for the attachment point of each occurrence ceded to the contract to be much higher than that of an aggregate contract. An example of an occurrence ILW will illustrate how the contract works. The fictitious contract we will examine has the following pertinent features.

Territory: the 50 states of the US plus territories and possessions (or US plus T&P).
Term: 12 months from January 1, 2002.
Limit: US$10,000,000.

❏ *Retention*: US$10,000.
❏ *Warranty*: US$20,000,000,000.
❏ *Index*: PCS.
❏ *Rate-on-line*: 15%.
❏ *Reinstatement*: one at 100% as to time, pro rata as to amount.
❏ *Premium*: payable in full at inception.
❏ *Perils covered*: all natural perils.
❏ *Reporting period*: 36 months from the date of loss.

This contract will only cover property catastrophe losses that are caused by a natural peril where the original insured industry loss in the US (plus T&P) is equal to or greater than US$20 billion. The client would recover US$10 million under this contract once the warranty has been satisfied and the client has US$10,010,000 in ultimate net losses. In the event the reported loss by PCS is US$19 billion, the client has 36 months from the date of loss to make a recovery if the original insured loss develops to satisfy the warranty. PCS is the index that is used and in order for a loss to be paid, it would have to be PCS who report that the original insured industry loss is equal to or exceeds US$20 billion.

A variation on the occurrence contract is the window contract, which is also known as the corridor contract. In this instance, a recovery is made only if the original insured industry loss is equal to or greater than X and less than Y. The advantage of a window contract for a reinsurer is that there is no recovery once the loss reaches a certain level. As such, it does not aggregate with other contracts that the reinsurer has that attach at a level higher than the exhaustion point of the window contract. The advantage of a window ILW for a buyer is the reduction in price. Buyers of window contracts usually have protection in excess of the upper level of the window cover.

Aggregate contracts
Aggregate covers are used to protect a buyer against the frequency of losses. It is usual that the attachment point of each occurrence ceded to the contract has a low attachment point. Additionally, there is no reinstatement provision as coverage is provided in the aggregate rather than on an occurrence basis. The key element of an aggregate ILW is the definition of events to be covered under the contract as well as the aggregate retention. An example will help to illustrate these distinctions. The fictitious contract we will examine is detailed as below.

❏ *Territory*: the 48 contiguous states of the US.
❏ *Term*: 12 months from January 1, 2002.
❏ *Limit*: US$10,000,000
❏ *Retention*: US$10,000.

❑ *Warranty*: original insured industry losses less than US$1,000,000,000.
❑ *Aggregate retention*: US$6,000,000,000.
❑ *Index*: PCS.
❑ *Rate-on-line*: 18%.
❑ *Premium*: payable in full at inception.
❑ *Perils covered*: all natural perils excluding earthquake and ensuing fire loss.
❑ *Reporting period*: 36 months from the expiration of the contract.

This contract will only cover property catastrophe losses that are caused by a natural peril (other than earthquake and ensuing fire) where the original insured industry loss is less than US$1 billion. In order for a recovery to take place, the aggregate loss amount will need to equal or exceed US$6 billion. Any individual loss that is equal to or greater than US$1 billion at the end of the reporting period will not be included in the calculation of the aggregate losses. Logical deduction dictates that there will need to be a minimum of seven individual loss occurrences in order to satisfy the aggregate retention. The client would recover US$10 million under this contract once the aggregate retention has been satisfied and the client has US$10,010,000 in ultimate net losses. The reporting period is 36 months from the end of the term of the contract; however, the buyer is entitled to make a provisional recovery for actual paid losses recoverable under this contract as soon as the aggregate retention has been satisfied.

Payoff options

The payoff under occurrence and aggregate contracts is either *binary or pro rata*. Greater than 90% of ILWs have *binary* triggers, meaning that the reinsurer pays out 100% of the limit once the warranty has been reached, assuming that the buyer has an ultimate net loss that is equal to, or greater than, the limit of the contract plus the retention. A number of buyers have been concerned about the original insured industry loss being reported just below the attachment level of the contract purchased. Sellers have also been concerned about the original insured industry loss coming in just above a particular trigger. Historically, buyers and sellers have dealt with this concern by buying and selling ILW contracts at various attachment points.

In response to these concerns, a new structure has been developed where the payoff is directly proportional to the level of the original insured industry loss. These are called pro rata or layered ILWs. An example will illustrate how the *pro rata* payoff works.

Assume that the structure is US$10 million, a part of US$10 billion excess of US$10 billion – for an ILW protecting against earthquakes in California.

Table 3 shows the recovery under various scenarios, assuming the buyer has sufficient ultimate net loss.

Table 3   Recovery under a US$10 million part of US$10 billion excess of US$10 billion ILW

Original insured industry loss	Percentage recovery	US dollar recovery
US$10,000,000,000	0%	US$0
US$15,000,000,000	50%	US$5,000,000
US$20,000,000,000	100%	US$10,000,000
US$25,000,000,000	100%	US$10,000,000

Pricing

Pricing for ILWs is primarily derived from the market. The laws of supply and demand dictate the pricing, and the prices fluctuate from one week to the next. No two sellers have the same pricing and the level of pricing varies, sometimes by a considerable margin. Underpinning the law of supply and demand is the calculation of the minimum price that a seller of ILWs is willing to accept for the assumption of the risk. This is a combination of the historical loss cost and scientific calculations based on the perceived chance of a loss. The formula used for the scientific calculation by a number of sellers is as follows:

minimum price = loss cost + risk load + expense factor + profit requirement

where:

❏ the lost cost is the annual probability of a loss. Sellers use a variety of computer models to calculate what the loss cost is and the result may vary for each seller depending on the model(s) used and the underlying assumptions used in working with the model.
❏ the risk load is usually expressed as a percentage of the standard deviation. Determining the percentage to use is a function of how volatile the class is perceived to be by the seller, how much capacity the seller has available and other opportunities available to the seller.
❏ the expense factor is a calculation that is unique to each company and varies widely based on the seller's cost structure.
❏ the profit requirement is also an internal calculation for each company and it too is a function of the minimum requirements for a seller, the amount of capacity available for sale and other opportunities available to the seller.

In most instances, a seller of ILWs will not offer their minimum price when requested to offer a quotation for a particular ILW. Most sellers will try to set the price as high as possible to ensure that they do not leave any money

Table 4 Access Re indicative ILW pricing grid (as of 1 April, 2002)[10]

First event covers with reinstatement 1 @ 100 (indications may still apply without a reinstatement.)

Trigger point	Nationwide natural perils	Nationwide wind	Nationwide quake	Florida wind	California quake	New Madrid quake	Georgia to Maine wind	Texas wind
US$1 billion	N/A	N/A	N/A	N/A	N/A	N/A	N/A	N/A
US$1.5 billion	N/A	N/A	N/A	N/A	N/A	N/A	N/A	N/A
US$2 billion	N/A	N/A	N/A	N/A	N/A	N/A	N/A	11.00%
US$3 billion	N/A	N/A	N/A	N/A	N/A	N/A	N/A	9.00%
US$5 billion	35.00%	26.50%	18.00%	20.25%	14.50%	4.00%	9.00%	6.00%
US$10 billion	25.00%	19.00%	12.00%	14.50%	10.25%	2.50%	5.00%	4.00%
US$12.5 billion	21.75%	16.50%	11.50%	12.50%	9.25%	2.00%	4.50%	3.25%
US$15 billion	18.50%	13.75%	10.00%	11.00%	8.00%	1.75%	4.00%	2.75%
US$20 billion	14.50%	10.00%	6.50%	7.75%	6.25%	1.50%	3.00%	2.00%
US$25 billion	12.00%	8.50%	5.25%	6.25%	5.25%	1.40%	2.25%	1.75%
US$30 billion	9.50%	6.50%	4.50%	5.25%	4.25%	1.30%	1.75%	1.50%
US$40 billion	7.50%	5.50%	4.00%	4.25%	3.50%	1.20%	1.50%	1.25%
US$50 billion	5.00%	4.25%	3.00%	4.00%	3.00%	1.00%	1.00%	1.00%

Trigger point	Japan			Europe	Caribbean	Rest of the World
	Natural perils	Quake only	Wind only	Natural perils	Natural perils	Natural perils
US$1 billion	N/A	N/A	N/A	N/A	30.50%	25.00%
US$1.5 billion	N/A	N/A	N/A	N/A	22.00%	17.50%
US$2 billion	N/A	N/A	N/A	N/A	16.00%	12.50%
US$3 billion	26.00%	15.50%	14.50%	27.00%	10.00%	8.00%
US$5 billion	14.00%	7.00%	6.50%	14.00%		
US$7.5 billlion	11.50%	6.00%	5.25%	11.50%		
US$10 billion	6.50%	4.75%	4.25%	6.50%		
US$12.5 billion	6.00%	4.00%	3.50%	6.00%		
US$15 billion	5.25%	3.00%	3.00%	5.25%		
US$20 billion	4.00%	2.00%	2.00%	4.00%		

Second event covers – indicative prices – no reinstatement

Trigger point	Nationwide natural perils	Japan natural perils	Europe natural perils
US$1 billion	N/A	N/A	N/A
US$1.5 billion	N/A	N/A	N/A
US$3 billion	12.00%	7.50%	8.00%
US$5 billion	5.75%	3.50%	4.00%
US$10 billion	4.75%	1.50%	1.50%
US$12.5 billion	3.50%		
US$15 billion	2.50%		
US$20 billion			

on the table. Therein lies the value of a good experienced broker who is knowledgeable on the supply and demand in the market as well as the pricing of deals done recently. A good broker will know where to go to get the best price for a given amount of capacity, what terms and conditions can be negotiated with a seller as well as where to go to sell capacity. A seller may want to sell discretely. A good broker can facilitate this. History tells us that there is a considerable variation in the price that may be paid for a contract at a given warranty level.

Until the late 1990s the majority of buyers and sellers of ILWs calculated the price based on the historical profitability in conjunction with their perceptions of future loss activity. One of the earliest ILWs purchased was in 1987. The contract protected against all property losses worldwide with a warranty of US$4 billion and paid a rate-on-line of 10%.

A number of multi-year contracts offer a profit commission feature. In the event the contract runs loss-free or the sum of the premiums exceed the losses over a given term, then a profit commission is payable.

Figure 2 provides a synopsis of the pricing levels during the period from 1998 to 2002 for the four most popular attachment points.

The general pricing trend since 1999 is upward. This is the result of a number of losses in the marketplace over this time, these being Hurricane Georges in the Caribbean in 1998, European storms Lothar and Martin in 1999, and the terrorist attacks in New York and Virginia in 2001.

Shown in Table 4 is a snapshot of pricing for various ILWs split by attachment level and by territory. (Please note that these prices are indications only and are based on contracts placed by the author.) Prices for pro rata ILWs closely track the prices for binary ILWs. A good benchmark to use when pricing a pro rata ILW is to take the midpoint of the layer and

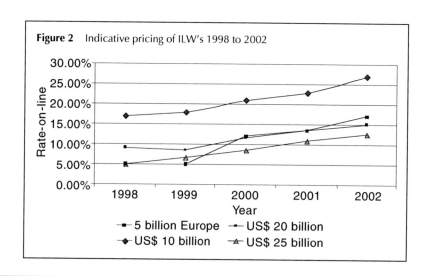

Figure 2   Indicative pricing of ILW's 1998 to 2002

compare it to the price of a binary ILW at that attachment point. The pricing will usually be close to that price.

Current trends
Over the last five years, ILWs have become more mainstream. Primary insurance companies have purchased them as a complement to traditional reinsurance protections. The more primary company buyers that become comfortable with the exposures in their portfolio, the odds of using ILWs as part of their risk management strategy increases.

In the past ILWs were universally viewed as "no tears" reinsurance, with no long-term commitment between the buyer and the seller. This perception is changing as buyers are purchasing and reinsurers are selling ILWs on a more consistent basis. Additionally, the majority of reinsurers are participants in the ILW market. Therefore, they are looking for a stable marketplace in the long term to sell their capacity.

CONCLUSION
In this chapter we have discussed how ILW's have become a key tool for insurance, reinsurance and other companies in the risk management toolkit. In particular they are viewed to be a complementary way of transferring risk in conjunction with more traditional forms of reinsurance to allow buyers to manage their net exposures to both severe losses and to the accumulation of smaller losses.

Innovation in ILW products continues. Recent innovations include the layered ILW and window/corridor contracts. Given the flexibility of ILWs it is expected that their use will continue to increase and innovations in product structure and pricing will persist.

1   http://www.nhc.noaa.gov/pastcost.html
2   http://quake.usgs.gov/info/1906/
3   http://www2.sunysuffolk.edu/mandias/38hurricane/
4   http://www.hurricanecity.com/betsy.htm
5   http://www.mathstat.usouthal.edu/~lynn/hurricanes/camille.html
6   The attachment point is the retention under the contract. ILWs have two attachment points, the low retention for the ultimate net loss and the original insured industry loss level where the contract begins to pay out or pays out in full if the ultimate net loss has been satisfied.
7   See www.iso.com/aisg/index.html
8   See www.iso.com
9   Basis risk is generally defined as the risk of varying fluctuations of the spot and the futures price between the moment at which a position is opened and the moment at which it is closed.
10 For updates email enda@accessre.com

5

Risk Swaps

Yuichi Takeda

Tokio Marine Management

Controlling risk is a never-ending theme in the insurance and financial community. Among the various risk management tools and techniques developed, financial swaps are by far the dominant risk management product in the global financial market; according to a report of the Bank of International Settlements, the notional amount of interest swaps at June 2001 reached more than US$61 trillion.[1] Since the early 1980s, a history of increased volatility urged market participants to utilise swaps as an effective tool to weather the turbulence of financial markets. Like banks, insurance companies also use swaps; in the area of asset and liability management, for example, they exchange a floating interest rate with a fixed one, in order to manage the risk of falling interest rates.

INTRODUCTION

In terms of volatility, insurance risks are no exception. In the past, catastrophic events such as Hurricane Andrew in 1992 and the Northridge earthquake in 1994 created hardening markets; reinsurers had to raise their premiums significantly, often reducing their capacities at the same time. The terrorist attack of September 11, 2001 created another significant volatility. Almost regardless of the memory of past insurance crises, the public again raised the concern of the availability of private insurance. Such experiences and comparisons with the financial markets call into question why the insurance markets, as professional communities of shared risks for centuries, have been behind the development of financial markets in creating alternative solutions to cope with the significant turbulence of insurance pricing and capacity.

The convergence between insurance and financial markets provided an opportunity to create alternative risk solutions. In addition to the emergence of insurance risk securitisation, a limited number of insurance and reinsurance companies have recently started to exchange natural catastrophe (cat) risks, in a similar fashion to financial swaps. This insurance version of swap – called a "risk swap" in this chapter – retains the spirit of reciprocity, together with the flexibility of insurance contracts and the fundamentals of finance. This chapter will discuss the concept, rationale, background and application of risk swaps.

WHAT IS A RISK SWAP?

Risk swaps were developed as one of the financial applications of exchanging insurance risks. As their name indicates, risk swaps involve two or more different insurance risks being exchanged. Following the principles of finance, both risks are clearly defined and quantified to be on a parity condition; extensive modelling analysis of insurance risks is almost prerequisite. On the other hand, risk swaps can be designed to tailor to the specific needs of the counterparties and to allow a flexibility to draft contracts. Instead of using the International Swaps and Derivatives Association (ISDA) form, a pair of two reinsurance contracts can also effectively constitute a risk swap transaction.

Deal Examples

1. One-on-one risk swap

In March 2000, Tokio Marine and State Farm exchanged earthquake risks of US$200 million each. Tokyo and New Madrid earthquake risks were exchanged between the two primary insurers for five years, with a pair of parametric triggers designed to equalise the loss probabilities of each party. Parametric triggers define the loss event by physical parameters such as earthquake magnitude within a pre-defined occurrence area, as opposed to loss amount as traditionally used in reinsurance contracts. To ensure the effective protection for larger catastrophe losses, a pair of sliding scales between magnitude and recovery ratio in an ascending manner was also established. For example, Tokio Marine would recover a full US$200 million from Tokyo earthquake with a 7.7 plus magnitude (as measured by the Japan Meteorological Agency (JMA)) but only a fraction of US$200 million from earthquakes with a magnitude of 7.2–7.6.

2. Multi-risk swap

In July 2001, Swiss Re, Tokio Marine and its reinsurance unit, Tokio Millennium Re, arranged a US$450 million catastrophe risk swap, by exchanging three separate risk pairs of US$150 million each: Japan earthquake for California earthquake, Japan typhoon for Florida hurricane, and Japan typhoon for France storm. Indemnity loss levels, reference portfolios and industrial indices were used to set trigger points, which define the amount at which of each pair of the swap transaction begin to recover losses. This swap transaction is annually renewable but expected to continue for several years.

It is important to note that risk swaps are regarded to be an effective tool for managing risk capital rather than a mere alternative to reinsurance. Risk swaps help insurers to reduce the risk exposure and take uncorrelated risks at the same time. Therefore risk swaps are more meaningful as part of insurance risk capital management – which is conducted in line with the financial strategy of insurance companies, as they control the overall insurance risk of portfolios.

The economic benefit of risk swaps is easily understood in a framework of managing risk capital. Suppose two companies agree to exchange each fraction of their independent extreme risks, such as natural catastrophe risks. To simplify the example, assume those two risks are equivalent in terms of incurring monetary loss probabilities, and associated costs such as brokerage fees are neglected. Figure 1 illustrates this transaction. Their peak risks decrease once they complete the proposed exchange and at the same time the probability of ruin for each company becomes much smaller. In addition, because this risk swap does not harm any existing profits, capital efficiency should improve. Now the companies may be able to use their new excess capital, if any, to expand another profitable business.

TRANSFORMING CONCEPTS INTO PRACTICE

The rapid growth of the financial swap market in recent years may give the initial impression that the idea of swapping risks is a new one. In fact, the economic benefits of risks swaps have been considered and tested for a

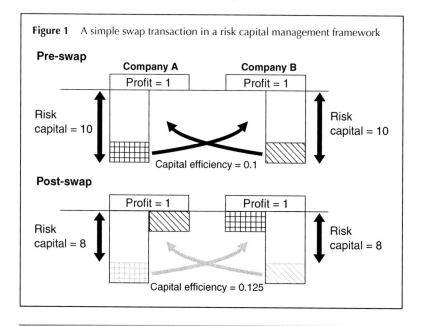

Figure 1   A simple swap transaction in a risk capital management framework

long time in insurance industry. The concept itself was always simple but transforming it into reality proved difficult; insurers found the application of the concept in the area of managing extreme risks a problem. Recently though, a series of developments led some insurers and reinsurers to reach an alternative version of reciprocal agreements, the details of which are described in this section.

The structure of risk swaps is a product of past developments in the insurance and financial markets. They are:

❑ reciprocal reinsurance arrangements;
❑ the growth of the financial swap market;
❑ catastrophe risk modelling as pricing information;
❑ insurance-linked securities and international diversification;
❑ insurance derivatives and non-indemnity index; and
❑ emergence of insurance capital and portfolio management tools.

Reciprocal reinsurance arrangements

The notion of exchanging primary insurance risks for commercial use was developed and implemented in the late 1800s with a form called the "reciprocal arrangement". An American insurance company catalogues this beginning,

> The first reciprocal insurer was formed in 1881 by six retail merchants in New York City who were dissatisfied with their stock insurers. They felt little or no consideration was accorded to the merchant's financial strength, commercial record and moral hazard, or to the discipline, care and cleanliness maintained in the premises, or to the precautions taken to prevent or minimize losses. These merchants agreed to reciprocally insure each of the others for $2,000 indemnity against fire. In this way, each of the six received $10,000 of insurance to augment the coverage they were carrying with other Stock and Mutual companies.[2]

Mutual insurance companies have the same goal. The strong presence of mutual insurers can still be witnessed in many regional markets, supported by the faith of policyholders. Perhaps the only concern of such regional insurers has been the geographical concentration of risks. There was also the similar idea of primary insurers and reinsurers helping each other, but it proved largely unsuccessful. The textbook *Reinsurance* fully explains the detailed background to the circumstances in which reciprocal arrangements might have failed.[3]

In short, reciprocal reinsurance arrangement was not necessarily used to manage risks, but often used as a tool for profit opportunities. Trying to obtain better risks by ceding worse risks could not provide a real reciprocal environment. Among the other reasons for failure were disappearance of tariff markets, lack of risk analysis skills or reinsurance expertise, significantly uneven risk exchange, and fear of disclosing business secrets among counterparties. It should be fully recognised that risk swaps serve well as a risk capital management tool for primary insurers, rather than a profit opportunity.

The growth of the financial swap market
While reciprocity arrangements in the insurance industry were not totally successful, the financial swap market has demonstrated spectacular growth over a relatively short period – the early 1980s to now. Unlike reciprocal reinsurance arrangements, financial swaps require counterparties to exchange risks on a parity condition. If the two risks exchanged are equivalent, each party should take the responsibility to settle later any overpayment that has occurred by the time of the expiration (as happens almost without exception), as agreed in the contract. The ISDA swap format was developed and widely used as a guardian of standardised trades.

Along with market growth, corporate financial managers recognised the importance of using swaps as a major vehicle of financial risk management tools. The most remarkable factor to encourage the growth was the active involvement of financial institutions as a user, not as an intermediary. Banks and securities firms, initially only serving as intermediaries of swap transactions between corporations, later started to participate in currency and interest swaps to manage their own risk exposures. They took advantage of their expertise to model the risks and thus expanded their business opportunities. Interestingly enough, this experience may also suggest the possible role of reinsurers in the area of risk swaps.

In the 1980s, insurers and reinsurers were not able to capture such opportunities in their core business of underwriting insurance risks; financial swaps were only used in their investment operations. Insurance risks are generally still very hard to quantify and even more difficult to standardise. With that reality in mind, insurers and reinsures still have to trade risks with the principle of *uberrimae fidei* – utmost good faith. Some unquantifiable risks have been traded in the form of finite reinsurance, a blending of funding and limited risk transfer.

Catastrophe risk modelling
Perhaps the first catalyst of the idea of swapping insurance risk was the development of insurance risk modelling technologies, particularly in the area of natural catastrophes. Natural catastrophe modelling firms have made a great contribution to improve the transparency of risk analysis among insurers, reinsurers, reinsurance intermediaries and even capital market investors. It is interesting to note that a series of sophisticated credit risk modelling technologies was also developed (mostly) simultaneously by some of the advanced practitioners such as RiskMetrics and KMV. The goals of modelling expertise in both natural catastrophe and credit risks are

essentially the same, as the risk analyses are designed to retain more transparency in quantifying the nature of the extreme risks.

Given the impossible challenge of predicting an "act of God", catastrophe risk modelling may not be a forecasting tool. Regardless of the accuracy, catastrophe risk modelling could work as a tool to form a consensus in the insurance and reinsurance pricing process. This function is similar to a financial option-pricing model in the financial market. From a technical point of view, those models also possess some similarities. The stochastic event-tree analysis, for example, is performed in a similar manner to that used for developing lattice models in finance.

Insurance-linked securities and international diversification

The second catalyst to directly improve the feasibility of swapping insurance risks was the introduction of insurance-linked securities. Readers may note that the first insurance-linked option to be invented was traded at Chicago Board of Trade (CBOT). However, the option did not materialise in a large scale. Perhaps this was because using CBOT cat options for the purpose of hedging insurance portfolios was effectively similar to using FRAs (Forward Rate Agreements) without knowing the interest sensitivities of loan portfolio at banks. Without the knowledge and experience of insurance portfolio management including basis risk control, using cat options was a difficult exercise.

The second wave of insurance-linked securitisation in the late 1990s enabled indemnity risks to be securitised. The significant contribution though was the disclosure of insurance risks to be securitised based on US Securities and Exchange Commission Rule 144a.[4] The detailed risk analysis is presented in an offering circular to investors, including underwriters in the insurance industry. Catastrophe risk modelling techniques are absolutely necessary to perform the analyses to provide investors with the default probabilities of insurance-linked securities. The attachment, mean and exhaustion probabilities of a particular insurance risk portfolio are the standard set of risk analysis results.

Another contributing aspect of insurance-linked securitisation was that it promoted international diversification of insurance risks. Capital market investors participating in the transactions welcomed the opportunity to invest in zero beta assets. Insurers also realised the potential benefits of investing insurance risks internationally. Almost at the same time, some primary insurers with a strong domestic presence started assuming international risks, using professional advice and the latest catastrophe modelling technologies.

Insurance derivatives and non-indemnity index

The third catalyst of developing risk swaps was the introduction of another version of the financial swap based on the underlying insurance-linked securities. This particular financial swap was primarily used to capture the additional reinsurance capacity from capital market investors, not as a diversifier of risk exposures. Thanks to the risk disclosures of insurance-linked securities, insurers with a limited risk analysis expertise could obtain the additional capacity from capital markets. Underlying insurance-linked securities shortened the time needed to structure and complete the financial swap deals.

At this time, the insurance-linked financial swap was introduced following the issuance of underlying insurance-linked securities, and the emergence of insurance-linked securitisation finally entered the first stage witnessed in the original financial swap market in the early 1980s – detaching the risks from the underlying securities and structuring them as a tool for managing risk capital.

Parametric index (or parametric trigger) was also used to structure insurance-linked securities and the synthetics. Based on physical risk triggers such as earthquake magnitude and hurricane wind speed measures, sponsors of insurance-linked securities designed a handful of parametric indices and sold them in the capital markets with help from investment bankers. Among the various advantages of parametric index, the most fundamental one is its ability to eliminate the complexities of analysing insurance risk by capital market investors. Investors could use their resources only for physical-event risk analysis, in which a field of scientific experts stand neutral between investors and issuers.[5] Indeed, most of the recent insurance-linked securitisation transactions were structured more on parametric triggers.

On the other hand, non-indemnity index also presents a challenge for insurers. Sponsors of insurance-linked securities should in turn perform a basis-risk analysis and reach the best structure of the index for themselves, as the parameterised risk portfolio does not completely match the original risk exposure. When using parametric triggers, insurance sponsors need to analyse basis risk and become experts in the subject themselves. Although basis risks can be traded in reinsurance, insurers may prefer to retain them if they fall within a tolerance level.

Capital and portfolio management tools

The last catalyst was the introduction of capital and portfolio management tools for insurers. Capital management concepts such as Dynamic Financial Analysis (DFA) or P&C RAROC (Property and Casualty Risk Adjusted Return on Capital) were introduced in the late 1990s.[6] Although these concepts and potential benefits were largely recognised in most of the insurance industry, the real applications were neither developed nor used, except by a small number of highly sophisticated professionals.

Many insurers may find difficulties in developing and implementing the capital management framework for many reasons (the complexity of developing models and using enormous amount of unassembled data, for example). However, the potential benefit may be greater than expected, depending on the scope of the analysis and management priorities. While it is generally not a good idea to be either too ambitious or conservative, applying the concept to natural catastrophe risks may be a suitable first step for many insurers.

Benefits of such analysis include the ability to:

❏ provide estimates of risk exposures for a group of businesses or a particular risk category such as natural catastrophe risk;
❏ provide a selection of required capital estimates given a range of confidence intervals or other extreme value measures;
❏ analyse "what if" scenarios by changing business, portfolio mix and external inputs such as reinsurance prices and correlation matrices among risks; and
❏ provide additional clues to manage company capital and the business lines analysed.

In terms of structuring risk swaps, capital management and portfolio analysis of the counterparties are almost prerequisite. For example, it is essential to work iteratively to see how a series of risk swap transactions can be beneficial for the company's risk landscape and the use of capital. This also makes it possible to prepare for the adverse environment when assumptions do not match the reality of the market.

From a capital market investor's view, applying modern portfolio theory to natural catastrophe risks may not work as effectively as it used to in the traditional financial markets; securitised insurance risks may be too skewed to fit in the mean-variance analysis, and even catastrophe risk modelling has its limits of use when investors want to rely on the single output of the mean loss estimate; the insurance market is competitive, but not efficient enough to apply modern financial theories fully. For that reason, recent advanced theories in the area of extreme value analysis and credit risk modelling are expected to play an important role in the analysis of investment portfolios including financial and insurance (or event) risks, as those theories explore the complex nature of extreme events and fill the gaps between the traditional theories and the realities of the risks explained.

A modern version of insurance risk exchange

By reading the previous sections, it is possible to follow the concept of risk swaps as an evolving process. Although the concept began in the area of natural catastrophe risks, the same structures can be used in credit and weather risks; a pair of Japanese utility companies – Tokyo Electric Power Company and Tokyo Gas Company – already tested a weather risk swap transaction in 2001, by exchanging summer temperature risks, causing the companies to incur an opposite profit and loss profile. Risk swaps are indeed the modern version of insurance and event risk exchanges.

The cost of risk management may be an additional factor to promote risk swaps. With the tremendous pressures to reduce operational expenses to sustain competitive advantages, sophisticated risk management is necessary but the additional significant cost may not be easily accepted, so insurers need to keep the cost of risk management at a minimum. The best alternative strategy should improve the benefit of risk management and cost reduction in the foreseeable time horizon. The greatest appeal of a risk swap is obvious: it reduces risk while keeping the risk reduction cost close to zero on average; risk swaps make risk work as another form of currency to purchase the cover needed. The transactional costs (risk modelling, intermediary costs, etc) should be decided by the values of the appropriate services provided to an insurer.

IDENTIFYING OPPORTUNITIES OF ENTERING RISK SWAPS

The concept of risk swaps is simple, as are the principles of identifying the opportunities for their implementation. There are three principles to consider:

1. Find a less diversified, or a regionally concentrated partner.
2. Swap high layers to reduce the required risk capital.
3. Swap for a long period.

Perhaps risk swaps work most efficiently when two partners can exchange their extreme risks, as such extreme exposures are often much above the existing reinsurance layers. This is another advantage because existing reinsurance programmes and risk swaps work together by managing different layers of the risks.

In all cases, capital management and portfolio analysis are necessary to identify the opportunity of entering risk swaps. It is not advisable to treat risk swaps separately from other reinsurance and capital market alternatives because risk swaps constitute the integral part of a risk financing programme; risk swaps should be used as a supplement to reduce risks, by enhancing the overall efficiency of the programme including the existing reinsurance arrangements.

Dynamic consideration for future insurance business plans and for changing key risk exposures is also a necessary step to identify opportunities. For example, a primary insurer may wish to expand its business in a certain region where a major natural catastrophe risk is apparently present. Alternatively, an insurer may plan to gradually reduce the natural catastrophe exposure in a particular region as the company foresees less profitability in the years ahead and therefore does not wish to incur significant risk management costs.

Either way, a long-term strategy is carefully developed to limit the natural catastrophe exposure within a given range, depending on the time-line and the budget constraints for the insurance business plans.

Insurers with such a constantly changing business environment may want to hedge the exposure with a parametric index format so that they can later reduce or increase the volume of the hedges by entering another parametric-based trade. Their counterparties may find the same reason. Because the risk analysis is transparent, selling risks by parametric trigger may be much easier and faster to complete than doing so by traditional reinsurance. In fact, dynamic control of the hedged portfolio is one of the key advantages to entering an insurance-linked financial swap transaction.

Finding an appropriate swap counterparty is perhaps the most difficult task for many insurers. There are more experts in this field, including rein-surance intermediaries, reinsurance companies and investment bankers, all of whom are quite knowledgeable about the potential needs and feasibility of the alternative solutions. Insurers can benefit by entering a risk swap with such experts as partners.

Reinsurance brokers

Reinsurance brokers are very familiar with the risk management issues and the ongoing challenges of primary insurers. Today, reinsurance brokers providing alternative risk solutions are a group of diverse experts in the field of risk analysis, reinsurance and financial management. Seasoned reinsurance intermediaries capitalise on a strong client network and their scope of expertise to match the isolated needs of different insurers and reinsurers, and propose the most beneficial structure of risk swaps.

Reinsurers

Reinsurers may also realise the tremendous opportunity in entering into risk swaps to strengthen long-term partnerships with insurers as well as to benefit from their own risk management strategy. With the most advanced level of knowledge on the particular risks and portfolios traded, profes-sional reinsurers are best positioned to help primary insurers manage their risks. In the future, reinsurers may often find opportunities to enter risk swaps for their own purposes, as did the banking and securities firms who entered the financial swap market to manage their risk exposures.

Investment Banks

Insurance risk alternative solutions are often not a mere substitute of rein-surance, but are instead a tool for managing insurance risk capital. Investment banks propose a variety of integrated insurance and financial solutions for insurers and reinsurers. Through the process of securitising insurance risks, they emerged as another powerful group of experts in structuring and executing insurance risk trades. In addition, they are experts of capital management for all industries. Insurers can benefit from investment banks' experience and their advanced technologies to manage both financial and insurance risks.

Risk modelling firms and risk consultants

Risk modelling firms also have a great advantage in providing risk analysis. They know insurance clients on a global scale and continue to upgrade models, adding new functions for advanced analysis purposes. Some companies already offer insurance capital management consulting via – for example DFA analysis – using a combination of natural catastrophe and financial modelling, which can be beneficial to insurers.

A HYPOTHETICAL CASE ANALYSIS OF MANAGING RISK CAPITAL WITH RISK SWAPS

In this section, an example examining the economic benefit of risk swaps is presented. Portfolio risk analysis is one of the core elements of developing risk management strategy for insurers. Looking at an image of the skewed and peak risk of insurance portfolios may provoke an idea of how to manage exposures by using risk swaps. However, in considering risk swap opportunities, the size of transactions can become very large. The strategic and the economic advantages of risk swaps often lead to an exchange of a fairly large amount of risks, as large as US$200–US$450 million per transaction. Portfolio analysis has a significant value to evaluate such opportunities.

In this section, a hypothetical case study is presented to describe the benefit of risk swaps using a DFA system developed at Tokio Marine group, led by Tokio Millennium Re Ltd. Readers may note that an actual case requires much more detailed analysis than this example, often with much larger numbers.

An appropriate measure of risk exposure should be discussed. Traditionally many insurance companies have used different risk measures to evaluate the riskiness depending on the particular line of operations. For example, investment departments usually use value-at-risk (VAR), while insurance underwriting departments may prefer to use probable maximum loss (PML) for reinsurance and accumulation control purposes.

In terms of measuring extreme risks such as natural catastrophe, we can use expected shortfall over VAR, or other threshold measures.

The major advantage of using expected shortfall is that it considers the possibility of extreme losses outside of the confidence boundaries (a range of thresholds defining exceedence probabilities of loss).[7] Monte Carlo simulation, for example, can calculate an expected shortfall value defined as a probability-weighted average of extreme losses outside of a predefined threshold. Conservative insurance risk management would prefer the Monte Carlo measure because the nature of extreme value modelling for natural catastrophe risks may amplify the uncertainties of tail-end estimates of the loss distribution.

The setting

US Wind Co, US EQ Co and EU Wind Co are a set of three insurers – two US-based regional primary insurers and a Europe-based primary insurer – each exposed to natural catastrophe risks in a US East Coast hurricane, a Californian earthquake and a European storm, respectively. Their net assets are all assumed to be equal to a 99.9% expected shortfall of each company exposure, to measure the benefit of risk swaps.

A hypothetical set of annual exceedence probability (AEP) curves is shown in Figure 2. As a standard scenario, correlations among all three risks are all set equal to zero.

Major observations are as follows:

❏ The 99.9% expected shortfall value of the sum of the all regions' insured losses (US$106.9 million) is much less than the sum of the company's risk capital (US$224.5 million), reflecting the benefits of diversification. Should those companies work together at least in the natural catastrophe risk management business, between them they would save more than US$100 million of risk capital for other purposes.

❏ Extreme losses increase dramatically beyond a certain threshold range. Similar situations in the natural catastrophe modelling results can often be observed. Dramatic trend changes may call for a further research; there may be modelling risks in addition to the risks of capricious Mother Nature.

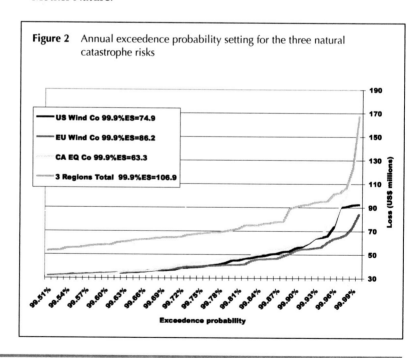

Figure 2 Annual exceedence probability setting for the three natural catastrophe risks

A set of risk swap transactions is structured so that each primary insurer will exchange risk by the following method: US Wind Co and EU Wind Co swap stop-loss covers. Each layer has risk of a 0.1% attachment probability of incurring insured loss. CA EQ Co swaps a layer with EU Wind Co. That layer has an attachment and exhaustion probability of incurring insured loss of 0.1% and 0.5%, respectively. EU Wind Co cedes the same risk layer to CA EQ Co. We also assume that CA EQ Co purchase a stop-loss cover over the 0.1% attachment level from a third party, or that it enters another risk swap transaction.

Results and further analysis

Figures 3 and 4 show the result of a risk swap between US Wind Co and EU Wind Co. As expected, the 99.9% expected shortfall values decreased dramatically in the standard scenario. Changing the correlation coefficient between the two risks, as in Figure 4 (from zero to 0.7 and 0.9) dramatically changes the results. Both immense wind risks may happen at the same time in the US and Europe. Note that EU Wind Co is hit by extreme US hurricane risks three times. In light of uncertainties regarding natural cata-strophe risks such as global warming, model users may need to perform several stress tests.

CA EQ Co and EU Wind Co swap lower layers than the first case between US Wind Co and EU Wind Co. Figure 5 shows more striking results, further lowering EU Wind Co's and CA EQ Co's expected shortfall.

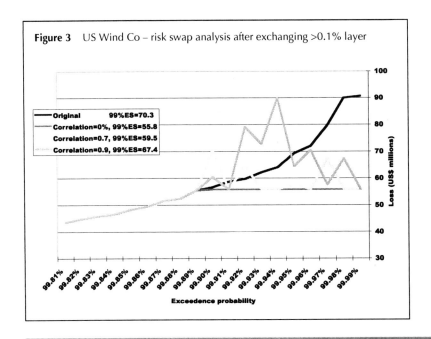

Figure 3   US Wind Co – risk swap analysis after exchanging >0.1% layer

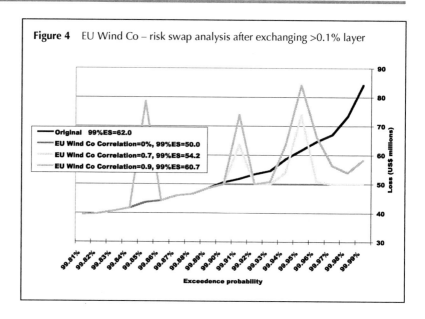

Figure 4 EU Wind Co – risk swap analysis after exchanging >0.1% layer

Because we exchange different risks that have the same probability of loss, the overall expected loss of the three portfolios does not change after risk swaps.

One of the implications from this later analysis is that a risk swap of only one layer without stop-loss also makes a difference. The case in Figure 6 shows the result, lowering the expected shortfall by approximately 30%. In reality, an insurer may wish to swap a much lower layer such as the one with a 1% attachment level, or even lower. Either way, it is important to see what strategy would make a significant contribution to the current insurance risk capital management.

There should be a choice over the threshold of expected shortfall. A 99.9% expected shortfall might be on a very conservative side among the insurance industry. The choice of a threshold depends on the management preference toward the balance between the profitability, economic solvency and perhaps the claim-paying ability ratings.

Because of the simplified assumptions, this example produced some obvious results. The key question is whether such an analysis can work in a real setting. There are several layers of many reinsurance programs including quota shares, excess loss, and even alternative solutions such as insurance-linked securitisation and risk swaps. It is important to be able to analyse the whole picture based on the actual risk management programmes, always testing the feasibility of alternative solutions for comparative purposes. To give an analogy, this analysis resembles an institutional investment portfolio where sponsors and money manage-

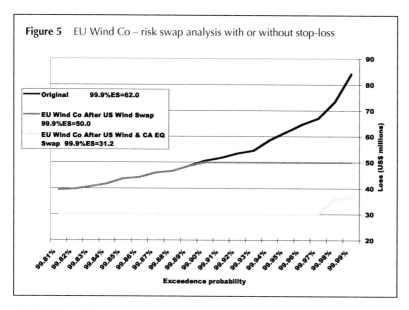

Figure 5 EU Wind Co – risk swap analysis with or without stop-loss

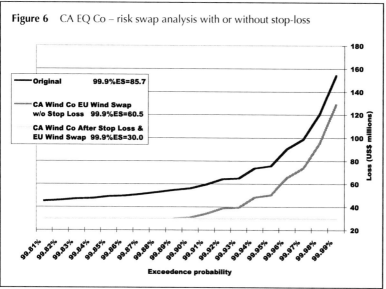

Figure 6 CA EQ Co – risk swap analysis with or without stop-loss

ment consultants evaluate various options of investment strategies. An insurer who wishes to manage its own exposure and use risk management expertise should be also prepared to perform a series of portfolio analyses.

DESIGNING A RISK SWAP TRANSACTION

Designing a risk swap transaction in a real setting of course requires a series of discussions between the counterparties. Practical considerations to design risk swap transactions include:

1. Understanding strategic objectives

The party needs to fully understand the strategic objective and risk capital management practice of each company. Risk exposures, financial management policy for the insurance risks and reinsurance strategy of each party are key elements likely to be discussed. The party then prioritises the objectives of entering a risk swap, so that the transaction would benefit both parties in light of their risk management strategy. One of the tremendous advantages is that the discussion does not end with the exchange of risk itself but also incorporates learning the ways those risks are managed by different companies; exchanging strategic objectives and risk management strategies is a tremendous learning process for the parties involved.

2. Risk selection and definition

Each company has its own priority of which risk to swap. As seen in the previous example, two companies may wish to match the nature of the risk – US hurricane to European storm, for example. Each company plays a role of both a cedent and a reinsurer or an investor of insurance-linked securities.

Each party should determine which parts of risk layers will be exchanged, based on the portfolio analysis and risk capital management needs. They also exchange the preferences over various types of risk definitions (including indemnity loss, modelled indemnity loss, industry loss and parametric triggered loss). If the parties would like to exchange a pair of indemnity losses, data analysis may be a huge burden to quantify the risks as the details of each insurance programme within the risk layer should be fully analysed and discussed, taking much more time to run the complex modelling analysis for both parties. On the other hand, the party can agree to exchange different risk formats. For example, one may take industry loss, while the other takes parametric trigger loss.

3. Amount and durations of risk swap

This reflects the desire of each party – how much they wish to swap in a transaction and how long they wish to continue the contractual relationship. Because of the significant benefits of structuring a particular risk swap transaction, the party may want to swap as large amount as possible. Alternatively, a party who wishes to maintain a network of partnerships may wish to swap with a modest amount. Either case may be beneficial.

4. Modelling analysis

Each party must decide how to agree on the valuation of risks using one or multiple modelling analyses. Depending on the choice of risks to be managed, they may be able to borrow an analysis that was already performed and used in the reinsurance programme, or they may need to rerun a model based on exposure. The parties may even want to take advantage of investing in the insurance-linked securities, where they obtain information with regard to the risks to be exchanged. Choices of the specific models and the evaluations between the parties may create another aspect that the parties need to discuss. While the different views on a particular modelling analysis may contain a risk that would cause the transaction to fail, the discussion examining two different risks together should itself be beneficial in that it enhances the detailed understanding of world's natural catastrophe risks in different markets that would otherwise not be instantly available.

5. Contract Period

The true spirit of reciprocal agreement may call for an almost perpetual contract as long as the two parties survive. In practice, a variety of choices are available. For example, a reinsurer may elect a one-year risk swap transaction because the company needs to monitor the change of its risk exposure and may wish to negotiate other terms and conditions at the next renewal season. A primary insurer may choose a period between five and 10 years to place the transaction in line with the timeline of its business plan which supports the risk management strategy.

6. Recovery Options

Risk swaps can transform the spirit of reciprocity into the contract by granting a recovery option. For example, this option can be drafted so that each party, after a first claim payment in the swap transaction, may elect to extend or renew another period under the same terms and conditions. This option can reasonably provide each party with a greater opportunity to receive a claim payment by the next loss in the swap agreement.

Depending on the pricing complexities, various types of recovery options can be considered. Examples include a tilted recovery option where the first claim payment receiver of the transaction may be eligible to recover only a fraction of the original amount should a second loss event occur.

7. Credit risk considerations

As is the norm with swap transactions, credit risks should be also considered. This condition may vary among the contracts, reflecting the mutual understanding of the companies involved, credit risk management policy and the absolute levels of their claim payment ability ratings. If there is a significant difference in their ratings, the party may agree to arrange a credit support.

8. Documentation

Risk swaps can be drafted either as a financial contract or a pair of reinsurance contracts. The choice depends on the parties' regulatory, accounting and possibly tax considerations. In some cases, the organisational structure of the parties may play a greater role; reinsurance departments of primary insurers normally deal with only reinsurance documents, while professional reinsurers have more flexibility to work with both formats.

9. Tax, regulatory and other legal considerations

Whenever the new transaction is structured, the parties need to carefully review the draft to confirm compliance with the rules and regulations. For example, a taxation code may require a cedent to have a reinsurance contract in less than six years, whereas a risk swap based on the ISDA format may not allow a cedent to qualify as a reinsurance contract for solvency margin purposes.

There are many choices when designing a risk swap contract. Many different paths are possible when trying to reach the final terms and conditions. This is a challenging but worthwhile process to build a consensus toward the mutually beneficial goal of diversifying and reducing risks while keeping the cost of risk management at a minimum. In practice, many often find a simpler structure works much better than a complex one.

IMPLICATIONS FOR THE FUTURE

Effectively, risk swaps have just been born and are still emerging. To date, the numbers of risk swap transactions are limited but the amount of risks swapped per transaction may be one of the biggest figures compared with the average size of reinsurance transactions. The concept of swapping risks is simple and the economic and strategic advantages can be significant.

Convergence of insurance and financial expertise

The first and most distinctive feature of risk swaps is that the structure embodies the convergence in insurance and financial markets. While the current scope of risk swap applications is mostly limited in the area of natural catastrophe risk management, another area of extreme risks, such as credit and weather risks, can be used more widely. Modelling technologies developed in credit risks, natural catastrophe risks and other financial risks may be used together, or even integrated, to analyse and manage entire risks embedded in a single balance sheet of insurance company.

Integrated risk management

Because a risk swap is designed to assume a different, non-correlated risk, it is not a substitute for an outgoing reinsurance program. It is a tool of managing risk capital combining both the features of reinsurance and diversification of insurance risks. As the advanced future applications of risk analysis will allow insurers to analyse risks much faster and more effectively, the process of the analysis will be more integrated with the broader risk exposure landscape.

Wider market to trade insurance and financial risks

The financial swap market has contributed to the widening of the scope and depth of trading financial risk. The risk swap market also has a potential to develop in a similar fashion. Because the insurance market is not an efficient market, there will be ongoing needs to swap various risks among the wide array of candidates. By doing so an insurer can become an expert in managing both standard and extreme risks – essential as insurance is a business of managing risks. The expertise accumulated on behalf of its own risk management can be also used for client needs.

Realistic negatives

Lastly, a list of caveats remains; no new products are immune from pitfalls. We need to learn from the lesson of the reciprocal reinsurance arrangements; risk swaps can be excellent risk management tools but may not be suitable for a profit opportunity. Instead, they can use the reduced risk capital for another profitable business.

Risk swaps require the traditional insurer to take a very different perspective. Taking a non-local risk may mean additional time-consuming work and furthermore lead to a series of extra losses. Primary insurers as a distributor of retail insurance products, not as a diversifier of retail insurance risks, may find it difficult to engage in risk swap transactions. On the other hand, even a leading primary insurer in its local market may want to think twice before entering this trade, particularly if they are not well prepared to put real effort into actively managing its exposure. That said, the challenge of creating more efficient and rational risk management strategies using risk swaps should ultimately gain the support of policyholders, stockholders and others such as ratings agencies, especially in an environment of intense industry competition. Given the strategic and economic benefits and the pitfalls of risk swaps, the entire balance should rest on the consciousness toward the vision of the future of insurance and financial markets. After all, any alternative solutions should seek to find a more efficient state of the market.

CONCLUSION

Risk swaps are an emerging tool of managing insurance risk capital. With a sound background, the structure of risk swaps utilises the latest developments in the convergence of insurance and finance. As a supplement to traditional reinsurance, risk swaps can add a significant value by diversifying risks, keeping the cost of risk management at a minimum, and immunising the ceded risk from the future turbulence of reinsurance supply and demand conditions. Implementing risk swap strategy calls for an advanced insurance risk portfolio and capital management. It ultimately leads to a wider landscape of integrated risk management including both the asset and the liability side of insurance companies. The expertise of managing extreme risks will continue to be a core competitive advantage for insurers and financial institutions.

1 Bank of International Settlements, the global OTC derivatives market at end–June 2001.
2 Erie Insurance Group Homepage.
3 Carter *et al.*, *Reinsurance*, pp. 98–101.
4 Rule 144a of the Securities Act 1933 states the private resale of securities to qualified institutional buyer without the registration of the securities.
5 Physical-event risk analysis deals with events such as earthquakes and winter storms, but not the insured losses triggered by such physical events themselves.
6 See Nakada *et al.*, (1999) for a detailed discussion of this topic.
7 For a detailed discussion on expected shortfall values, see Yamai and Yoshiba (2001).

BIBLIOGRAPHY

Bank for International Settlements, 2001, "The Global OTC Derivatives Market at End-June 2001", Press release, 20 December.

Carter R., L. Lucas and N. Ralph, 2000, *Reinsurance*, Fourth Edition, (London: Reactions Publishing Group in association with Guy Carpenter & Company), pp. 98–101.

Crouhy, M., D. Galai and R. Mark, 2000, *Risk Management*, (New York; McGraw-Hill).

Erie Insurance Group, company website, URL: http://www.erieinsurance.com/reinsurance/reinsaboutus.html>.

Nakada, P., H. Shah, H. U. Koyluogle and O. Collignon, 1999, "P&C RAROC: A Catalyst for Improved Capital Management in the Property and Casualty Insurance Industry", *The Journal of Risk Finance*, 1(1), Fall.

Yamai, Y. and T. Yoshiba, 2001, "On the Validity of Value-at-Risk: Comparative Analyses with Expected Shortfall", Institute for Monetary and Economic Studies, Bank of Japan, Discussion Paper 2001-E-4.

6

Contingent Capital and the Art of Corporate Finance

Christopher L. Culp[*]

CP Risk Management LLC and The University of Chicago

Contingent capital is an alternative risk transfer (ART) product through which corporations can issue new debt or equity after the occurrence of some specific risk-related loss, often on pre-loss financing terms.[1] Similar in design to knock-in put options, contingent capital facilities usually involve the direct acquisition of capital from a (re)insurance company. As low-cost off-balance sheet alternatives to paid-in capital that enable firms to integrate their corporate financing and risk management decisions, these facilities are classic examples of the recent convergence of insurance and capital markets – and, more fundamentally, of corporate finance with risk management.[2]

The relation between a company's financing and risk management decisions has long been recognised by corporate finance academics,[3] but only recently has begun to pervade the thinking of corporate treasurers and chief financial officers (CFOs). With the explosion of recent interest and activity in ART and alternative risk financing, however, companies have now begun to realise that arguments for integrating risk management and corporate finance do not just belong in the realm of financial theory – the *practice* of corporate finance now attests to the sensibility of this approach.

INTRODUCTION

This chapter provides an introduction to contingent capital in the theory of corporation finance. We begin with a brief introduction to how corporations utilise financial capital. We then review the distinctions between paid-in and contingent capital. The following section presents a discussion of some of the specific appeals of contingent capital. We then turn to

---

[*] The author is grateful to Angelika Schöchlin and Tom Skwarek for useful comments on this chapter, although the usual disclaimer applies and they remain blameless for any remaining errors or omissions.

explore and analyse some of the more interesting contingent capital structures to have been completed in the last few years, first in the area of risk
finance and then in risk transfer. We conclude with a discussion of how
contingent capital is most likely to help firms reduce their cost of capital by
mitigating problems arising from a "pecking order" in capital structure and
by relying on contingent capital providers as delegated monitors of their
users' investment decisions.

CORPORATE UTILISATION OF FINANCIAL CAPITAL

"Capital" has multiple meanings in economics and finance.[4] Especially
confusing is that these meanings apply to both sides of a firm's balance
sheet. "Real capital" includes those assets in which a firm invests as part of
its primary business, whereas "financial capital" is the collection of liabilities issued by a firm in order to fund its acquisition of investment capital.

Financial capital can be defined quite broadly as the collection of contracts and claims that the firm needs to raise cash required for the operation
of its business as an ongoing enterprise.[5] Operating a business *as an ongoing
enterprise*, however, often – if not usually – involves more than just raising
money to pay employees and finance current investment expenditures. It
also includes keeping the business going, and doing so efficiently, in a business environment fraught with risk and uncertainty.

Firms may demand financial capital for at least six reasons, which are
discussed below.[6]

Investment

Fama and French (1999) find that an average of about 70% of all spending
on new investments by publicly traded non-financial US firms from 1951–96
was financed out of those firms' net cash earnings (*ie*, retained earnings
plus depreciation).[7] The remaining 30% had to come from outside the firm.

To generate the funds required to close such deficits between net cash
earnings and target investment spending, firms issue financial capital
claims. In exchange for providing firms with current funds, investors in
those claims receive certain rights to the cash flows arising from the
investments of the firm. In other words, by issuing financial capital claims,
corporations can fund their investments and get cash today by promising a
repayment in the future that will depend on how the firm's investments
turn out.

Ownership and control

Financial capital claims also serve as a method by which the ownership of a
firm – or, more specifically, ownership of the real capital assets that define
the firm – can be transferred efficiently.[8] In lieu of selling individual
plants, machines, and employees, firms can sell *claims* on those real assets.

In turn, financial capital assets convey some form of control rights and governance responsibilities on the holders of those claims. By receiving a financial claim on the firm's real capital, investors naturally want some say in how the firm *uses* that real capital – including its acquisition of new real capital through its investment decisions.

Risk mitigation

Some firms find it in the interest of their security holders to hold *risk capital*. All firms issue financial capital claims as investment capital, but not all firms require risk capital. Not surprisingly, risk capital thus is virtually always capital held *in excess* of that required just to finance investment spending.

Merton and Perold (1993) define risk capital as the minimum amount of funds the firm must set aside and invest in order to protect the *firm's net assets* (*ie*, gross assets minus non-debt liabilities)[9] from a decline in value relative to the value of an investment of those net assets in risklesss bonds. Risk capital can be externally provided through risk transfer products like (re)insurance and derivatives *or* it can be provided by the holders of financial claims on a firm.[10]

Risk capital is principally intended to help companies reduce the expected value of *costly* financial distress – *ie*, the costs times the probability of encountering distress.[11] Although such costs include the out-of-pocket expenses associated with any formal (or informal) reorganisation, more important considerations are the diversion of management focus, loss of valuable investment opportunities, and potential alienation of other corporate stakeholders (customers, suppliers and employees) that can stem from financial trouble. Especially if financial distress costs increase disproportionately as a firm gets closer to insolvency, the more likely it is that the firm may need to use financial capital as a "buffer" against incurring those distress costs.

Financial slack

Many firms also hold capital above the amount required to finance their investment spending for liquidity risk management purposes, or, as Myers (1984) puts it, to maintain an adequate amount of *financial slack*. Liquidity risk capital or financial slack can be defined as the minimum amount of financial claims the firm must issue to fund a reserve of liquid assets that the firm needs to maintain in order to finance all anticipated positive net present value (NPV) investment opportunities.

When a firm's external borrowing costs rise as the firm's leverage rises but the firm's internal borrowing cost does not, the firm will prefer to finance investment spending out of internal funds – just as Fama and French (2000) and other evidence suggests they usually do.[12] When high cash flow volatility causes internal funds to be depleted, external financing might even be so high as to force the firm to reject otherwise positive NPV investment opportunities.[13] Maintaining a buffer stock of internal funds thus often makes sense for a firm.

Although often associated with financial distress, a firm's desire to maintain adequate financial slack may simply trace to informational asymmetries between a firm's managers and external investors. Akerloff (1970) developed the notion of "adverse selection" in his study of the used car market, which led to his becoming a co-winner of the 2001 Nobel Prize in Economics. As his work suggests, when information is asymmetric across car buyers and sellers, sellers know the true quality of the cars they are selling. Buyers do not. And because used car buyers cannot ascertain whether or not they are buying "a lemon," they will demand a price discount based on the assumption that at least *some* of the used cars being marketed are lemons. This price discount, however, creates a disincentive for sellers of *good* used cars to come to the market. The discounted price buyers are willing to pay believing some cars to be lemons is below what the *good* cars are worth. Consequently, the only sellers that show up really *do* have a lot of lemons. Buyers know this, too, of course. In what is known as a "rational expectations equilibrium," buyers expect lemons, pay for lemons, and get lemons.

The securities sold by firms can also be perceived as lemons when insiders like the senior managers of a firm know the true quality of the firm's real investment decisions but outsiders do not. Investors will assume that insiders come to outsiders only when they have lemons to offer. External investors thus discount the price they are willing to pay for the firm's securities. In turn, firms with good information refuse to come to market because the price they will receive is too low. The result is that indeed securities are only issued by firms when they are lemons. As in the case of cars, securities investors expect lemons, pay for lemons, and thus get lemons.

The result is a "pecking order" in which firms strictly prefer to finance new investments with internal funds rather than issuing external securities.[14] As a result, firms may issue financial claims as liquidity risk capital to fund a balance of internal funds that helps firms avoid seeking external funding.[15]

Signalling

Some firms hold financial capital over and above that required to fund their investment expenditures quite simply to prove that they can. Beginning with Ross (1977), Leland and Pyle (1977), and Miller and Rock (1985),[16] financial economists have argued that a firm's financial capital can be used to "signal" information about the firm's true earnings to investors when insiders are better informed than outsiders.[17] Similarly, Nelson (1970,1974) and Milgrom and Roberts (1986) argue that firms sometimes "burn money" on things like advertising in order to signal their financial and product market strength. Spence (1973) finds a comparable benefit for signalling even when the signal is not money burning but actually conveys value, such as seeking a graduate education. In both cases, expenditures can be an important signal to the market of a firm's credibility and quality.

In the same spirit, Shimpi (2001) suggests that the *amount* of capital held by a firm may be an informative signal of its financial condition. Especially if securing the capital requires a firm to undergo a costly credit evaluation or due diligence process, the successful procurement of capital can go a long way toward informing investors of the true quality of the firm's business decisions when that quality is otherwise not perceptible to outside investors.

Regulatory compliance

A final reason for some firms to issue financial capital is because they have no choice if they wish to comply with the regulations to which they are subject. Banks, insurance companies, securities broker/dealers, savings institutions, and other firms are all subject to "minimum capital requirements".

Especially in banking and insurance regulatory regimes, capital requirements pertain both to the *amount* of financial capital a firm must hold to support its risk-taking activities, and the type of claims used to raise that capital. Under the Basel Accord promulgated in 1988 by the Bank for International Settlements (BIS), for example, banks are required to compute "risk weights" for all their credit-sensitive assets, as well as some of their interest rate-sensitive and market risk-sensitive positions. A bank's regulatory capital then must not fall below 8% of its risk-weighted assets, thus defining a minimum level of capital for the bank. In addition, the Accord requires that at least *half* of that amount must be satisfied with "Tier I" capital, which includes equity, perpetual preferred stock, disclosed reserves, and minority interests in subsidiaries. In addition, subordinated debt used to satisfy the remaining capital requirement may not exceed more than 50% of Tier I capital. The type of claim the firm issues to meet its capital requirement thus can be just as important as the absolute minimum capital level.

THE SUPPLY OF FINANCIAL CAPITAL

In order to raise funds for the reasons discussed in the prior section, firms can issue any of several types of financial capital claims, any of which can be classified as either *paid-in* or *contingent* capital. The salient differences between these alternative sources of funding are discussed in this section.

Paid-in capital

Paid-in capital includes equity, debt, and hybrid securities.[18] "Paid-in" implies the immediate creation of a claim on all net cash flows of the firm following the issuance of the claim. In return, an immediate infusion of cash money occurs. The types of paid-in financial capital claims that a firm issues, together with the "priority" of each of those claims in the event of insolvency, define a company's classical or securities capital structure.

Paid-in capital from an options perspective
Paid-in capital can either be a residual claim on the net cash flows of the firm, a fixed claim, or a mixture of the two. Residual claims – better known as equity – include unrestricted and restricted common stock, partnership shares, preferred stock, and the like. If the net assets of a firm (ie, gross assets less non-debt fixed liabilities) have a market value of A(T) on some date T when the firm is liquidated, the value of the firm's outstanding equity claims is

$$E(T) = max[A(T) - FV, 0]$$

where FV is the total amount of the firm's debt.

Debt, in turn, represents a *fixed claim* on the net cash flows of the firm because the promised payoff to debt holders is fixed.[19] If the firm liquidates its assets for A(T) > FV, debt holders will receive the promised FV and no more. But just because the *promised* repayment is fixed does not mean the *actual* repayment is fixed. If the liquidation of the firm's assets generates insufficient cash to pay off debt holders, the creditors to the firm as a group will receive only A(T) < FV on a pro rata basis. Accordingly, the liquidation value of all debt claims issued by the firm at time T is equal to

$$D(T) = min[FV, A(T)]$$

The value of the firm at time T, V(T), is equal to the market value of the net assets of the firm A(T). Expressed in terms of the firm's financial capital, the market value of the firm is equal to the sum of the market values of its debt and equity, or

$$V(T) = A(T) = E(T) + D(T) = max[A(T) - FV, 0] + FV - max[FV - A(T), 0]$$

As the above equations suggest, the equity and debt claims issued by a firm can be usefully viewed as types of options written on the net assets of the firm. All of the above expressions are payoffs on the firm's claims at *liquidation*, but the options perspective certainly works for earlier dates, as well. Specifically, the total equity issued by the firm has a value at any time t that can be denoted

$$E(t) = C(t, A(t), FV, T)$$

where A(t) is the current market value of the firm's net assets, T is the "maturity date" for these options that is either the next principal repayment date on the firm's debt (assuming all debt matures at the same time) or the liquidation date of the firm, and C(·) is the price of a European call option.

Viewed from an options perspective, the debt of a firm is equivalent to a risk free bond with face value (FV) and an option written to equity that gives residual claimants the right to exchange the assets of the firm A(T) for the riskless loan FV. When A(T) < FV, shareholders will exercise that option. The option by debt holders that allows equity holders to exchange FV for A(T) is synthetically equivalent (from debt's perspective) to owning a riskless loan with a face value of FV and selling a put option on the net assets of the firm:

$$D(t) = e^{-r(T-t)}FV - P(t, A(t), FV, T)$$

where r is the riskless interest rate, and P(·) is the price of a European put option. We can re-express the value of debt at maturity the same way:

$$D(T) = min[FV, A(T)] = FV + min[A(T) - FV, 0] = FV - max[FV - A(T), 0]$$

The components and payoffs of debt viewed through this option lens at maturity are shown in Figure 1.

Once we realise that equity and debt can be viewed as options on the firm's net assets, we can express the value of the firm at any time t as

$$V(t) = A(t) = C(t, A(t), FV, T) + e^{-r(T-t)}FV - P(t, A(t), FV, T)$$

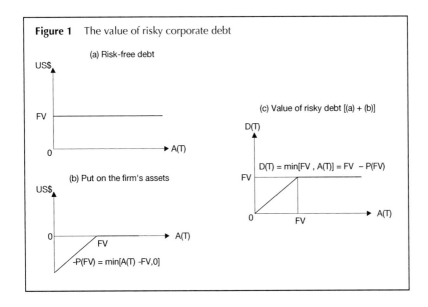

Figure 1   The value of risky corporate debt

(a) Risk-free debt

(b) Put on the firm's assets

(c) Value of risky debt [(a) + (b)]

If we re-arrange terms to express the market value of the firm's debt as the residual of the market value of the firm's assets less the market value of its equity, we can see that the relation between the value of a firm's debt, equity, and assets is the same as the usual expression for European put-call parity:

$$A(t) - C(t, A(t), FV, T) = e^{-r(T-t)}FV - P(t, A(t), FV, T)$$

In Figure 2, we can now put the pieces together to express the whole firm as a portfolio of options on liquidation date T. When the firm's assets are worth A(T) and that amount is less than the face value of the debt, the firm is worth the only value of the assets. Debt holders then receive a pro rata distribution of those assets, and residual claimants receive nothing. When A(T) has a market value greater than FV, debt holders receive FV, equity holders receive a pro rata distribution of the surplus in asset value above FV, and the firm is again worth A(T). In either case, the value of the firm is equal to the value of its assets. The nature of the two types of claims issued by the firm to obtain capital to acquire those assets does not change the nature or value of the assets themselves.

Fixed and residual claims can be combined to form hybrid claims that have features of both debt and equity. Typical hybrids include convertible debt, preferred stock, collateralised preferred stock, and trust-preferred stock. All of these products can also be viewed as options or portfolios of options.

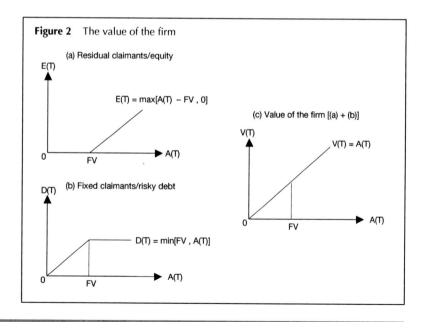

Figure 2 The value of the firm

(a) Residual claimants/equity

E(T)

E(T) = max[A(T) − FV , 0]

0   FV   A(T)

(b) Fixed claimants/risky debt

D(T)

D(T) = min[FV , A(T)]

0   FV   A(T)

(c) Value of the firm [(a) + (b)]

V(T)

V(T) = A(T)

0   FV   A(T)

Consider, for example, a typical convertible bond that allows holders to convert what begins as a debt instrument into equity under some pre-specified conditions and at a specified conversion price. The net value at time T to the convertible bond holders is the *maximum* of the values of the two components. As before, the debt component is a put on the assets of the firm struck at the face value of the debt FV plus a riskless loan of FV, and the equity component is a pro rata claim on α proportion of the firm's net cash flows or asset values A(T). For values of the firm's assets A(T) ≤ X*, the bond holder would prefer to receive FV than the αA(T) resulting from a conversion into share equity, where α is the proportion of total equity into which all convertible holders can switch. But for A(T) > X*, the bond holder is better off surrendering the repayment of FV in return for αA(T). The net position thus is equivalent to a short put on the assets of the firm struck at FV, a riskless loan of FV, and α long calls on the firm's assets struck at X*. Figure 3 shows the aggregate payoff at time T to all convertible holders.

Priority and the securities capital structure
The classical "securities capital structure" of a firm is characterised by the mixture of financial claims the firm issues *and* the seniority of those claims, or the priority in which they are paid off in the event of insolvency. Equity claims are sometimes called "soft" claims because their seniority in the capital structure of the firm varies based on the other securities that the firm issues. In an all-equity firm, equity holders are first in line at the asset liquidation, but in most situations equity holders are last – having a *residual* claim after all the bills *and* all the debt are paid off.

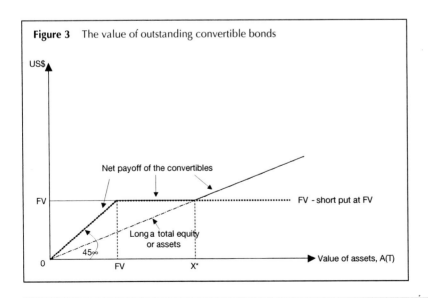

Figure 3   The value of outstanding convertible bonds

The priority of debt depends on the firm's use of "me-first" rules to classify debt into different categories of priorities. Senior debt is unsecured debt for which "me first" rules gives the lenders to a firm priority on the remaining assets of the firm *vis-à-vis* other classes of debt holders in the event the assets of a corporation are liquidated. Senior debt often comes in the form of bank loans made directly by commercial banks to corporations. Subordinated debt is debt in which "me first" rules give lenders a *pro rata* share of the cash proceeds from liquidated assets *only after* senior lenders have been paid off.

Subordinated debt is sometimes called "mezzanine finance". Highly subordinated mezzanine issues are sometimes considered hybrids rather than pure debt, especially by banks and insurance companies. Such perceptions arose both because the interest rate on mezzanine issues is usually closer to the equity return than the rate on senior debt and because mezzanine debt is often accompanied with an issue of detachable warrants.

When a firm issues securities whose classes have different priorities, the options perspective still proves a useful lens through which to view the value of the firm. Consider a firm that issues unrestricted common stock, enters into senior bank loans with a total principal amounting to K_1, and issues subordinated debt with principal K_2. Equity is still a call on the value of the firm, but now with a strike price equal to the sum of all outstanding fixed obligations – $K_1 + K_2$. Unless the value of the firm's assets upon liquidation exceeds this amount – ie, $A(T) > K_1 + K_2$ – the firm's equity holders get nothing in insolvency.

To model the debt using options only requires that the proper strike prices be identified to characterise each class of security (*ie*, priority). First consider the senior debt. At time T, senior debt holders are whole as long as $A(T) > K_1$. Otherwise, senior creditors have a pro rata claim on whatever is left of $A(T)$. Just as above, senior debt thus can be viewed as the combination of a riskless loan of K_1 plus a short put on the firm's net assets struck at K_1.

Now consider the subordinated debt. The face value of the debt is K_2. Because subordinated debt is junior to senior debt, however, junior creditors are only made whole if the assets of the firm are worth enough to pay off *both* classes of debt holders. If $A(T) – K_1 > K_2$, there is more than enough for junior creditors to be fully repaid *after* senior debt has been paid off. But if $K_1 < A(T) < K_1 + K_2$, there is enough to repay senior debt but not all of junior debt, which must ratably split $A(T) – K_1$. If we stopped here, we might conclude that junior debt is equivalent to a riskless loan of K_2 plus a short put on the firm's net assets struck at $A(T) – K_1$. But that is not enough. If $A(T) < K_1$, we need an additional feature to ensure that the holders of the subordinated debt cannot get to any of the residual assets to which they do not have priority. A long put bought by sub debt holders from senior debt and struck at K_1 does the trick. The resulting payoff on junior debt at maturity is thus

$$\min[K_2, A(T) - K_1] + \max[K_1 - A(T), 0] = K_2 - \max[K_2 - (A(T) - K_1), 0]$$
$$+ \max[K_1 - A(T), 0]$$

Subordinated debt thus can be viewed as a riskless loan of K_2 plus a short put struck at $K_1 + K_2$ plus a long put struck at K_1.

Contingent capital

Contingent capital is an option on paid-in capital. Specifically for purposes of this chapter, contingent capital is a contract or structure that gives a firm the right but not the obligation to issue a paid-in financial capital claim on or before a certain date.[20] Contingent capital is almost always off-balance-sheet until the contingency feature allows the owner of the facility to "exercise" or "draw" it – ie, turn it into balance-sheet paid-in capital.

Contingent capital from an options perspective

Consider a firm that has common stock, senior debt, and subordinated debt in its capital structure. The firm will be wound up on date T, and the face values of the two classes of debt are K_1 and K_2, respectively. The values of the firm's securities are as follows on date T:

$$
\begin{aligned}
E(T) &= \max[A(T) - K_1 - K_2, 0] \\
D^1(T) &= K_1 - \max[K_1 - A(T), 0] \\
D^2(T) &= K_2 - \max[K_2 - (A(T) - K_1), 0] + \max[K_1 - A(T), 0]
\end{aligned}
$$

where D^1 and D^2 denote the market values of senior and sub debt, respectively. Prior to time T, the values of these securities can be written in terms of the market prices of European calls and puts as:

$$
\begin{aligned}
E(t) &= C(t, A(T), K_1 + K_2, T) \\
D^1(t) &= e^{-r(T-t)}K_1 - P(t, A(T), K_1, T) \\
D^2(t) &= e^{-r(T-t)}K_2 - P(t, A(T), K1 + K_2, T) + P(t, A(T), K_1, T)
\end{aligned}
$$

where the arguments in parentheses of the option prices represent the current time, the underlying of the option, the strike price of the option, and the maturity of the option, respectively.

First consider a contingent debt option that a company buys entitling it to issue subordinated debt at the price of Z^D. For simplicity, suppose the facility is European and may be exercised only on date $0 < \tau < T$. Suppose further that the facility has no additional triggers and that the debt issued underlying the option has a subordination level that places it behind all existing classes of debt holders.[21] At maturity, the option is worth

$$\Phi^D(\tau) = \Psi\max[Z^D - D^2(\tau), 0]$$

If the current market price of debt at time τ is below the strike price Z^D, the option is in-the-money and the firm can issue new debt at a savings *vis-a-vis* the then-current market price. We can re-write this for any time $t < \tau$ as

$$\Phi^D(t) = \max[Z^D - e^{-r(T-t)}K_2 + P(t, A(t), K_1 + K_2, T) - P(t, A(t), K_1, T), 0]$$

Clearly the contingent capital facility can be viewed as a compound put option with a striking price of Z^D and an underlying of the subordinated debt of the firm.

The market value of a similar contingent capital facility on the firm's common stock with strike price ZE can be expressed as follows as of any time $t < \tau < T$:[22]

$$\Phi^E(t) = \Psi\max[Z^E - E(t), 0] = \Psi\max[Z^E - C(t, A(t), K_1 + K_2, T), 0]$$

where Ψ is an adjustment to take into account the dilution of existing common stock holders.[23] The contingent equity facility thus can be viewed in a manner similar to warrants, with the important difference that the option is now controlled by the firm.

A few things are immediately noteworthy about even this over-simplified contingent capital facilities. First, contingent capital facilities are always put options no matter what the underlying security because they are always options *issue* securities. The option to buy back securities at a fixed price may exist, but this does *not* provide the firm with an alternative source of funds.

A second notable feature is that, when viewed through the option lens, the market price of a contingent capital facility at any given time is a function of the *current* market price of the firm's assets net of debt liabilities. These are not "path-dependent" and do not depend on the way that the firm's assets evolve over time.

Finally, realise that all of the above hold without regard to the option pricing model that might be used to estimate the theoretical option prices $C(\cdot)$ and $P(\cdot)$. In other words, viewing the models as options from a financial engineering standpoint does not require us to make any modelling assumptions.

Typical features of contingent capital
Just like a regular option, contingent capital can be characterised by its underlying, exercise style, tenor, and strike price. The "underlying" of a contingent capital facility is a fixed, residual, or hybrid capital claim. More specifically, a contingent capital facility is essentially a commitment by a capital provider to provide paid-in capital on pre-agreed terms if the buyer of the facility chooses to exercise that right on or before the expiration of the contingent facility.

Because financial capital claims are themselves options on the net assets of the firm, however, the true economic underlying of contingent capital viewed as a compound option on the net assets of the firm is also still the net assets of the firm. The connection between the claim held by contingent capital providers and the firm's net assets is one step removed from the rights and priorities of paid-in capital providers, but the economic factors that influence the *value* of the contingent capital option are still the same factors that influence the net asset value of the firm. Although the holder of the option differs, the control and valuation issues raised by the issuance of warrants by a firm are similar.[24]

The exercise style of a contingent capital facility concerns the timing with which the purchaser of the contingent claim may convert that claim into paid-in capital. Like regular options, a contingent capital facility may entitle its buyer to utilise the facility and obtain paid-in capital only on a few specific dates (*ie*, Bermuda exercise style), only when the contingent capital facility expires (*ie*, European-style), or on any date up to its expiration (*ie*, American-style). Most contingent capital facilities are American-style, possibly subject to some restrictions on exercise at the very beginning of the life of the option.

The tenor of the contingent claim is the period during which the firm has access to the paid-in capital. Care must be taken not to confuse the tenor of the contingent claim with the tenor of the underlying. A contingent debt facility, for example, may have a tenor of a year but an underlying with five years to maturity. In this case, the firm buying the contingent capital has purchased a one-year American option on five-year debt – *ie*, at any time over the next year, the capital provider has agreed to purchase five-year debt from the firm at a pre-defined price. A contingent equity facility, by contrast, may have a tenor of a year despite the fact that if exercised, the resulting paid-in claim is *perpetual*.

The contingent capital facility also includes the analogue of a "strike price," or the terms on which the paid-in capital will be transferred if the buyer exercises its right to draw upon that paid-in capital.

The second trigger
Apart from the standard features all option contracts contain, contingent capital also almost always involves what is known as a "second trigger," or an additional condition that must be activated before the option can be exercised – the first condition/trigger being that the option is in-the-money. In this sense, contingent capital facilities appear similar to a type of barrier option called a "knock-in" put option.

A knock-in put has all the features of a normal put option, including a strike price, but *also* includes an "instrike" defined in terms of the price of the underlying on which the option is written. Until the underlying price falls below the instrike, the put option is not exercisable. Once the barrier is breached, the exercise value of the option is based on the original strike price, not the instrike.

Figure 4 shows the payoff (net of any premium paid) on both a traditional put (the dashed line) and a knock-in put with instrike X (the heavy black line). Both have strike price K and maturity date T, and both payoffs are shown for date T as a function of the underlying asset price at maturity, A(T). The traditional put is in-the-money for any A(T) < K and increases in value one-for-one with declines in the underlying price below K. For values of A(T) greater than X and less than K, the knock-in put is *also* in-the-money, but because A(T) is still above instrike X, the option cannot be exercised. When the second trigger is activated at A(T) = X, the option thus immediately is worth A(T) – K = X – K, resulting in a payoff for the knock-in option that is discontinuous at point X.

Despite a strong resemblance to barrier options, however, one important feature distinguishes most contingent capital facilities from a knock-in put on a traded asset. Namely, the second trigger on many barrier options is defined in terms of the same variable as the first trigger – *ie*, the underlying asset price.[26] This is not true for most contingent capital facilities.

As an ART form specifically designed to integrate risk management with a financing decision, the second trigger for most contingent capital facilities is usually tied to a specific business or financial risk facing the firm – *eg*, the risk of unexpected losses on a business line, the risk of declining cash balances, the occurrence of an accident or peril, and so forth. This risk may be

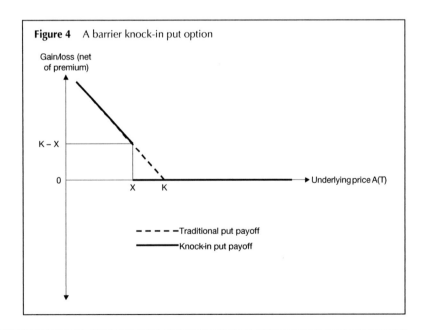

Figure 4   A barrier knock-in put option

expressed either in terms of an event (*eg*, a California earthquake above seven on the Richter scale) or an associated loss arising from the event (*eg*, property claims arising from a California earthquake above seven on the Richter scale).

If the second trigger is defined in terms of a loss rather than a discrete event, the trigger may either be based on the *actual losses* incurred by the firm purchasing the contingent capital or may be based on a *proxy for losses*. In other words, the second trigger may or may not be under the control of the purchaser of the facility. This gives rise to an important trade-off facing both providers and buyers of contingent capital – moral hazard.

When the second trigger of a contingent capital facility is tied to a discrete event or a loss proxy (*eg*, an industry loss index) outside the firm's immediate control, the purchaser cannot "game" the exercisability of the product – the second trigger is totally exogenous. This has the effect of introducing something akin to "basis risk" into the structure.

Consider a contingent equity put that can only be exercised when losses on the Property Claims Services (PCS) of California earthquake losses is over US$50 million in a reporting year. The purchaser of the contingent put – presumably an insurer or reinsurer with property exposure in California – is at best one of many firms reporting losses in this index and thus cannot influence whether or not the trigger is activated. At the same time, if the insurer's own losses greatly exceed those on the index, it is possible the option will not be triggered even though the purchaser of the contingent put has sustained damage well above the trigger threshold.

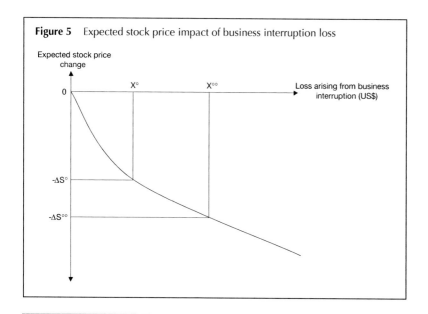

Figure 5   Expected stock price impact of business interruption loss

Triggers tied to a variable under control of the firm do not have such basis risks, but they do create moral hazard problems that can give purchasers perverse risk management incentives. To help visualise this distinction, we can follow Doherty (2000) and associate second trigger loss levels with the price of the security underlying the contingent capital facility so that the product looks more like a traditional knock-in put. Suppose, for concreteness, a telecommunications firm purchases the contingent capital facility. The facility entitles the firm to issue preferred stock at fixed strike price K per share on date T.[26] The stock will be issued if the time T stock price S is below K *and* if the firm has experienced a business interruption resulting in US$X° of economic damage sustained. Figure 5 shows the relation between damage sustained from business interruption and the decline in the stock price *expected to result* for each loss.[27]

Figure 6 now shows the *expected* payoff of the contingent equity at maturity date T put as a function of the *expected* price per share of the telecom's common stock. In other words, Figure 6 *assumes* that the relation shown in Figure 5 between actual business interruption losses and expected stock price changes will prevail, thus allowing us to express the *actual* loss trigger US$X° in terms of a stock price change ΔS. If the firm's preferred stock is worth S_1 per share on date T *and* the firm has sustained business interruption losses of exactly US$X°, the contingent capital facility cannot be used. The stock price $S_1 - \Delta S$ is still above the strike price of the option, K.

Now suppose the time T stock price is S_2 so that the contingent capital facility is just out-of-the-money absent any business interruption loss. If a reported loss of US$X° occurs and the stock price declines as expected to $S_2 - \Delta S$, now the option *can* be exercised – a business interruption loss of at least US$X° has occurred *and* the stock price is below the option strike K.

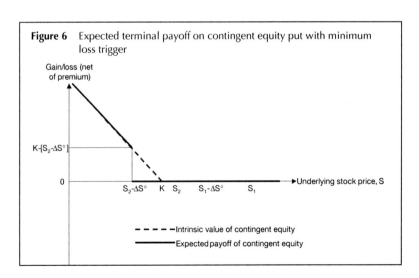

Figure 6 Expected terminal payoff on contingent equity put with minimum loss trigger

In a traditional barrier option, the expected exercise value of the option is based entirely on where the time T stock price is relative to the instrike. For the contingent capital facility, the expected exercise value is based instead on where the time T stock price is relative to the actual option strike. For a business interruption loss of US\$X° resulting in a stock price decline of ΔS, the option has an intrinsic value of $K - (S_2 - \Delta S)$.

As was the case with a traditional knock-in option, the contingent equity put has a payoff that is discontinuous at point $S_2 - \Delta S$. But unlike the barrier option in which the discontinuity is determined by the fixed instrike, the location and size of the discontinuity in the contingent capital payoff changes with the current stock price. If the time T stock price is exactly $K + \Delta S$ when the loss of US\$X° occurs and the *actual* stock price change is equal to the *expected* stock price change, the option will be just at-the-money, and further stock price declines will result in the usual dollar-for-dollar gain in the value of the put. For any stock price *greater* than $K + \Delta S$, the loss will be inadequate to knock the option in. And for stock prices *less* than $K + \Delta S$, the option moves from zero intrinsic value to a positive intrinsic value by exactly the amount that the stock price is below $K + \Delta S$. The values in between zero and that number are never realised.

Doherty (2000) emphasises that this "discontinuous gain" can create serious moral hazard problems. If the stock price is just above $K + \Delta S$ when the loss occurs, the put owner has an incentive to over-state or exaggerate the effects of the loss in an effort to get the *actual* stock price decline to exceed ΔS and nudge the put into-the-money.

Now return to Figure 5 and suppose the second trigger is no longer defined as any loss above US\$X° but rather as any business interruption loss in the *range* between US\$X° and US\$X°°. Figure 7 now shows the expected value of the contingent equity at expiration assuming again that the relation between business interruption losses and expected stock price changes holds. The dashed line shows the payoff to a traditional put, and the heavy line shows the expiration value of the contingent equity for a starting stock price of S_1. As shown in the dashed line, the intrinsic value of this option is increasing in stock price declines for all prices below K, but the *exercise* value is increasing in stock price declines only for prices below $S_1 - \Delta S°$ *and* above $S_1 - \Delta S°°$. Notice that the payment upon exercise is still relative to K, but the payment cannot be received unless the second trigger is active.

Insurance companies often include a policy coverage limit to mitigate moral hazard problems. Recognise here, however, that the source of moral hazard comes not from the *payoff*, but from the *trigger*. The upper trigger US\$X°° thus is *not* a policy limit. Indeed, the inclusion of this upper trigger arguably even *exacerbates* the moral hazard problem *vis-à-vis* the minimum loss trigger depicted in Figure 6. For losses that are just under US\$X°, the firm may have an incentive to over-report or exaggerate the impact of

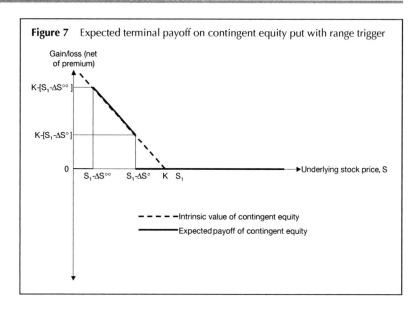

Figure 7   Expected terminal payoff on contingent equity put with range trigger

losses just as before in order to activate the lower trigger. But now, as losses approach the upper range of the loss trigger US\$$X^{\circ\circ}$, firms may be tempted to *under*-report losses. The put owner thus has moral hazard problems "on two sides"!

One way suggested by Doherty (2000) to keep the second trigger of the facility as a single minimum loss but mitigate moral hazard is to set the strike price of the contingent debt K so that the facility is at-the-money *immediately before* the loss. The goal is to avoid situations where the option is in-the-money but has not knocked in because the loss event falls just short of the required amount, thus giving the holder of the put an incentive to nudge the reported loss upward. By using the market price of the stock just before the loss occurred, most of the discontinuity in the expected pay-off is eliminated.

APPLICATIONS OF CONTINGENT CAPITAL

Now that we have the basic theoretical framework in place for under-standing how contingent capital is structured and compares to paid-in capital, we turn briefly to consider the basic applications of contingent capital facilities. This will provide us with an important means by which the actual contingent capital structures observed in the market place can be distinguished from one another. Specifically, contingent capital structures have been designed and can be used by firms for three reasons: risk trans-fer, risk financing on a pre-loss basis, and post-loss risk finance.

Risk transfer

If a firm's equity holders do not wish to bear the impact of a risk to which the firm's primary business naturally exposes it, one possibility – *risk transfer* – is for a firm to shift the impact of losses arising from a risk to one or more other firms. Because risk capital is defined to be the minimum amount of capital investment required to guarantee the value of the firm's net assets against a loss relative to a comparable riskless investment, the demand for risk capital is inversely related to the firm's net asset risk.

Risk transfer through the use of financial instruments, ART forms, or balance sheet operational hedging are ways to reduce net asset risk without changing the securities capital structure of a firm.[28] But the use of contingent capital that performs a risk transfer function at the same time as changing the firm's capital structure can make sense in at least two situations.

First, risk transfer decreases the firm's risk capital required, and thus increases its debt capacity – *ie*, the firm can issue new debt without exposing the firm to higher net asset risks and an increased risk capital requirement. The *combination* of a new capital issue with a risk transfer element in a contingent capital facility can potentially provide firms with a lower cost of capital relative to either a pure risk transfer solution or an unrestricted new issue of paid-in capital.[29]

Second, risk transfer also provides firms with a means of avoiding "underinvestment" problems associated with a "debt overhang". When the benefits of a positive NPV project accrue mainly to debt holders of a firm but the firm's managers are acting mainly on behalf of shareholders, valuable investment opportunities can be foregone simply because too many of the project's benefits accrue to debt holders while leaving equity holders with all the risks.[30] By increasing debt capacity, this underinvestment problem is mitigated.

Importantly, the debt overhang problem can also lead to underinvestment in the firm's primary business line *if* that business involves customer liabilities.[31] Because risk transfer reduces net asset risk, it increases the opportunities for the firm to extend additional customer liabilities without incurring higher expected financial distress costs. Consider a reinsurance company whose revenues are related to the amount of business the firm underwrites. By reducing the probability of insolvency for any given net asset value, risk transfer increases the firm's *premium capacity* – *ie*, it has greater underwriting capacity for a given expected financial distress cost.

Increasing underwriting volumes, however, often require an increase in *regulatory* capital of a certain kind to support the new risk of the business. In that case, pure risk transfer alone will not be enough to support the higher volume of customer business. In that case, a *combined* risk transfer/ capital acquisition can make good sense.[32]

Risk finance

If a firm does not transfer a risk, the risk either is neutralised through operational hedging or it is "retained".[33] An unexpected loss on a retained risk can impact the firm's value, cash flows, and earnings. Although a firm may be comfortable retaining a risk in a value and earnings context, it may *not* be comfortable with the liquidity risk created by a retention for reasons noted earlier – namely, a desire to avoid underinvestment and costly external financing in a pecking order context.

Risk finance is the process by which firms manage the *cash flow* dimension of their retained risks. *Pre-loss financing* involves securing funds at a price determined before the loss occurs, whereas in a *post-loss financing* the firm pre-arranges *access* to funds but not the price.

Pre-loss risk finance

In pre-loss finance, actual funds may not be obtained until after a loss event, but they will be obtained at a pre-loss price. Pre-loss financing can be accomplished using contingent capital by specifying the strike price underlying the contingent put option when the facility is first arranged.

A primary motivation for firms to engage in pre-loss finance is to avoid cash flow-related underinvestment problems.[34] In other words, pre-loss financing through contingent capital vehicles can act as a critical source of financial slack or liquidity risk capital for the firm. In that case, the underlying of the contingent capital facility will likely involve a low-risk debt security, preferably one that is senior in capital structure.[35]

Post-loss risk finance

Like pre-loss finance, *post-loss* risk financing is a firm's pre-arrangement of access to cash. But unlike pre-loss finance, the price at which that cash will be obtained is not specified in advance. As such, the price paid for the funds does not matter to the firm, and post-loss financing products thus may involve the issuance of securities of *any* priority.

The key distinguishing feature of a contingent capital facility used for post-loss financing is that the strike price of the contingent capital option is defined to make the option at-the-money at the time of exercise. This guarantees that the contingent capital facility is "worthless" to both parties upon exercise in a value sense. Even for contingent equity, if the strike price is set equal to the market price of equity at the time of exercise, the exchange is zero NPV – every dollar in cash paid by capital providers to the firm results in exactly a dollar's worth of equity.

Despite being a zero NPV transaction, post-loss contingent financing structures to date have involved the payment of a positive premium by the firm to the capital provider indicating *some* value of the facilities beyond the intrinsic value of the option.[36] One possibility is that firms may use post-loss financing facilities to help satisfy regulatory capital requirements. In order to avoid the possibility of being undercapitalised after a major loss, firms may be willing to pay some "insurance premium" for access to regulatory capital. The structures do not in any way help the firms avoid the long-run costs of their losses, but they do help ensure that a firm will not be in violation of its minimum capital requirements over the short-term post-loss period.

Apart from the risk of a regulatory sanction arising because a firm is undercapitalised, companies also face the risk of an unexpected business interruption if their financial slack is completely depleted. Unexpectedly large adverse shocks to cash flows that wipe out current internal funds, for example, can force a shutdown to the extent that the firm does not have access to ready external liquidity. To avoid this situation, post-loss financing can help. Firms may not mind paying up to get liquidity, but they need some form of pre-commitment from a liquidity supplier *simply to ensure the liquidity is there*. Otherwise, the firm's primary business could be disrupted based mainly on a lack of current liquid funds.

In both above, the underlying fear that drives post-loss financing contingent capital purchases seems to be fear of a liquidity squeeze. The issue is not the price paid for funds, but rather the actual *supply* of those funds.

CONTINGENT RISK FINANCING STRUCTURES
We turn now to consider several examples of contingent capital deals whose primary purposes seem to have been pre- or post-loss risk finance. Importantly, these structures involve *virtually no risk transfer* from their purchaser to the capital provider(s), with the exception of liquidity risk transfer.

Committed letters and lines of credit
A common example of contingent debt claim is a committed letter or line of credit (LOC), in which a lender – usually a bank – accepts a fee from a corporation and in return agrees to lend the corporation money at a subsequent time of the corporation's choosing, as long as the firm still meets certain criteria specified by the borrower.[37] If the corporation draws on the LOC, the contingent claim turns into an actual fixed claim in which the firm now owes interest and principal on the loan back to the bank. In a committed LOC, the interest rate is pre-determined when the facility is first arranged, thus making a committed LOC a very common form of pre-loss finance.

Although a committed LOC usually does not include an explicit second trigger, they usually contain a major restriction that allows the capital provider to escape its loan commitment in certain circumstances, leading many to criticise LOCs on the grounds that they are usually not available at exactly the times they are most needed.

Specifically, LOCs contain restrictions known as "material adverse change" clauses, or "MAC" clauses. A typical MAC clause states that a firm can draw on its letter of credit at any time *unless* the firm has experienced a MAC in its financial condition or credit quality. Unfortunately, this means that LOCs tend to be available to firms as actual sources of funds *only* when the firm does not experience an adverse event that eats away at its paid-in capital.

Uncommitted letters and lines of credit

An *uncommitted* LOC behaves much like a committed LOC except that the strike price of the contingent debt put is set to make the facility at-the-money upon exercise. In other words, the loan is extended to the borrower at prevailing interest rates as the line is drawn.

Uncommitted LOCs generally are much cheaper than committed LOCs – hardly surprising given that their NPV appears to be zero upon exercise. Nevertheless, uncommitted LOCs are popular vehicles for firms concerned about ensuring access to liquid funds – subject, of course, to the same MAC clause that committed LOCs inevitably contain.

Event-contingent surplus notes

Insurance companies define their regulatory capital as "surplus." A "surplus note" is a type of debt instrument issued by an insurance company in which the insurer borrows directly in exchange for making a fixed principal and interest repayment.[38] Some insurance companies have issued *event-contingent* surplus notes. These products represent put options on surplus notes, where the option includes a second trigger tied to an adverse insurance event – usually a catastrophe or catastrophic loss.

Contingent surplus notes are designed almost exclusively to satisfy regulatory capital requirements faced by insurers. Accordingly, the strike price of the put option is usually set to be at-the-money at the time of exercise. In other words, contingent surplus notes are a form of post-loss finance whose principal rationale seems to be regulatory capital compliance.

Three major contingent surplus notes done to date include structures issued by Nationwide, Hannover Re, and Arkwright.[39] In these structures, investors in the contingent notes place funds into a collateral account. The proceeds are taken by a collateral manager and invested in Treasuries. As long as the insurer does not exercise its option to issue surplus notes, the investors earn the Treasury interest, in addition to a fee paid by the insurer to investors (ie, premium) for their commitment to hold surplus notes later. If the triggering event occurs, the insurer may, at its discretion, "exchange" its own surplus notes for the Treasuries. From that point on, investors receive interest and principal from the insurer's surplus notes.

Event-contingent equity financing

Event-contingent equity financing products are equity shares that may be issued by an insurance company in exchange for cash if a triggering event occurs – again, usually a catastrophic insurance loss or related event. This product represents a put option held by the insurer on its own preferred stock.

Despite involving an equity issue, event-contingent equity financing structures are intended to serve essentially the same post-loss financing purpose as event-contingent surplus notes and thus involve virtually no risk transfer. As with contingent surplus notes, the strike price of the option held by the insurance company is set to be at-the-money at the time of exercise, so investors always exchange cash for preferred stock with a value equal to the cash paid. The issuer benefits by securing a supply of committed post-loss financing, and a small option premium is paid to investors to compensate them for bearing the liquidity risk of the insurer.

CONTINGENT RISK TRANSFER STRUCTURES

Cleanly separating pre-loss financing from risk transfer products is essentially impossible. If the security underlying the contingent facility is risky at all, there is clearly some element of both. When the underlying security is equity, for example, the providers of contingent capital must purchase a residual claim upon exercise of the facility. Although the risks to which this exposes them are not confined to the risks enumerated in the structures, the contingent equity purchasers – like existing equity holders – bear *all* the residual risks of the firm after taking ownership of their shares. In cases where the underlying has been debt, the debt is often investment-grade and thus contains less risk exposure to the firm's future performance. Nevertheless, as with any corporate debt instrument, some performance risk still exists.

Loss equity puts

Apart from the event-contingent equity financing products discussed in the risk finance section, most contingent equity structures fall generally under the rubric of "loss equity puts." In a typical loss equity put, the firm essentially pre-negotiates an equity private placement with a single counter party (or syndicate) in the form of a put allowing the firm to issue and sell new stock directly to the counterparty.

The underlying may be preferred or common stock. If the stock is preferred, the dividend rate can either be comparable to the rate paid on other preferred stock or can be fixed. The former behaves like equity and thus can be a source of risk transfer. The latter, by contrast, makes the preferred shares function more like perpetual fixed-rate debt and thus represents more of a hybrid between risk finance and risk transfer.[40]

Loss equity puts have been issued with a wide range of second triggering events, some based on variables under the capital purchaser's control and others on proxies. Most loss equity puts have second triggers that allow them to be associated with managing a specific type of risk. Swiss Re, for example, offers loss equity puts triggered by business interruption and other operational risk-related losses. Similarly, a loss equity put option on preferred stock whose second trigger is a natural disaster (or a catastrophe-related loss) is known as a "CatEPut". This has been designed by Aon and is issued mainly by insurance companies with catastrophic exposures.

The loss event serving as the second trigger is usually highly correlated with changes in stock prices. If a property loss following an earthquake is the second trigger, for example, it makes sense for the loss level that activates the loss put option to be sufficiently large that a decline in the stock price can *also* be expected. This helps ensure that the option is providing access to equity capital on favourable terms at a time when it is genuinely needed either for risk finance or risk transfer.

Committed long-term capital solutions (CLOCS)

A highly successful ART form provided by Swiss Re is its committed long-term capital solutions or CLOCS. Unlike the loss equity puts just discussed, CLOCS can be structured as contingent *debt* as well as contingent equity. In addition to the usual benefits and applications of contingent capital, CLOCS have also received regulatory blessings from some quarters. Most notably, a CLOCS giving its purchaser the right to purchase preferred stock at a pre-determined price constitutes Tier I regulatory capital for banks under the Basel Accord.

To date, Swiss Re has placed CLOCS in three major sectors of the economy – commercial banking, non-financial corporations, and the insurance industry. Three major CLOCS issues across those industry lines are discussed below.

Royal Bank of Canada

In October of 2000, Swiss Re negotiated a committed capital facility with the Royal Bank of Canada ("RBC") in which Swiss Re would provide C$200 million (US$133 million) to RBC in exchange for preferred stock in RBC at the spread prevailing on October 27, 2000 – the date the CLOCS deal was negotiated. The triggering event is tied to RBC's loan portfolio and is activated when the bank incurs "exceptional" credit losses that are in high loss layers but that are not so high as to expose the firm to default risk.[41] The C$200 million would result in Swiss Re owning about 1% of the firm's total equity if the facility was exercised, keeping control concerns minimum – *ie*, neither Swiss Re nor RBC had to worry that Swiss Re would be "running the company" because of RBC's exercise of the facility. The small size of the deal relative to RBC's total equity also kept moral hazard problems to a minimum.

The committed capital facility appears to have helped RBC in several ways. First, it gave RBC a lower cost of pre-loss funding its loan-loss reserves. As RBC executive David McKay indicated, "It costs the same to fund your reserves whether they're geared for the first amount of credit loss or the last amount of loss ... What is different is the probability of using the first loss amounts vs the last loss amounts. Keeping [paid-in] capital on the balance sheet for a last loss amount is not very efficient."[42]

By covering the upper layers of RBC's loan loss reserves, the CLOCS structure also helped RBC improve its financial ratios. Swapping balance sheet reserves for contingent capital increases RBC's return on equity, for example. In addition, RBC was apparently using the facility for capital well above regulatory minimums. Although the facility would convert into Tier 1 regulatory capital under the Basel Accord if drawn, having the undrawn facility be contingent rather than paid-in Tier 1 capital in the surplus capital zone created a major cost savings for the firm.

In addition, if the pecking order theory of capital structure as noted earlier is truly descriptive of firms like RBC, adverse selection costs should be greatly reduced by obtaining equity capital from a single capital provide with a conservative due diligence and credit evaluation process (*ie*, Swiss Re). The CLOCS acquired by RBC thus played a type of delegated monitoring or signalling role in addition to serving a risk finance/transfer purpose.

From Swiss Re's perspective, the risk of the deal includes the risk that a correlated shock to the Canadian economy could adversely impact loss developments on RBC's loans. To address this risk, Swiss Re undertook a due diligence and risk modelling effort until it was satisfied with the risk/pricing tradeoff. Swiss Re did not syndicate or reinsure any of the RBC deal.

Compagnie Financière Michelin
Together with Société Générale ("SocGen"), Swiss Re also placed a CLOCS facility with Switzerland's Compagnie Financière Michelin, the financial and holding company for French tyre maker Michelin. The deal has been heralded as one of the most innovative and successful corporate financing transactions of the last decade.

The Michelin deal is actually part bank debt and part CLOCs. SocGen granted Michelin for five years the right to draw a long-term, deeply subordinated bank credit facility, and Swiss Re wrote Michelin a five-year put option on subordinated debt maturing in 2012.[43] The bank line is a single trigger, exercisable any time Michelin wishes and it is in the money. The CLOCS option contains a second trigger: the put can be exercised only when the combined average growth rate of GDP across the European and US markets in which Michelin is active falls below 1.5% from 2001–2003 or below 2% from 2004–2005. Michelin's earnings are highly correlated with GDP growth in these markets, but because GDP growth is a variable outside the direct control of Michelin management, moral hazard risks are mitigated.

The linking of the deal to low earnings is based on several ideas. The first is that the firm is more likely to restructure in a low earnings environment, and additional capital would facilitate any such restructuring. In addition, the contingent capital will give Michelin access to adequate funds to exploit potential acquisition opportunities – *ie*, to avoid the cost and difficulty of having to issue new equity in a low earnings environment in order to exploit positive NPV investment opportunities.

If undrawn, Michelin pays a commitment fee of 35 basis points per annum and 30 basis points for the banking and insurance facilities, respectively. The higher price on the banking facility owes to the absence of a second trigger.[44]

Unlike the RBC deal, Swiss Re syndicated the Michelin deal by bringing its transaction to both insurance markets like Credit Suisse's Winterthur and to major European banking markets. This had the effect of increasing the supply of capital so much that the overall cost of the transaction to Michelin became very attractive. Indeed, the deal probably never would have been placed in either the traditional bank syndication or Eurobond markets, especially given that virtually no transactions in these markets have tenors above 10 years as compared to the initial tenor of the Michelin deal of 12 years.

MBIA

Swiss Re's third CLOCS transaction, concluded in December 2001, was placed with AAA/Aaa-rated US monoline insurer MBIA Insurance Corporation (MBIA). Monoline insurers are so named because they provide only one type of insurance – credit insurance or "wraps" to bonds that guarantee timely principal and interest repayment. As of September 2001, MBIA was the largest monoline insurer, having provided about US$450 million in bond guarantees, the majority of which are provided to municipal bond issues.[45]

The Swiss Re CLOCS provides US$150 million in cover to MBIA. The second trigger is tied to significant losses on MBIA's existing guarantees. Upon exercise of the facility, Swiss Re purchases sub debt that converts to perpetual preferred stock over time. As in the Michelin deal, Swiss Re syndicated its exposure to other (re)insurance players.

The purpose of the facility from MBIA's standpoint is clear. Default and solvency risk are *not* the main concern for bond issuers and investors that purchase credit wraps from the likes of MBIA. The major risk is instead the risk that MBIA looses its AAA/Aaa rating. The monoline business is essentially driven by firms that want to "rent" a AAA/Aaa rating for a bond issue and go to the monolines to do it. Because of the importance played by ratings, the monolines work closely with rating agencies to help ensure that deals will not trigger rating concerns *before* the deals are done.

So much of the monoline wrapping business is AAA/Aaa-dependent that many market observers believe that the loss of a single letter in their ratings would cause business to dry up that it would force the monoline into almost immediate insolvency. Another large monoline insurer apparently suffered rumours that a downgrade might be possible several years ago. So concerned were the users of that firm's credit wraps that two of the firm's leading investors apparently stepped in with new capital to ensure a downgrade did not occur.[46]

A key attraction of CLOCS to MBIA thus clearly is the access it gives the firm to additional capital on pre-loss terms after taking a major hit on its guarantee business, thereby providing MBIA with a significant cushion against a rating downgrade.

Reverse convertibles

A conversion of debt into equity can help a firm achieve some relief for post-loss financing problems by reducing the firm's leverage following a loss. At market prices, however, this conversion would have no benefit apart from outright post-loss financing – the debt and equity prices, after all, will both already reflect the loss.

If a firm wishes to swap debt for equity on pre-loss terms, the firm can issue a *reverse convertible*. A reverse convertible functions like a convertible bond by allowing debt to be switched for equity at a pre-specified strike price. The important difference is that *the issuing firm* determines when the conversion occurs, not the bond holder. The firm will exercise this option when the value of the firm's stock falls below a point where the shares offered have a lower value than the debt from which the shares have been converted.

Exercising a reverse convertible can make sense for an issuing firm following a large loss for two reasons. The first is that the optimal exercise policy involves converting only when the debt has a higher value than the equity. The conversion thus forces a shift in its capital structure toward a cheaper source of capital. The difference in the prices helps offset/fund the costs of the adverse loss. In addition, the conversion decreases the outstanding debt in the firm's capital structure and thus reduces the firm's leverage, thereby reducing expected distress costs and increasing effective debt capacity at a time when such shifts would have the highest benefit to the firm's security holders at the margin.

Putable catastrophe (cat) bonds

All of the contingent capital facilities explored thus far have involved the combination of a put option on a traditional security with a risk-based second trigger. The risk transfer thus occurs through the risk of holding the underlying security itself and the timing of the new issue. Now we consider two deals in which the timing of the issue is not specifically tied to a risk, but the payoffs of the underlying securities are.[47] The risk transfer accomplished with these products thus owes to the nature of the underlying security rather than the second trigger.

Reliance III Optionable Note[48]

In early 1998, Reliance National purchased a contingent debt option from investors entitling it to issue cat bonds at any time during the 1998–2000 period. The primary purpose of the Reliance III contingent capital facility (*ie*, "Reliance III") was to give Reliance National access to additional reinsurance capacity for certain business lines in the event of a hardening in the reinsurance market. The strike price of the option was set slightly out-of-the-money so that, if exercised, the Reliance III cat bonds would be purchased by option holders at a slightly below-market price. The price Reliance paid to investors to secure their commitment to purchase cat bonds if exercised was further reduced by the inclusion of a deductible in the bond underlying the option facility.

From 1997–8, Reliance National had issued two early and pioneering cat bonds. The first one, issued in early 1997 with the assistance of Sedgewick Lane Financial and INSTRAT (UK), was the first cat issue based on multiple business lines. Reliance II also involved multiple business line exposures. Not surprisingly, the cat bond underlying the Reliance III contingent debt facility mimicked Reliance I and II in this regard.

Specifically, 20% of potential note holders' principal in Reliance III would be at risk from losses on each of five enumerated Reliance underwriting lines: property losses in the US above US$6.5 billion; property losses in the "rest of the world" over US$4.5 billion; Japanese or American aviation losses resulting in 250 or more fatalities; offshore marine losses over US$500 million; and more than two failures from a list of 12 eligible "rocket launch" events.[49]

Allianz Risk Transfer/Gemini Re putable cat bond

Allianz Risk Transfer developed a structure similar to Reliance III for its German parent – insurance giant Allianz – that provides contingent capital to Allianz for catastrophe reinsurance through the issuance of cat bonds whose principal and interest payments were tied to reported losses on European windstorm damage. Concerned that a major catastrophic loss would lead to a hardening in the regular reinsurance market, Allianz sought to place a cap on its future reinsurance costs by using the option on future cat bond issue.

The option was sold to investors in 1999 by the special purpose vehicle (SPV) Gemini Re and gave Allianz three years during which that option could be exercised. If exercised, the writers of the option to Allianz agreed to purchase three-year notes whose principal and interest payments were linked to losses on European windstorms and hailstorms. Called *subscription agreements*, the options knock in when wind and hail losses reach a specified triggering amount. In exchange for pre-agreeing to purchase the notes at a specified price, the option writers receive an annual commitment fee (*ie*, put premium).

The notes underlying the option were for an original principal of US$150 million. If the options are exercised by Allianz and trigger a purchase of the notes, the structure functions much like the ones we have explored already. The note proceeds are placed in a collateral account in Gemini Re and are invested in reserve assets to fund insurance claims. As usual, Gemini Re engages in an income swap to smooth the actual investment income on the investment portfolio into a LIBOR-based cash flow stream suitable for servicing the notes.

Gemini Re in turn entered into a retrocession agreement with Allianz Risk Transfer, itself a retrocessionaire for Allianz AG.[50] The holders of the notes issued by Gemini Re receive a basic interest payment of LIBOR plus a risk spread unless the retrocession agreement between Gemini Re and Allianz Risk Transfer results in claims payments. In that case, both the interest and principal of the notes may not be completely paid off. The structure is shown in Figure 8.

THE COST OF CAPITAL
Recognising that a firm can issue new securities independently from whether or not it engages in risk transfer or risk finance, there are some distinct advantages to combining the corporate finance and risk management

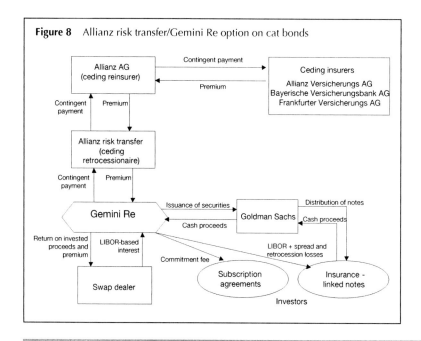

Figure 8   Allianz risk transfer/Gemini Re option on cat bonds

solutions in a single structure. Some of these have already been mentioned, such as the efficiency of combining risk transfer and a new capital issue for meeting regulatory requirements or for optimising the firm's costs in choosing to guarantee or transfer away the firm's net asset risks.

One major apparent attraction of contingent capital is potential cost savings that result if unnecessary paid-in capital does not have to be raised. If a firm is unsure whether it *needs* paid-in capital, then to raise it makes little sense, especially if information asymmetries between investors and managers lead to adverse selection costs of new external security issues. Consider the Royal Bank of Canada CLOCS deal. Raising paid-in capital to fund a loan-loss reserve is *highly* inefficient relative to the CLOCS alternative. Under the CLOCS facility, capital never simply sits idly by waiting to cover a distant loss.

Another attraction of contingent capital is the "delegated monitoring" it can engender. In the context of signalling theory, the successful placement of contingent capital can be a very positive signal to the market. Because the credit evaluations and due diligence of (re)insurance providers is so stringent, successfully securing a contingent capital commitment from such a firm – a firm whose very business depends on avoiding a rating downgrade – the (re)insurer can act as a delegated monitor for other creditors to the firm. Other creditors will observe the placement or renewal of a contingent capital facility and conclude that the investment activities and risks of the firm must be reasonable, thereby reducing the adverse selection costs of external funding.[51]

The above rationales for contingent capital depend critically, of course, on how the contingent structures affect the firm's overall cost of capital. If contingent capital can enable a firm to import the lower cost of capital of some other firm, then it is almost certainly a preferable solution for the firm. But how does the firm's *overall* cost of capital or weighted-average compare to the traditional formulation?

Shimpi (2001) suggests a framework for analysing a firm's cost of capital when some of the capital is obtained through contingent sources. His concept ties closely into the concept of an "economic balance sheet" in which the economic value of the firm is equal to the value of its assets, in turn equal to the value of *all* the firm's claims.[52] In this context, we can write the value of the firm as follows:

$$V(t) = A(t) = E(t) + D(t) + CC(t)$$

where $CC(t)$ is the time t market value of the contingent capital sources committed to the firm at time $t - 1$ *plus* any new commitments of contingent capital at time t. In this equation, the values of the contingent capital facilities are the values of *options on the claims underlying those facilities* using the appropriate option pricing methods. In other words, they are presumed not to be drawn as of date t. Once drawn, the contingent capital shows up as either debt or equity, but until then has only option-like features.

The value of the firm can be written even more simply as

$$V(t) = A(t) = \Phi(t) + \phi(t)$$

where the uppercase $\Phi(t)$ denotes the market value of the firm's *paid-in capital* at time t and where the lowercase $\phi(t)$ denotes the market value of the firm's *options on paid-in capital* (*ie*, contingent capital) at time t.

Taking all the firm's sources of capital into consideration, the firm's weighted average cost of capital (WACC) can be written as follows:

$$R_{WACC}(t) = \frac{D(t)}{V(t)} R_D(t) + \frac{E(t)}{V(t)} R_E(t) + \frac{\phi(t)}{V(t)} R_\phi(t)$$

where
$$
\begin{aligned}
D(t) &= \text{market value of debt at t} \\
E(t) &= \text{market value of equity at t} \\
\phi(t) &= \text{market value of contingent claims at t} \\
V(t) &= A(t) = D(t) + E(t) + \phi(t) \\
R_D(t) &= \text{cost of debt capital} \\
R_E(t) &= \text{cost of equity capital} \\
R_\phi(t) &= \text{cost of contingent capital}
\end{aligned}
$$

The cost of contingent capital is the total premium paid for the unexercised contingent capital options. The type of capital underlying the facility is known, but what is not known is whether the resulting paid-in capital claim will be exercised. Happily, using the appropriate option pricing methods to value undrawn contingent debt and equity facilities will give us the right result. The price of an option is, after all, the discounted expected NPV of future cash flows and thus takes into account the probability of exercise.

Consider for a moment the simplified world of Black and Scholes (1976). In their famous option pricing equation, the term N(d1) is essentially the probability the option will expire in-the-money. In a contingent capital context, that component of the option price thus would represent the probability that the facility will be drawn.

Merton and Perold (1993) propose a method for the valuation of risk capital that could be used in the expression above. Their method applies to risk capital supplied through traditional securities placements, but works equally well for contingent facilities and provides a very useful basis for comparing the costs of external risk financing and transfer solutions.

CONCLUSION

Contingent capital lies at the heart of the recent trend in the convergence of insurance and capital markets – a trend that more fundamentally indicates an increasing desire by firms to address corporate financing and risk management issues in an integrated fashion. Contingent capital can be a useful means for firms to engage in pre-loss financing to manage underinvestment or regulatory capital risks, post-loss financing to assuage liquidity concerns, and risk transfer to reduce expected financial distress costs, to mitigate underinvestment problems, and to increase debt or premium capacity.

At the heart of any firm's risk management and financing decisions is its cost of capital. If paid-in capital seems too expensive, then contingent capital will not necessarily provide a free lunch alternative. But especially in a world where corporate managers have information that investors do not, contingent capital can provide an important way around the "pecking order" problem of capital structure. These facilities also can have a signalling benefit that turns the providers of these structures into additional delegated monitors for their users.

1 ART forms include the large and growing collection of contracts, structures, and solutions provided by (re)insurance companies that enable firms either to finance or transfer risk in a non-traditional way. *See* Culp (2002a).

2 The convergence of financial and risk management policies is explored in detail in Culp (2002a), on which much of this chapter relies heavily.

3 See, for example, Mayers and Smith (1982) and Smith and Stulz (1985).

4 *Cf.* Fama and Miller (1972), Hicks (1973), Lewin (1999), and Garrison (2001).

5 See Fama and Miller (1972).

6 I only offer five reasons in my recent book, Culp (2002a), where "risk" and "liquidity" capital were essentially combined. For this chapter, however, it is clearer to distinguish between them as separate corporate uses of financial capital.

7 This finding is consistent with statistics reports in Eckbo and Masulis (1995) and elsewhere.

8 See Harris and Raviv (1991) for a survey of capital structure theories tracing to this particular corporate demand for capital.

9 This is the definition of "net assets" that will be used throughout this chapter.

10 For example, a firm's senior debt holders can effectively "sell insurance" to the firm's subordinated debt holders. See Merton and Perold (1993) and Merton (1977).

11 As the italics are meant to suggest, the possibility of financial distress is not necessarily value-reducing for all firms; in fact, for mature companies with large and stable operating cash flow and limited investment opportunities, high leverage, which of course raises the probability of financial distress, is likely to a value-increasing strategy. See Culp (2002b).

12 This empirical regularity can be easily confirmed by looking at the Federal Reserve's flow of funds data each year for the nonfarm nonfinancial corporate sector.

13 See Froot, Scharfstein, and Stein (1993).

14 See Myers (1984) and Myers and Majluf (1984).

15 Evidence for and against this "pecking order" theory is provided in Fama and French (2000).

16 In the Miller and Rock (1985) model, for example, higher dividends signal high-quality investments, whereas any public security issue signals low-quality investments.

17 For a comparison of the theories of asymmetric information that lead to signalling capital and those leading to a pecking order, see Harris and Raviv (1991) and Culp (2002a).

18 We avoid making purely legal and institutional distinctions arising mainly from different international conventions. Depository instruments, for example, are just considered "debt" for the purpose of this chapter.

19 Floating-rate debt is also, strictly speaking, a "fixed" claim because it can be viewed as a fixed-rate bond plus an interest rate swap. Of the two, the only specific claim on the firm is the debt component, which is fixed.

20 Note that this definition excludes products like insurance (or, more recently, "guarantees") and derivatives, which sometimes are considered contingent capital. True, those products involve the payment of funds to the firm contingent on an event such as the realisation of property damage or an interest rate increase, but those payments involve cash money. Such financial instruments do *not* involve an exchange of funds for a claim on the future net cash flows of the firm. If no claim on the firm's *future* net cash flows is issued in return for cash, then the product is not considered contingent capital for the purpose of this chapter. Having said this, risk transfer and risk finance products like derivatives, (re)insurance, and many ART forms often function as *substitutes for* financial capital. See Culp (2002a,b).

21 If me first rules do not put these new debt holders into a new priority class, dilution effects may need to be considered.

22 This valuation expression assumes that the firm will indeed issue *new shares* of common stock when the contingent capital facility is exercised.

23 Specifically, $\Psi=N/(N+m)$ where N is the number of shares of common stock outstanding before the new issue and m is the number of new shares issued.

24 See, for example, Galai and Schneller (1978).

25 Although most barrier options have both exercise triggers defined in terms of underlying price, not all do. A knock-in put on three-month LIBOR, for example, might have a second trigger defined as a decline in the five-year CMT rate below some instrike.

26 Assume the preferred stock is in a priority class of its own so that dilution issues can be ignored for the examples.

27 These figures are based on those presented in Doherty (2000).

28 Balance sheet or operational hedging involves the "internal hedging" or netting of risks across assets and liabilities (*eg*, a British firm with dollar-based revenues can neutralise a large part of its exchange rate risk by issuing dollar-denominated debt).

29 Contingent capital may also allow the firm to fine-tune its relative distribution of risk capital across different classes of security holders in the sense of Merton and Perold (1993). See Culp (2002c).

30 Myers (1977) calls this the "agency cost of debt".

31 See Merton and Perold (1993).

32 Risk transfer and the new capital issue could, of course, be done separately. Some cost savings associated with bundling the two thus is still implied.

33 How a firm distinguishes between risks that are transferred and those that are retained is discussed in Culp (2001,2002a).

34 The classic underinvestment model and rationale for hedging is Froot, Scharfstein, and Stein (1993).

35 In a pecking order world, when firms are forced to raise funds externally by issuing new financial capital claims, they prefer lower-risk claims like senior debt to higher-risk claims like equity because lower-risk claims are less sensitive to the revelation of new information (information that originally created the knowledge gap between managers and investors and that led to the pecking order in the first place). See Myers (1984) Myers and Majluf (1984), and Fama and French (2000).

36 A contingent capital facility whose terms *define* the exercise value to be zero by setting the strike to equal the market price of the underlying *also* has no time value. The transaction is thus zero NPV *on all dates* (or so it would seem).

37 LOCs are not considered "alternative" risk transfer/finance products.

38 Surplus "notes" can also take the form of preferred stock, but we confine our discussion to debt for simplicity.

39 See Froot (1998).

40 The subordination of the issue means that some risk transfer is still involved, although not necessarily of the risk that activates the second trigger.

41 The RBC deal is discussed in Banham (2001).

42 Banham (2001).

43 The details of the Michelin deal are discussed in "Swiss Re and SocGen in $1 bn Loan," *Reactions* (September 2000), Schenk (2000), and Banham (2001).

44 See Schenk (2000).

45 The other big monolines are Ambac Assurance Corporation (Ambac), Financial Guaranty Insurance Company (FGIC), and Financial Security Assurance, Inc. (FSA). See Knepper (2002) and Schorin (2000).

46 Knepper (2002).

47 Lane (1999) briefly discusses a third deal done by Aon for Yasuda Fire and Marine in 1998 that is similar in spirit to the two deals discussed in this section.

48 All of the analysis in this section is based on Lane (1999). This section merely summarises the salient features of the deal. For a real analysis of the structure, see Lane (1999).

49 The reported loss numbers on which these exposures were based was the loss reported by *Sigma*, a publication (and loss index) of Swiss Re. In most of the risk categories, losses on the Reliance III notes were based on a schedule rather than a complete loss of 20% principal if the trigger was activated. USA property losses, for example, were tied to the 20% principal at risk in the optionable note as follows: a 5% principal reduction for any loss in 1998 over $6.5 billion, with the proportion of principal reduction increasing up to a maximum of 20% for a US$15 billion or greater loss. See Lane (1999) for all the details.

50 When an insurance company buys reinsurance, the risk transfer is called a cession and the seller of that reinsurance is called a resinsurer. When a reinsurance company buys reinsurance, the risk transfer is called a retrocession or "retro" and the seller of the second layer of resinsurance is called a retrocessionaire. See Culp (2002a).

51 This is similar to the delegated monitoring role provided for many years by banks as senior creditors to corporations. See Diamond (1984,1991).

52 See Merton and Perold (1993) and Culp (2002a).

BIBLIOGRAPHY

Akerlof, G., 1970, "The Market for 'Lemons': Qualitative Uncertainty and the Market Mechanism," *Quarterly Journal of Economics* 43, pp. 448–500.

Banham, R., 2001, "Clocs Ticking to New Market," *Reactions* (April).

Culp, C. L., 2001, *The Risk Management Process: Business Strategy and Tactics* (New York: John Wiley & Sons).

Culp, C. L., 2002a, *The ART of Risk Management: Alternative Risk Transfer, Capital Structure, and Convergence in Insurance and Capital Markets* (New York: John Wiley & Sons).

Culp, C. L., 2002b, "The Revolution in Corporate Risk Management: A Decade of Innovations in Process and Products," *Journal of Applied Corporate Finance* 14, 4, forthcoming.

Culp, C. L., 2002c, "Contingent Capital and the Theory of Risk Capital", *Journal of Applied Corporate Finance* 15, 1, forthcoming.

Culp, C. L., and M. H. Miller, 1995a, "Metallgesellschaft and the Economics of Synthetic Storage", *Journal of Applied Corporate Finance* 7, 4, pp. 62–76.

Culp, C. L., and M. H. Miller, 1995b, "Hedging in the Theory if Corporate Finance", *Journal of Applied Corporate Finance*, 8,1, pp. 121–7.

Diamond, D., 1984, "Financial Intermediation and Delegated Monitoring", *Review of Economic Studies*, 51, pp. 393–414.

Diamond, D., 1991, "Monitoring and Reputation: The Choice Between Bank Loans and Directly Placed Debt", *Journal of Political Economy*, 9, 9pp. 689–721.

Doherty, N. A., 2000, *Integrated Risk Management* (New York: McGraw-Hill).

Eckbo, B. E, and R. W. Masulis, 1995, "Seasoned Equity Offerings: A Survey", *Handbooks in Operations Research & Management Science, Vol. 9, Finance* (Amsterdam: Elsevier).

Fama, E. F., and K. R. French, 2000, "Testing Tradeoff and Pecking Order Predictions About Dividends and Debt", Graduate School of Business, The University of Chicago, Center for Research in Security Prices, *Working Paper No 506*.

Fama, E. F., and M. H. Miller, 1972, *The Theory of Finance* (New York: Holt, Rinehart, and Winston).

Froot, K., 1998, *The Evolving Market for Catastrophic Event Risk* (New York: Marsh & McClennan Securities Corp. and Guy Carpenter Special Report).

Froot, K. A., D. S. Scharfstein, and J. C. Stein, 1993, "Risk Management: Coordinating Investment and Financing Policies", *Journal of Finance*, 48, 5, pp. 1629–58.

Galai, D., and M. I. Schneller, 1978, "Pricing of Warrants and the Value of the Firm", *Journal of Finance*, 33, 5, pp. 1333–42.

Garrison, R. W., 2001, *Time and Money: The Macroeconomics of Capital Structure* (London: Routledge).

Harris, M. and A. Raviv, 1991, "The Theory of Capital Structure", *Journal of Finance*, 46, 1, pp. 297–355.

Hicks, J., 1973, *Capital and Time* (Oxford: Clarendon Press).

Knepper, L., 2002, "Unwrapping the Wrappers, ", *Barclays Capital Securitisation Research*.

Lane, M. N., 1999, "An Optionable Note: The Reliance III Case Study", *Lane Financial LLC Trade Notes*.

Lewin, P., 1999, *Capital in Disequilibrium: The Role of Capital in a Changing World* (London: Routledge).

Mayers, D., and C. W. Smith, Jr., 1982, "On the Corporate Demand for Insurance", *Journal of Business*, 55, 2, pp. 281–96.

Merton, R.C., 1977, "An Analytic Derivation of the Cost of Deposit Insurance and Loan Guarantees: An Application of Modern Option Pricing Theory", *Journal of Banking and Finance* 1 (June), pp. 3-11.

Merton, R. C., and A. F. Perold, 1993, "Management of Risk Capital in Financial Firms", in *Financial Services: Perspectives and Challenges* (Boston: Harvard Business School Press).

Milgrom, P., and J. Roberts, 1986, "Price and Advertising Signals of Product Quality", *Journal of Political Economy*, 94, 4, pp. 796–821.

Miller, M. H., and K. Rock, 1985, "Dividend Policy Under Asymmetric Information", *Journal of Finance*, 40, 4, pp. 1031–51.

Modigliani, F., and Miller, M. H., 1958, "The Cost of Capital, Corporation Finance, and the Theory of Investment", *American Economic Review*, 47, pp. 261–97.

Modigliani, F., and Miller, M. H., 1963, "Corporate Income Taxes and the Cost of Capital: A Correction", *American Economic Review*, 53, 3, pp. 433–43.

Myers, S. C., 1977, "The Determinants of Corporate Borrowing", *Journal of Financial Economics*, 5, pp. 147–76.

Myers, S. C., 1984, "The Capital Structure Puzzle", *Journal of Finance*, 39, 3, pp. 575–92.

Nelson, P., 1970, "Information and Consumer Behavior", *Journal of Political Economy*, 78, 2, pp. 311–29.

Nelson, P., 1974, "Advertising as Information", *Journal of Political Economy*, 82, 4, pp. 729–54.

Ross, S., 1977, "The Determination of Financial Structure: The Incentive Signaling Approach", *Bell Journal of Economics*, 8, 1, pp. 23–40.

Schenk, C., 2000, "Michelin: Setting the Standard", *Alternative Risk Strategies: Special Supplement to Risk Magazine* (December).

Schorin, C., 2000, "Monoline Bond Insurers: Are All AAAs Created Equal?", *Morgan Stanley Dean Witter Special Report* (January).

Shimpi, P., 2001, *Integrating Corporate Risk Management* (New York: Texere).

Smith, C. W., Jr., and R. M. Stulz, 1985, "The Determinants of Firms' Hedging Policies", *Journal of Financial and Quantitative Analysis*, 20, 4, pp. 391–405.

Spence, M., 1973, "Job Market Signaling", *Quarterly Journal of Economics*, 87, pp. 355–74.

Stulz, R. M., 1996, "Rethinking Risk Management," *Journal of Applied Corporate Finance*, 9, 3, pp. 8–24.

Tufano, P., 1996, "Who Manages Risk? An Empirical Examination of Risk Management Practices in the Gold Mining Industry", *Journal of Finance* 51, 4, pp. 1097–137.

7

Contingent Covers

Bryon Ehrhart

Aon Re Services, Inc

Contingent covers are generally the most esoteric of the coverages that are considered as the enterprise's risk management programmes are structured and restructured from time to time. Most corporate risk management programmes do not include contingent covers as they are defined in this chapter.

INTRODUCTION

This chapter explores the use of contingent covers by corporate risk managers and insurers. The contingent covers to be discussed here are generally those insurances and reinsurances that provide new coverage in the event that any existing arrangement becomes unrenewable or exhausted. In addition, this chapter includes those insurances and reinsurances that are appropriate in only those limited circumstances when substantial aggregate retentions are exhausted or other unrelated events – such as a general stock or bond market decline – occurs in addition to the occurrence of substantial otherwise insurable events.

Consideration of contingent covers

The use of contingent covers is very limited beyond the reinstatement terms that are generally included in both traditional insurance and reinsurance contracts. This is discussed further in the section on reinstatement provisions. Risk managers and insurers tend to purchase few back up or contingent covers because the cost, even though it can be a fraction of the original cover, is an apparent additional cost that their competitors might not want to assume. In addition, the events typically considered for contingent covers tend to be those that are considered unexpected by Wall Street analysts and rating agencies.[1] Further, such events also tend to affect the entire peer group, as many will not have provisioned cover for such events. Management groups generally do not feel that the benefit of being an out performer in the peer group for events experienced by the entire sector, is greater than the cost of the contingent cover. Nevertheless, some contingent covers are purchased and this chapter explores some of the more common forms of them.

The following discussion is segregated into a section devoted to those contingent covers that are typically utilised or considered by corporate customers that are not insurers. The later section is devoted to the contingent covers that are utilised by insurers and reinsurers. As discussed later, the type of cover needed will differ between the two.

Contingent insurance covers

Surety bonds

Surety bonds have emerged as a form of contingent credit risk management for a significant portion of the financial services industry. The surety bonds that fit within the definitions we set out earlier in this chapter are those that operate largely as financial guarantees. These surety bonds have generally been restricted to what is generally referred to as the commercial surety bond sector, which are bonds that guarantee financial performance of larger companies, most of which have independent ratings or substantial intrinsic value. A simple example of commercial surety bonds is a bond required by state insurance statutes for companies that self-insure their workers' compensation exposure. A more complex example is the use of commercial surety bonds to guarantee the receipt of interest and principal on bonds, notes or receivables within the loan portfolio of a bank or financial institution. This more complex example really fits the definition of a contingent cover because banks and financial institutions generally had retained, limited or otherwise diversified their exposure to significant single name credit exposures until they began utilising commercial surety insurance as a risk management tool in the 1998–9 era. As the US economy began showing signs of weakness in late 1999 and 2000 the use of commercial surety insurance grew significantly. A glimpse of the significance of this practice is the nearly US\$3 billion of commercial surety coverage alleged to have been in place by several financial institutions on the now bankrupt Enron and Enron-related entities including several of its vilified off-balance sheet partnerships. For example, reports of such transactions between JP Morgan and Enron.[2]

Financial institutions that found efficient pricing in the commercial surety market vs the pricing available in the credit default market prior to the Enron bankruptcy, have been – at the time of writing – finding it very difficult to develop meaningful surety bond capacity at reasonable prices.

In effect, in the aftermath of Enron the commercial surety market has had to re-evaluate the fundamentals of its business.

Representations and warranties coverage
In connection with mergers and acquisitions it is reasonably common for significant contingencies to be included in contract representations or warranties. Buyers and sellers have found it beneficial to manage some of the credit exposure – and in some cases the contingencies – themselves through insurance contracts. These contingent covers generally respond in addition to any other insurance that may apply in the circumstances. A simple example is an acquirer that is concerned that environmental exposures of the seller may exceed some reasonable threshold. In this case, a seller may be asked to escrow proceeds. A seller that does not wish to escrow proceeds may offer to provide an insurance contract that provides similar protection to the buyer. The buyer may also purchase additional coverage or pay to completely rid itself of the contingent liability.

These contracts remain a popular commercial solution to issues that regularly arise in connection with sales of businesses.[3]

Adverse development programmes
Frequently corporations, often through special or – in Wall Street vernacular – non-recurring charges, recognise liabilities related to contingencies from their past. For example, organisations have taken charges related to their role in activities that may have damaged the environment, manufacturing or distributing defective products such as asbestos, various medical devices or consumer products. In many cases, these organisations have substantial excess insurance programmes in place to cover such losses. However, courts have often ruled that each and every act or sale constitutes an "occurrence" as defined in the insurance policy exposing the corporation's retention to each "occurrence". In many cases, corporations have sought to limit their aggregate exposure to additional claims through the use of adverse development insurance programmes. These programmes generally provide an aggregate limit of coverage for future claims related to specified contingencies or classes of potential claims, for example asbestos or environmental exposures. These programmes generally are disclosed by corporations at the date that the charges are taken. By using these programmes, management usually tries to assure investors that the announced special or non-recurring charges plus the new insurance coverage is sufficient to cover any further exposure that the corporation may be subject to relating to the covered events.

These contingent covers have been widely utilised. In relatively limited circumstances – as corporate risk managers aim to fully extinguish their exposure – these contracts take the form of a "liability buy-out" wherein an insurer agrees to cover any and all additional exposure the corporation may have to a particular series of claims. Both of these areas of contingent covers have been substantially affected by the 1999 Financial Accounting

Standards Board adoption of Appendix D Topic No. D-79, which substantially limits the accounting benefit that a corporation may reflect from placing transactions that cover any past event exposures when they are not carried out in connection with a merger or an acquisition.[4]

Risk management professionals can often struggle to differentiate adverse development covers – as discussed, those that provide additional coverage for exposure to past events – from new "prospective" covers that provide "claims made" coverage. Generally, such claims made coverage provides limits for events that are reported during the upcoming year that may occur during the upcoming year or may have occurred years earlier but not before the retro date.[5] In theory, the accounting prescribed in Topic No. D-79 would apply to all "claims made" covers as well. Almost no corporation follows this accounting prescription and this is an emerging issue within the industry. If the prescription were to be enforced, the need for substantial additional prospective insurance covers and contingent covers would be increased.

Aggregate retention protection programmes

The prior section discussed adverse development covers that refer to contingent covers placed after events occurring that result in financial liability to the company. Generally these adverse development covers are placed when it is clear to the corporation that it either does not have insurance or it has obtained insufficient insurance. These experiences from the past have prompted many risk managers to consider supplementing their prospective insurance programmes with coverage that responds when certain retention thresholds are exceeded. These, structures in particular, can be placed to cover the accumulations of retained exposure from, for example, all product liability claims that occur during the upcoming year or – in the case of corporations with a relatively stable product mix and highly estimable exposures of all product liability claims arising from new products or substantially altered products during the upcoming year. Risk managers are routinely interested in exploring the costs of programmes given the increasingly litigious business and consumer environment.

During the softest cycles in the insurance industry – for example in the early eighties and late nineties – it is not uncommon to find that substantial coverage beyond a relatively low aggregate retention is essentially "thrown-in" or provided at very low cost for standard coverages including workers' compensation, auto and general liability (excluding products). This coverage quickly evaporates or becomes very expensive during cycles where underwriters are forced to properly value the exposures they insure after losses.

Insurance price caps

In the most recent soft market in the late nineties risk managers generally understood that the insurance industry was, in many cases, substantially underpricing its capital. (For example, the poor underwriting performance in every insurance and reinsurance sector which can be seen in underwriting results at Lloyds North America and Europe – where there are many examples – from 1999 up until the time of writing.) While insurers may have had competent reasons for doing so, some risk managers saw the opportunity to buy protection from the risk that the cost of insurance might rise dramatically. In most cases the resulting product was even better than simply a price guarantee because insurers simply sold multiple year policies that assured the risk manager that important terms other than price would not change. This was especially true in the directors' and officers' liability market and with the substantial turn in the economic environment in the United States, insurers have uniformly sworn-off this habit and blamed it for the prolonged period of poor underwriting results. However, multiple year policies were not the only form of price protection sold. Certain insurers did offer separate coverage for potential price increases referencing coverage terms that are no better than contracts that are about to expire. Amazingly, few risk managers purchased this coverage even though pricing appeared to be very efficient. The rationale for not buying the separate price risk coverage often involved an explanation that the expense was unbudgeted as well as a core belief that the insurance industry would never really regain pricing power because of the continuous flow of capital after significant events.

The outlook for these products does not seem optimistic as few risk managers think it is productive to pursue price caps in "hard markets". However, even a more tightened insurance industry appears to provide accretive capital to substantial segments of the economy and risk managers that recognise this fact will benefit their organisations by accessing this capital.

Earnings per share protection

Perhaps the most interesting contingent cover of all time, earnings per share (EPS) protection, was discussed in the late 1990s.[6] In these heady days the thought that risk managers could insure everything that might affect earnings per share seemed plausible to certain insurers. While it appears that no such transactions occurred as they were deemed not feasible (and the insurer that made headlines for introducing the product later became insolvent for apparently unrelated reasons) the idea did focus the minds of many risk managers that had previously grappled with "enterprise risk management" processes and solutions. While the prospect for EPS insurance probably always was dim, the idea of applying insurance capital to more business development and operational contingencies is alive and well. Generally risk managers and chief financial officers understand that insurance is another form of capital and its efficiency relating to the management of business risks can be evaluated against all other forms of capital. As mentioned before, even in "hard markets" for insurance, insurers may continue to provide accretive capital to many industries.

As a closing note to this section, the significant progress the risk management industry has made since the early nineties that now allows direct comparison of the pricing and efficiency of insurance capital to all other forms of capital available, sets the stage for substantial expansion of contingent covers as defined in this section. While EPS insurance will not be the focus, the "enterprise risk management" process has matured beyond a, 'scrap all that has been done before and do a new combined limit programme' concept, to one that focuses upon how existing efficiencies can be improved or expanded to address the needs of the corporation. Contingent covers can represent a good business for both the insurers and the insured.

Contingent reinsurance covers
Reinstatement provisions
The most common forms of contingent covers in the reinsurance sector are the reinstatement provisions that are included in many traditional reinsurance contracts. For example, the reinstatement provisions in a property catastrophe contract provide that upon exhaustion of any part of the occurrence limit, this limit shall be reinstated after each occurrence until the value of the original occurence limits has been fully exhausted. In a property catastrophe layer of US$10 million in excess of US$10 million, the traditional terms provide for an aggregate limit of US$20 million while only US$10 million is recoverable from any single occurrence. Following on this example, if the insurer sustains US$25 million of direct insured catastrophe losses in one occurrence, US$10 million will be recoverable. Upon the payment of the reinstatement premium (generally offset against the losses paid from the first event) an additional US$10 million of limit in excess of US$10 million will be available to cover occurrence losses originating from any subsequent occurrence or occurrences. The premiums paid by insurers to reinstate catastrophe covers are generally priced at the original price for the layer, multiplied by the proportion of the occurrence limit that is exhausted to the original limit. No discount is typically given for the expiration of any portion of the annual term prior to the date of the loss occurrence.

Reinstatement premium terms for property catastrophe covers are the easiest to generalise as we have done above. Meanwhile reinstatement premium terms for property risk covers and casualty covers are highly variable and the subject of extensive negotiation.

Reinstatement provisions (both pricing and limits) are among the fastest to change in hardening reinsurance markets. For example, prior to

Hurricane Andrew, it was common for reinstatement premiums to be reduced to recognise any time that had expired within the annual term prior to the date of the loss occurrence. The elimination of this provision was simply made to reduce the size of the covered loss. The impact of this change has meant that it does not make sense to buy catastrophe coverage at rates on line greater than say 30% given that upon the occurrence of a loss, the cedent will only recover a net 40% of the loss after considering the initial and reinstatement premiums. The traditional contract generally provides two times the occurrence limit in each layer regardless of the probability of attaching the layer. Generally the reinstatement provisions are considered to be worth less to the cedent as they are provided further and further up the coverage ladder. However, in years with multiple loss occurrences, cedents are pleased to have the reinstatement limits throughout the programme. In certain circumstances after the occurrence of several significant events during an annual period, cedents exhaust the traditional limits and must seek additional reinsurance cover to reduce their exposure to any subsequent events. Seeking additional capacity under these circumstances can be very expensive given that reinsurers have recognised limit losses on the programme. The desire to stay clear of this negotiating position is the basis for the existence of the market of the "third aggregate limits" described in the next sub-section.

Third aggregate limit covers
Third aggregate limit covers are often referred to as second event or third event covers. However, because most are purchased to supplement the traditional reinsurance contract that – as discussed in the previous sub-section – includes two full occurrence limits these covers are at least third event covers. In the securitisation market for catastrophe covers the term second event covers tends to be used to describe the limits that become available to a cedent in lower layers of an annual period following a year with significant losses. Several transactions have included these provisions with the underlying thought that in years following significant catastrophe losses, coverage may either not be available at all or at efficient prices. Few insurance placements are done on this basis. The pricing and capacity in the securitisation market for this coverage is more fully discussed in other sections of this text. In the reinsurance market few reinsurers have spent much time developing pricing models or allocating capacity to the segment. This appears to be due to the lack of predicable interest from cedents. Cedents recognise that sufficient catastrophe capacity at reasonable prices has been available following Hurricane Andrew, the Northridge Earthquake and the events of September 11 2001.[7]

Third and fourth aggregate limits alongside property catastrophe retentions are routinely considered by cedents with significant exposure to tornado, hail and Winter storm losses such as those that occurred in the US in 2001. This is especially true given the unusually high level of tornado hail losses since 1998. Reinsurers have not uniformly embraced these routine enquiries with efficient pricing or capacity in the author's experience. These products have been most useful to small to medium size regional insurers who have the need for extra capital due to the frequency of events.

Run-off options in expiring treaties

An interesting development within the reinsurance community has been the practical implications of a uniform elimination of reinsurance capacity for terrorism on commercial insurance contracts. With cedents forced by statue to continue to insure losses resulting from terrorism, they have looked to their expiring contracts for continued coverage. Under contingent coverage provisions generally used by cedents that wish to exit certain lines of business, cedents have been able to trigger the run-off option within these expiring treaties. The result for the ceding insurer is coverage at the expiring terms (including terrorism) for the unexpired term of all policies in force at the end of the treaty term. In the majority of cases, the pricing of this contingent coverage is at or slightly above expiring terms. Many reinsurers are unhappy that this provision has been used to continue their exposure to terrorist attacks in the authors experience; however, cedents would hardly be prudent ignoring this coverage option given the dearth of other alternatives.

While this form of contingent cover may not be plentiful after the 2002 renewal season, as the market recovers clients will still need treaty options to run-off discontinued lines of business. This need may result in a new range of contingent covers if reinsurers continue their course of withholding this coverage option.

Adverse development reinsurance covers in mergers and acquisitions

Since the statutory and generally accepted accounting principles (GAAP) benefits of retroactive reinsurance are substantially limited by the statement of statutory accounting principles (SSAP) 62 and the statement of financial accounting standards (SFAS) 113, respectively, there is very little activity in the adverse development or contingent loss reserve development cover market.[8] This statement excepts companies that are nearing significant statutory risk based capital levels where – despite the unfavourable book accounting – a benefit is allowed. Adverse development covers placed in connection with mergers and acquisitions are really the only area where substantial accounting benefit is allowed (GAAP only not statutory). This benefit was not originally given within the context of SFAS 113 when it was released in December of 1992. The benefit was finally allowed through a separate interpretation of the accounting for analogous guarantees made by non-insurers in connection with mergers and acquisition transactions. Non-insurer acquirers are allowed to account for guarantees made by the seller as if they were prospective insurance agreements, which allow for a current accounting benefit at the time that the guarantee is used. Given this analogy, the emerging issues task force (EITF) documented its conclusion that insurers should be allowed similar credit for guarantees made by sellers of insurance companies even when such guarantees are purchased by the seller from reinsurers that are not affiliated with the seller.[9]

Today there is hardly a merger or acquisition of an insurer or reinsurer that does not include a Topic D-54 qualifying adverse development cover. These contingent reinsurance covers are really the only way insurers have been able to cap the exposures written by prior owners of insurers. The benefits to the industry have been enormous. Significant reinsurers such as Berkshire Hathaway, Munich Re, Ace and XL have made the provision of these covers a significant component of their business plans. Given the financial condition of a significant portion of the industry the outlook for writing these merger and acquisition related contingent covers is bright.

Reinsurance price caps
Options to control the price volatility of reinsurance would seem likely given the sophistication of a number of reinsurance buyers. However, very few transactions have occurred despite the availability of the product at several points during the soft reinsurance market. The lack of interest of buyers seems to be related to the fact that those that would provide the price caps tend to want to control the placement of the reinsurance if the cap were triggered. This feature violates the relationship based on buying trends used by most cedents. Cedents that have a significant desire to control reinsurance costs over time tend to enter into multiple year agreements rather than purchase price caps. Even though there are inefficiencies related to doing multiple year reinsurance deals – largely due to the loss of about a third of the market because they either refuse or cannot do multiple year deals – this is the route most often taken. The outlook for reinsurance price caps, while still intellectually interesting, is not positive.

Double trigger covers
Contingent covers with recoveries that are subject to two triggers are an interesting thought but are hardly ever transacted. The more notable transactions are those that provide excess property catastrophe coverage only when significant property catastrophe losses occur in the same year that a significant decline in the equity markets occurs. While conceptually these covers should be substantially cheaper than traditional reinsurance contracts with only an event trigger, few reinsurers have been willing to discount traditional pricing enough to attract significant cedent interest. The equity market volatility has occurred since the two lead transactions in

this area were completed by North American insurers exposed to earthquake and hurricane risk. This has not encouraged reinsurers to think more seriously about discounting traditional pricing more significantly. The outlook for the availability of attractively priced double trigger products linked to the equity markets is not positive.

Double trigger products that respond only in the circumstance of significant property catastrophe events in more than one zone during an annual period continue to be discussed within the industry – particularly in the retrocession market. While these covers are rarely placed they remain more efficiently priced than products with second triggers that are associated with the equity markets. The outlook is more favourable for these products given the otherwise hard retrocession market.

Contingent finite stop-loss

Beginning in earnest in 1995, large multiple division property and casualty carriers began to use finite stop-loss reinsurance contracts that provided little economic risk transfer but significant GAAP and statutory accounting benefit. The accounting benefit arose from the fact that reinsurers would charge premiums that reflected the time value of money vs the reserves insurers need to post, which are generally not discounted. The time value of money was significant since stop-loss treaties require the reinsurer to pay the cedent only when paid losses exceeded the planned loss ratio – these programmes sometimes attached above or below plan as well. For commercial lines insurers this payment lag could be as long as 10–15 years. The premium cedents needed to pay, including reasonable margins to the reinsurer, given that the significant discounting period was often substantially less than the undiscounted losses ceded (say 35% to 60% of the undiscounted losses ceded). The insurance and reinsurance market generally softened from 1995 and, as management groups continued to establish plans based upon unattainable loss ratios, more and more losses were ceded to these covers. The covers continue to mask the poor underwriting results attained by some of the larger commercial insurers during the soft market of the late 1990s.

In about 1998, Wall Street analysts began to catch on to the fact that the earnings reported by larger commercial insurers were significantly improved by finite stop-loss reinsurance contracts. These analysts began to pound the table about the "mortgaging of the company's future" effect that was created by these products. This "mortgage" is created by the loss of investment income on the ceded premiums that was not so significant in the year of the ceded losses but became meaningful as future earnings were adjusted to reflect lower investment returns. This is particularly significant for companies that ceded significant losses year after year to such programmes. Analysts valued significant finite stop-loss users differently than those that did not have such "mortgage" obligations.

Rather than stop using these agreements all together, commercial insurers began entering into contingent finite stop-loss agreements that were to be used – not to hide bad underwriting results from continued under pricing of workers compensation and other casualty lines but – to smooth unexpected volatility from retained property losses. The notion of "contingent" finite stop-loss comes from the normal transaction style that only the margin was paid at inception and the full premium due would be paid at the time, and only if losses were ceded to the programme. This practice seemed to be not only accepted but also preferred by Wall Street analysts through 2001.[10] There is, however; a building taint associated with companies that maintain any stop-loss reinsurance. The claim is that it mortgages the future earnings for a current benefit that is not entirely transparent. Few insurers plan to continue this type of earnings smoothing cover.

Risk excess programmes with significant annual aggregate deductibles
Commercial insurers recognise new levels of uncertainty surrounding casualty lines that have previously performed within reasonable parameters. Many believe that the current rating environment is attractive but would like catastrophe protection within, what are in many cases, larger risk retentions. Given the taint associated with contingent finite stop-loss agreements, clients are interested in true risk transfer transactions. One significant source of such risk transfer is the traditional casualty excess reinsurance market. The contingent form of cover is assembled by placing new layers, within the higher retentions now taken, while retaining significant annual aggregate deductibles within the new layers. The annual aggregate deductible can be set well in excess of planned layer losses. The coverage beyond the annual aggregate deductible acts as contingent protection. Many cedents will explore this type of protection during the current cycle.

Contingent capital
The previous chapter introduced contingent capital as an additional source that allows insurers and reinsurers to optimise their capital structures.

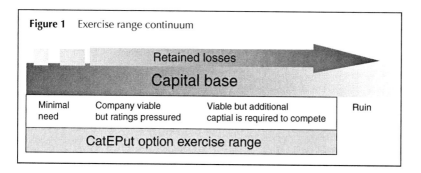

Figure 1 Exercise range continuum

Retained losses

Capital base

| Minimal need | Company viable but ratings pressured | Viable but additional captial is required to compete | Ruin |

CatEPut option exercise range

Contingent capital has been utilised by most government catastrophe pools and several insurers and reinsurers. These transactions largely stemmed from these entities' inability to obtain sufficient or efficient traditional reinsurance coverage in advance of losses, but they could obtain efficient financing following losses by pledging their assessment rights to lenders or bondholders. Similar programmes for private insurers have generally backstopped the balance sheets of these organisations without providing income statement protection. The transactions are simple in structure, allowing insurers (options buyers) to put their capital securities to investors (option writers) upon the occurrence of certain pre-defined events. The CatEPut, developed by Aon in the wake of Hurricane Andrew and the Northridge Earthquake continues to be the most popular transaction format. These arrangements continue to be attractive alternative arrangements in the current – at the time of writing – hard market.

Losses that exceed the reinsurances acquired by entities consume capital on a dollar for dollar basis ignoring tax effects. Small amounts of retained losses generally do not generate the need to replace capital. However, as losses consume greater proportions of the capital of the entity reinstating the capital structure – at reasonable terms – becomes more and more important. In CatEPut transactions, the right of the option holder to access capital to reinstate their capital is pre-negotiated. The exercise range is generally fairly wide as depicted in Figure 1; however, in instances where the option owner is no longer an attractive counterparty even after considering the additional capital – a ruin condition – the option cannot be exercised.

The transaction structure is simple as depicted in Figure 2. This demonstrates an uncollateralised transaction. In a collateralised transaction a trust would become the option writer and investors would hold notes in an amount equal to the principal contributed to the trust. The majority of the contingent capital transactions that have been completed to date, have been

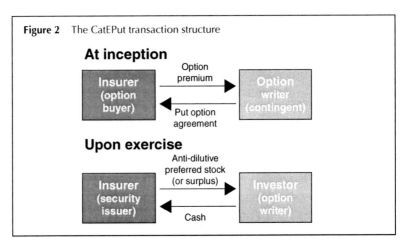

Figure 2 The CatEPut transaction structure

uncollateralised. Most of the uncollateralised transactions call for collateral upon significant ratings downgrades of the option writers.

CONCLUSION

This chapter has focused upon some of the most esoteric covers that are considered by risk managers and reinsurance buyers. While there are other contingent covers in the market place, the most common forms have been summarised herein. The goal of this chapter has been to simply define what contingent covers are and to address some of the current uses and the prospects for their use in the future. Contingent insurance products, contingent reinsurance products and contingent capital have been used to complement the capital structures of industrial corporations and insurers. These products will continue to evolve in the ever-changing insurance, reinsurance and capital markets. Ultimately, it is clear that these products can be an accretive form of capital to a variety of organisations.

1   Such as windstorms Lothar and Martin.[For more information on this instance see: http:www.rms.com/Publications/Lothar_Martin_eventreport.asp]
2   For further information on Mahonia transactions see: Wall Street Journal, 2002.
3   For example, claims made on health-related grounds as in asbestos exposure cases against Turner & Newell (see http://www.ibas.btinternet.co.uk/lka_imp_tn_admin.htm).
4   See EITF Abstracts 2001 : A Summary of Proceedings of the FASB Emerging Issues Task Force (Financial Accounting)
5   A retro date is a fixed date that precludes events occurring prior to such date from being covered by the policy.
6   For more information on earnings per share see, for example, http://www.nunews.com/archives/pc_archive/1999/p02-[n]08/06earnings.asp
7   Approximately US$8 billion of capital was raised following the 1992-4 sequence of property cat losses and approximately US$ 14 billion of equity capital was raised following the events of September 11th.
8   SFAS and SSAP are pronouncements that prescribe accounting for reinsurance in the US.
9   Appendix D, Topic D-54 of the EITF minutes.
10 This was borne out in real time during insurance company conference calls with Wall Street analysts during 2001.

Finite Risk Insurance and Reinsurance

Oscar Tymon
Centre

Finite: Limited, bounded, not infinite

Risk: Chance or possibility of danger or other adverse consequences

These two words combine to create a term that, in the last 15 years, has successfully integrated itself into insurance, reinsurance and indeed financial parlance.

INTRODUCTION

This chapter will attempt to shed some light on the emergence of the significant and powerful risk management tool of finite risk and will focus mainly on prospective coverage. Loss portfolio transfers and other retrospective structures are dealt with elsewhere in this book.

HISTORY

Steven Gluckstern and Michael Palm, the two founders of Centre Reinsurance, which commenced operations in 1988, are generally credited with the creation of the concept of finite risk. Gluckstern and Palm gained access to some 20 years' worth of treaty reinsurance experience of one of the major US broking companies. The data were analysed carefully and some very important conclusions were made.

Treaty reinsurance is usually bought and sold over long periods of time. At the outset, the buyer and the seller typically have an idea of the expected range of financial outcomes over the life of the contract. There is often the stated intention that the buyer expects the reinsurer to make a reasonable profit over the long-term. Rarely does one party deliberately set out to exploit the other.

When the data were analysed, they showed that, in well over 80% of cases, the outcome was within the boundaries of reasonable financial expectation. Some contracts were loss-free – 100% profit for the reinsurer.

These were often contracts where the risk reinsured was a natural peril or some other short-tail event that did not occur during the period of coverage. At the other end of the spectrum, however, a small group of contracts went disastrously wrong. So much so that, in some cases, the results bankrupted the reinsurer and severely threatened the reinsured. Even when considered as part of a spread portfolio, the profits from the contracts that went well were inadequate to compensate for those with very poor outcomes.

What was learned from this analysis? Quite simply that reinsurers are not compensated sufficiently to take on an unlimited or infinite risk. The transactions that had been financial disasters contained no overall limit of liability whatsoever, apart from the financial strength or capital resources of the reinsurer.

So the concept of finite risk was born; if the pot is not large enough to pay for unexpected horrors then some limitation of liability has to be incorporated. Consequently, all finite risk structures contain an overall aggregate limit of liability. There is also the more practical question as to whether any underwriter has enough knowledge and skill to take on an unlimited risk, but that is for another book.

Finite risk and financial reinsurance

From another perspective, it can be argued that finite risk grew out of "financial reinsurance", a term used to describe contracts of reinsurance that were purely financial in nature with no real transfer of risk between buyer and seller. The only practical risk assumed was that of the creditworthiness of the two contracting parties.

Prior to 1993 these financial arrangements were in widespread use. It was, in fact, their *abuse* that lead to some significant accounting changes in the US at the beginning of 1993 – Financial Accounting Standards Board (FASB) regulation 113, followed soon after by Financial Reporting Standard (FRS) 5 in the UK. At the heart of these standards was the definition of "risk transfer" for the purposes of deciding whether a particular contract should be accounted for as (re)insurance, with premium deductible for tax purposes, or deposit accounted as a banking transaction would be treated, where any benefit would only be earned over time.

There was some interesting, perhaps anecdotal, evidence supposedly unearthed by the Securities and Exchange Commission (SEC) in the aftermath of Hurricane Andrew, a severe hurricane that devastated large parts of Southern Florida in August 1992. When the US property and casualty insurance industry filed its annual reports at the end of 1992, the SEC found a "hole" of around US$4 billion. The insured cost of hurricane Andrew was known, yet this appeared to be understated in the books of certain insurance companies when the reported losses were tallied.

A significant element of this shortfall is believed to have arisen as a result of the accounting treatment of certain of the aforementioned financial rein-surance contracts. Some of these policies were taken out at the beginning of 1992. In effect, a limit of indemnity was granted over the five years. For this illustration we shall call it 100 units. An annual premium was payable of 20 units per year. If we ignore interest earned on the premium received by the reinsurer, over the five-year period, the limit would be fully funded. In the event of favourable experience, a substantial proportion of the premium was payable back to the reinsured by way of a profit commission. In the event of an early loss that resulted in a negative balance for the reinsurer (ie, losses were greater than premiums paid to date), the contract provided for additional premium/interest to be paid so as to make the reinsurer whole over the period of the contract.

Hurricane Andrew caused a total loss to many of these policies. If we take contracts that had only started in 1992, we have a situation where the entire limit of indemnity had been exhausted (100 units taking the work-ings above) but only a small percentage of the overall premium (20 units) had been paid. As there was no future limit available or value left in these contracts for the buyer, all the future premiums should have been accrued with the result that the effect of the contract would have been broadly neu-tral with no real volatility, either in cash or accounting terms, transferred from reinsured to reinsurer. However, in some cases, the accounting accrual for these future premiums was conveniently "ignored". As a con-sequence, for the year-end 1992 accounts, it was possible to have ended up with a gain of 80 (100 of limit minus the first year's premium of 20). On the face of it, it looked as though 80 units of volatility had been transferred to the reinsurer. In fact, the reinsured still owed 20 units of premium in each of the next four years and there was no cover left. Failing to properly account for this future obligation created part of the hole cited above and naturally caused widespread concern especially among those whose task it was to present a true and fair view.

The FASB in the US decided that, in order for contracts to receive insur-ance and reinsurance accounting treatment (as opposed to being deposit accounted) and for the premiums paid to be tax deductible, there had to be a meaningful amount of risk transferred under the contract. In their stan-dard 113, which came into effect at the beginning of 1993, the FASB set out to define what constituted risk transfer for accounting purposes.[1] However, as a result of the use of words like "significant" in the definition, without any further qualification, more practical, quantifiable guidelines emerged.

The best known of these was the so-called "10:10 rule": there had to be at least a 10% probability of the reinsurer having a loss equal to or greater than 10% of the premium it had received, calculated on a present value basis. This relatively crude standard has become one of the most popular benchmarks to decide whether there is a transfer of risk in insurance and reinsurance contracts.

This accounting standard became effective some five years after finite risk had been born. Those companies that had been concentrating on developing and selling finite risk contracts to their clients in many ways welcomed the new accounting rules: as the "finite" concept entailed the limited (but nevertheless some) transfer of risk, the new risk-transfer guidelines were easily met. On the other hand, certain companies selling the type of financial reinsurance arrangement outlined above found it difficult to adapt to the levels of risk transfer now required for their contracts to receive the desired accounting treatment.

Since the early 1990s, the use of the term "finite" has grown to embrace structures that were called "financial" or "funded". In practice, many programmes sold today are structured in such a way so as to meet the minimum risk-transfer requirements but little more. The important point here is that many clients are seeking structures that receive insurance accounting treatment and are, therefore, able to transfer accounting and cashflow volatility in the event of loss but where the margin (the fee paid to the insurer/reinsurer) is minimised.

BLENDED FINITE CONTRACTS

There is a variation of finite cover called "blended finite". The name derives from the structure being a blend of finite and traditional excess insurance. The cover is integrated into a single policy but is typically more leveraged than a pure finite cover. The use of the term "leveraged" in this instance refers to the relationship between the maximum premium payable and the total limit provided, usually described as the "upside–downside" relationship. In finite covers, this relationship is usually between 1:1.25 and 1:3 – for a potential upside (profit) of one unit there is the risk of losing between 1.25 and three units. In blended covers, this ratio may increase to 1:5 or more. This upside–downside relationship can often have a significant bearing on the perceived value for money from the standpoint of the buyer.

FINITE RISK – OTHER STRUCTURAL FEATURES

After the aggregate limit of liability, perhaps the most important structural feature of a finite cover is the explicit recognition of the time value of money. This is of particular importance for contracts covering long-term liabilities, where a long but potentially volatile time gap exists between the receipt of premium and the payment of loss. Typically, a high proportion of the premium paid (50%–90%) is allocated to an "experience account". Losses are first deducted from this experience account but if the balance is positive, it would attract interest, typically based on three-month or one-year US treasury rates (or other appropriate major government security). In the event of the balance in the experience account becoming negative, an interest debit is typically provided for. It is relatively straightforward to perform a scenario-based, discounted cost-benefit analysis of a finite programme as all the pricing parameters are set out for the (typically three- to five-year) term of the contract. It is difficult to do the same for traditional annual cover because so much depends on general market changes from year to year. The experience account would be available for return to the buyer upon commutation of the contract. In this process, the reinsurer is relieved of all further liability as a *quid pro quo* for the payment of the (positive) balance in the experience account to the client.

The arrival of the finite risk specialists brought with it other worthwhile additions to the cultural armoury of the reinsurance industry, namely a genuine problem-solving mentality together with contracts that were tailored to the specific requirements of each individual customer. This is not surprising as finite covers are often considered as an alternative to, and a replacement for, standard, off-the-shelf reinsurance coverage. Sometimes a carefully structured finite programme could replace dozens of individual layers of coverage previously purchased. It is also important to note that traditional reinsurance capacity has been, and to an extent still is, quite fragmented. Until a few years ago it would have been common to have over 100 individual participants on a catastrophe excess of loss programme for a major US insurer. Moreover, each of those 100 or more participants would in turn be heavily reliant on its own ability to hedge or reduce its risk positions through further reinsurance.

In contrast, finite programmes are often entirely underwritten by a single carrier and the position is held net by the finite reinsurer – no further reinsurance is purchased to protect the position. From this simple comparison it is easy to understand how much easier it is to tailor a finite programme to suit the (often-changing) needs of individual clients.

Cost, although by no means the only consideration, is a major factor determining whether a finite programme might be attractive to a buyer. A sudden tightening of the insurance and reinsurance markets often stimulates creativity and "alternatives". Useful examples of this are the medical malpractice crisis in the US in the mid-1970s and the General Liability crisis around 10 years later. The former stimulated the creation of the so-called "bedpan mutuals". Here, doctors and other medical professionals were forced to organise themselves into regional insurance companies in the absence of any realistic alternative in the conventional insurance market. The thin capital base of these companies was then supplemented by reinsurance capacity.

In the latter example, the world's largest corporations were faced with severe capacity shortages and price increases. The excess liability carriers ACE and XL were born out of this crisis, and were initially structured more along the lines of mutual companies. A condition of coverage was a one-off contribution to surplus as well as annual premiums.

Supplementing these broader industry solutions, finite-risk programmes brought flexibility. When traditional pricing is high, buyers seek alternatives. Finite programmes typically span a number of years, so they allow terms and conditions to be fixed over a wider part of the pricing cycle. This addresses a number of major concerns for buyers: cost, continuity and levels of risk retention. As we will see, the cost is addressed through profit sharing and continuity and consistent retention through the fixed, multi-year contractual term.

In severe market conditions or in particular client circumstances, the available choice is often reduced to two options. Either doing nothing – keeping the risk – or using some form of tailored finite approach.

FINITE RISK EXAMPLE
In contrast to the wider financial world, where significant publicity and disclosure surround important transactions, relatively few finite reinsurance structures reach the public domain. Perhaps insurance companies are more secretive than other types of corporation!

The case chosen here is a three-year alternative to traditional annual catastrophe cover purchased by an insurance or reinsurance company to help mitigate the effect of a major natural peril event. Covers of this type are being bought and sold at the time of writing as a result of tightening market conditions in the wake of the World Trade Center tragedy. This type of approach lends itself to a broad range of business and is certainly not restricted to natural perils.

It should be borne in mind, when considering this example, that finite risk is axiomatic to the central theme of this book – "alternative". One of the fundamental concepts of finite risk is that it represents an alternative to what might *traditionally* have been done, executed or purchased. The main reason why these alternatives are created is because buyers are seeking solutions that are unavailable, too expensive or fundamentally undesirable for some reason.

The cost and availability of coverage that insurance and reinsurance companies buy to protect themselves against natural and man-made catastrophes can be volatile. Immediately following a major catastrophe, such as Hurricane Andrew in 1992 or the World Trade Center tragedy, markets typically react by raising deductibles, increasing pricing and restricting coverage. A major event also alters people's perception as to the correct probability of the same, or indeed other events happening in the future.

Traditional coverage is typically sold on an annual basis. Finite risk structures, as mentioned above, can have a fixed, contractual term of three years or more. Table 1 provides an outline of a three-year finite structure with notes as to where the major differences lie compared with conventional, annual cover.

Table 1   Finite risk example, summary of major terms

Reinsured:	XYZ Insurance Company
Term:	Three years commencing January 1, 2002[2]
Business covered:	All Property business written by the reinsured
Exclusions:	Reinsurance assumed, liability[3]
Retention:	US$20 million per event
Limit:	US$20 million per event
Annual limit:	US$40 million per year, in the aggregate.
Overall aggregate limit:[4]	US$60 million in all over the term of the contract.
Annual premium:	US$8 million per annum (assume that the cost of conventional cover would have been US$6 million per annum)
Additional or reinstatement premium:[5]	50% of Aggregate Losses paid between US$15 million and US$30 million
Experience account:[6]	50% of Annual Premiums minus losses paid
Commutation:[7]	At the option of the reinsured, 12 months following the expiry of the contract and annually thereafter for a further three years until all losses are settled

COMPARATIVE ANALYSIS AND CONCLUSIONS

One of the factors determining whether a client would choose traditional annual cover or a finite approach would be the relationship between the base or annual cost and the client's estimation of the probability of loss. In a hard market, the pricing summarised in the outline terms contained in Table 1 might apply to events that have an annual probability of around one in 10. If this were true, the client is likely to be attracted to the reduction in cost for the finite structure in favourable (low-loss) scenarios compared with the relative high cost of traditional cover in the no-loss case. In a soft market, pricing tends to move much closer to the technical probability of loss, with little or no margin for profit. Taking this to the extreme, in the above example, if the cost of traditional cover were only US$2 million per year (as opposed to the US$6 million cited) then clearly it would be more attractive as the price equates to the technical probability of loss. At traditional pricing of US$6 million the theoretical profit, before costs, is US$4 million – 67% of the premium paid.

Table 2 shows comparative summary results/costs for annual probabilities of loss of both 10% and 15% per annum. The probabilities reflect the fact that coverage is limited to a maximum of two losses per year. Note that as the probability of loss increases from 10% to 15%, the relative cost advantage of the finite programme reduces.

This example ignores the time value of money (not significant in short-

ALTERNATIVE RISK STRATEGIES

Table 2 Probability weighted cost analysis of finite vs traditional approach

10% probability of loss in any year, maximum two events per year

Number of losses	Traditional three-year cover			Finite three-year cover		
	Probability (%)	Cost (US$ 000s)	Weighted cost (US$ 000s)	Probability (%)	Cost (US$ 000s)	Weighted cost (US$ 000s)
0	70.5	18,000	12,689	70.5	12,000	8,460
1	23.8	4,000	951	23.8	6,500	1,545
2	5.0	-10,000	-505	5.0	-8,500	-429
3	0.6	-24,000	-152	0.6	-28,500	-181
4	0.1	-44,000	-25	0.1	-28,500	-16
5	0.0	-64,000	-2	0.0	-28,500	-1
6	0.0	-84,000	0	0.0	-28,500	0
			Total **12,695**			Total **9,378**

15% probability of loss in any year, maximum two events per year

Number of losses	Traditional three-year cover			Finite three-year cover		
	Probability (%)	Cost (US$ 000s)	Weighted cost (US$ 000s)	Probability (%)	Cost (US$ 000s)	Weighted cost (US$ 000s)
0	56.7	18,000	10,199	56.7	12,000	6,800
1	30.8	4,000	1,233	30.8	6,500	2,003
2	10.2	-10,000	-1,021	10.2	-8,500	-868
3	2.0	-24,000	-483	2.0	-28,500	-574
4	0.3	-44,000	-122	0.3	-28,500	-79
5	0.0	-64,000	-15	0.0	-28,500	-6
6	0.0	-84,000	-1	0.0	-28,500	0
			Total **9,790**			Total **7,275**

tail business at 2002 interest rates) and assumes that the traditional cover is available at exactly the same terms and conditions throughout the three-year period. After losses in years one and two, this is unlikely to be the case and would result in it being relatively more expensive compared to the finite option, where the cost is known over the three-year period. On the other hand, it could be argued in the event of no losses in years one and two, the cost may go down. What the finite option does bring is predictability of cost and coverage.

The probabilities of having four, five or six losses are very remote, supporting the point made above that the client is hardly more exposed limiting the maximum number of losses to three over the three-year period.

The straightforward cost comparison shows the finite programme being US$3,578,000 cheaper than traditional cover over the three years. This reduces to US$2,515,000 if one assumes the annual probability of loss increases from 10% to 15%. The main saving is in the no-loss case. So this type of structure is likely to find favour with a buyer who attaches a high probability to there being no losses.

This is not an actual case study (for reasons of confidentiality) but it is intended to represent differentials that one might expect in the real marketplace. Perhaps the most important point to draw from the example is that there are always going to be a large number of tradeoffs involved and it is a question of what is attractive to the particular client at the time that will ultimately determine the route chosen. It is also at the higher end of the risk transfer or leverage range – mentioned above – being nearly 1:2.4 (that is the maximum loss is 2.4 times the maximum gain). It would be possible to structure the cover in a less leveraged way so as to make the relationship between the upside and downside less extreme. In that case, the total premium in relation to aggregate limit would increase and the percentage profit share would increase – the reinsurer is taking less risk and therefore needs less of the premium as a margin.

The case is, however, typical of the finite approach and has found its way into many applications including whole account stop-loss covers and specialist areas such as aviation and the corporate sector. In the latter case, many large corporates have their own captive insurance companies and finite covers have been used to increase the exposure the captive is able to assume without having to inject further capital. The more sophisticated of these structures combine many different lines of insurance (some non-correlating) into a single limit and possibly contain credit and other coverages that are subsequently hedged in the capital markets by the insurer.

THE FINITE APPROACH – FURTHER AFIELD

The reference to "capital" at the end of the last paragraph is an important one. It is the leading finite insurers and reinsurers that have largely helped to put insurance on the map as a legitimate and flexible form of capital over the last decade or so. Prior to this, very few people really thought of insurance as capital in the same way that debt and equity are considered capital. However, by extending contractual coverage over a number of years, it becomes possible to measure the relative attractiveness of insurance vs other traditional forms of capital.

An excellent example of this emerged from the housing crisis in the UK in the late 1980s. At the time, most mortgage business was conducted by building societies. These societies were legally obliged to seek recourse to other third-party collateral in circumstances where individual loan to values exceeded 75%. A mortgage indemnity insurance product grew out of this requirement. Although there was no limitation in coverage, experience for the insurers was acceptable, as potential losses were often mitigated or eliminated by high inflation in times of crisis – until the late 1980s.

In this latter crisis, inflation was conspicuously absent. Traditional mortgage indemnity insurers lost huge sums. How did they respond? Claims were investigated and in some cases denied. Premiums skyrocketed, coverage became restricted and, perhaps most important of all, the building societies were required to carry a co-insurance piece – a share of the risk that they were seeking to insure – for themselves. What could the building socities do with this risk? Up to that point, regulation did not allow building societies to own more than 15% of an insurance company. This was changed with respect to insurance companies for mortgage indemnity risks only. Many of the large lenders set up their own offshore captive insurers to manage, initially, the co-insurance piece imposed. Soon they started to consider whether it might be more efficient to manage the *entire* mortgage indemnity risk in these companies. However, there was the issue of capital.

The Bank of England and the Building Societies' Commission, recalling the huge claims suffered by insurers from the late 1980s crisis, were very keen to ensure the financial robustness of these new offshore insurance vehicles. The new guidelines required that these new captive insurance companies had sufficient capital to be able to withstand at least three years' worth of the worst experience ever suffered by their parent organisations. In practice, this meant circumstances even more adverse than those that existed during the 1988–90 period. It required considerable capital which many societies did not readily possess, or were keeping in reserve, pending demutualisation and floatation.

Enter finite reinsurance. There were many different programme designs. One of the most popular was a 10-year, non-cancellable reinsurance structure to protect these captive companies for up to three years of catastrophic coverage any time in the next 10-year period. The cost of providing this cover was spread over monthly or quarterly instalments throughout the 10 years. From a regulatory perspective, the limits of liability and the promises to pay under these programmes acted as a substitute for the substantial permanent equity capital that would have been required. Instead of paying a huge lump sum, the cost was spread. Moreover, these finite programmes provided for profit sharing in the event of favourable long-term experience.

Although it was impossible to measure the cost comparison between the finite and permanent capital accurately, evidence at the time pointed to it being between 30% and 50% cheaper.

CONCLUSION

Until the mid 1990s, finite coverage was mainly concerned with what could be described as "repackaging the otherwise insurable" – creative, efficient restructuring of risks that were traditionally covered by the insurance industry. However, at this time corporations were seeking ever-greater balance sheet efficiency. A manifestation of this was the desire to lease as opposed to own outright, large operational assets such as real estate, ships and aircraft. This desire pushed volatility and other risks onto the wider financial community, parts of which turned to the insurance industry.

In response to these new demands, many finite insurers developed residual value coverage for a range of different assets. Most typically, these programmes guaranteed the asset's value or the balloon repayment at the end of a contractual lease term. Subsequently these programmes became more sophisticated, providing real-time coverage of the asset in the event of lessee default, this cover was typically provided either through the right to put the asset to the insurer at any time or the insurer providing some form of liquidity facility to the lessee to cover payment default. These residual value programmes were increasingly considered as a form of financial enablement. Today, in conjunction with the wider convergence of the insurance, banking and capital markets, finite risk insurers have developed more sophisticated forms of credit enhancement that often constitute vital parts of the financing structures for projects, major assets, securitisations or similar future-flow-type transactions. Recently, coverage has been provided to guarantee receivable streams from intellectual property – in one case pharmaceutical royalties. No doubt the creative, problem solving, multi-disciplined team-based approach of these finite companies will be turning their skill and capital to even more interesting risk-based challenges in the future.

The top finite insurers and reinsurers represent a new breed of financial company. They have developed their own definitions of risk and reward and sit in the middle of the traditional disciplines, work practices and nomenclature of the insurance, banking and capital markets. Their real strength today lies in the varied skills of their employees together with a culture that combines entrepreneurial judgement with rigorous analysis.

1   The detail of this is well written up elsewhere. Standard 113 from the FASB would provide further information, as would contacting any of the major accounting firms who are likely to have a wealth of material on this subject.
2   Traditional cover would typically be for a period of only one year.
3   The finite approach may be more flexible in its treatment of excluded classes than the traditional market, which is made up of dozens of individual participants who need to come to agreement on coverage.
4   There is an important difference with regard to the overall limit afforded under the finite approach compared with traditional cover. Usually, annual cover contains one reinstatement per year – two limits per year. Over three years that amounts to six limits, more than is really needed. Nevertheless, cover has to be purchased each year as it is not known in advance how losses will fall. If we assume, for the purposes of this example, that the probability of having a full limit loss is 10% – a one in 10 annual event – the probability of having six events in three years is extremely remote – considerably less than 1%. Thus, it could be quite strongly argued that the reinsured in this instance is buying more cover than is needed over the three years. The finite approach provides three limits over three years, which should be sufficient for all foreseeable circumstances and as we shall see later, "trades" this apparent reduction in cover available for a reduction in cost in the no-loss or low-loss scenarios.
5   The reinstatement premium in the conventional annual cover would typically be 100% of the base or annual premium in the proportion that the actual paid loss bears to the per event limit of liability. There is some further commentary below on the cost/benefit comparisons between the two approaches.
6   This is the amount available to the reinsured as a profit commission in the event of favourable experience – when total losses are less than US$12 million, this being 50% of the total annual premiums.
7   The commutation process involves the reinsured releasing the reinsurer from any further liability in return for receiving any positive balance in the experience account.

9

Captives

Paul Wöhrmann and Christoph Bürer

Zurich Financial Services

Corporations are primarily concerned with increasing their value. As a consequence, they engage in entrepreneurial activities to exploit promising opportunities and inevitably face a myriad of risks. These are typically dealt with by means of a particular mix of individual risk management measures which can be broken down into four basic elements: risk avoidance, risk reduction, risk transfer and risk retention.[1]

Risk transfer and risk retention are usually referred to as "risk financing" and are aimed at securing the availability of funds to control financial consequences of events with adverse effects. As such, they are capital resources and form part of a firm's capital structure.[2] Aimed at improving the efficiency and overcoming the limitations of traditional techniques, alternative risk-financing solutions have been developed. "Captives", a well-established and wide-spread alternative risk-financing instrument, frequently form an essential part of risk management programmes.

INTRODUCTION

This chapter offers an elaboration on the captive concept. It begins with a review of the background, the main benefits and drawbacks of captives. It then sheds light on the most important aspects of this instrument. The following sections discuss the rent-a-captive and protected cell company as the most widely used variations of the captive concept. Finally, actual structures with captive involvement are explored.

THE CAPTIVE CONCEPT
Background
A captive[3] is an insurance company that is wholly owned by a non-insurance company and provides coverage for risks of the parent company and its affiliates.[4]

Historically, there were two related driving forces behind the emergence of captives. First, scarcity of insurance capacity forced corporations that were desperately seeking coverage to find and use alternative routes. In many cases, corporations were not able to lay off risks on to the market and therefore used captives to manage retained risks efficiently.

Second, corporations investing heavily in risk management measures and, in turn, experiencing good loss experience found that, over time, premium payments far exceeded claims payments. More importantly, they formed part of a portfolio of insureds that was priced on the basis of the loss history of a particular industry. As a result, such companies supported other risks of bad quality and, in effect, even subsidised competitors. As insurers were not able to respond to the requirements of adequate rates reflecting fair value for the specific risk profiles of such corporations, captives were perceived to be a viable option. There was a clear trend towards individually priced and structured solutions, making the captive concept increasingly popular.

Beneficial tax effects of captive structures accelerated this development. Frequently, tax optimisation was even the primary motivation. This changed over time, however, due to both a clear understanding of the true role of the captive concept in the context of risk management and greater scrutiny by tax authorities. Today, the primary focus is on the use of a captive as a risk management instrument as a part of an overall risk management strategy. Nevertheless, captive structures are regularly designed in a tax-efficient way.

Benefits

Captives offer corporations various distinct benefits. The most prominent one is probably the reduction of cost; if a corporation enjoys a stable favourable loss development, a captive can offer coverage on appropriate (and generally favourable) terms. In effect, risks are being priced individually and spread over time as well as within the group's portfolio, rather than within the one of an insurer. The company can effectively share in the underwriting profit of its business. As the insured participates in its loss experience directly, it obviously has a strong incentive to further improve risk management and enhance risk awareness as well as loss prevention and control. A corporation may even influence loss settlement and control cost directly. This alignment of interest between both parties, the insured and the insurer, potentially diminishes the latter's concerns over moral hazard. This may have a beneficial effect on the capacity available on the market. On the other hand, the insurance industry would face adverse selection problems should only poor risks be shifted to the insurance market. Appropriate measures may be required.

Moreover, investment income can be generated on premiums, reserves and capital. In this respect, particular appeal lies in continuous favourable loss experience and long-tail types of business where a longer period between receipt of premiums and claims payments allows the exploitation of investment opportunities. A further cost reduction can be achieved through direct access to the reinsurance market. In this market, cheaper capacity is available as reinsurers operate under simplified regulation, have a small-scale sales force and – in general – lean overheads. They also have well-diversified portfolios. Therefore, they need comparatively less capital to support their operations.

Cost savings are further enhanced as a captive potentially operates on low cost levels and does not necessarily have to build a profit portion comparable to professional insurers into its premium or, at least, keeps it within the group. With a captive, a corporation also is equipped with a structure that enables it to retain commissions within the group. Captives further allow self-retention to be optimised on a group level, while defining local retentions according to the financial strength of the individual business units. On this basis, a worldwide co-ordinated insurance programme can be designed, tailored to the corporation's specific risk profile and appetite.

By accumulating premiums, it is possible for capacity to be created that could extend cover to previously uninsurable or uninsured risks. The potential stabilisation of pricing works along the same lines; funds created over time allow swings in the insurance market price cycles to be evened out. A strong captive may even offer the option to pursue a flexible and opportunistic risk management strategy with respect to the insurance industry, eventually focussing on the purchase of complementary services rather than insurance. Captives also facilitate a centralised and comprehensive risk management. With detailed statistics, greater transparency can be achieved. This forms the basis for accurate measures and further improvement of risk management.

Moreover, underwriting profits and investment return traditionally left to the insurance industry can be retained within the group and improve its cashflow. The latter can also be accelerated as funds accumulated in the captive can be returned to the parent in the form of dividends or can be employed in the core business via inter-company-loans, ie, credits granted by the captive to other units within the organisation.

It should be borne in mind that a captive has the formal status of an insurance company and that it is commonly accepted that the nature of insurance business requires specific reserving methods, ie, the setting of provisions for claims not yet incurred. Hence, retained risks can be managed considerably more efficiently via a captive rather than on the parent's balance sheet. Generally, captive programmes are regularly structured in a tax-efficient way. This adds to the efficiency of the overall mechanism.

Potential drawbacks

Conversely, there are potential drawbacks associated with the captive concept. First of all, a captive needs to be capitalised, not only in order to comply with solvency regulations, but also from an economic and actuarial point of view. As a result, funds are tied up in the insurance operation of a firm and hence withdrawn from its core business. Therefore, opportunity costs are incurred. Similarly, costs associated with the formation and the ongoing operation of the captive add up to a substantial amount. Running a captive can also involve substantial management capacity.

While a captive is one way to partly take advantage of a broad risk portfolio of a corporation, the portfolio of the captive, as opposed to the one of a professional insurer, obviously has a limited spread of risks. As a result, captives are highly sensitive to substantial losses particularly in the early stages of operation when sufficient funds have not been accumulated. As a consequence, the definition of an adequate level of captive retention is key and the purchase of carefully structured reinsurance cover – where available – may be imperative, particularly to manage the potential of severe losses and random fluctuations. At the same time, the investment activities require attention. Care needs to be taken not only in managing the risks related to the investment but also in ensuring that sufficient solvency is maintained, taking into account loss scenarios and respective pay-out patterns. Underwriting and investment losses may coincide if a subsidiary that is funded with assets of the captive suffers a severe loss. Finally, changes in the legal environment of the various jurisdictions involved are a threat to the success of a captive solution.

Critical requirements

In order to ensure the long-term success of a captive, a corporation must be able to maintain a sustainable positive loss experience. Consequently, superior active risk management and loss control are prime requirements. Similarly, a sound underwriting practice is imperative.

From the above reasoning, it is also easy to recognise that a sufficient premium volume to be written by the captive is a necessity. Furthermore, adequate financial resources are required. A corporation needs considerable capacity to bear a significant portion of its own risk exposure via the captive, which needs to be capitalised accordingly. Other requirements include an open attitude to alternative approaches to risk financing, the willingness to assume a share of its own risk, and the management's commitment in general. Needless to say, a captive has to be run professionally. Finally, the legal and political environment of the entities involved must be suitable for captive solutions.

When considering a captive, the potential benefits and drawbacks have to be weighed up and all the different parameters taken into consideration.

Forms of captives[5]

The natural form of a captive would be a direct insurance company. Insurance, however – due to considerations of consumers and market protection – is a regulated business and direct insurers have to comply in general with rigid legislation pertaining to capitalisation and solvency, reporting, investment, management, etc. In addition, specific expertise in the area of risk assessment, pricing and claims handling is required. Obviously, these services can be outsourced against corresponding fees.

Furthermore, the geographic reach of a direct insurance operation is limited as licenses are restricted to the area of the respective country or region. Non-admitted business usually is not allowed. Consequently, it takes a tremendous effort and a major financial commitment to run one or a number of direct insurance captives properly. However, they may be the solution for corporations with large values and risks in one specific territory; firms based in the European Union, in particular, may enjoy the benefits of the freedom of services and the single license principle.

Not surprisingly, the majority of captives have been implemented on the reinsurance level. By this means, corporations take advantage of the highly deregulated nature of the reinsurance business. Moreover, to further exploit the benefits of the captive concept, corporations have been seeking offshore domiciles for both their lenient regulation and low tax – or even tax-free – environment. This way, the burden of high capitalisation, administration cost and other cost related to rigid legislation can be eased. At the same time, the profit potential can be further enhanced as underwriting profit and investment return are taxed at low rates, if at all.

The typical and most simple form of a captive is a reinsurance company closely held by a single parent as illustrated in Figure 1. As a rule, captives used to only accept risks of affiliated companies. Later though, some broadened their activities to underwrite third party risks and even developed further to become real profit centres. These moves were largely driven by tax and portfolio considerations as well as the aim to further improve profitability.

A captive comes to fruition only in the case of a substantial business volume. The sponsoring firm must also be in a position to put considerable capital at stake. Very similar to the early developments and basic principles of insurance, such an approach requires a larger pool for the purpose of achieving both a minimum spread of risks and sufficient capacity. Rather than establishing their own captive, many companies join forces and opt for captives with a multiple-parent structure and partner within an industry or association. These captives work on the basis of a common captive with a certain degree of risk-sharing among the participants. The design of such a mechanism involves some degree of solidarity and poses very specific challenges.

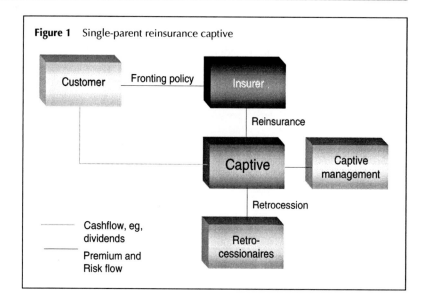

Figure 1 Single-parent reinsurance captive

Fronting

As discussed above, most captives are licensed as reinsurance companies. As a rule, legislations require that insurance coverage be provided by a locally admitted carrier. With the reinsurance captive typically unable to issue local policies, the risks are initially being underwritten by a fully licensed local direct insurer. Subsequently, the risks assumed by the direct insurer are, to a certain extent, passed on to the captive on a reinsurance basis. This process is usually referred to as "fronting".

The local insured and the "fronter" enter into a direct insurance contract. The fronter issues the policy, collects the premium, handles and settles the claims. Yet, as a distinctive feature, the fronter and the captive simultaneously conclude a contractual relationship and define the terms of the reinsurance the captive is providing. Accordingly, the fronter cedes the defined risk share and forwards the corresponding premium collected to the captive. Local insurance regulation does not always permit the cession of 100% of the risks assumed on the direct insurance level and the fronter may have to retain a certain portion of the risks.

The fronter may cede the captive retention exactly or the captive may underwrite the total exposure via reinsurance and, in turn, lay off some or all risk assumed on to the market, possibly focussing on the commission income. Often, the fronter also acts as the excess insurer of the corporation, either on the direct or the retrocession level. In either case, the fronter retains the premium portion corresponding to the risk assumed and charges a fee for the fronting arrangement. This fee covers the usual range of services rendered. Most notably a charge is made for the capital being tied up for the fronting business assumed and subsequently reducing the direct insurer's underwriting capacity for other business. Conversely, including an acquisition component is not justified as the context of a captive structure is slightly different to the one of common reinsurance business.

A very important aspect of fronting is the services that the fronter provides. In order for a corporation to make the most out of a captive solution, the fronting services must be of high quality. This requires a worldwide network and a well-organised and well-equipped infrastructure primarily on the fronter's, but also on the insured's side. Customers expect delivery of statements evidencing claims and financial flows on all levels with clear evidence of the erosion of defined aggregates and the costs incurred.

The accounting and statistics overviews provided by the fronter to the captive are a major source of information. Based on these statements, the captive sets reserves and initiates cashflows. Moreover, the corporation gains insight into the loss development on an aggregate level. Detailed loss information will enhance transparency and, in a risk management context, benefit the corporation at large.

The fronter should be able to transfer premium from the local level to the captive in an efficient and speedy manner. This means distilling multi-currency cashflows down to aggregated payments to the captive, effected in one currency. The most efficient way for administering fronting arrangements has proved to be the structure of an international programme led by one programme manager (as shown in Figure 2). Structures under which every insurer involved cedes to the captive individually are characterised by complex processes and obvious redundancies.

From an economic perspective, the role of an insurer in a fronting arrangement is gradually developing from that of risk carrier to service provider. Nevertheless, the fronter assumes the unconditional obligation to pay for losses covered under the policy up to the total exposure or limit, respectively. Consequently, the fronter retains the counterparty credit risk of the captive failing to pay its respective share under the reinsurance agreement and subsequently incurring a financial loss. Therefore, the captive's ability to pay claims due is of overriding importance. As a general policy matter, the solvency of captives is being appropriately recorded, assessed and monitored. As the financial strength of many captives does not meet minimum requirements, fronters require collaterals to secure the fronting transaction.

Cash call agreements are also integrated in the reinsurance contracts. The purpose of such clauses is to enable the direct insurer, in the event of a large loss, to demand the proportion reinsured with the captive without delay after it has paid the claim under the direct insurance contract. The most widely used security arrangements are parental guarantees, letters of credit, escrow accounts and simultaneous payment clauses. However,

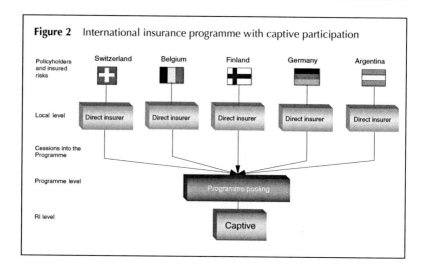

Figure 2 International insurance programme with captive participation

corporations often are reluctant to provide these types of collaterals, primarily due to cost, accounting and tax reasons.

Captive Management

As compared to the majority of risk-financing instruments, captives are insurance companies and formal legal entities. As such, they need their own management. In terms of administration organisation, a distinction has to be drawn between the board of directors and the actual management. The board's primary duty is the assumption of a supervisory function while the management assumes responsibility for daily operations.

A thorough management requires a broad range of services. A first category covers general corporate affairs such as the maintenance of accounts and statistics, the handling and supervision of banking and payment transactions, the preparation of annual accounts and the arrangement of the respective audits, the convening, holding and minuting of board meetings and the general assemblies as well as dealing with tax authorities. A second category encompasses aspects specific to insurance business, including assistance in designing insurance and reinsurance protection, underwriting, administration and servicing of contracts, claims handling, cash management, placing and monitoring investments, dealing with regulatory bodies, monitoring the creditworthiness of retrocessionaires and possibly providing actuarial reserve studies. Particular attention has to be paid to the risk selection and the investment activities. For the underwriting decisions, however, the captive's interests are often outweighed by the needs of the parent from a group perspective. The management will usually report to the board in meetings held on a regular basis and facilitated with detailed documentation covering a business report, financial statements and specific premium, loss and investment information.

For the typical sponsoring corporation, managing a captive means activities in a field in which it has no significant expertise. Evidence for this expertise, however, is a precondition for the captive to obtain a license as authorities also place a special emphasis on the necessary management capabilities. While the board is regularly composed of representatives of the parent and necessary local representatives, only a minority of captives are effectively self-managed or administered by the sponsoring organisation itself. Usually, professional management organisations that are licensed as captive managers are contracted to perform the effective management. Predominantly, captives appoint broker firms and insurance companies as their management service providers. Insurers, being full-scale insurance carriers, are obviously very well suited to manage captives successfully; they are in a position to serve the client with their expertise, infrastructure, resources and long-standing experience.

Taxation[6]

While not the primary reason for captive formation, taxation aspects of captive solutions are a major factor. Basically, taxation considerations address three levels: the units paying insurance premium, the captive and the parent or holding company. These positions must not be considered in isolation and can be put into perspective, as in Figure 3.

Generally, premiums paid to an insurance company are recognised as a deductible expense for tax purposes. Many tax authorities have

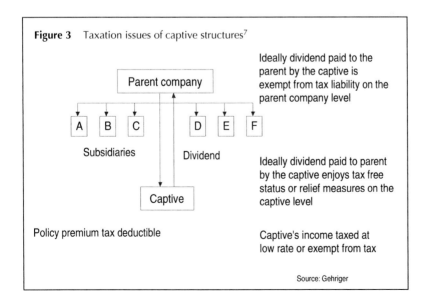

Figure 3 Taxation issues of captive structures[7]

Ideally dividend paid to the parent by the captive is exempt from tax liability on the parent company level

Ideally dividend paid to parent by the captive enjoys tax free status or relief measures on the captive level

Captive's income taxed at low rate or exempt from tax

Parent company

A B C D E F

Subsidiaries

Dividend

Captive

Policy premium tax deductible

Source: Gehriger

challenged this view in the context of captive solutions. They argue that such a payment would have to be considered as a mere inter-company transaction from an economic point of view as the premiums would not leave the group. Hence, the reduction of tax payments would not be justified.

The question of the acknowledgement of the deductibility of insurance premiums paid to a captive ultimately centres around the determination of an appropriate premium level and is largely dominated by underwriting and arm's length considerations; premium payments to captives should be justified from an underwriting perspective and comparable to premiums negotiated between unrelated parties, thus reflecting fair market levels. Further issues taken into account are the ownership structure of the captive and the amount of unrelated business a captive is writing. Both the stance of the various tax authorities and the structures responding to them are rich and diverse.

Another issue that has to be dealt with from a tax perspective is the taxation of the captive as such. Tax can be optimised in two respects: first, depending on the choice of domicile, the captive's profits are either taxed at a low rate or exempt from tax; second, as an insurance company the captive can build substantial reserves, thus reducing any profit. In an attempt to attack this kind of tax optimisation, some high-tax countries have introduced controlled foreign company (CFC) legislation. In simple terms, the holding company of a captive that enjoys an income tax rate below a certain level is sanctioned by additional tax payments. The precise response to these challenges is locating captives in domiciles offering tax rates that do not trigger the sanctions of the CFC rules while being lower than the parent company's ordinary tax level. An alternative is a domicile with a relatively high tax rate exceeding the level determined by the CFC rules and which grants the possibility to set aside large reserves that effectively offset any profit.

Cashflows from the captive to the parent in the form of dividends or loans should also be structured in a tax-efficient way. In this respect, double taxation treaties between the countries of residence of captive and parent are of overriding importance. Often, the overall tax burden is further reduced as the holding company takes advantage of tax relief measures related to income arising out of shareholdings.

Other tax issues include taxes levied on the issue of shares at the incorporation stage or subsequent increases of capital, possible capital taxes, the payment of insurance premium taxes and withholding taxes on various forms of investments. Normally, these aspects do not cause severe problems. Nevertheless, potential impacts have to be examined carefully and can have a significant bearing on the structure of captive programmes.

Captive Locations[8]

The incorporation and operation of a captive as a legal entity involves the selection of a location. Various criteria require careful consideration. First, the domicile should be of legal, economic and social stability. Second, the location should provide a sound regulation that supports the wellbeing of the business and the credibility of the domicile. Ideally, at the same time the supervisory regime would not be too stringent as far as capitalisation requirements, formation and licensing processes, reservation treatment, investment activities and reporting are concerned. The local tax level and related considerations such as the existence of double taxation treaties are also among the most important facets.

Another critical factor is the availability of services. This includes insurance capacity, banking infrastructure, investment services and auxiliary services such as legal, tax and accounting advice. Further criteria are the absence of restrictions on capital transactions and inter-company loans or the domicile's reputation.

Finally, the captive location is preferably situated conveniently relative to the sponsor's domicile in geographic terms. Sufficient evidence for local substance of the captive has to be provided for tax purposes. Therefore, board members have to attend board meetings on a regular basis. This duty can tie up a considerable amount of senior management time if the captive's domicile cannot be reached easily. When taking the location decision, each criterion needs to be analysed individually in order to determine the location best suited to the parties and jurisdictions involved.

Historically, offshore locations have been chosen as they provided for commercial freedom and low taxation. Their regulatory framework limit the efforts required and keep costs of captive solutions at a minimum. They also provide for an environment in which beneficial effects of the captive concept may best be exploited.

Undisputedly, Bermuda has been the leading captive location, followed by Cayman and Guernsey. However, increased tax scrutiny and reputation pressure has lead to onshore formations. This is particularly true for Vermont, which accommodated a substantial number of US-parent-sponsored captives. Indeed, the number of onshore formations has increased significantly and a trend to locate captives onshore has crystallised. This development is made up of both new incorporations and re-domiciliation transactions. Against this backdrop, the potential of leading financial services marketplaces like Switzerland have been recognised. These locations offer considerable capacity in the field of insurance, banking and Alternative Risk Transfer (ART). In addition, a wide array of ancillary services is also available. Moderate taxation can be an added advantage. It becomes clear that the friendly business climate of traditional finance centres may serve well as a captive domicile.

THE "RENT-A-CAPTIVE" CONCEPT

The captive concept is fundamentally attractive. Nevertheless, medium-sized companies may perceive the cost of this mechanism to be prohibitively expensive. Similarly, large corporations are often somewhat reluctant to introduce such a formal structure. Aimed at further spreading captive solutions and making this option available to medium-sized companies, insurance companies launched the "rent-a-captive" concept. Rather than forming its own captive, a corporation joins the existing infrastructure of an insurance or reinsurance carrier and rents such a facility. In effect, the company is provided with an instrument similar to a captive.

Technically speaking, the insurer opens an individual account for the customer internally and a defined proportion of risk participation is allocated to it. Premium payments and investment income are credited; claims payments, management and other expenses are debited to this separate account. If, at the end of the term of the facility, a positive balance results, the profit flows back to the client. Conversely, the client has to settle a negative balance.

The benefits of a rent-a-captive structure are similar to those of a captive. The particular attraction lies in the main distinction to the captive concept: the corporation enters a flexible contractual relationship that is relatively easy to implement rather than incorporating a legal entity. Therefore, no capitalisation is needed. The costs of risk retention are further reduced as administration expenses are spread among the participants. With this aspect of mutuality, however, the rent-a-captive services provider is not in a position to offer the same degree of freedom and influence as a single-owned captive.

The preconditions for a rent-a-captive solution are very much the same as the ones for a captive, the most important probably being a positive long-term loss experience. However, as the financial commitment is limited and smaller volume is sufficient, the step into risk retention with a formal structure may be realised more easily with a rent-a-captive facility.

Again, most rent-a-captives operate on the reinsurance level, as depicted in Figure 4. The framework of contracts is as follows: the risk flow is reflected in a direct insurance contract between the corporation and the direct insurer acting as fronter. The fronter, in turn, cedes a defined share of risk and premium to the rent-a-captive service provider under a reinsurance contract. Besides this, the corporation arranges a rent-a-captive agreement with the rent-a-captive service provider. In this agreement, the principles, terms and conditions of the account are defined. In addition, the rights and duties of both parties are stipulated. While the client is predominantly obliged to pay the funds necessary to settle any negative balance, the service provider has to provide the necessary infrastructure and render various services: underwriting and reinsurance administration, claims

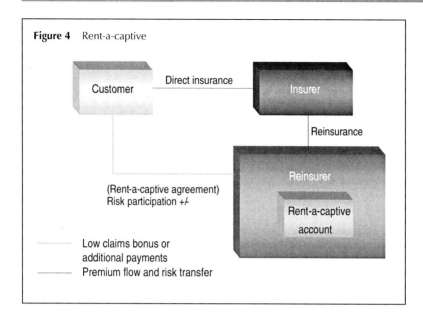

Figure 4   Rent-a-captive

Customer

Direct insurance

Insurer

Reinsurance

Reinsurer

Rent-a-captive
account

(Rent-a-captive agreement)
Risk participation +/‑

.... Low claims bonus or
additional payments
——— Premium flow and risk transfer

handling, investments, statements, accounts and statistics as well as corporate administration for the carrier.

When dealing with the external parties, the service provider acts in its own name as the account is based on a contractual arrangement and is not an incorporated entity. For this reason, the fronter's counterparty risk is usually lowered as it deals with the service provider, the solvency of which is usually of superior quality. The credit risk lies much more with the service provider as he expects the participating client to extinguish obligations as they appear. As a result, the sound financial standing of the customer is a vital prerequisite and the service provider has to scrutinise the participants' financial strength. In most cases, however, fronting and rent-a-captive services are offered as a package provided by entities belonging to the same organisation.

Through positive experiences with rent-a-captive solutions, corporations with sufficient business volume become more accustomed to formal risk retention approaches and decide to form their own captive. In such a case, the portfolio of a rent-a-captive account can be transferred to the newly incorporated captive quite easily. In essence, the captive substitutes the rent-a-captive carrier and assumes all rights and liabilities of the service provider under the reinsurance structure. Simultaneously, a payment is made to the captive based on reported and expected claims.

For the most part, numerous accounts of participating corporations are operating within the frame of the carrier acting as the rent-a-captive service provider. If one of the participants is hit by a severe loss in such a manner that the funds available in the rent-a-captive account are not sufficient to offset the loss and subsequently the customer is not able to settle the negative balance, then theoretically the accounts of other participants may be adversely affected. This is – as pointed out above – due to the rent-a-captive carrier being a legal entity who must answer to third parties. As a consequence, all assets attributable to the carrier are available to meet its obligations to third parties. The participants face the risk of losing their assets accumulated in the rent-a-captive account, in which they have a contractual claim only if the carrier is insolvent.

It therefore does not come as a surprise that insurers offering rent-a-captive services have superior credit ratings. On top of that, they carefully assess the prospective participants' creditworthiness, as well as their risk management policy, and design insurance and reinsurance programmes cautiously.

THE PROTECTED CELL COMPANY CONCEPT[9]

In response to the concerns raised above, flexible offshore legislations, considering accommodating captive business to be a core business activity, introduced an evolution of the rent-a-captive concept, the protected cell company (PCC).

The PCC is a new type of corporate structure that is a single legal entity consisting of a core and an unlimited number of individual cells, whereby the cells are statutorily segregated from each other. Consequently, as the main characteristic, each cell and its assets and liabilities is separated from the other cells and protected by statute. Thus, the nature of segregation claims to be effective against third parties. Creditors, although entering into contracts with the legal entity of the PCC as a whole – which contracts on behalf of an individual cell explicitly – only have access to the assets of the designated cell and, under certain circumstances, to the assets of the core.

The usage of a PCC structure is not limited to the captive concept illustrated in Figure 5. Other applications include usage as a platform for investment funds or securitisation transactions. Applied in the context of financing risk retention and designed for participants to share in their own risk and repatriate generated profits, this novel concept effectively combines the benefits of captive and rent-a-captive solutions. Most notably, a separate facility can be established with low capital commitment and limited operating costs. The PCC concept offers considerable potential for captive structures that can be customised to the participating corporations' organisational structure. Particularly, operating units can sponsor their own captive programmes. This kind of organisation also results in higher flexibility for a corporation as separate divisions with stand-alone risk-financing programmes can be created for merger and acquisition purposes.

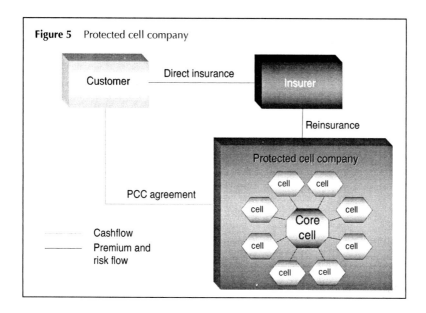

Figure 5   Protected cell company

Nevertheless, there are also some doubts about the blessing of the PCC concept. A potential disadvantage for the ceding party obviously is the limited pool of assets which is accessible for recourse. Again, the ceding party needs to have a clear understanding of the solvency of the counterparty with which it is dealing. Furthermore, it is questionable whether the concept would stand up in court in the context of a complex international case with the involvement of jurisdictions that do not have legal provisions similar to the PCC concept. In practice, however, the principal focus of PCCs is on prudent management. As a result, exposures are regularly requested to be secured with collaterals. This makes actual solutions more expensive than conceptually envisaged.

Having emanated from Guernsey and spread to Bermuda, Cayman and other leading captive locations, the PCC structure has seen quite a successful launch. This success is mirrored by the introduction of PCC legislation in the US. Still, many companies feel more comfortable going down the rent-a-captive route with reasonably structured programmes, placed with solid carriers.

ACTUAL STRUCTURES AND DEVELOPMENTS
Structuring a risk-financing programme can be looked at as an optimisation process.[10] High frequency, low severity risks can easily be paid for out of a company's cashflow. Any insurance arrangement would merely be an inefficient exchange of money flows incurring unnecessary transaction costs. It is therefore advisable to retain these kinds of risks and pay for

them out of the current cashflow. Catastrophic losses usually exceed a company's risk bearing capacity and can normally be transferred to the insurance market for a moderate premium. These disastrous loss potentials are therefore less attractive to retain. In certain periods of short capacity in the insurance industry it may be necessary to tap the capital markets for capacity. In some instances, it may even be necessary or appropriate to retain catastrophe risk.

Medium risks are characterised by reduced frequency and increased loss costs. The aggregate loss potential, however, is fairly predictable in the medium-term. Spread over time, these risks are suitable to be retained with appropriate structures such as the scope of captive solutions.

Apart from compulsory coverages, there are no major restrictions with respect to suitable lines to be ceded to captive facilities. However, property and liability risks have proved to be the preferred lines. The inclusion of traditionally uninsurable risks is moderately spread yet does not account for a major portion of captive business.

In principle, the reinsurance programmes the captives are writing can adopt all the common forms of reinsurance. Many customers prefer non-proportional structures; favouring the generation of fair amounts of premium in return for risks assumed.[11] In many cases, they also limit the captive's exposure by means of the definition of an annual aggregate and the purchase of stop-loss covers in order to prevent the captive from suffering from random fluctuations. It is also true that the majority of captive programmes form part of international insurance programmes.

Some giant companies of particular financial strength focus on buying insurance-related services rather than risk transfer and use their captives as a funding tool, primarily serving as an instrument to manage retained risk efficiently. This indicates a clear trend towards employing captives as a financing vehicle.

The development into the life and employee benefit business has not yet become mainstream, which may primarily be due to high regulation standards. A particularly interesting move has been captive-backed insurance provided for customers and suppliers, facilitating the efficiency of both the buying and selling process. This has been shown, for example, in the extension of product warranties to promote the sales process. These types of solutions reflect a shift from pure loss financing to a contribution for the parent's core business, improving competitiveness.

Of course, companies also exploit other alternative risk-financing instruments and often combine them with captive structures. Retrocession is increasingly being taken out on an alternative basis. Finite-risk solutions, for example – structured as reinsurance behind captives – offer the client the ability to participate in a favourable loss experience with the potential profit share flowing to the captive.

Despite a long period of soft markets, the number of captives has been growing consistently; there has clearly been a certain saturation in the segment of large companies and some captives have had very little involvement given the market conditions. As the first signs of a hardening market appeared, some companies entered captive arrangements in order to prepare for future premium increase and to have the captive readily available. Indeed, recent trends created a scarcity in capacity and, in conjunction with the economic slowdown, left corporations facing increased cost pressure and hardening rates. As a necessity, firms opted for higher retentions in their programmes, which are often borne by the captive. Others promptly responded by implementing the flexible rent-a-captive structure.

Recent developments also had a severe impact on captives themselves. They suffered badly due to substantial underwriting losses and due to the fact that depressed capital markets only allowed for a moderate performance. In such an environment, fronters tend to be very cautious about the credit risk associated with fronting transactions. This attitude normally affects the conditions under which fronting services are available.

Merger and acquisition activity also affected captive business. When more than one party involved has a captive in operation to facilitate risk financing (as is often the case), it is easily concluded that these facilities are condensed into one single entity. The most widely used technique to do so is probably one existing captive assuming all business by means of loss portfolio transfers. In this context, corporations are increasingly asking for liquidation and run-off services, a demand to which captive service providers are challenged to respond.

Captive solutions, as a whole and concerning their structure, need to be constantly reviewed and possibly refined. The focus of such considerations lies on their risk-financing role, but they must also address more rigid accounting and tax standards.

CONCLUSION

While captives are predominantly considered as an instrument representing risk retention, they may also be implemented as a pure risk transfer mechanism. In most instances, however, they reflect a cross of the typical forms of risk retention and risk transfer, applying funding and hedging techniques at the same time. As a unique form of capital, they embody dedicated capacity to facilitate formalised self-retention and selective risk transfer, enhancing the efficiency of risk financing and, ultimately, strengthening corporate value.

1 Haller and Ackermann (1992), pp. 9–10.
2 Shimpi (1999), pp. 25–53.
3 The term "captive" indicates that this type of insurance company is closely held by its parent and places emphasis on the traditional origin and nature of the business written.

4   See Bawcutt (1997), pp.1–2.
5   For an overview see Best (2001), p. xiv.
6   See Gehriger (2001) and Skaar (1998).
7   See Gehriger (2001), p. 654.
8   See Wöhrmann and Bürer, (2000).
9   See Wöhrmann and Bürer, (2001).
10 See Lehmann and Jutzi (1991), pp. 326–7.
11 This has been seen in transactions assisted by Zurich Continental Europe Corporate in a European context.

BIBLIOGRAPHY

Best, A. M., 2001, *Captive Directory,* 2001 Edition, (New Jersey: AM Best Company).

Bawcutt, P., 1997, *Captive Insurance Companies,* Fourth Edition, (London: Whiterby & Co Ltd).

Gehriger, P. O., 2001, "Besteuerung von Captives und Steuerplanung mit Captives", in: *SteuerRevue,* 10, pp. 642–59.

Haller, M., and W. Ackermann, 1992, *Versicherungswirtschaft – kundenorientiert,* (Zürich: Verlag des Schweizerischen Kaufmännischen Verbandes).

Lehmann, A., and M. Jutzi, 1991, "Risikofinanzierung – wachsende Bedeutung als Teilaspekt im Risikomanagement", in: *Zeitschrift für Versicherungswesen,* (Hamburg: Allgemeiner Fachverlag Dr Rolf Mathern GmbH), pp. 325–7.

Shimpi, P., 1999, *Integrating Corporate Risk Management,* (New York: Texere LLC).

Skaar, A. A., 1998, *Taxation Issues Relating To Captive Insurance Companies,* (Amsterdam: IBFD Publications BV).

Wöhrmann, P., and C. Bürer, 2000, "La Suisse Attire les Assurance Captives", in: *Banque Assurance,* 6, November/December, pp. 48–50.

Wöhrmann, P., and C. Bürer, 2001, "Instrument der alternativen Risikofinanzierung", in: *Schweizer Versicherung,* 7, July, pp. 14–17.

Part 2

The price of risk and its volatility

10

Catastrophe Risk Pricing in
the Traditional Market

John A. Major and Rodney E. Kreps

Guy Carpenter & Co., Inc.

If the assumptions of typical financial economics models were true, there would not be either an insurance – or even less so – a reinsurance industry. There is no liquid market. Most of the "trading" between customers and insurers and between insurers and reinsurers occurs on a quarterly cycle, not daily, much less minute-by-minute as apposed to market-traded securities such as stocks and bonds. Insurance buyers usually purchase annually, or possibly semi-annually. Reinsurance, while technically operating year round, finds its busiest times at the beginnings of the four quarters. Broker-dealers can trade a particular stock daily, and specialists, who constantly monitor their positions, adjust them by buying and selling many times a day. Moreover, there is no expectation of one's being able to "unwind" a risk-bearing position by selling back into the market. (For example, a purchaser of bonds who no longer desires to hold them expects to find a ready market of buyers willing to take the risk off his hands.) Reinsurance is not a commodity, although syndication on an individual contract results in all the members of the reinsurance syndicate getting the same rate.[1] In particular, since there are effectively no hedges and no derivatives, the so-called "law of one price" is unhelpful. Nevertheless, there is competition.

INTRODUCTION

For these reasons, it seems that the best way to understand the pricing of catastrophe (cat) risk is to go "behind the curtain" and find out how it is actually done. We have conducted a series of interviews with underwriters and pricing actuaries at major broker-market reinsurers.[2] The aims of the interviews have been to understand their pricing methodologies and solicit their views on related topics such as cat models and the role of underwriter judgement. At the same time, we performed a data analysis on hundreds of treaties to supplement our understanding of the essential issues behind cat pricing. Some of these findings have been presented in an oral report to

The Bond Marketing Association's 2001 Conference on Risk-Linked Securities.

Naturally, one should expect the events of September 11, 2001 to cause something of a discontinuity in the capacity and appetite for risk, as well as the price of risk, in reinsurance markets. Nonetheless, we feel that the logic and methodology of cat pricing will not change radically. Rather, it will continue its gradual evolution.

PART I: NORMATIVE
Use of cat models

All interviewees have had experience with multiple cat models and most use more than one model concurrently. A few like to run and compare multiple models on the same submissions; most are content to use one model primarily and another one or two for special purposes. No single model appears to dominate.

Roughly a quarter of the respondents have their own internally developed cat models. Reasons given for this include: to get more global coverage; to model the more complex treaties better, and to more definitively sample the upper tail of the risk curve. ("Off-the shelf models bring a lot of useless info, [where only] 10 points [are] in the tail out of 1400".) One respondent organisation used their internal model as a consulting tool: "Our model allows us to bring an alternative perspective, since we can customise it to specific features of a client portfolio, and not just tweak the knobs". Many saw their experience and knowledge of multiple models as a strategic weapon. As one respondent put it, "We offer a multimodel optimisation service. We understand the rating agencies (who are our de facto regulators) and how their models work".

Most respondents are well aware of the differences in model results, and that such differences are heavily dependent on geography and peril. At one extreme, Florida hurricane results are very similar from one model to the next, typically within 10%. Long Island/New England results tended to be somewhat further off, and New Madrid (central USA) earthquake results could differ by a factor of three. At the extreme, California "fire following earthquake" results sometimes disagree by nearly an order of magnitude.[3] At the same time, the models seem to be converging over time – upwards.[4] One respondent remarked favourably on a modeller's presentation showing how more sophisticated treatments in modelling tended to raise the estimates of risk. He opined "As time goes on, expect to see the models ratchet upwards as we all discover the world is more dangerous than we imagined". Another, a highly respected modeller himself, stated, "We believe the worldwide expected annual loss for cat is in excess of $20 billion." Note: this is not the expression of an extreme; it is the annual average! As to the effect that cat models have had on the marketplace, respondents were generally positive:

❏ "It's harder now to justify a rate increase. It puts the industry in a band, but also preventing rates from coming down too far. We still see a lot of volatility in marine and aviation, but more stability in property".

❏ "I'll tell you in 2–3 years after we have a $10–15 billion event. That will be the real test".

❏ "The consistent thing we know about cat models is one hasn't been right yet. But they're state of the art, and they're an objective benchmark".

❏ "It has introduced some sort of floor that has saved the reinsurance market from destroying itself. It has also reduced uncertainty. And helped the primary markets introduce cat loads".

As to the phenomenon of pricing below expected loss (EL) in other parts of the world, respondents offered a variety of explanations:

❏ "Models are less accepted in Europe. The models are based on low quality data, applied to lower quality data and less of it. They are more relationship-driven".

❏ "The Japan wind market is soft because a significant event has been too long ago".

❏ "We write some business we would not write in the US, just to maintain a presence".

❏ "Bad management. We also see some [quotes below EL] in US. People need to fill up the bucket".

❏ "Everyone is pricing for Martin/Lothar as the biggest event, but now models show 1/80 for that with 1/500 results to knock your socks off. Our non-US underwriters still want to price off one event; our US underwriters know better".

Pricing theory

Two complementary approaches to measuring risk tend to be cited in the available literature.[5] The volatility approach is concerned with measuring the typical variation from average or expected results. Extreme variations, which, by definition, are rare, are considered exceptions and not of particular concern save insofar as they contribute to the overall measure of variation. The ruin theoretic approach, on the other hand, is specifically concerned with quantifying the rare, extreme cases, and regards "normal variation" as something to be ignored.

The volatility of a financial index (eg, return on equity (ROE)) can be defined either as its standard deviation (square root of the average of the squared differences between the index and its overall mean) or mean absolute deviation (average of the absolute values of the differences between the index and its overall mean). It is symbolised by the Greek letter σ (sigma). In the case of return on equity, volatility is heavily influenced by leverage, ie, changes in the denominator (equity).

The ruin probability can be defined as the probability that, over a specified time horizon, financial results emerge in such a way that the firm becomes insolvent, ie, its equity becomes negative. Alternatively, other, more stringent constraints on equity can be used as the definition of ruin, eg, equity goes below some statutory threshold level, induces a ratings downgrade, etc.[6] The amount of equity that is held at the start of the period in question obviously has a direct effect on the risk of ruin.

Typically, management will set a volatility or ruin probability target and then arrange its financial affairs to meet that target. Changing the amount of equity capital is a direct means of affecting either – increasing it will reduce the volatility of ROE as well as the risk of ruin, but it will also lower the overall mean ROE, usually another important financial criterion.

Risk and return criteria are translated into requirements for profit margins and business volume and, ultimately, pricing. In reinsurance, price is usually expressed as rate on line (ROL) which is the reinsurance premium to be charged divided by the limit of insurance to be covered. Thus, if a US$10million limit of insurance is to be covered for a premium of US$1million, the price is 10% ROL.

Traditional actuarial pricing formulas include standard deviation load and variance load. We may add a third of utility load from the economics literature, such as Ingersoll.

The standard deviation load formula sets the price as follows:

$$ROL = EL + k\sigma$$

where EL is the actuarially expected value of the reinsurance payment and σ is the standard deviation of that payment. The coefficient k is a constant chosen to meet the financial requirements of the firm writing the business. This formula has ties to both volatility and ruin theory.

The variance load formula is similar:

$$ROL = EL + h\sigma^2$$

where h is a (different) constant, appropriately chosen. The advantage of this formula is that if two reinsurance contracts are statistically independent (eg, property catastrophe covers in two separated geographic areas), then the formula respects the "law of one price," setting the same ROL for the combined contracts as it would for the sum of the separate contracts. It, too, has mathematical ties with volatility and ruin theory.

The utility formula, suggested by economic theory (Ingersoll, 1987), puts:

$$ROL = EL + E[g(L)]$$

Where L represents the loss random variable (the payout under the reinsurance contract), the $E[\ ]$ operator represents mathematical expected value, and g is the so-called utility function, expressing the risk-aversion of the reinsurer. While this formula has many theoretical advantages, it is sel-dom used in practice because it is extremely difficult to estimate the utility function g in real-world situations. Numerous problems have been recog-nised with these traditional formulas.

First, whose risk is being measured? The standard deviation of the rein-surance contract payment is more a measure of the cedent (purchaser) risk than the risk of the reinsurer. The most important risk the reinsurer faces is *parameter* risk, the risk that the estimate of EL is wrong.

Even if estimates are correct, the *process* risk (direct risk of loss) should be measured in incremental terms. What is the marginal impact on the rein-surer's total risk, and what does that imply for a marginal change in capital requirements? Such calculations are notoriously compute-intensive to per-form in practice. Moreover, there is a theoretical problem with incremental impact of renewals – the order in which contracts are considered makes a difference in their incremental risk measures, and if all contracts are mea-sured as "last-in," then the sum of the incremental risks will not equal the total risk.

Investment-equivalent pricing

A more recent approach to pricing is the "investment-equivalent" method developed by one of the authors of this chapter (Kreps) in the 1990s. The objective here is to treat the prospect of writing a reinsurance contract on the same footing as any other risky investment. A special-case algorithm, allows any investment criteria of return and risk to be applied to a combi-nation of the reinsurance contract and financial techniques (see Kreps, 1999).[7] In that paper, the contract is considered standalone, not part of an addition to a portfolio. The methodology relates to both volatility and ruin-theoretic approaches.

The algorithm predicts the existence of minimum premiums for rare event contracts, and generally suggests reduction in risk load for pooling across contracts and/or years. Three major applications are: pricing indi-vidual contracts; packaging a reinsurance contract with financial techniques to create an investment vehicle; and providing a tool for whole book management using risk and return to relate investment capital, underwriting and pricing.

The inputs are the investment criteria, the loss distributions, and a crite-rion describing a reinsurer's underwriting conservatism (risk aversion). In order to stay in business, the reinsurer should prefer writing a reinsurance contract to committing the same funds to a traditional investment. Therefore, the expected return and volatility on a reinsurance contract should meet benchmark criteria expressing what alternatives are available in the capital markets. In addition, the reinsurer should desire to hold suffi-cient funds to guarantee reinsurance payments on the contract (if called for) with a certain level of probability. This is, in effect, avoiding ruin at the level of the standalone contract. The level of funds and the requisite probability describe this ruin criterion. Finally, a statistical description of the likely behaviour of the reinsurance contract is needed to complete the analysis.

The outputs are the required ROL and the time-zero assets allocated to the contract.

Figure 1 depicts the cash flows. At time zero, the cedent pays a reinsurance premium which consists of an amount equal to the discounted present value of expected loss payments plus an additional risk load. (One of the objectives of the formula is to determine what that risk load should be.) The reinsurer in turn places those monies as well as an additional amount of assets (surplus) allocated for a safety margin, into a fund.

While there are several variations that can be studied, we will focus here on the simplest case where the fund is invested entirely in risk-free instruments.

Symbolically,

$$P = R + EL / (1 + f)$$

expresses the reinsurer's time zero proceeds from the reinsurance contract where, again, EL is the expected loss (reinsurance payout), f is the risk-free rate, R is the risk load, and P is the total reinsurance premium. The funding is represented by

$$F = P + A$$

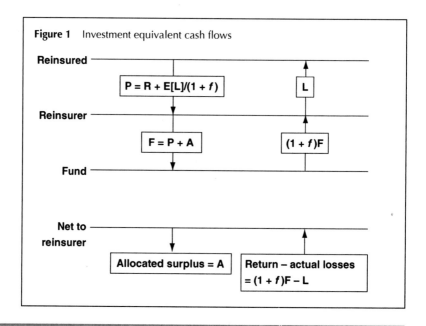

Figure 1   Investment equivalent cash flows

Reinsured

$$P = R + E[L]/(1 + f)$$

L

Reinsurer

$$F = P + A$$

$$(1 + f)F$$

Fund

Net to reinsurer

Allocated surplus = A

Return – actual losses
= $(1 + f)F - L$

where P is as before, A is the allocated surplus, and F is the total amount devoted to the fund. On a net basis, at time zero, the reinsurer experiences an outflow of the allocated surplus A.

At time one, the reinsurer cashes out the fund, receives a total return $(1 + f)F$, and uses it to pay whatever is due on the contract, L. The reinsurer's net outflow at time one is therefore $(1 + f)F - L$.

The investment criteria can be stated as three inequalities. First, the expected return on allocated surplus should be at least as high as a specified alternative investment threshold rate of return y:

$$(1 + f)F - EL \geq (1 + y)A$$

Second, the volatility of the return, $\sigma((1 + f)F - L)$ (which mathematically equals the volatility of the losses $\sigma(L)$) must be no greater than that of the specified alternative investment, σ_y (scaled to the invested amount A):

$$\sigma(L) \leq \sigma_y A$$

Finally, the ruin criterion (referred to in the paper as the "safety criterion") is expressed by noting the minimum required terminal fund amount, S:

$$(1 + f)F \geq S$$

Solving these inequalities simultaneously allows us to determine the minimum risk load R. A more complicated situation arises when, instead of a risk-free investment, the fund proceeds are used to buy a put option on a risky investment (eg, stock). See Kreps, 1999, for details.

The above methodology leaves open several questions. What is the probability distribution of losses L and how is it to be determined? This is where cat modelling comes into play. What is the alternative benchmark investment and what are its expected return y and volatility σ_y? These crucial parameters can only be set by considering the fundamentals of insurance financial management. What is the definition of "ruin" in this context, and what is its desired maximum probability? In particular, since the method treats each contract as a standalone entity, the answer cannot be obtained by referring to the financial situation of the firm. A deeper question then, is, how can one apply this method "on the margin," in terms of the incremental impact of a contract on the firm? Kreps 1990, addresses this point.

Pricing practice

All respondents indicated they used a more-or-less formal pricing methodology, by this we mean a written, computer-controlled, or otherwise codified procedure, promulgated throughout the organisation, specifying how pricing is to be done. For the vast majority, the underwriter has a "walkaway price" in mind, below which no deal will be done. In particular, they generally would not write below the EL level, unless, perhaps, it was "to oblige" – that is, to gain a share of a compensating (profitable) other piece of business. A few respondents claimed that they would not even do that. One respondent said 'There were one or two instances where we took a sliver of cat (a contract priced below EL) to get the surplus (a different but associated contract above EL). We try to do everything we can not to. You can count them on two fingers". Another said "It used to be that we would not write any business below EL. We didn't quite succeed. But walkaway prices are exceptionally well defined".

The routine is generally as follows:

1. Run a quality assurance (QA) check on the submission data.
2. Run cat models to calculate actuarial statistics.
3. Run the pricing model. This varied in sophistication (this is detailed in the paragraph below).
4. Decide what to believe (see section on underwriting judgement below).
5. Adjust the results for circumstances (see section on underwriting judgement below) and effects not considered in models (eg, portfolio effects, unusual contract features).
6. Load for uncertainty/ignorance (see below).
7. Load or discount for capacity constraints/availability.

The level of complexity of the pricing methodology varied greatly between respondents. The majority used the basic "expected loss (EL) plus fraction of standard deviation (sigma)" formula or some slight enhancement thereof. That fraction of sigma is usually "tuned" to reflect overall ROE requirements, typically 15–20%, which are generally handed down from the parent corporation. A few respondents varied this factor by region, peril, and attachment point and – at the time of interview – another was studying the issue to see whether it made sense to do so.

A few of the more sophisticated respondents attempt to assess the incremental impact a new contract would have on the capital needed to support the overall portfolio of business, and set a price accordingly. Most respondents expressed a wish that they could do that formally, but lacked the analytical skills or the brute force computing power needed to accomplish it.[8] This area is plagued by philosophical problems as well. As mentioned previously, while the theoretically correct way to assess the impact of new business on capital use is fairly clear, the treatment of renewals remains a subject of controversy. Difficulties notwithstanding, several respondents do attempt an informal incremental analysis, at least in special cases where there may be justification for moving away from the technical rate.

One actuarially interesting issue is the question of minimum rates on line

(ROL). As a risk gets more remote (eg, a higher and higher attachment point for the same limit), and, as a result, the expected loss gets lower and lower, the walkaway ROL shrink to zero, too, or does it reach a floor value?[9] Over half the respondents suggested that there definitely is a floor value, and it seems to be around 3%. Other responses opposed this view implying that, that is why you have human judgement. One respondent had in fact done a deal at 0.5% ROL for a very unlikely and geographically remote property risk.

Another issue is "charging for uncertainty". Most respondents said that if they are missing exposure data – because it is not available from the cedent or they are pricing an industry loss warrantee (ILW), or they are dealing with a situation where the models are less reliable or don't exist at all – they need to compensate by charging more. Several have a formal methodology for pricing "parameter risk," but most deal with it informally. One respondent summarised the general view, saying, "[Data quality] becomes the ability to *consider* business. We want to understand what's going on".

Portfolio management

All respondents, however, are sensitive to the overall composition and accumulation risk of their portfolios. Most snapshot it quarterly and control aggregates by zone.[10] Typically, there are about 10 to 12 US zones and 40 to 50 worldwide.[11] The exposure is managed to a particular probable maximum loss (PML) horizon, typically a 100–250-year return period.[12] As one respondent put it, "We want to survive and thrive at the 250-year level, post-event." Another, more ambitious respondent, said, "We want to be the last man standing there when everyone else is blown away". Snapshot management is considered a stopgap technique, however, by a few who want to move towards real-time portfolio management.

Another respondent said "The top 5% tail of the risk is driving our capital needs; that is the area where one loss could amount to 15–20% of our equity. This basically means South-east US Wind". This is probably more-or-less true of most respondents.

Our own internal hurricane studies show that most of the EL from hurricanes comes from the "major" hurricanes (category III and higher), which have an occurrence rate of 0.66 per year making landfall in mainland USA and a rate of 0.34 per year in the group comprising Florida, Alabama and Mississippi. The figures are 0.18 and 0.08 respectively, for the more intensely damaging category IV+ hurricanes.[13] Florida is the fourth highest-ranking state in the US in terms of population, behind California, Texas and New York.[14]

All of our respondents had substantial US exposures. However, as one put it, despite accumulation control, "We really are [betting the company at some probability level] although we don't know it".

Underwriting judgement

With the increasing use of models and formal pricing procedures, the role of the underwriter has evolved as well. Respondents indicated a wide range in the autonomy they give underwriters to set prices. In some cases, underwriters are closely tied to the technical rate and need to justify any substantial deviations. In other cases, they are given wide latitude and discretion. Will they ever leave money on the table? Not usually, but one respondent pointed out, "There may be good reasons to leave money on the table, like market differentiation in maintaining more [pricing] consistency".

Underwriter judgement is used to set parameters for the technical calculation (deciding which model is most appropriate to use, setting factors for demand surge and fire following, etc) and deciding the influence of non-modelled, but relevant, issues. Those might include future growth prospects of the cedent and their claims management standards, or allowances for difference-in-conditions (DIC), managing general agency (MGA) business, and other operational risks. The basic issue is: are the company and its submission to be trusted?

To some respondents, relationships still matter, at least to some extent. One said, "We prefer steady buyers, where we can build a relationship. A long-term client with a clean history will not get as big a bump after a loss". Another rebutted, "Not sure 'partnership' plays out in property cat – it's adversarial because the directs are not such a factor". A third countered, "We don't look at every transaction as a short-term maximisation. We look for relationships. We take advantage of other [markets'] rapacious pricing".

PART II: EMPIRICAL
Source data

Do the markets behave in a way that is consistent with their stated ideals? We studied 180 cat layers sold between 1999 and 2001, representing 32 distinct cedents. Multiple cat model results were available on 44 contracts. Auxiliary rating factors were examined, allowing us to examine the relative importance of various items on the price of risk.[15] This is discussed in more detail below.

Regression models

As expected, by far, the most important factor in explaining rates was the expected loss as determined from a cat model. Figure 2 displays this data. Each symbol (small square) represents one layer. There may be several layers displayed that are associated with the same contract. The horizontal axis represents the actuarial expected loss to the layer, as estimated by a cat model (or the average if more than one cat model is used), as a fraction of the total dollar limit of the layer. The vertical axis represents the price of the

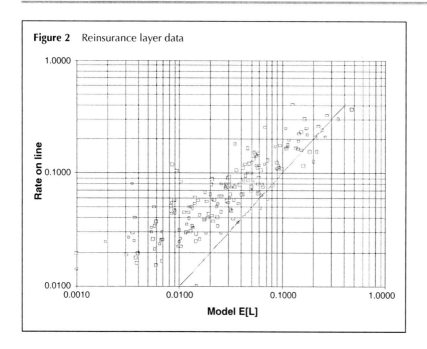

Figure 2   Reinsurance layer data

layer as a "rate on line" – dollar of reinsurance premium per dollar of limit. Both axes are rendered in a logarithmic scale.

The diagonal line indicates where layers would fall if the price were the same as the actuarial cost. For most of the layers, the price was greater than the actuarial cost, which should be expected. As is the case in insurance, the sellers (here, reinsurers) receive compensation beyond an actuarial break-even level for taking the risk. What is surprising is that a substantial number of layers seem to be selling at less than cost. This may be due to a lower cost estimate from the particular cat model that was used for pricing, vs the result calculated here. It may also reflect an actual underpricing "to oblige" a different, more profitable, layer associated with it. This was discussed in the section "pricing practice" above.

There is more structure evident in this diagram. The symbols tend to cluster in a broad diagonal swath that lies above, but not parallel to, the diagonal line. Figure 3 displays the same data with two additional lines.

The thin, straight line is the result of a regression of the logarithm of ROL on the logarithm of EL and corresponds to the formula: ROL = $(0.47)(EL^{0.53})$. It crosses the price = cost line around 19%. This indicates that so-called "working layers," where losses are frequent and more predictable, are actuarially "fairly" priced. This makes sense, as customers can seriously consider retaining the risk and do not want to pay substantial premia above the actuarial cost.

The most common pricing model (as discussed in the section "pricing

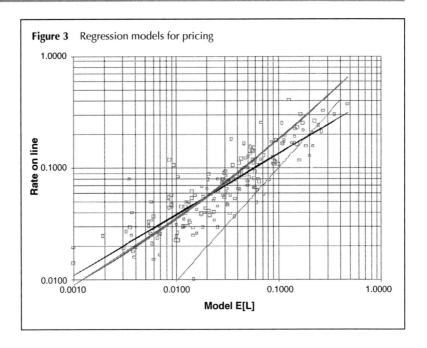

Figure 3 Regression models for pricing

theory" above) uses the "standard deviation load". The thicker, curved line in Figure 3 is the best-fitting version of this model. It corresponds to the formula: $ROL = EL + 0.25\sigma$. Of necessity, this formula always produces a price greater than EL. Thus, it does not do a good job of representing the data in the high-probability working layers. However, it does just about as good a job as the regression line on the rest of the data.

Nevertheless, there is a substantial degree of variation in actual pricing around either theoretical line. This is discussed further below.

Cat bond comparison

We had sufficient information from 46 cat bond tranches to draw comparisons with the reinsurance layers. This is shown in Figure 4. Here, a new set of symbols – large, solid diamonds – has been added to represent the cat bond tranches. The regression line from Figure 3 remains, but the curve representing the sigma-load has been removed.

Two generalisations can be made. First, cat bonds tend to cover the low-probability area: most of the tranches are estimated to have less than a 1% EL rate and only four have loss rates over 2%. The average loss rate of the reinsurance layers, in contrast, is 5.4%. Second, the cat bond tranches tend to be more expensive than the reinsurance layers. The regression line passes through the centre of the cloud of reinsurance symbols, dividing them approximately in half. By contrast, only five of the cat bond tranches lie below the regression line. For expected losses around 1%, the average

Figure 4 Cat bond comparison

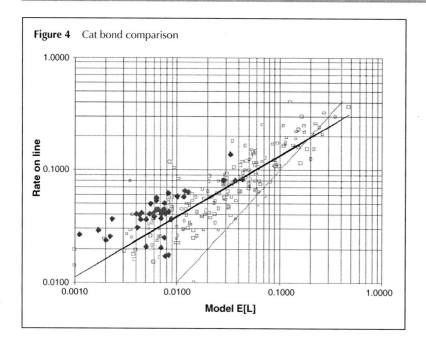

ROL for reinsurance contracts is about 4%. The equivalent price of a cat bond layer (based on its spread over Treasuries) is more in the range of 5% to 6%. At the 0.5% expected loss level, reinsurance is around 2.5% and cat bonds are more like 4%.

Differences among cat models

Part of the risk in pricing reinsurance (or cat bonds) is the uncertainty with regard to the true values of the probabilities involved. Figure 5 illustrates this uncertainty by comparing expected loss computations from several cat models operating on the same reinsurance layers.

Forty-four layers had multiple model results. Each layer is represented by a horizontal stripe. The vertical position of the stripe corresponds to the rate on line at which the layer was sold. The horizontal range covered by the stripe represents the minimum to maximum estimates of EL produced by the cat models. The two diagonal lines represent the regression and the price/cost equality as before. The median ratio between max and min is 1.5:1. About a third of them show ratios in excess of 2:1.

This potential for disagreement between cat models is well known to our survey respondents. Moreover, it is not a random or haphazard phenomenon. Mostly, it is driven by specific geographically focused differences. Perhaps because of the efforts of the Florida Commission on Hurricane Loss Projection Methodology, cat models tend to be the closest together in their estimates of Florida and South-eastern US hurricane risk.[16] In the Gulf

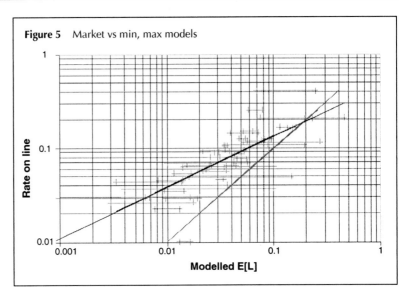

Figure 5   Market vs min, max models

region (Texas through western Florida), our data reveals typical differences of about 50% in EL estimates. For well-diversified worldwide or US-wide books of business, differences are typically in the 30–40% range, probably because the largest component of risk tends to be centred on Florida. As one moves away from the south-east, the cat models tend to diverge. North-eastern risks show estimates off by as much as a factor of three in our data, and Mid-western risks (driven by the New Madrid region earthquake potential) by as much as a factor of ten. Recall our interviewees told us that fire following earthquake risk in California can be even worse, but this could not be confirmed in our data.

An important note concerning model differences: input matters. These models are highly sophisticated, but also flexible in dealing with limited data. Preferably, the data describing the risks will be accurate and precise in locating the properties to a specific latitude-longitude point on the ground. All too often, the available data is aggregated to a ZIP code (postcode) or even county level. While the models can deal with this by making assumptions about the distribution of properties within units of geography, a degree of precision is necessarily lost. If different models make different assumptions, or one model must make them while another does not, then it should be no surprise that estimates diverge. Of course, errors in the input data will have adverse effects on the quality of the model estimates, too.

Analysis of pricing

To distinguish various influences on pricing, we fit a generalised linear model (multiple regression) of the form:

$$\ln(ROL) = a + b(BUSMIX) + c(INCEP) + d(GEOCODE) + e(COINS)$$
$$+ f(LEAD) + g(SHORT) + h(MODEL) + k*\ln(EL)$$

where $\ln(.)$ is the natural logarithm, a is a constant, $b(.)$ through $h(.)$ are fixed effects on the various levels of the explanatory variables (itemised below) and k is a constant.

Table 1 itemises the variables (pricing factors). They are discussed individually below.

Table 1 Pricing factors		
• EL	=	expected loss
• BUSMIX	=	line of business
• INCEP	=	inception date
• GEOCODE	=	geographic location and diversification
• COINS	=	coinsurance per cent
• LEAD	=	lead reinsurer
• SHORT	=	shortfall (failure to fully place)
• MODEL	=	cat model used
• Also examined:		client specifics

Expected loss (EL)

We hypothesised that the most important factor would be the cat model result, specifically the EL to the layer. Further, we expected to see that while lower ELs imply lower prices, it would not be a one-for-one relationship; a higher relative price (or load) would be applied for lower ELs. This was confirmed in the data, as discussed previously. The coefficient k in the regression equation was 0.53 (with a standard error (se) of 0.02). This can be interpreted in econometric terms as an elasticity coefficient. Since it is very close to one-half, it offers evidence in favour of the standard-deviation load equation.

Business mix (lines)

We hypothesised that commercial and multiline coverages would be more expensive than personal lines due to the increased model uncertainty. This appeared not to be the case, with line of business differences being only borderline statistically significant for a relationship in the other direction.
Specifically, we coded for:

1. Personal lines
2. Commercial lines, and
3. Multilines.

About two thirds of the cases were multilines. Personal lines appeared to be associated with log-ROL of 0.13 higher (se 0.10) than multilines, and commercial with 0.12 lower (se 0.07). While contrasts with the multilines group were not significant, personal was significantly higher than commercial.

Inception date

Most of the layers in our dataset had inception dates of 2000 or 2001, and were split about evenly; only six were from 1999. The contrast between 2000 and 2001 was not statistically significant, with 2001 rates associated with a log-ROL 0.11 (standard error 0.07) higher than for 2000 rates. The few 1999 policies were associated with log-ROL of 0.50 (se 0.18) higher than 2000. While that contrast was statistically significant, the data cannot claim to represent a wide class of 1999 reinsurance layers.

Geography

Geographical diversification would argue that worldwide and national exposures would be less expensive than regional or local exposures, everything else being equal. However, the reality was the reverse: worldwide and national exposures were about 20% more expensive than regional risks, and this was statistically significant.

Specifically, we coded for:

1. Worldwide risk portfolio
2. US nationwide,
3. North-east, Mid-Atlantic, and Mid-western US concentrations, and
4. Gulf, South-east, and Florida concentrations.

Categories one and two had a little less than a quarter of the cases each, category three had half as many, and category four had twice as many. Categories one and two were associated with log-ROL of 0.20 (se 0.09) and 0.17 (se 0.07), respectively, greater than category four. Category three was not significantly different from category four.

Coinsurance

Like some insurance, reinsurance can also come with a coinsurance percentage. We hypothesised that a low coinsurance, implying the buyer's unwillingness to shoulder a portion of the risk, would result in a higher premium rate, other things equal. This turned out not to be statistically significant, although the results leaned in that direction.

Specifically, we coded for:

1. No coinsurance,
2. Coinsurance between 0% and 10%, and
3. Coinsurance greater than or equal to 10%.

Category two had over half the cases in it, with another third going in category three. In isolation, this factor had significant explanatory power, but because it was correlated with other factors, its significance is questionable. Having no coinsurance was associated with log-ROL of 0.12 (se 0.09) higher than the majority category two. Higher coinsurance was indistinguishable from the majority.

Lead reinsurer
In most cat contracts, cover is supplied by more than one reinsurer. Sometimes a particular reinsurer will "take the lead" in analysing and pricing the contract, and other reinsurers will "follow the lead" and sign on to participate. In other cases, several reinsurers will actively participate in the analysis and a consensus price will emerge. We hypothesised that having a lead reinsurer would be associated with a higher price, as the consensus-building process would be associated with more bargaining power on the part of the buyer. This turned out to be correct and highly significant.

Specifically, we coded:

1. Consensus cases,
2. Cases where a particular lead reinsurer was identified, and
3. Cases where our data did not indicate which situation held.

The first two categories were roughly equal in numbers, with the third being half the size. Named leads were associated with log-ROL of 0.28 (se 0.08) higher than consensus cases. This means pricing for named leads was 32% higher, all other things equal. Category three (unknown) cases appeared to be 0.09 (se 0.1) higher than consensus, but this was not statistically significant.

Shortfall (placement success)
We hypothesised that shortfall, the inability to find sufficient sellers to fill the order, would signify a "difficult" risk, not particularly desirable from the sellers' point of view, therefore commanding a higher price. Here, we were wrong – placement success is a result, not a determinant, of pricing. The relationship was in the opposite direction, and highly significant. Evidently, a shortfall arises from severe mispricing, averaging about 26% low. Specifically, cases coded with a shortfall were associated with log-ROL of 0.30 (se 0.09) lower than those fully placed.

Cat model used
Between the big three vendors – AIR,[17] RMS,[18] and EQECAT[19] – their software offerings, and the versions of those offerings that have been used over time, we had dozens of distinct models represented in the data. To attempt to draw any inferences, we divided them into vendor groups, with one

vendor split into two categories representing two substantially different models. This was a highly significant explanatory variable, due to the substantial differences among models discussed in a previous section.

Client-specific effect

From earlier studies of the Guy Carpenter Catastrophe Index, we anticipated there would be specific attributes of the client, not captured by the other rating factors, that would be taken into account in the pricing. This was confirmed, with highly significant effects averaging plus or minus 0.10 in the log-ROL between clients.[20]

Conclusions

Our discussions led us to summarise the state of cat reinsurance as being in transition, midway between the relatively unsophisticated "old school" approach driven by relationships and rules of thumb, and a nearly visible ideal future where information technology drives risk quantification, liberating human creativity to add value to the client relationship. This is depicted in Table 2.

Our data analysis revealed that pricing decisions depended on much more than an estimate of actuarial cost plus "rule of thumb" risk loading. The complexity of cat risk suggests that the human element, in particular the knowledge and insight that distinguishes the important from the irrelevant, will continue to be integral to the pricing process for some time to come.

Table 2 The evolving state of cat reinsurance

	Old school	Present reality – heterogeneous transitional	Ideal future
Models	Unsophisticated: burning cost, share of event.	Partial, inconsistent, varying degrees of sophistication and credibility by geography and peril. Still need to review old models/ methods, too.	Global, credible consistent probability distributions.
Portfolio control	Zonal aggregates.	Recognition of portfolio effect, range of formality and sophistication in dealing with it. Snapshots of portfolios; still pay attention to zonal aggregates.	Falls naturally out of real time incremental impact pricing.
Relationships with clients	Banking and payback period.	Quality assurance (understanding the risk).	Value-added consulting
Underwriting judgment	Picking a rate.	Deciding what model to apply.	

1   Syndication can be explained roughly as a group of reinsurers each of whom takes on a portion of the entire risk being reinsured. For example, two reinsurers may each take 50% of the liability of a particular reinsurance contract and receive 50% of the premium. This is not to be confused with a Lloyd's syndicate, which is a particular legal form of reinsurance organisation.

2   We met with staff of eight major reinsurers with offices in the US and Bermuda. Each meeting included senior management and underwriting and/or actuarial personnel. In half the meetings, the chief operating officer, chief underwriting officer or head of reinsurance operations was present. In the other meetings, at least one senior vice president was present. Typically, pricing actuaries, underwriting management, and cat modelling analysts were also present. All quotes included here were made by, or were made in the presence of senior management.

3   This was told to us by interviewees and confirmed by our own cat modelling people.

4   This was a statement by an interviewee.

5   Volatility is usually discussed in the framework of mean-variance analysis; ruin is sometimes approached from the concept of "value at risk"(VAR). See Daykin, C.D., Pentikäinen, T. and Pesonen, M., 1994, *Practical Risk Theory for Actuaries* (London: Chapman & Hall); Ingersoll, J.E. Jr., 1987, *Theory of Financial Decisionmaking* (Maryland, USA: Rowman & Littlefield); Jorion, P.,1997, *Value at Risk: The New Benchmark for Controlling Market Risk* (Chicago: Irwin).

6   Value at risk, a measure familiar to the banking world, is related to the ruin approach. It fixes the threshold probability of an undesirable outcome and measures how low the equity will get with that probability.

7   See Kreps 1990, for treatment of the impact on marginal surplus.

8   One respondent pointed out another, more fundamental, difficulty: "It is hard to argue on renewal that your price went up because we wrote more *other* business in your area."

9   This behaviour is a logical consequence of the "EL + fraction of sigma" price formula, if the fraction is a fixed number.

10 By "snapshot" we mean taking an accounting statement at one point in time and using it for decision-making purposes throughout a subsequent period of time, even though the reality portrayed may have changed since the date of the accounting statement.

11 Outside the US, cat management is typically based on CRESTA zones. CRESTA (Catastrophe Risk Evaluating and Standardizing Target Accumulations) was originally developed as a joint project of Swiss Reinsurance Company (Zurich), Gerling-Konzern Globale Reinsurance Company (Cologne) and the Munich Reinsurance Company (Munich). For more information, see http://www.europa-tech.com/cresta.htm

12 Originally, PML was a subjective concept; see Strain, R.W., 1980, *Reinsurance* (Texas: Strain Publishing) and Launie, J. J., Lee, J.F., and Baglini, N.A., 1977, *Principles of Property and Liability Underwriting* (Pennsylvania: Insurance Institute of America). With the emergence of catastrophe models, it has acquired a probabilistic interpretation equivalent to value at risk; see Woo, G.,1999, *The Mathematics of Natural Catastrophes* (London: Imperial Press).

13 Source: National Oceanic and Atmospheric Administration, National Hurricane Center, http://www.nhc.noaa.gov/paststate.html.

14 Source: US Bureau of the Census, http://www.census.gov/population/cen2000/tab04.txt.

15 It also allowed us, to some extent, to examine the relationship of models to one another. This confirmed the impressions our respondents gave us, as discussed earlier in this chapter.

16 "In an effort to overcome some of the problems involving the evaluation of complex models and the treatment of proprietory information, the Florida Legislature created the Florida Commission on Hurricane Loss Projection Methodology, a body independent of both the insurance industry and the regulator. The commission is comprised of eleven individuals with expertise in disciplines used in hurricane modelling. These independent experts thoroughly reviewed all aspects of the catastrophe models, including those sections deemed proprietary by the vendors". Musalin, R. 1998, *Computer Modeling of Catastrophic Losses*

(Florida: Florida Insurance Council). [Available as http://www.ffbic.com/actuary/papers/modeling.pdf]

17 Applied Insurance Research (http://www.air-boston.com)

18 Risk Management Solutions (http://www.rms.com)

19 EQECAT, Inc. (http://www.eqecat.com)

20 Technically, the client-specific random effect had a variance component of 0.0108.

BIBLIOGRAPHY

Ingersoll, J. E. Jr., 1987, *Theory of Financial Decisionmaking* (Maryland, USA: Rowman & Littlefield)

Kreps, R. E., 1990, "Reinsurer Risk Loads from Marginal Surplus Requirements", *Proceedings of the Casualty Actuarial Society*, Volume LXXX, pp. 196–203.

Kreps, R. E., 1999, "Investment-Equivalent Reinsurance Pricing", in O. E. Van Slyke (ed), *Actuarial Considerations Regarding Risk and Return in Property-Casualty Insurance Pricing*, pp. 77–104, (Alexandria, VA: Casualty Actuarial Society).

11

Pricing of Catastrophe Bonds

Shaun Wang
SCOR

The editor of this volume, Morton Lane, started his prize-winning paper on the pricing of catastrophe (cat) bonds with the following question:

> "Should the pricing of reinsurance catastrophes be related to the price of the default risk embedded in the corporate bonds?
> If not, why not?
> A risk is a risk is a risk, in whatever market it appears. Shouldn't the risk prices in these different markets be comparable? More basically perhaps, how should reinsurance prices and bond prices be set? How does the market currently set them?"[1]

INTRODUCTION
In this chapter we will first explore these questions, then, present a universal pricing framework for financial and insurance risks, and finally, test this framework, using recent market-transaction data.

Cat bonds are insurance-linked securities (ILS) that translate referenced cat risk into credit risk borne by outside investors. In the event of a cat loss, investors, as holders of cat bonds, risk future coupon payments, and redemption of underlying principal. For detailed product information about cat bonds as an asset class, the reader may consult the chapter by Mocklow, DeCaro and McKenna in this volume.

On the investor side
From 1999 to 2002, the domestic investing environment has been characterised by:

1. Weak stock markets following the burst of the NASDAQ bubble;
2. Low interest rates amid economic recession;

3. Credit and accounting debacles in the corporate and high-yield debt sectors; and
4. High correlation between credit losses and equity losses.

These factors have contributed to growing interest in non-correlated assets, such as cat bonds. Indeed, cat bonds are quickly gaining investor acceptance because of their historically strong performance and very low correlation with other asset classes.

On the insurance side

At the same time, many property-casualty insurers and reinsurers have found themselves in a weak capital position due to:

1. Years of under-pricing, resulting in severe underwriting losses;
2. High litigation costs related to asbestos, requiring more loss reserves;
3. Inadequate loss reserves as a means of delaying a full recognition of a depressed financial condition;
4. Large losses from the September 11, 2001 terror attack, the collapse of Enron, and the credit defaults of large telecommunications firms; and
5. Poor investment returns of insurer's assets, not offsetting the above underwriting losses.

All of these factors have contributed to the recent contraction of the retro-cession market, and significant rate increases in catastrophe insurance rates.[2]

Over the past few years, some primary and reinsurance companies have successfully issued cat bonds, surmounting old challenges of data collection and cat exposure aggregation. With reinsurance rates and retrocession costs rising, primary and reinsurance companies are relying more on the capital markets for risk transfer than ever before.[3]

A burgeoning cat bond market will need a commonly accepted pricing model, where investors can compare the risk-return trade-off of cat bonds with that of other asset classes comprising a diversified portfolio, like stocks, bonds, currencies, or commodities.

The need for a universal pricing theory

Cat bonds lie at an intersection of two different approaches: a capital markets approach for pricing assets in a trading environment, and an actuarial approach for pricing liabilities in an underwriting environment. The pricing of cat bonds requires a fundamental reconciliation between these two approaches.

In a 2001 industry roundtable discussion on the main factors driving the alternative risk transfer (ART) in the coming years, Michael Leybov commented that a universal pricing theory is a key factor:[4]

"Also, from the technical, internal point of view, it's important to have people who can do pricing – both the way insurance companies do it, and capital markets do. And that they can reconcile one way of pricing with the other one. So far it has been two very different areas. But if you're standing between these markets, you also have to bridge it from the technical point of view."

The cat bond market calls for a universal pricing theory for insurance and credit risks.

Aspects of cat bond pricing
Both cat bonds and corporate bonds are subject to default risks characerised by:

❑ Frequency of default, and
❑ The recovery rate, given default.

For corporate credit risk, there are documented statistics on:

❑ Historical default probabilities by bond rating classes (eg, Standard and Poors, Moody's), and
❑ The recovery rate by debt seniority (eg, see Carty and Lieberman, 1996).

For cat bonds, investors are generally provided with loss-exceedance curves that are obtained either:

❑ By running company exposure data through commercially available cat modelling software, or
❑ By designing payoff functions along some parametric indicators (eg, the Richter Scale of an earthquake at a specified location, an aggregate industry loss index, etc).

For investors, it is desirable to compare the relative attractiveness of the yield spread between cat bonds and corporate bonds. To accomplish this, one needs a universal pricing theory that can quantify the risk-return trade-off between yield spread and the frequency/severity of bond default.

For issuers, it is desirable to compare the cost of issuing a cat bond to that of purchasing equivalent reinsurance protection. The excess yield spread over the risk-free rate for a cat bond can be translated into risk premium dollars for an insurance contract providing the same cat protection.

The perspective of the capital market vs an individual investor or issuer
Before proceeding, it is important to make a clarification: this chapter shall focus on how the market – that is, an integration of both the capital market and insurance market – prices a risk, instead of how an individual investor

or insurer evaluates a risk. For an individual investor or insurer, the cost of accepting a new risk generally depends on its existing portfolio composition. For instance, due to risk concentration concerns, an insurer may demand more than twice the risk premium for taking twice the amount of exposure for a given cat risk. However, in a market setting where there are many participants, proportionality of price with respect to risk is a reasonable expectation. Note that cat bonds are sold to capital markets where investors themselves are holding diversified portfolios. Therefore, our pricing approach will focus on the market perspective, instead of that for an individual player.

PRICING THEORIES FOR CAT BONDS
Zero beta of cat bond and CAPM theory

Many financial economists contend that cat bond losses are generally uncorrelated with changing economic and market conditions, thus such losses should have *zero beta* with respect to the capital market portfolio.[5] According to CAPM, assets with "zero beta" should not command any risk premium. Obviously, this theory fails to explain the significant risk premiums contained in observed cat bond transactions. This risk premium puzzle has caught the attention of some researchers (see Bantwal and Kunreuther, 1999).

The Embrechts chapter in this volume sheds some light on the meaning of "zero beta". As a single-summary statistic of linear correlation, "beta" itself may not hold enough information on correlations at the extreme tail of loss distributions. Thus, for pricing catastrophe events, it may be misleading to rely on "beta" in calculating risk premiums.

Morton Lane's pricing model

Instead of debating with the zero beta CAPM theory for cat bonds, Lane (2000) focused his effort on fitting empirical yield data for a dozen cat bond transactions in 1999.

Lane introduced the following terminologies:

❑ Probability of first loss (PFL): the expected annual frequency of incurring a loss.
❑ Conditional expected loss (CEL): the average severity as percentage of principal given that a loss occurs.
❑ Expected excess return (EER): the adjusted spread over LIBOR, further net of expected loss (that is, PFL × CEL).[6] Expected excess return represents the risk loading.

Motivated by empirical data, Lane proposed the following pricing model for cat bond default risk:

$$EER = \gamma \, (PFL)^{\alpha} \, (CEL)^{\beta} \qquad (1)$$

The Lane model is appealing in that it explicitly reflects the frequency and severity of catastrophe losses. It is a big step forward from the traditional methods based on standard deviation or variance. As pointed out by Lane, his pricing model in Equation (1) is similar to the Cobb–Douglas production function in economics. Lane showed that his model, as shown in Equation (1), fit reasonably well to empirical prices for a dozen cat bond transactions in 1999, for which the best-fit parameters were $\gamma = 55\%$, $\alpha = 49\%$, and $\beta = 57\%$. Lane has also updated the fitted model parameters to incorporate recent data on cat bond transactions from 2000.[7]

Insurance pricing methods
Over the past century insurers have developed a number of pricing methods. The Kreps and Major chapter in this volume provides a good survey of these methods. In general, insurance pricing methods start with objective loss data, calculate an expected loss (burning cost), and then load for risk margin and expenses. The most commonly used method for loading risk margin is the standard-deviation principle:

Price = (expected value of loss) + λ (standard deviation of loss), where λ is a loading multiplier.

Despite its popularity, this standard-deviation principle has suffered criticisms for

❏ Failing to reflect the skew of a loss distribution (in fact, standard-deviation loading may unwittingly penalise upside skew, while ignoring downside skew), and
❏ Failing to produce additive prices when a large risk is split into smaller layers (tranches).

The drawbacks of the standard-deviation method have pushed researchers to develop various alternatives. A major research breakthrough is no-arbitrage pricing of reinsurance layers, see Venter (1991) and Wang (1996).

Probability distortions
In reinsurance, a large risk is often subdivided into several layers. A layer in reinsurance is comparable to a call-spread in option trading, or a tranche in a cat bond series.

Let $G(x) = Pr\{X > x\}$ be the exceedance curve for a cat loss X. The exceedance curve is related to the cumulative distribution function (CDF) by $F(x) = 1 - G(x)$.

The expected value of loss X is equal to the total area under the exceedance curve $G(x)$:

$$E[X] = \int_0^\infty G(x)dx$$

Let $X_{(a,\,a+h]}$ denote a layer with limit h and attachment point a. The loss to the layer $X_{(a,\,a+h]}$ is related to the ground-up loss X by the following relationship:

$$X_{(a,\,a+h]} = \begin{cases} 0, & \text{if} & X < a; \\ X - a, & \text{if} & a \leq X < a + h; \\ h, & \text{if} & a + h \leq X. \end{cases}$$

It can be verified that

$$E[X_{(a,\,a+h]}] = \int_a^{a+h} G(x)dx$$

In other words, the expected loss to the layer $X_{(a,\,a+h]}$ equals the area under the loss exceedance curve over the interval $(a, a+h]$

When the layer limit h is sufficiently small, the expected loss to the layer is

$$E[X_{(a,\,a+h]}] \approx G(a) \cdot h$$

Suppose that we have an observed price, $E^*[X_{(a,\,a+h]}]$, for a small layer $(a, a+h]$. Note that the layer price $E^*[X_{(a,\,a+h]}]$ often contains a risk load in addition to the expected loss $E[X_{(a,\,a+h]}]$. From the layer price $E^*[X_{(a,\,a+h]}]$ we can infer a price-implied loss exceedance probability:

$$G^*(a) \approx E^*[X_{(a,\,a+h]}] \cdot \frac{1}{h}$$

We can expect that $G^*(a) \geq G(a)$. Indeed, observed market prices by layer imply a *direct* transform of the loss exceedance curve from $G(x)$ to $G^*(x)$.

It was with this insight that Venter (1991) argued that no-arbitrage pricing always implies a transformed distribution.

The remaining question was: what kind of mathematical relationship connected $G(x)$ and $G^*(x)$? Inspired by Venter's observation, Wang (1996) first studied a class of probability distortions:

$$G^*(x) = g[G(x)]$$

where $g[0,1] \to [0,1]$ is increasing with $g(0) = 0$ and $g(1) = 1$

A particularly simple distortion is the proportional hazards (PH) transform:

$$G^*(x) = G(x)^{1-\lambda}, \text{ with } 0 \leq \lambda < 1$$

The PH transform method turned out to be similar to a traditional premium calculation method used by a Swiss reinsurer. However, the PH transform is not directly relatable to modern financial pricing theories (like the CAPM and Black–Scholes formula), since the PH transform of a normal distribution is no longer a normal distribution.

The Wang transform

Motivated to link actuarial pricing theories with modern financial pricing theories, Wang (2000) proposed the following probability distortion:

$$G^*(x) = \Phi(\Phi^{-1}(G(x)) + \lambda) \tag{2}$$

Here Φ represents the standard normal cumulative distribution function; the parameter λ is identical to the "market price of risk" and the well-known Sharpe ratio for fund managers. In various industry presentations Equation (2) is referred to as the Wang transform.

For a given loss variable X with objective loss exceedance curve $G(x)$, the Wang transform (2) produces a "risk-adjusted" loss exceedance curve $G^*(x)$. The mean value under $G^*(x)$, denoted by $E^*[X]$, will define a risk-adjusted "fair value" of X at time T, which can be further discounted to time zero, using the risk-free interest rate.

One important property of the Wang transform, as shown in Equation (2) is that normal and lognormal distributions are preserved:

❑ If G has a normal (μ, σ^2) distribution, G^* is also a normal distribution with $\mu^* = \mu + \lambda\sigma$ and $\sigma^* = \sigma$.
❑ For a loss with a normal distribution, the Wang transform (2) recovers the traditional standard-deviation loading principle, with the parameter λ being the constant multiplier.
❑ If G has a lognormal (μ, σ^2) distribution such that $\ln(X) \sim$ normal (μ, σ^2), G^* is another lognormal distribution with $\mu^* = \mu + \lambda\sigma$ and $\sigma^* = \sigma$.

Note that there is no restriction on the loss distribution $G(x)$. Indeed, the Wang transform (2) can be applied to any computer-generated distribution and it is fairly easy to compute numerically. Many software packages have both Φ and Φ^{-1} as built-in functions. In Microsoft Excel, $\Phi(y)$ can be evaluated by NORMSDIST(y) and $\Phi^{-1}(y)$ can be evaluated by NORMSINV(y).

Unified treatment of assets and liabilities

A liability with loss variable X can be viewed as a negative asset with gain variable $Y = -X$, and vice versa. Mathematically, if a liability has a market price of risk λ, when treated as a negative asset, the market price of risk will be $-\lambda$. That is, the market price of risk will have the same value but opposite signs, depending upon whether a risk vehicle is treated as an asset or liability. For an asset with gain variable X, the Wang transform (2) has an equivalent representation:

$$F^*(x) = \Phi[\Phi^{-1}(F(x)) + \lambda] \qquad (3)$$

where $F(x) = 1 - G(x)$ is the cumulative distribution function (CDF) of X.

The following operations are equivalent:

1. Apply transform (2) with λ to the exceedance curve $G(x)$ of the loss variable X,
2. Apply transform (2) with $-\lambda$ to the exceedance curve $G(y)$ of the gain variable $Y = -X$, and
3. Apply transform (3) with λ to the CDF $F(y) = 1 - G(y)$ of the gain variable $Y = -X$.

Their equivalence ensures that the same price is obtained for both sides of a risk transaction.

Stock prices are often modelled by lognormal distributions, which implies that stock returns are modelled by normal distributions. Equivalent results can be obtained by applying Equation (3) either to the stock price distribution, or, alternatively, to the stock return distribution.

Although the Wang transform in Equation (3) was derived from insurance pricing, it has close connections with financial pricing theories. In the Appendix we show that Equation (3) recovers CAPM for pricing underlying assets and Black–Scholes formula for pricing options. This makes the Wang transform (3) a universal pricing formula, and a good starting point for pricing cat bonds.

A variation of the Wang transform

For normal distributions, the Wang transform as shown in Equation (3) represents a location-shift while preserving the volatility. As a variation of Equation (3), we can simultaneously apply a location-shift and a volatility-multiplier:

$$F^*(x) = \Phi[b \cdot \Phi^{-1}(F(x)) + \lambda] \qquad (4)$$

When $F(x)$ has a normal (μ, σ^2) distribution, Equation (4) represents an adjustment of the volatility by $\sigma^* = \sigma/b$, and a shift in the mean by

$\mu^* = \mu + \lambda\sigma$. For most applications we would like to have $0 < b < 1$, so that $\sigma^* = \sigma/b$ is greater than σ (in other words, the volatility is being inflated).[8]

Adjustment for parameter uncertainty

So far we have assumed that probability distributions for risks under consideration are known without ambiguity. Unfortunately, this is seldom the case in real-life risk modelling. Parameter uncertainty is part of reality in an incomplete market. Even with the best data and technologies available today, there are parameter uncertainties in the modelling of catastrophe losses, see Major (1999).

Consider the classic sampling theory in statistics. Assume that we have m independent observations from a given population with a normal (μ, σ^2) distribution. Note that μ and σ are not directly observable, we can at best estimate μ and σ by the sample mean $\bar{\mu}$ and sample standard deviation $\bar{\sigma}$. As a result, when we make probability assessments regarding a future outcome, we effectively need to use a student-t distribution with $k = m - 2$ degrees of freedom.

The student-t distribution with k-degrees of freedom has a density

$$f(t; k) = \frac{1}{\sqrt{2\pi}} \cdot c_k \cdot \left[1 + \frac{t^2}{k}\right]^{-(0.5k + 1)}, -\infty < t < \infty$$

where

$$c_k = \sqrt{\frac{2}{k}} \cdot \frac{\Gamma((k + 1) / 2)}{\Gamma(k / 2)}$$

In terms of density at zero we have $f(0; k) = c_k \cdot \phi(0)$, where $\phi(0)$ is the standard normal density at $x = 0$. Student-t has a lower density than standard normal at zero. As the degree of freedom k increases, the factor c_k increases and approaches one:

k	3	4	5	6	7	8	9
c_k	0.921	0.940	0.952	0.959	0.965	0.969	0.973

The student-t distribution can be generalised to having fractional degree of freedom.

Following the statistical sampling theory that uses a student-t distribution in place of a normal distribution, we suggest the following technique of adjusting for parameter uncertainty:

$$F^*(x) = Q\left(\Phi^{-1}(F(x))\right) \tag{5}$$

where Q has a student-t distribution with degree of freedom k.

Note that Equation (5) is an extension of the classic sampling theory, since there is no restriction imposed on the underlying distribution $F(x)$.

It may be argued that the adjustment in Equation (5) represents a more objective view of the risk's probability distribution, instead of a form of profit loading. Empirical evidence suggests that market prices do often contain an adjustment for parameter uncertainty.

A two-factor model

Let $G(x)$ be a best-estimate probability distribution, before adjustment for parameter uncertainty. The combination of parameter uncertainty adjustment in Equation (5) and pure risk adjustment using the Wang transform in Equation (2) yields the following two-factor model:

$$G^*(y) = Q\left(\Phi^{-1}(G(y)) + \lambda\right) \tag{6}$$

where Q has a student-t distribution with degree of freedom k.

The two-factor model in Equation (6) can also be written in terms of adjustments of local volatilities:

$$F^*(x) = Q\left[\Phi^{-1}(F(x)) + \lambda\right] = \Phi\left[b \cdot \Phi^{-1}(F(x)) + \lambda\right] \tag{7}$$

where the multiplier b depends on the value of $F(x)$, rather than being a constant.

As shown in Figure 1, the implied b-values in Equation (7) depend on the value of $F(x)$. In the middle range of a risk probability distribution, the implied b-values are closer to one, indicating relatively smaller "volatility adjustment".

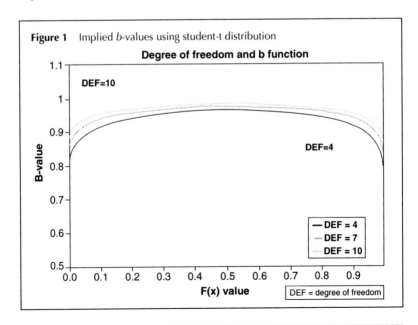

Figure 1 Implied b-values using student-t distribution

At the extreme tails of a risk probability distribution, the implied b-values deviate further below one, showing an increasing adjustment at the extreme tails. The extreme tails may represent many different pricing situations: deep out-of-money options, low-frequency but high-severity catastrophe losses, or, markets where risk vehicles are illiquid, benchmark data sparse, negotiations difficult, and the cost of keeping capital reserves is high.

If we choose Q being a student-t without rescaling in the two-factor model in Equation (7), the degree of freedom will affect the simultaneous estimation of the Sharpe ratio λ.

To overcome this drawback, we can choose Q in Equation (7) being a rescaled student-t distribution that matches the standard normal density at $x = 0$. This rescaled student-t distribution has a density function:

$$q(t; k) = \frac{1}{\sqrt{2\pi}} \cdot \left[1 + \frac{x^2}{k \cdot c_k^2} \right]^{-(0.5k + 1)}, -\infty < x < \infty$$

An advantage of using rescaled student-t is to ensure a more robust estimate of the Sharpe ratio λ. This can be of importance if a fund manager is comparing the Sharpe ratio for various asset classes.

Symmetry vs asymmetry

Insurance risks are characterised by having skewed distributions. As Lane had put it:

> "Any appraisal of the risks contained in insurance or reinsurance covers must take into account the fact that the statistical distribution of profit and loss outcomes may be severely skewed. Conventional risk measurement (ie the standard deviation) deals with random outcomes that are symmetric in nature. Price volatility is usually viewed as symmetric. Event or outcome risk (a characteristic of insurance) is not. How is the asymmetry to be captured? What are the components of event risk and how they factor into price?"[9]

Although the distributions Φ and Q are symmetric themselves, the Wang transform in Equation (3) and the two-factor model in Equation (7) automatically reflect the skew in the input distribution G(x). This ability to reflect the skew is an advantage over the standard deviation loading.

As an example, consider two bets with the following gain/loss probability distributions.

Bet X has a probability distribution of gain/loss:

x	−1	0	1	19
f(x)	0.29	0.6	0.1	0.01

Bet Y has a probability distribution of gain/loss:

y	−19	−1	0	1
f(y)	0.01	0.1	0.6	0.29

Both X and Y have the same mean = 0 and variance = 4. While X has an upside skew, Y has a downside skew.

1. Apply the Wang transform in Equation (3) with $\lambda = 0.3$, we get fair values of $E^*[X] = -0.26$ and $E^*[Y] = -0.36$. Note that $E^*[X] - E^*[Y] = 0.10$. The one-factor Wang transform (3) differentiates slightly the upside skew from the downside skew.
2. Using a Student-t adjustment as the second factor, as in Equation (5), for parameter uncertainty with a degree of freedom of $k = 6$, we get fair values $E^*[X] = 0.36$ and $E^*[Y] = -0.36$. The Student-t adjustment in Equation (6) clearly reflects the direction of the skew. We have $E^*[X] - E^*[Y] = 0.72$.
3. Using the two-factor model, as in Equation (7), with $\lambda = 0.3$ and $k = 6$, we get fair values of $E^*[X] = 0.04$ and $E^*[Y] = -0.78$. We have $E^*[X] - E^*[Y] = 0.82$, approximately equal the combined differences under Equations (3) and (5).

Risk premium for higher moments

In classic CAPM where asset returns are assumed to follow multivariate normal distributions, the "market price of risk", $\lambda = (E[R] - r)/\sigma[R]$, represents the excess return per unit of volatility.

The classic CAPM has gone through important enhancements in modern finance and insurance research. In addition to risk premium associated with volatility, there is strong evidence of risk premium for higher moments (and/or for parameter uncertainty). This evidence has spurred extensions of classic CAPM, to include higher moments. In their recent paper, Kozik and Larson (2001) give a formal account of an n-moment CAPM. The authors offer insightful discussions on the risk premium for higher moments, pointing out that a three-moment CAPM significantly improves the fit of empirical data; however, there is little marginal gain by including higher moments beyond the third moment.

Obviously, the risk premium for higher moments has direct implications in pricing property cat insurance, high excess-of-loss insurance layers, credit default risk, and way-out-of-the-money options. From a risk management point of view, the cost of cushion capital increases with gearing and parameter uncertainty, as though they were extreme tail events.

The one-factor Wang transform (3), which can be viewed as an analogue to the two-moment CAPM, does not produce sufficient risk adjustment at the extreme tails of the risk probability distribution.

The Student-t adjustment, as in Equation (5), captures two opposing forces that often distort investors' rational behaviour, namely *greed* and *fear*. Although investors may fear unexpected large losses, they desire unexpected large gains. As a result the tail probabilities are often inflated at both tails; and the magnitude of distortion normally increases at the extreme tails. This distributional adjustment at both tails increases the kurtosis of the underlying distribution. The mean value of the transformed distribution under Equation (5) reflects the skew (asymmetry) of the underlying loss distribution.

The two-factor model in Equation (7), however, as a combination of Equation (3) and Equation (5), provides risk premium adjustments not only for the second moment, but also for higher moments, and for parameter uncertainty.

Dynamics of the price of risk
In the two-factor model shown in Equation (7), the pricing parameters λ and k are indicators of the risk-return trade-off. Note that λ and k may change as market dynamics (aggregate supply and demand) change. Indeed, a weakened capital position for the insurance industry due to losses from September 11 had increased the demand for issuing cat bonds, which had further pushed the price of risk up. On the other hand, increasing acceptance by the investor community can have an offsetting effect on the price of risk.

EMPIRICAL FINDINGS
A natural question is how well various pricing models fit with observed transaction prices for cat bonds and corporate bonds. We shall use the cat-bond transaction data compiled by Lane (2000).[10]

Figure 2 shows the fitting result of the two-factor model from Equation (6) to the yield spreads for a dozen cat bond transactions, see Lane (2000). Based on minimising the mean squared error, the best-fit parameters were $\lambda = 0.453$, and $k = 5$ (for the student-t degrees-of-freedom).

As shown in Table 1, the two-factor model in Equation (6) showed a smaller mean-squared error than did the three-parameter model of Lane (2000).

Figure 3 shows the fit of the two-factor model in Equation (6) to the grid of yield spread for corporate bonds with various credit ratings.[11] With parameters $\lambda = 0.453$, and $k = 6$ (for the student-t degrees-of-freedom), we get approximately the best fit.

CONCLUSIONS
The one-factor Wang transform generalises CAPM for pricing equities and the Black–Scholes formula for pricing options. By incorporating an adjustment for moments, extreme values, and parameter uncertainty, the two-factor Wang transform provides a unified theoretical framework for

Table 1 Comparison of model yield spread with empirical yield spread

1999 cat bond transaction	Empirical spread	Two-factor model	Lane model
Mosaic 2A	4.06%	3.88%	3.80%
Mosaic 2B	8.36%	10.15%	11.83%
Halyard Re	4.56%	4.82%	5.01%
Domestic Re	3.74%	4.36%	4.45%
Concentric Re	3.14%	4.01%	3.97%
Juno Re	4.26%	4.15%	4.16%
Residential Re	3.71%	4.08%	4.03%
Kelvin 1st Event	10.97%	12.80%	15.34%
Kelvin 2nd Event	4.82%	3.25%	3.02%
Gold Eagle A	2.99%	2.81%	2.51%
Gold Eagle B	5.48%	4.82%	5.03%
Namazu Re	4.56%	5.20%	5.52%
Atlas Re A	2.74%	2.35%	1.92%
Atlas Re B	3.75%	3.15%	2.90%
Atlas Re C	14.19%	11.01%	12.90%
Seismic Ltd	4.56%	5.13%	5.38%
Sum Squared Error		0.22%	0.41%

pricing both insurance and credit risks with extreme values and parameter uncertainties.

The two-factor Wang transform provides good fit to cat bond transaction data and corporate credit yield spreads. The lambda parameter, called "the market price of risk", is directly linked to the Sharpe ratio, a familiar concept to fund managers. With this universal pricing formula, investors can compare the risk-return trade-off of risk vehicles drawn from virtually any asset class.

Market transaction data in Lane (2000) indicated that cat bonds and corporate bonds offered similar risk-return trade-offs in terms of Sharpe ratio. However, cat bonds and corporate bonds showed different student degrees-of-freedom, $k = 5$ and $k = 6$, respectively. In other words, investors demanded higher risk-adjustment for parameter uncertainty for cat bonds than for corporate bonds.

These empirical findings have very interesting implications. Corporate bond defaults are highly correlated, because issuers are subject to the same economic upturns and downturns that facilitate the payment of solemn obligations. In contrast, cat bond risks have almost zero correlation with an

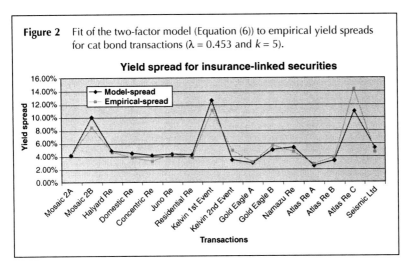

Figure 2 Fit of the two-factor model (Equation (6)) to empirical yield spreads for cat bond transactions ($\lambda = 0.453$ and $k = 5$).

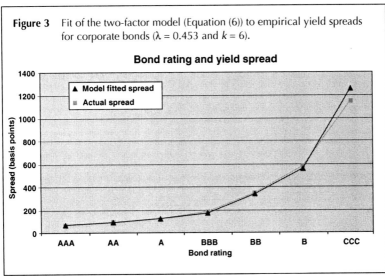

Figure 3 Fit of the two-factor model (Equation (6)) to empirical yield spreads for corporate bonds ($\lambda = 0.453$ and $k = 6$).

expanding or contracting economy. Cat bond risks with different geographic regions and referenced perils also have low correlations. Pooling cat bond exposures can yield lucrative diversification benefits. In summary, there is great potential benefit for sophisticated investors to include cat bonds in their asset portfolios.

BIBLIOGRAPHY

Bantwal, V.J. and H.C. Kunreuther, 1999, *A Cat Bond Premium Puzzle?*, The Wharton School, University of Pennsylvania, working paper, 99–26.

Black, F., and M. Scholes, 1973, The pricing of options and corporate liabilities, *Journal of Political Economy*, May/June, 81,pp. 637–59.

Mocklow, D., J. DeCaro and M. Mckenna, 2002, this volume.

Butsic, R. P., 1999, Capital allocation for property-liability insurers: a catastrophe reinsurance application, *Casualty Actuarial Society Forum*, Spring Reinsurance Call Papers, 1–70.

Carty, L. V. and Lieberman, D., 1996, *Defaulted bank loan recoveries*, Global Credit Research, Special Report, Moody's Investors Service.

Crouhy, M., Galai, D., and Mark, R., 2000, A comparative analysis of current credit risk models, *Journal of Banking & Finance*, 24, pp. 59–117.

Embrechts, P., 2002, this volume.

Hull, J. 1997, *Options, Futures, and Other Derivatives*, Third Edition (New Jersey: Prentice Hall).

Kozik, T. J. and A. M. Larson, 2001, The N-Moment Insurance CAPM, *Proceedings of the Casualty Actuarial Society*, Volume LXXXVIII.

Kreps, R. and J. Major, 2002, this volume.

Lane, M. N., 2000, Pricing risk transfer transactions, *ASTIN Bulletin*, Vol. 30, 2, pp. 259–93.

Lane, M. N., 2001, *Analyzing the pricing of the 2001 risk-linked securities transactions*, Lane Financial LLC Trade Notes, July 31, [Available from:http://www.LaneFinancial LLC.com.]

Major, J., 1999, The Uncertain Nature of Catastrophe Modelling, *Natural Disaster Management*, by Tudor Rose and in association with the IDNDR Secretariat of the United Nations.

Merton, R. C., 1973, An intertemporal capital asset pricing model, *Econometrica*, 41, pp. 867–80.

Merton, R. C., 1974, On the pricing of corporate debt: The risk structure of interest rates, *Journal of Finance*, 28, pp. 449–70.

Venter, G. G., 1991, "Premium implications of reinsurance without arbitrage," *ASTIN Bulletin*, 21, 2, pp. 223–30.

Wang, S. S., 1996, "Premium calculation by transforming the layer premium density," *ASTIN Bulletin*, 26, 1, pp. 71–92.

Wang, S. S., 2000, "A class of distortion operators for pricing financial and insurance risks", *Journal of Risk and Insurance*, Vol 67, 1, pp. 5–36.

Appendix

Linking Wang transform with financial pricing theories
In this appendix we will show how the Wang transform Equation (3) is related to the financial pricing theories, behind CAPM and the Black–Scholes–Merton option formula.

Recovering CAPM
Consider an asset i on a one-period time horizon. Assume that the return R_i for asset i has a normal distribution with a standard deviation of σ_i. Applying the Wang transform (3) to the distribution of R_i, we get a risk-adjusted rate-of-return:

$$E^*[R_i] = E[R_i] - \lambda\sigma_i \qquad (A1)$$

In a competitive market, the risk-adjusted return, $E^*[R_i]$ in Equation (A1), should be equal to the risk-free rate, r. Therefore we can infer that $\lambda = (E[R_i] - r)/\sigma_i$, which is exactly the same as the market price of risk in classic CAPM. With λ being the market price of risk for an asset, the Wang transform reproduces the classic CAPM equation.

Pricing of contingent payoffs
For an underlying risk X and a function h, we say that $Y = h(X)$ is a derivative (or contingent payoff) of X, since the payoff of Y is a function of the outcome of X. If the function h is monotone, we say that Y is a co-monotone derivative of X. For example, a European call option is a co-monotone derivative of the underlying asset; in (re)insurance, an excess layer is a co-monotone derivative of the ground-up risk.

Theoretically, the underlying risk X and its co-monotone derivative Y should have the same market price of risk, λ.

In pricing a contingent payoff $Y = h(X)$, there are two ways of applying the Wang transform:

❏ Method I: apply the Wang transform to the distribution F_X of the underlying risk X. Then derive a risk-adjusted distribution F_Y^* from F_X^* using $Y^* = h(X^*)$.
❏ Method II: first derive its own distribution F_Y for $Y = h(X)$. Then apply the Wang transform to F_Y directly, using the same λ as in Method I.

Mathematically it can be shown that these two methods are equivalent. This important result validates using the Wang transform for risk-neutral valuations of contingent payoffs.

Implied λ and the effect of duration

For a traded asset, the market price of risk λ can be estimated from observed market data. We shall now take a closer look at the implied market price of risk and how it varies with the time horizon under consideration.

Consider a continuous time model where asset prices are assumed to follow a geometric Brownian motion (GBM). Consider an individual stock (or a stock index). The stock price A(t) satisfies the following stochastic differential equation:

$$\frac{dA(t)}{A(t)} = \mu dt + \sigma dW \tag{A2}$$

where dW is a random variable drawn from a normal distribution with mean equal to zero and variance equal to dt. In Equation (A2), μ is the expected rate of return for the asset, and σ is the volatility of the asset return. Let $A(0)$ be the current asset price at time zero. For any future time T, the prospective stock price $A(T)$ as defined in Equation (A2) has a lognormal distribution[12]

$$A(T)/A(0) \sim \text{lognormal} \,(\mu T - 0.5\sigma^2 T,\, \sigma^2 T) \tag{A3}$$

Next we apply the Wang transform to the distribution of $A(T)$ in Equation (A3) and we get

$$A^*(T)/A(0) \sim \text{lognormal} \,(\mu T - \lambda\sigma\sqrt{T} - 0.5\sigma^2 T,\, \sigma^2 T) \tag{A4}$$

For any fixed future time T, a "no arbitrage" condition (or simply, the market value concept) implies that the risk-adjusted future asset price, when discounted by the risk-free rate, must equal the current market price. In this continuous-time model, the risk-free rate r needs to be compounded continuously.

As a result, we have an implied parameter value:

$$\lambda = \lambda(T) = \frac{(\mu - r)}{\sigma}\sqrt{T} = \sqrt{T} \cdot \lambda(1) \tag{A5}$$

The implied λ in Equation (A5) coincides with the market price of risk for the stock as defined by Hull.[13] This implied λ is also consistent with Robert Merton's inter-temporal, continuous-time CAPM, see Merton (1973).

It is interesting to note that the market price of risk λ increases as the time horizon lengthens. This makes intuitive sense since the longer the time horizon, the greater the exposure to unforeseen changes in the overall market environment. This interesting result has applications in quantifying risk-premiums for multi-year contracts.

Applying the Wang transform with the λ in Equation (A5), the stock price has a risk-adjusted distribution

$$A^*(T)/A(0) \sim \text{lognormal}(rT - 0.5\sigma^2 T, \sigma^2 T) \qquad \text{(A6)}$$

where both the market price of risk λ and the expected stock return μ have dropped out from the transformed distribution $F^*(x)$.

Recovery of the Black–Scholes formula

An European call option on an underlying stock (or stock index) with a strike price K and exercise date T is defined by the following payoff function

$$Y = \text{Call}(K) = \begin{cases} 0, & \text{when } A(T) \geq K, \\ A(T) - K, & \text{when } A(T) > K \end{cases}$$

Being a non-decreasing function of the underlying stock price, the option payoff, Call(K), is co-monotone with the terminal stock price, $A(T)$; thus it has the same market price of risk as the underlying stock. Therefore, the same λ as in Equation (A5) should be used to price the option Call(K). In other words, the price of an European call option is the expected payoff under the transformed (risk-neutral) stock price distribution $F^*(x)$, where the expected stock return μ is replaced by the risk-free rate r. The resulting option price is exactly the same as the price obtained by Black–Scholes formula.

Corporate bond defaults

According to Robert Merton (1974), a default event for a corporate bond is triggered when corporate asset value falls below the level of corporate debt. This establishes an option-based framework for valuing corporate defaults (see for example the distance-to-default approach by the KMV Corporation).[14]

Assume that corporate asset value $A(t)$ follows geometric Brownian motion as in Equation (A2). At horizon T, the asset value $A(T)$ has a lognormal distribution with an expected rate of return μ, as in Equation (A3). We have shown that, using the lambda in Equation (A4), the risk-adjusted lognormal distribution has an expected rate of return r, as in Equation (A6). Therefore, the objective default frequency p and the risk-neutral default frequency p^* have the following relation:

$$p^* = \Phi\left(\Phi^{-1}(p) + \frac{\mu - r}{\sigma} \sqrt{T} \right) \qquad \text{(A7)}$$

Crouhy, Galai and Mark (2000) derive the same relation (Equation (A7)) for corporate bond defaults under Merton's optioned-based model. When $\mu > r$ we have $p^* > p$. The risk-neutral probability of default, after adjusting for the price of risk, is greater than the actual probability of default. The difference, $p^* - p$, reflects the magnitude of risk adjustment.

Note that Merton's corporate default model provides a direct justification for using the Wang transform as a starting point for pricing default risks. The Wang transform goes beyond relation Equation (A7) in that:

1. Relation (A7) is obtained by assuming a geometric Brownian motion for the underlying asset value. In contrast, the Wang transform in Equation (2), as a probability distortion function, is mute about the assumptions on the underlying asset value.
2. The relation shown in Equation (A7) represents a risk-adjustment to the default frequency only, while the Wang transform is always applied to the whole distribution $G(x)$.
3. The two-factor model in Equation (6), as an important enhancement of the one-factor Wang transform in Equation (2), was made possible in the context of probability distortions.

1   See Lane, (2000), pp. 259.
2   When a reinsurer itself transfers part of its risk to other (re)insurers, it is called a retrocession.
3   SCOR issued new cat bonds in early 2002. California Earthquake Authority is also – at the time of writing – thinking of issuing cat bonds to reduce its reliance on the insurance market.
4   Alternative risk strategies round table 2000. (Available from: http://www.financewise.com/public/edit/riskm/art/art-roundtable_q4.htm)
5   For example, David J. Cummins, presentation at the Fields Institute of Toronto, 2000.
6   London Interbank Offered Rate (LIBOR).
7   See http://www.lanefinancialllc.com
8   In an unpublished result, John Major and Gary Venter fitted model (7) to a set of observed cat layer prices. Robert Bustic (1999) applied both a location-shift and a volatility-multiplier to a lognormal cat loss distribution.
9   (2000, p 261)
10 Readers are referred to the Lane Financial Publications website for more detailed descriptions of these cat bond transactions. An update of the 2000 cat bond transactions can be found in Lane (2001). (See: http://www.lanefinancialllc.com).
11 The corporate bond data used is taken from Table 7 of Lane (2000).
12 See Hull (1997) p. 229)
13 (1997, p. 290)
14 See KMV Corporation publication, available from: http://www.kmv.com/Knowledge_Base/public/general/white/Merton_Prediction_Power.PDF

Implications of Market Shocks: Capacity, Price Volatility and the Value of Transparency

Joan Lamm–Tennant

GeneralCologne Re Capital Consultants

Using seminal theories of risk as a foundation, this chapter will discuss the practical implications of shocks to the insurance markets in terms of capacity, price and demand for risk transfer. The focus of this chapter is to provide relevant information to risk managers as they manoeuvre through times of crisis and build profitable portfolios of risk alongside appropriate hedge strategies. The chapter begins by developing a theoretical framework for thinking about the insurance market following a shock to capital. The theoretical framework establishes the interrelationships between price, capital and demand for risk transfer. Using financial theory as a motivation, we then look to specific firms and their respective risk/capital management strategies to discuss possible "signalling" to the financial markets. We conclude by rendering practical recommendations to risk managers regarding effective risk and capital management strategies following extreme shocks to the market. We ask and explore the following questions.

❑ How can theoretical underwriting cycle models, such as the capacity constraint model (Gron, 1994 and Winter, 1988), assist us in anticipating the market's response to shocks?
❑ Has management "signalled" information to the financial markets through their explicit risk and capital management strategy and through their behaviourism (transparency) following September 11, 2001?
❑ How can risk managers fortify their company, build profitable portfolios of risk and establish appropriate risk hedge strategies following market shocks?
❑ What are the implications of September 11 to risk managers?

INTRODUCTION

The events surrounding September 11, and their impact on the insurance/reinsurance markets, present an opportunity to evaluate the effect of market shocks on the capacity and the price of risk transfer. While September 11 represents an extreme shock to the insurance/reinsurance markets, previous shocks of lesser magnitude encouraged practitioners, regulators, researchers and analysts to consider the market response to such events.[1] Since the 1950s, there have been seven episodes referred to as "insurance crises". These crises give way to property/casualty underwriting cycles – alternating periods of rising and then falling underwriting profits. The "bottom" of the underwriting cycle is typically characterised by withdrawal of insurers from some markets resulting in an availability crisis. Whereas the period of rising underwriting profitability is characterised by increased entry of insurers and expanded coverage.

In structurally developed and competitive financial markets, underwriting cycles would not be expected. Explanations for cycles follow two schools of thought. The first explanation is motivated by the premise that insurance markets operate irrationally (Venezian, 1985) and/or exhibit market imperfections (Gron, 1994 and Winter, 1988). The second explanation emphasises rational markets that are interrupted by institutional irregularities. These irregularities include:

- ❏ institutional, regulatory and accounting characteristics such as cash flow underwriting;
- ❏ exogenous shocks to surplus attributed to natural catastrophes, unexpected increases in claims costs, or shifts in loss distributions;
- ❏ interest rate changes coupled with changes in equity values; and
- ❏ uncertainties in the market environment.[2]

In Section 1, we re-visit the capacity constraint model as a framework for evaluating the market response to shocks, and in particular to the shock of September 11. We consider the literature addressing rational markets with institutional irregularities, to better understand the market's reactions to September 11. Price and capital implications are also evaluated. Section 2 evaluates firm-specific risk/capital management strategies. Using financial theory, we explore the possibility of "signalling" – does management "signal" relevant information to the financial markets about their future ability to generate profits through their chosen strategy and degree of transparency? Our objective is not to test the efficiency of the capital markets, but more so to "look through" stock price movements to draw inferences about the effectiveness of various firms' risk and capital management strategies. Some of the risk and capital management strategies considered include pre-loss risk hedging (ie, reinsurance), share buybacks, floatation of debt vs issuance of equity and transparency with the markets. As risk managers, we care about the financial market's perception of our decisions. Risk managers may not be directly responsible for managing stock values but risk managers do care about the market's perception of their decisions. Based on a series of hypotheses motivated by financial theory, we evaluate the observed cross-sectional differences in firm strategy alongside of the financial market's short-term response. We then conclude by providing practical insights intended to assist risk managers in building profitable portfolios of risk and manoeuvering through extreme events such as September 11.

SECTION 1: THEORETICAL FRAMEWORK – UNDERSTANDING THE EFFECTS OF MARKET SHOCKS

The capacity constraint model was initially developed to better understand underwriting cycles. This model offered an alternative to "arbitrage" theories that suggests that cycles are simply a consequence resulting from institutional interference such as reporting practices. To the contrary, the capital constraint model suggests that a systematic relationship does, in fact, exist between capacity (capital) and price (profitability). Empirical tests of the capital constraint model suggest that unanticipated decreases in capacity cause higher profitability resulting from increased prices which eventually result in a replenishment of capacity.

In Figure 1, a), the supply curve for risk is illustrated as having a kink. The industry can accept risk at the long-run equilibrium price up to its level of net worth (Q). The long-run equilibrium price of risk is simply the present value of the expected losses plus expenses.[3] If the industry continues to accept risk at the long-run equilibrium price beyond its net worth or if the industry prices risk beneath the equilibrium price, then insolvency risk is increased. Consequently, for a given level of net worth and insolvency risk, the insurer can sell more insurance (extend capacity) if and only if they receive a higher price, resulting in kink and an upward-sloping

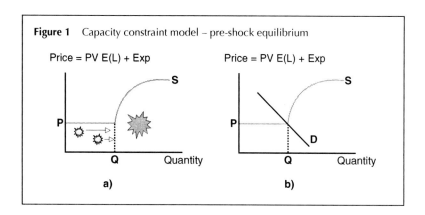

Figure 1   Capacity constraint model – pre-shock equilibrium

supply curve. The higher price, in essence, attracts additional net worth. In Figure 1, b), the demand curve for risk is overlaid on top of the supply curve. The demand curve is downward sloping suggesting that price must fall to increase the demand for risk. In equilibrium, the supply and demand intersect to determine price – this intersection occurs at the appropriate level of capacity and at the "fair" price. This is a long-run equilibrium model where 'life is in harmony".

Now let us consider what happens in the short-run when capacity is shocked by an extreme event such as the World Trade Center (WTC) event. Figure 2, a), illustrates that a shock to capacity caused by an unanticipated loss shifts the "kink" in the supply curve to the left. This shift is an immediate response to the event and the magnitude of the shift depends on the size of the loss. Shifting the "kink" in the capacity curve to the left results in a rise in price from P to P*. In time the increase in price results in an increase in profitability and likewise a natural, orderly replenishment of capital through retained earnings. Note that if the industry extends capacity post-shock at the pre-shock price, then insolvency risk would increase. In the case of the WTC event, capacity was not only shocked but risk aversion was heightened. Behaviours or attitudes, not only financial capital was affected. Figure 2, b), illustrates an increase in risk aversion, which causes the increase in the demand for risk transfer. An increase in the demand will exacerbate the price increase from P* to P** and expedite the replenishment of capital through profitability and retained earnings.

Let us now turn our attention to what actually occurred post September 11 in terms of capital and price. We will observe that the capacity constraint model provides a framework for not only understanding but also anticipating the effect of extreme shocks on capital, price and demand. While this framework is useful, we did experiences some departures from the theory. We offer some possible explanations for the divergences.

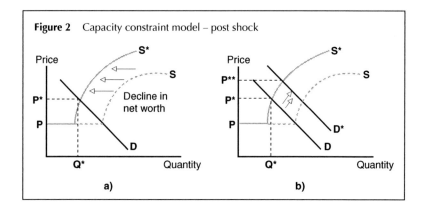

Figure 2   Capacity constraint model – post shock

Capital Considerations

A relevant question is how quickly will the supply curve return to long-run equilibrium and what will be the effect of new capital from external sources? Generally, external capital is more expensive than internal capital, therefore the regeneration of capital is "expected" to be an orderly process largely driven by internal replenishment. An interesting and unexpected occurrence resulted from the WTC event. Soon after September 11, the industry was bracing itself for price increases in both commercial and personal lines. Commercial lines were hardest hit by the WTC event but due to the reduction in capital, even personal lines would experience a rationing of capital and hence an increase in price. As price increases were being implemented, a sudden and significant inflow of new capital from external sources occurred. According to a report by Morgan Stanley as of January 2002, US$22.4 billion in new capital was completed with an additional US$8.6 billion pending, totalling US$31 billion of new capital. While partially speculative, some of this capital was acquired through hedge funds and carry a required rate of return in the range of 20 to 25%, greatly in excess of the 12 to 15% implied cost of internal capital for the insurance industry. This influx of new capital results in the proverbial paradox since price increases will be dampened the faster the capital flows back into the industry.

What might explain this counter-intuitive capital event following September 11? Why was theory defied? While theory provides us with a framework to evaluate market shocks – it is merely theory and not necessarily reality. The departures between theory and reality provide fertile grounds for consideration. By considering these departures we may better understand why our markets behave dysfunctionally, and perhaps set forth a plan for change. Some suggest that the rate at which capital adjusts following a shock depends on other factors aside from the relation between the cost of internal capital and external capital. Other suggestions include the availability of capital in the marketplace, the perceived magnitude of the opportunity (size effect of the price increase), opportunistic behaviour resulting from information asymmetry and the increase in information flows and technology. Certainly 2001 represents a period whereby capital was available and in pursuit of attractive investment returns. This is largely attributed to the rise and subsequent fall of the equity markets as well as the withdrawal of numerous hedge funds from the market. The general consensus was that September 11 was a mega event with expected mega price implications. The following report appeared in the September 15, 2001 issue of Barrons which suggests the strength of the forthcoming pricing power.

> Typically, after a large catastrophe, insurance companies have to raise prices
> to rebuild reserves. But for some of the smaller, weaker players, that will not

be an option this time around; huge losses will push them out of business. And as the huge payouts shrink the industry's capital base, the amount of new insurance that can be sold will be limited. Yet even as capacity shrinks, demand for insurance should remain the same and possibly grow. The result: greater pricing power.

A third argument for the immediate flow of external capital following the WTC event is opportunistic behaviour resulting from information asymmetry. On September 28, 2001 March & McLennan announced that it would privately raise US$1 billion in capital to set up a new Bermuda-based insurer. The new insurer, Axis Specialty Ltd., will specialise in classic London market lines such as marine, property and aviation products – the lines expected to tighten most severely as a result of the WTC event. As of October 2, 2001, Renaissance Re announced that it filed a shelf registration for US$400 million. Morgan Stanley stated that "given that the company's losses for the WTC attack are expected to be relatively minor, we view this move as an opportunistic way to fund potential growth". The concept of information asymmetry provides additional impetus for the opportunistic behaviour – when information is not shared evenly between the buyer and the seller then the party with the best information possesses an advantage. Insurance, by its very nature, is rid with information asymmetries. Also, improved information flows and technology expedite the flow of capital once it begins.

A more pragmatic view as to why the insurance markets may have experienced departures from process set forth by the capital constraint model is that price is not totally dependent on supply and demand in a regulated market. Also, in reality we never really know P or even P* since it takes years of development to estimate the expected loss with accuracy. This lack of clarity in P gives way to divergence in opinion between buyers and sellers as to where current price is relative to equilibrium price – sellers tend to believe that current price is beneath equilibrium price and vice versa. Also providers of capital may have reconsidered their appetite for risk, shifting Q to the left.[4]

Pricing Considerations

The WTC event did not create the hard markets. The hard market had already begun following a steady decline in return on equity and deteriorating economic value added (difference between return on equity and cost of capital). Figure 3 reports that the US property-casualty insurance industry reported return on equity (ROE) from 1993 to 1999. Aside from 1997, the industry experienced a steady decline in ROE – reporting 11.2% ROE in 1993 vs 4.3% ROE in 1999. Throughout this period, the reported ROE is below the industry's cost of capital which ranges from 12 to 15%, depending on the source of capital and the risk level of the insurer. Some believed the industry was overcapitalised prior to September 11 causing a drag on

ROE. In a study by Lamm-Tennant (1999), the EVA was calculated for 90 publicly traded property-casualty insurance companies for each year beginning in 1994 up to 1998. Figure 4 reports the distribution of economic value added values across company, by year. The median EVA peaked in 1997 at 11.7% and then declined to 4.5% in 1998. In 1998 the EVA for firms in the 5th percentile is –19.0% vs 24.4% for firms in the 95th percentile. American International Group (AIG), the one property-casualty insurance company which, trades at an attractive multiple to earnings, performed consistently above median. Clearly, from the reported ROEs and estimated EVAs, the property-casualty industry experienced difficult times in the 1990s. The industry began to recover by imposing rate increases in

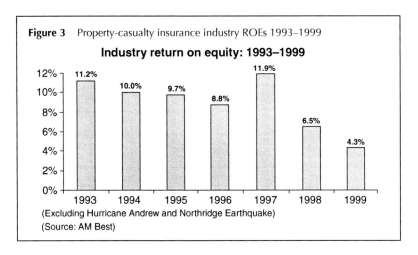

Figure 3 Property-casualty insurance industry ROEs 1993–1999

Industry return on equity: 1993–1999

(Excluding Hurricane Andrew and Northridge Earthquake)
(Source: AM Best)

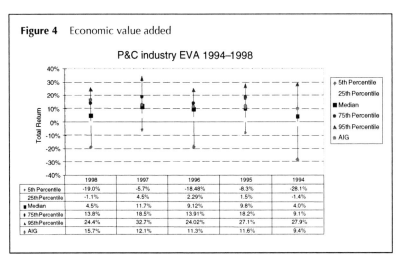

Figure 4 Economic value added

P&C industry EVA 1994–1998

	1998	1997	1996	1995	1994
5th Percentile	-19.0%	-5.7%	-18.48%	-8.3%	-28.1%
25thPercentile	-1.1%	4.5%	2.29%	1.5%	-1.4%
Median	4.5%	11.7%	9.12%	9.8%	4.0%
75thPercentile	13.8%	18.5%	13.91%	18.2%	9.1%
95thPercentile	24.4%	32.7%	24.02%	27.1%	27.9%
AIG	15.7%	12.1%	11.3%	11.6%	9.4%

2000. Swiss Re Sigma estimates that the average worldwide rate increases at January 2001 renewals was 16%. Benfield's Paragon US catastrophe-pricing index indicated that rates were up 7.2% during 2002 – the first increase since 1984. Figure 5 reports that results from a survey of commercial accounts prepared by the Council of Insurance Agent and Brokers. The percent of respondents indicting price increases in excess of 10% are noted for small vs medium vs large accounts from third quarter 2001 to fourth quarter 2001. In the third quarter of 2001 31% of respondents for large accounts indicated a price increase in excess of 10% vs 97% in fourth quarter 2001. The increase in respondents indicating price increases in excess of 10% was similar for small and medium accounts.

While price increases were clearly underway prior to September 11 the question now challenging the industry is whether or not the price increase will continue and, if so, with what momentum? Will the inflow of new capital provide a ballast to the price increases? In the current environment, how many new contributors of capital are committed to building franchises and how many are short-term investors looking to profit from the recent upturn in the property/casualty pricing cycle? While only time will tell, we can look to stock price performance of insurance companies to infer what the financial markets might be anticipating. Figure 6 reports the change in stock price for large capitalisation property-casualty insurers (exposed to large commercial lines risk) for two time periods – year to date through December 31, 2001 and from the WTC event through December 31, 2001. Figures 7 through 9 report similar information for small capitalisation companies (exposed to small commercial lines risk), personal line writers and international companies. For large capitalisation property-casualty companies the change in stock price year to date is largely negative; whereas the change in stock price following the WTC event is largely positive. Although many confounding factors are at play, this might be an

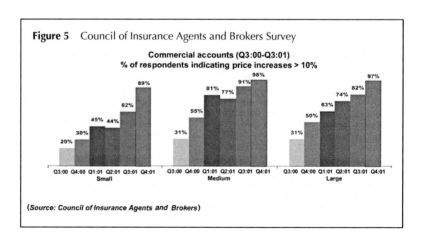

Figure 5 Council of Insurance Agents and Brokers Survey

Commercial accounts (Q3:00-Q3:01)
% of respondents indicating price increases > 10%

(Source: Council of Insurance Agents and Brokers)

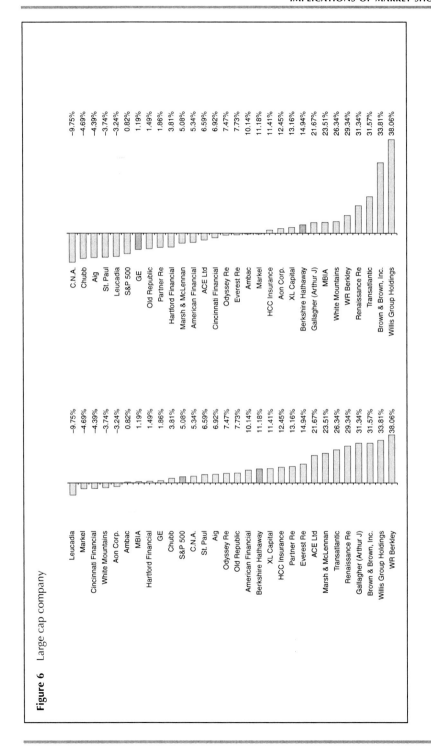

Figure 6 Large cap company

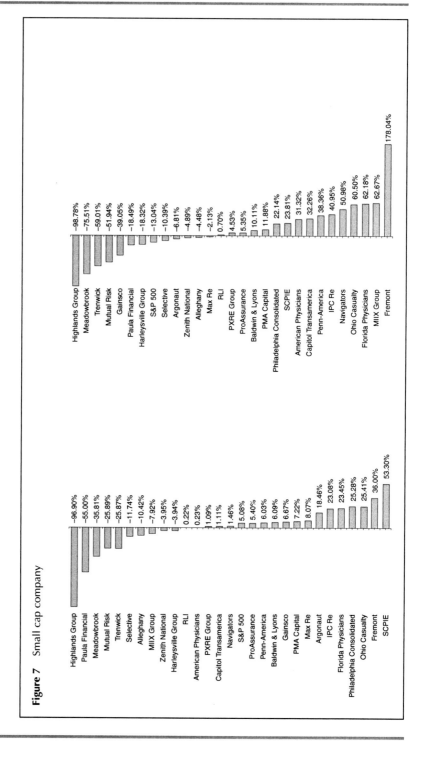

Figure 7 Small cap company

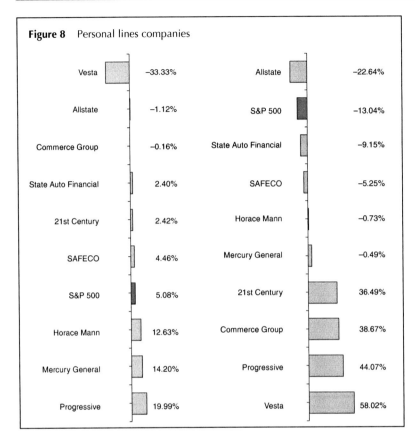

Figure 8   Personal lines companies

Vesta	−33.33%
Allstate	−1.12%
Commerce Group	−0.16%
State Auto Financial	2.40%
21st Century	2.42%
SAFECO	4.46%
S&P 500	5.08%
Horace Mann	12.63%
Mercury General	14.20%
Progressive	19.99%

Allstate	−22.64%
S&P 500	−13.04%
State Auto Financial	−9.15%
SAFECO	−5.25%
Horace Mann	−0.73%
Mercury General	−0.49%
21st Century	36.49%
Commerce Group	38.67%
Progressive	44.07%
Vesta	58.02%

indication of the market's expectation of rising profitability attributed to an expectation that the increase in the price of risk will continue, especially in commercial line business written of large companies. The inference drawn from small capitalisation companies (Figure 7) is mixed. Personal lines companies reported in Figure 8 may benefit from an increased price for risk post-WTC event, although the benefit for personal lines may not be as significant as that expected for writers of large commercial accounts. In fact, personal lines are hardening because of capital rationing (redirecting capital away from personal lines into commercial lines with higher net present values (NPVs)) rather than due to recent loss experience. Generally, international companies (many of which are Lloyd's syndicates) reported in Figure 9 continue to experience a negative change in stock price following the WTC event, perhaps due to solvency problems, which will limit their ability to book significant amounts of new business regardless of the price.

Figure 9 International companies

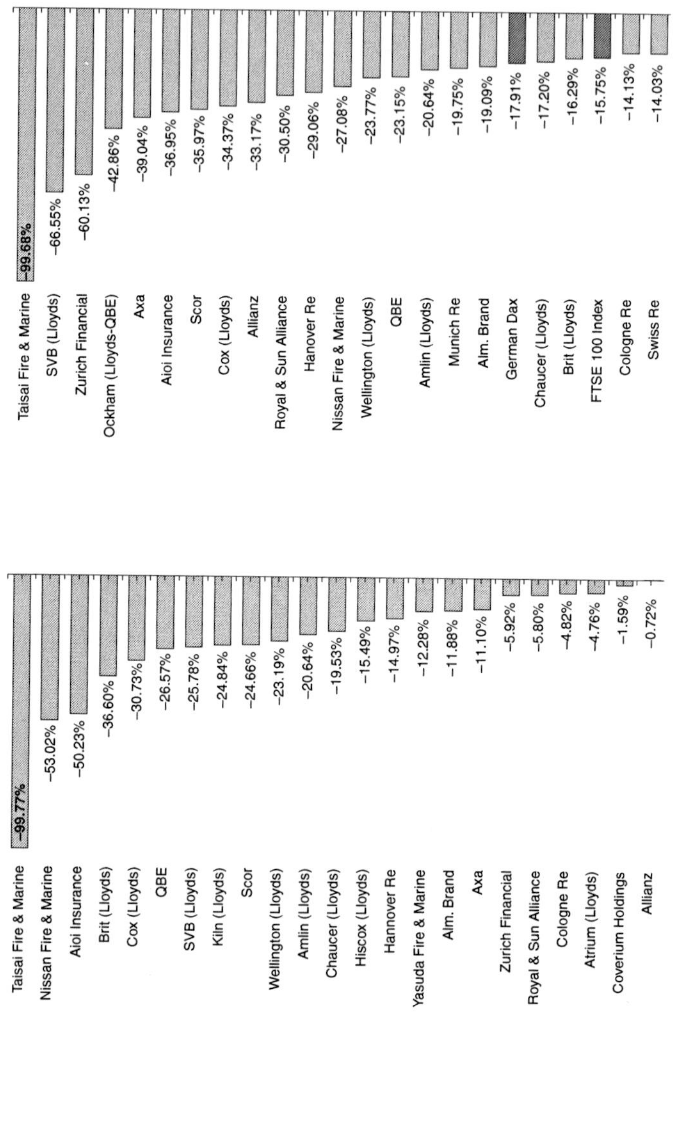

SECTION 2: RISK AND CAPITAL STRATEGIES POST SHOCK EVENT

Let us now turn our attention to the risk and capital management strategies of specific insurance companies. The strategies employed by companies include not only specific transactions such as pre-loss hedge strategies, leverage adjustments through share repurchases, floatation of debt, and issuance of equity but also their transparency with the financial market. We begin by looking to financial theory to draw inferences about risk and capital management. Financial theory will help us motivate a series of hypotheses regarding the effect of the various strategies and how these strategies send "signals" to external constituents. Then we select a sample of companies grouped into four categories – large capitalisation insurance companies (both domestic and international), personal line insurance companies, reinsurance companies and reinsurance brokers. We provide antidotal evidence about specific risk and capital strategies employed by these companies surrounding September 11 and observe stock market reactions. We conclude by discussing a more robust empirical test of cross sectional differences in firm-specific strategy by Doherty, Lamm-Tennant and Starks (2002). The objective is to understand the integration of risk management with capital management and to observe near term market response. It is important to emphasise that we are only observing the near term market response and the true underlying value to the firm-specific strategy may yet be realised.

Part A: risk and capital management strategies: hypotheses

While the capital constraint model is helpful in thinking about the pricing and capacity issues attributed to market shocks, other financial theories such as agency theory, risk overhang theory, pecking order theory, and hedging theory provide insights that are helpful in understanding specific firm strategies. Let us begin by developing a series of hypothesis from these theories to set forth a framework for thinking about the implications of firm-specific strategies.

Paramount to the capital constraint model is the belief that the economic loss attributed to an extreme event is not merely the loss itself, but the ability of the firm to capitalise on the new investment opportunities (due to increase demand) at higher NPVs (due to hardening markets). We can draw a series of hypothesis from this theory suggesting differences in firms' response to September 11 when the markets opened as well as their recovery in stock price following September 11.

> *Hypothesis 1: Large capitalisation insurers (most of which had significant exposure to the WTC event) would suffer from a significant decline in stock value, holding the general market effect aside. Following September 11, the stock values of large capitalisation insurers will behave differently depending on their ability to capitalise on the hardening markets. (Note: the differences in their ability to capitalise on hardening markets will be further specified by agency theory and the pecking order theory.)*

Hypothesis 2: Personal lines insurers not only avoided the loss attributed to WTC but also experience less post-event price hardening. Personal line insurers will experience less stock price volatility relative to large capitalisation firms, holding the general market effect aside. That is, personal lines firms avoided the loss by the very nature of the risk they write, but are faced with less profitable investment opportunities post-event.

Hypothesis 3: The majority of the loss attributed to September 11 will be borne by reinsurers due to the nature of the non-proportional reinsurance contract. Therefore, holding the market effect aside, reinsurers will experience an even greater decline in stock value relative to large capitalisation insurers. Similar to large capitalisation insurers, the reinsurers' stock values will behave differently following September 11 depending on their ability to capitalise on the hardening markets. (Note: the differences in their ability to capitalise on hardening markets will be further specified by agency theory and the pecking order theory.)

Hypothesis 4: Brokers are not insurable risk-takers. Therefore, general market effects (versus company effects) will explain the decline in stock price around September 11. Brokers are positioned to profit following the WTC event since they can capitalise on higher brokerage fees due to higher prices for insurance/reinsurance. Therefore, following the immediate stock market effects of September 11 brokers will experience rising stock prices.

Agency theory suggests that conflicts and mis-aligned incentives between the "agents" (shareholders, creditors, policyholders, employees, etc) in the business model will result in the loss of economic value. Shock events will exacerbate the consequence of the mis-alignment in incentives. For example, if an extreme shock event renders the firm "solvency impaired" the conflict between shareholders and creditors or policyholders will be ignited. Each agent will have an incentive to render decisions in their own self-interest. For example, the firm may fail to exploit subsequent investment opportunities with positive 'NPV's value because the value provided would not accrue to the contributors of equity capital but instead would simply prop up the debt otherwise in default. This dysfunctional investment behaviour results in the loss of economic value and is attributed to agency conflicts exacerbated by shock events. A hypothesis motivated by agency theory postulates the following:

Hypothesis 5: The ability of the firm to recover after September 11 will be negatively related to their post-loss leverage. That is, firms that are capital constrained following September 11 (ie, firms with the most significant loss due to the event and/or the greatest pre-loss leverage) will have the weakest recovery.

The pecking order theory (Myers and Majluf, 1984) suggests that insurers will respond to an extreme event by reducing capacity and slowly building surplus internally since internal capital is less expensive than external capital. The cost differential in capital is attributed to agency problems (previously discussed) as well as information asymmetries. But informational asymmetry (management having access to more information than external contributors of capital) coupled with an extraordinary opportunity for profitable investment that cannot be postponed will cause management to seek new capital in the external markets. The pecking order theory suggests information is "signalled" by the corporation's choice of external capital (debt vs equity). For example, if management anticipates "dark clouds on the horizon", then they will acquire new capital by issuing equity; whereas if management anticipates prosperity, then they will acquire new capital by issuing debt. If prosperity is anticipated, the corporation will prefer debt capital to equity capital because all the residual benefit resulting from the unusually large number of investment opportunities with positive NPVs will accrue to the initial shareholders. The signalling effect is heightened the less transparent the business, ie, the more likely information asymmetries. That is, asymmetry is greatest in industries whose cost structure is less obvious, such as insurance. On the contrary, if management anticipates difficult times ahead, they will elect to acquire new capital via the equity markets. An incentive exists such that the corporation would dilute the effect of bad times on existing shareholders by inviting in new shareholders.

Pecking order theory suggests that due to information asymmetry and agency costs, corporations will issue new shares if they anticipate "dark clouds on the horizon" or in situations where management thinks the shares are overvalued. Alternatively, management will elect to issue new shares in the unlikely event that they have extraordinarily profitable investments that cannot be either postponed or financed by debt. Issuing new shares of stocks therefore signals the following:

(1) the shares are overvalued, or
(2) dark clouds are on the horizon, or
(3) they have profitable opportunities ahead but could not access the debt markets; all of which are negative signals.

Since investors recognise these signals, the stock price will be driven down by the announcement of an equity offering regardless of the profit potential ahead. As of January 2002, Morgan Stanley reported that 44 property-casualty insurers/reinsurers have completed capital raising activities following the WTC event and an additional 18 attempts are pending (at the time of writing). Of the completed transactions, 13 involved the issuance of debt or hybrid financing, five involved both debt and equity and the remaining 26 transactions involved stock issuance. Of the pending transactions, nine involve both debt and equity while nine involve stock issuance. According to Morgan Stanley's Insurance and Risk Briefing dated February

8, 2002, eleven property-casualty insurers/reinsurers have announced share repurchases. Two hypotheses are motivated by pecking order theory as following:

Hypothesis 6: The ability of the firm to recover after September 11 will be negatively related to the pursuit of new "equity" capital post event. To the contrary, the ability of the firm to recover after September 11 will be positively related to the pursuit of new "debt" capital post event subject to the prior hypothesis regarding post-event leverage.

Hypothesis 7: Since companies will issue new shares if they believe that the existing shares are overvalued then the corollary is true – the company will repurchase existing shares if they believe those shares are undervalued. Also, share repurchases may be motivated by the absence of profitable investment opportunities or by the desire to change the firm's capital structure.

Two models explaining why firms manage risk or why firms hedge (Doherty, 1985; Froot, Scharfstein and Stein, 1992) provide insights relevant to understanding the effect of hedging. (In the case of an insurance company, reinsurance is a pre-loss hedge.) There is "duality" associated with risk management – that is, management can either remove the risk (ie, hedging) or remove the consequence of the risk (ie, de-leveraging the firm). Therefore, we think of a hedge as having the same benefits previously discussed with regards to capital management – hedging allows the firm to finance new investment opportunities with internal funds because the cost of the extreme event is borne by the counterparty to the hedge. In the case of September 11, insurance companies that hedged the cost of the event by buying reinsurance are capable of transferring the cost to the reinsurer; and consequently these firms can finance post-loss investment opportunities with internal funds. Doherty argues that pre-loss hedging offers additional advantages in contrast to post-loss external funding. Hedging permits managers to avoid the monitoring associated with external funding of post-loss investment choices. Firms that hedged the risk associated with September 11 do experience some unique confounding events making it difficult to draw hypothesis from the theory. Many insurance companies heavily reinsured the loss of September 11 and therefore reported significant gross-net ratios. Nevertheless, the credit quality of the reinsurance recoverables became an issue since some reinsurance companies may have been impaired. In addition, the nature of the hedge is somewhat unclear – that is, excess of loss (non-proportional) reinsurance can be perceived as a "loan" of capital as opposed to a transfer of risk. There may be some expectation of payback on the part of the reinsurer. These expectations are largely subject to the verbal agreement, more so than the precise language of the contract. Therefore holding aside the credit quality of the reinsurer as well as the payback consequence of the agreement, hedging theory would lead us to postulate the following:

Hypothesis 8: The establishment of a pre-loss hedge is positively related to the firm's ability to recover following the event.

Gron and Winton (2001) extended the work of Froot, Scharfstein and Stein (1993) by considering how the structure of the insurer's existing book of business will affect its ability to recover from an extreme shock. Their concept of "risk overhang" suggests that insurers with risky, long-tailed lines of business will be hardest hit and will experience greater difficulty in recovering from an extreme shock because the "risk overhang" exacerbates the agency problems. Furthermore, the lack of transparency attributed to the risk overhang (ie, the risky, long-tailed book of business) will make it difficult for these firms to raise capital post-event. Risk overhang may explain cross sectional differences in the depth of the response and the speed of recovery of individual firms to September 11.

Hypothesis 9: Insurers with the greatest concentration in high-risk, long-tailed lines will be affected more severely and will recover more slowly than firms with concentration in short-tailed lines.

Collectively these theories carry a set of predictions about the impact of September 11 across insurance companies. Let us now focus on behavioural issues such as differences in the degree of transparency across firms. Firms behaved differently in communicating with the financial markets following September 11. In the days following the WTC event, the economy plunged into what has been coined the "fear economy". The financial markets confirmed the fear of uncertainty. When the stock market opened on September 17, the DJIA dropped 7% by end of day with an additional 1.8% drop in the following two days – the DJIA reached it lowest level since December 1998. The equity market reaction spanned the world markets. In the week ending September 19 the percentage change in the DJIA was -8.8% vs -7.0% for the S&P 500, -3.3% for London FTSE 100, -5.5% for Paris CAS 40, and -6.8% for Frankfurt DAX.[4] Unlike other catastrophic events, the fear surrounding WTC event did not end on September 11. The world remained in lingering fear of future attempts and the looming war on terrorism. The estimate of loss associated with the WTC event range from a low of US$25 billion by Goldman Sachs to a high of US$100 billion with the average estimate of US$45.3 billion. Expected losses vary widely primarily due to the difficulties in estimating the loss associated with business interruption and workers compensation.[5]

Increased uncertainty gave rise to both the demand for transparency and to opportunistic behaviour.[6] Some insurance companies were vigilant in reporting estimated net losses prior to the market opening on September 17 while other insurers either delayed or may have withheld information. Thirty-seven insurers/reinsurers/Lloyds associations estimated net losses totalling US$13.6 billion before the markets opened on September 17. These "early reporters" revised their loss estimates numerous times (generally upwards) and eventually additional insurers reported their net loss. As of February 2002, approximately 150 insurers/reinsurers/Lloyds associations have reported losses totalling US$25.8 billion. Eventually, firms began reporting not only their net loss estimate but also their gross exposure. As of February 2001, 56 primary insurers have reported an average gross loss of US$30.4 billion with an average net of US$10.6 billion. The average of the gross-net ratio is 2.87. Twenty-six reinsurers have reported an average gross loss of US$18.8 billion with an average net loss of US$11.6 billion (average gross-net ratio of 2.19). Clearly, these estimates suggest that as of February 2002, has not accounted for total industry losses. The vagaries in accountability for losses coupled with concerns surrounding the likelihood of reinsurance recoverables and the financial well being of Lloyd's result in a heightened need for transparency.

We therefore derive a series of hypothesis regarding transparency. We believe firms will be rewarded for transparency. That is, firms will be rewarded for early announcement of net losses. With regards to gross losses, we recognise the uncertainty regarding reinsurance recoverables. On one hand, a high gross-net ratio may indicate the savvy of the insurer in arranging for a pre-loss hedge. On the other hand, recoveries from the pre-loss hedge may not be collectible depending on the credit quality of the reinsurer. We recognise what may be a "lemons" problem. Firms will early announce gross losses if and only if their reinsurance was placed with high quality reinsurers. A delay in announcing or unwillingness to announce gross losses infers the opposite – poor credit exposure to reinsurers. Hence the size of the gross-net ratio is not meaningful, but instead the act of announcing gross losses is

> *Hypothesis 10:* *While firms with higher net losses would have greater stock price decline, early announcement of net losses will ballast the decline in stock price – that is, firms would be rewarded for transparency.*

> *Hypothesis 11:* *Firms that announce gross losses regardless of the size of gross loss relative to net loss will ballast the decline in stock price.*

Part B: risk and capital management: evidence

We select a sample of companies and grouped them into four categories – large capitalisation insurance companies (both domestic and international), personal line insurance companies, reinsurance companies and reinsurance brokers. For each company we have prepared a stock price graph illustrating the cumulative percentage change in stock price from July 3, 2001 to December 31, 2001. The stock price charts for each group of industry participants appear in Figure 10 through Figure 13. We then provide antidotal evidence about specific risk and capital strategies employed by these companies. Using this antidotal evidence and the hypotheses derived from financial theory, we attempt to understand both the signals sent by management as well as the financial markets response. We conclude Section 2, Part B by summarising a more robust empirical test of cross-sectional differences in firm strategy by Doherty, Lamm-Tennant and Starks (2002). It is important to emphasise that we are only observing the near term market response and the true underlying value to the firm-specific strategy may yet be realised.

Figure 10a and 10b illustrate the cumulative percentage change in stock price for four large capitalisation property-casualty insurers. Figure 10a illustrates the stock price graphs of American International Group (AIG) and Chubb, both whose stock prices declined immediately following September 11 but subsequently increased. Figure 10b illustrates the stock price graphs of Royal & SunAlliance (RSA) and AXA Group (AXA), both whose stock price declined immediately following September 11 and

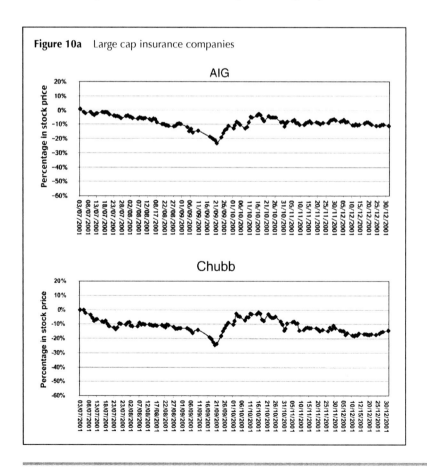

Figure 10a   Large cap insurance companies

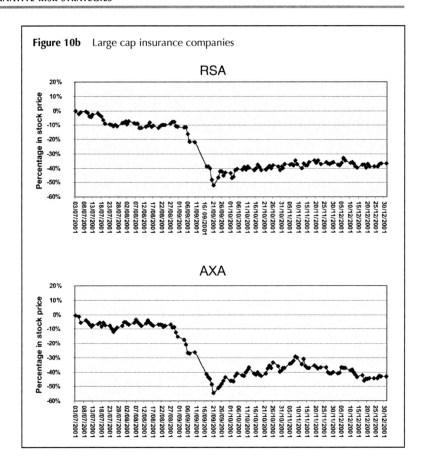

Figure 10b Large cap insurance companies

whose stock price remained depressed thereafter. Given that all four insurers were significantly exposed to losses due to the WTC event, we are not surprised by the immediate decline. One might question the underlying factors explaining the recovery of AIG and Chubb vs the sustained depressed stock value of RSA and AXA. Between 1991 and 2000, AIG's stock price performance increased an average 29% per year vs a 17% average annual rise in the Standard & Poor's 500. From January 1, 2001 up to the WTC event, AIG 's shares lost 25% of their value due to investor concerns over the effects of slowing economies in Asia and potential liabilities in the US. On September 14 2001, AIG's board authorised a stock buyback of 40 million shares (approximately US$3 billion) in excess of the 10 million shares authorised on September 5 2001. The share repurchase followed an announcement of a US$500 million expected net loss which was released on September 13. The estimate of the net loss was subsequently revised upward to US$820 million with a gross loss estimate of US$2.1 billion released on October 9 (gross-net ratio equal to 2.56). On October 12, AIG announced that its board revoked its previous authorisation to purchase shares in the open market in excess of 10 million shares. Two weeks following the WTC attack, AIG announced that it would write aviation war risk and hijacking liability coverage. On November 11, AIG completed a US$1 billion issuance of convertible debt. AIG, along with Chubb and Goldman Sachs sponsored the Bermuda start-up, Allied World Assurance Co. Ltd. AIG's stock price performance is aligned with the hypothesis derived from financial theory. Their capital raising activities and, in particular, their choice of debt capital is consistent with signalling management's anticipation of good news on the horizon. AIG was quick to embrace new business – especially risky new business having high expected returns. AIG announced net losses prior to the market opening on September 17 and signalled to the market that although the gross was many multiples times the net, the credit quality of the reinsures was exceptional. Chubb announced US$150 million net losses on September 17 and then revised the net loss estimate to US$550 million on September 20 and to US$645 million on October 30. Chubb announced a gross loss of US$3 billion on November 2 (gross-net ratio of 4.65). While the gross-net ratio is one of the highest in the industry, Chubb reported the information early along with a statement assuring the investment community of the reinsurer's credit quality. Chubb also participated in the Bermuda start-up, Allied World Assurance Co. Ltd. Chubb's transparency with the financial markets in spite of the significance of the loss, along with their capital activities, is consistent with the stock price recovery hypothesised by financial theory.

AXA and RSA have yet – at the time of writing – to recover from the initial decline following September 11. Neither company announced share repurchases since the WTC event. RSA has not participated in debtor equity capital raising activities since September 11 and AXA announced, although has not completed, a stock offering of US$223 million. AXA reported net losses in the amount of US$350 million and revised the estimate on September 21 to US$550 million. AXA has not reported gross loss estimates. RSA reported US$220 million net losses on September 17 and revised the estimate to US$300 on October 10. On November 9, RSA reduced their estimate of net losses to US$294 million and reported their gross loss estimate equal to US$1.090 billion. While RSA did eventually report gross estimates, they were late to the market with the estimate – many estimates of gross loss were released in early October. While RSA and AXA did report net losses in a timely fashion to the financial markets, they were less transparent with regards to gross figures. AXA's pending stock offering would be consistent with the belief that issuance of equity (as opposed to debt) signals bad times on the horizon. RSA refrained from raising capital in the financial markets. Also international property-casualty insurers are notorious for carrying a greater proportion of invested assets in the equity markets than do domestic insurers. Given that September 11 was both an insurance market event and a capital market event, RSA's and AXA's position in equities along with their liability exposure resulted in an aggregation of risk across the balance sheet. According to financial theory, these activities and behaviourism would be consistent with a decline in stock price without a subsequent recovery.

Figure 11 illustrates the cumulative percentage change in stock price for two personal line property-casualty insurers – Progressive and Allstate. Both insurers experienced a modest decline immediately following September 11 that could be attributed to general market effects. Consistent with the hypotheses set forth by financial theory, September 11 was less of an event for personal line insurers than for commercial line insurers. Following September 11, both Progressive and Allstate enjoyed a modest stock price rally – also consistent with the hypotheses set forth by financial theory.

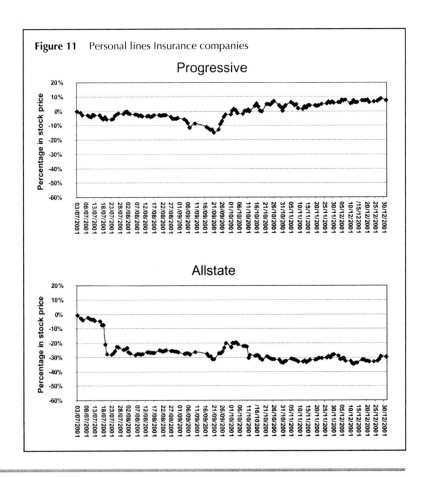

Figure 11   Personal lines Insurance companies

Figure 12a and 12b illustrates the cumulative percentage change in stock price for five reinsurers. Figure 12a illustrates the stock price graph of Berkshire Hathaway (General Reinsurance), Swiss Re and Munich Re whose stock prices declined immediately following September 11, but

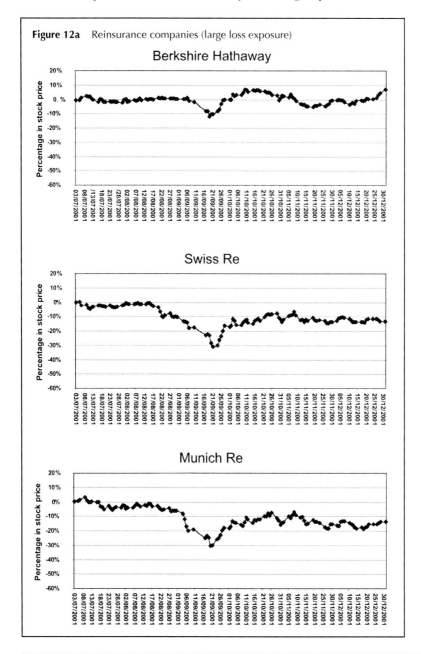

Figure 12a Reinsurance companies (large loss exposure)

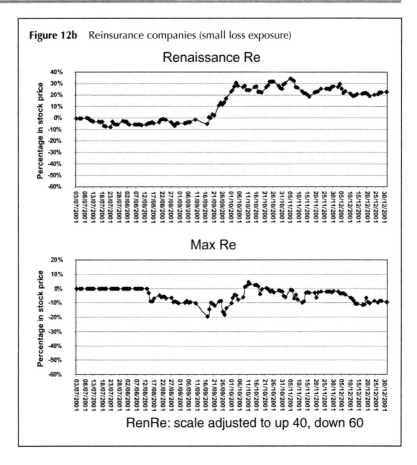

Figure 12b   Reinsurance companies (small loss exposure)

Renaissance Re

Max Re

RenRe: scale adjusted to up 40, down 60

subsequently increased. Figure 12b illustrates the stock price graphs of Renaissance Re and Max Re whose stock price was largely enhanced by the events surrounding September 11. Given that the three reinsures illustrated in Figure 12a were significantly exposed to losses due to the WTC event, we are not surprised by the immediate decline. Renaissance Re and Max Re were unaffected by losses due to the WTC event but engaged in opportunistic behaviour following September 11 along with capital raising activities. Berkshire Hathaway, Swiss Re and Munich Re reported net losses prior to the market opening on September 17 and subsequently revised their estimates. Berkshire Hathaway was the only company to report losses as a per cent of total, although the financial press mapped the estimate into US dollar losses. The net exposure for Berkshire Hathaway was estimated to be US$1.2 billion as of September 17 and latter revised to US$2.2 billion as of September 20 and eventually US$2.48 billion along with a gross loss approximately equal to the net. Swiss Re reported a net loss of US$720 million on September 17 and revised the estimate to US$1.25

billion on September 20 and US$1.615 on September 28 (the gross was esti-
mated to be equal to the net). Munich Re (including American Re) reported
a net loss of US$910 million on September 17 that was revised to US$2 billion on September 20 alongside of a gross loss estimate of US$3 billion.
Swiss Re completed capital raising activities totalling US$1.6 billion using
both debt and equity markets on November 11. Neither Munich Re nor
Berkshire Hathaway reported capital raising activities. To the contrary,
both Max Re and Renaissance Re actively engaged in capital activities.
Renaissance Re was the first to complete the acquisition of new capital. On
October 15, Renaissance Re completed the issuance of US$233 million of
equity. On November 14, Renaissance Re completed the issuance of
US$150 million of preferred debt. Renaissance Re along with State Farm
announced the formation of a Bermuda start-up, DaVinci Reinsurance Ltd.
Max Re announced a share repurchase on September 17 up to US$15 mil-
lion and again on September 27 up to US$25 million. Neither Max Re nor
Renaissance Re experienced significant exposure to the WTC event – Max

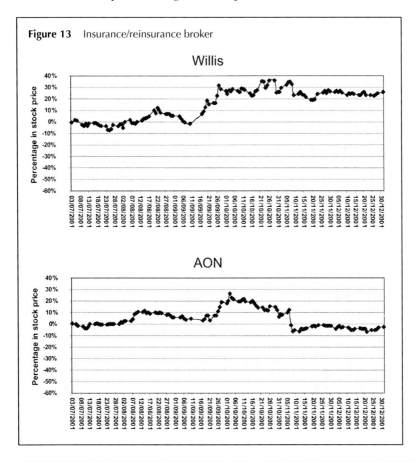

Figure 13   Insurance/reinsurance broker

Re reported a net loss of US$4 million and Renaissance Re reports US$48 million net loss. Financial theory suggest that the aggressive capital management activities as well as the modest loss exposure of Max Re and Renaissance Re may account for the rise in stock price following September 11.

Figure 13 illustrate the cumulative percentage change in stock price for two insurance brokers – Willis and Aon. Both brokers experienced a modest decline immediately following September 11. This decline could be attributed to general market effects. Consistent with the hypotheses set forth by financial theory, September 11 was a positive event for brokers since they will enjoy the benefits of higher brokerage fees due to hardening insurance/reinsurance prices. Following September 11, both Willis and Aon enjoyed a healthy stock price rally – also consistent with the hypotheses set forth by financial theory.

Doherty, Lamm–Tennant and Starks (2002) employ a more robust empirical methodology to evaluate cross-sectional differences in risk and capital management strategies and stock prices surrounding September 11. Using 95 publicly traded insurers/reinsurers/brokers along with daily stock price data and time-dated announcements of losses and capital market activities; Doherty, Lamm-Tennant and Starks (2002) provide preliminary evidence in support of many of the previously cited hypotheses. At the time this book is published, the analysis by Doherty, Lamm–Tennant and Starks is preliminary. Nevertheless, their analysis is indicative of the differences between large capitalisation insurers, personal line insurers, broker and reinsurers. In addition, they report evidence in support of the value of transparency as well as the importance of being early to the market with information – that is, the value of transparency declines for late reporters. Their analysis also supports the hypothesis regarding leverage. Firms with the greatest post-event leverage experienced the weakest recovery in stock price.

Section 3: practical implications for risk managers

While the risk manager is not directly responsible for stock price, they do value the stock market's reaction to their decisions. Most importantly, risk and capital management is an integrated set of decisions. We cannot separate risk management strategy from capital management strategy. Duality does exist – we can either remove the risk (risk management) or eliminate its effect (capital management). Second, the financial markets do appear to be rational in differentiating between the risk and return opportunities of commercial insurers, personal insurers, reinsurers and brokers. Commercial insurers were initially penalised relative to net losses. Given evidence of opportunistic behaviour supported by capital raising activities, a recovery in stock price was experienced. Personal insures were largely unaffected by Sept 11 – exonerated from losses but subsequent price increases are limited. Brokers had everything to gain – not exposed to the loss but positioned to profit from increasing brokerage fees. Decline in stock price for reinsurers was dependent on their loss exposure and the subsequent risk was fuelled by opportunistic behaviour coupled with capital market activities. Third, transparency is rewarded. All things equal, the decline in the stock price for firms that were early announcers of losses enjoyed a buffer in the decline in stock price. The buffer or reward for reporting diminished for firms that reported late. Fourth, firms were rewarded (stock price decline was buffered) who actively participated in the acquisition of new capital post WTC event or who announced share buy backs immediately following the WTC event. Fifth, firms with higher post loss leverage may fail to exploit post-loss investment opportunities dampening the stock rally post WTC event. Sixth, firms that hedged risks (buying reinsurance) are able to fund post-loss opportunities internally vs acquiring capital externally after the event when the cost of capital is high. Consequently, the market did not penalise firms with high gross-net ratios. Seventh, risk asymmetry (fearing losses more than loving gains) may dampen their desire to exploit post WTC event opportunities and therefore dampened the subsequent stock rally.

CONCLUSION

September 11 was an extreme event that was unanticipated yet the market responded expediently and rationally. Consistent with the capital constraint model, the shock to capital was followed by price increases and by a subsequent inflow of new capital. This was not a single risk event but linked risk events – business risk, hazard risk, and capital market risk. Therefore, risk managers have a heightened interest in understanding the correlations and aggregations across risk classes. Also, the awareness of risk management and capital management is heightened and the role of the risk manager is more visible. Finally, corporate governance will be more active with increased interest in rigorous risk/capital management and in stress testing the assumptions as well as imaginative solutions.

1   The terrorist attacks on the World Trade Center towers will be the most costly man-made catastrophe in US history, according to the Insurance Information Institute. The 1993 World Trade Center bombing caused US$510 million in insured losses. The 1995 Oklahoma City bombing resulted in insured losses of US$125 million. The Los Angeles riots of 1992 resulted in insured losses of US$775 million, previously the most costly insured man-made disaster at the time of writing. As of January 11, 2002, the Morgan Stanley estimate of the loss attributed to the World Trade Center towers ranged from US$50 billion to US$55 billion (including both life and non-life). Estimates are rendered by numerous sources with the average loss estimate for non-life insurers being US$45.3 billion.

2   Lamm–Tennant and Weiss (1997) provide a review of the literature regarding international underwriting cycles, empirical evidence of the existence of underwriting cycles internationally and across numerous lines of business and empirical support attributing cycles to institutional interventions.

3   While the model sets price equal to the expected value of losses plus expenses, this is an over-simplification. A profit expectation for the insurer must also be recognised. This reward for risk assumption is a function of the insurer's utility or appetite for risk and perhaps the portfolio effect of the specific risk.

4   By October 24 the world markets recovered somewhat with the percentage change in the index from September 10 to October 24 being –2.0% for the DJIA, –0.0% for the S&% 500, –0.0% for London FTSE 100, +1.5% for Paris CAS 40, +2.0 for Frankfurt DAX. The US US$18 trillion bond markets experienced difficulty in settling and clearing trades when it reopened two days after the WTC attack – volume was 50% of normal yet the market extended the time for settling bond trades to five days from one day and dealer spreads sharply widened. The US high yield spreads on B-rated debt widened to 948 basis points on September 30 vs 300 basis points in 1997 (1000 basis points during the 1990–91 recession). Moody's annual default rates for speculative grade corporate debt increased to 8.29% in September 2001 vs a 30-year average of 3.9% (peaked at 10.5% in 1991).

5   Even property losses estimates vary due to pending litigation needed to determine whether the event is consider a single event or multiple events.

6   The collapse of Enron in the fourth quarter of 2001 heightened the value of transparency.

BIBLIOGRAPHY

Doherty, N., 1985, *Corporate Risk Management: A Financial Exposition*, (McGraw Hill).

Doherty, N., Lamm-Tennant, J. and Starks, L, 2002, "Market Shocks and The Value of Transparency", Working Paper.

Froot, K., Scharfstein, D. and Stein, J., 1993, "Risk Management: Coordinating Corporate Investment and Financing Policies," *Journal of Finance* 48, pp. 1629–58.

Gron, A, 1994, "Capacity Constraints and Cycles in Property-Casualty Insurance Markets," *Rand Journal of Economics* 25, pp. 110–27.

Gron, A and Winton, A, 2001, "Risk Overhang and Market Behavior," *Journal of Business* 74, pp. 591–612.

Lamm-Tennant, J. and Weiss, M., 1997, "International Insurance Cycles: Rational Expectations/Institutional Intervention," *Journal of Risk and Insurance*, 64 (3), pp. 414–39.

Lamm-Tennant, J., 1999, "Economic Value Added of the Property-Casualty Insurance Industry," Working Paper.

Myers, S. and Majluf, N., 1984, Corporate Investment and Financing Decisions When Firms Have Information That Investors Do Not Have," *Journal of Financial Economics*, 13, pp. 187–222.

Winter, R., 1988, "The Liability Insurance Crisis and The Dynamics on Competitive Insurance Markets." *Yale Journal of Regulation*, 5, pp. 455–99.

Venezian, E., 1988, "Ratemaking Methods and Profit Cycles in Property and Liability Insurance, *Journal of Risk and Insurance*, 52, pp. 477–500.

Part 3

Assessing individual risks by modelling

13

Natural Catastrophe Loss Modelling

Mahmoud Khater and Dennis E. Kuzak

EQECAT Inc

The purpose of this chapter is to provide the reader with an introduction to the concepts and the technical methodology employed in natural catastrophe (cat) loss modelling. The development of the insurance-linked catastrophe securities markets could not have occurred without the rigorous risk quantification provided by the use of such models, as investors and rating agencies place significant (but not total) reliance on modelled results in assessing risk of loss and required pricing. These models have therefore become an essential ingredient in structuring these securities, and assisting ceding companies in managing their overall catastrophe risk positions.

INTRODUCTION

First, this chapter will ask the question of why we need such models, and why they take a probabilistic vs deterministic form. This will be followed by a survey of the general types of perils and regions in the world in which models have been developed to date. The main part of the chapter discusses the probabilistic modelling methodology, reviewing the various modules including the hazard and damage modules, defining the portfolio of risks, estimation of financial losses, and typical outputs. The balance of the chapter will discuss model uncertainty considerations, and demonstrate the role of cat models in an Alternative Risk Transfer (ART) example. Finally, the chapter will conclude with a section on alternative loss triggers in ART transactions, and how these models are being used in this newly evolving aspect of the market.

WHY DO WE NEED NATURAL CATASTROPHE MODELS?

A simple example that vividly demonstrates the case for why we need catastrophe models is Hurricane Andrew, 1992. At that time, catastrophe models were only beginning to be developed and were not generally available within the insurance industry. Instead, insurance rates, which are

based on the expectation of future claims costs, were traditionally estimated by extrapolating loss results from the past. Prior to Hurricane
Andrew, in Florida, an "excess wind procedure" model was used by
Insurance Services Office (ISO) to estimate the additional costs to property
insurance associated with hurricane events. This approach relied on a 30-
year historical average of storm losses, which were assumed to occur at the
same rate in the future. Underlying this future expectation were implicit
assumptions that the prior 30-year storm pattern was "normal", that population (and property) distributions were constant, and that construction
quality was consistent. Reviewing those assumptions, almost 10 years after
Hurricane Andrew, shows that they were grossly in error; the 1960–1990
storm pattern was abnormally low, when viewed in the context of 100
years of Florida hurricane data, which resulted in an underestimation of
loss frequency. Furthermore, the population surged, especially in high hazard coastal areas, and was accompanied by less than acceptable housing
construction practices.

Thus the loss severity potential also was significantly understated. In one
event, Hurricane Andrew shocked the insurance industry out of its com-
placency towards catastrophic risk. In 1992, ISO using the traditional
excess wind procedure model calculated a hurricane provision for Florida
homeowners' writers of US$80 million annually. At that premium rate, it
would take the industry over 100 years to recover their losses from
Andrew and they would still not be able to provide for premium for other
future storms. Twelve insurers became insolvent, and other major property
insurers (principally personal lines companies) threatened to withdraw
from the market, precipitating a rate crisis that still has politicians searching for a solution other than higher rates.

Hurricane Andrew demonstrated a number of risk characteristics that
were not being recognised by traditional actuarial methods, which rely on
historical loss data. First, insurance rates are based on future loss occurrences, but developed on past experience. Large cat events, (ie, low
probability and high severity) fortunately occur only infrequently, but
yield only limited loss data, making it difficult to use past experience to
establish adequate rates. Second, the low frequency of events provides no
assurance that future scientifically credible events may occur, even though
they have not occurred in the past. Also, the future loss vulnerability is a
function of changing building and land use development practices (ie, zon-
ing) which historical information does not capture.

Therefore, what is needed is a model that is prospective in risk estimation, not retrospective. In addition, considerable scientific and engineering
uncertainty is involved, partly due to the inherent randomness of the physical events and partly due to the lack of complete understanding on the
precise quantification of damage and loss. In addition, the large number of
computational factors, such as frequency, wind speed, peak gust wind

speed, building damageability, are not necessarily independent; correlation between these may alter the loss severity expectations. Hence a model using single-point parameters (ie, a deterministic) for simulation of future losses will not be able to adequately estimate the risk associated with these events, or the loss potential to investors. Most models have utilised a probabilistic construction, which treats many of the loss parameters as random variables. This permits simulating potential loss events over a wide range of parametric variations, which is characteristic of the underlying physical aspects of natural catastrophes. The resulting loss estimates from a probabilistic model include probabilities of losses exceeding a specified value (attachment probability), the probability that the loss would exceed some upper limit (exhaustion probability), and the expected loss to this risk, defined as level between the attachment point and exhaustion point. These loss measures are very similar to the credit market parameters of default probabilities and expected loss recoveries. The models, in essence, provide the risk-bridge between insurance-related risks and credit market risks, enabling insurance-linked securities to receive credit ratings that are essential in the fixed-income debt markets.

TYPICAL MODELLED PERILS
Initial development of probabilistic cat models were directed at the insurance and reinsurance industry and focused on regions of high insurance exposures to perils that had the potential of producing very large, Hurricane Andrew-style losses. Hence, the first models logically focused on the United States. In terms of loss-potential regions, "Florida/East Coast Hurricane" and "California Earthquake" generated the most cat exposures and loss potential and hence were modelled first. Subsequently, models were developed for other high loss-potential regions including "Japan Earthquake and Typhoon", "European Windstorm", and "US Tornado". Over time, probabilistic flood models for the US and Europe have evolved, as well as earthquake models for the southern and eastern Mediterranean, Middle East, Canada, and Latin America. Other modelled regions include Australia, New Zealand, South East Asia, Taiwan and China. In most cases, insurance and reinsurance exposures have dictated the priority and robustness of the country/peril model. Model uses include underwriting and risk screening, portfolio risk management, claims management, solvency analysis (in conjunction with financial planning models), pricing, and risk transfer (reinsurance or retro covers). Naturally, the models were also relied on to provide the risk analysis necessary in the ART markets, especially insurance-linked securities.

MODELLING METHODOLOGY
This section describes the methodology typically found in probabilistic cat loss models. Since multiple vendors as well as large reinsurers have created

such models, the following description cannot characterise all such models. But it is believed that most probabilistic models have the same general approach and model outputs. However, each vendor or model builder will approach the risk quantification in a different manner. Therefore, model results may vary from one model to another, with equally credible alternate assessments of the same risks.

Defining exposures

The first step in modelling cat losses is to determine what is subject to loss. Software models can usually handle various levels of information, as illustrated in Figure 1. The location of a portfolio of properties may be defined at the country level or it can be defined at the site level, ie, the longitude and the latitude (long/lat) of every site in the portfolio is defined. Also the total sum insured (TSI) can be defined for the entire portfolio at the county level or for every site in the portfolio separately.

This flexibility is usually built into the software since the available policy information varies between insurance companies. Some companies can provide detailed location and insurance information and others are only able to provide general information. The data provided by the insurance company can be analysed on an individual risk basis or aggregated in a number of ways (by geographical locations, by occupancy, and by structural type, for example), in order to meet specific needs. However, as shown in Figure 1, increasing levels of exposure information reduce the level of uncertainty in the analysis. In ART deals involving indemnity loss triggers, minimal standards of information have been developed which

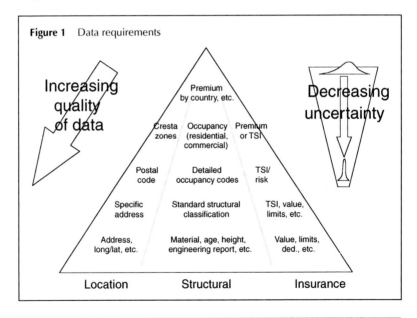

Figure 1 Data requirements

Increasing quality of data

Decreasing uncertainty

Location	Structural	Insurance
	Premium by country, etc.	
Cresta zones	Occupancy (residential, commercial)	Premium or TSI
Postal code	Detailed occupancy codes	TSI/ risk
Specific address	Standard structural classification	TSI, value, limits, etc.
Address, long/lat, etc.	Material, age, height, engineering report, etc.	Value, limits, ded., etc.

would be acceptable to the rating agencies and investors. Typically, this includes minimum standards for information on risk locations, value-at-risk, and primary insurance policy information.

OVERVIEW OF NATURAL DISASTER RISK ASSESSMENT

Once the assets at risk have been identified, the loss assessment methodology follows a general pattern, regardless of the kind of natural hazard being investigated (earthquake, tropical or extra-tropical cyclone, tornado, flood, for example). First, the hazard phenomenon is modelled based on historical and scientific information. The hazard intensity at the source is then propagated to hazard intensities at different sites away from the event location using attenuation models, eg, ground-motion attenuation models for earthquakes and time decay models for hurricanes (maximum wind speed decays with time). Once the intensity of the hazard (shaking intensity or gust wind speed) is estimated at a site, the induced damage to the property is quantified using vulnerability models. A prerequisite for assessing damage is to have appropriate inventory information, ie, as much information as possible on the physical characteristics of the assets. Losses are then computed based on the amount of damage and the characteristics of the insurance policy (deductibles and limits). Each step of the process involves dealing with stochastic or random variation associated with all aspects of the modelled phenomena. Consequently, the estimated damage and losses are defined probabilistically, ie, in terms of a probability distribution, moments, and/or probable maximum damages and losses. The process may be performed for a single event, eg, a scenario event, or repeated to analyse the effects of all possible events in a given time period, such as one year. In the latter case, the individual damage and loss estimates for each possible event are probabilistically aggregated to estimate the overall loss exceedance probabilities, expected (annual) damage and loss, and associated variability in damages and losses between events.

Overview of methodology

When assessing the risk (structural, content and business interruption (BI)), to which a property (or a set of properties) is exposed due to a possible natural disaster, the three modules of the model shown in Figure 2 (hazard, damage and loss) are used to perform a series of analyses.

Hazard module

The first phase of the analysis, the hazard module, involves estimating the hazard potential. Historic information, such as the frequency, location, and magnitude of past events, is used together with scientific information regarding the possible causes of the disaster. The hazard is estimated using either a semi-probabilistic or a full probabilistic definition of the disaster event. In the first case, a given scenario (eg, a repeat of a significant past

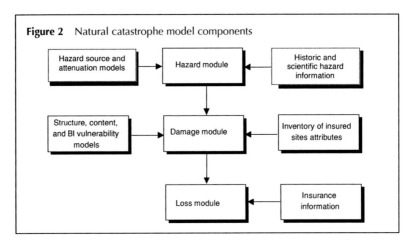

Figure 2 Natural catastrophe model components

event, a maximum possible event without consideration of its probability of occurrence, or an event with a certain probability of occurrence), or a series of scenarios, is selected and simulated. In the second case, a probabilistic analysis of all the major sources and magnitudes of the hazard is carried out, leading to a probabilistic description of occurrence of the hazard intensity through hazard curves. A hazard curve typically defines the probability of exceedance of a hazard intensity level in a given duration of time, usually one year.

The effect of an event of a given magnitude and its attenuation or amplification as it propagates from the source to a particular site is estimated as a function of the distance between the site and the event location, ie, the earthquake epicentre or hurricane landfall. These functions, called attenuation relations, are based on statistical studies, and are a function of the physical characteristics of the geology and terrain between hazard sources and sites. Local characteristics of the site are also accounted for in the attenuation relations. For example, local soil type and depth are included in ground-motion models and topographical variables are included in hurricane decay models. Probability distributions (as presented by the probability density function (PDF) in Figure 3) are derived for a hazard intensity variable at the site (eg, peak ground acceleration in the case of earthquakes, or gust wind speed for hurricanes), as shown in Figure 3.

Damage module
The second phase of the analysis, the damage module in Figure 2, involves two databases of input information and an estimation of the damage induced by the hazard at each site. One database is the inventory of insured site attributes; it contains all the relevant information of the portfolio members, including location (street or postal address, or latitude and longitude coordinates), value-at-risk, structure type (wood frame, rein-

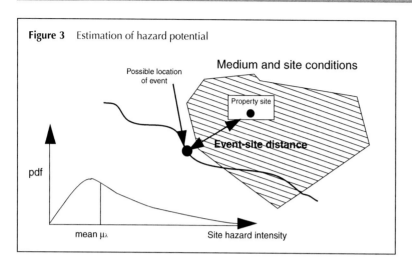

Figure 3 Estimation of hazard potential

forced concrete shear wall, etc), condition (quantified by a quality factor), occupancy, or use. This information is used in determining the potential damage. Development of this information is very important as the quality and accuracy of the information provided will have a significant effect on the level of uncertainty contained in the final loss estimate. For example, if the site address is known, the latitude and longitude coordinates of a portfolio member can be determined accurately, as can the soil characteristics at the site. On the other hand, if only the state location is known, more generic and less accurate soil conditions must be used. Between these two extremes, a range of data quality exists. Similarly, for the structural data, the best situation is when detailed information is available regarding material, age, design code, etc. However, it might be that the only data available is the occupancy type. As the quality of the information increases, so does the accuracy and quality of the damage estimates.

The second database provides inputs relevant to determining the relative vulnerability of buildings, contents and/or operations to the hazard intensity at the site of the property. Vulnerability is measured in terms of the damage factor, D, which is the ratio of the repair cost and the total insured value (TIV). Depending on the type of structural system (eg, frame or walls), the method and time of construction, the materials, etc, specific vulnerability models are defined, as shown in Figure 4.[1]

A vulnerability model consists of a vulnerability function – describing the mean or expected vulnerability as a function of the hazard intensity – and a coefficient of variation (COV) or standard deviation, describing the variation of the vulnerability given the hazard intensity, which is generally also a function of the hazard intensity.

Vulnerability functions typically have been developed on the basis of analyses of claims data from catastrophe events throughout the world,

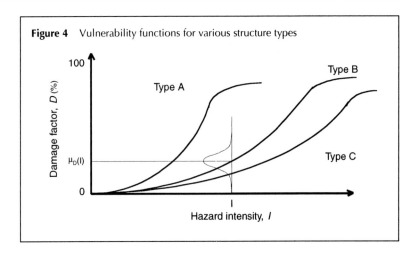

Figure 4   Vulnerability functions for various structure types

engineering-based analytical studies, expert opinions, testing, or a combination of all these. Vulnerability functions have been developed for
structural damage, as well as for business interruption losses and damage
to contents.

The potential hazard, vulnerability models, and site attributes are combined in the damage module to estimate the potential damage to
individual properties and the portfolio. For a particular value of the intensity of the hazard, and the type of structural system, a damage factor is
derived for each individual property. This factor expresses the relative cost
of repair that the structure is likely to need – in respect to its insured value
– if the property is hit by a hazard of a given intensity. The hazard module
yields a PDF of the hazard intensity at the site (eg, the hurricane wind
speed), as shown in Figure 5. For a given value of the hazard intensity, I, a
mean damage factor, $\mu_D(I)$, is obtained from the vulnerability function,
with its corresponding standard deviation, $\sigma_D(I)$, derived from the associated COV curve. Combining the vulnerability assessment over all values of
hazard intensity results in a probability distribution for the damage factor
described by the PDF in Figure 5. From this distribution the mean value,
μ_D, and standard deviation, σ_D, for the damage factor of a particular structure, contents, or BI can be obtained. The level of damage is calculated by
adjusting the damage factor by a quality factor (to account for any specific
structural characteristic of the site) and multiplying by the TIV. The damage for the entire portfolio is the statistical combination of the damages for
each individual property taking correlation into account.

Loss module
The third phase of analysis, the loss module in Figure 2, involves estimating the losses to the insurers. An important element of this calculation is

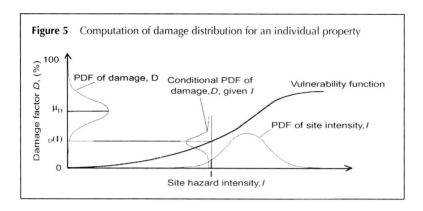

Figure 5 Computation of damage distribution for an individual property

the insurance information, which is, in general, expressed in terms of deductibles (d), limits (l), and TIV. The quality of the insurance data can vary from being crude to being very detailed, which will affect the level of uncertainty in the estimation of losses. The gross loss at a property or group of properties is a function of damage and the insurance information, d, l, and TIV, relevant to the properties. Figure 6 shows a typical relation between loss and damage, d, l, and TIV, for any given property. Combining the insurance information with the probability distribution of damage using the loss relation gives the analysis represented by the loss module in Figure 2. The probability distribution of gross loss is derived from the loss model (Figure 6) and the damage distribution (Figure 5).

Net loss to a primary insurer and losses to reinsurers are further calculated based on the insurance information relevant to facultative reinsurance and treaties. In all cases the relevant probabilistic information, (eg, the expected loss of a treaty layer) is based on the probabilistic information of the gross loss and the relation between the loss of interest, (eg, treaty layer loss) and gross loss.

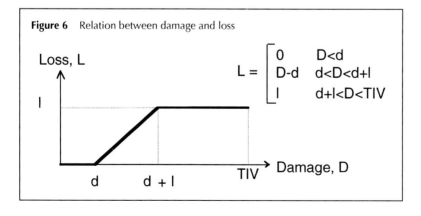

Figure 6 Relation between damage and loss

$$L = \begin{bmatrix} 0 & D<d \\ D-d & d<D<d+l \\ l & d+l<D<TIV \end{bmatrix}$$

Correlation

An important element in the analysis process is the consideration of the inherent correlation associated with many of the stochastic variables characterising potential losses due to catastrophic natural events. Correlation is a factor in the hazard due to a catastrophic event at various sites in a portfolio, as well as in the damage induced by the event. In the case of earthquake hazards, the shaking intensity at the various sites depends on the earthquake source variables (eg, magnitude, depth, epicentre location), the geological conditions of the travel path of the seismic waves, and the local soil conditions. It can be expected that the travel path and the local soil conditions at sites in close proximity to each other will be similar. Thus, it can be expected that the variability (deviation from its expected value) in the stochastic shaking intensity, ie, hazards, at sites close together to be more highly correlated than the ground-motions at sites some distance apart, which may be geologically quite different.

Similar expectations exist for hurricane hazards. The time decay of hurricane winds and the variation in wind speeds across the storm track once the hurricane has hit landfall is a function of several variables, including the radius of the hurricane, maximum wind speed, translational velocity (the hurricane forward speed), and the atmospheric conditions and terrain along its track. Again, it can be expected that the variability of wind speeds at sites close together will be more highly correlated then the variability of wind speeds at sites some distance apart. Correlation in the hazard between sites can be modelled in a probabilistic analysis by accounting for correlation in the development of sample vectors (across sites) of hazard intensities. For damage assessments, given a hazard's intensity, it can be expected that the variability of the damage for similar structures (ie, structures of the same type, material, age, etc), will be more similar than the variability of the damage for dissimilar structures. The same can be expected for damages between structures close to each other as compared to damages of structures that are some distance apart. For example, homes built by the same builder in the same housing development will be more correlated as compared to homes built by separate builders in widely scattered locations in different years; correlation of damage will be a function of structure type, material, age, and distance between site locations.

Not accounting for correlation in the assessment, either in the hazard or the damage, results in unrealistically low estimates in the standard deviation of losses aggregated over multiple sites, (eg, portfolio losses). This is because, if hazard correlation is not considered, (eg, the hazard intensities at multiple sites are assumed to be independent), the assessment process assumes that a relatively high hazard (relative to its expected value) at one site and a relatively low hazard at an adjacent site are equally likely as relatively high and relatively low hazards at the two sites. Whereas, with correlation considered, the latter two outcomes would be more likely. When the losses are computed, the assumption of independence yields lower probabilities within the extreme high and low loss levels of the distribution. Thus, based on the independence assumption, the distribution of losses over all sampled ground-motion vectors will be less variable (a lower standard deviation) than the distribution based on the realistic correlation assumption. A similar effect occurs when the correlation of damage to structures of the same type, material, age, etc, is not considered. Again, the independence assumption results in lower loss probabilities with the extremes of the aggregated losses. The bottom line is that the correlated analysis will produce higher, and more realistic exceedance probabilities for large losses.

DAMAGE AND HAZARDS
Seismic hazard models
The peril of earthquakes has many potential agents of damage or hazards, including: fault rupture, shaking, liquefaction (conversion of soils with high water content into a liquefied state as a result of strong ground shaking), land sliding, fire following earthquake, hazardous material release, tsunami and inundation. The most important of these hazards is shaking, not only because of the potential for damage to a large number of properties, but also because it is also the underlying initiator of the other hazards. A graphical description of the elements of the seismic hazard model is shown in Figure 7. The ground motion shaking at a sight is a function of the earthquake magnitude, M, the distance of the site to the fault rupture plane, d, the soils stiffness and regional geology.

The seismic hazard model, which corresponds to the hazard module of Figure 2, consists of three parts (as shown in Figure 8), with each part contributing to the final ground-motion estimates.

Seismic sources
Depending on the information available regarding the tectonics of the region under consideration, point or area source models (in which thrust faults or zones of unknown geological structure are modelled), or a line source model (in which strike-slip faults (a fault in which the movement is parallel to the plane of the fault) are modelled) can be adopted to represent the regional seismotectonics, as shown in Figure 9. In a point or area source model the earthquake epicentre can be located anywhere in a given area, whereas in the line source model the seismic event is modelled as a fault rupture of a given length (the rupture in turn can be located anywhere along a given fault). In some models, faults can be modelled in three-dimension to accommodate non-vertical faults (dipping) and blind thrusts (dipping faults at depth).

Earthquake models typically build in seismotectonic databases, which contain detailed information on all major active faults in the region of interest.

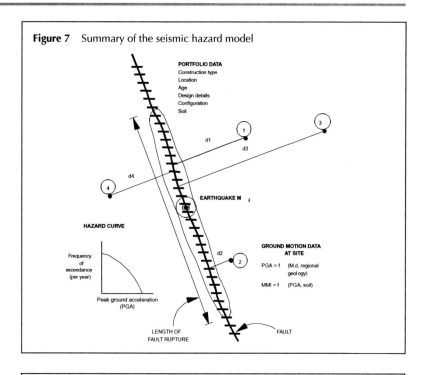

Figure 7 Summary of the seismic hazard model

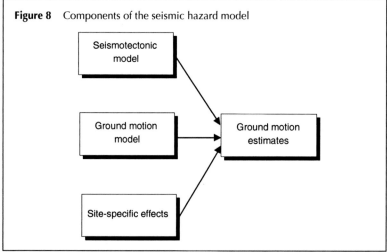

Figure 8 Components of the seismic hazard model

Ground motion models

The locations of the sites in a portfolio can be translated from street or postal code addresses to absolute geographic references (latitudes and longitudes) using internally developed and/or third-party software. If a site street address is not known, the site postal code centroid (the population centroid of the postal code) can be used as an approximation. Using the site latitude/longitude, the distance from the site to the relevant earthquake faults or area sources can be determined. Based on the event magnitude and the distance to the fault rupture or earthquake epicentre, attenuation relations are used to determine the ground-motion, eg, the peak ground-motion acceleration (PGA), or spectral acceleration at the site. Thus, for a given event magnitude, the distance of the site from the fault determines the magnitude of the shaking hazard at the site. This is illustrated in Figure 10.

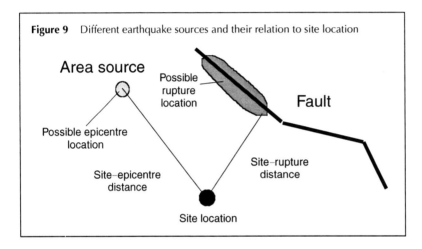

Figure 9 Different earthquake sources and their relation to site location

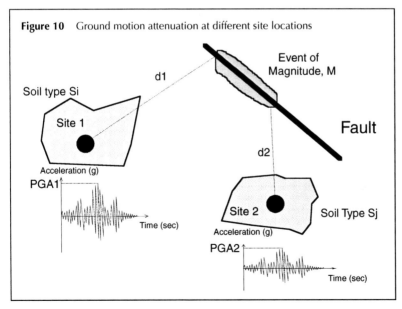

Figure 10 Ground motion attenuation at different site locations

The attenuation relations are based on statistical studies of earthquake data. They differ from region to region. Most models will contain a library of ground-motion attenuation models and use multiple models, as appropriate for each region.

Site soil conditions

Once a site's latitude/longitude has been established, soil databases are accessed to determine the site soil conditions. The soil databases characterise soil stiffness in a location, with stiffer soils denoting lower surface shaking than soft loose soils. A simple classification consisting of the four soil types is listed in Table 1.

For each site, for a given event magnitude and rupture location, the PGA and spectral acceleration obtained from the region's attenuation relation are adjusted (increased or decreased) using local soil characteristics in terms of shear wave velocity, which is a physical measure of a soil's stiffness.

Hurricane hazard models

Development of the wind hazard is the first phase of the analysis depicted by the hazard module (seen in Figure 2). Given the parameters and attributes of the hurricane, the wind hazard model is used to estimate the sustained maximum wind speeds at a portfolio of locations, as described in the following sections.

Hurricane attributes and models

A hurricane usually appears as a fairly organised spiral of clouds. The centre of a hurricane, or eye, follows a path or track with a varying translational speed. The shapes of most hurricanes in the northern hemisphere share some common traits. Hurricanes are born in the tropics at sea in late summer, and tend to move steadily toward higher latitudes while also moving in a westerly direction. As a general rule, the higher the latitude, the higher the probability that the hurricane track will begin to travel

Table 1 Soil types (abbreviated list)

Soil type	Description
S1	A rock-like stiff or dense soil (good soil)
S2	A soft-medium stiff soil (average soil)
S3	A saturated alluvium soil (poor soil)
S4	Artificial fill (very poor soil)

Table 2   Saffir–Simpson intensity scale

Saffir–Simpson Intensity (SSI)	Central pressure (mb)	Maximum sustained winds (mph)	Storm surge height (ft)	Damage
1	≥980	74–95	4–5	Damage mainly to trees, shrubbery and unanchored mobile homes
2	965–979	96–110	6–8	Some trees blown down; major damage to exposed mobile homes; some damage to roofs or buildings
3	945–964	111–130	9–12	Foiliage removed from trees; large trees blown down; mobile homes destroyed; some structural damage to small buildings
4	920–944	131–155	13–18	All signs blown down; extensive damage to roofs, windows and doors; complete destruction of mobile homes; flooding inland as far as 6 miles; major damage to lower floors of structures near shore
5	<920	>155	>18	Severe damage to windows and doors; extensive damage to roofs of homes and industrial buildings; small buildings overturned and blown away; major damage to lower floors of all structures less than 15ft above sea level within 500m of shore

clockwise towards the east, while the high velocity rotational winds move in a anti-clockwise direction. The actual mechanisms, which steer tracks, are quite complex; the description above serves only as a general rule.

Storm intensity is measured using the Saffir–Simpson damage potential scale, or Saffir–Simpson Intensity (SSI). The SSI was developed in 1975 and serves to rate storms based on a scale of 1–5, with 5 being the most damaging. Storms are rated on observed maximum sustained wind speed, given in miles per hour, within ranges.

Time decay model
When moving over land, hurricane maximum wind speed along the track decays with time. To estimate the barometric pressure decay of hurricanes as they travel over land, a model estimates the decay as an exponential function, where the pressure decay is given as a function of the time spent, since landfall, by the storm over land. This model, characterised in Figure 11, was based on an exponential regression analysis of data available from 13 East Coast America storms.

Since the storm decay is assumed to be a function of time elapsed, the assumed storm translational speed strongly affects the storm decay. If the storm translates at a very high speed it will travel a great distance inland before it decays. It may also be assumed that storms translate at a speed that is a function of latitude, atmospheric pressure and water temperature.

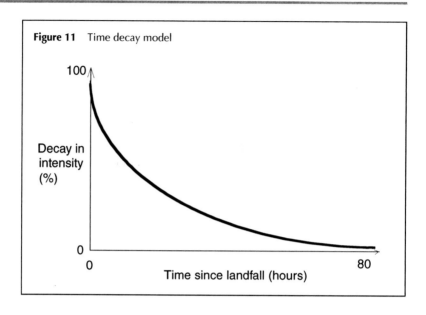

Figure 11   Time decay model

Attenuation of wind speed with distance from hurricane

A typical hurricane model is usually based on the model developed by the National Oceanic and Atmospheric Administration (NOAA) (which may be supplemented by a wind speed decay model). While the eye of the hurricane follows the selected track, the typical hurricane model estimates rotational and translational wind speeds at all distances away from the eye.

The parameters of interest for the computation of wind speed include storm-specific and site-specific information. Storm-specific data includes: landfall location; radius of maximum winds (the radial distance from the hurricane centre to the band of strongest wind, as a function of latitude and central barometric pressure); translational velocity (a function of the latitude); a pressure-velocity conversion factor, K, (dependent on latitude); the coriolis parameter, f, (dependent on latitude); the angle between the storm track and the shore; and the ratio of maximum wind to gradient wind speed.

Site-specific information includes: the site topography; the control point (the location of the storm track which produces maximum wind speed at the site); distance, d, from landfall to the control point along the track; and distance from the site to the control point, r. The eye is the point of lowest barometric pressure, which increases in correlation to the distance from the eye. Furthermore, there is a negative correlation between barometric pressure and wind speed; therefore, as a general rule, the further a site is located from the eye, the lower the maximum observed winds.

With exact hurricane and site information able to be defined, the pressure difference between normal barometric pressure away from the storm, and the barometric pressure at the control point is computed (as explained in the preceding section). Then, the maximum wind speed for a stationary hurricane is evaluated. From the wind speed at the control point, the wind speed at a site is then evaluated.

Site-specific adjustments
The coefficient of the attenuation of the wind speed from the control point to a site depends on the corresponding distance, d, and the radius of maximum wind speed, r. In the case of attenuation of over-water wind to onshore wind, a terrain conversion factor must be considered. This factor is a function of the wind direction and the onshore topography, eg, terrain (dry ground with tree growth, or hills), flat non-inundated land, or rough terrain, such as urban areas or dense forests.

Gust wind effects
The damage at a site is a function of the gust winds (temporary increases in wind speeds arising from the chaotic dynamics within a hurricane) rather than the maximum sustained wind speed. Therefore, assuming that the ratio of gust to maximum sustained wind speed is constant, the site maximum sustained wind speed is adjusted for gust effect.

VULNERABILITY MODULES
Vulnerability models have been developed from a number of sources. The primary sources are studies of past earthquakes and hurricanes and the damage they have caused to structural and architectural building systems, contents, equipment, stock and supplies, as well as the losses incurred due to loss of use or business interruption (BI). Vulnerability models also can address other non-structural loss sources such as workers compensation and general liability. The vulnerability models also consider modern building codes and engineering analyses of numerous structures representative of common construction categories.

Seismic vulnerability models
Structures and buildings
Specialised techniques have been developed for identifying differences in relative earthquake damage potential for similar or different types of buildings in different parts of the same geographic areas. Relative damage potential is based on differences in building practices arising from different dates of construction and differing building codes.

Models will usually rely on a database of buildings that have been analysed in detail to estimate the structural vulnerability. Based on the extent of available information, a specific building is characterised by its material, lateral-force-resisting system, geometry, height, and other measures of its size and complexity. The building is then assigned to a class for which a vulnerability function has been developed based on analysis of similar buildings. Models include vulnerability functions for a wide variety of building types representing occupancy, age and type of construction.

The vulnerability function is a measure of the expected cost of repairs of a structure belonging to a specific class (eg, ductile moment frame mid-rise). The function is modified by a quality factor based on the value, age, complexity and other specifics of the building. Figure 12 shows an example of a building vulnerability function for a particular type of reinforced concrete structure. Given the hazard intensity for a site, the vulnerability function provides an estimate of the mean damage factor for the structure. The damage factor is an estimate of the cost of repairs, expressed as a percentage of the total insured value of the building.

Vulnerability functions, similar to the ones described above, exist to identify damage potential to the contents of buildings. These functions have been developed based on analysis of performance in past earthquakes.

Business interruption

Business interruption (BI) is a significant component of loss, especially for commercial policies. Therefore models need to have algorithms to estimate BI, which usually are based on damage to a structure. The BI is evaluated in number of days lost, as a function of the damage factor of the building

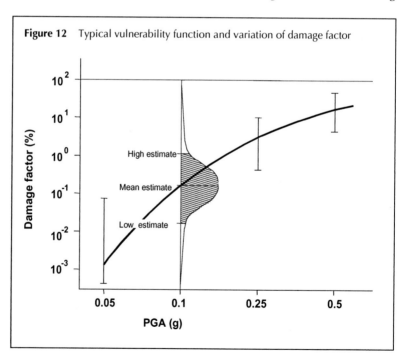

Figure 12   Typical vulnerability function and variation of damage factor

(between 0 and 100%). For residential properties, this calculation yields the additional living expense portion of the loss settlement.

Fire following earthquake
Very large insured losses from earthquake-induced fires, while rare, have the potential to result in losses many times greater than from the shaking damage. This was demonstrated by the large conflagrations in the Great Kanto Earthquake in Tokyo in 1923 and the 1906 San Francisco Earthquake. Therefore, fire following loss algorithms are usually included in earthquake models and are based on the amount of shaking damage, building construction type, and building density, as well as the regional supply of water and fire department resources. In general, these estimates become quite important when considering very large events, since fire ignition probabilities rise as the impacted area grows, while the fire fighting resources are limited.

Hurricane vulnerability models
Structures and buildings
Hurricane damage to a structure type is most influenced by four general attributes.

1. Facility use: residential buildings, especially single-family units, tend to be non-engineered, thus are seen to be more vulnerable structures; commercial and industrial buildings tend to be engineered, thus are deemed less vulnerable structures.
2. Building height: the taller the building, the more vulnerable it is to wind loads.
3. Structural system: heavier building materials (concrete, heavy steel, masonry) tend to resist extreme wind loads better than lighter building materials (light steel, timber).
4. Cladding system: cladding is the structure's external covering. If it is breached, then wind and rain can cause extensive damage to the building's interior and contents. Cladding is categorised as strong, (eg, cast-in-place or precast concrete panels, masonry and heavy veneers, such as marble) or weak (eg, glass, metal and wood panelling).

Based on the extent of available information, a specific building is characterised by its use, material, lateral-force-resisting system, geometry, height, and cladding system. The building is then assigned to one of the classes of structures for which a vulnerability function has been developed. The vulnerability function is a measure of the expected cost of repairs of a structure belonging to a specific class (eg, wood frame). It may be modified by a quality factor based on the age, complexity and other specifics of the building.

Figure 13 shows a typical residential building's vulnerability curve. It refers to damage to structural and architectural components. Fifty percent damage refers to the median (50th percentile) damage to the structural system and architectural components. Total damage means the building will be demolished to the foundation and rebuilt. Partition walls, ceilings, ducts and electrical fixtures damaged by wind are considered part of the structural damage. The damage factor is expressed as a percentage of the insured value of the building.

Vulnerability functions, similar to the ones described above, exist to identify damage potential to the contents of buildings. Figure 14 shows a typical vulnerability curve for the contents of a residential building. Building contents include furniture, carpets, draperies, works of art, decorations, office machines, computers, files and books. Loss is assumed to be total if these items get wet. The factor is expressed as a percentage of the insured value of the contents.

Business Interruption

Potential hurricane BI is estimated in a manner similar to seismic damage. Given the wind damage, a model estimates – via special algorithms – the number of days lost as a function of the damage factor of the building (between 0 and 100%).

BI can also be correlated to the area infrastructure damage, as shown in Figure 15. In other words, although a structure and its content may not have suffered any damage, the business located there may suffer a costly interruption if the utilities (eg, electric power) are damaged.

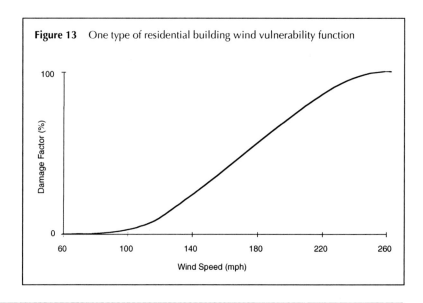

Figure 13 One type of residential building wind vulnerability function

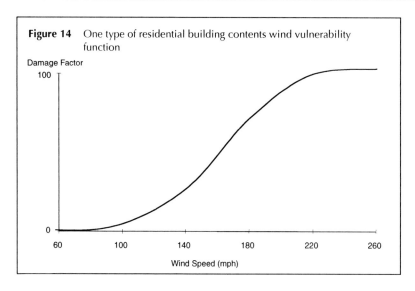

Figure 14 One type of residential building contents wind vulnerability function

Damage Factor

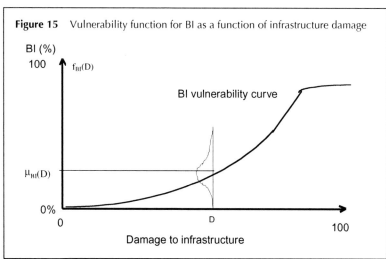

Figure 15 Vulnerability function for BI as a function of infrastructure damage

DAMAGE COMPUTATION
Seismic Damage Assessment
The seismic hazard model estimates the peak ground acceleration and spectral acceleration at the site. Given the hazard intensity and the information specific to each property, the vulnerability model provides an estimate of the degree of damage for each individual asset. This is expressed in terms of an estimate of the mean and standard deviation of damage.

To estimate the damage for a given property for each relevant earthquake scenario, two sources of stochastic or random variation associated with the damage calculation are considered. First, the damage sustained by a structure is subject to a number of sources of variation, such as, variation in coupling of the ground-motion to the structure, quality of construction, local soil conditions, etc. Thus, the damage at a site, given the shaking intensity, is modelled by a probability distribution. Second, the shaking intensity at the site is also subject to random variation, as described by the hazard intensity distribution. The damage for a given property is calculated by combining the variation in damage with the variation in peak wind speed values, which is shown in Figure 5.

Portfolio (or other aggregations of properties) damage estimates, eg, the portfolio normal expected damage (NED) – the damage that the portfolio is typically expected to sustain on average – are calculated by aggregating the damage over all properties in the portfolio. The portfolio NED and standard deviation are based on combining the individual property mean and standard deviation, accounting for correlation between damages at various sites. Thus, a probabilistic analysis provides a complete picture of the damage outcome for individual properties and for aggregations of properties.

Hurricane damage assessment
Given the peak wind speed at the site (provided by the hurricane hazard model) and information specific to each property, the vulnerability model provides estimates of the degree of damage for each individual asset. This is expressed in terms of the mean and standard deviation of damage.

Analogous to the seismic damage assessment model, the hurricane damage model typically recognises two sources of random variation associated with the damage calculation. First, variation in damage sustained by a structure is subject to local wind turbulence, quality of construction, site conditions, etc.

Second, the peak wind speed at the site during a hurricane is also subject to random variation, such as, variation in wind speed decay, wind speed gradient attenuation, translational speed of the storm, radius of maximum wind speed, etc. As in the earthquake analysis, the damage for a given property is calculated by combining the variation in the damage function with the variation in peak wind speed values.

INSURANCE LOSS COMPUTATION
When the damage estimates are known, the next step in the risk assessment process is to estimate the potential insurance losses. This involves subjecting the damage estimates to the constraints imposed by the insurance loss model, such as policy level deductibles and limits, facultative reinsurance and treaty attachment points and layer amounts, and special catastrophic loss settlement factors. The initial loss calculation involves estimating the

gross loss, which considers the effects of policy deductibles and limits. The algorithm for calculating gross loss is based on the relation of loss to damage as shown in Figure 6. Both site level and policy level constraints are considered. The probabilistic information for gross loss is calculated using the damage-loss relation and the probabilistic information developed for damage. Similar calculations are performed to develop probabilistic information for the net loss (to the primary insurer) and ceded losses to reinsurers, based on the amount and layers of any reinsurance in place. The basic probabilistic information is based on deriving the probability distribution of the loss if a hazard event occurs.

Losses are characterised in several ways. For a given hazard scenario, eg, a repeat of a significant past event, or a series of specified hazard scenarios, the primary measures of loss are the expected annual loss (EAL) and the loss distribution associated with each hazard scenario. For a probabilistic analysis, eg, considering all possible hazard scenarios, the primary measures of loss are the EAL and the per-occurrence and aggregate loss exceedance curves (described in the next section).

The EAL reflects both the loss, given an event occurs, and the frequency per year that an event occurs. For a given hazard scenario, the EAL measures the average aggregated loss per year associated with the given scenario. For a probabilistic analysis, the EAL takes into account the losses and frequencies of occurrence of all foreseeable earthquake magnitudes on all faults and seismic zones or all foreseeable hurricane scenarios affecting each site.

The primary reinsurance results are the EAL, ie, risk premiums by reinsurance treaty layer and by reinsurer. Additional results for each reinsurer include the EAL, standard deviation of the annual loss, and the probabilities of penetration and exceeding the monetary loss for each layer. Also, the damage and the gross loss (to the reinsurer) exceedance curves are developed for each layer.

PROBABILISTIC LOSS EXCEEDANCE CURVES

In addition to characterising loss in terms of the expected and probable maximum losses, loss (or risk) exceedance curves are developed in the probabilistic analysis. A loss curve is a useful way of quantifying the variability of losses and the potential of significant losses. One such curve is the "annualised per-occurrence loss exceedance" curve shown in Figure 16. This curve quantifies the probability that the largest per-occurrence loss – per year – exceeds a value, x, as a function of loss. The curve expresses the probability that the annual per-occurrence loss exceeds specified loss thresholds in 1, 10, 25, 50, etc, years.

Figure 16 shows the per-occurrence loss exceedance curves for two sites. The curve for site two has a longer tail than site one, which indicates that

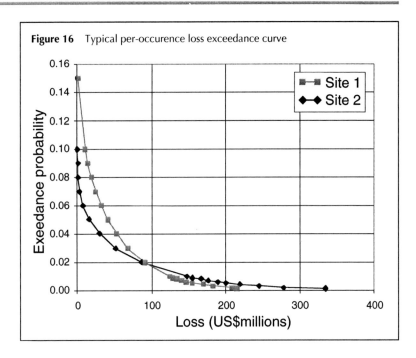

Figure 16   Typical per-occurence loss exceedance curve

site two is affected by high severity low frequency events more than site one.

An alternate curve is the aggregate loss exceedance curve. This curve quantifies the probability that the aggregate loss, per year (ie, the sum of the losses for all events per year) exceeds a value, x, as a function of loss. In general, this curve will have the same shape as the per-occurrence curve, but will have higher loss probabilities for a specific loss amount since it includes losses from all potential events, as opposed to the largest single loss event.

MODELLING UNCERTAINTY

There are two types of variability that can be included in the probabilistic analysis: aleatory and epistemic variabilities. Aleatory variability is natural randomness associated with the prediction of a parameter from a specific model, assuming that the model is correct. Specification of the standard deviation (σ) of a mean ground-motion attenuation relationship is a representation of aleatory variability since it is a measure of the natural variation in observed ground motion. Epistemic variability, or modelling uncertainty, accounts for incomplete knowledge in the predictive models and the variability in the interpretations of the data used to develop the models. Aleatory uncertainty can be estimated better, but it cannot be reduced through scientific advances. This contrasts with epistemic uncertainty, which arises from imperfect information and knowledge, which is potentially reducible through data acquisition.

Aleatory variability is usually included directly in the probabilistic analysis calculations by means of simulation or mathematical integration. Epistemic uncertainty on the other hand, is included in the probabilistic analysis by explicitly including alternative hypotheses and models. For example, epistemic uncertainty can be accounted for through the evaluation of several alternative attenuation models or through the formulation of a logic tree that includes multiple alternative hypotheses in a single model. Each alternative hypothesis, indicated by a branch of the logic tree, is given a subjective weight corresponding to its assessed likelihood of being correct. The logic tree allows a formal characterisation of uncertainty in the analysis by explicitly including alternative interpretations, models and parameters. The proposed alternative hypotheses account for uncertainty in ground motion or other parameters such as earthquake source zonation, maximum magnitude, earthquake recurrence rate, location and segmentation of seismogenic faults, style of faulting, and distribution of seismicity between faults and area sources. Logic tree models may be exhaustively evaluated, or adequately sampled through Monte Carlo or other simulation techniques, which permit quantification of the variance in model outputs due to variability in model parameters.

USE OF MODELS IN ART TRANSACTIONS – A CASE STUDY

This section aims to demonstrate the use of catastrophe modelling in a typical insurance-linked securitisation, California Earthquake. California represents one of the largest sources of catastrophe risk in reinsurer's portfolios, and hence alternate risk market sources are appealing. Since 1997, five California Earthquake securitisations totalling over US$700 million have been placed. In addition, several more multi-peril and multi-region deals that included California Earthquake have also been completed.

A typical transaction involves a reinsurer with excess California Earthquake exposures who wishes to hedge its exposure to large events, such as a repeat of the 1906 California Earthquake. Since the company's reinsurance portfolio is likely to be sourced from a large number of primary insurance companies with California Earthquake exposures, their losses are expected to be highly correlated with reported industry losses. So, instead of using their own portfolio, the company would select an index based on the Property Claims Service, which regularly reports insured US property losses from catastrophic events.

In such a transaction, the ceding company would retain the services of the risk modelling company to perform the analysis on the portfolio – earthquake-insured exposures in the state of California, in this case. The modelling company would compile an estimate of current earthquake insurance written by all insurers in California using data from the

California Department of Insurance, California Earthquake Authority, and private insurers. The modeller would then create a portfolio of insured properties by postal code, using a database of building inventory constructed from tax assessor and census information. The portfolio defines the type of occupancy, location, underlying insurance policy coverages, such as deductibles, limits, sub-limits, etc.

The portfolio is analysed using a probabilistic earthquake model, as previously described, and the loss exceedance curve is obtained from the model. Based on the reinsurers desired level of protection and correlation with the industry loss, the reinsurer selects the level of coverage desired. The resulting attachment and exhaustion probabilities are determined from the curve, and integrating the area under the curve between those two points derives the expected loss for the layer. Figure 17 shows the curve from a typical transaction.

The expected loss to the layer becomes the base estimate for pricing the security. Moody's Investor Service and other rating agencies have developed criteria to rate insurance-linked notes based on comparing model-based loss probabilities with historical credit default and loss. Following a series of stress tests by the rating agencies, the agency determines a bond rating, which then becomes the basis for pricing based on interest rate spreads over Libor (London Interbank Offered Rate – a short-term lending rate offered by major banks in London) for equivalent rated securities.

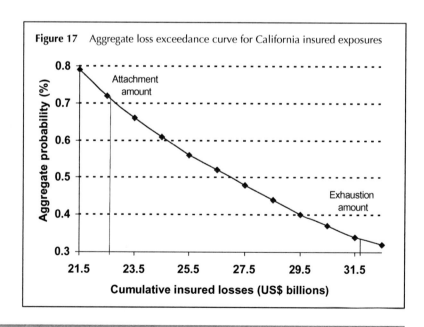

Figure 17   Aggregate loss exceedance curve for California insured exposures

ALTERNATE LOSS TRIGGERS

Initial insurance-linked transactions were structured to mimic excess of loss reinsurance coverages. Thus the bondholders paid out incurred monetary losses above an attachment point. However, due to investor concerns related to moral hazard and data quality issues, the ceding company was required to retain a portion of the risk. Hence, in some circumstances, reliance on reported industry losses became a more attractive loss determinant since specific company underwriting or claims procedures would not be of concern to the investor. Furthermore, an industry loss measure would be attractive if the ceding company did not have detailed policy information, or did not want to publicly disclose their book of business to competitors.

In some situations, insurers do not have sufficient detailed information on risks to meet the data standards necessary to structure an indemnity transaction, yet they still wish to access the capital markets; thus the concept of a parametric trigger was conceived, in which bond payments would be triggered by the event occurrence, and not the ensuing monetary loss. The first such transaction was for Tokio Marine's, risks centred on Tokyo Bay. The loss trigger was defined by a minimum earthquake magnitude occurring within two rectangular areas. Instead of using the entire probabilistic loss model, the event probabilities were calculated by using only the first portion of the hazard module; the investor assumed only the event risk, while Tokio Marine still retained the uncertainty of actual damage and loss. The resulting basis risk carried by Tokio Marine is an inevitable by-product of non-monetary loss triggers.

Further variations on non-monetary loss triggers have also been introduced, including loss triggers based on modelled losses. When an event takes place, the loss to investors is calculated by inputting event parameters into the same model used to perform the risk estimate. (In order to protect the investor, the model is placed into escrow for the duration of the term of the security.) The model then calculates the payoff to the issuer.

A further variant of non-monetary triggers has been recently introduced, called "second generation parametric triggers". In these deals, the loss trigger is defined by a specific physical parameter, such as peak ground velocity or peak wind speed gust, and measured (or calculated) at a defined series of locations in the vicinity of the insured exposures. In many cases, the physical parameters are available on the Internet within minutes of the event, permitting investors and issuers to quickly determine if a payoff is forthcoming.

Non-monetary triggers still rely upon portions of the loss models to estimate the loss exceedance probabilities, thus creating a simple structure for investors to understand. This also reduces issues of moral hazard and uncertainty in damage and loss payments. Of course, the issuer then retains those risks in the form of basis risk. Probabilistic loss models have become an essential ingredient to ART catastrophe insurance transactions, either for monetary or non-monetary loss triggers.

CONCLUSION

This chapter demonstrates why there is a need for catastrophe models. Prior historical loss-based approaches cannot anticipate very large catastrophes that have yet to occur. Yet with advances in science and engineering, the probability of future large credible loss events can be estimated through the use of catastrophe models. Construction of the models follows a logical sequence of:

1. defining the natural hazard in terms of frequency and severity;
2. estimating physical damage to structures and contents of a portfolio of properties; and
3. estimating insured losses by considering such insurance policy features as deductibles and limits.

Since substantial uncertainty exists in scientific phenomenon and building damage, models must consider the variability in many of the loss parameters. This is typically achieved by use of a probabilistic analysis, which permits parameters to assume a wide range of values that are consistent with the natural randomness found in nature and the limits of scientific understanding.

The ability to rigorously quantify catastrophe insurance risk through the use of cat models has provided the bridge to link insurance risks with the much larger fixed-income capital markets. For the first time, capital markets investors can directly participate in such risks in lieu of making equity or debt investments in insurance or reinsurance companies. And finally, such models can assist in the disaggregation of catastrophe risk into event risk and insured loss, through the analysis of parametric loss structures, which are now growing in popularity in the ART market.

1 It should be noted that in Figure 4 a type C structure has the lowest expected damage factor or vulnerability, whereas a type A structure has the highest vulnerability.
2 Property Claims Services, a division of ISO Services, www.iso.com/AISG/pcs.

BIBLIOGRAPHY

ATC-13, 1985, *Earthquake Damage Evaluation Data for California* (Redwood City, CA: Applied Technology Council).

FEMA 366, 2000, *HAZUS 99 Estimated Annualized Earthquake Losses for the United States* (Washington, DC: Federal Emergency Management Agency).

Florida Insurance Council, 1998, *Computer Modeling of Catastrophic Losses*, February, Fact Book URL: http://www.flains.org/newfic/mediapublic/).

Freeman, J. R, 1932, *Earthquake Damage and Earthquake Insurance* (New York: McGraw-Hill)

HAZUS99, 1999, "Earthquake Loss Estimation Methodology HAZUS 99 Service Release 2 (SR2)", Federal Emergency Management Agency Washington, DC and National Institute of Building Sciences Washington, DC.

Hwang, H. H. M., H. Lin and J.-R. Huo, 1997, "Seismic Performance Evaluation of Fire Stations in Shelby County, Tennessee, *Earthquake Spectra*, 13(4), pp. 759–72.

Kircher, C. A. *et al.*, 1997, "Estimation of Earthquake Losses in Buildings", *Earthquake Spectra*, 13(4), pp. 721–38.

Moody's Investor Service, 1997, Approach to the Rating of Catastrophe-Linked Notes, Special Report, September.

NOAA, 1972, "A study of Earthquake Losses in the San Francisco Bay Area", National Oceanographic and Atmospheric Administration of the Department of Commerce for the Office of Emergency Preparedness, Washington DC.

Petak, W. J., and A. A. Atkinson, 1982, *Natural hazard risk assessment and public policy: anticipating the unexpected*, (New York: Springer).

Scawthorn, C., M. Khater and C. Rojahn, 1993, "Seismic Vulnerability and Impact of Disruption of Lifelines in the Conterminous United States", National Earthquake Conference, Memphis, TN.

Scawthorn, C., and M. Khater, 1992, "Fire Following Earthquake – Conflagration Potential in the Greater Los Angeles, San Francisco, Seattle and Memphis Areas", Natural Disaster Coalition, EQE International, San Francisco.

Steinbrugge, K.V, 1982, *Earthquakes, Volcanoes and Tsunamis, An Anatomy of Hazards* (New York: Skandia America).

Thompson, W., 1891, *Popular Lectures and Addresses* (London: Macmillan and Co).

Whitman, R.V. *et al.*, 1997, "Development of a National Earthquake Loss Estimation Methodology", *Earthquake Spectra*, 13(4), pp. 643–62.

Wiggins, J. H., 1979, "Estimated building losses from U.S. earthquakes", Second US National Conference on Earthquake Engineering, Earthquake Engineering Research Institute, Berkeley, pp. 253–62.

14

Quantifying Insurance Terrorism Risk

Gordon Woo

Risk Management Solutions

The World Trade Center (WTC) disaster in 2001 was a stark reminder to the insurance industry of the potentially dire consequences of accumulating high concentrations of insured value and underestimating a hazard to which they are exposed. By imposing strict coverage limits, or stopping to offer terrorism cover for large commercial policies, initial steps can be taken to address the accumulation problem. Subsequently, exploration of the impact of some hypothetical future terrorist scenarios can guide the control of risk accumulations.

However, estimating loss potential, as well as the pricing of terrorism risk, also requires the hazard issue to be addressed. This will never be resolved as effectively as for hurricane or earthquake hazard, but some insight into its ranking as a peril is urgently needed. With the insurance industry struggling with the uncertainty of how to deal with terrorism risks, hopes will be placed on a reduction of the terrorist threat now that there is a global determination to combat terrorism. Terrorism hazard is considered here in the wake of this international governmental resolution. The frequency and severity of attacks depends crucially on organisational structure. To minimise detection by counterterrorist forces, the terrorists may take advantage of alternative forms of network architecture, such as those adopted by drugs syndicates, pirates, and other criminals, within which sporadic pulsing swarm attacks (Ronfeldt and Arquilla, 2001a) might be effectively launched.

The constraints of this network architecture, with sustained pressure from counterterrorist forces, will influence the relative likelihood of different scenarios being favoured by terrorist groups. A terrorism cost function, involving planning time, technical difficulty, and consumption of resources, may be defined to quantify relative scenario likelihood, and thereby allow a loss severity curve to be derived. As part of the task of normalising this curve to strike frequency, a logical event-tree is outlined for computing the probability that a planned attack will be successful. Any probabilistic framework for quantifying terrorism risk, however logically designed, will ultimately have to involve a measure of expert judgement. Extensive expert consultation exercises have already been commissioned by the Pentagon, (Reeve, 1999) and should prove as insightful for the insurance industry as for government agencies.

QUANTIFICATION OF TERRORISM RISK

On September 11, 2001, the worldwide insurance community suffered its worst ever loss. The shock of such an enormous loss was compounded by the realisation that this was a loss stemming from a risk which was accepted, but not quantified. Rough calculations on risk exposure may have been made on the basis of past claims. But, as with all low frequency, high severity perils, whether natural or man-made, a rudimentary actuarial approach to risk quantification, based upon historical loss experience data, is inadequate for a variety of reasons: in particular, the questionable relevance of much of the historical record, and the disparity between its short length and the return period of extreme events.

Every catastrophic loss teaches a hard lesson in risk management: to underwrite a catastrophe peril ignorant of the scale of the risk is to invite further financial trouble. Where catastrophe risks are underwritten, a diligent attempt should be made to quantify them, challenging though this task may be. The major property insurance losses of recent times, such as Hurricane Andrew and the Northridge earthquake (Woo, 1999), have not merely been outlying statistics on a loss–experience plot, they have propelled forward methodological advances in risk modelling. Terrorism cover will continue to be provided after 2001, and from Ground Zero will have to rise up quantitative methods for modelling terrorism risk.

This chapter addresses the challenge of quantifying terrorism risk. The classic definition of risk is that it is a product of hazard and vulnerability. The second factor deals with the loss inflicted if a specific terrorist scenario were to occur. Such a scenario might involve the crash of a plane into an urban area, a city bomb blast, an explosion of a liquefied natural gas (LNG) ship in harbour, detonation of a nuclear device, etc. Modelling a specific scenario is essentially a complex engineering problem, not dissimilar, in principle, to the scenario analysis conducted for natural perils such as windstorms and earthquakes. Given the dynamics of the energy source and the geometry of energy dissipation, the vulnerability of engineering construction of different types may be evaluated. Modelling studies of various hypothetical terrorist scenarios are in progress by Risk Management Solutions (RMS).

For natural perils, hazard modelling may be technically and computationally demanding, but modellers can take comfort from Einstein's dictum that "Nature may be subtle, but is not malicious"(Pais, 1983). Terrorists, on the other hand, may be both subtle and malicious. So how can a hazard model for terrorism be developed? Obviously, a different approach is required from the traditional reductionist bottom-up approach used for modelling the inanimate world of engineering physics.

A suggestion by RAND (see Ronfeldt and Arquilla, 2001a) is to focus on the network behaviour of a terrorist organisation, and its capacity to wage a netwar. A theoretical framework for this modern mode of conflict does exist, based on the principles of complexity (see eg, Waldrop, 1992), which shows how key features of the organisational structure of complex interacting systems emerge. This theory has been successful over the past decade in pioneering quantitative understanding of many aspects of the social behaviour of biological organisms. Doubtless as oblivious of the finer mathematical points of complexity theory are the seasoned net war practitioners among the criminal fraternity; drugs, immigration, and smuggling racketeers. It is a basic tenet of complexity theory that network characteristics are not consciously moulded by its components, but rather emerge spontaneously from their individual actions.

In applying the broad ideas of complexity theory to the sociological context, account must be taken of human factors such as intelligence and social interaction. As sociologists have remarked (Kennedy and Eberhart, 2001), through learning from experience and emulating the successful behaviour of others, people are able to discover relatively optimal patterns of attitudes, beliefs and behaviours. For social groups, in which individuals learn from, emulate, and adapt to other group members, there is thus a collective intelligence, which is geographically distributed. This collective dispersed intelligence is a prime facet of terrorist organisations; a hydra-like feature which makes them inherently more threatening, powerful and evasive than lone terrorists.

The concept of swarm intelligence has been developed to describe populations which exhibit certain basic collective patterns of behaviour, arising not so much from leadership direction, but rather emerging from the actions of individual members. The social insect metaphor has been a powerful tool in exploring some crucial characteristics of social organisations, including flexibility, robustness, distributed functioning and autonomy.

Although originally developed in the context of cellular robotic systems, the foremost paradigm for swarm intelligence is that of the ant colony, which has the remarkable capability of collectively arriving at solutions to almost intractable mathematical problems (Bonabeau, Dorigo and Theraulaz, 1999). Edward Wilson's deep fascination with the way that the mass organised behaviour of ant populations may be understood from a single ant's behaviour drew him towards a theory of sociobiology (Wilson, 1975). Of course, ants are not human beings. Ants are genetically programmed to dedicate themselves to their pre-assigned tasks; to kill and be killed rather like automatons; to be as prepared to die for the colony as to live.

If the ideas of swarm intelligence are applicable to any group of human beings, it would be to zealous and fanatical terrorists, bound together as one by a bond of brotherhood; as absolute as that shared by blood relatives. Such a terrorist group could not be adequately represented simply as a set of single-minded individuals, espousing a common cause. Much of their special strength resides in the unusual qualities of their collective swarm intelligence, which govern the group's fearsome capability of executing extreme acts of terror and escaping prior detection. Accordingly, in order to understand the nature of terrorism hazard: its spatial and temporal characteristics, the frequency and severity of attacks; it is necessary to comprehend the structure of terrorist organisations.

STRUCTURE OF TERRORIST ORGANISATIONS

An immediate observation made in the aftermath of September 11, 2001 was the meticulous planning and precise execution of the surprise assault on the United States. The inference was that this well-coordinated assault had to have been masterminded by a highly organised terrorist network. However well resourced and armed, terrorist groups can never match the economic and technological capability of nation states. As in all conflicts involving an imbalance of military assets, the lesser party can only hope to achieve its objectives through efficiency and smartness of organisation and deftness of manoeuvre. Despite being vastly inferior in overall numbers and weaponry, at the moment of attack, terrorist forces may coalesce to form an overpowering danger.

The effectiveness of attacks which a terrorist group might be capable of launching depends largely on the structure of its organisation. The less centralised and hierarchical, the more resilient the organisation will be to counterterrorist action (Ronfeldt and Arquilla, 2001a). Hamas, for example, is much less centralised than the Palestine Liberation Organisation (PLO), (Ronfeldt and Arquilla, 2001a) so the detention or death of its members causes little disruption to its capability of launching numerous attacks, most of which are comparatively modest in scale. Although a hierarchical army-style organisation is more vulnerable to counterterrorist action, for as long as its command and control centre is functional, it may have the potential to launch highly destructive raids of military proportions. Accordingly, the frequency and severity of attacks by terrorists depends on their organisational structure.

The names by which terrorist groups are known reflect the manner in which they are collectively organised. Some may be self-styled as liberation or freedom-fighting organisations, armies, brigades or fronts, but no appellation is as frustrating to national security services as that of the network, most notably as in the late 1990s with the al-Qaeda network. Spanning several continents, an international network prospers from national differences in the tolerance of foreign terrorists, and in the liberality of laws of asylum and extradition.

Dispersed over a multitude of host countries, al-Qaeda is in fact a hybrid of hierarchical and network forms of organisation; a terrorism conglomerate with both vertical and horizontal command elements (Ronfeldt and Arquilla, 2001b). Although it is notorious for the leadership of Osama Bin Laden, within al-Qaeda there are also semi-autonomous groups which have horizontal coordination. If al-Qaeda had a standard hierarchical army structure, then the capitulation or removal of its leadership might signal its demise as a terrorist force. If this were the case, then the hazard stemming from al-Qaeda would be greatly reduced. This may be wishful thinking. There are a variety of alternative network architectures that al-Qaeda, or any of the other dozen major terrorist organisations, might adopt. Each architecture poses a different challenge to the security services, and to life and property. To avoid the targeting of leaders, a network design may encourage the spatial diffusion of leadership, minimising the dependence on central control.

MULTI-HUB NETWORKS

One possible architecture for a terrorist network involves multiple independent hubs, each serving as a control centre for a number of satellite cells. To maximise the chance of surviving concerted counterterrorist action, these hubs may be dispersed over different countries, if not continents. This multi-hub structure is illustrated in Figure 1. The cells attached to a given hub would, for security of information reasons, be isolated from one another, with instructions restricted to a "need-to-know" basis. But the cells might be linked up for major operations. Traditional terrorist organisations, such as the Irish Republican Army (IRA) and the Basque separatist

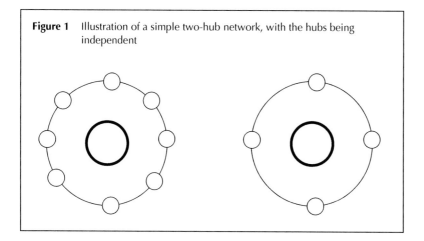

Figure 1   Illustration of a simple two-hub network, with the hubs being independent

group ETA developed complicated cell structures to combat infiltration and monitoring by the security services (Ronfeldt and Arquilla, 2001b).

This hub architecture is partly hierarchical, in that financial, logistical and training support for the peripheral cells are centrally sourced, and strategic planning would be directed from the hubs. However, much of the tactical strike planning, cell recruitment and management would be handled locally. This kind of network architecture would, through the ambition of the hub leadership and continuity of the senior high command, enable centralised planning to be conducted on a long-term basis, and facilitate the coordination of complex operations. Ultimately, this would tend to cut the failure rate of attempts at major spectacular attacks.

However, rather like giant battleships in a naval war, hubs are high profile targets, the elimination of which can lead to rapid military defeat. Of course, the more hubs there are, the more redundancy there is, and the harder the network is to defeat. The al-Qaeda network architecture that existed prior to September 11, 2001 may well have been adapted in order to survive the subsequent declaration of war on terrorism. The international safe havens where al-Qaeda could operate its hubs without hindrance may now disappear, forcing al-Qaeda to assume another organisational guise.

SWARM INTELLIGENCE NETWORKS

A more elusive and resilient type of network architecture has no hub, but consists simply of a set of terrorist cells, which may comprise one or more individuals. As perceived by RAND strategists, these cells may be geographically spread over a wide area, or even around the world, but would be capable of swarming in for a coordinated terrorist attack. This kind of architecture is illustrated in Figure 2. The possibility for complex move-

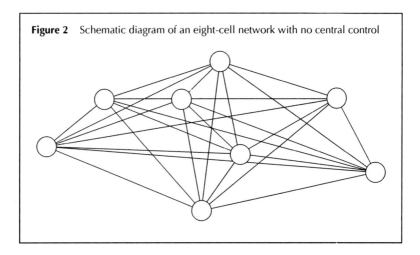

Figure 2 Schematic diagram of an eight-cell network with no central control

ments of large numbers to be coordinated without any central command and control is familiar from the flocking of birds, and the swarming of insects. Some aerobatic flocking displays seem remarkable without the presence of a lead bird to guide the others. Astonishing feats of spatial intelligence are also achievable by colonies of ants, following an equally elementary set of individual behavioural rules.

In the realm of human conflict, an analogy may be made with the predatory tactics of the German U-boat fleet during the Second World War. The submarines were dispersed over thousands of square kilometres of the North Atlantic. When a merchant ship was spotted by one of the submarines, information was communicated by radio to the rest of the fleet, and those within range swarmed in for the kill (Ronfeldt and Arquilla, 2001b).

With no specific hub to aim at, counterterrorist forces face a greater challenge in trying to root out all the individual cells making up a swarm intelligence network. The cells would each tend to have a lower security profile than a hub. At this time, according to the BBC, Iraqi reports claim that a score of trained terrorists are dispersed around the world, prepared to launch a concerted terrorist strike against Western interests. Such terrorists constitute at least a tangible search target for counterterrorist forces, even if special intelligence resources would be needed to locate them. Tough as this challenge may be, more problematic would be a swarm cluster which emerged more or less spontaneously (Wilkinson, 1995). Such a cluster would be very difficult to identify, and security services would have little warning of its operations.

EMERGENT SWARM CLUSTERS

Where cells exist with a definite geographical locus, they may become progressively vulnerable to surveillance operations, and infiltration, by counterterrorist forces. For protection and survival, the dynamics of cell formation may have to be adapted. Harder for security services to thwart would be an attack from an alternative network: one which emerged almost spontaneously from the complex behaviour of peripheral sympathisers of the terrorist cause. A swarm attack would be mainly manned not by long-term terrorist suspects, whose movements may be tracked via regular surveillance, but by newer recruits to the terrorist cause, unknown to the security forces.

The most difficult type of network architecture to deal with is one which has the superficial appearance of random disorganisation, with components moving in an apparently chaotic manner, but which actually displays a high degree of spatially distributed intelligence. What would be especially puzzling to security forces is the apparently haphazard variation in the commitment of a specific individual to the terrorist cause. Such individuals would not be classified as hard-liners, and would soon disappear from the terrorist radar screen. The charter of the Jihad movement, as expressed in the Islamic radicalism of Sayyid Qutb (Mousalli, 1993), is freely available on the Internet; therefore, attendance at mosques to hear radical imams might be rather sporadic. Grounds for prior arrest or detention as a potential terrorist suspect would accordingly be very thin.

Swarming is an image borrowed from the natural world of three space dimensions. A swarm of bees, for example, is defined by spatial clustering. However, swarming may be defined in any number of dimensions, including non-physical dimensions such as support for extremist groups, disdain for Western culture, etc. For simplicity, these other dimensions may be collapsed to a single dimension defined by commitment to participate in a terrorist act. The greatest challenge to security forces would arise from swarming in this virtual terrorism dimension, by individuals who might physically be geographically dispersed all over the world. This is illustrated schematically in Figure 3.

These individuals may not themselves have any prolonged history of links with radical groups, so they would be hard to identify in advance as

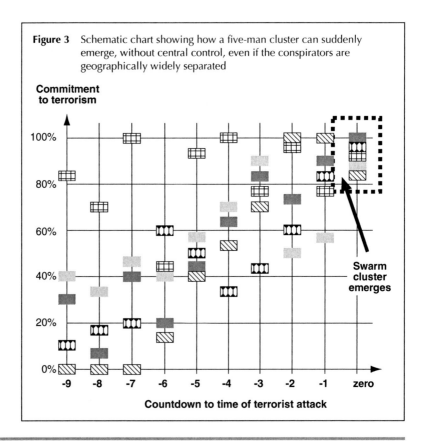

Figure 3 Schematic chart showing how a five-man cluster can suddenly emerge, without central control, even if the conspirators are geographically widely separated

potential suspects. They may be motivated through public exhortations to violence on the radio, television, or the Internet. A cluster of like-minded individuals, who may never have actually met, could collectively contrive a terrorist act, using global communications such as the Internet. Being spontaneously generated, such a group would be almost impossible to infiltrate. An emergent network is essentially a virtual one, in respect of both physical presence and web-based communication. The capability of militant anarchists and anti-capitalists to mass together and cause mayhem at the economic summits in Seattle and Genoa (Ronfeldt and Arquilla, 2001a,b) shows the potency of an emergent network.

The commitment of an individual to participating in terrorism is gauged in percentage terms, and graphed as the ordinate on the plot. Clustering is in this dimension, rather than in actual space dimensions, so the detection of a cluster by security services, in advance of the zero hour for attack, would be extremely difficult. The formation of attack swarms can be computer simulated, using algorithms drawn from the modelling of other emergent swarm intelligence phenomena (Kennedy and Eberhart, 2001).

Since cell membership may fluctuate widely from time to time, terrorists would be hard to track down by security forces. The attacks perpetrated by an emergent network would be difficult to prevent, even if intensive counter-swarm measures were implemented to catch nests of terrorists. Given the comparatively low reliability of attack detection, (Reeve, 1999) the number of attacks, therefore, might proliferate. However, given the shorter training time available for the attacks, and the involvement of less experienced personnel, the damage inflicted in any action is unlikely to be as extensive as in attacks planned carefully over many years. Nevertheless, the remote possibility exists that an emergent network, might be capable of delivering a strike involving weapons of mass destruction (WMD). The danger is that, in the distorted perception of al-Qaeda, this might be viewed as the perfect network for such a mission.

THE FREQUENCY OF PLANNED ATTACKS

For as long as Jihad is used to support or excuse fanatical suicide missions, (Qutb, 1991) others will follow in the footsteps of the British-educated Ramzi Yousef, master-bomber of al-Qaeda, who imagined he was advancing the Palestinian cause by plying his terrorist trade around the world (Reeve, 1999). As with the IRA's terror campaign in Britain, (www. BelfastTelegraph. co. uk) the frequency of Islamic terrorist attacks may be expected to fluctuate with the swings of political fortune and progress in peace negotiations. Exasperation with the political process may encourage the proliferation of attacks.

In the days before television, terrorists could signal their presence by means of an intensive bombing campaign: the IRA exploded 127 devices in Britain during the late 1930s (www.BelfastTelegraph.co.uk). In contrast,

IRA political frustration with the Ulster peace process was vented in 1996 by a showpiece bomb blast at Canary Wharf, London's equivalent of the WTC (www.BelfastTelegraph.co.uk). As appreciated by the IRA, publicity and fear go together and these are maximised if terrorists choose not just political and financial targets, but a wide range of targets, including infrastructure, shops, bars, government offices, as well as commercial buildings. This diversity in targeting is some consolation to property insurers, who would not be heavily exposed to loss from all attacks.

For a hierarchical terrorist organisation, the rate of planned attacks should be proportional to the number of mature active cells. This number would thus be drastically curtailed by sustained global counter-terrorist action to seek and destroy these cells. However, the spontaneous formation of less detectable emergent terrorist cells would permit quite frequent attacks to be launched, in guerilla style, on a multiplicity of targets around the world. Attack frequency would not be restricted by the number of cells, since these would rapidly form and disperse. The numbers of planned attacks ie, the rhythm of terror, might ultimately be determined as much by publicity goals as by the size of the terrorist ranks. As exemplified by the IRA campaign, well-publicised occasional moderate bomb damage suffices to perpetuate a reign of fear.

THE SPATIAL DISTRIBUTION OF HAZARD
The distributed spatial intelligence of transcontinental terrorist networks allows attacks to be made across the globe, by operatives of many nationalities, at locations which may be far away from any cell. From the bombing of the Khobar Towers in Saudi Arabia in 1996, to the Nairobi and Dar es Salaam US Embassy bombings in 1998, to the bombing of the USS Cole in 2000 and the WTC disaster of 2001, al-Qaeda have developed a swarm-like campaign of pulsing attacks from different nodes of its global network (Ronfeldt and Arquilla, 2001a,b).

Unlike natural perils, whose hazards are spatially concentrated around geological faults, coastlines, flood plains etc, the free mobility of terrorists means that there is no fixed geography for terrorism hazard. There is an earthquake engineering adage that an earthquake will expose the weakest link in a building (Coburn and Spence, 1992). But, if a number of structures are randomly distributed in a region, the pattern of seismicity does not alter so that the weakest structure is most likely to be shaken. Yet, with a terrorist threat to a number of prize targets, the most vulnerable may have the highest probability of being attacked. Other things being equal, less planning time and fewer resources should be needed to launch a successful raid. The dependence of hazard location on vulnerability introduces a non-linear feedback in risk computation, which would tend to escalate the loss potential.

Should a terrorist organisation aim to cause maximal economic disruption, it might preferentially target spatially distributed infrastructure networks of telecommunications, power, water supply and transportation. Not only is there little redundancy in these systems, but they are also highly vulnerable. US critical infrastructure suffers historically from serious neglect by regulatory and law enforcement agencies (Flynn, 2001). The potential consequences of a breach of security are enormous. If the USS Cole attack were replicated against a tanker docked at the main terminal in Long Beach, California, the economy of southern California would be crippled in days through lack of oil supplies (Flynn, 2001). Similarly, if Port Everglades in Florida were shut down through terrorist action, millions of southern Florida residents would suffer an almost immediate fuel shortage (Flynn, 2001).

EVENT-TREE FOR THE DETECTION AND THWARTING OF PLANNED ATTACKS

In common with other long-tail risk phenomena, such as aviation or marine accidents, the task of characterising the tail of the terrorism loss distribution is assisted by exploration and analysis of the statistics of the more common "near miss" events, which narrowly failed to be significant disasters. In the context of terrorist attacks, near misses arise because they were thwarted by counterterrorist forces, security checks, or because of some technical or logistical misadventure. Nobody familiar with the prolific professional bombing career of Ramzi Yousef would be content to assess risk on the basis of actual losses alone. In 1993, he came close to toppling one of the towers of the WTC; he bombed a Philippines airliner in 1995, and subsequently plotted to bomb as many as eleven jets over the Pacific (Reeve, 1999). Even though Yousef was jailed, he was a member of a terrorist network, (Reeve, 1999) and prudent underwriters might well have double-checked their exposure to multiple WTC and civil aviation disasters.

Apart from the 1993 attack itself, the possibility of the WTC being targeted for terrorist action might have been apparent to underwriters, if not also to the security forces, from other developments. The concept of using a fuel-laden commercial airliner as a missile had occurred to Algerian terrorists in 1994, who hatched a plan to crash a plane into the Eiffel Tower in Paris (Reeve, 1999).

Not all planned attacks succeed in causing a notable loss. Terrorists may be defeated through good intelligence; good security and policing, and some good fortune. Yousef's audacious multiple airliner bomb plot was foiled through an accidental fire breaking out during the bomb-making process (Reeve, 1999). The Eiffel Tower still stands because the plane hijacked by Algerian terrorists was stormed by French commandos, while being refuelled.

In the probabilistic risk assessment (PRA) of nuclear installations, which provides the methodological basis underlying insurance natural catastrophe modelling (Woo, 1999), and more recently civil aviation risk modelling, the damage consequences of initiating a hazardous event are logically charted via a multi-branch event-tree. The process of systematically disaggregating risk into component elements, through an event-tree, is an important aspect of structuring a risk analysis.

The event-tree can be used in the present context to estimate the probability that a planned terrorist attack results in a notable loss. The success of a planned attack is contingent on certain events either occurring or not occurring. These events are the procurement of intelligence about the attack, resolution to act based on any intelligence, interdiction by police or other security officials and technical or logistical operational failure. A basic event-tree, constructed around these events, is shown in Figure 4.

To parameterise this event-tree, four basic conditional probabilities need to be quantified.

1. Given that an attack is planned, what is the probability that there is some prior intelligence about it?
2. Given that an attack is planned, and there is some prior intelligence about it, what is the probability that the intelligence is acted upon?
3. Given that an attack is planned, and either no intelligence exists or else is not acted upon, what is the probability that the attack is nevertheless detected by border guards, police or other security personnel?
4. Given that an attack is planned, but remains completely undetected, what is the probability that it fails to cause significant loss due to technical or logistical shortcomings?

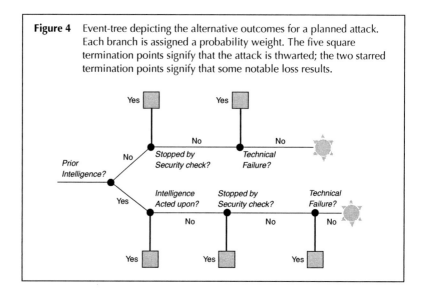

Figure 4   Event-tree depicting the alternative outcomes for a planned attack. Each branch is assigned a probability weight. The five square termination points signify that the attack is thwarted; the two starred termination points signify that some notable loss results.

These key questions of probability are elaborated below.

1. Availability of intelligence
Even with a hub network structure, which is comparatively accessible to surveillance, intelligence on al-Qaeda has been poor. Whatever the enhancement of counterterrorist intelligence, Pentagon officials (Reeve, 1999) admit that future attacks planned by emergent local networks will be "very, very difficult to stop". Terrorists may never actually meet, except to carry out a specific operation, with all the planning and the vetting of individuals taking place through the Internet. Thus the chance that intelligence about such an attack would be forthcoming is very slight.

2. Action on intelligence
False alarms are the bane of intelligence services. The more disinformation and bogus threats there are, the smaller the probability that intelligence about a specific threat will be acted upon. In the six months following the US Embassy bombings in East Africa, (Bergen, 2001) US diplomatic facilities around the world were inundated with 650 credible threats from al-Qaeda (Bergen, 2001). These threats were garnered from a range of sources, including informants; telephone surveillance, sightings of a terrorist in a city, and embassy videotaping. Finite resources for checking the reliability of threats greatly restricts the number which can be adequately acted upon (Bergen, 2001). Furthermore, as with other natural peril hazard alarms, the high cost of the disruption resulting from a false alarm has to be weighed against the expected benefit from sounding a correct alarm.

In common with the international transport of illegal immigrants, intelligence is vital. But unless this intelligence is sound, the time and expense of stopping and searching can be inordinately high. In the case of the cargo ship MV Nisha, purportedly carrying sugar from Mauritius to London, via Djibouti, the detention of the vessel for several days at the end of 2001 turned out to be a false alarm. According to newspaper reports, no evidence of explosives was found. Given practical tolerance limits to the economic disruption induced by rigorous security checks at borders, searching for terrorist needles in a transportation haystack may well prove to be a largely futile exercise.

3. Security barriers
Even if no prior intelligence exists about a planned attack, or if any such intelligence is ignored, there is still a chance that it would be detected at some stage by border guards, police, customs officers, or another security barrier. However, recognising the coarse mesh of the global security net, this chance may be comparatively low. Given the vast traffic flows across international borders, tracking terrorists effectively without unacceptable delays to others may be nigh impossible.

At the world's busiest commercial land border crossing, which is the Ambassador bridge between Michigan and Ontario, US customs officers have no more than two minutes for each truck (Flynn, 2001). Despite security deficiencies, sometimes terrorists do manage to get themselves caught at border crossings, as happened when the sweating Ahmed Ressam was arrested on a ferry arriving from Canada. In his car were 130 pounds of explosives intended for a Millennium Eve bombing (Flynn, 2001).

4. Technical or logistical failure

The track record of terrorist miscalculations, bungles, and other miscellaneous mishaps provides some relevant experience data on mission failure. One of the longest data series, covering a number of decades, comes from the IRA campaign in Britain (Bowyer Bell, 2000). In attacks on political targets, the IRA succeeded in several political assassinations, and came close on several occasions, in 1984 and 1991, to assassinating a group of senior government ministers (www.BelfastTelegraph.co.uk). In attacks targeted at the public, car and truck bombs have taken their toll of bars, shopping centres and offices. But apart from those bombs which have caused notable damage, others have either only partially exploded, failed to detonate, or detonated prematurely. Failures have also occurred for logistical reasons such as in the theft of cars or trucks for bomb transport (www. BelfastTelegraph.co.uk).

Public sources of information from media reports provide some guide as to the proportion of undetected bombing attempts which failed to make a significant impact for technical or logistical reasons. However, allowance needs to be made for those technical or logistical failures which never attracted public attention. In principle, the failure ratio might be assigned on a scenario basis, but this complication may be avoided by using a generic value.

The systematic assignment of probability weights remains to be undertaken, but preliminary estimates (Ronfeldt and Arquilla, 2001a,b) suggest that the overall chance of a planned attack being successful would be high for an emergent network. Weaknesses in the defensive shield against such terrorist attacks will be hard to rectify. Whatever the international will to fight terrorism, a substantial residual risk is likely to remain.

LOSS SEVERITY DISTRIBUTION

Before war was declared on terrorism, al-Qaeda could afford to take time, and devote resources, to plan attacks which would perpetuate their reign of terror, and also inflict substantial loss. It is possible that the larger the loss, the more likely the scenario would have been chosen. With this positive feedback, the loss severity distribution prior to September 11, 2001 would have been skewed towards heavy losses; a risk characteristic consistent of course with the WTC attack.

Adapting from a hub structure to an emergent network architecture, al-Qaeda may become less visible to the spreading force of counterterrorists, but the organisation would pay a penalty: it would be hampered with more coordination and supply problems. The impairment of coordination and restriction of resources should make it more difficult for spectacular massive single-site strikes to be successfully delivered, and more tricky to synchronise contemporaneous strikes at different locations. Furthermore, the non-linear feedback dependence of scenario likelihood on loss will be much diminished; high loss scenarios may be attractive to al-Qaeda, but they may also be especially hard to execute under pressure. Counting synchronised strikes as a single event, the relative likelihood of one event generating enormous losses is correspondingly reduced with the hubless swarm network architecture. In earthquake parlance, one would say that the emergent network architecture yields a higher b-value of the Gutenberg–Richter magnitude–frequency relation; the b-value being a measure of the relative frequency of small to large events (Woo, 1999).

This argument can be made computationally explicit when expressed in terms of an ensemble of realistic terrorism scenarios, which are the basic building blocks of a terrorism stochastic model. Geographic Information Systems (GIS) tools for mapping the geography of exposure, developed originally for natural hazard applications, are being adapted by RMS to map the spatial footprint of loss across a spectrum of high-publicity showpiece terrorist scenarios, considered as realistic in terms of their potential attraction to terrorist groups. This mapping procedure is quite arduous and lengthy, because these scenarios can be quite diverse in their initiating event, and in their urban impact.

For an emergent network, under constant pressure from international counterterrorist forces, the types of attacks which can be attempted will be constrained by available resources, and limited by lack of planning time. The campaign against the IRA provides illustrations of the effectiveness of heightening security, and cutting off supplies of armaments, in reducing the options for terrorist action (www.BelfastTelegraph.co.uk). In future, terrorist groups will have more of an operational research allocation problem to solve: to achieve their high-profile publicity goals, subject to fairly stringent time and resource constraints. Thus, whatever the personal predilections of the individual terrorists, the relative likelihood of a show-piece scenario, (missile strike, LNG tanker explosion, nuclear device detonation or whatever), will be governed by a cost function. This is a measure of the overall difficulty in execution, allowing for a variety of factors, such as planning time, personnel effort, technical problems, and consumption of financial and material resources. (For martyrdom missions, there is of course no cost consideration for danger to the terrorists themselves.)

By quantifying relative likelihood on the basis of the cost function, a value of which is assigned to each realistic scenario, a loss severity distribution can be constructed by ranking the terrorism scenarios according to loss. Clearly, the form of this loss severity distribution will depend on the choice of the cost function. But, since the cost function is used for assigning relative rather than absolute frequencies, the final risk results should be reasonably robust against changes, the effect of which, in any case, can be explored in sensitivity studies.

LOSS EXCEEDANCE PROBABILITY ESTIMATION

Once the loss severity distribution is parameterised, the annual loss exceedance probability may be calculated. This is done by using a best estimate, (or hypothetical time-dependent distribution), for the overall frequency of planned attacks and the event-tree estimate for the probability of an attack being thwarted. This risk calculation inevitably involves a number of subjective probability assignments. These may be made informally by in-house risk analysts, but, in order to maintain the principles of fairness, neutrality and accountability (Cooke, 1991), these are best made through eliciting the expert judgement of terrorism experts.

The procedure for eliciting expert judgement indeed has its origins in assessments made of Cold War threats in the 1960s, by the RAND corporation, and its use in the present terrorist context closes a circle of application. This reference to RAND's expertise in strategic thinking is particularly apposite, because the seminal ideas of netwar which underpin this chapter originate from RAND experts (Arquilla, Ronfeldt and Zanini, 2000). Since the 1960s, the expert elicitation procedure has been used widely in natural hazard risk studies, including the most rigorous site-specific analyses of engineering seismic hazard. It has also been used to assess the risk of malicious intrusion into a radioactive waste disposal site (Woo, 1989). The theft of radioactive material, and its dispersal in an urban population centre, has a terrorist precedent in the Chechen campaign against Russia, and is very much a major concern for the future.

The value of consulting a group of leading terrorism experts was clearly demonstrated in a secret study called *Terror 2000*, conducted by the Pentagon, intended to help the intelligence world meet the terrorism threat. This study was facilitated by the president of Forecasting International, who involved forty leading experts, including a former KGB head; a senior official from Mossad, and Professor Paul Wilkinson, the noted British terrorism analyst. One of the prescient conclusions of the study was that terrorists would soon try to conduct simultaneous bombings, perhaps in different countries, to maximise the devastation and publicity. This was just one of a number of findings which recipients of the report, both in government and industry, found to be unrealistic as well as unpalatable.

Knowledgeable as these experts would have been of the foiled Algerian attempt to crash a plane into the Eiffel Tower, had they been asked in 2000 to assign a probability to an aviation attack on the WTC, the answer would surely have prepared insurers better, both commercially and pyschologically, for the disaster of the following year. Loss potential values maintained by some insurers for the WTC would have been tenable only if the probability were minuscule.

In order to provide insurers with a quantitative guide as to the extent of terrorism exposure, the probabilistic framework outlined here for quantifying terrorism risk could be parameterised systematically with the assistance of a convocation of international terrorism experts. Simple calculations suggest that, despite international counterterrorist action, the risk is currently substantial, as indeed it was before September 11, 2001.

CONCLUSION

Although insurance is provided against many types of criminal behaviour, quantifying terrorism risk is recognised as a formidable task for the insurance industry. Yet it should be remembered that the challenge of assessing human factors, such as fraud, vandalism, sabotage and human error is met in the course of many industrial probabilistic risk assessments.

An approach to tackling the terrorism risk quantification task has been outlined, from which the following principal observations may be drawn.

❑ The frequency and severity of planned attacks will depend critically on the network architecture of the terrorist organisation.

❑ Pressurised increasingly by counterterrorist forces, terrorist organisations may adapt to form emergent swarm clusters. These rapidly forming virtual cells, communicating via Internet, will be very hard to detect and stop.

❑ Emergent networks will facilitate the execution of more frequent, but less ambitious and generally less damaging, planned attacks.

❑ An event-tree may be constructed to estimate the probability that a planned attack will succeed, depending on the availability and usage of intelligence; the effectiveness of security barriers and technical and logistical mishaps.

❑ The loss severity distribution may be derived by mapping losses from realistic showpiece terrorism scenarios, and assigning a cost function to each. The cost function reflects practical logistical factors such as planning time, technical difficulty, and consumption of scarce resources.

❑ The overall computation of a terrorism loss exceedance curve can be achieved, provided that the assignment of subjective input probabilities is made using the formal elicitation of expert judgement, such as has been invoked already by government security agencies.

As with any risk analysis, the derivation of probabilistic loss exceedance curves for terrorism is not an end in itself, but an aid for insurers to make better decisions under uncertainty. Even if these loss curves themselves are uncertain, general guidance on the steepness and scale of these loss curves, and their sensitivity to model assumptions, would be welcome technical support for insurers in setting loss potential values and in pricing terrorism cover.

BIBLIOGRAPHY

Arquilla, J., D. Ronfeldt and M. Zanini, 2000, "Information-age terrorism", *Current History*, Vol. 99, pp. 179–185.

Bergen, P. L., 2001, *Holy War, Inc.* (London: Weidenfeld and Nicholson).

Bonabeau, E., M. Dorigo and G. Theraulaz, 1999, *Swarm Intelligence*, (Oxford University Press)

Bowyer Bell, J., 2000, The IRA, 1968–2000 (London: Frank Cass & Co.)

Coburn, A. and Spence, R., 1992, *Earthquake Protection*, (Chichester: John Wiley & Sons).

Cooke, R. M., 1991, *Experts in Uncertainty* (Oxford University Press).

Flynn, S. E., 2001, "The Unguarded Homeland", in: J. F. Hoge and G. Rose (eds), *How Did This Happen?* (Oxford:PublicAffairs Ltd.).

Johnson, S., 2001, *Emergence* (London: Allen Lane, the Penguin Press).

Kennedy, J., and R. C. Eberhart, 2001, *Swarm Intelligence* (San Francisco: Morgan Kaufmann Publishers).

Moussalli, A. S., 1993, *Radical Islamic Fundamentalism: The Ideological and Political Discourse of Sayyid Qutb* (NY: Syracuse University Press).

Pais, A., 1983, "Subtle is the Lord: the Science and the Life of Albert Einstein", (Oxford University Press).

Qutb, S., 1991 "Milestones", (American Trust Publications.)

Reeve, S., 1999, *The New Jackals,* (London: Andre Deutsch).

Ronfeldt, D., and J. Arquilla, 2001a, "Networks, Netwars, and the Fight of the Future", *First Monday,* 6(10).

Ronfeldt, D., and J. Arquilla, 2001b, "Networks and Netwars: The Future of Terror, Crime and Militancy", (Washington: RAND Corporation).

Waldrop, M. M., 1992, *Complexity* (London: Viking Press).

Wilkinson, P., 1995, "Terrorism, motivation and causes", (Canadian Security Intelligence Service, Commentary No. 53.)

Wilson, E. O., 1975, *Sociobiology* (Cambridge, MA: Harvard University Press).

Woo, G., 1989, "Is the risk of human intrusion exaggerated?", in: Proceedings of NEA workshop on: *Risks With Human Intrusion at Radioactive Waste Disposal Sites,* (Paris: OECD).

Woo, G., 1999, *The Mathematics of Natural Catastrophes* (London: Imperial College Press).

15

Weather Risk Modelling for Improved Weather Risk Management

Mark Gibbas and S. Ming Lee

Applied Insurance Research, Inc (AIR)

Nearly US$2 trillion of the US economy – from gas and electric utilities, airlines and snowmobile manufacturers to beer and bathing suit makers – is sensitive to temperature, precipitation and other weather variables according to the US Department of Commerce.[1] Globally, weather has an astronomical impact on corporate bottom lines. Although meteorologists have not yet figured out how to control the weather, the "weather market" has come up with ways to manage weather risks through the use of weather derivatives: financial contracts that allow companies whose bottom lines are affected by the weather to hedge their weather risk. For example, a warmer than normal winter could result in less revenue for a natural gas utility or heating oil distributor. However, a company can buy a contract to receive a contingent payment, the amount of which is based on how much warmer the winter season turns out to be, and thereby hedge against the risk of a warmer winter.

Who is involved in the weather market? The primary players in the weather market are customers, market makers, insurers and reinsurers, investment banks and brokers that interface between these groups. Customers are the companies that need to protect their earnings from undesirable weather outcomes – for example, the gas or electric utilities, ski lodges, or summer resorts which lose business when the weather is too hot, too cold, too rainy, or when there is not enough snow. Market makers, traditionally energy trading companies, structure and offer weather derivatives to customers and are responsible for providing liquidity in the market. Insurers and reinsurers provide insurance and other weather risk products to customers and also provide liquidity in the market. Traditionally, investment banks provided their clients – the market makers, insurers and reinsurers – capacity by providing them access to the capital markets. Recently, some investment banks have started directly trading weather derivatives. Finally, brokers bring market players together, and in the case of insurance brokers, introduce customers to insurers for a fee. Brokers also help find new participants and, among other functions, help structure and price deals and maintain anonymity of the counterparties, when that is important.

Players in the weather market have different perspectives and need to evaluate risk, value transactions, and track and manage portfolios in their own way. Since weather contracts rely on the weather observed at particular weather stations, market participants require high quality meteorological data from the relevant stations in order to quantify the weather risk, perform analyses, and make good decisions.

In order to execute a weather contract, a number of items need to come together. First, customers (at-risk companies) need to quantify the impact of weather in financial terms as accurately as possible. Second, the market maker and the customer need to agree on the structure and cost of a suitable contract. Access to high quality weather data is critical to understanding the risk and appropriately structuring and pricing a contract. These data provide the basis for deriving probability distributions that describe the range and relative frequency of weather that has occurred at the weather station of interest. In addition, climate forecasts that incorporate the weather expected over the course of the contract may be used to fine-tune the probability information.

Between November 1997 and March 2001, nearly 5,000 contracts, with a total notional value of US$7.5 billion, were transacted, according to the Weather Risk Management Association.[2] However, in comparison with the value of all financial derivatives traded worldwide, the weather market has not grown as rapidly as its advocates would have liked. One key factor limiting the growth is the accessibility and quality of the weather data used for modelling. Ultimately, the market depends on the ability of all parties to quantify weather risk reliably.

INTRODUCTION

This chapter explores the critical role of high quality weather data and climate forecasts in pricing and structuring weather derivative deals, and the issues surrounding historical data and forecast quality. We conclude that the advent of sophisticated weather data improvement methodologies, and the introduction of robust climate forecasts, will help the weather market achieve its growth potential.

THE ROLE OF WEATHER DATA

Suppose that we manage the operations of a large office tower in New York, and that in recent years our electricity bills have soared dramatically because of increased air conditioning needs during hotter than normal summers. Given our obligation to meet certain financial goals, we are willing to pay a predetermined amount (a premium) to hedge our risk against having to pay unexpectedly high electricity bills should summer temperatures be hotter than normal.

To start the process, we need to quantify the weather risk and understand the type of contract structure that might be useful. The risk of the weather being too hot can be measured in terms of a probability distribution of cooling degree days or CDDs. (See Panel 1). Figure 1 below shows an example of a CDD distribution.

The CDD distribution is, in this case, a Gaussian distribution fitted to the historical frequency of CDDs for the month of July over the last 30 years. From this distribution, it can be determined that the mean is 520 CDD. Of course, varying qualities of historical time series will lead to varying qualities of derived distributions. Thus it is clear that we need to start with

---

PANEL 1

Calculating HDD and CDD

Heating degree days (HDD) and cooling degree days (CDD) are indices used by the energy industry to measure demand for energy for heating and cooling purposes.

HDD and CDD are calculated by finding the average temperature for the day by adding the daily minimum and maximum temperatures together and dividing by two. The result is then compared to a temperature that is considered "comfortable". In the US this threshold is 65°F. In many other countries this threshold is 18°C.

Only positive results are counted. Negative values are set to zero. Subtracting the daily average temperature from 65 gives the daily value of HDD. Again only positive results are counted and negative values are set to zero. For example, in January, if the average temperature on a given day were 35°F, this would translate into 30 HDD, which can be equated to how much energy is needed to keep living spaces comfortable on that day.

Daily CDD and HDD are then combined into monthly or seasonal aggregates by adding together the daily values.

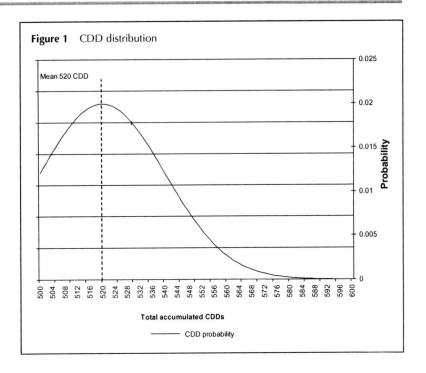

Figure 1   CDD distribution

highest quality temperature data in order to quantify the weather risk accurately.

In the next step of the process, we need to decide how much protection is needed and how much we are willing to pay for it. We then determine that an extremely uncomfortable summer season will cost several hundred thousand US dollars in additional air conditioning costs. Through consultation and negotiation with a market maker or broker, we can agree on a deal for a CDD call option (see Figure 2). In this case, the strike is set at 530 CDD. The cost of this contract is US$120,000, and for that premium we will be paid US$10,000 per CDD above 530. The contract is capped at a maximum payoff of US$500,000. Accounting for the cost of the contract, the revenue line starts at -US$120,000 and has a limit of US$380,000 due to the cap.

Assuming the CDD distribution properly represents the probability, there is an 86% chance that the contract will not pay out. However, should the weather be unusually hot, such that the contract settles in the warm 14% region of the distribution, payoff from the contract can be used to offset increased cooling expenses.

While the above example is somewhat simplified, it does illustrate the basic constructs of weather derivatives. Beyond calls, there can be other types of contracts such as puts, collars and dual-trigger contracts.

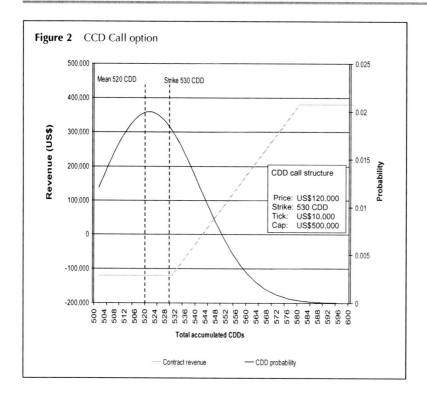

Figure 2   CCD Call option

Regardless of how simple or complex a contract is, the starting point is good quality weather data.

WEATHER DATA QUALITY ISSUES

Data collected over a number of years at weather stations serve as the primary means of estimating probability distributions upon which weather contracts are structured and priced. In order to derive representative distributions it is important that the data be accurate (no erroneous values), continuous (no data gaps) and homogeneous (ie, the data are temporally consistent with current observation behaviour).

To ensure data are of high quality it is essential that the data originate from first-order stations that are professionally staffed and equipped with high quality, dependable instrumentation. Continuity is important because missing data will cause serious errors when weather parameters are aggregated. For example, if when creating a time series of January HDD in one particular January there were a number of missing observations, the total HDD for that January would turn out to be much smaller compared to HDD totals from Januarys with complete observations. Finally, when a distribution is derived from the January HDD time series, it would not be representative of actual conditions.

Non-meteorologists can appreciate the need for data continuity, but may not realise the need for data homogeneity. After all, if data are collected from a single station, shouldn't the data be homogenous? Unfortunately, changes to a station over time can result in a time series that is temporally inconsistent. Two events that can cause shifts in time series are instrument changes and station relocations. Additionally, trends such as global warming and urbanisation can also render the time series temporally inconsistent. Any inconsistencies that are not corrected would result in probability distributions that do not accurately represent the weather conditions observed at the station.

Instrument Changes

Weather thermometers are instruments designed to measure the temperature of the air. Like any sensing device, thermometers do not measure temperatures with perfect accuracy. In fact, it is common for most thermometers to produce biased measurements. If only one thermometer is used over the history of a station, and if the bias in the instrument is constant over time, then as long as there were no other inconsistencies, the time series would be homogeneous and may therefore be acceptable for contract structuring and pricing.

However, consider a case when one thermometer is replaced by another. Suppose the original thermometer, on average, recorded temperatures that were half a degree colder than the actual temperature at that station. Now, suppose that a new thermometer that records temperatures half a degree warmer than actual temperatures recently replaced this thermometer. All other things being constant, if the majority of the time series was recorded with the first instrument, the distribution derived from the time series would be about a degree colder than what is being recorded on average with the new instrument. Returning to the example CDD call option, assume that the change in instruments occurred as described above and that the weather during the period of the contract was normal. Given that the new thermometer is recording observations that are one degree warmer than the old thermometer, the new thermometer will generate 30 more CDD during the month such that even if the ambient weather was normal, the total number of CDD would be closer to 550, as opposed to the expected mean of 520 CDD. The seller of the contract would have to pay out US$200,000 that it would not have had to if better data had been used to structure the contract. The risk of poorly structured contracts emphasises the need for the use of high quality data that has been specifically conditioned for structuring sound, robust contracts.

Station Relocations and Changes to Station Surroundings

Occasionally, weather stations need to be relocated. Primary weather stations, often located at airports, get moved when airports expand. Weather modernisation programs also cause station relocations. During the 1990s, many primary weather stations in the US were moved when the National Weather Service (NWS) migrated to a new meteorological observation system known as the Automated Surface Observing System (ASOS). ASOS represented not only a change in instrumentation for all primary weather stations; it also often prompted a change in location of the weather stations, as existing locations often did not meet the requirements of the new ASOS instrumentation.[3]

Station relocations cause inhomogeneity in weather data because the nature of the surroundings in the immediate vicinity of a station can influence the observed temperature. Changes in elevation, soil type, vegetation, and proximity to bodies of water can significantly affect temperatures at the instrument location. To complicate matters, the shift experienced is almost never constant. Moving a station close to a body of water, for example, has the effect of lowering temperatures in the summer and warming temperatures in the winter. Another reason why a station may experience a move-like shift is when the station's surroundings change while the station remains fixed. Sudden shifts have been identified in stations resulting from changes to the surrounding environment, such as the appearance of a new lake formed by the construction of a nearby dam. For rooftop stations, dramatic shifts have occurred resulting from re-tarring of the roof.

Figure 3 illustrates a shift in observational readings resulting from a move of the Orlando, Florida station.[4] The top chart shows the time series of averaged January minimum temperature for the period before (in dark grey) and after (in light grey) the station move. The difference in the mean between the before and after portions of the time series is approximately 6°F. The lower panel shows distributions derived from different portions of the time series. The dark grey distribution was derived from the period before the move and the light grey distribution was derived from the period after the move. The distribution represented by the black dashed line was derived from the whole 1976–2000 time series.

With respect to structuring weather contracts, it can clearly be seen from this example that data inhomogeneities such as this can lead to very inappropriate distributions, thus emphasising the fact that such inhomogeneities must be corrected and made consistent with current observations.

Trends

Some long-term trends can be considered another source of data inhomogeneity, since it can be assumed that the trends will continue into the foreseeable future. Examples of long-term trends are global warming and,

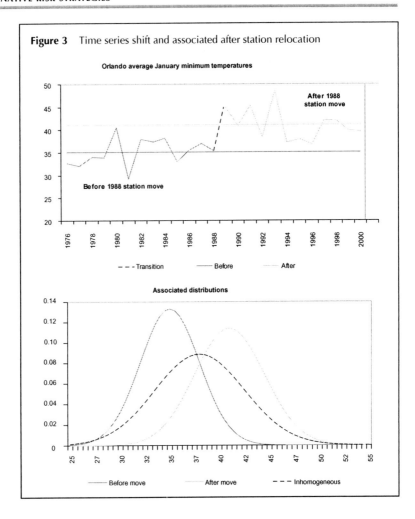

Figure 3 Time series shift and associated after station relocation

for many locations, urban warming which is induced by the growth of urban infrastructure and increased emissions.

CLEANING AND RECONSTRUCTING THE DATA

Given the significant financial implications of poor quality weather data, it is critical that the inconsistencies in the underlying weather data be corrected in order to facilitate accurate contract structuring and pricing. The basic steps that must be performed to prepare a temperature time series are data cleaning, de-shifting and de-trending.

Data Cleaning

Data cleaning involves filling in missing observations and replacing erroneous observations with high quality estimates derived from highly correlated surrounding stations. Cleaning the data of a target station involves the use of surrounding station data to validate and correct the daily minimum and maximum temperature values observed at the target station. As illustrated in Figure 4,[5] this is accomplished by identifying nearby stations whose temperature observations correlate highly with those of the target station, and building regression equations based on the relationship from the target station to each surrounding station. Then for each observation in time, the observations from the surrounding stations

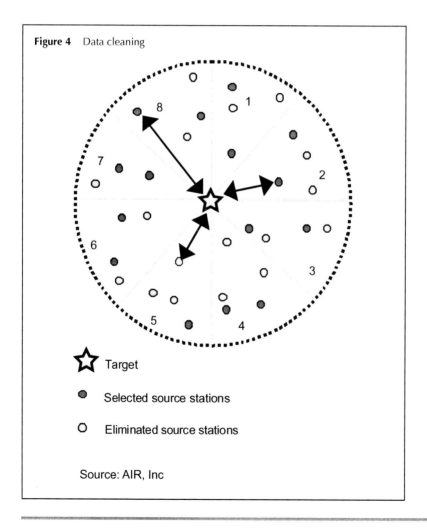

Figure 4 Data cleaning

☆ Target

◉ Selected source stations

○ Eliminated source stations

Source: AIR, Inc

are used with the regression equations to produce a set of estimates that predict the daily temperature values at the target station.

The target observation is then tested against the collection of estimates obtained from the highly correlated surrounding stations. A number of different tests are performed to ensure the observed values at the target station are consistent with the temperature pattern of the region. If the target observation passes all testing criteria, the observation is considered valid. If the observation at the target station fails any single test, the observation and surrounding data are reviewed by an expert meteorologist and corrected if necessary. In the event that the target observation fails all the tests, it is considered an erroneous value and a replacement value is generated based on regression estimates from the highest correlated stations. Similarly, if the target observation is missing, it is filled in using an estimated value generated by the same technique.

It is critical that the quality of estimates generated by the cleaning methodology be rigorously tested. This is done by artificially removing validated daily temperature observations, and replacing them with estimates derived using the cleaning algorithm. The generated time series of estimates are then tested against the original validated data. If the estimates closely follow the validated observations, the root mean square error (RMSE), a standard statistical measure of error, should be low. RMSE tests of the cleaned estimates are consistently less than 1°F, indicating the high quality of the estimates generated by the cleaning algorithm. This is demonstrated in Figure 5.

De-shifting

De-shifting is the process of identifying and removing shifts in the data time series, such as those caused by instrument changes and station moves. Starting with cleaned temperature time series from the target and surrounding stations, the shift identification process begins by creating a set of time series of mean difference in temperature between the target station and each highly correlated surrounding station. These time series are then analysed to find points at which the majority of time series demonstrate a similar shift. For example, if each time series had experienced a simultaneous two degree change, then this is evidence that a two degree shift took place at the target station. Once a potential shift has been identified, the value is recursively tested and adjusted to converge on a shift solution.

The de-shifting algorithm is based on an objective analytical process and thus does not rely on information, such as station logs, to identify station changes. According to the US National Climate Data Center (NCDC), only about 30% of major station changes have been properly recorded.[6]

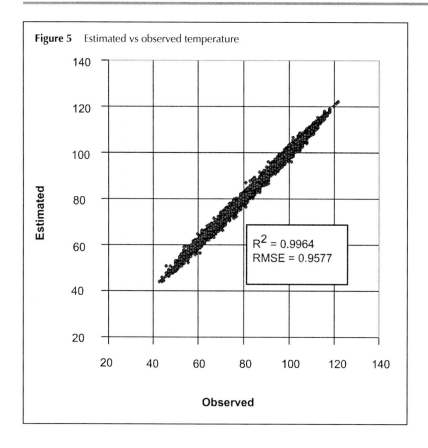

Figure 5 Estimated vs observed temperature

De-trending

De-trending is the process of removing trends from a time series. Starting with the cleaned de-shifted data, the standard de-trending process is designed to remove only long-term trends, such as those resulting from global warming and urbanisation. To accomplish this, a set of low-order cubic splines are used to compute the trend in the data. Once the trend is computed the data are adjusted to remove the trend signal. This conservative approach is suitable for most purposes, however more aggressive de-trending can be performed to meet specific requirements.

PERFORMANCE TESTING OF RECONSTRUCTED DATA

Applied Insurance Research, Inc (AIR) refers to cleaned data that has been de-shifted and de-trended as "reconstructed" data. Reconstructed data are carefully tested for performance in generating accurate estimates of temperature. The results provide a measure of confidence that the reconstructed data are robust and appropriate for pricing contracts. This is accomplished by extracting the "reconstruction adjustment signal", which represents how the observations have changed over time at the target station. This signal can be used to make a station's observations consistent with any particular point in time. For example, a reconstructed time series can be produced to be consistent with observations made in the year 1980. In other words, the time series will behave as if the station had observed its entire history of weather using the 1980 location and instrumentation. The ability to produce reconstructed data sets consistent with any year allows recursive backtesting to be implemented.

One of the standard backtests measures the performance of reconstructed data in generating accurate estimates of monthly average maximum and minimum temperatures. (By testing maximum and minimum temperatures directly instead of degree day variables, the tests can evaluate performance in all months, and not just the months where heating degree days or cooling degree days are common.) Tests are conducted on data representing a 21-year period. Each set of estimates is derived from the 20 years of previous data. Thus, the standard test for a station uses a total of 41 years of reconstructed data.[7]

To understand the process, it is best to work through an example, shown schematically in Figure 6. The test begins by using cleaned data and the reconstruction adjustment signal to create a reconstructed temperature time series consistent with 1980 (Step 1). The resulting monthly average

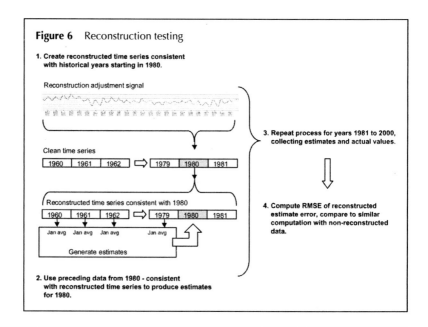

Figure 6 Reconstruction testing

1. Create reconstructed time series consistent with historical years starting in 1980.

Reconstruction adjustment signal

Clean time series

| 1960 | 1961 | 1962 | ⇨ | 1979 | 1980 | 1981 |

Reconstructed time series consistent with 1980

| 1960 | 1961 | 1962 | ⇨ | 1979 | 1980 | 1981 |

Jan avg   Jan avg   Jan avg   Jan avg

Generate estimates

2. Use preceding data from 1980 - consistent with reconstructed time series to produce estimates for 1980.

3. Repeat process for years 1981 to 2000, collecting estimates and actual values.

4. Compute RMSE of reconstructed estimate error, compare to similar computation with non-reconstructed data.

maximum and minimum temperatures of each January from 1960 to 1979 is used to estimate the average maximum and minimum temperatures for January 1980 (Step 2). The same procedure is followed for the remaining months of the year. The same process is repeated for 1981, 1982, and so on, up to the year 2000 (Step 3). In addition, a similar calculation using cleaned, non-reconstructed data generates similar estimates for each month for the same set of years from 1980 to 2000. At the end, there are 252 estimates of monthly average maximum and minimum temperatures (21 years times 12 months per year) based on the reconstructed data, 252 estimates from cleaned, non-reconstructed data, and 252 actual observations of monthly average maximum and minimum temperatures.

The next step in the test (Step 4) is to compute the RMSE by comparing the estimates produced by the reconstructed data and by the cleaned, non-reconstructed data to the actual observations. If the RMSE of the reconstructed data is smaller then the RMSE of the cleaned data, the reconstructed data is more accurate.

A convenient way to view this information is to look at the "performance ratio", which is the ratio of the reconstructed data RMSE divided by the cleaned (non-reconstructed) data RMSE. If the RMSE for the reconstructed data is smaller (more accurate) than the non-reconstructed RMSE, the performance ratio will be less than 1.0. Again, smaller ratios indicate that the reconstructed data are more accurate.

Table 1 shows an example of the monthly RMSE scores for reconstructed (Rcn) and cleaned (Cln) monthly average maximum and

Table 1 Summary of RMSE scores by month for Atlanta (1980–2000)[8]

| Month | RMSE scores by month | | | | Performance ratios | | |
	Rcn min	Cln min	Rcn max	Cln max	Rcn min/ Cln min	Rcn max/ Cln max	Avg ratio
Jan	4.530	5.378	4.957	5.731	0.842	0.865	0.854
Feb	4.266	5.465	4.619	5.508	0.781	0.839	0.810
Mar	3.544	4.347	4.204	4.876	0.815	0.862	0.839
Apr	3.783	4.378	4.391	5.008	0.864	0.877	0.871
May	4.265	5.012	4.720	5.423	0.851	0.870	0.861
Jun	3.843	4.950	5.134	6.058	0.776	0.847	0.812
Jul	3.932	5.053	5.904	6.907	0.778	0.855	0.816
Aug	3.698	4.619	5.024	5.847	0.801	0.859	0.830
Sep	3.234	3.975	4.491	5.078	0.813	0.884	0.849
Oct	4.183	4.809	4.132	4.432	0.870	0.932	0.901
Nov	4.575	5.197	4.530	4.898	0.880	0.925	0.903
Dec	4.776	5.273	4.901	5.205	0.906	0.942	0.924

Source: AIR, Inc

minimum temperatures for the Atlanta weather station. (Note that performance ratios for each month in Table 1 are all less than 1.0.)

Another convenient way to assess the accuracy of the reconstructed data is to use an average ratio. The average ratio is the average of the maximum and minimum performance ratios. Again, an average ratio of less than 1.0, as for all months in Table 1, indicates reconstructed data that is more accurate than the cleaned data.

Table 2 provides examples of performance ratios across 21 of the most prominent primary NWS weather stations by averaging the monthly ratios into a single averaged performance ratio. In all cases, as indicated by the average ratio, the reconstructed data have outperformed the cleaned, non-reconstructed data.

The ability to quantify the performance of historical data in producing accurate estimates is critical in evaluating their use in pricing weather derivatives. Quantifying the accuracy of historical data allows weather contracts to be structured with confidence.

CLIMATE FORECASTING

While historic weather data serve as the primary means for estimating the climatological probability of potential weather at a station, the resulting

Table 2 Performance data from 20-year hindcast estimation tests from 1980 to 2000[9]

ICAO	Station name	Min Rcn/ Cln ratio	Max Rcn/ Cln ratio	Avg ratio
KATL	ATLANTA/HARTSFIELD INTL AP	0.832	0.877	0.855
KAUG	AUGUSTA FAA ARPT	0.854	0.852	0.853
KATT	AUSTIN WSO AP	0.888	0.935	0.912
KBOI	BOISE WSFO AIRPORT	0.681	0.902	0.792
KCMH	COLUMBUS WSO AIRPORT	0.872	0.901	0.886
KDFW	DAL-FTW WSCMO AP	0.797	0.953	0.875
KDTW	DETROIT METRO WSCMO	0.840	0.984	0.912
KERI	ERIE WSO ARPT	0.823	0.881	0.852
KFAT	FRESNO YOSEMITE INTL	0.836	0.963	0.899
KLAS	LAS VEGAS WSO AIRPORT	0.759	0.983	0.871
KSDF	LOUISVILLE WSFO AP	0.880	0.943	0.911
KLGA	NEW YORK LAGUARDIA WSCMO AP	0.875	0.917	0.896
KPHL	PHILADELPHIA WSCMO AP	0.826	0.944	0.885
KPHX	PHOENIX WSO AP	0.629	0.956	0.793
KRDU	RALEIGH DURHAM WSFO AP	0.891	0.933	0.912
KRNO	RENO WSFO AIRPORT	0.695	0.936	0.816
KSFO	SAN FRANCISCO WSO AP	0.832	0.921	0.877
KSHV	SHREVEPORT WSO AP	0.868	0.949	0.908
KTPA	TAMPA/INTL ARPT	0.872	0.955	0.913
KTOL	TOLEDO EXPRESS WSO AP	0.891	0.937	0.914
KTUS	TUCSON/INTL ARPT	0.931	0.842	0.887

Source: AIR, Inc

distributions are often quite broad due to the inclusion of a diverse range of weather including that caused by El Niño, La Niña and other weather regimes. To get a more focused view of the expected climate variability over future months and seasons, many weather traders and weather risk managers utilise seasonal climate forecasts.

We are all familiar with weather forecasts, but what exactly is a climate forecast? Climate forecasts differ from traditional weather forecasts in that they forecast the probability of what the average weather should be over the course of months and seasons, as opposed to attempting to predict the details of specific weather events. For example, a short-range climate forecast (a forecast for the season ahead) may say that there is a significant probability that the next winter will be unusually warm or that the frequency of heat waves will be higher than normal next summer.

Specific weather events can be well predicted on the scale of days due to the fact that the evolution of the atmosphere on the scale of days is fairly linear. However, when trying to make predictions beyond a couple of weeks, the chaotic nature of the atmosphere leads to increasing divergence in the number of possible solutions. This makes it almost impossible to forecast specific weather events beyond a couple of weeks. But even though specific weather events cannot be predicted accurately beyond a couple of weeks, predictions about the expected distribution of possible weather outcomes can be made months and seasons ahead. Based on the distribution of possible outcomes, climate forecasts provide probabilistic information about what the average weather should be over a period of time. A probabilistic climate forecast can offer, therefore, another probability distribution that can be used to help structure and price weather contracts.

In order to effectively use a climate forecast one needs access to:

1. the probability distribution derived from the forecast output; and
2. a quantitative assessment of the skill, or accuracy, of the underlying forecasting system.

Based on this information, the user would be able to determine the appropriate weight that should be assigned to the forecast.

Quantification of the skill of a forecasting system is usually conducted by the forecast provider. This involves a comprehensive evaluation of the accuracy of the system based on a set of previously made forecasts or "hindcasts". Hindcasts are simply forecasts that were made using historical data as opposed to real-time data. In climate prediction, skill studies are often conducted with hindcast data because it would take several years to generate and evaluate a sufficient number of forecasts that are based on real-time data. Typically, forecast skill is evaluated by examining how well the forecasts did compared with climatological distributions in explaining what actually occurred. (At AIR, forecasts are compared with climatological distributions based on reconstructed data since these have been shown to be more skilful than those from non-reconstructed data.) In other words, does the forecast provide better guidance than climatological distributions derived from historical data?

One objective means of answering this question is by computing the linear error in probability space (LEPS) score.[10] Essentially LEPS scores are normalised between –100% and 100%. Positive scores indicate that the climate forecasts have performed better than climatological distributions. A score of 0% means that the climate forecasts have had the same skill as climatological distributions, and negative scores indicate that the climate forecasts performed worse than climatological distributions. To be useful at all, climate forecast systems must demonstrate positive LEPS skill, otherwise it is best to use climatological distributions derived from reconstructed historical data.

Depending on the specific application, climate forecast distributions and distributions derived from reconstructed historical data could be merged to create a suitable distribution for the contract. Obviously, the higher the LEPS score of the forecast system, the more weight should be given to the forecast distribution.

Over the past decade, numerous climate forecasting methodologies have been developed.[11] The various methodologies can essentially be divided into either statistical or dynamical modelling systems. Statistical models leverage lagged correlations in historical time series between pre-

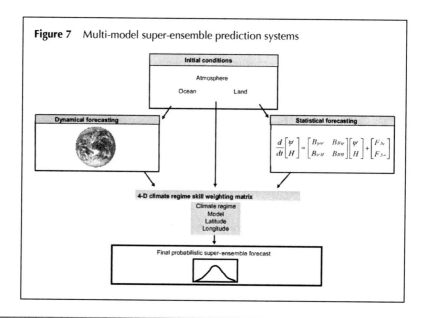

Figure 7   Multi-model super-ensemble prediction systems

dictors (sea surface temperature, sea level pressure, etc) and predictants (surface temperature, precipitation, etc) to produce forecasts. Dynamical models, on the other hand, are based on mathematical representations of the physics of the earth's climate system, and produce forecasts by initial-ising the system with observed climate data and evolving the climate model forward in time. Regardless of the type of model used, the climate model is typically run in *ensemble mode* to produce a distribution, or ensemble, of possible outcomes. To do this, the model is run numerous times with slightly different sets of initial conditions that are consistent with the current climate, yet cover the range of uncertainty inherent in the initial conditions.

While both statistical and dynamical models have their own strengths and weaknesses, both are capable of producing skilful forecasts. It has been shown in various studies, however, that the most accurate forecasts are made by incorporating guidance from a number of skilful dynamical and statistical climate models.[12] Climate forecasting systems that utilise multi-ple models and numerous ensemble members are called multi-model super-ensemble prediction systems (see Figure 7).

As shown in Figure 7, in this forecast system, initial conditions are used to initialise a number of dynamical and statistical models. The initial con-ditions are also used in a post process model weighting application, where outputs from the various models are weighted based on their historic skill in forecasts from climate regimes similar to the current regime. For instance, if the current climate is dominated by El Niño conditions, and model A has demonstrated that it has performed 50% better than model B under these conditions, than model A would have 50% more weight than model B in contributing to the final forecast distribution. By taking advan-tage of the demonstrated strengths from each model, the forecast is optimised.

CONCLUSION

Weather can pose significant financial risk to corporate bottom lines around the world. Weather derivatives are specifically designed to help at-risk companies manage weather risk. To ensure that weather market players have the most accurate information available to quantify risk, per-form analyses and structure contracts, new data improvement and climate forecasting technologies have been developed to produce reconstructed data and probabilistic multi-model super-ensemble climate forecasts.

Weather derivatives, together with reconstructed weather data and advanced climate forecasts, give risk managers the critical tools and infor-mation needed to effectively manage their weather risk. Now, with no excuse for not doing a better job of managing weather risk, especially given today's competitive environment and pressure to meet profit goals, the weather market will finally achieve its projected growth.

1 See Clemmons (2002).
2 See PricewaterhouseCoopers Report (2001).
3 See Federal Coordinator for Meteorological Services and Supporting Research (1994).
4 US National Climatic Data Center.
5 Personal communication with NCDC.
6 Original research conducted by AIR, Inc.
7 See Potts *et al.* (1996).
8 For further reading, see Barnston *et al.* (1994), Barnston (1994), Cane and Zebiak (1987), Graham *et al.* (2000), Ji, Kumar, and Leetmaa (1994b), Ji *et al.* (1993), Kirtman *et al.* (1995), Shukla (1981), and Krishnamurti *et al.* (2000).
9 See Krishnamurti et al. (2000).

BIBLIOGRAPHY

Barnston, A. G., 1994, "Linear statistical short-term climate predictive skill in the Northern Hemisphere", *Journal of Climate*, 7, pp. 1513–1564.

Barnston, A.G., H.M. van Dool, S.E. Zebiak, T.P. Barnett, M. Ji, D.R. Rodenhuis, M.A. Cane, A. Leetmaa, N.E. Graham, C.R. Ropelewski, V.E. Kousky, E.O. O'Lenic, and R.E. Livesey, 1994, "Long-lead seasonal forecasts-where do we stand?" *Bulletin of American Meteorological Society*, 75, pp. 2097–2114.

Cane, M., and S.E. Zebiak, 1987, "Prediction of El Niño events using a physical model", in H. Cattle (ed), *Atmospheric and Oceanic Variability*, pp. 153–182 (London: Royal Meteorological Society Press).

Clemmons, L., 2002, "Weather risk management: practical uses in industry", Presentation to the MIT Sloan Energy and Environmental Finance Club.

Federal Coordinator for Meteorological Services and Supporting Research, 1994, "Federal standard for siting meteorological sensors at airports", FCM-S4-1994, Washington DC.

Graham, R.J., A.D.L. Evans, K.R. Mylne, M.S.J. Harrison, and K.B. Robertson, 2000, "An assessment of seasonal predictability using atmospheric general circulation models", *Quarterly Journal of the Royal Meteorological Society*, 126, pp. 2211–2240.

Ji, M., A. Kumar, and A. Leetmaa, 1994, "An experimental coupled forecast system at the national meteorological center: some early results", Tellus, 46A, pp. 398–419.

Ji, M., A. Kumar, A. Leetmaa, and M.P. Hoerling, 1993, "Coupled ocean-atmosphere climate forecast system for ENSO predictions", *Proceedings of the Workshop on Numberical Extended Range Weather Prediction*, Airlie, Virginia, pp. 141–144.

Kirtman, B.P., J. Shukla, B. Huang, Z. Zhu, and E.K. Schneider, 1995, "Multiseasonal predictions with a coupled tropical ocean/global atmosphere system", *Monthly Weather Review*, 125, pp. 789–808.

Krishnamurti, T.N., C.M. Kishtawal, T. LaRow, D. Bachiochi, Z. Zhang, C.E. Williford, S. Gadgil and S. Surendran, 2000, "Multi-model super-ensemble forecasts for weather and seasonal climate", *Journal of Climate*, November.

Potts, J.M., C.K. Folland, I.T. Jolliffe, and D. Sexton, 1996, "Revised "LEPS" scores for assessing climate model simulations and long-range forecasts", *Journal of Climate*, 9, pp. 34–53.

PricewaterhouseCoopers, 2001, Report: "The weather risk management industry: survey findings for November 1997 to March 2001".

Shukla, J., 1981, "Dynamical predictability of monthly means", *Journal of Atmospheric Science*, 38, pp. 2547–2572.

16

The ART of Dependence Modelling: The Latest Advances in Correlation Analysis

Peter Blum[1], Alexandra Dias[2] and Paul Embrechts

Department of Mathematics, ETH – Swiss Federal Institute of Technology

From a methodological point of view, for instance, Alternative Risk Transfer (ART) aims at securitising risk from a typically more specialised market (the property insurance market, say) to the broader market of finance, something that is broached in greater detail in other chapters of this title. From a marketing point of view, ART products are claimed to have a number of benefits for the portfolio manager:

1. They are products from markets that are very different from the usual financial markets.
2. They have low correlation with (even termed "independent from" by some of the sellers) other traditional instruments leading to low beta or even zero beta from a portfolio theory point of view.[3]
3. They achieve a better diversification effect when included in a portfolio.
4. They have lower risk and yet yield higher returns, hence piercing the traditional efficient frontier.

Products with such marketing advantages include funds-of-funds (also referred to as hedge funds or non-traditional funds), private equity, securitised insurance risk, and weather and energy derivatives. To these, and others, some of the above diversification arguments may apply over some period of time. We have, however, also learned that the diversification effect may break down especially in periods of financial distress, the key example coming from the hedge fund crisis in 1998, triggered by the collapse of Long-Term Capital Management (LTCM).

INTRODUCTION
However one looks at the history of ART, at the basis of both its successes as well as its failures lies the notion of dependence; when the returns on an ART product are (close to) independent from the returns of other portfolio

instruments, it pays to add these products to one's investment portfolio. (There is, however, a crucial difference between "independent" and "uncorrelated"; a difference that lies at the heart of understanding the potential of ART methodology and one which will be especially stressed in this chapter.)

Although the notion of low (zero) beta plays an important role at both the design and pricing stages of ART products, for these non-standard products, the interpretation of dependence through linear correlation (and hence the portfolio-beta language) becomes dubious, as we shall see in the following. Much of what is stated in this chapter alludes to the problems of model risk, ie the risk encountered when using a specially fitted model. However, the field of model fitting as a whole is a diffuse one indeed, allowing for the existence of many different alternative models, some of which are dealt with in this chapter.[4]

The first section of this chapter reviews some of the new tools (like copulas) to handle the measurement of dependence in ART products, giving a brief statistical introduction. The second section concentrates on a particular stylised example from the realm of property insurance, and the final section applies the findings of previous sections to more general ART products. This chapter will generally focus on some of the methodological issues underlying the pricing and portfolio theory of specific ART transactions.

MEASURING DEPENDENCE THROUGH COPULAS

The copula of a vector of risks describes the interdependence between the vector's various components. It yields a canonical way to link (or "couple") the individual behaviour of the risks to their global, joint behaviour. (A precise, more technical definition is given below.) By now, the history and current development of copula theory is well-established; papers on applications of copula techniques to finance and insurance now appear very regularly (see for instance Schmidt and Ward (2002) for a recent example).[5] This chapter will highlight some of the basic results of copula modelling, mainly through examples. For the purpose of clarity, in this chapter we concentrate on d 1–period, dependent risks $X_1, \ldots, X_d$, where the dimension $d \geq 2$. In order to price a financial instrument $\Psi(\mathbf{X})$ on $\mathbf{X} = (X_1, \ldots, X_d)^T$, ideally one would need full information on the joint probability distribution

$$F_{\mathbf{X}}(\mathbf{x}) = \mathbb{P}(X_1 \leq x_1, \ldots, X_d \leq x_d), \mathbf{x} \in \mathbb{R}^d$$

From this, the distribution function $F_{\Psi(\mathbf{X})}$ of $\Psi(\mathbf{X})$ can be calculated, and hence the position $\Psi(\mathbf{X})$ priced. However, as we typically only have partial information on a model for $\mathbf{X}$, no exact solution can be obtained. Often one knows the distribution functions (or a statistical estimation of) $F_{X_1}, \ldots, F_{X_d}$, the marginal risks, where $F_{X_i}(x) = \mathbb{P}(X_i \leq x)$, $x \in \mathbb{R}$, together with "some information" on the dependence between the risks $X_1, \ldots, X_d$. For ease of notation, we denote $F = F_X$ and $F_i = F_{X_i}$. To avoid technicalities, we assume that F_is are continuous, strictly increasing. From a mathematical point of view, a copula is a distribution function C on the hypercube $[0, 1]^d$ with uniform – $(0, 1)$ marginals. A copula provides the natural link between F and $(F_1, ..., F_d)$ in the following:

$$
\begin{aligned}
F(\mathbf{x}) &= \mathbb{P}(X_1 \le x_1, ..., X_d \le x_d) \\
&= \mathbb{P}(F_1(X_1) \le F_1(x_1), ..., F_d(X_d) \le F_d(x_d)) \\
&= \mathbb{P}(U_1 \le F_1(x_1), ..., U_d \le F_d(x_d)) \\
&= C(F_1(x_1), ..., F_d(x_d))
\end{aligned}
\tag{1}
$$

Here we used the mathematical property that the random variables $F_i(X_i)$ have a uniform – $(0, 1)$ distribution, a result used daily for simulation purposes in every bank or insurance company. The link between X_i and U_i is also referred to as "quantile transformation".[6] The converse representation to Equation (1) is for all $u_i \in (0, 1)$, $i = 1, ..., d$,

$$
C(u_1, ..., u_d) = F(F_1^{-1}(u_1), ..., F_d^{-1}(u_d))
\tag{2}
$$

Equations (1) and (2) form the basis for all copula modelling.

Hence C in Equation (1) links the marginals F_i, $i = 1, ..., d$, to the joint distribution F. Numerous joint models can be considered when we keep the F_is fixed and vary the copula, C. Via Equation (2) we can extract, at least theoretically, the copula function from any joint distribution (ie, model) F. Suppose for instance that the risk factors $X_1, ..., X_d$ are jointly normally distributed with covariance matrix Σ; for convenience we assume that the marginal means are zero and the variances are one so that Σ corresponds to the correlation matrix of $\mathbf{X}$. Hence for each $i = 1, ..., d$, $F_i = N$, the standard (one-dimensional) normal distribution function, whereas F corresponds to the above multivariate normal distribution. Hence C in Equation (2) can be calculated numerically leading to the so-called "Gaussian copula" $C = C_\Sigma^{Ga}$. A special choice corresponds to the equicorrelation case where we assume that all correlations ρ_{ij} are equal, to ρ say, in which case we write C_ρ^{Ga}. Another important example is the t-copula, extracted via Equation (2) from the multivariate t-distribution on v degrees of freedom and a positive-definite matrix Σ, which for $\mathbf{x} \in \mathbb{R}^d$ has density

$$
f_{\mathbf{X}}(\mathbf{x}) = \frac{\Gamma\left(\frac{v+d}{2}\right)}{\Gamma\left(\frac{v}{2}\right)\sqrt{(\pi v)^d |\Sigma|}} \left(1 + \frac{(\mathbf{x} - \boldsymbol{\mu})^T \Sigma^{-1}(\mathbf{x} - \boldsymbol{\mu})}{v}\right)^{\left(-\frac{v+d}{2}\right)}
\tag{3}
$$

Note that, for $v > 2$, the covariance of $\mathbf{X}$ equals $\text{Cov}(\mathbf{X}) = \frac{v}{v-2}\Sigma$. The normal case above corresponds to the limiting case $v = \infty$. The resulting copula is denoted by C_Σ^{tv} and C_ρ^{tv} in the equicorrelation case.

Besides these two natural examples of copulas, whole families of interesting ones can be constructed. For instance, for $d = 2$ the following copulas are useful:[7]

- Gumbel copula:

$$C_\beta^{Gu}(u, v) = \exp\left\{-\left[(-\ln u)^\beta + (-\ln v)^\beta\right]^{1/\beta}\right\}, \beta \in [1, \infty)$$

- Frank copula:

$$C_\beta^{Fr}(u, v) = -\frac{1}{\beta}\ln\left(1 + \frac{(e^{-\beta u} - 1)(e^{-\beta v} - 1)}{e^{-\beta} - 1}\right), \beta \in \mathbb{R}\setminus\{0\}$$

- Clayton copula:

$$C_\beta^{Cl}(u, v) = \max\left((u^{-\beta} + v^{-\beta} - 1)^{-1/\beta}, 0\right), \beta \in [-1, \infty)\setminus\{0\}$$

- Farlie–Gumbel–Morgenstern (FGM) copula:

$$C_\beta^{FGM}(u, v) = uv + \beta uv(1 - u)(1 - v), \beta \in [-1, 1]$$

At the moment, the main virtues of copula modelling are:

❑ Pedagogic, ie, opening up the mind of the user to think about dependence beyond linear correlation.[8]
❑ Stress testing (typically using simulation) the pricing of financial (one-period) products on multivariate financial or insurance underlyings (typical examples in finance include basket options and credit derivatives; in insurance, we may think of multi-line products).

To illustrate some of the key features of copulas, some simulation examples are given.[9] Figure 1 contains three models each having standard normal marginals ($F_1 = F_2 = N$), illustrated by the marginal histograms. Moreover, all three models have the same linear correlation of 50%, but the copula changes. In Figures 1a–1c, $C = C_{0.5}^{Ga}$, $C_{0.5}^{t4}$ and C_β^{Gu}, respectively, where β is chosen in such a way that the resulting bivariate distribution has 50% correlation. In each plot we have simulated 1,000 points and empirically estimated the linear and Kendall τ rank correlation.[10] A key feature to be observed is the change from a perfectly elliptical cloud with few joint extremes (beyond two, say) in Figure 1a, over a two-sided elongated cloud with more extremes (both top right and bottom left) in Figure 1b, to a teardrop shape in Figure 1c with peak (joint extremes) mainly in the top right corner. These important model differences *cannot* be explained on the basis of marginals and linear correlations alone; these are identical across

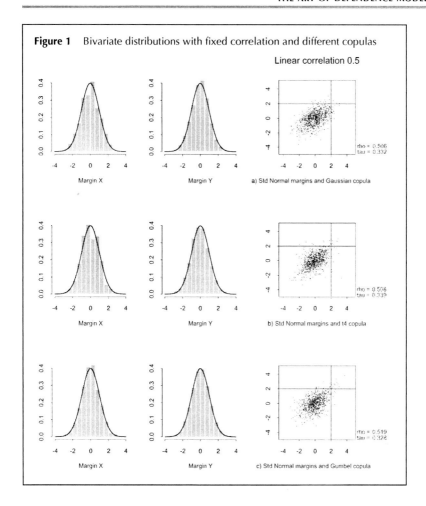

Figure 1 Bivariate distributions with fixed correlation and different copulas

Linear correlation 0.5

a) Std Normal margins and Gaussian copula

b) Std Normal margins and t4 copula

c) Std Normal margins and Gumbel copula

the figures. Figure 2 further stresses the point; the lines drawn in each plot correspond to univariate quantiles, q, of the marginal distribution so that $\mathbb{P}(X_1 > q, X_2 > q) = 0.99$, added only for illustrative purposes in order to indicate a "danger zone" in the joint distribution. In Figure 2a we again have $F_1 = F_2 = N$, $\rho = 50\%$ (the bivariate normal case). Note the less pronounced extreme joint moves (top right and bottom left). Joint extreme moves appear much more pronounced in Figure 2d, the case of a bivariate t (see Equation (3)) with $\nu = 4$, $\rho = 50\%$. In the latter case, $F_1 = F_2 = t_4$. Moving from Figure 2a to 2c we keep $F_1 = F_2 = N$ but if (by using Equation (1)) we superimpose the copula $C_{0.5}^{t4}$ on F_1, F_2, we then see points clustering more into the top right and bottom left corners. Between Figures 2a and 2b we change the marginals from N to t_4, but keep the copula fixed ($C_{0.5}^{Ga}$). Making the marginal tails much longer (from N to t_4) but keeping the

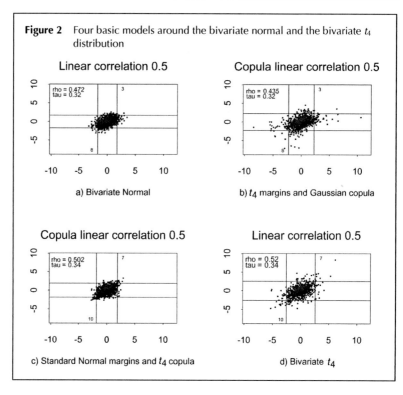

Figure 2 Four basic models around the bivariate normal and the bivariate t_4 distribution

copula Gaussian does not yield pronounced joint extremes. From these figures we get the impression that joint extremes are more a copula property than one of the marginal distribution.[11]

Figures 2a and 2d correspond to the class of so-called "elliptical distributions". In Figures 2b and 2c, the resulting models fail to have a correlation of 50%, though the estimated values show that the deviation is fairly small. We could have calibrated these models differently by changing $v = 4$ to achieve a theoretical value of 50% for ρ. It is especially this flexibility gained by separately modelling the marginals (F_1, F_2) and the copula, C, that allows the discovery of models that reflect the qualitative behaviour of multivariate loss data more closely. One could call this approach "copula engineering". The next section gives an illustrative example of this technique based on some real insurance loss data.

AN EXAMPLE: THE DANISH FIRE DATA

For the purposes of this chapter, it is important to realise that the data (n = 2,493 observations) are three-dimensional ($d = 3$).[12] For the Danish industrial dwellings fire data, the losses consist of X_1 = loss to buildings, X_2 = loss to contents, X_3 = loss to profits. For the data which have for each component a strictly positive loss amount (resulting in a reduced sample size of

$n = 517$ obeservations), the histograms are plotted for the log-transformed variables (as in Figure 3), where $Y_i = \log(X_i)$, $i = 1,2,3$.

From Figure 3a heavy-tailedness (beyond lognormality) can be clearly seen in the marginal data, further exemplified in Figure 4.

The data are clearly dependent, as can be seen from the three-dimensional (Figure 5) and two-dimensional (Figure 6) scatter plots.

Suppose, as an example, that one would be interested in a bivariate model for log contents (Y_2) versus log profits (Y_3) (see Figure 6c). A very important property of a copula is that it is invariant under continuous and strictly increasing transformations (like the logarithm) of the underlying variables,[13] hence making no difference between fitting the copula to the data (X_i) or to the logarithms of the data (Y_i). Linear correlation does not have this invariance property.[14] One possibility for obtaining a statistical model would be by using a so-called "pseudo-likelihood" approach (as discussed in Genest et al., 1995). In this method one replaces the unknown copula C by a parametric copula family C_θ (the Gumbel family, say) and estimates the marginal distributions (here, F_2, F_3) empirically. An optimal choice among several competing parametric models for C can for instance be obtained through the minimisation of some information criterion, as with Akaike's Information Criterion (AIC). Of course, several parametric or

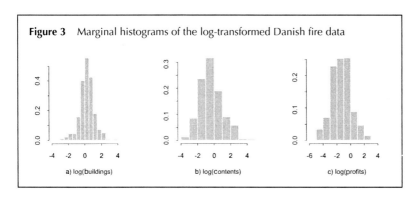

Figure 3 Marginal histograms of the log-transformed Danish fire data

a) log(buildings)   b) log(contents)   c) log(profits)

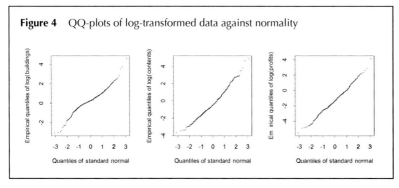

Figure 4 QQ-plots of log-transformed data against normality

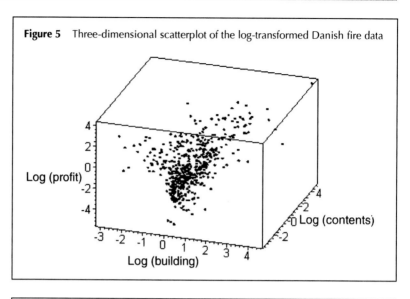

Figure 5 Three-dimensional scatterplot of the log-transformed Danish fire data

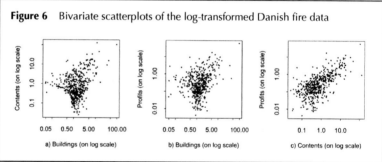

Figure 6 Bivariate scatterplots of the log-transformed Danish fire data

semi-parametric models for the marginal fitting may also be used, possibly based on extreme value theory (EVT).[15]

By way of an example, below we have used the pseudo-likelihood approach to fit some copulas to the (X_2, X_3) data. The results are summarised in Table 1. The fit based on the Gumbel copula has the lowest AIC value so should be chosen (according to this criterion). According to the AIC, the Clayton family performs worst (fits least well) and the Gaussian and Frank copulas perform similarly. The Farlie–Gumbel–Morgenstern family is not appropriate for fitting data exhibiting strong dependence, as is the case in our example. This is confirmed by the estimate close to the β-parameter boundary $\beta = 1$. Further diagnostic checks could be added.

We can use these estimates to price positions $\Psi(X_2, X_3)$ based on the variables (X_2, X_3). Four payout functions are considered in a simulation study using the six fitted models together with the model that assumes independence. The following payout functions are chosen:

Table 1   Parameter estimates for various copula models for (X_2, X_3)

Copula family	Parameter space	$\hat{\beta}$		AIC
Gumbel	$\beta \geq 1$	1.8569		−319.51
Clayton	$\beta \in [-1, \infty)\backslash\{0\}$	1.0001		−107.73
Frank	$\beta \in \mathbb{R}\backslash\{0\}$	5.0008		−262.75
FGM	$\beta \in [-1, 1]$	0.9996		−165.84
		$\hat{\rho}$	$\hat{v}$	
t	$\rho \in [-1, 1], v > 0$	0.6456	9.1348	−268.55
Gaussian	$\rho \in [-1, 1]$	0.6323	−	−262.06

- $\Psi_1(X_2, X_3) = X_2 + X_3$
- $\Psi_2(X_2, X_3) = (X_2 + X_3 - 10)_+$
- $\Psi_3(X_2, X_3) = (X_2 + X_3) \cdot 1_{\{X_2>5, X_3>5\}}$
- $\Psi_4(X_2, X_3) = 1_{\{X_2>5, X_3>5\}}$

Ψ_1 corresponds to the combined loss, whereas Ψ_2 is like a stop-loss treaty on Ψ_1. The position Ψ_4 can be viewed as a digital, ie, taking the value to be one whenever both X_2 and X_3 are larger than five, otherwise the value zero is obtained. Position Ψ_3 pays out the combined loss Ψ_1 only if triggered by Ψ_4.

Monte Carlo estimates of the fair premium $\mathbb{E}(\Psi_i(X_2, X_3))$ under each of the seven fitted models are obtained through 500,000 simulations and are given in Table 2 (see the $\hat{\mathbb{E}}_{\hat{F}}(\Psi)$ column). A combination of the estimates for the mean ($\hat{\mathbb{E}}_{\hat{F}}(\Psi)$) and the standard deviation ($\hat{\sigma}_{\hat{F}}(\Psi)$) for each position can be used to construct an actuarial (standard deviation) premium principle.

Note that the values in Table 2 are derived from specific models fitted to the data. Table 3 summarises some empirical estimates of the most important quantities, hence no model fitting is taking place here. The various standard error (SE) estimates listed in Table 2 can be used to further discuss model risk and fitting adequacy (goodness-of-fit), although these values have been included for completeness rather than for further commentary. Recall that the Gumbel model was chosen as the best fitting model (according to AIC); this choice is also largely confirmed when we compare the estimated mean values and standard deviations in Tables 2 and 3. Also note that, in some cases, large differences exist between the estimated fair premiums. Careful modelling of the dependence can make a huge difference in the quoted prices. On the basis of this fairly preliminary analysis, we would choose the Gumbel model for the copula, superimposed via Equation (1) on the marginal empirical distributions, ie,

$$\hat{F}(x_2, x_3) = C^{Gu}_{1.8569}(\hat{F}_{2,n}(x_2), \hat{F}_{3,n}(x_3))$$

Table 2 Monte Carlo analysis for four positions on the (X_2, X_3) data from seven different models

$$\Psi_1(X_2, X_3) = X_2 + X_3$$

Copula model	$\hat{\mathbb{E}}_f(\Psi)$	$\widehat{SE}(\hat{\mathbb{E}}_f(\Psi))$	$\hat{\sigma}_f(\Psi)$	$\widehat{SE}(\hat{\mathbb{E}}_n(\Psi))$	$\widehat{SE}(\hat{\sigma}_n(\Psi))$
Gumbel	3.231	0.015	10.772	0.458	3.060
t	3.224	0.013	10.009	0.445	2.768
Frank	3.205	0.013	9.188	0.409	2.235
Gaussian	3.232	0.014	9.853	0.424	2.516
FGM	3.245	0.013	9.120	0.398	2.254
Clayton	3.243	0.013	9.137	0.409	2.262
Independence	3.234	0.013	8.985	0.397	2.234

$$\Psi_2(X_2, X_3) = (X_2 + X_3 - 10)_+$$

Copula model	$\hat{\mathbb{E}}_f(\Psi)$	$\widehat{SE}(\hat{\mathbb{E}}_f(\Psi))$	$\hat{\sigma}_f(\Psi)$	$\widehat{SE}(\hat{\mathbb{E}}_n(\Psi)$	$\widehat{SE}(\hat{\sigma}_n(\Psi))$
Gumbel	1.134	0.013	9.525	0.406	3.240
t	1.066	0.012	8.711	0.389	2.927
Frank	1.001	0.011	7.801	0.346	2.368
Gaussian	1.072	0.012	8.522	0.367	2.655
FGM	0.970	0.011	7.773	0.346	2.382
Clayton	0.970	0.011	7.789	0.349	2.388
Independence	0.927	0.011	7.686	0.340	2.350

$$\Psi_3(X_2, X_3) = (X_2 + X_3) \cdot 1_{\{X_2>5, X_3>5\}}$$

Copula model	$\hat{\mathbb{E}}_f(\Psi)$	$\widehat{SE}(\hat{\mathbb{E}}_f(\Psi))$	$\hat{\sigma}_f(\Psi)$	$\widehat{SE}(\hat{\mathbb{E}}_n(\Psi)$	$\widehat{SE}(\hat{\sigma}_n(\Psi))$
Gumbel	1.118	0.014	10.382	0.456	3.518
t	0.727	0.011	8.067	0.348	3.187
Frank	0.303	0.006	4.201	0.196	2.183
Gaussian	0.657	0.010	7.336	0.322	2.943
FGM	0.142	0.004	2.793	0.123	1.791
Clayton	0.146	0.004	2.805	0.128	1.794
Independence	0.077	0.003	2.128	0.097	1.643

$$\Psi_4(X_2, X_3) = 1_{\{X_2>5, X_3>5\}}$$

Copula model	$\hat{\mathbb{E}}_f(\Psi)$	$\widehat{SE}(\hat{\mathbb{E}}_f(\Psi))$	$\hat{\sigma}_f(\Psi)$	$\widehat{SE}(\hat{\mathbb{E}}_n(\Psi)$	$\widehat{SE}(\hat{\sigma}_n(\Psi))$
Gumbel	0.0227	0.0133	0.1489	0.0064	0.0209
t	0.0160	0.0121	0.1255	0.0053	0.0209
Frank	0.0095	0.0001	0.0968	0.0043	0.0229
Gaussian	0.0015	0.0119	0.1229	0.0054	0.0218
FGM	0.0048	0.0108	0.0689	0.0031	0.0266
Clayton	0.0049	0.0108	0.0700	0.0031	0.0268
Independence	0.0025	0.0107	0.0023	0.0502	0.0289

Table 3 Empirical estimates for four positions on the (X_2, X_3) data

Payout	$\hat{\mathbb{E}}_n(\Psi)$	$\widehat{SE}\,(\hat{\mathbb{E}}_n(\Psi))$	$\hat{\sigma}_n(\Psi)$
	Sample statistics		
$\Psi_1(X_2, X_3)$	3.2330	0.4670	10.6240
$\Psi_2(X_2, X_3)$	1.1490	0.4110	9.3350
$\Psi_3(X_2, X_3)$	0.8190	0.3670	8.3380
$\Psi_4(X_2, X_3)$	0.0213	0.0064	0.1444

Similar analyses can be performed for the other bivariate claims, as well as for the trivariate data.

For the pair (X_1, X_2) we notice the special wedge-like behaviour near zero in Figure 6a. In order to come up with a good statistical model in this case, we would have to consider so-called "censoring techniques" as discussed in Shih and Louis (1995). In the case of (X_1, X_3) we notice a clear diagonal asymmetry in the scatter plot of Figure 6b, implying that we have to look for non-exchangeable copulas (see Genest *et al.*, 1998 and Joe, 1997). For a good trivariate model one would have to combine the above approaches.

THE IMPORTANCE OF COPULA TECHNIQUES FOR ART

How do the above techniques reflect on the modelling of ART products? Traditionally, insurance companies have managed each risk separately, eg, by buying reinsurance for a certain line of business (insurance risk factor), or by setting up hedges for a foreign currency (financial risk factor). The quantitative analysis of such isolated risk management tools did not (or did only rarely) require a deep understanding of dependence between the various risk factors.

While these isolated risk management tools are relatively easy to handle and easy to analyse, they do not necessarily offer the most cost-effective protection if one looks at the company as a whole. The fact that a company depends on various stochastic risk factors creates the possibility for diversification, ie, the use of offsetting effects between the risk factors. This fact has been widely known for a long time, for example in insurance through the work of de Finetti in 1942 or Borch's Theorem in the late sixties (see Bühlmann, 1970, for both) and in finance through Markowitz's portfolio theory from 1952 (see, for example, Brealy and Myers, 2000). However, it was only recently that insurance companies began to capitalise on this diversification potential, driven by factors such as:

❏ Increased pressure from the investors for better overall results and, thus, better returns on the risk capital that they were providing to the insurers.

❏ Lack of capacity in some reinsurance markets, and hence the need to use available capacity more efficiently or to open up new capacity.

In fact, an insurance company does not need to protect itself against adverse outcomes in single risk factors; it is basically sufficient to protect the company's bottom line while taking into account the diversification potential emanating from the variety of the risk factors.[16] New types of risk transfer solutions – ART products – were created in response to these new approaches to risk management.[17]

Practical ART solutions tend to be highly customised and rather complicated, partly due to regulatory, accounting and tax implications, and it is well beyond the scope of this chapter to treat detailed examples. Instead, we investigate some simple, stylised classes of ART solutions in order to reinforce the point that proper understanding and modelling of dependence structures among the risk factors is essential for any related quantitative analysis.

1. *Finite risk covers* are normally aimed at spreading the risk of one (insurance) risk factor over time, which is outside the scope of this chapter. However, given the long time horizons of such deals, it is fairly commonplace to incorporate investment income into the pricing, which – in turn – requires the understanding of possible dependence between investment return and insured risk.

2. *Multi-line products* cover the total risk of several risk factors, with whole account stop-loss treaties being a simple and popular example. Understanding the dependence structure of the included risk factors is therefore essential for understanding the behaviour of the total risk. Multi-line deals are often underwritten for several years, which makes it sensible to incorporate investment income, including – of course – possible dependences with the other risk factors.

3. *Multi-trigger products* (knock-in options being a popular example from finance) provide payments only if several conditions are fulfilled simultaneously. Although pure multi-trigger products are only rarely underwritten in insurance, multi-trigger structures are regularly part of other products. Multi-trigger structures allow the triggering of payouts only if they are actually necessary, eg, a large insurance loss would only be paid if the company has simultaneously suffered losses on its asset side, indicated by stock and bond indices going below some threshold. This reduces the probability of payouts and thus the premium for the cover. Obviously, sensible design and pricing of such products is only possible if the dependence between the triggering risk factors is well understood.

4. *Securitisation products*, eg, Catastrophe (cat) bonds can be based on multiple lines, or they can have multiple triggers (in order to avoid moral

hazard, for example). Dependence modelling is important for another reason: as stated earlier, these products are sold to investors in the capital markets with the marketing argument that they have low, or even negative, correlation with the usual investment assets and thus provide good diversification of investment portfolios.

Recall that $\mathbf{X} = (X_1, \ldots, X_d)^T$ denotes the vector of random risk factors and $a = (a_1, \ldots, a_d)^T \in (\mathbb{R} \cup \{\pm\infty\})^d$ is a constant vector. We can easily formalise the payouts of the types of stylised ART products mentioned above as being a function of the aggregate sum, ie,

$$\Psi(\mathbf{X}) = f\left(\sum_{i=1}^{d} g(X_i)\right)$$

or as being contingent on the risk factors assuming certain values, ie,

$$\Psi(\mathbf{X}) = c \cdot 1_{\{X_1 > a_1, \ldots, X_d > a_d\}}$$

or as being combinations thereof, eg,

$$\Psi(\mathbf{X}) = f\left(\sum_{i=1}^{d} g(X_i)\right) \cdot 1_{\{X_1 > a_1, \ldots, X_d > a_d\}}$$

where, sometimes, we are only interested in conditional distributions, eg, the distribution of

$$f(X_1, \ldots, X_d) \text{ given that } X_1 > a_1, \ldots, X_d > a_d$$

Note that the payout functions $\Psi_1, \ldots, \Psi_4$ from the previous section all belong to one of the above classes of stylised payout functions. It (almost) goes without saying that the distribution of the payout $\Psi(\mathbf{X})$ depends in all cases on the joint distribution F of the risk factors, ie, on the marginal distributions of the single risk factors $X_1, \ldots, X_d$ as well as on their dependence structure (copula).

Moreover, it is important to remember that the risk factors $X_1, \ldots, X_d$ typically include pure insurance risks (downside only) as well as financial risks (double-sided). Therefore, in ART set-ups we are unlikely to face risk vectors $\mathbf{X}$ for which an element of the class of elliptical distributions is a sensible model. Elliptical distributions can be thought of roughly as a generalisation of the multivariate Gaussian distribution. However, in these cases where the joint distribution of the risk factors $\mathbf{X}$ is non-elliptical, the usual linear correlation is not a viable means for describing the dependence structure between the risk factors. See Embrechts *et al.* (2002) for more details on these issues. Therefore, we have to revert to more sophisticated concepts for dependence modelling, like the copula approach described in the previous two sections.

Another aspect is that, in many cases, ART products are designed in such a way that they are hit with only relatively low probability (eg, cat bonds). Hence, whatever the exact structure of such products may be, the interest often lies on "rare" or "extreme" events of the joint distribution of the risk factors. Therefore, dependence modelling must be particularly accurate in the related regions of the joint distribution function F. All the more so in view of the observation that dependence structures that prevail for the "usual" course of events of the risk factors tend to change under more extreme events. This can be thought of in terms of two risk factors, X_1 and X_2, that are almost uncorrelated for high-probability events, but tend to assume particularly high values jointly, as, for example, in Figure 1c. For instance, a small fire destroys some furniture in a commercial building, but does not cause a business interruption. A large fire, however, generates a high claim from destroyed furniture and, moreover, is likely to also cause a major business interruption with an associated large claim.[18]

Classical portfolio theory along the lines of Markowitz and the Capital Asset Pricing Model (CAPM), as described for instance in Brealy and Myers (2000), are closely related to the use of linear correlation for the measurement and modelling of dependence between the considered classes of assets. Therefore, the arguments given above suggest that it may not be optimal to use classical portfolio theory to justify the usefulness of insurance-linked securities (like cat bonds) to the investor, since the joint distribution of insurance risks and financial risks is not likely to be elliptical. A possible alternative approach based on VAR and copulas for the dependence modelling is given in Embrechts *et al.* (2001).

Returning to the data example will provide an idea of the impact of dependence modelling on the distributions of some stylised ART payouts and hence on the pricing of such products. Putting the results of the computations for the different models and payout function examples from the previous section together, we obtain the following results for the expected values of the payouts:

Model	AIC	$\hat{E}(\Psi_1)$	$\hat{E}(\Psi_2)$	$\hat{E}(\Psi_3)$	$\hat{E}(\Psi_4)$
Gumbel	−319.51	3.231	1.134	1.118	0.0227
t	−268.55	3.224	1.066	0.727	0.0160
Frank	−262.75	3.205	1.001	0.303	0.0095
Gaussian	−262.06	3.232	1.072	0.657	0.0015
FGM	−165.84	3.245	0.970	0.142	0.0048
Clayton	−107.73	3.243	0.970	0.146	0.0049
Independence	−	3.234	0.927	0.077	0.0025

and for the standard deviations of the payouts:

Model	AIC	$\hat{\sigma}(\Psi_1)$	$\hat{\sigma}(\Psi_2)$	$\hat{\sigma}(\Psi_3)$	$\hat{\sigma}(\Psi_4)$
Gumbel	−319.51	10.772	9.525	10.382	0.1489
t	−268.55	10.009	8.711	8.067	0.1255
Frank	−262.75	9.188	7.801	4.201	0.0968
Gaussian	−262.06	9.853	8.522	7.336	0.1229
FGM	−165.84	9.120	7.773	2.793	0.0689
Clayton	−107.73	9.137	7.879	2.805	0.0700
Independence	−	8.985	7.686	2.128	0.0023

Recall that all models use the same marginal distributions (ie, any difference in the result is due to the choice of the different dependence structures). The AIC is a measure for the goodness-of-fit, where lower values indicate a better fit, ie, the results are ordered in descending order of goodness-of-fit (except for the independence assumption). We can observe the following:

1. There are indeed significant differences between the estimates generated under the various dependence models. In particular, there are also significant differences between the best fitting models and the independence assumption. In particular, the estimates under the independence assumption usually correspond well with estimates from models with poor goodness-of-fit values.
2. The differences between the estimates usually correspond well with the differences in goodness-of-fit. In particular, models with similar goodness-of-fit values usually produce similar estimates.

Figure 7 shows the estimated cumulated distribution functions of the payout $\Psi_1(X) = X_2 + X_3$ for two different dependence models and under the assumption of independence. From this figure it can also be seen that whether or not to account for dependence – and if so, how – can make a significant difference in the resulting profit-and-loss distribution.

CONCLUSION

The fact that the pricing of insurance and ART products relies heavily on the expectation of the payouts and their dispersion leads to the conclusion that the accurate measurement and modelling of dependence between risk factors is a crucial ingredient for being able to determine effective product structures and viable prices. Through its examples, this chapter has shown that it is necessary to go beyond the notion of linear correlation in order to capture the true dependence underlying typical insurance (and indeed finance) data. The notion of copula can help to achieve a better under-

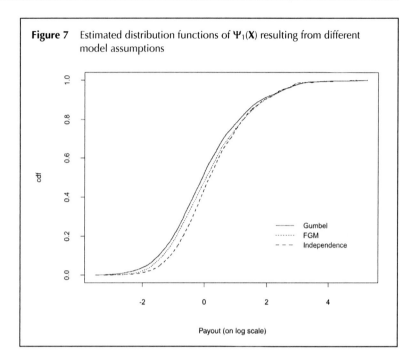

Figure 7   Estimated distribution functions of $\Psi_1(\mathbf{X})$ resulting from different model assumptions

standing of the role that dependence plays in the realm of ART. It should be stressed that this chapter has only focused on some of the underlying issues; no doubt considerable additional work in this area is needed.

1 Supported by Converium Reinsurance Ltd, Zurich, Switzerland.
2 Supported by Fundação para a Ciência e a Tecnologia and Faculdade de Ciências e Tecnologia, Universidade Nova de Lisboa, Portugal.
3 The beta of a security measures its sensitivity to market movements. Beta measures the amount that investors expect the stock price to change for each additional change of one percentage point in the market; see Brealy and Myers (2000).
4 An excellent example of a model risk analysis for a specific ART product is to be found in Schmock (1999) and Gisler and Frost (1999). For a more general discussion on model risk within finance, see Gibson (2000).
5 An influential paper importing copulas into mainstream risk management is Embrechts *et al.* (2002). The paper contains numerous references to basic publications in the copula field. For an in depth discussion, see the above paper and for instance Nelsen (1999) for a textbook treatment.
6 See Lemma 4.1.9 in Embrechts *et al.* (1997).
7 For generalisations to $d > 2$, see for instance Nelsen (1999) or Embrechts *et al.* (2000). These publications also explain how to prove that the stated functions are indeed copulas.
8 See Embrechts *et al.* (2002) for several examples on this.
9 Although some of the key advanced facts of copula modelling are addressed below it is important to acknowledge that the key issue remains how to find the copula that best models the dependence structure of real multivariate data. Though this chapter partly addresses this issue, it is important to state that giving an answer is essentially as difficult as estimating the

joint distribution F in the first place, hence for the dimension d large this will be extremely difficult, if not impossible.

10 For a definition of the Kendall τ rank correlation see Embrechts *et al.* (2002).

11 This crucial fact is indeed true and can be shown mathematically; see for instance Embrechts et al. (2002).

12 For a one-dimensional discussion of these data, see Embrechts *et al.* (1997), Example 6.2.9 and further. See also Rytgaard (1996), from whom the data in this chapter were obtained, and McNeil (1997) for an early extreme value analysis.

13 See for example Proposition 2 in Embrechts *et al.* (2002).

14 For this, and further shortcomings of linear correlation, see Embrechts *et al.* (2002), Section 3.2.

15 See, for example, McNeil and Frey (2000).

16 We tacitly assume here that corporate governance structures are set up in such a way that they do not penalise adverse results of a single line of business if they are due to an integrated risk management structure that focuses on protection of the overall bottom line only.

17 An easily accessible account on the trend towards the integrated management and transfer of risks as well as descriptions of the most important types of ART products is given in Shimpi (1999).

18 A worked-out example with data from finance as well as a theoretical result on copula convergence for tail events given in Juri and Wüthrich (2002) provides further evidence for this.

BIBLIOGRAPHY

Brealy, R. A., and S. C. Myers, 2000, *Principles of Corporate Finance*, Sixth Edition, (New York: McGraw-Hill).

Bühlmann, H., 1970, *Mathematical Methods in Risk Theory*, (Berlin: Springer-Verlag).

Embrechts, P., A. Hoeing and A. Juri, 2001, "Using Copulae to Bound the Value-at-Risk for Functions of Dependent Risks", Working Paper, ETH Zurich.

Embrechts, P., C., Klüppelberg and T. Mikosch, 1997, *Modelling Extremal Events for Insurance and Finance*. (Berlin: Springer-Verlag).

Embrechts, P., F. Lindskog and A. J. McNeil, 2000, "Modelling Dependence with Copulas and Applications to Risk Management", forthcoming in: *Heavy-Tailed Distributions in Finance*, 2002, S.T. Rachev (ed), (Amsterdam: North Holland).

Embrechts, P., A. J. McNeil and D. Straumann, 1999, "Correlation: Pitfalls and Alternatives", *Risk Magazine*, 5, pp. 69–71.

Embrechts, P., A. J. McNeil and D. Straumann, 2002, "Correlation and Dependence in Risk Management: Properties and Pitfalls", in: *Risk Management: Value at Risk and Beyond*, M. Dempster (ed), (Cambridge University Press) pp. 176–223.

Genest, C., K. Ghoudi and L.-P. Rivest, 1995, "A Semiparametric Estimation Procedure of Dependence Parameters in Multivariate Families of Distributions", *Biometrika*, 82(3), pp. 543–52.

Genest, C., K. Ghoudi and L.-P. Rivest, 1998, "Commentaire sur l'article de E. W. Frees et E. A. Valdez intitulé "Understanding relationships using copulas"", *North American Actuarial Journal*, 2, pp. 143–9.

Gibson, R. (ed), 2000, *Model Risk: Concepts, Calibration and Pricing*, (London: Risk Books).

Gisler, A., and P. Frost, 1999, "An Addendum and a Short Comment on the Paper from U. Schmock, "Estimating the Value of the WinCAT Coupons of the Winterthur Insurance Convertible Bond: A Study of the Model Risk"", *ASTIN Bulletin*, 29(1), pp.165–71.

Joe, H., 1997, *Multivariate Models and Dependence Concepts*, (London: Chapman & Hall).

Juri, A., and M. Wüthrich, 2002, "Copula Convergence Theorems for Tail Events", in *Insurance: Mathematics and Economics*, Forthcoming.

McNeil, A. J., 1997, "Estimating the Tails of Loss Severity Distributions Using Extreme Value Theory", *ASTIN Bulletin*, 27(1), pp. 117–37.

McNeil, A. J., and R. Frey, 2000, "Estimation of Tail-Related Risk Measures for Heterocedastic Financial Time Series: An Extreme Value Approach", *Journal of Empirical Finance*, 7, pp. 271–300.

Nelsen, R. B., 1999, *An Introduction to Copulas* (New York: Springer-Verlag).

Rytgaard, M., 1996, "Simulation Experiments on the Mean Residual Life Function $m(x)$", in: *Proceedings of the XXVII ASTIN Colloquium*, Copenhagen, Denmark, 1, pp. 59–81.

Schmidt, W., and I. Ward, 2002, Pricing Default Baskets, *Risk Magazine*, 1, pp. 111–14.

Schmock, U., 1999, "Estimating the Value of the WinCAT Coupons of the Winterthur Insurance Convertible Bond: A Study of the Model Risk", *ASTIN Bulletin*, 29(1), pp. 101–63.

Shih, J. H., and T. A. Louis, 1995, "Inferences on the Association Parameter in Copula Models for Bivariate Survival Data", *Biometrics*, 51, pp. 1384–99.

Shimpi, P. (ed), 1999, *Integrating Corporate Risk Management*, (New York: Swiss Re New Markets).

17

Economic Modelling: The Residual Valuation and Lease Income Streams of Aircraft Fleets

Derrell Hendrix and Neil Hohmann

RISConsulting

Aircraft-related financial risk extends far beyond the owners of aircraft. Aircraft hull and engine manufacturers, banks, insurance and reinsurance companies, lessors, airlines and the investment community are all exposed to a wide variety of aircraft-related risks through obligations that are tied to the financial performance of aircraft values and income streams. Insurers and manufacturers, for example, routinely guarantee the future value or income levels of aircraft to facilitate sales or to protect owners against value declines. Aircraft lessors are naturally exposed to changes in the lease income they receive on their fleets as a result of supply and demand and credit factors. Manufacturers are also known to provide banks and other providers of aircraft financing with guarantees against customer default in order to credit-enhance weaker buyers. Finally, with the evolution of securitisation as a mainstream financing technique, investors are playing a large and critical role in financing the assets and assuming the asset-related risk of airlines and operating lessors, providing billions of US dollars in cash and risk capacity on an annual basis. All of these activities are based on inexact assessments of aircraft market value and lease income risks, confounded by the lack of transparency and liquidity in the industry. Active management of these risks increasingly requires industry participants to employ more accurate risk assessment and pricing tools based on an analysis of the macroeconomic and industry factors that drive aircraft market values and lease income streams.

INTRODUCTION

This chapter provides an introduction to the economic factors that influence movements in aircraft values and lease income streams and outlines a framework for the assessment of aircraft financial risks related to these movements. The first section reviews the sources of increasing demand for risk mitigation as well as the particular difficulties associated with the assessment and transfer of aircraft-related risks. The second section explores in depth the economic sources of risk in aircraft market values, including macroeconomic movements, industry conditions, depreciation patterns and technology. The following section introduces the aircraft lease cycle and examines the various components of the lease income stream for an aircraft. A framework for the economic modelling of these risks is given in both sections. The final section emphasises the importance of incorporating contract-level data and portfolio-level effects into the assessment of aircraft financial risks.

BACKGROUND

Until recently, direct and indirect exposures to aircraft financial risk have, in general, been poorly understood and seemingly immeasurable. Aircraft are large, high- value assets with a specialised application and a narrow market. As such, they are illiquid assets and do not trade with great frequency. When market transactions do occur, the related price data is often unavailable or unreliable, and very often incorporates services or extraneous financial considerations (eg, tax benefits) that distort the true economic value of the asset. In addition, the aircraft industry is oligopolistic on both the supply (eg, manufacturer and lessor) and the demand (eg, airline) ends of the market spectrum, and data is closely held in all quarters. All of these factors have complicated and impeded the development of an open, transparent and, hence, liquid aircraft market. Such complexity and opaqueness has also limited the assessment and quantification of aircraft related risks and limited industry practitioners to evaluating risk through a fairly crude process (by today's risk management standards) of projecting expected future aircraft values and incomes (based more on accounting norms than market information) and applying deterministic stresses to these levels.

The limitations of deriving a sound understanding of an aircraft risk are increasingly perceived by both industry insiders and outsiders to be conflicting with current trends and demands in risk management. These emanate from senior managers, analysts, investors and counterparties and regulators, and call for, among other things, greater transparency, truer accounting, more precise risk assessment and capital adequacy. Firms in other industries, such as banking and insurance, have made significant strides in the past decade or two towards implementing more rigorous risk measurement techniques, as well as risk management procedures and systems. They require timely, accurate, and detailed information on not only the value of assets and liabilities but their volatility over future time horizons. As a result of the tools and transparency that have been derived from this evolution, new trading instruments such as catastrophe (cat) bonds and credit derivatives have developed, creating new sources of liquidity and capital for these markets. Today, banks trade exotic derivatives with capital market investors using universally available models, enabling both sides to value and mark-to-market transactions and portfolios and to forecast future volatility. This is not the case in aircraft, where management is seeking to achieve similar capabilities and benefits driven by a growing desire to manage actively (ie, to transfer), in order to strengthen and to preserve company balance sheets and market value.

Lacking the regulatory impetus of the banking and insurance industries, the aircraft industry, like many others, has been slow at evolving new risk management practices. The stock market has performed this role to a limited extent by rewarding companies (by raising their valuations) that proactively address complex and poorly understood risks such as the portfolios of manufacturer residual value guarantees and contingent liabilities (concepts which will be explained in detail later). While their scrutiny is far from sophisticated, markets are becoming increasingly interested in the valuation and disclosure of these risks. In the absence of a developed trading market for an asset class growing at over US$40 billion in annual sales that is largely supported by weak industry balance sheets, these portfolios will only continue to increase in size.

The tragic events of September 11, 2001 have dramatically magnified the aircraft industry's risk management problems. The sharp drop in passenger revenue has led to a corresponding drop in virtually all aircraft values, leading those exposed to re-evaluate the likelihood and severity of portfolio losses. Investors and risk capacity providers, such as the alternative risk transfer (ART) branch of the reinsurance market, have responded by significantly raising spreads and risk premiums, or exiting the aviation market altogether. What little liquidity there was in the market prior to the event has all but vanished, leaving the industry's future more uncertain than ever, particularly given the lingering threat of future acts of terrorism.

Under these conditions, the demand for better risk assessment and pricing tools for aircraft-related assets is pronounced. Companies want to know where they are now in terms of value and to gauge the direction and magnitude of potential future changes. They also want to know, with more clarity, what will drive the direction and magnitude of these potential changes in values and incomes, as well as how specific assets or asset types will be affected.

Over the past five years, The RISConsulting Group LLC has been active in assisting a number of leading industry participants in developing a rigorous framework for measuring and managing aircraft-related financial risk. RISConsulting's efforts in this regard have directly supported the raising of over US$5 billion in risk capacity covering over US$10 billion in underlying financial risk. For this to have occurred, given the complexity of the risk and the amounts involved, it has been essential to accommodate the requirements of not only manufacturing company clients – who were shifting large, diversified portfolios of risk – but also many of the most sophisticated reinsurance companies as well as the leading rating agencies. In the process, RISConsulting developed valuable experience in identifying the factors that drive industry risk and considerable expertise in assessing and modelling aviation residual value and lease income risk, supported by a wealth of portfolio and market data. The balance of this chapter elaborates on these economic modelling methods, which are the key to the development of a modern risk management platform for the aviation industry.

DRIVERS OF AIRCRAFT-RELATED FINANCIAL RISK

Apart from the relatively small scrap value of an aircraft's aluminium, steel and other physical components, its primary value derives from its present and future capability to provide a service – the transportation or "lift" of passengers and cargo from one location to another. Like any other good or service, the stream of value of future lift services for a particular aircraft is determined in a marketplace and is subject to fluctuations in supply and demand. Unlike consumable goods and services, however, an airplane provides its services over a life that may span 25–40 years. The current value of an aircraft, whether new or in service, depends on current and expected future market for lift. The current operating lease rate – which is essentially the rental rate that a lessee, such as an airline, pays an aircraft owner for temporary usage (typically 3–7 years) – is more reflective of current market conditions. Both market values and lease rates are fundamental, but different, measures of an aircraft's lift services. This section describes the market factors that shape both aircraft values and lease income streams, and it provides a framework for modelling their future behaviour.

Aircraft Revenue

The value of an aircraft to its owner or lessee over some period of time, t, is its potential net income, I_t, ie, the revenue generated by paying passengers (or cargo receipts) less the costs of operating the aircraft. (The costs of financing the purchase of the aircraft are considered separately and are not included in operating costs.) Operators set ticket prices to maximise revenues for a given flight, not necessarily to fill the aircraft. Revenue maximisation is enhanced by practices such as price discrimination or discounts among customers with different demands (eg, two-week restricted fares vs business class) and fleet management (switching aircraft among routes to optimise profitability). At its base, however, an aircraft's revenue is a function of passenger demand for the routes the aircraft flies.

Revenues for time t (R_t) can be decomposed into two basic industry measures:

$$R_t = RPM_t \times RY_t,$$

where RPM_t is the total number of miles flown by customers (revenue passenger-miles, RPM) in period t, and RY_t is the average revenue per RPM flown – revenue yield (RY) during t. Both of these summary measures have historically been highly sensitive to the prevailing demand and supply conditions at macroeconomic and industry levels.

Passenger-miles, an indicator of the number of people who fly, are tied closely to the strength of domestic and international economies. For example, Figure 1 illustrates the particularly tight relationship within the US between annual RPM growth and US GDP growth. Other factors affecting RPM include industry deregulation trends (positively), as well as security concerns in the aftermath of the Gulf War and the September 11 terrorist attacks (negatively).

RY measures the average amount collected from each paying passenger. Yield increases tend to follow inflation. Inflation at the producer level (measured by the Producer Price Index, PPI) is reflected in higher aircraft operating costs (such as aviation fuel, crew and administrative salaries, and benefits) that are passed, at least partly, to passengers. Inflation at the consumer level – measured in the Consumer Price Index (CPI) results in higher prices for flight substitutes such as automobiles and trains, raising the relative demand for air travel and, subsequently, yields.

Imbalances of demand and supply for seats also affect yields. Such imbalances might occur on flights to and from particular destinations or could apply to the entire industry over several years. For a particular route, the demand is balanced against the number and frequency of flights. While airlines may add planes to overbooked routes, airport gate restrictions and regulatory constraints can limit those adjustments. For example, limited airport size or regulations may reduce competition for a route, leading to

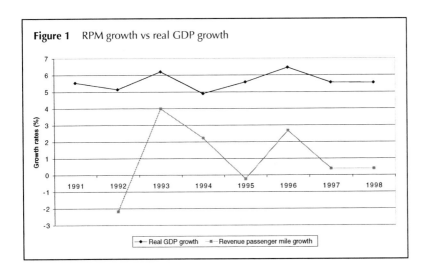

Figure 1   RPM growth vs real GDP growth

the exercise of market power in pricing, and, consequently, higher yields. Alternatively, the introduction of new capacity to a route by a growing airline, such as Southwest Airlines, can depress prices for all airlines.

At an industry level, individual route situations may not be relevant, but other factors contribute to long-running imbalances in demand for and supply of air travel. Because a significant portion of an airline's costs are fixed (eg, aircraft purchased, gate fees, and employee salaries), airlines have an incentive to offer flights that cover variable operating costs, even if they do not book a profit. Such scenarios can continue until airlines' cash on hand and sources of funding evaporate. Large airlines and national flag carriers may even be able to operate indefinitely in the red as a result of significant subsidies from their home countries. These factors can contribute to an oversupply at the industry level. Supply imbalances also may be exacerbated by the multi-year production cycle for passenger jets, which sometimes results in aircraft deliveries peaking during soft demand; too many planes chasing too few passengers depresses yields. RY will return to balance only when demand recovers, some airlines fail, or older assets are retired.

To summarise all of these determinants of an aircraft's revenue stream over a given period, t, let us express R_t as a function of economic growth, inflation, demand factors and supply factors:

$$R_t = RPM_t(GDP_t, u_t) \times RY_t(CPI_t, PPI_t, RPM_t, S_t, v_t)$$

where GDP_t, CPI_t, and PPI_t are economic growth rates, consumer inflation rates and producer inflation rates, respectively all over the period, t. S_t measures the supply of comparable aircraft and u_t and v_t represent the collective effects of several idiosyncratic factors such as security issues, airport capacity constraints, regulatory changes, and airline bankruptcies. In the short-run, this revenue formulation applies at the individual route level. However, because aircraft can be reallocated among routes and operators, it is longer-run industry supply factors, such as the percentage of comparable aircraft in the world fleet that are idle and available, and demand factors, such as countrywide or worldwide economic growth, that determine lease rates and aircraft values. This chapter will focus throughout on these longer-run factors.

Aircraft Operating Costs and Net Income

The cost (C) of operating an aircraft in period t, C_t, includes the variable costs of flying the aircraft plus a pro-rated portion of the airline's fixed costs required to ticket and board passengers and maintain the aircraft. The variable costs consist primarily of the cost of fuel and the salaries of the crew (to the extent that staffing levels are flexible). Crew costs are sensitive to changes in labour market conditions that form a component of the PPI.

Fuel price movements are also an important component of the PPI, but because of their relative importance, it is helpful to consider their effect independently of the PPI. The fixed cost component is highly sensitive to drops in passenger-miles as these fixed costs must be spread over fewer passengers. Other factors that can influence operating costs include airport security changes, aircraft-specific airworthiness maintenance directives from the Federal Aviation Administration (FAA), and higher airport fees.

We summarise the determinants of an aircraft's anticipated operating costs as

$$C_t = C_t(FI_t, PPI_t, RPM_t, w_t)$$

where FI_t denotes fuel price inflation rates and w_t represents idiosyncratic factors that influence operating costs. It is important to note that any costs associated with buying the aircraft are not considered operating costs. Operating costs include only those costs that an operator must incur in order to fly the aircraft.

It is now possible to define the value, I_t, of the stream of services provided by an aircraft in period t as revenues less operating costs:

$$I_t = R_t - C_t = RPM_t(GDP_t, u_t) \times RY_t(CPI_t, PPI_t, RPM_t, S_t, v_t)$$
$$- C_t(FI_t, PPI_t, RPM_t, w_t).$$

The value of the lift services that an individual aircraft therefore can provide over a period depends on: macroeconomic conditions (including fluctuations in fuel prices) in the period, the current demand for air travel, the supply of comparable aircraft, and the myriad other idiosyncratic factors that influence industry supply and demand.

The above is a *structural* equation for determining an aircraft's value. It shows the decomposition of total revenues into RPM and RY, includes RPM as an independent term and as an explanatory factor in RY and C and suggests relationships between RPM, RY and C and their underlying factors. This complex and recursive equation is an accurate and informative description of an aircraft's net income in a period. For purposes of analysis and estimation, however, it is helpful to rewrite the structural equation in terms of its underlying factors solely, or

$$I_t = I_t(GDP_t, CPI_t, PPI_t, FI_t, S_t, e_t),$$

where e_t is the combined effect of the idiosyncratic factors u_t, v_t, and w_t. This equation is called the "reduced form". It includes all of the information implicit in the structural equation and also clearly expresses the combined effect of the underlying factors on the net income in period t. Based on the reduced form, it is possible to identify the expected combined effect of each of the factors on net income. Table 1 displays the expected effect on income of several of the described factors.

Modelling the Macroeconomy

We have suggested that movements in macroeconomic variables – such as economic growth, consumer and producer inflation, fuel prices and interest rates – are key determinants of potential income streams from aircraft. (We shall see the importance of interest rates below.) In addition to affecting net income – and, by extension, current market values and lease rates – the macroeconomy strongly influences several other measures that can affect aircraft leasing cashflows: lease terms, downtime between leases, the proportion of fleet that is idle and the probability of operator default. An aircraft value model is incomplete without an understanding of the links between economic factors and market outcomes as well as an ability to forecast the likely behaviour of these macroeconomic variables.

A proper macroeconomic model should incorporate an econometric analysis of future macroeconomic variable trends, volatility and correlation from a base of current and past macroeconomic conditions and accommodate the simulation of macroeconomic variables forward in a consistent fashion. Naturally, the question arises of which macroeconomy should be modelled. As this chapter focuses on the long-run industry-wide determinants of income, the macroeconomic performance of large well-defined markets is most relevant here. For the aircraft industry macroeconomic performance in the US, European Union and Asian markets, as well as for the world in aggregate, are useful measures. The particular choice of variables for modelling income of a particular aircraft should be based on the missions and markets that the aircraft and its comparables fly. For example, due to its international use, the income of workhorses such as Boeing's 747 is particularly sensitive to aggregate global GDP growth.

Having identified the appropriate markets and variables to model, a macroeconomic model is typically estimated from historical data for each of the variables, on either a quarterly or annual basis. The model takes the form of an equation for each variable identifying its expected future trend,

Table 1   Impact on macroeconomic and industry factors on aircraft net income

Factors	Net income (+/–)
GDP growth	+
Fuel price increase	–
Supply of comparable aircraft increase	–
Inflation	generally +

its volatility and its correlation with each of the other variables. Regression approaches are generally used for and are well-suited to the estimation of these equations, although the estimation process is more art than science. Figure 2 illustrates one system of equations for US quarterly variables estimated on a historical data set using a vector autoregression framework.

Based on the model equations, the mean and probability distribution of future macroeconomic conditions can be simulated, conditional on current conditions. As the following sections demonstrate, future macroeconomic movements drive future market values and lease income streams.

Aircraft Residual Values

The value (V) of an aircraft to its operator in the present period, denoted t, is its potential net income I_t. The total current value, V_t, of the aircraft to the operator is the discounted stream of expected future net income over its remaining useful life,

$$V_t = E_t \left[\sum_{s=t}^{t+l} \delta_s I_s (GDP_s, CPI_s, PPI_s, FI_s, S_s, e_s) + \delta_{t+l+1} S \right] \qquad (1)$$

where l is the remaining useful economic life of the aircraft (eg, 11 years), δ_s is a discount factor that applies to I_s, the income in some future period, s. S is the scrap value of the aircraft, and $E_t[\ ]$ is the expectations operator indicating that V_t is the discounted *expected* future income stream based on information available in period t, rather than the actual stream of future incomes I_s. Examination of this equation reveals the source of important features of aircraft value behaviour, which are explored below.

Industry-wide factors and competition among operators limit the range of values that different operators have for the same aircraft, but in practice V_t does differ somewhat among potential operators. In the long-run, the

---

Figure 2 Equations for macroeconomic model

Real GDP gdp_t $= -0.186 + 0.198gdp_{t-1} - 0.084InfCPI_{t-1} - 0.183InfPPI_{t-1}$
$- 0.062FF_{t-1} + 0.032EC_{t-1} + \varepsilon_{gdp_t}$

CPI $InfCPI_t = -0.156 + 0.015gdp_{t-1} - 0.119gdp_{t-2} + 0.037InfCPI_{t-1}$
$+ 0.00003InfCPI_{t-2} + 0.188InfPPI_{t-1} + 0.135InfPPI_{t-2}$
$+ 0.194FF_{t-1} - 0.141FF_{t-2} + 0.025EC_{t-1} + \varepsilon_{InfCPI_t}$

PPI $InfPPI_t = -0.098 + 0.030gdp_{t-1} - 0.065gdp_{t-2} + 0.458InfCPI_{t-1}$
$+ 0.150InfCPI_{t-2} + 0.127InfPPI_{t-1} + 0.152InfPPI_{t-2}$
$+ 0.109FF_{t-1} - 0.134FF_{t-2} + 0.016EC_{t-1} + \varepsilon_{InfPPI_t}$

FF Rate FF_t $= -0.043 + 0.234\beta_2gdp_{t-2} + 0.060gdp_{t-2} - 0.181InfCPI_{t-1}$
$+ 0.295InfCPI_{t-2} + 0.210InfPPI_{t-1} - 0.074InfPPI_{t-2}$
$+ 1.079FF_{t-1} - 0.166FF_{t-2} + 0.007EC_{t-1} + \varepsilon_{FF_t}$

---

market value – the price at which the aircraft would trade in the market, whether new or in service – will tend to reflect the highest valuation V_t held for the aircraft by any potential operator because this operator has an incentive to purchase or lease the aircraft away from an operator with a lower valuation. Because it reflects an operator's valuation, the market value is subject to the same macroeconomic and industry effects that we have examined above. In the remainder of the chapter, an aircraft's valuation will refer to its market valuation.

Depreciation
Depreciation is the period-by-period deterioration of the aircraft's value, as for any asset with a fixed useful life. The causes of this deterioration are clear in Equation (1); as the remaining useful life, l, runs out, the discounted stream of future income falls to zero. The amount of depreciation in monetary terms is $\Delta V_t = V_{t+1} - V_t$. The rate of depreciation, $d_t = \Delta V_t / V_t$, tends to rise as the remaining life runs out, assuming the periodic future income I_t is constant or declining. For example, if future income over the remaining life of the plane and the periodic discount factor are constant (ie, $I_s = I$, $\delta_s = \delta^s$, and $S = 0$), then $d_t = \delta^l / (1 + \delta + \dots + \delta^l)$. The rate of depreciation rises even more quickly with age if anticipated income declines as the plane nears the end of its useful life. Figure 3 illustrates sample depreciation rates for an aircraft assuming both constant and declining income with age. A typical appraiser depreciation forecast is included for reference.

A certain rate of depreciation for an aircraft can be expected based on its income-generating potential and its remaining life. These predicted rates

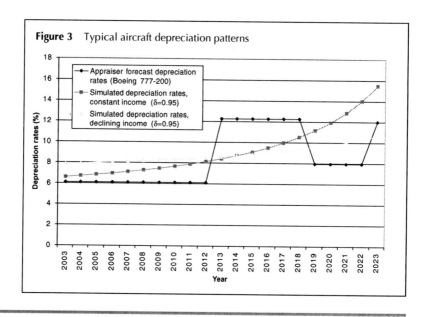

Figure 3   Typical aircraft depreciation patterns

are estimated, for example, by appraisers, and they form the basis of simple baseline financial analyses of aircraft future values. The *risk* to a holder of an aircraft value-linked asset, however, is unexpected depreciation. An unpredicted acceleration in depreciation may result from business cycle effects (ie, macroeconomic forces), technological obsolescence, competition or industry-level shocks such as security concerns. The following sections explore the modelling of these risks.

Business Cycle Effects

Macroeconomic shifts are a primary source of unexpected depreciation. Deviations from the long-run expected level of GDP growth or inflation can lower residual vales because of their effect on present and future income streams. One way to examine this effect is to break the monetary amount of depreciation ΔV_t into two terms, based on the market value equation:

$$\Delta V_t = -I_t(GDP_t, CPI_t, PPI_t, \ldots) + V_{t+1}(GDP_{t+1}, CPI_{t+1}, PPI_{t+1}, \ldots)$$
$$- \delta_{t+1} E_t[V_{t+1}(GDP_{t+1}, CPI_{t+1}, PPI_{t+1}, \ldots)] \qquad (2)$$

The first term, $-I_t$, is simply the net income paid out in period t. Like a stock dividend, after period t income's is paid out, the value of the aircraft asset declines in reflection of the payment. Unexpected business cycle movements that raise current income, such as higher economic growth, will result in an elevated amount of depreciation through this first term. This counter-intuitive response occurs because the positive income effect, based on information on economic conditions available in period t, has already been incorporated into the value V_t, ie, the higher depreciation is simply taken off a higher base level.

The second and generally dominant term, often abbreviated to $V_{t+1} - \delta_{t+1}$ $E_t[V_{t+1}]$, represents the market revaluation of future income streams from period t + 1 forward that results as the actual observed economic conditions in period t deviate from their expected levels at the beginning of the period. The effect on depreciation is straightforward; if macroeconomic developments result in future income levels that exceed the expected levels, the value of the aircraft rises and depreciation for the period lessens. It is important to note that current economic conditions *per se* may not drive depreciation rates – it is often the implications for future conditions that drive depreciation. For example, one might expect the announcement of a sharply higher US inflation rate to have a positive impact in the short-run on aircraft residual value, lowering short-term depreciation rates. In fact, the possibility of a sharp Federal Reserve Bank response and a concomitant recession in the following years may actually accelerate market value declines below their expected levels.

Economic growth and inflation affect market values and depreciation through their effect on present and future aircraft income. The market value equation (Equation (2)) above introduces the important effect of current and future interest rates on market values. Interest rates enter primarily through the discount factors δ_{t+k}, which represent the degree to which the market discounts future expected income streams. The discount reflects the opportunity cost of an investment in assets other than the aircraft. The discount factor, δ_{t+k}, that applies to income k periods in the future can be expressed as:

$$\delta_{t+k} = 1/(RF_t(k) + RP)^k$$

where $RF_t(k)$ is the k-period maturity annual risk-free rate at time t and RP is a periodic risk premium, reflecting the excess return available for alternative investments with a risk profile similar to aircraft. A rise in the expectation of future interest rates therefore results in immediate depreciation as the valuation of future income streams falls. A rise in the risk premium has the same effect. At least part of the sharp drop in aircraft market values after September 11, 2001 can be attributed to higher risk premia.

Competition, Technology and Obsolescence

Over their long useful lives, aircraft are exposed to a variety of industry developments that may affect their value. In addition to business cycle and other macroeconomic movements, technological innovations and aircraft production patterns can greatly affect the value of existing aircraft.

In the shorter run, say one to three years from present, the fleet numbers of comparable aircraft are largely fixed. Future deliveries are set with manufacturers as supply implications for a given aircraft's income depend on the number of similar planes that are available for purchase or lease. Thus supply considerations in the short-run on the whole will be captured by the percentage of similar mission-capable aircraft that are idle.

In the medium-term, say four to eight years, supply adjusts to accommodate demand through the order and delivery of comparable aircraft types. However, the planned introduction of new plane types may devalue existing models. Newer plane types that compete with existing aircraft types for the same routes are likely to have operating cost advantages based on newer technology. Examples of such advances include lower fuel consumption, smaller crew requirements and reduced maintenance. Over time operators may switch their fleets to a newer successful aircraft type, shifting demand away from existing types. This shift in demand away from existing plane types as a result of newer technology is called "obsolescence" and is to be distinguished from the inevitable depreciation that accompanies any asset of fixed life. Introductions of new technologies, particularly the introduction of an entirely new plane class, carry their own risks; the markets may reject a new aircraft type that fails to live up to its expectations, resulting in rapid depreciation of the new aircraft. In general, however, the introduction of a new aircraft type causes a corresponding acceleration in the depreciation of older types competing in the same market niches. These introductions are planned and announced years ahead, so the risk of unexpected depreciation of existing types is limited to market acceptance of the new type.

Finally, in the longer run, even the introduction of new technologies is not predictable. History is a less precise guide to aircraft residuals 10 or more years in the future, though it does provide certain lessons. Plane types with widely established user bases are less likely to suffer obsolescence than those with smaller niche markets. For example, Boeing 747 and 737 aircraft command a large market share for the missions they fly, and there are a large absolute number of both models still in operation. They are likely to weather, with some deterioration, the introduction of newer competing types. On the other hand, markets for several smaller turboprop aircraft have begun to dry up with the introduction of competing regional jets. Perhaps just as important as newer technologies in planes is continued reductions in manufacturing costs for new aircraft, lowering the replacement cost of similar aircraft types and generally accelerating obsolescence for all existing types.

Estimation and Simulation

To summarise the potential impact of business cycle movements, inflation, interest rates, short-run aircraft idle rates, longer-term new model type introductions and the variety of other idiosyncratic industry factors that affect depreciation rates and market values, it is helpful to rewrite a future market value as a function of future depreciation rates and future depreciation rates as a function of new information made available at that time:

$$V_{t+k} = d_{t+k} \, d_{t+k-1} \ldots d_{t+1} \, V_t \text{ and}$$

$$d_{t+k} = d_{t+k}(GDP_{t+k}, CPI_{t+k}, PPI_{t+k}, FI_{t+k}, S_{t+k}, IR_{t+k}, TI_{t+k}, l_{t+k}, e_{t+k}) \quad (3)$$

where TI_{t+k} is an indicator of new-type announcements or introductions on or around period t+k, l_{t+k} is the number of periods remaining in the aircraft's useful life, and the other variables are as defined for Equation (2). Because market values drift away from their expected levels only in response to new information (surprises), the depreciation rate in any one period can be treated as largely independent of the depreciation in the following period. The depreciation rate d_{t+k} is expressed in its reduced form. The sensitivity of the depreciation rate to each of these variables can be estimated in a regression framework using historical depreciation rate values. The observable macroeconomic and supply variables often explain over half of the period-to-period variation in depreciation rates. The remainder of the variation can be attributed to the idiosyncratic industry factors accounted for in the term e_{t+k}. Figure 4 demonstrates a typical relationship between depreciation rates and three of the observable variables within historical data. Based on the estimated sensitivities to observable factors and the estimated patterns of volatility and correlation in the remaining idiosyncratic variation, it is possible to simulate a consistent set of future depreciation rates for an aircraft. By applying these depreciation rates to the current market values, future market values are simulated.

Aircraft Lease Income

Many aircraft-linked assets are sensitive to the lease income flows of an aircraft rather than to the plane's market value. Examples of such assets include lease income securitisations, lessor balance sheets and lease income guarantees made by asset managers. Operating lease income flows are generated by the lease of an aircraft by its owner to an operator for a term (often three to five years) at an agreed lease rate, typically a fixed or floating periodic payment to the owner. The owner may act as the lessor or may use a servicer to market and place the aircraft.

A lessor is exposed to several risks with respect to leasing the aircraft and must price these risks into the terms of the lease, particularly into the lease rate. First, a lessor is exposed to the length of aircraft downtimes between the lease placements, when the lessor makes no income on the aircraft. Second, although lessees are required to perform scheduled maintenance at their own expense, the lessor is responsible for refurbishing

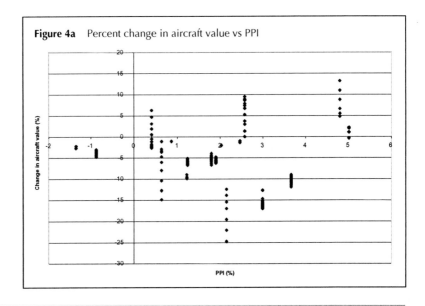

Figure 4a   Percent change in aircraft value vs PPI

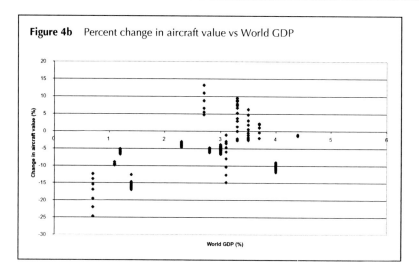

Figure 4b   Percent change in aircraft value vs World GDP

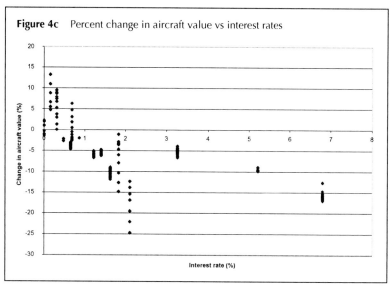

Figure 4c   Percent change in aircraft value vs interest rates

and remarketing the aircraft at the end of the lease. Finally, a lessor faces the possibility that an operator defaults on its lease obligations, resulting in a premature return of the aircraft to the lessor and lost lease income. Although security deposits and maintenance reserves generally are required of poor credit quality lessees to cover repossession costs, lost lease income and overdue maintenance, the typical turnaround times on aircraft returned on default are longer than otherwise and the security deposits may be insufficient to cover expenses.

On the other hand, the lessor locks in an established lease rate for a certain period (of several years), isolated from the risk of short-term fluctuations in the aircraft's operating income. The present value of a typical lease income stream, LI_t, for a leased aircraft with two future leases remaining in its useful life might be:

$$LI_t = LR_t(1 + \delta_{t+1} + \ldots + \delta_{t+t1}) - RC_{t+t1} + LR_{t+t1+dt1}(\delta_{t+t1+dt1+1} + \ldots + \delta_{t+t1+dt1+t2})$$

where LR_t is a fixed lease rate assigned at time t for a term of t1 for the first lease and t2 for the second lease, dt1 is the length of downtime after the end of the first lease, and RC_t the cost of refurbishing the aircraft between leases. The longer the downtime between leases and the shorter the term of the leases, the lower the cumulative lease income stream. Even ignoring the complication of maintenance and security deposits, the lease income stream is still quite complicated to model because of the variability in downtimes, lease terms and the possibility of default. The next section describes the factors that drive lease rates, terms and downtimes.

Lease Rates, Lease Terms and Downtimes

The lease rate will be a function of lease term, probability of default, lessee characteristics such as creditworthiness and the host of factors that drive aircraft net income over the term of the lease, examined above. Longer lease terms result in lower rates for two reasons. First, the plane's potential income often drops as time passes. A longer fixed lease will be associated with a lower mean aircraft income over its term. Second, a longer lease term shifts more of the risk from the lessor onto the lessee, and the lessee receives a discount to compensate for this increase in risk. On the other hand, leasing to an operator with a poor credit rating raises the likelihood

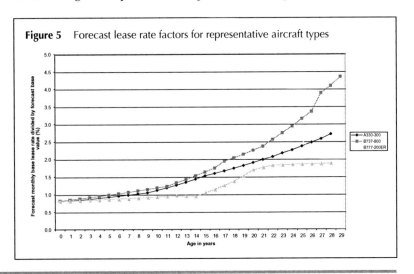

Figure 5   Forecast lease rate factors for representative aircraft types

of expensive downtime, so the lessor may command a premium for leasing to such high-risk operators. Finally, the lease rate that the market will bear is linked to the periodic income I_t that an operator can earn using the asset over the period of the lease. Therefore, lease rates share the same types of sensitivities to movements in macroeconomic, supply and idiosyncratic variables, as do I_t and V_t.

The expected future levels of lease rates for a given aircraft are traditionally projected using lease rate factors that express lease rates as a percentage of the prevailing market value. These lease rate factors often slope upwards with the age of the aircraft, indicating that the potential lease rate for the aircraft declines more slowly than the aircraft's depreciation rate. Figure 5 illustrates sample lease rate factors for several representative aircraft types. While these expected future lease rates may allow a baseline analysis of future lease income, this approach yields little insight into the volatility of future lease income streams. Modelling the volatility of future lease income around its expected level is best accomplished by modelling both the response of lease rates to the above factors (credit, macroeconomic, etc) then estimating and simulating from the probability distribution of lease terms and downtimes.

Scheduled lease terms are also sensitive to the economic cycle. Tough times tend to result in shorter leases because lessors do not want to lock in low rates for an extended period. Downtimes are yet more sensitive to economic conditions. When demand for aircraft is high, operators are quickly replaced at lease end and downtimes are limited to return and refurbishment times. When demand is low, it may take longer to find a lessee for the returned aircraft, leading to longer average time on ground. Oversupply and obsolescence also can lengthen downtimes on particular aircraft types. If demand flags to a sufficient degree, some older aircraft may be retired to the desert, effecting essentially permanent downtime.

Because lease terms and downtime lengths are duration variables, their modelling is somewhat different to that of lease rates or market values. First, and particularly for lease terms, the scheduled length of a current lease term might not be yet be publicly available. Instead, only its conditional duration up to the present time may be known. Second, historical duration data typically is characterised by a distribution that differs from a normal bell-shaped curve – it is bounded below by zero and can have a large degree of skew in its right tail. For this reason, it is useful to model these variables in a duration framework that accommodates non-normal distributions. The estimation approach should also allow the distribution of lease lengths and downtimes to shift with macroeconomic conditions. A variety of parametric regression approaches (eg, a Weibull parameterisation) and non-parametric approaches (eg, the Cox proportional hazard model) accommodate both the unusual features of duration data and allow for co-movement with macroeconomic and industry factors.

CONTRACTS: THE FUNDAMENTAL SOURCE OF AIRCRAFT TRANSACTION AND PORTFOLIO RISK

Accurately simulating the future distributions of market values and lease income for an aircraft-linked investment is only part of a risk assessment exercise. It is also essential to consider the contractual structure of payment obligations or an asset's returns with respect to market values and lease income. For example, an operator that owns an aircraft is exposed to any change in market values, up or down. The writer of a deep out-of-the-money residual value guarantee on the same aircraft, on the other hand, bears only the small probability of payment due to market values declining below the strike value at the strike date. An aircraft lessor may be fully exposed to swings in the lease income associated with a leased aircraft, while an investor in the A-class (the senior-most tranche of a lease portfolio securitisation) may be exposed only to extreme movements in the systematic component of the aircraft's lease income. Given this potential diversity of responses to the same underlying values, any risk modelling that does not capture the detail of individual contracts is likely to be incomplete.

The range of assets and contingent liabilities that are linked to movements in aircraft value or income is wide but can be classified into categories. The classes of these aircraft-linked derivatives include asset value guarantees (AVGs), credit guarantees, purchase options, lease income guarantees and collateralised debt obligations. Each of these contingent liabilities is exposed in a different fashion to aircraft value and income, depending on the contractual terms.

Asset Value and Lease Income Guarantees

The provider of an AVG guarantees the value of the aircraft at a pre-agreed strike price over an exercise window. The AVG is similar to a put option on the value of the aircraft and may, like an option, have exercise windows that take on European, Bermudan or American form.[1] However, AVGs differ from traditional options in their likelihood of exercise and in the illiquidity of the underlying asset. For example, a European option is valued based on an assumption that the option will be exercised if it is in-the-money. For an AVG, there are a variety of reasons that an in-the-money option might expire unexercised: exercise may require the sale of the aircraft, which would interfere with an operator's fleet planning; the AVG holder may have passed a necessary notification date with no action. In many cases, the likelihood of exercise of even in-the-money options is well below one. Risk assessment for AVGs must consider these mitigating factors.

Even assuming that an AVG is exercised based solely on a financial basis, its valuation is considerably more complex than the valuation of traditional options. Aircraft markets are illiquid, so it is difficult to infer a market risk premium from sparse or nonexistent recent price data on a given aircraft type. Furthermore, it is important to incorporate future expected depreciation and age-specific volatility into any valuation exercise. Both of these goals, however, are accomplished with significant modifications to a standard binomial tree simulation approach.[2]

A lease income guarantee is written to guarantee a certain periodic level of lease income flows, typically over the length of a particular lease. Because the value of an aircraft is the discounted value of its future income flows, the potential losses in an AVG and on a lease income guarantee on the same aircraft are highly positively correlated. The lease income guarantee spreads the risk in value movements over a longer period of time and diversifies over short-term movements. However, the lease income guarantee entails a longer duration guarantor exposure than the AVG.

Purchase options and credit guarantees
Two other value-linked derivatives are purchase options and credit guarantees. A purchase option allows an option owner to purchase the aircraft under certain conditions in the future and resembles a call option on the aircraft. Credit guarantees are often written by a manufacturer to enhance the credit of a poorly rated or unrated operator in order to facilitate purchase financing. It is a guarantee to meet the obligations of the purchaser should they default on payments. For example, suppose that the obligation of the guarantee provider is the repayment of remaining loan principal and accrued interest in the event of the operator's default. Then the credit guarantee can be treated as an AVG that is contingent on a default of the operator and the strike being equal to the obligation at time of default. The valuation of the credit guarantee requires the simultaneous modelling of both trigger events, ie, the future credit migration of the operator and the future value of the aircraft. As these events are likely to be correlated over time through industry conditions, it is important to consider the common factors that drive both.

Collateralised Debt Obligations
The final category of aircraft-linked assets is collateralised debt obligations (CDOs). Broadly speaking, CDOs include any debt instruments that are secured by aircraft values or lease incomes. Examples include leveraged leases, enhanced equipment trust certificates (EETCs), and lease portfolio securitisations. The debt in these structures is often tranched, enabling different investor classes to have different degrees of protection on the basis of the same underlying assets. Investor exposure in CDOs is highly dependent on the structure of the program.

A key feature of these investments is the collateralisation of a portfolio of aircraft, rather than a linkage to a single aircraft. Lease portfolio securitisations, in particular, are collateralised by the aggregate lease income produced by a portfolio of aircraft, while EETCs are backed by the market value of an aircraft portfolio. Modelling the risk in the aggregate value of an aircraft portfolio is quite a different task from modelling the individual risk on the aircraft in the portfolio; the capital requirements against value fluctuation for the individual aircraft in the portfolio sum to a much higher amount than those for the aggregate value of the portfolio. This occurs because the correlations between value fluctuations for different planes are not perfect, resulting in diversification benefits to pooling collateral. For example, the estimated degree of correlation in value movements over time is highest among planes of the same type, lower among planes of the same airframe size, and least among aircraft of different airframes. Modelling portfolio effects requires these levels of correlation among aircraft be identified and estimated. One method for estimating these correlation levels is an "error components regression framework" that decomposes the residual variation over time in aircraft values (after controlling for economic factors) into common effects associated with different levels of aircraft characteristics, such as the airframe type, aircraft type, year of build, etc. For example, the residual variation e_t at time t is decomposed into $e_t = u_t + v_t + w_t$, where u_t, v_t, and w_t are period t changes in value common to all planes of a certain airframe, type, and year of build respectively.

The ground-up stochastic modelling of a lease portfolio securitisation requires almost all of the economic modelling components that have been discussed in the article above. These include the factor-based modelling of the macroeconomy, idle rates of portfolio aircraft types, lease rates, operator default probabilities, downtimes, lease lengths, market values (for scrap value calculations), correlations among different plane types (for both market values and lease rates), and the correlation between lease rates and market values. Such a modelling exercise, while containing many components, demonstrates that the risk behind even complex securitised transactions involving portfolios of aircraft can be rendered transparent by the thorough application of economic modelling.

CONCLUSION

Current methods of assessing aircraft-related risks are inadequate to address the growing demand among industry participants for transparency and liquidity with respect to their complex portfolios of aircraft-linked assets and liabilities. In response, RISConsulting has, over the past several years, developed an economic modelling framework that provides contract and portfolio level assessments of aircraft-related risk, based on aircraft-level contractual detail and modelled responses to changes in macroeconomic and industry conditions. Aircraft values depend on their future income streams, which are in turn highly sensitive to macroeconomic factors including economic growth, inflation and interest rates. Industry factors are similarly important – the supply of aircraft, technological improvements, the competitiveness of airlines – all affect the value of particular types. The volatility of future value movements and their sensitivity to macroeconomic and industry factors can be estimated from historical transaction data and simulated into the future.

Future lease income depends on additional factors associated with the lease cycle, such as lease rates, lease lengths, and downtimes, but can be similarly simulated based on econometric analysis of historical lease cycle data. Finally, the actual exposure to risk in a portfolio depends not only on the volatility of movements in the underlying value and lease income streams, but also in the correlation of these value movements across different aircraft and on the detailed structure of financial contracts that depend on the underlying value and lease income streams of aircraft. Thorough economic modelling can provide the level of transparency in risk assessment of aircraft-linked assets and liabilities for which industry participants are increasingly yearning.

1   Each of these forms has a unique mixture of strike prices and exercise windows: the European tends to have a single exercise date, the Bermudan a series of distinct exercise windows and strike prices, and the American tends to have an open exercise window of some duration with strikes set within that interval.
2   For further information, see Hull (1993).

BIBLIOGRAPHY

Hull, J., 1993, *Options, Futures and other Derivative Securities*, Second Edition, (New Jersey: Prentice-Hall).

Part 4

Industry-specific practices and solutions

18

Industry-Specific Practices and Solutions: Credit Solutions Provided by Insurance Companies

Uwe E. Remy and Daniel Grieger*

Swiss Re – Credit Solutions and Asset Re

Credit-related instruments such as credit derivatives or financial guarantees have been the fastest growing area of what many people refer to as alternative risk transfer (ART). While the favourable regulatory treatment of credit portfolio transfers from banks to insurance companies has initially fuelled growth in this area, other motivations such as economic capital held against various asset classes by banks become ever more important as banks strive to make most efficient use of their capital. The rapid expansion of insurance companies into innovative capital market credit solutions is leading to a reconsideration of the separate regulation of insurance companies and banks, and to a discussion on how credit risks should be underpinned with capital. Popular questions also raised are: what should be the role of an insurance company in the credit arena and is there a natural role for insurance companies in the credit business?

INTRODUCTION

This chapter responds to these questions. We give an overview of the players, clients and solutions provided in the various fields in which insurance companies are active. As different credit risk transfer instruments serve different needs it has become ever more important to understand the differences between them and the purpose that they serve. Further, we will show that the much-cited term of "convergence" between the banking and insurance industry stands for something that is not entirely new. We will point out that assuming credit risk is by no means new for the insurance industry, and only a few areas exist where insurance companies have entered new markets. Finally, we will describe how the portfolio credit

---

* The opinions expressed herein are solely the ones of the authors and do not represent the opinion of Swiss Re.

default swap business has evolved over time, and we will also discuss the developments and trends that we expect to see for insurance companies active in credit capital market solutions.

For the remainder of this chapter the term "insurance company" also comprises reinsurance companies unless otherwise specified.

OVERVIEW OF THE ESTABLISHED CREDIT LANDSCAPE: PLAYERS, CLIENTS AND INSTRUMENTS

Pointing out the various business fields where insurance companies take on credit risk is not an easy task. Like many other industries, the insurance industry has become a diverse and specialised area where many companies focus only on one single type of asset or risk transfer instrument. Insurance companies with multiple business lines have most often separated their credit business from their traditional life and non-life business, with their own organisational standing and infrastructure (an organisational separation that until some years ago was a regulatory requirement in many countries).

One possible distinction between the various instruments of credit risk transfer is the split between capital market instruments and insurance market solutions. Typical insurance market solutions are credit insurance, financial guarantee and surety. They cannot be traded in the capital market, but they are bought by the insurance companies' clients and are held until the cover expires. On the other hand, capital market solutions such as credit derivatives, credit-linked notes and asset-backed securities are instruments that can be bought and held by investors such as insurance companies, but can also be actively traded. While the provider of an insurance market solution can only be an insurance company, the provider of a capital market credit instrument can be any other company that is allowed to enter into such a transaction. Figure 1 illustrates the various credit risk transfer instruments and also names substitutes to the insurance market solutions that are provided by non-insurance companies such as banks.

What exactly are the various credit risk transfer instruments and how do they work? Starting with credit insurance, financial guarantees and surety, these solutions are hybrid products that have been offered by insurance companies and banks alike. They will be detailed in the following paragraphs.

Credit insurance

Credit insurance is a well-established risk transfer instrument and the trade credit insurance is one of the oldest forms of credit risk protection provided by the insurance industry. Credit insurance mainly deals with trade receivables and is a protection against a customer not paying for goods or services provided on credit by the supplier, whether through insolvency or protracted default. Historically, credit insurance has been more popular in Europe than elsewhere with Coface, Gerling NCM Credit and Finance, Euler

Figure 1 Overview of credit risk transfer instruments

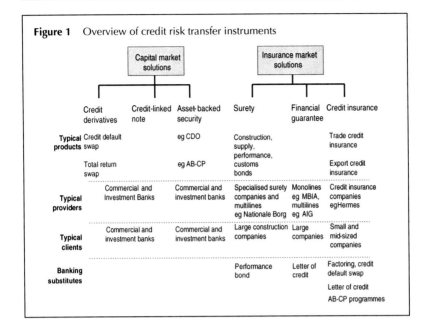

and Hermes being the leading four companies worldwide in terms of premium volume.[1] In the US, credit insurance has not become as popular as in Europe, as most large US companies maintain credit departments that are actively engaged in debt collection and debt recovery or sell receivables directly to a factor.[2] The reason for this could be a difference in credit culture or risk mentality. In the US, credit risk is seen more as a business risk that should be managed within an organisation's own credit department rather than by the whole turnover policy of a credit insurer.

Competitive conditions have pushed credit insurers to enter new markets and provide new products and services, such as credit information, debt collection services and protection for commercial Internet purchases. Credit insurers have significant expertise in credit risk assessment and own large proprietary databases on millions of companies worldwide. They are among the first to know about any payment delays or changes in payment patterns, which are early warning indicators for credit deterioration. Given the short tenors of the receivables, credit insurers have time to use this information and to take appropriate measures. This expertise and information on companies is the basis for underwriting credit risk and can be used to provide new services to credit departments of corporate companies. From the selling company's point of view the main advantages are:

❑ the transfer of the risk associated with the default of a buyer;
❑ the service of the continuous monitoring of the default risk of the buyer;
❑ support in a workout situation if a default has occurred;

❏ consulting on payment terms; and
❏ access to cheaper financing, as banks honour the benefit of credit insurance of receivable portfolios.

A description of the trade credit insurance industry is incomplete without mentioning the state export credit insurance. Given the unwillingness of the private sector to assume certain risks associated with exporting in the early 20th century, the state export agencies were established with the objective of helping firms finance the overseas sales of domestic goods and services. Over the years, many state export agencies have been privatised and many private insurers have entered the political risk insurance market, so that currently state export credit agencies provide export credit insurance partly as a substitute, and partly as a complement to the private credit insurers.

Asset-backed commercial paper programmes

Asset-backed commercial paper (ABCP) programmes are becoming a relatively new substitute for the traditional trade credit insurance. ABCP programmes see receivables of sellers sold to a credit enhanced special purpose vehicle (SPV), which then issues a short-term commercial paper. The seller immediately obtains cash (note the similarity to factoring) at a lower price than borrowing from a commercial bank but it must pay fees and set-up costs. ABCP programmes may change the role of credit insurers as their expertise could be used to assess the quality of the receivables and to credit enhance the SPV.

Credit derivatives

Credit default swaps (CDS) could potentially become another substitute for credit insurance as the universe of names traded in the CDS market grows.[3] Credit derivatives emerged as a response to the need of banks to transfer isolated credit risk as opposed to interest rate or currency risk. The transfer of the credit risk and return of the underlying asset (the "reference asset"), without transferring the asset itself, is also referred to as "synthetic risk transfer". One big advantage to this kind of risk transfer is that the bank can maintain the client relationship without notifying the bank's client about the transfer of default risk, which is not possible in the case of a non-synthetic risk transfer, such as a traditional securitisation. Particularly in the mid-1990s the commercial banking sector started to transfer the credit risk as portfolios of names from their corporate loan book to other sectors such as the insurance industry. Important players from the insurance industry have been globally diversified insurance companies such as AIG, General Re, XL, Chubb or Swiss Re (through its proper affiliates) and monolines such as Ambac. The importance of insurance companies as protection sellers has grown over the last few years, as the regularly published study of the British Bankers Association (BBA) on the credit derivatives market shows.[4]

The CDS has become the standard and most liquid credit derivative market instrument, with an estimated outstanding notional exposure in excess of US$1 trillion. It is a bilateral contract that enables an investor to buy protection against the risk of default of securities that are issued by a specified reference entity. The contract is typically specified using the confirmation document and legal definitions produced by the International Swaps and Derivatives Association (ISDA).[5] Following the legally defined credit event, the buyer of protection receives a payment linked to the loss incurred on the reference entity. In return for this protection, the protection buyer pays a fee – known as the "default swap spread" – as a regular stream of cashflow that will terminate at default or at maturity, whichever occurs first. The default swap spread depends on the credit quality of the reference security. Following a credit event, the default swap contract is settled either in cash or via physical delivery of the reference asset. Physical settlement has now become the market standard for single-name CDS, as has cash settlement for portfolio CDS.

CDS and credit insurance differ in terms of maturities and that the CDS indemnifies the "insured" based on standard default events, with the severity rate as a function of a market-traded asset. Therefore, CDS leave a certain basis risk to the "insured". Credit insurance, however, indemnifies the insured on the incurred loss; a basis risk does not exist. Table 1 further details the differences.

Surety
Suretyship is a contingent credit business. A surety issues a bond to the beneficiary that guarantees the performance of the principal in accordance with the provisions of the underlying contract or the compliance with legal or regulatory requirements. A surety does not provide an insurance cover but rather acts against the payment of a fee as a guarantor, which enhances the credit quality of a debtor. Contrary to credit insurance, a surety bond is a banking rather than an insurance product, and consequently both banks and insurance companies are active in this area. Whenever acceptable to the beneficiary, the principal tries to provide a surety bond from an insurance company in order to ease the strain on current credit lines available from the banks.

Unlike credit insurance, suretyship is more popular in the US. The market is regulated and only specialised surety companies are allowed to write a large variety of different surety bonds.

Financial Guarantee
"Financial guarantee" is a term used to describe a wide range of contracts. Its main difference to trade credit insurance and surety is that the underlying insured contract is not a delivery of goods or services, but is the pure financial obligation itself. Often the purpose of a financial guarantee is not

Table 1 Credit insurance and credit default swaps compared

Criteria	Credit insurance	Credit default swap
Insured obligation	Insurance for a specific obligation	No specific obligation but reference entity
Tenor of underlying risk	Underlying risks are trade receivables with typically 30–180 days maturity	Underlying risks are corporate loans of bonds with maturities of several years
Determination of payment	Insurance payments only if insured has a loss and files a claim. Payment is then equal to actual sustained loss up to the sum insured	Settlement and payment of the swap is triggered by a specific credit event of the reference asset; no deductible applied; no proof of loss
Jurisdiction	Usually country of credit insurer	Usually London or New York
Settlement	Payment is in cash	Settlement is either physical (single-name CDS) or cash (portfolio CDS)
Effect of settlement	Loss event does not necessarily cancel insurance contract	Settlement closes swap contract
Accounting	Reserve accounting applies	Mark-to-market accounting applies (FASB 133)
Transferability	Policies are not traded but can be reinsured	Contracts can be traded
Information requirements	No need for publicly available information to file a claim	Credit event has to be publicly available information

credit protection, but a financial service such as enhancing the credit rating. The most common financial guarantee known in the capital markets that provides such a service is called "credit enhancement" or "credit wrap". To lower the cost of funding, borrowers pay the insurer a premium for providing an "unconditional and irrevocable guarantee" of the principal and interest payments on insured obligations such as bonds or asset-backed securities when due. The demand for financial guarantee and actual premium rates depends on the cost of alternative funding possibilities, which closely follows market credit spreads; the higher the market credit spread differential, the greater the opportunity for financial guarantors.

This market has traditionally been dominated by the US-monoline financial guarantee insurance companies (monolines) such as the AAA/Aaa-rated MBIA, Ambac, FGIC and FSA.[6] Multiline companies also play an important role, most often through the reinsurance of monoline-insured business. For insurance regulatory reasons, monoline companies have limited themselves to guaranteeing highly rated investments, such as municipal bonds – a practice they started in the early 1970s that would later allow them to be seen as the real "pioneers" of convergence. Previously, this business was dominated by AAA/Aaa-rated banks that provided letters of credit to enhance municipal bond issues. Today, monolines – but also multilines – see opportunities elsewhere, such as credit enhancement of asset-backed securitisations. With their involvement in credit enhancements of securitisations, monolines are playing the important role of a catalyst for the securitisation market as they give comfort to investors for new asset classes where investors may not be willing to invest without a AAA-credit wrap. It is more efficient if – similarly to rating agencies – monolines assess new and complex risks where a potential investor may lack expertise or resources for a diligent underwriting.

A description of the financial guarantee would be incomplete without stressing financial guarantees' difference to traditional credit insurance contracts. In 2001, a high profile case took place between a large American multiline insurance company and a multinational investment bank. The multiline, acting as credit enhancer on a securitisation programme rejected to pay a claim, citing fraud/misrepresentation/breach of warranty which resulted in an immediate downgrade of the enhanced transaction, and two other transactions from AAA to below investment grade. This case made particularly clear the difference between "traditional" insurance policies, which are typically issued by multiline insurers, and the "financial guarantee" insurance policies typically provided by monoline insurance companies; while under traditional insurance, usually the right is reserved to adjust a claim before actual payment, and if warranted, litigate the validity of a claim before actual payment is made. The spirit of a financial guarantee insurance is the unconditional obligation to pay a claim in a timely fashion, as it is key for structured finance transactions.

Asset-backed securities and collateralised debt obligations
Over the past few years, the possibility of transferring assets synthetically has developed dramatically and market participants have developed ways of securitising various types of assets; asset-backed securities (ABS), for example, particularly in the form of collateralised debt obligations (CDOs) (ie, collateralised bond and loan obligations), have enjoyed tremendous growth.[7] The term "CDO" refers to a debt obligation issued by a SPV secured by the assets transferred to the vehicle. The assets can be traditional corporate loans, bonds, swaps or more exotic assets such as project finance loans. The portfolio of these assets is then tranched into different layers of risk according to the allocation of losses and recoveries in case of defaults. In this way, the bottom tranches are leveraged to the default risk in the entire portfolio, but they also offer very high returns if losses within the portfolio are well managed.

Even though the traditional CDO resembles other asset-based securitisations, the CDO structure is increasingly being applied to credit derivatives. Many market participants are combining their traditional cash CDO business with their credit derivative businesses. As such, CDOs need to be understood in the context of the overall credit derivatives market, and not simply as another fixed-income product. For example, with a financial guarantee there is no acceleration of payments in case of default, while with a CDS payment it is usually due after an agreed number of days after default. This difference makes the CDS more risky in terms of liquidity risk as a substantial upfront cash call and the market value-based claim could be significantly different from the ultimate underlying credit loss on the insured obligation. Besides the multiline insurance companies, many monoline companies have entered the market of insuring the higher-rated tranches of CDOs through transformer vehicles, which they use as they are not allowed to enter into credit default swaps directly for regulatory reasons.[8] Insurance companies entering this market need to be aware of the differences between CDOs and traditional fixed-income products and the accumulation issues which can arise when participating in many CDOs at the same time. We explain the underwriting requirements and credit risk management and monitoring procedures for portfolio credit default swaps in more detail below.

Credit-Linked Notes
Credit-linked notes CLNs are structured notes with an embedded CDS. Typically, a high-rated debt instrument and a default swap (or a portfolio of credit default swaps) are placed in a SPV, which then issues the CLN. If a credit event occurs on the CDS, the investor sustains a loss based on the reference asset's loss. In effect, the investor is selling protection on the reference asset and receives a premium in the form of an attractive yield spread. The issuer of the note, on the other hand, is purchasing default protection on the reference asset. CLNs are attractive due to their non-derivative nature because investors who are unable to enter into a derivative transaction can still enter into a CLN. From a regulatory standpoint, banks that purchase CLNs must hold capital against the face amount of the note according to the risk weighting of the underlying reference asset. Banks that issue CLNs linked to loans in their portfolios can potentially receive off-balance sheet treatment for these assets if the embedded default swap is effectively a guarantee, and the credit risk is effectively cash-collateralised by the proceeds from selling the CLNs.

THE PORTFOLIO CREDIT DEFAULT SWAP BUSINESS FROM AN INSURER'S PERSPECTIVE

Taking a closer look at the CDS portfolio business as an example for a capital market solution in which banks and insurance companies found an area of synergy, it is interesting to see how this business has developed over time and has become, within a few years, a commoditised business. This section first shows the evolution of this business, and then describes the underwriting process of such a portfolio CDS transaction from the insurer's perspective.

The Development of the Portfolio Credit Default Swap Business

How does today's portfolio CDS business compare to the transactions carried out in the mid-1990s when the first portfolio CDS were executed between insurance companies and banks? The possibility to transfer credit risks via CDS on a portfolio basis from banks to insurance companies for capital relief purposes was discovered at the right time for the insurance industry for three reasons. First, the insurance market for traditional property and casualty business was weak and the market for credit business presented attractive premiums. Second, low interest rates favoured the development of structured credit products providing better rates of return through CLNs or CDOs. Third, although statistically difficult to prove, there seems to be a low correlation between traditional insurance risks, such as property and casualty risks, and credit risks, which makes credit risks interesting from a diversification perspective. Also, from the bank's perspective, the timing was right: to create more value for shareholders, credit portfolios had to be managed more efficiently and expensive capital using credit facilities could be placed with insurance companies and banks to free up regulatory capital.

In the beginning of the portfolio credit default swap business, participants concentrated on balance sheet-driven transactions with well diversified portfolios and high-rated and frequently traded (ie, liquid) corporate names as reference assets. Portfolios were negotiated openly between the protection buyer and the protection seller, and name disclosure was standard. The subordination retained by the originating bank allowed for several names to default before the attachment point was reached, and the risk taker would take the risk of the whole transaction above the attachment point.

Much has changed since then. Soon after this time, investment banks started to intermediate and promote the portfolio CDS, thereby attracting more insurance companies and banks to the market. With increasing competition from new insurance companies entering the market and due to the increasing commoditisation of the portfolio credit default swap business, the transaction parameters changed. While in the beginning the motivation for banks had been pure regulatory capital relief, more and more transactions marketed by banks were no longer balance sheet-driven, aimed at regulatory capital relief, but became structured to achieve a return from arbitrage. Investment banks in particular – but also insurance companies – started to structure portfolios synthetically, ie, portfolios were formed without having the interest-bearing assets on their balance sheet, which they then placed in the market, thereby earning a spread from the arbitrage. In regard to balance sheet-driven transactions, underlying assets became less standard and therefore a larger proportion of names no longer had a public rating, but were internally rated by the originating bank's credit risk management team. A CDS involving names of companies with few or no publicly traded debt instruments raises the question of the underlying deliverable in case of default. With regard to synthetic arbitrage deals, the arranger assembles a basket of liquid names, where a relative value between the protection sold on single names and the protection bought on layers of the whole structure is the greatest. In these arbitrage structures the arranger particularly seeks to hedge the mezzanine layers that are the most expensive to keep on their own books from a risk-return perspective, and therefore consume most of the economic capital.

Table 2 compares the two concepts of balance sheet and synthetic arbitrage portfolio CDS.

Building on the successful experience of corporate loans for large companies as reference assets, market participants moved forward into other asset classes, such as small and medium-sized companies, residential or commercial mortgage or project finance. Geographically, the interest widened to transferring reference assets with domiciles other than Western Europe or North America.

Underwriting Requirements for Portfolio Credit Default Swaps

In the rapidly growing area of credit securitisation insurance companies have recently been criticised by regulators, as they see the risk of insurance companies loading credit risks on their books through synthetic investments. In the past, insurance companies have encountered difficulties due to mispriced trades, poor exposure control, poor monitoring and inadequate reserves. This sometimes led to the conclusion that insurance companies may not be the right investor for credit capital market risks (a conclusion with which the authors disagree).

As a general – and obvious – rule, each participant in any risk market

---

Table 2 Balance sheet CDS and synthetic arbitrage CDS compared

Criteria	Balance sheet portfolio CDS	Synthetic arbitrage portfolio CDS
Motivation	Regulatory capital relief, fee income in case of intermediary	Income from arbitrage
Intermediation	20% risk weighted intermediary necessary for insurance companies to achieve regulatory capital relief for the bank	No 20% risk weighted intermediary necessary as capital relief is not the motivation
Underlying assets	Assets can be illiquid and do not have to be traded in the CDS market	Assets are liquid and tend to be traded in the CDS market
Risk transferred	Protection is bought for the entire portfolio above equity layer	Entire portfolio is hedged
Portfolio composition	Often negotiable, exclusion of names often possible, replenishment mechanism, revolving character	Often driven by equity investor. Portfolio composition for investors in higher layers usually not negotiable, portfolio is static

should understand the nature of risk that is underwritten. Besides the necessary expertise to structure and model a risky transaction, the right infrastructure (such as capital market carriers) and organisational set-up in terms of the independent underwriting control, exposure control, limit and transaction approval process is key. Standards for this evolve over time and can certainly change. While infrastructure and organisational requirements for players in insurance market solutions and capital markets may differ, it is vital for every player in any market to keep track of changes or establish best practices. For every financial market innovation it is clear that not everyone participates from the beginning and particularly new market entrants have to make sure that they have the right expertise at hand before taking the first step. The example below gives an idea of what should be the process for any insurance company entering into a structured credit transaction, in particular a portfolio CDS with the reference assets being corporate companies. While this example is only a summary of the many different tasks and processes to be followed, we believe that it gives a good indication of what kind of expertise may be required.

Example: Underwriting a corporate loan portfolio
A bank and an insurance company enter into negotiations regarding a CDS. The bank has identified a portfolio of corporate names that it seeks to transfer through the CDS to a 20% risk weighted entity. The goal is to achieve regulatory capital relief and hedge against losses above a certain threshold. The portfolio contains reference names of companies domiciled in European and North American countries. Some names are not rated by a rating agency but are internally rated by the bank's credit risk management unit.

Important points that need to be clarified between the bank and the insurer in terms of overall portfolio characteristics and structure are:

❏ full name disclosure and exclusion of certain asset types;
❏ diversification of reference asset pool: obligor domicile, industry, country, etc;
❏ ranking, tenor and nature of underlying assets (syndicated loans, loans, bonds);
❏ average rating and portfolio layering;
❏ legal final maturity, call provisions;
❏ amortisation schedule of the portfolio;
❏ pool dynamics: is the pool static or dynamic? - meaning can assets be removed or substituted?;
❏ credit events, eg, exclusion of certain credit events such as restructuring and to what type of asset the credit event will be applied (bonds or loans/borrowed money/payment obligations);
❏ will the CDS allow for ongoing cash settlement or can the cash payment be made at the maturity of the deal?;

❏ what will be the procedure and timing for determining the severity of loss?; and

❏ will the intermediation or carrier achieve 20% risk weighting?

The following risk management considerations are important to be made on the insurer's side:

❏ credit risk assessment on single-name basis and possibly exclusion of certain names for credit risk considerations;

❏ due diligence on bank's internal rating system and mapping of internal ratings to public ratings; and

❏ exposure accumulation check and possibly exclusion of certain names for capacity reasons or hedging in CDS market on single-name basis immediately after execution.

After the modelling and pricing of the portfolio, the agreement with the bank on price, internal approval and execution, the transaction needs to be monitored closely. Important tasks are the following:

❏ continuous monitoring of portfolio on a regular basis and mark-to-market valuation;

❏ in the case of portfolio migration, possibly restructuring of portfolio, elimination of names which are migrated to improve portfolio quality; and

❏ in the case of defaults, settlement to fix amount which has eaten into subordination.

Some conclusions can be drawn from the example: starting with the underlying risks, it is clear that full-name disclosure is a must. In the market, many transactions are handled on a blind basis, ie, without name disclosure but with disclosure of industry or domicile characteristics. Accumulation control is crucial and without full disclosure of the reference assets, insurers put themselves at a disadvantage that is usually not compensated by a higher premium. The example also demonstrates that the closing of a transaction is by no means the end of the involvement of the dedicated underwriter; constant monitoring, hedging of single names (if necessary) and the mark-to-market of the risk is necessary on a continuous basis to ensure that measures are taken if the portfolio deteriorates in quality or defaults occur.

CONCLUSION

Looking at current developments in the credit arena in the context of the insurance industry is interesting for several reasons:

1. The current economic downturn with high profile bankruptcies is testing all credit instruments' ability to function, particularly of the younger ones such as the CDS.
2. The revision of the capital requirements for banks is leading to discussions about capital adequacy frameworks and credit modelling.
3. The large amounts of credit risks assumed by insurance companies have led to a discussion about systemic risks within the financial services industry coming from the insurance industry.
4. High-profile cases where insurance companies refused claim payments under certain credit instruments led to a discussion about the effectiveness of these credit instruments.

While this may seem to be giving mixed signals, there are a couple of conclusions that can be drawn from these observations: credit risk has moved more into the focus of all market participants and regulators, and insurance companies are – as already mentioned – under scrutiny because of the credit risks on their books and because of the instruments used. Recent high-profile mishaps have shown that a full understanding of the documentation employed to transfer the credit risk is key. Financial guarantee, credit insurance, surety and derivatives are very different from each other, and each one is the solution for a specific problem, as proved over years, if not decades. Problems arise if these instruments are used for solutions other than their traditional and established business purposes. Recently, many clients of insurance companies have started to ask for a credit derivative solution instead of a financial guarantee. While this may be understandable as a spontaneous reaction to recent mishaps in connection with surety and traditional insurance policies, using CDS documentation for every kind of credit risk transfer would lead to less efficient solutions. It should be clear that in the future the best solution can only be found if the full range of credit risk transfer instruments is put to use and the underlying documentation is well understood.

With respect to the future development of CDS and synthetic securitisations, a further broadening of the underlying asset classes is foreseeable. The portfolio modelling technology developed in the CDO business will influence other ABS areas and alternative investment instruments such as hedge funds and private equity. Despite its rapid development, the CDS is far from perfect. The effectiveness of the settlement mechanism is particularly tested in times of frequent defaults and will be further improved. As the market is always looking for the cheapest instrument to deliver in the case of settlement, recovery rates are volatile, which leaves a basis risk with the protection seller. While the CDS makes all debt instruments of a borrower equal, the underlying loan documentation can differ considerably in terms of covenants and loan structure, which may also influence the future development of CDS.

1 Earned premiums in 2000 were: Coface: €670.9 million; Euler: €1028.9 million; Hermes Credit €525.3 million; and Gerling Kredit Speziale: €608 million who merged in 2001 with NCM (€528 million).

2 Factoring is the business of buying trade receivables at a discount and thereby providing immediate financing to the originator of these receivables.

3 The term "name" refers to the name of the reference entity or company that represents the default risk.

4 Further information can be found on the BBA's website, http://www.bba.org.uk

5 Further information can be found on the ISDA's website, http://www.isda.org.

6 Municipal Bond Insurance Association, American Municipal Bond Assurance Corporation, Financial Guaranty Insurance Company, and Financial Security Assurance.

7 Looking at the European CDO market only, the market volume in 2001, measured in terms of credit risk transferred, was at US$98 billion – over 55% more than the year 2000 volume (US$63 billion), according to Coleman, 2002.

8 The term "transformer vehicle" relates to transforming capital market products to insurance products and vice versa. Typically the transformer enters into a CDS on the asset side and is covered by a financial guarantee on the liability side.

BIBLIOGRAPHY

Barry, M., J. C. Mezzanotte, and F. Phillip, 2001, "Use of Insurance Policies as Credit Enhancement in Structured Finance", Fitch Special Report on Structured Finance, June, Fitch Ibca, Duff & Phelps.

Carl, U., 2002, "Financial Guaranty and Credit Securitisation", ART Academy Presentation 2001, Swiss Re internal paper presented to ART Academy, p. 2.

Cheng, V., 2001, "Credit Derivatives – A Good Thing if Done Right", US Financials Strategy Research 13/2001, Fox-Pitt, Kelton Group.

Coleman, E., 2002, "2001 Review and 2002 Outlook – Collateralized Debt Obligations in Europe: Bigger and Bigger it Grows", International Structured Finance, January.

Dorer, J., S. Rouyer, and L. Levenstein, "Financial Guaranty Industry Outlook", Global Credit Research January 2002, Moody's Investor Service.

Hottensen, R., G., M. S. Hodges, J. Lustbader, and J. Simon, 2001, "Specialty Finance: Financial Guarantors", Goldman Sachs Global Equity Research December 2001, Goldman Sachs.

Kessler, M., and L. Levenstein, 2001, "Credit Default Swaps versus Financial Guaranties – Are the Risks the Same?", Global Credit Research June 2001, Moody's Investor Service.

O'Kane, D., 2001, "Credit Derivatives Explained: Market, Products and Regulations", Lehman Brothers Structured Credit Research March 2001, Lehman Brothers.

Punjabi, S., and J. F. Tierney, 1999, "Synthetic CLOs and their Role in Bank Balance Sheet Management", Fixed Income Research March 1999, Deutsche Bank Research.

Raturi, M., and B. Schmolck, 2000, "Trade Credit Insurance: Globalisation and E-business are the Key Opportunities", Sigma 7/2000, Swiss Reinsurance Company.

Veno, D., 2001, "Bond Insurance and Credit Default Swaps", Standard & Poor's Bond Insurance Book 2001, pp. 28–29 (New York: McGraw-Hill).

19

Securitisation of Life Insurance Businesses

Michael J. Millette, Shiv Kumar, Omar J. Chaudhary, Jacqueline M. Keating and Steven I. Schreiber

Goldman, Sachs & Co. and Milliman USA

Since 1987, securitisation has been a promising but slow-developing technique allowing life insurers to raise capital and hedge risk. Activity appears to be accelerating. Over the past few years several companies have employed securitisation as a critical element in their business strategies. At the end of 2001, nearly US$2 billion of securities based on the traditional life-insurance business of Prudential Life Insurance Company were placed, signalling a phase change in this activity. It is now clear that the constituencies of the capital markets – investors, rating agencies and bond insurers – can understand and finance blocks of life insurance business directly and on a scale that makes it possible to treat securitisation as a feasible business model.

The development of securitisation has been motivated by the structure of the industry. Life insurance companies compete directly with other classes of financial institutions for consumer and institutional savings accounts. They add value to these products by including protection features such as book value withdrawal rights, guaranteed minimum benefit rights and mortality and morbidity payments. As a result, their products are more complicated and costly to originate, although subsequent margins may be higher.

The complexity of products and their high origination costs lead to balance sheets that are among the most leveraged and intricate in the financial services industry. As margin pressure and market return expectations have intensified, life companies have focused on the development of less capital-intensive ways to manage their businesses.

Many companies have become interested in the potentially transformative possibilities of securitisation. Rather than simply accumulating assets and liabilities, companies now consider the possibility that they can develop blocks of business that may be analysed, rated, then "sold" to investors through leveraged, non-recourse structures. Companies may then redeploy capital to new blocks of business. Interest in these developments has been global. The Prudential transaction is an interesting working model for future structures.

In the US, market pressure to increase and maintain returns on equity along with consolidation and demutualisation activity have driven interest in capital redeployment. Outside the US, the development of "embedded value" (EV) as an accounting concept has driven interest as companies seek ways to monetise these values. Life reinsurance has expanded, but the scale of EVs present in the industry challenges the capacity of the reinsurance market and calls for an alternative.

Although the reinsurance industry has been able to offer ample capacity for pure risk transfer transactions to date, interest in alternatives in this area has also increased, particularly relating to longevity and catastrophic mortality risks.

INTRODUCTION

The first section of this chapter will review the development of securitisation techniques and motivations from 1987 through the late 1990s. This will be followed by detailed review of the large 1998 National Provident Institution transaction, and the 2001 Prudential transaction. The final portion of the chapter reviews the attempts to securitise mortality and longevity risks, as well as prospects for the market.

BACKGROUND – 1988 TO THE MID-1990S

The notion of securitising life insurance business developed in the mid-1980s in tandem with a massive expansion in types and amounts of assets being securitised. The asset-backed securities market (distinct from the mortgage-backed securities market) grew from US$7 billion in issuance in 1985 to US$103 billion in 1990 and nearly US$1 trillion in 1997.[1] Life insurance policies generate an array of cashflows over their lives and some of these appeared to be natural candidates for this developing technology.

In 1988, Citicorp completed a US$75 million transaction for General American through which rights to future life insurance premium loadings (the spread between the premium paid by the policyholder and the premium deposited into reserve) were isolated and purchased by commercial paper-funded conduits.[2] Ernst & Whinney reviewed the transaction from a statutory accounting perspective.[3]

Several such transactions, covering whole life, universal life, industrial life and variable annuities, were completed during the following year. In order to make these cashflows qualify as assets for conduit purposes, uniform commercial code filings were made against the policy contracts and reserve tables themselves – the fees and loadings were paid into lockboxes.[4]

The risks assumed by the conduits in these transactions included the lapse of underlying life insurance policies (the possibility that policyholders would cease to pay premiums and ultimately terminate their policies) and the termination of premium payments upon death of a policyholder. These risks were analysed by determining historical premium termination rates and applying a multiple to these rates to generate a conservative advance rate. The high rate of policy terminations and withdrawals instigated by the high interest rate environment in 1979–83 provided a ready downside scenario – these transactions were designed to pay out fully, with room to spare given a repeat of such rate levels. Extraordinary risks, such as the possibility of a change in tax law that would drive non-historical levels of premium termination, were also considered. The life insurers retained the residual cashflows and risk in each transaction.

The creditworthiness of the insurer was also considered a risk as it was assumed that deterioration of the financial condition of the insurer would drive down persistency and that regulators could choose to terminate cashflows to the conduit upon a seizure of a company.

A number of commercial banks including Citicorp and Chase Manhattan also developed facilities that lent against policy fees and loadings to "levellise" (ie, to covert a lump sum payment into a series of level instalment payments stretched over many years) commissions and other new business origination costs. Banks took on the financing burden for new business generation by funding companies that paid such costs and that were repaid by life insurance companies over time, subject to the policy continuing in force and the life insurance companies remaining solvent. These companies were sometimes referred to as "super-agents".

A key objective for all of these transactions was to allow the securitisation proceeds to be treated as regulatory surplus. United States' regulatory accounting requires that all insurance policy acquisition expenses (including agents' commissions and underwriting analysis costs) be charged off as incurred, resulting in a great deal of "surplus strain" for growing companies. Securitisation was seen as a potential remedy, particularly for mutual life insurers lacking other means to access the capital markets for surplus formation.[5]

Initially, regulators in several states (starting with Missouri) recognised that the emergence of these cashflows to repay financings relied on the continuing payment of premiums, and they granted regulatory surplus treatment. However, on 13 March, 1989, the State of New York Insurance Department sent out a circular letter stating that it believed surplus treatment to be inconsistent with statutory accounting principles.[6] The National Association of Insurance Commissioners endorsed this view soon afterwards.[7] The regulators did not explicitly lay out criteria for securitisation transactions that would result in surplus treatment but they did suggest that surplus treatment should be limited to transactions that removed all risks against a block of business from the company – in other words, transactions that securitised embedded profit.

Also in 1988, Prudential Bache Capital Funding and Morgan Stanley completed a different type of life insurance securitisation with a US$455.6 million private placement of future cashflows from the policy loan portfolio for Prudential Insurance Company. These securities were whimsically tagged "death-backed bonds" by the market because any unpaid balances would simply be net against death benefits if a policyholder had not repaid by that point. Assuming that Prudential was a continuing entity, only immortality would stand in the way of ultimate repayment. The transaction was successfully placed on mortgage-backed security-style sequential tranches, with Prudential providing some support on timing risk. A banker at Prudential Bache Capital Funding reported that the financing required two years of actuarial work and 300 hours of computer time to process.[8] This transaction was simply an asset-based financing so it generated liquidity but not surplus.

Life insurers typically enjoy abundant liquidity and this was the chief benefit of all such transactions following the regulatory limitation on surplus treatment, so activity diminished in the early 1990s. The relatively small but growing variable life and annuity business provided the only exception to this trend. Unlike other types of "general account" life insurance business in the US, nearly all of the premium and annuity inflows arising from a variable policy must generally be placed into a mutual fund at origination, resulting in a financing requirement to cover policy acquisition costs. Companies specialising in variable business, such as North American Security Life (NASL), continued to create asset-backed bank facilities to support this financing need.

Outside the US, the development of EV reporting generated conceptual interest in securitisation as companies considered ways to monetise these values. Royal Life began reporting EV – the present value of future profit on in-force business plus shareholder equity – in 1984. Most remaining UK companies had adopted this practice by 1994, and many large life groups in Europe, South Africa, Australia and Canada joined over the following five years. Companies reporting EV typically also report the incremental EV created over the immediate past year, which allows equity analysts to estimate the value of the company's future business production by applying a multiplier. Generally accepted accounting practice (GAAP) in the US occasionally allows EV reporting through "present value of profit" assets that are created in the course of acquisitions, sometimes referred to as "value of business acquired" (VOBA). Deferred policy acquisition costs (DPAC) are also constrained by EV.

Under EU legislation, life insurers have been allowed in some cases to count a limited amount of EV as an asset for solvency purposes.[9] Regulatory apprehension that these amounts would not be realisable combined with company reluctance to broadcast what may be interpreted as a sign of weakness to independent agents limited the booking of such embedded assets. Companies have realised these amounts through reinsurance but regulators have put pressure on companies to make certain that provisions in the reinsurance agreements do not reduce the transfer of risk.

Growth in variable products, desire to monetise EVs, and capital pressures would ultimately instigate another round of life securitisation activity in the mid-1990s.

GROWTH IN SECURITISATION ACTIVITY, 1995–2000
The American Skandia transactions
American Skandia Life Assurance Company's (ASLAC) variable annuity business was experiencing significant growth by the mid-1990s, resulting in the financing strain usually associated with this product. In 1996, the company entered into a private placement called ASLAC Funding Trust 1996 through which Dillon Read placed US$41.925 million of notes collateralised by the cashflow associated with mortality and expense (M&E) fee income and contingent deferred sales charges (CDSCs) payable to ASLAC according to the specifications of designated variable annuity contracts. The rights to 80% of this fee income and CDSCs were sold to the trust by ASLAC. A number of life insurance companies as well as other private placement investors purchased the transaction. Duff & Phelps rated the notes BBB "based on statistically derived cash flow scenarios and other qualitative and quantitative factors".[10]

This was the first packaging of such cashflows into security (albeit private placement) form since the Prudential Policy Loan Transaction, and the first rated securitisation of future cashflows on a block of life insurance. This may have been the first life insurance securitisation supported by an independent actuarial modelling study, in this case authored by Robert J. Schwartz, Consulting Actuary. The introduction of an actuarial study allowed investors that did not have actuarial departments themselves (or intimate relationships with the issuers as in the case of banks) to understand the risks in such financings. The template created through this transaction proved durable – ASLAC completed numerous additional placements over the following several years. In 1999, the company announced a US$97.315 million placement by Putnam, Lovell, de Guardiola & Thornton, Inc. Its year-end 2000 statutory statement disclosed a total of 13 such transactions.

The Hannover Re transactions
Hannover Re re-engaged bank interest in life securitisation with a series of transactions entitled "L1"–"L4", completed in collaboration with the RISConsulting Group LLC over the period 1998–2000.

Hannover Re's 1998 L1 transaction provided the company with the option to transfer 75% of defined life reassurance treaties up to DM100 million to Dublin-based Interpolis Re, a Rabobank reinsurance subsidiary, in order to finance acquisition costs. Rabobank financed the facility through an asset-backed loan, where the subsidiary retained mortality and persistency risks. The structure was able to accommodate multiple currencies.

The 1999 DM250 million L2 transaction was specifically designed to allow Hannover Re's cedent clients to realise EVs from closed blocks of business. Like L1, this transaction involved Interpolis Re and could accommodate multiple currencies and lines of business. The bank was not disclosed. In effect, this transaction allowed financing to be transformed to reinsurance through Interpolis and Hannover Re.

The €50 million L3 transaction, completed at about the same time, was designed to finance Hannover's acquisition of blocks of business in emerging markets. Rabobank provided the financing.

The €200 million L4 securitisation, completed in 2001, financed the acquisition of unit-linked life and annuity reinsurance business from Austria and Germany, originated primarily from Aspecta Leben. Financing banks for this transaction included Landesbank Hessen-Thuringen (Helaba), Caja Madrid, Landesbank Baden-Wurttemberg (LBBW) and Nordduetsche Landesbank.

National Provident Institution (NPI) – Mutual Securitisation plc
In early 1998, NPI raised £260 million, which qualified as capital for solvency purposes, through an innovative securitisation that synthesised a number of the ideas developed over the previous 10 years. NPI's underwriters – SBC Warburg Dillon Read, Goldman Sachs International, Dresdner Kleinwort Benson, and other advisors – created "Mutual Securitisation plc", a special-purpose Irish company to issue £260 million of limited recourse bonds and lend the proceeds to NPI. This loan's repayment was limited to profits emerging from a specified block of NPI life insurance policies (the "securitised block"). If this EV proved to be insufficient to repay the loan, a reserve account funded with £40 million from the proceeds could be used to cover shortfalls. Ultimately, failure of profit to emerge could generate a loss to investors.

Two amortising sequential tranches were issued: £140 million Class A1 limited recourse bonds, due 2012 (7.39%, December 2006 Gilt + 140 basis points (bp)) and £120 million Class A2 limited recourse bonds, due 2022 (7.59%, December 2015 Gilt + 170bp). Moody's and Standard & Poor's rated the two classes of bonds A3 and A, respectively, based on NPI's claims-paying ability. NPI retained the ability to issue an additional £30 million until year-end 2000 subject to various valuation and rating conditions ("further bonds"). These additional bonds were never issued.

The securitised block contained a total of £4.08 billion in policy values,

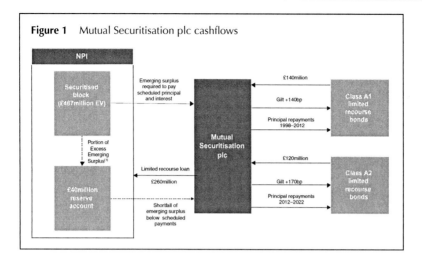

Figure 1 Mutual Securitisation plc cashflows

with an EV of £487 million indicating a loan-to-value of approximately 45% (when the £40 million reserve account is netted out of the proceeds). There were 505,000 individual and group policies, 35% unit-linked and 65% unitised with-profit policies, of which 72% were single premium and 28% were regular premium.

The transaction structure is illustrated in Figure 1.

Investors bear four major insurance-related risks:

1. Given that management charges, levied by NPI on policyholders, are calculated as a percentage of investment fund values, fluctuations in value create risks for investors.
2. Policy termination rates affect future cashflows via (i) the future stream of management charges, less (ii) future expenses linked to policy benefits in the securitised block and (iii) termination penalties payable to NPI by the policyholder; the net effect of an increase in termination rates is a decrease in future emerging surplus.
3. Inflation has a direct impact on administrative expenses, which have a negative effect on total emerging surplus although it is partially offset by an increase in investment returns over the long-term.
4. Changes in mortality rates have differing effects on the block; certain policies become less profitable when rates increase whereas others are similarly affected when there is increased longevity due to ongoing retirement benefits; the net effect is that an increase in mortality rates yields a small decrease in future emerging surplus.

Watson Wyatt completed an actuarial study that was included in the offering circular to aid investors in understanding these risks.

The sensitivity analysis summarised in Figure 2 illustrates the level of

Figure 2 Mutual Securitisation plc sensitivity analysis

	Aggregate emerging surplus (£ million)	Total proceeds*/aggregate emerging surplus (%)
Base case	486.614	60
Higher mortality	478.868	61
Higher early termination	449.884	64
Lower investment returns	394.320	74
Immediate fall in market value of investments	477.924	61
Higher expense inflation	471.275	62
Higher mortality and early termination rates with lower investment returns	362.300	80

* Includes Further Bonds as these were considered in structuring and rating the transaction.

protection against these risks available to investors. The aggregate emerging surplus is the EV of the business. In effect, NPI retained 40% subordination in the EV for this business, and the most severe sensitivity only required 20% subordination. The reserve account provided additional subordination. NPI retained a large equity tranche.

The policies continued to be housed in NPI, so investors bore the risk of NPI's continuing solvency. The ratings of the transaction were limited to NPI's ratings as a result. Unlike most asset securitisations, there was no "true sale" of the insurance policies from NPI to the special purpose vehicle (given the sensitivity analysis results, the ratings could have theoretically been higher if a true sale had been achieved). To provide some protection against this solvency risk, the transaction included a "trigger event" causing all cash emerging from the business to be trapped in the reserve account if the securities were downgraded to Baa1/BBB+. The closing of NPI to new business following its acquisition by AMP resulted in such a

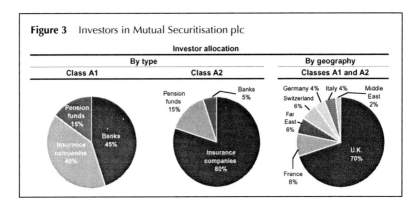

Figure 3 Investors in Mutual Securitisation plc

downgrade due to an ongoing-business rule maintained by Standard & Poor's.

Investors included life insurers and mutual funds, mainly in the UK. The transaction was completed as a Regulation S offering and was not marketed in the US. There has been a modest amount of secondary trading activity. Despite limitations in distribution and liquidity, this transaction introduced many investors outside of bank and private placement circles to life-insurance securitisation.

PRUDENTIAL'S CLOSED BLOCK SECURITISATION
Overview
Prudential Financial succeeded in extracting and redeploying nearly US$2 billion in EV from its traditional participating life insurance business through a securitisation of this business in December 2001 simultaneous with the company's demutualisation. The form of this transaction was consistent with the emerging class of "operating company securitisations" or "whole business securitisations", through which an entire operating business is isolated, its operations codified in servicing agreements, and its cashflows dedicated to investors.[11] This approach proved far more flexible and consistent with regulatory objectives than previous attempts to securitise life business either by filing legal claims against existing cashflows (General American and ASLAC) or by creating contractual cashflows against which to file claims (super-agents, NPI). It also allowed cash to be raised at a holding company level, which facilitated redeployment to other businesses.

In this transaction, Prudential Holdings, LLC, a newly formed intermediate holding company, raised US$1.75 billion of total funds (Intermediate Holding Company (IHC) Debt) based on Prudential Insurance's traditional, participating business (the "Closed Block Business"). Scheduled principal and interest payments were designed to match the emergence of cashflow from this business, which is housed in Prudential Insurance. Prudential Financial, Inc also issued a second class of stock (Class B Stock, a tracking stock) totalling US$175 million, which is entitled to the residual cashflows from the business. Goldman Sachs was the advisor to Prudential on the structuring of this transaction and placement of the Class B shares.

Another element of Prudential's demutualisation transaction was the transfer of the non-life insurance companies in the group – asset management, securities brokerage, property and casualty, international and other businesses – from Prudential Insurance to Prudential Financial. This "destacking" transaction effectively isolated Prudential Insurance from the various non-life insurance activities of Prudential Financial. Prudential Holdings LLC was designed to be non-consolidated in bankruptcy with the balance of Prudential Financial, which provides further credit-remoteness to the life insurance group. The Closed Block Business was further isolated

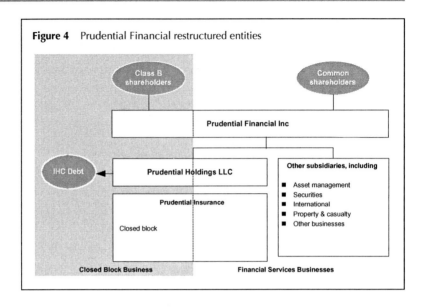

Figure 4   Prudential Financial restructured entities

within the life insurance group, though – as in the case of the NPI transaction – it does remain exposed to that group's solvency.

The transaction structure and reorganised entities are shown in Figure 4.

All of the future cashflows of the Closed Block Business, aside from those dedicated to policyholders, were sold to either IHC debtholders or Class B tracking stock shareholders, so Prudential presented the income statements and balance sheets of the Closed Block Business separately from the ongoing Financial Services Businesses in its disclosure documents. This separation of the inherently low-growth Closed Block Business allowed shareholders of the publicly traded common stock to focus on the results of the growing Financial Services Businesses, which was intended to enhance shareholder value.

Prudential Holdings issued US$332,850,000 of Series A floating rate insured notes, due in 2017, US$776,650,000 of 7.245% of Series B fixed-rate insured notes, due in 2023, and US$640,500,000 of 8.695% of Series C fixed-rate notes, due in 2023. The diverse tranches were offered so as to appeal to various types of capital markets investors – in particular those from both the investment grade corporate and asset-backed universes. The notes were senior, secured indebtedness of Prudential Holdings, LLC, with limited recourse to the Financial Services Businesses of Prudential Financial. Series A and B notes were insured through a financial guarantee insurance policy provided by Financial Security Assurance, Inc (FSA). FSA guaranteed the timely payment of scheduled interest and principal on the notes and wrapped all net swap payments of Prudential Holdings to the swap counterparty.

Background: closed block description

In the US, when a mutual company converts to stock ownership through demutualisation, a regulatory closed block is generally established as a mechanism to provide for continuing dividends to participating policyholders, reflecting their mutual experience. As suggested by the term "closed block", no new policies are added to the block after the demutualisation's effective date. These policyholders also generally receive shares in the new company or else cash or enhanced policy values in lieu of shares.

Following demutualisation, dividends continue to be declared by the company's board of directors based on the underlying experience of the policies in the closed block but subject to the constraint that dividends should be set at a level that would result in full pay out of closed block assets at the point in time that the last policy terminates. The company manages its dividend rate to prevent outcomes in which the last surviving owners of closed block policies receive dividends that are substantially higher or lower than those previously received by other owners of closed block policies.[12]

The initial value of assets set aside for the closed block is determined by an iterative modelling process, illustrated in Figure 5, such that the projected amount of assets will equal zero when the last policy is projected to terminate.

The assumptions used in this modelling process are derived from the experience-based rates underlying the dividend scale in effect in the year in which the company's board adopted its demutualisation plan. The experience-based rates include earnings rates on the portfolio of assets backing the policies included in the closed block, and mortality rates and termination (or lapse) rates on closed block policies as well as other factors. The amount of assets set aside at the establishment of the closed block is determined such that there should be sufficient cashflow to pay all benefits, contractual expenses and taxes, contractual as well as policyholder dividends at current levels, if current experience continues.

Taking the above approach, Prudential began operation of its closed block, consisting of ordinary life business and industrial life business plus a

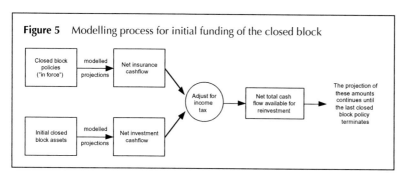

Figure 5   Modelling process for initial funding of the closed block

small number of old retirement annuities, on 1 July, 2000, with total statutory assets of US\$48.7 billion and total statutory liabilities of US\$50.8 billion. Prudential's board of directors adopted Prudential's plan of reorganisation in 2000, so the closed block funding was based on the 2000 dividend scale and the experience underlying that scale.

The initial value of assets in Prudential's closed block was less than the initial value of statutory liabilities for the closed block policies. This difference relates to the fact that the laws, regulations and accounting standards governing the calculation of these liabilities for statutory balance sheet purposes generally require the use of conservative discounting assumptions and methods. The actual cost of fulfilling all obligations with respect to the closed block policies, including future policy dividends, is expected to be less than the amount held as a liability. Funding the closed block with assets less than liabilities is consistent with the funding of the closed blocks established in connection with the demutualisations of other life insurers in the US.

Closed Block Business description

An insurer with a closed block, such as Prudential, needs to hold assets outside of the closed block to cover the shortfall between the statutory closed block assets and closed block liabilities, as well as to meet capital requirements relating to policies included in the closed block. These amounts are referred to as the "Surplus and Related Assets".[13] In the case of Prudential, the amount of such assets was approximately US\$3.7 billion. Prudential's Surplus and Related Assets are released over time as the policies in the closed block runoff and these released amounts, plus investment income on the Surplus and Related Assets, generate statutory net gain for the Closed Block Business within Prudential Insurance. These gains may

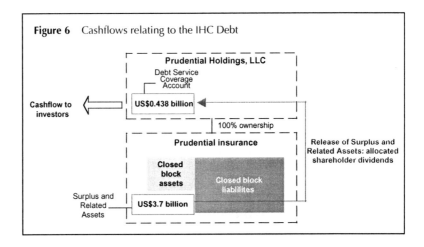

Figure 6   Cashflows relating to the IHC Debt

generally be paid as dividends to Prudential Holdings and used to service debt, subject to the constraints discussed below.[14] The securitisation of the Surplus and Related Assets' runoff has no effect on the benefit or dividend payments on closed block policies. The present value of the release of such cashflows may be regarded as the EV of the closed block.

To allow for the continued payment of principal and interest to debtholders in case of any interruption of the flow of dividends from Prudential Insurance, 25% of the IHC Debt proceeds (initially US$437.5 million) were placed in a Debt Service Coverage Account (DSCA) within Prudential Holdings. This amount is available for use by the IHC debtholders, but is not the property of the Closed Block Business. Following debt repayment, it would be returned to the Financial Services Businesses.

The release of the Surplus and Related Assets in any period is constrained by the shareholder dividend capacity of Prudential Insurance, a New Jersey regulated life-insurance operating company.[15] Even though Prudential Insurance has been separated on an accounting basis between the Closed Block Business and Financial Services Business, regulators still regard the operating company as a single regulated entity and apply one set of tests to the entire company. Moreover, the company is subject to regulatory capital requirements that further constrain dividends.

An objective allocation formula was developed to isolate the cashflow to debtholders and class B shareholders (the Closed Block Business) from the cashflow due to Prudential Financial shareholders (the Financial Services Businesses). In effect, the New Jersey rule and a risk-based capital test are applied to the Closed Block Business within Prudential Insurance as if it were a freestanding life insurer, and the overall company dividend is divided proportionately based on the dividend capacity arising from the Closed Block Business vs the dividend capacity arising from the company as a whole. This approach also prevents the Closed Block Business from "leaning on" the dividend capacity of the whole company – its cashflow is based separately on application of regulatory dividend rules. It is possible that Prudential Insurance would dividend less than its dividend capacity in order to support growth. This would in turn reduce the dividend allocated to debtholders. The allocation rules allow Prudential Insurance to do so, but provide a mechanism to allocate the reduced dividends first to the Closed Block Business if certain tests are met in order to align interests of the two businesses.

The Surplus and Related Assets and DSCA funds are the primary sources of cashflow to service the IHC Debt. To ensure the security and income generation of these funds, a detailed investment policy guideline is applied to the respective asset portfolios. The Surplus and Related Assets must be invested in a minimum of 90% investment grade assets. There are also disclosed limitations on investment in commercial mortgages, privately placed bonds, derivatives, emerging markets and exposure to single issuers. All of the DSCA assets must be invested in investment grade securities; additional single-issuer exposure and derivative restrictions exist.

Releasing the EV associated with the closed blocks of demutualised life insurers had been a focus for many companies. In the year prior to the Prudential transaction, both Metropolitan Life and John Hancock completed modified coinsurance transactions in order to release the bulk of the required capital associated with their closed blocks. By securitising the emergence of value from the difference between statutory assets and liabilities as well as the regulatory capital requirements of the closed block, Prudential created access to more EV. In addition, the Prudential transaction was completed at the holding company level where capital allocation is executed, rather than at the life insurer level.

Unlike the NPI transaction, Prudential did not retain the economic equity in this business, but rather sold it to the Class B shareholders. The apparent retention of equity (the difference between the securities proceeds on the one hand and the Surplus and Related Assets on the other) is illusory – although there was approximately US$3.7 billion of Surplus and Related Assets at closing, it takes many years for this amount to become distributable to Prudential Holdings, which greatly reduces its present value.

Structural considerations

The closed block remains within Prudential Insurance. The Closed Block Business entered into contracts with the Financial Services Businesses within Prudential Insurance and other Prudential financial entities to continue to administer the policies and invest the assets of the business. The board of directors of Prudential Insurance retains the right to set policyholder dividends each year. To balance this discretion, a portion of the administrative servicing fee charged to the closed block may be retained in an additional reserve account if policyholder dividends are set in such a fashion that the closed block deviates from the expected stream of asset and liability values in future years.

The Closed Block Business entered into a tax agreement with the Financial Services Businesses, under which it pays or receives its share of tax for each legal entity. Moreover, the Closed Block Business agreed to hedge its interest rate risks through swaps.

Security interest/collateral

IHC debtholders have a perfected security interest in certain assets of the Closed Block Business including the DSCA, certain additional reserve account amounts, amounts due under the tax agreement, and any net swap payments.

The debtholders also receive a pledge of approximately 15% of the shares of Prudential Insurance as additional security. The exact amount is calculated as 125% of the book value of the IHC Debt (US$2.187 billion) subject to a limit.

Bondholder protections/trigger events

The first set of bondholder protections relates to the characteristics of the underlying regulatory closed block of participating policies. There is certainty about the quality of new business as the Closed Block Business is structured as a closed system to which no new business can be added. Regulatory approval is needed to (i) terminate or amend the closed block or (ii) change the purpose of the assets held for the block. Further, regulators need to agree to alter operations of the closed block, which are precisely limited by the closed block memorandum (which was part of Prudential's reorganisation plan).[16] Full disclosure of management's ability to adjust policyholder dividends to reflect changes in investment, mortality, surrender and other experience factors reduces bondholders' concern that the company may not be willing to reduce dividends in poor performance years. The formulaic basis of administrative and overhead expenses reduces concern that the issuer is funnelling cashflow to itself by overpaying expenses. The Financial Services Businesses mitigate litigation risk through indemnification of the Closed Block Business.

Numerous debt covenants were included to ensure that Prudential Holdings, and implicitly the overall public company, acts in the interest of bondholders. A selected few are listed here:

❏ Prudential Holdings will cause Prudential Insurance to seek to maintain a shareholder dividend policy that is sufficient to service the IHC Debt;
❏ following demutualisation and related transactions, Prudential Insurance will not dividend or transfer subsidiaries or assets without receiving fair value in exchange;
❏ all Prudential Holdings and Prudential Insurance transactions with affiliates are to be for reasonable value;
❏ Surplus and Related Assets and DSCA will be managed according to specified investment policies;
❏ Prudential Holdings, LLC may not incur indebtedness other than for securities lending activities or subordinated, unsecured indebtedness to Prudential Financial, Inc, which is subordinated to the notes;
❏ Prudential Holdings will be subject to limitations governing transfers between the Closed Block Business and the Financial Services Businesses; and
❏ Prudential Insurance will only engage in businesses similar to those engaged in at the time of demutualisation (following destacking).

Several other non-consolidation covenants have been included to ensure that, in a bankruptcy scenario for Prudential Financial, its creditors will not be able to capture funds held in the DSCA. Provisions of the transaction that are typically found in whole business securitisations include:

❏ management of the business via a servicing contract;
❏ hedging of all interest rate risk;
❏ isolation from other aspects of the company's business;
❏ constraints on additional financing or asset sales;
❏ presence of insured bonds;
❏ amortising structure of bonds;
❏ bondholder covenant not to petition for bankruptcy; and
❏ non-consolidation in bankruptcy.

Risks to investors of closed block securitisation

Liquidation or rehabilitation of the insurance company

Given that it is not legally possible in the US to separate a closed block from the regulated insurance operating company, investors are exposed to the risk that the assets held ultimately to service their bonds would be claimed by all other creditors of the insurance company. This includes both the assets used to fund the closed block and the assets held to support the block (Surplus and Related Assets).

Investment performance of Surplus and Related Assets

Surplus and Related Assets, similar to the assets held in a closed block, are invested assets. Given that the primary source of cashflow to debtholders is from the income and principal of this pool of assets, investors are also exposed to investment risk on these assets. In particular, managers of these assets bear risk as they could potentially invest in low quality fixed-income securities or in riskier equity and real estate investments. This risk is mitigated through the disclosure of a restrictive investment policy statement that places bounds on the asset manager's discretion.

Timing risk

Closed blocks are normally established on very mature blocks of business, so future insurance cashflows are fairly predictable. To the extent that experience does deviate from that expected at the time of closed block funding, the company can adjust the dividend scale to reflect such changes in experience, thereby bringing the actual runoff of the closed block (and the runoff of the Surplus and Related Assets) back into line with the expected runoff. A risk to the investors of the closed block securitisation is that the company allows the actual runoff of the closed block (and the corresponding runoff of the Surplus and Related Assets) to deviate significantly from the expected runoff.

Inadequacy of closed block assets to meet all guaranteed closed block benefits

If the assets allocated to the closed block along with the investment cash-flows from those assets and the revenues from closed block policies are not sufficient to pay the guaranteed benefits under the closed block policies, the company would have to pay the guaranteed benefits from the Surplus and Related Assets and from other company general funds.

Such a situation could only occur if there were a significant deterioration in actual experience (such as a deterioration in asset earnings due to increased defaults or losses on equity assets, a decline in rates available on new fixed-income investments, or a significant deterioration in mortality experience). The company would reduce policyholder dividends if actual experience deteriorates, so it is important for potential investors to know the size of the policyholder dividend "cushion". Typically, in US demutualisations, the dividend cushion provides significant protection against a possible inadequacy of closed block assets.

To test the sensitivity of the closed block to changes in future experience rates, potential investors should be interested in whether the policyholder dividend scale can be managed to offset fairly extreme changes in experience over the term of the investment. Such sensitivity tests could include changes in various assumptions, such as changes in investment earnings rates, default rates, mortality rates and lapse rates. In each of these scenarios of future changes in experience, the policyholder dividend scale is adjusted based on direction from the company as to how such dividends might be adjusted in the future if experience emerged as projected under the sensitivities. If the sensitivity tests show that policyholder dividends can be managed to offset the changes in the experience of the closed block under particular scenarios, the assets of the closed block should be adequate to pay the guaranteed benefits on the closed block policies. Surplus and Related Assets or other general account assets should not be needed to pay closed block guaranteed benefits under such scenarios.

Milliman USA provided an expertised modelling analysis covering the initial funding level for Prudential's closed block as well as various sensitivity tests. The funding analysis showed that there was a significant dividend cushion (the after-tax present value of future policyholder dividends assuming no change in future dividend scales was about 60% of the initial closed block assets) that could be used to offset potential future adverse experience while still allowing the closed block to pay all guaranteed benefits.

The sensitivity analysis tested various changes in future experience and possible policyholder dividend actions in response to those changes in future experience. The scenarios tested included changes in:

❏ investment earnings from interest rates, equity returns and default costs;

❏ mortality rates; and
❏ persistency rates.

The closed block is charged expenses according to a fixed schedule, so there was no need to test changes in expenses. The sensitivity testing showed that the investment earnings of the closed block was the key driver of future policyholder dividends on closed block policies. The scenarios tested included a 3% drop in interest rates, a 3% increase in interest rates, historical equity returns, and historical default losses. Scenarios that produced lower investment returns than those assumed in the initial funding of the closed block required a cut in dividends. Lower interest rates result in lower earnings rates on closed block assets as the cashflows of the closed block are invested over the lifetime of the closed block. Most of the closed block assets are fixed-income assets, so closed block dividends are sensitive to falling interest scenarios. Conversely, scenarios that produced higher investment earnings from higher interest rates, higher equity returns and lower default costs result in increases to dividends.

The analysis compared the aggregate effect of policyholder dividend scale changes with the original dividend scale by comparing, for each scenario, the present value of policyholder dividends after reflecting the modelled dividend actions with the present value of dividends projected to be paid under the original (year 2000) dividend scale. The sensitivity testing showed that, for each scenario tested, Prudential's closed block policyholder dividend scale could be managed to offset changes in experience and to keep the closed block on a path consistent with the original glide path.

This analysis made the technical life insurance risks embedded in the closed block understandable to a wide array of investors.

Investor pricing and risk

The Milliman analysis provided a starting point for analysis. Investors could then use the Milliman sensitivity analysis to develop a probabilistic analysis by undertaking a four-step process:

1. Attribute probabilities to the sensitivities in the Milliman analysis by using historical distributions reflecting the underpinnings of the loss scenario (rates, credit, mortality, etc).
2. Adjust the probabilities to reflect the fact that none of them generated a loss in the closed block, so the probability of loss for each scenario would be less than the scenario probability.
3. Develop income and loss probabilities for the Surplus and Related Assets based on their investment policy and include them in a debt model to determine incidence of default.
4. Factor in the impact of Prudential Insurance credit risk.

The business continued to be housed within Prudential Insurance so the continued solvency of that company (as in NPI) was important to investors and the rating agencies placed a ceiling on ratings based on the company's debt ratings. The debt was subordinated to policyholder obligations, so the relevant rating benchmark for this risk was the company's surplus notes. Both agencies rated this debt on an unwrapped basis at or above the surplus note ratings, so it is reasonable to assume that the charge attributed to other risks was extremely low.

Theoretically, if the business could be distanced from the credit risk of the insurance entity, the risk could be lower and the price as a multiple of risk could be higher, all while providing lower cost funds to the issuer. There are several ways to achieve such true-sale or near-true sale treatment, including reinsurance and policyholder consent processes. These alternatives share a great deal of incremental regulatory scrutiny and problematic execution, however.

Investor placement
The IHC Debt placement by Goldman Sachs and Lehman Brothers validated the notion that investor appetite exists for securitised life insurance risk. A wide variety of capital market investors were members of the final order book including banks, fund managers and insurers. The majority of the bonds were allocated to US firms, especially for the series C notes. The length of the bonds, timing of the transaction and familiarity with the Prudential franchise were key factors driving relative demand in the US vs Europe. Figure 7 shows the allocation by both investor type and geography.

The Class B Stock was privately placed with American International Group and Pacific Life, who were attracted by the stability of the Closed Block Business, a target dividend and the potential for upside through the residual cashflows following the repayment of the debt.

MORTALITY AND LONGEVITY RISK SECURITISATION
Following the unexpectedly high levels of insured loss caused by Hurricane Andrew in 1992, property and casualty companies and their reinsurers began exploring ways to spread super-catastrophe risks through the much larger capital markets through securitisation and derivative transactions. Early transactions by Hannover Re in 1994 and St Paul Re in 1996 laid the groundwork for an expansion of activity in 1997. Several dozen transactions have been completed since, resulting in the securitisation of risks ranging from Japanese earthquakes to European windstorms.

As risk securitisation developed in the second half of the 1990s, mortality risk appeared to be a natural candidate. The basic structure of catastrophe bonds could be employed (as in Figure 8). After some exploratory work, most potential securitisers moved away from bonds that would pay out

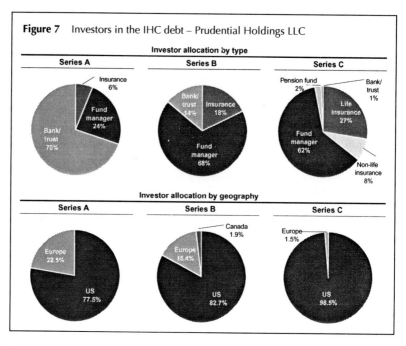

Figure 7   Investors in the IHC debt – Prudential Holdings LLC

based on the occurrence of actual death claims and toward bonds triggered by changes in death rates in aggregate. The required length of actual mortality-based bonds would exceed the investment horizon of most investors.

None of these bonds has yet been completed. Reinsurance prices have remained far below potential capital markets levels. Mortality risk does not appear to "peak" easily – it is diversifiable in that as more policyholders are added, the likely distribution of average loss tends to become tighter. This is quite different from catastrophe risk, in which the more exposed properties that an insurer adds to its portfolio, the more risk that it has. Catastrophic mortality risks (whether caused by plague or disaster) have generally been discounted by life insurers. Most companies routinely suffer more volatility from investment results than they would even from an epidemic on the scale of the 1918 influenza virus (the worst US mortality event of the past century and the one that life insurers often test against). Until September 11, 2001, most companies discounted the possibility of large-scale, single-event mortality outside of war.

It is more difficult to diversify away longevity risk. Particularly in Europe, life insurers perceive that potential losses due to lengthening life span on life-contingent annuity policies is the key insurance risk to the industry. A number of securitisation structures have been developed. These are generally based on the aggregate survival rate of a large book of business but may also be based on the average survival rate for a whole population. For example, based on a state's records of deaths vs population

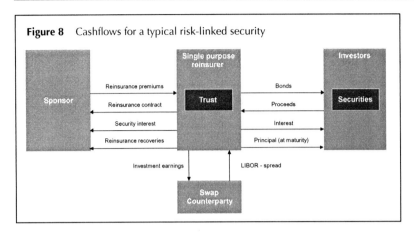

Figure 8   Cashflows for a typical risk-linked security

for any year, a bond structure may pay a claim to a protection buyer if the level of mortality exceeds a predefined "trigger" which has a relatively low probability of occurrence. A probability distribution with defined securitisation layers is illustrated in Figure 9.

A more exotic issue arises in this type of securitisation – anti-tontine legal risk. Tontines were a class of securities that were frequently available in the capital markets in the 18th and 19th centuries. These are securities that pay a fixed payment to all surviving owners over some period of time. As some owners die, the share of those surviving grows. They were eventually outlawed based on the notion that they gave an unrelated person an interest in the death of another. Longevity securitisations based on small pools or single long lives have a tontine aspect. This is another reason for indexed structures.

Reinsurance rates have been attractive relative to the capital markets rate for longevity risk coverage, but the difference between reinsurance and capital markets rates has been smaller than for mortality risk. This may lead to transactions in this segment as the capital markets experience with life insurance expands and issuance spreads lose some of their novelty premium.

The risk of catastrophic mortality at the workplace is compounded by

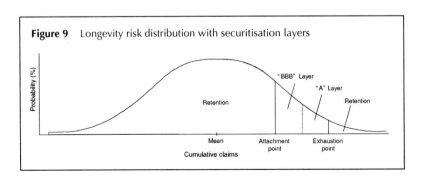

Figure 9   Longevity risk distribution with securitisation layers

the potential for "clash" risk involving individual insurance, group insurance, disability, corporate-owned life insurance (COLI) and workers compensation losses, all involving members of the same group. This risk did not appear to seriously damage the solvency of any one company in 2001, but the possibility of such losses has led companies to consider issuance to cover discrete catastrophic events.

A variant on mortality risk securitisation that has seen some activity over the years is securitisation of life insurance or viatical settlements. As policyholders seek ways to liquidate unneeded life insurance policies (rather than simply surrendering and sacrificing embedded mortality value) securitisation may provide a portion of the financing. This market has developed slowly as regulators grapple with the consumer sales practice issues around such transactions.[17] The development of life settlement securitisation could provide policyholders with a secondary market in their insurance policies.

ALTERNATIVES FOR CAPITAL GENERATION: PROSPECTS FOR SECURITISATION

The life reinsurance market is the backdrop against which the development of securitisation activity has played out. The development of the securitisation market has been interesting and shows some promise for future development, but the slow speed at which it has developed is a function of the ability of the life reinsurance market to meet the bulk of the needs of life insurers efficiently.

The life reinsurance market has experienced a great deal of growth in recent years. Increasingly, life insurers are configuring themselves as providers of feature-rich savings products and are ceding the bulk of mortality contingencies to reinsurers. It is estimated that, in the US, more than half of all life mortality risk is currently being ceded.

Consolidation and demutualisation/privatisation activity around the world has driven reinsurance activity. Consolidators often use reinsurance as a supplemental source of financing and as a post-merger asset disposition market (the assets being closed blocks of business for which they are paid the EV). Companies desiring to stabilise their earnings profile or to redeploy capital outside of mergers are increasingly turning to reinsurers. Specific regulatory changes including Regulation XXX, new accounting for modified coinsurance in the US, new solvency regulations, and the Insurance Groups Directive in Europe are driving the level of reinsurance activity.[18]

This activity level has attracted a great deal of new capital into the life reinsurance market. Large global life/non-life reinsurers have reallocated capital to life businesses in recent years in response to soft pricing on the non-life side. A number of new companies have been created offshore, notably in Bermuda, whose business model involves embedding a variety of investing strategies within stable books of life reinsurance business. Growth in spread lending via Euro-GIC (Guaranteed Investment Contract) and Euro-MTN (Medium-Term Note) issuance by several US companies has caused them to become net reinsurers of other types of policies in order to maintain target business mixes.

Explicitly or implicitly, some of this capital may have been reallocated back to non-life business since the attacks of September 11, 2001, and the consequent hardening in non-life insurance rates. This will become clearer with time.

This expansion in capital has generally been sufficient to provide adequate mortality and longevity reinsurance and to allow some extraction of EV from existing blocks of business by primary insurers. The scale of EV within the life-insurance industry are likely to exceed the scale of the life reinsurance market and drive more companies to the capital markets as primary companies seek to rationalise their use of capital by extracting it from existing blocks of business.[19] The favourable equity analyst response to such extraction that has occurred (notably for demutualised US life companies relative to their closed blocks) suggests that the time is near for this notion to be tested.

Securitisation via whole business structures can also resolve some frictions that exist within the reinsurance system today. Reinsurance represents a direct transaction with an operating insurer, so extraction of EV through reinsurance results in proceeds being paid to an insurance operating company rather than a holding company where it may be more flexibly redeployed. Moreover, reinsurance proceeds are taxable in many jurisdictions because they are treated as an expense reimbursement rather than a financing. Since the advent of SFAS 113 (Accounting for Reinsurance) in the US, there is no way to achieve accounting separation between reinsured and retained business under US GAAP without some form of policyholder consent to a legal transfer of the policy to the reinsurer (novation), a step that many insurers do not take because of its potential to undermine distribution, servicing or asset-management businesses. The mismatch between domestic insurers and global reinsurers shows up most often in letter-of-credit requirements that regulators impose on out-of-country transactions, adding a layer of expense. Finally, a great deal of surplus-generating reinsurance is transacted as a direct transfer of reserves between companies with little cash changing hands. If a company's objective is financing, this type of transaction is generally inapplicable.

The renewed interest in life securitisation has also sparked increased rating agency coverage. Both Moody's and Standard & Poor's have released reports profiling their analysis of the risk associated with these types of transactions. The focus has not only been on the ability of the securitisation structure to produce sufficient cashflow to meet obligations on the issued securities but also the financial strength of the underlying insurance company and the safeguards of the transaction structure. Ratings have been constrained by credit exposure to the host of insurer and regulatory risk.

Ultimately, as has been the case in catastrophe securitisation, life securitisation may prove to be most valuable as a tool for reinsurers who are acting as specialised capital providers in the life-insurance system. Because of their technical infrastructure and capital bases, they may be among the best positioned to pool risk and policies and issue more standardised instruments of various sorts, whether risk bearing or capital raising.

CONCLUSION

Securitisation is a tool that allows a pool of financial business to be packaged and directly capitalised by the debt market on a freestanding basis rather than through a company's balance sheet. Risk is transferred to the providers of debt capital. The development of securitisation technology and a knowledgeable investor base allows capital to become a less critical factor for success, and provides a vehicle to allow the highest-skill participants to lead the sector.

APPENDIX A – SELECTED LIFE INSURANCE AND ANNUITY SECURITISATIONS

Sponsor	Class of business	Transaction description	Size	Comments
MONY Holdings, LLC (2002)	Closed block of traditional whole life and related policies.	Closed block curve out; EV Sucuritisation.	US$300 million.	Rule 144A placement of debt; option to issue an additional US$150 million of debt.
Prudential Financial (2001)	Closed block of traditional whole life and related policies.	Closed block carve out; EV securitisation with sale of residual as tracking stock.	US$49 billion assets, US$51 billion liabilities, US$1.925 billion capital raised plus additional capital released.	Rule 144A placement of debt; three tranches totalling US$1.75 billion as well as a private tracking stock totalling US$175 million.
Hannover Re L4 (2001)	Unit-linked life and annuity reinsurance business from Austria and Germany.	Financial reinsurance securitisation for acquisition cost relief.	Up to €200 million.	Business originated primarily from Aspecta Leben, three-year facility.

Sponsor	Class of business	Transaction description	Size	Comments
Hannover Re L3 (1999)	All classes of life, health, personal and accident insurance originated in Asian emerging markets.	Financial reinsurance securitisation for acquisition cost relief.	€50 million.	Three-year facility.
Hannover Re L2 (1998)	Multi-currency life reinsurance.	Financial reinsurance	Approximately US$118 million.	Allows cedents of Hannover to release EV from blocks of life insurance.
NPI (1998)	Unit-linked, unitised with-profit life insurance.	EV securitisation.	£260 million proceeds.	Two classes (A1, 9.1-year average life, and A2, 19.9-year average life), both rated A3/A–, vehicle based in Ireland.
Hannover Re L1 (1998)	Multi-currency life reinsurance.	75% private EV securitisation: Interpolis Re absorbed mortality and lapse risk, and Rabobank provided liquidity.	DM100 million.	Three-year facility, facility based in Ireland.
American Skandia (1996–01)	Variable annuities, mortality and expense fees.	Securitisation of EV through private placements.	Over US$900 million in 13 separate transactions.	American Skandia received debt treatment for US GAAP but favourable Swedish regulatory accounting treatment for the parent company; rated BBB by Duff & Phelps.

Sponsor	Class of business	Transaction description	Size	Comments
Dignity Partners	Viatical settlements.	Securitisation of death benefits of terminally ill policyholders.	US$50 million.	
NASL (1994)	Variable annuity fees	Fee securitisation.	US$30 million	Bank financing; debt treatment.
Anchor National (SunAmerica) (1989)	Variable annuity fees.	Fee securitisation.	US$31.4 million. Citibank (conduit); surplus treatment.	Surplus treatment (grand-fathered).
Monarch Life (1988) "Maple Leaf"	Variable annuities.	Super-Agent: bank facility designed to pay agents' commissions and collect a repayment stream over time from the life insurer.	US$175 million.	Chase (bank financing); debt treatment.
Prudential Insurance Company of America (1988)	Policy loan.	Private placement asset securitisation.	US$445.6 million.	Debt treatment.
Fidelity Benefit Life (1988)	Fixed annuities.	Super Agent: bank facility designed to pay agents' commissions and collect a repayment stream over time from the life insurer.	Approximately US$25 million.	Citicorp (bank financing).
Washington National Life Insurance (1988)	Whole and industrial life.	Future premium loading securitisation.	US$30 million.	Citibank (conduit); surplus treatment (grand-fathered).

Sponsor	Class of business	Transaction description	Size	Comments
General American Life Insurance (1988)	Whole and universal life.	Future premium loading securitisation.	US$75 million.	Citibank (conduit); surplus treatment (grand-fathered).

APPENDIX B – GLOSSARY

Annuity	A contract that provides for periodic payments to an annuitant for a specified period of time, often until the annuitant's death. Most annuities involve a lengthy "deferred" period in which an annuityholder's original deposit accumulates interest.
Appraisal value	Embedded value plus the present value of future business.
Cash surrender value	Money that the policy owner is entitled to receive from the insurance company upon surrendering a life insurance policy with cash value.
Death benefit	Amount payable, as stated in a life insurance policy, upon the death of the insured. This is the face value of the policy plus any riders, less any outstanding loans and the interest accrued thereon.
Deferred policy acquisition costs (DAC or DPAC)	Commissions and other selling expenses that vary with, and are directly related to, the productions of business and that are deferred and amortised to achieve a matching of revenues and expenses when reported in financial statements prepared in conformity with generally accepted accounting principles.
Demutualisation	The process of conversion from mutual to stock ownership, generally involving the distribution of shares to certain policyholders and an initial public offering of additional shares.
Dividend scale	The formulae used to develop dividends for classes of participating policyholders.
Embedded value (EV)	Adjusted capital and surplus plus the discounted value of future distributable profits on in-force business (free cashflow).
Endowment policies	A type of life insurance including a benefit paid to the insured after a defined period of time.
Glide path	Projected statutory balance sheet of a closed block of business consistent with initial funding assumptions.
Guaranteed investment contract (GIC)	A group contract that guarantees a minimum rate of return, which may be fixed or floating, on the amount invested.

In force	Policies and contracts reflected on applicable records that have not expired or been terminated as of a given date.
Industrial life insurance	Older traditional whole life insurance policies with small face amounts where premiums historically were collected by the agent on a weekly or monthly basis. Because of the cost associated with premium collection on these small policies, many companies have made these policies "paid-up", ie, future premiums are no longer required to keep the policy in force.
Morbidity	The incidence of disease or disability in a specific population over a specific period of time.
Mortality	The number of deaths in a specific population over a specific period of time.
Participating policy or annuity	Policies and annuities under which the policy holder/contract holder has a right to participate in the divisible surplus of the insurance company to the extent dividends are apportioned thereon.
Persistency	Measurement of the percentage of insurance policies or annuity contracts remaining in force between specified measurement dates. Policies that do not persist are said to "lapse" or "terminate".
Premiums	Payments and considerations received on insurance policies issued or reinsured by an insurance company.
Reinsurance	The ceding by one insurance company (the "reinsured") to another (the "reinsurer") of all or a portion of a risk for a premium. The ceding of risk to a reinsurer, other than in the case of assumption reinsurance, does not relieve the original insurer (ie, the reinsured) of its liability to the insured without the notification and/or consent of the insured.
Reserves	Amounts recorded as a liability in order to provide for anticipated payoffs such as benefits, dividends or contingencies.
Riders	Additions to a basic insurance contract providing additional benefits (such as accident insurance additional limits for life insurance policies).
Statutory	Pursuant to state law.
Surrender charge	An amount specified in some insurance policies and annuity contracts that is charged to a policyholder or contract holder for early cancellation of or withdrawal under that policy or contract.
Tontine	A contract paying the survivors in a pool more as other pool members die.
Tracking stock	An additional class of shares of a company based on a business outside the core business of a firm.

Traditional whole life insurance	A life insurance policy that offers the beneficiary benefits in the event of the insured's death for the whole of life, provided premiums have been paid when due; it also allows for the build-up of cash value but has no investment feature under the control of the policyholder.
Universal life insurance	Interest-sensitive life insurance under which separately identified interest and mortality and expense charges are made to the policy fund, typically with flexible premiums.
Variable annuity	An annuity contract under which values during the accumulation phase fluctuate according to the investment performance of a separate account or accounts supporting such contract that is/are designated by the contract holder.
Whole business securitisation (also operating company securitisation)	A securitisation involving future cashflows resulting from the entire business of an operating company, generally accomplished through the isolation of that business from a bankruptcy perspective from the remainder of the enterprise and the offering of non-recourse debt by that entity.
Whole-life policy	Policy that remains in full force and effect for the life of the insured, with premium payments being made for the same period.

1 Securities Data Company.
2 Conceptually, such loadings were historically priced into policies to allow insurers to recover acquisition expenses. At the time, many insurers noted that pricing in the industry had fallen to such a level that the loadings were often negligible or negative, which would have limited such transactions.
3 Ernst and Whinney were one of the "big eight" accounting firms in the 1980s. They later merged with Arthur Young to become Ernst & Young.
4 Citicorp pointed out that it had been involved in securitising other assets for insurers (including non-admitted receivables, furniture and equipment) in this fashion for over 10 years, although it had not previously securitised elements of insurance policies themselves (Agostino and Cosgrove, 1990).
5 The transactions were viewed as an alternative to surplus-generating reinsurance, which itself has characteristics of privately placed securitisation. The key attraction of these transactions vs such reinsurance was the low cost of funds passed along through the CP conduits and the debt-treatment of such transactions for tax purposes. Reinsurance that generates surplus is treated as an acceleration of income and results in an acceleration of tax, although this may be offset in some cases in which a reinsurer is able to take and pass along the benefit of a corresponding deduction. Moreover, "surplus relief" reinsurance structures typically involve a transfer of reserves from the cedent to the reinsurer without the payment of cash, and some cedents preferred to receive cash financing through these transactions.
6 The department stated that a liability should be created in statutory accounting for such transactions. Terrence Lennon, then Chief of the Life Bureau of the New York insurance department commented that either the transactions were loans and therefore not surplus, or else they were reinsurance, which banks were not allowed to write. Lennon wrote an article on the topic in which he stated that "in an environment where profit margins are low, management structures are in need of rebuilding and the industry is increasingly leveraged,

this is the only possible answer (debt treatment). The margins must be addressed-an industry that chronically produces inadequate profits is ultimately an unhealthy industry" (Lennon, 1990).

7 The NAIC ultimately adopted the following language into its accounting manual: """Sale" of Future Revenues:' The immediate recognition of proceeds from certain transactions characterized as 'sale of future revenues in income and/or surplus is inconsistent with Statutory Accounting Principles. These transactions are sometimes characterized as selling 'deferred acquisition costs.' Accordingly, a liability should be established for the amount of the proceeds, which may be amortized over an appropriate period." Existing transactions were grandfathered. In order to provide other avenues for mutual life insurers to raise capital, regulators commenced a review of surplus notes.

8 See Ness (1988).

9 This practice is referred to as "zillmerisation" of future profits or hidden reserves. The cap on the value of implicit profit is the lesser of (a) 50% of the product of annual profit (trailing 5-year statutory average) and remaining policy average life (up to 10 years), or (b) present value of future profits. For most companies, non-implicit items must cover all liabilities and at least one-sixth of the required margin of solvency. These EU regulations are under review (Saunders, 2000).

10 ASLAC Funding Trust, Jones and Joseph Tuczak 1996, and Duff and Phelps, 1997.

11 Moody's defines operating company securitisations as "transactions in which a line of business (which may be a substantial portion of the assets of a company) is sold by the company to one or more limited-purpose, bankruptcy-remote vehicles, an affiliate of which issues securities backed by the assets. Typically, the original operating company (the sponsor) continues to manage the assets under the terms of a management agreement with the issuing vehicle." (Moody's 2002). The first transactions were completed in the UK in the mid-1990s, enabled by "creditor-friendly" aspects of UK bankruptcy law. Other sectors that have been securitised include licensed pubs, film and music rights, ferries, unique entertainment properties, water companies, motor service areas, nursing homes and food brands.

12 Any situation in which an individual is rewarded for surviving longer than other members of a group is known as a "tontine". The need to manage the dividend scale of a closed block such that policyholders are not rewarded in this way is driven by "anti-tontine" rules or laws.

13 Other industry terms for the assets held against the difference between statutory liabilities and assets for a closed block include "immobilised assets", "additional assets", and "deficit assets".

14 Note that other funds available for debt service include net tax payments from Prudential Financial to Prudential Holdings and net swap payments between Prudential Holdings and the swap counterparty. Moreover, the DSCA is initially funded with US$437.5 million but also may be "topped up" with an additional US$350 million on a contingent basis when certain triggers occur.

15 New Jersey limits shareholder dividends to the greater of 10% of the prior year's (capital and) surplus or the prior year's statutory net gain from operations.

16 A closed block memorandum is a regulatory document that the company prepares as part of the demutualisation describing how the closed block is structured and operated. Once accepted by the regulator, it becomes an effective operating policy and guide going forward.

17 As early as 1995, Dignity Partners had securitised US$50 million of viatical settlements (Saunders, 2000).

18 This regulation resulted in increased reserve requirements for certain long-term insurance policies.

19 Moody's recently estimated the embedded value of large European groups that report this statistic to approach €70 billion.

BIBLIOGRAPHY

Agostino, D. J., and W. J. Cosgrove, 1990, "The Securitization Solution", *Best's Review*, January, p. 44.

Arabeyre, V., and S. Hardwick, 2001, "From Embedded Value to Share Price", URL: http://www.towers.com/towers/publications/emphasis/emp2001-1/embedded.htm.

Borronow, G., and T. Mazzaferro, 1996, American Skandia Press Release, December 17.

Corcoran, J. P., 1989, Securitization of Future Premiums – Statutory Accounting Treatment, New York State Department of Insurance Circular Letter (1989-7).

Hannover Re, 1998, "Hannover Re Completes First-Ever Life Reassurance Transaction with Capital Markets", *Hannover Re Newsletter* (April 15).

Harris, S., 2002, Moody's Analysis of Life Insurance Embedded Values and Their Securitisation, Moody's Rating Report Publication, January.

Jones, J. G., and J. S. Tuczak, 1996, ASLAC Funding Trust, Duff & Phelps Credit Rating Agency Company Report.

Lennon, T., 1990, "Securitization: A Regulatory View", *Bests Review*, January, pp. 45–6

MetLife Inc, URL: www.sec.gov. SEC Form 10-K. March 14, 2001.

Macy, S. C., 2002, "Approach to Rating Operating Company Securitizations", Moody's Rating Agency Report, February 8.

Murray, J. B., D. J. Bennett, P. Headly, A. D. Affleck, N. Bauer, A. Rayner, 2001, Use of Embedded Values at United States and European Insurance Companies, Milliman Global Research Report.

Ness, I., 1988, "Pru Cashes in on Policy Loans" *National Underwriter*, February 15.

Ness, I., 1989, "New York Insurance Department Opposes Securitizations", *National Underwriter*, March 27.

Pfister, B., 2000, "Whole Business Securitisations: A Unique Opportunity for UK Assets", Moody's Rating Agency Report, October 19.

Prudential Financial, Inc, 2001, SEC Form S-1, December 12.

Puccia, M., 2001, "Reducing Risk Through the Creation of a Closed Block", *RatingsDirect Commentary*, September, URL: http://www.ratingsdirect.standardandpoors.com.

Reed, I., J. U. Dhru, J. Doona, J. Siberon and M. Puccia, 2001, "Interest in Life Insurance Securitization Heats Up", *RatingsDirect Commentary*, October 23, URL: http://www.ratingsdirect.standardandpoors.com.

Saunders, A. J., 2000, "Securitization and Other Financing Options Available to Life Companies", *Institute of Actuaries and Faculty of Actuaries*.

Shante, V. M., 1989, "Securitization and Sale of Future Revenue Streams", Prudential-Bache Capital Funding, Unpublished Paper.

20

The Origin of Contingent Liabilities

Stephen Hough

BAE SYSTEMS

In order to understand why BAE SYSTEMS became a leader in the development of innovative risk transfer schemes it is helpful to spend some time reviewing the company's history in the regional aircraft market.

INTRODUCTION

The aim of this chapter is to use the BAE SYSTEMS' experience in the regional aircraft manufacturing business as a case study of how the company successfully recognised and managed the transfer of the potential risks associated with contingent liabilities. It will demonstrate how such an exercise has, together with subsequent strategic decisions, allowed BAE SYSTEMS to draw a line under its exposures to regional aircraft manufacturing.

HISTORY

Leasebook exposure had accumulated rapidly in the 1980s to place the high production levels of jets and turboprops, which the then British Aerospace manufactured, into the regional aircraft market.[1] The aircraft concerned covered the full range in the regional aircraft market (see Figure 1).

This resulted in a leasebook exposure that was already in excess of £3 billion in 1994 and still growing at that time.

This production had in the main been financed through long-term head leases, or asset value positions guaranteed by British Aerospace and placed with airlines on what in reality turned out to be short-term operating leases. In addition, complexity of the head lease structures and the high values at which the aircraft were then being financed meant that there was limited flexibility in re-marketing the aircraft and little ability to unwind the financings economically. The types of structures used included classic UK tax leases, US leveraged leases in which the aircraft is owned by a grantor trust, and Japanese leveraged leases in which a special purpose vehicle (SPV)

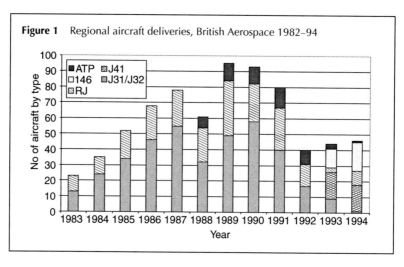

Figure 1 Regional aircraft deliveries, British Aerospace 1982–94

owns the aircraft financed with equity from tax-driven private investors and debt. By using these tax-driven structures there are likely to be jurisdictional restrictions on where aircraft can be leased and the termination values would be higher to account for the clawback of tax benefits (such as accelerated depreciation allowances built into the structure).

On balance the regional aircraft were being placed into a weak market overpopulated with competitors, where the financial strength of many of the airlines leasing the aircraft was invariably poor.

If the lenders were not happy with the credit risk of the airline they would require British Aerospace to act as the primary lessee under a head lease absorbing all the risk of default by the airline and the asset risk. Alternatively British Aerospace sometimes provided lease deficiency guarantees or put options or residual value guarantees. The lease deficiency guarantees would be provided for airlines who opted to obtain financing from third parties. They would be structured so that if the airline defaulted on its obligations to the financing party who would be leasing the aircraft to the airline, then the lessor would require British Aerospace to cover the airline's default, which it would do by effectively stepping into the airline's position as lessee or by acquiring the asset itself by paying off the outstanding obligations under the lease. Put options or residual value guarantees would be granted to airlines (or assigned to the party financing the aircraft for the airline) to enable them to sell the aircraft back to British Aerospace, providing the aircraft met the agreed return conditions and clear title could be granted, on specified dates and at specified prices. Such "windows" to sell the aircraft back would require the airlines to provide British Aerospace with notice of its intentions at a pre-agreed period of time in advance of the "window" to enable the aircraft to be remarketed prior to its return to British Aerospace.

The leasing of British Aerospace regional aircraft was, after 1990, primarily undertaken through the Trident Group. The Trident Group was independently owned and managed but funded using a combination of structured financing transactions, such as those described above, and a series of bank and export credit facilities that were in most cases fully guaranteed by British Aerospace.

The portfolio was therefore managed by three different lessor entities, the Trident Group, Jet Acceptance Corporation ("JACO", a wholly-owned subsidiary of British Aerospace in the US which acted as the head lessee/ sub lessor of aircraft financed through US leveraged leases) and British Aerospace itself acting as the head lessee/sub lessor of aircraft financed through UK tax leases.

The use of vendor finance by all aircraft and major component (ie, engine) manufacturers was, and indeed still is, taken as the expected norm in the civil aviation market and in this regard British Aerospace was not alone in responding to the requirements of its customers

In the early 1990s a substantial number of aircraft were returned, resulting in 44 BAe 146's and over 100 turboprops lying idle at the peak of the recession. At that time British Aerospace (like other manufacturing-led companies) had no organisation or methodology in place within the company to deal with such a substantial fleet of used aircraft.

British Aerospace was arguably the first aircraft manufacturer to recognise this issue and significant strategic actions were taken by the company to deal with these problems. These included the closure of the Hatfield UK factory and the transfer of production of the upgraded Avro RJ (successor to the BAe 146) to the Woodford facility near Manchester at a dramatically reduced production rate – from 42 aircraft a year to 18–20 aircraft a year.[2] Turboprop production was also substantially reduced – ATP production was cut from 24 a year to only eight and Jetstream from 72 aircraft to 30, before all turboprop manufacture ceased in 1997.

On the financial side, from the second half of 1992, British Aerospace made provisions to restructure its regional aircraft business, including recognition of its exposure to aircraft financing by marking-to-market the portfolio. The company also set out the full details of its aircraft contingent liability portfolio in a note to its Annual Report. The note reflected the fact that the liabilities were offset by income from sub-leasing activities and the realisation from time to time of the residual value of the aircraft through either the sale or re-leasing of that aircraft. Where income was not expected to fully match the liabilities, however, provisions were made. The overall provision established (which also included elements for site closures and rationalisation) was, at that time, the largest ever made by a UK corporate.

On the organisational side British Aerospace also reorganised a combined manufacturing/leasing business into separate businesses with their own focus with the creation of a specific asset management business.

The asset management business was established with a three-stage business plan – the so-called "three steps to heaven".

Phase one: Get the idle aircraft assets performing by offering keenly priced but shorter-term leases and by extending leases on imminent aircraft returns.

Phase two: Improve the lease rates, secure better quality leases (in terms of duration and value) and attract new quality customers to the portfolio through – among other things – the delivery of manufacturer support programmes to enhance the reputation of the aircraft with operators and to underpin the operating costs.

Phase three: Gradual, but planned, disposal of the aircraft in the portfolio through conventional asset sales or the sale of the lease receivables where appropriate.

Since 1993 this strategy has been implemented methodically and efficiently and phases one and two were largely implemented for the jet portfolio by the end of 1995 and for the turboprop portfolio in 1998. Phase three commenced in 1996.

In the process the team built the skills and tools of an aircraft leasing business from scratch. Realistic modelling and evaluation of customer revenue commitments provided the appropriate information for placement decisions. The creation of aircraft inspection and credit protocols plus the development of databases to monitor the aircraft portfolio created sustainable business processes. It has developed and refined its marketing, portfolio management, technical, financial and commercial techniques to industry-leading standards.

The result is that the jet portfolio now consists of quality airlines like Qantas, KLM UK, Air Canada Commuter, Aer Lingus, British European Airways, British Regional, Cityflyer and Eurowings. In six years the business has negotiated in excess of 260 new leases and lease extensions of the jet portfolio, giving a measure of the transaction-intensive nature of aircraft management activity.

Despite the more acute difficulties of the turboprop market the turboprop portfolio has made considerable progress. A three-year programme to stabilise the turboprop portfolio was completed in 1998 with the reduction in the idle fleet to only 31 aircraft out of a total turboprop portfolio of nearly 380 aircraft.[3]

The impressive asset management record now includes the successful management of over 1,000 individual leasing contracts and more than 150 sales. According to Airline Business February 2002 the asset management organisation is the world's

❏ Second largest regional jet aircraft portfolio servicer by fleet size and value (see Figures 2 and 3).
❏ Second largest turboprop aircraft portfolio servicer by fleet size and value (see Figures 4 and 5).
❏ Eighth largest jet aircraft portfolio servicer by fleet size (see Figure 6).[4]

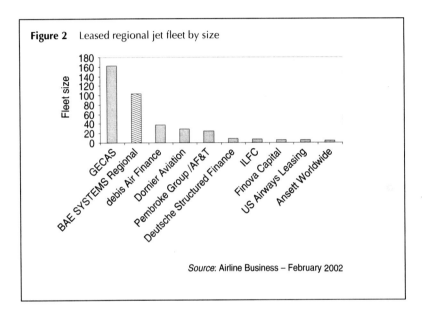

Figure 2   Leased regional jet fleet by size

Source: Airline Business – February 2002

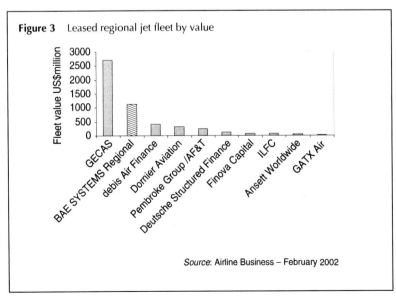

Figure 3   Leased regional jet fleet by value

Source: Airline Business – February 2002

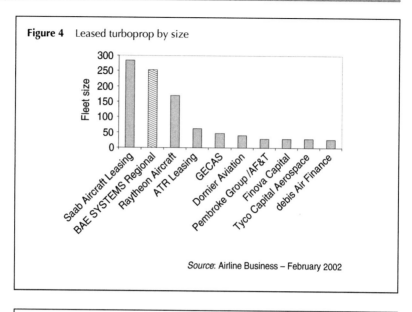

Figure 4 Leased turboprop by size

Source: Airline Business – February 2002

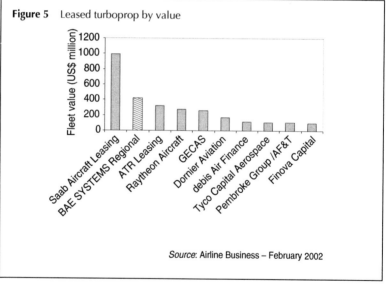

Figure 5 Leased turboprop by value

Source: Airline Business – February 2002

STRATEGIES CONSIDERED FOR MINIMISING THE RISK

As the portfolio became more balanced and its performance more predictable, BAE SYSTEMS started to explore options to remove any residual
volatility in the portfolio linked to external factors beyond its control and to
remove contingent liability exposure from its financial statements. To do so
would mean that BAE SYSTEMS' shareholders and future strategic alliance

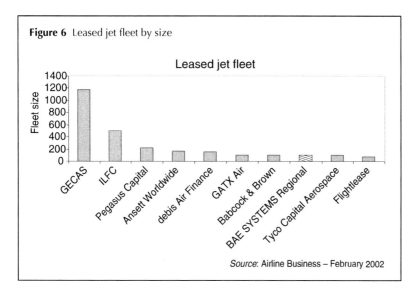

Figure 6 Leased jet fleet by size

Source: Airline Business – February 2002

parties need no longer concern themselves with the position that British Aerospace had faced in the early 1990s when the company as a whole had been threatened by the potential exposure in relation to its regional aircraft support obligations.

A number of alternatives were explored as to how best to eliminate, insure or hedge this exposure. This process started in 1996 with the establishment of a small team to investigate the feasibility of a block transaction in the financial markets to transfer the bulk of the risk in a single transaction, subject to acceptable cost. The author of this chapter was a member of that risk transfer team.

A full securitisation was ultimately ruled out for the following reasons.

❏ It required ownership of the assets to be transferred into a bankruptcy remote vehicle, which would have meant the early termination of a significant number of tax leases, and this would have been prohibitively expensive.
❏ The securitisation structure would be required to handle residual value guarantees or put options which allow the airlines to sell the aircraft back to BAE SYSTEMS at a given price and time.
❏ The securitisation structure would be required to handle a large number of US leveraged leases in which the aircraft is owned by a trust who is looking to realise the residual value itself to meet the desired economics of the deal for the equity party.
❏ BAE SYSTEMS was not looking upon the transaction as a capital or fund-raising exercise but rather as a way of transferring risk and eliminating any residual concerns with its regional aircraft portfolio.

❏ The complexity of the transaction caused concern over the timescale to transact and the fact this would lead to greater uncertainty of completion.

The team then considered a "virtual" or "synthetic" securitisation using the capital markets which would leave the ownership structures in place. Under this alternative, BAE SYSTEMS would enter into a risk transfer contract whereby if the amount of sublease income is less than a certain pre-determined amount, then BAE SYSTEMS could make a claim for the difference in order to meet its financing obligations under the structures used to finance the aircraft (as detailed in the history section of this chapter). In effect the risk transfer contract would have been structured to guarantee a certain pre-determined level of aircraft sublease income over the term of the risk transfer contract. The aggregate sublease income to have been guaranteed would have been used to determine the aggregate amount of funds that would have been raised from the capital market.

Whilst such a "virtual" or "synthetic" securitisation alternative met more of the team's initial criteria, the pricing was very high compared with a third alternative that was evolving. This third alternative had a number of advantages and in 1997 BAE SYSTEMS decided to pursue a risk transfer structure through the insurance markets.

FINANCIAL RISK INSURANCE PROGRAMME (FRIP)

BAE SYSTEMS approached the RISConsulting Group (RISConsulting) to evaluate the potential for developing an insurance programme to transfer the contingent liability risk.[5] RISConsulting proposed that a sophisticated financial model of the portfolio be developed and that the model be used to structure and price the insurance programme. The concept was tested with a select number of insurers and with Marsh & McLennan (Marsh) who brokered the transaction before the model building and transaction structuring began in earnest.

The structure using the insurance markets had a number of key advantages:

❏ it would be flexible in its application – BAE SYSTEMS could continue to actively manage the portfolio. For instance, it could sell aircraft when appropriate;
❏ it would be significantly less expensive than a capital markets solution;
❏ it did not involve an expensive rating process and on-going credit rating. (A shadow rating was sought for the least risky capacity layer, for the capacity providers' own capital adequacy purposes);
❏ the existing financing structures could remain in place; and
❏ it could handle the residual value guarantees or put options.

The insurance programme, which was given the name "financial risk insurance programme" or FRIP, was closed in October 1998. BAE SYSTEMS worked with its broker Marsh and RISConsulting as technical advisor and a number of highly-rated insurers based in Europe, North America and Bermuda to secure a risk transfer of approximately £2.2 billion. At the time of its completion, the FRIP was the largest alternative risk transfer (ART) transaction ever concluded.

The FRIP policy consisted of almost 550 aircraft, all BAE SYSTEMS manufactured, approximately 450 of which were leased aircraft and the balance of which were option aircraft with residual value guarantees and put option agreements.[6] It has an effective term of 15 years and is a non-cancellable, irrevocable policy – well outside insurance market norms at the time. The core strategy behind the FRIP transaction is to reduce volatility by smoothing the impact of unexpected market or industry-specific events over a long period of time and over a diversified portfolio of assets.

The FRIP provided a BAE SYSTEMS first loss retention amounting to 10% of the total portfolio. This retention was designed, among other things, to ensure that BAE SYSTEMS would continue to manage the fleet in such a way as to maximise value to protect the insurers from downside and, to a lesser extent, give insurers comfort that there was an alignment of interests between the parties.

Based on the output of the model, BAE SYSTEMS and the insurers agreed an aggregate limit of income from the portfolio to be protected over the term of the programme which took into account the cyclical nature of the regional aircraft business. The factor-based model developed by RISConsulting incorporated a rigorous analysis of historical regional aircraft price, income and cost data and a multi-layered Monte Carlo simulation approach to estimate the mean value of portfolio income and the distribution of income values around the mean. The model therefore measured the size and the likelihood of possible losses to the portfolio as a result of potential movements in the values of fundamental economic variables (eg, GDP growth rates and inflation rates) and industry variables (eg, lease term, lease rates, turnaround costs and downtime for aircraft) which affect regional aircraft values and income. Three independent, expert, external aircraft appraisal firms provided future lease rate projections that were used to establish a marketable basis for the future lease rates used in the model. An independent model review was carried out by KPMG who conducted a thorough audit of the functioning of the model.

The FRIP covers not only income associated with the portfolio of leased aircraft but also potential income relating to some 100+ aircraft where residual value guarantees or put options had been granted. The model was constructed to enable it to determine the potential market value underlying a residual value guarantee or put option at the date it could be exercised. If the option was in the money, the guarantee was assumed to have been called. The aircraft was simulated to have been put back to BAE SYSTEMS. If the option was out of the money, it was assumed that the guarantee lapsed and the aircraft was not put back to BAE SYSTEMS.

The FRIP guaranteed that if the actual income earned by the portfolio was less than a defined portfolio income by an amount exceeding the BAE SYSTEMS retention, the insurers would pay the difference. The defined portfolio income was set at policy inception to be equal to the mean value of the portfolio produced by running a simulation involving several thousand iterations of the model. Should subsequent actual income have over-performed against the defined portfolio income the insurers would be repaid any previous claims.

For the transaction to work it was essential that the on-going management and maintenance of the aircraft and the re-deployment of aircraft at the end of their lease terms would be conducted with the highest standards of care and professionalism. The insurers needed to get comfortable with BAE SYSTEMS' ability to continue to service the portfolio. To do this the insurers carried out due diligence by reviewing BAE SYSTEMS' processes and procedures, seeking information on past and current performance and meeting the management and operational staff in the asset management organisation. The insurers also employed their own industry adviser during this process.

The standard of servicing is a contractual obligation of BAE SYSTEMS and a servicing agreement was put in place which was based on market standard servicing agreements used in other aircraft securitisations. The servicer standard creates mechanisms to ensure BAE SYSTEMS' ongoing compliance with a defined level of service.

All the risks of the operating lease business are covered by the policy except for a few very limited exclusions, which by their nature were already covered by other policies or were entirely within the control of BAE SYSTEMS itself.

For BAE SYSTEMS the FRIP accomplished the following:

❑ It transferred lease income risk thereby underpinning its financial exposure to its regional aircraft portfolio.
❑ It allowed it to re-present the note to the accounts detailing the contingent liabilities.[7] (Endnote 7 shows the note to the annual report for 1998, the year of completion of the FRIP. This endnote also provides the previous year figures thus enabling the reader to see the re-presentation which the FRIP made possible.)
❑ It covered regional aircraft assets with a policy backed by insurance companies to a credit rating level not less than AA- (with some 63% underwritten by AAA insurers).
❑ Once understood there was a positive impact on the perception of BAE SYSTEMS within the financial and investor community. The contingent

liabilities had always been a difficult exposure to describe to analysts. Under the FRIP, BAE SYSTEMS transferred the risk and insured this exposure thereby ensuring that BAE SYSTEMS' future could not be threatened by one or a series of major adverse events affecting the value of the regional aircraft portfolio.

❏ It meant that the financial exposure to the regional aircraft portfolio was not an issue for discussion with future strategic alliance partners.

In completing the FRIP, BAE SYSTEMS developed an innovative risk management programme which represented a prudent and successful wholesale transfer of its financial liabilities on its historic portfolio of regional aircraft.

SAAB FRIP

As an example of how best practice can be employed, in 1999 Saab AB (a leading European manufacturer in the defence, aerospace and technologies industry) approached BAE SYSTEMS (a 35% shareholder) to investigate a FRIP solution for its portfolio of some 300 Saab 340 and Saab 2000 leased regional aircraft

Saab had created a financial provision in 1997 whereby the income from the portfolio was not expected to match liabilities and these liabilities were set out in a note to its accounts. The portfolio was serviced by Saab Aircraft Leasing AB. The major aspects of a successful risk transfer trans-action were therefore in place – that is an ongoing, professional management of the assets and the alignment of interest among the parties.

In November 2000 a FRIP was successfully closed for Saab AB. The insurance cover guaranteed income of US $1.17 billion after Saab's 10% first loss obligations. BAE SYSTEMS advised Saab AB on the transaction with Marsh acting as broker and RISConsulting as the technical advisor.

In the two weeks following the announcement of the Saab FRIP Saab's share price rose from 65SKr to 79SKr, an increase of over 20%, representing US$135 million in increased market value.[8] The movement of the Saab share price compared to that of the S&P500 Aerospace Defence Price Index over a two-month period prior to the announcement of the FRIP and over a seven-month period post the announcement is shown in Figure 7.

From Saab AB's perspective the deal was self-financing.

SYSTEMS 2001 ASSET TRUST

Having completed the FRIP, BAE SYSTEMS had isolated the performance of its portfolio of regional aircraft from lease income and asset value risk in the regional aircraft market. However, the FRIP did not address the financing requirements of the FRIP portfolio. BAE SYSTEMS was still responsible for funding the shortfall with the FRIP supporting its obligations to pay the head lease financings or the residual value guarantees it had written.

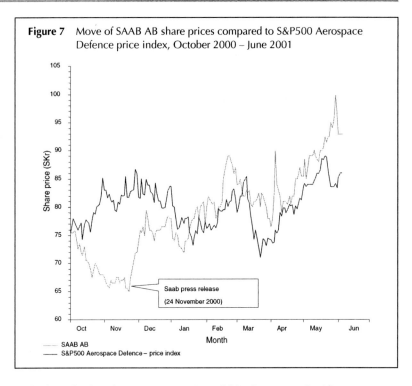

Figure 7   Move of SAAB AB share prices compared to S&P500 Aerospace Defence price index, October 2000 – June 2001

As described in the opening section of this chapter, a significant proportion of the financing of the portfolio was provided by banks lending through medium-term credit facilities guaranteed by BAE SYSTEMS. These medium-term credit facilities were not matched to the life of the assets and would therefore require to be re-financed over such a period, the so-called "re-financing risk". Also, whilst the FRIP covered the future lease income of the aircraft which had been put back to BAE SYSTEMS under residual value guarantees which had been called, it did not pre-fund BAE SYSTEMS' obligations to pay the residual value to the holder of the guarantee or put option.

Thus BAE SYSTEMS' credit capacity was continuing to be used for assets it had manufactured over the last 20 years and hence such capacity was not being used to secure new business opportunities in its core business as a systems company. As a result, BAE SYSTEMS looked to develop a structure which would efficiently recycle this credit capacity for use elsewhere in its business. The motivation was funding diversification. If the capital markets could fund its vendor finance portfolio of regional aircraft, BAE SYSTEMS could use its bank lines for other things. The structure would be required to ensure the continued off-balance sheet treatment of the aircraft.

What BAE SYSTEMS was looking to do was to complete the second leg of a two-phase exercise. The FRIP underpinned the future rental income assumptions on the aircraft portfolio and now it wanted to refinance those aircraft with amortising-matched financing freeing its bank lines once again for alternative use.

As already described, the underlying regional aircraft portfolio is financed through various different structures out of various jurisdictions, which were incorporated in three different portfolios. Consolidating the financing on these three portfolios in a way that enabled BAE SYSTEMS to achieve its objective of refinancing on a long-term basis to better match cashflows of the underlying assets was extremely complicated.

Nevertheless, in June 2001, BAE SYSTEMS successfully closed SYS-TEMS 2001 Asset Trust, a landmark-structured bond transaction, for approximately US$2.1 billion.

SYSTEMS 2001 Asset Trust securitised the lease receivables from the portfolio of regional aircraft lessees, refinanced existing BAE SYSTEMS guaranteed debt facilities and pre-funded obligations that BAE SYSTEMS has in respect of the residual value guarantees or put options.

The transaction which was lead managed by Salomon Smith Barney is essentially structured and secured on BAE SYSTEMS' credit risk. The rating on the US$883 million junior tranche was capped at BAE SYSTEMS' rating of A, but as a result of the security the US$1.189 billion senior bond was rated in the AA region before being raised to AAA rating by a wrap from AAA monoline bond insurer MBIA.

The structure incorporates a pool of unencumbered aircraft which at the outset of the transaction amounted to 89 aircraft which were previously debt-funded through the medium-term credit facilities now refinanced as a result of SYSTEMS 2001 Asset Trust. These aircraft formed a collateral pool which, for the purposes of the rating agencies and the wrap provider, MBIA, drive the loan-to-value ratio throughout the life of the transaction. This collateral pool is dynamic because as aircraft come to the end of their head lease financings, they would in many instances be placed into the structure as part of the collateral pool.[9] As time goes on, if aircraft on which BAE SYSTEMS has given residual value guarantees are returned, these would also be available to be added into the collateral pool.

The deal's primary obligor is BAE SYSTEMS. If it suffers losses, BAE SYSTEMS itself can then claim under the FRIP. The transaction does not transfer the FRIP to the capital markets.

The transaction was heavily over-subscribed with some US$9 billion of orders taken. The senior bond, the AAA rated G note, has a 6.9 year average life, a maturity of September 2013 and was priced at 6.664% or 150 basis points (bp) over Treasuries. The junior bond, the A rated B note, has an average life of seven years and a maturity of December 2011 and was priced at 7.156% or 200bp over treasuries. The bonds were all fixed-rate although swaps were put in place to hedge the floating element of the portfolio back into fixed.

THE FINAL STEP

BAE SYSTEMS regional aircraft business had been affected very significantly by the commercial aerospace market downturn post the events of 11 September, 2001. A rationalisation programme was announced in November 2001 which included the cessation of regional jet production. The measures announced draw a line under the company's exposure to regional jet manufacturing and the financial risks inherent in the regional aircraft market. The company's focus in the regional aircraft market in the future is primarily in providing full support for all its in-service regional aircraft.

CONCLUSION

This case study demonstrates how the application of a prudent and successful strategy can remove the potential risks to a company of one, or even a series of, major adverse events affecting the value of a portfolio of assets

In developing these sophisticated financial products to resolve a legacy which had required British Aerospace to take the largest UK corporate provision ever at that time, BAE SYSTEMS has now gained a reputation for being an innovator in the provision of financial solutions.

In the UK we have witnessed the growth of defence capability procurement through financial mechanisms such as public private partnership (PPP) and private finance initiative (PFI). In view of these developments BAE SYSTEMS core defence markets will increasingly need access to private sector financing. This has opened up new opportunities for BAE SYSTEMS with its proven track record in developing groundbreaking structured finance products and in January 2002 BAE SYSTEMS Capital (a wholly-owned subsidiary) was established to respond to BAE SYSTEMS' customers' long-term needs by offering them a new range of solutions together with innovative financing opportunities.

BAE SYSTEMS Capital will be backed by the full resources of BAE SYSTEMS, which will allow it to act as a highly credible originator and manager of financing transactions for BAE SYSTEMS' customers.

1 In November 1999, British Aerospace merged with Marconi Electronic Systems and was renamed BAE SYSTEMS. Though manufacturing and engineering remained at the heart of the company, the platforms themselves had become less important as the evolution of the systems they housed had become the dominant factor in the selection and acquisition of defence equipment. Defence contracts are now awarded to those who can demonstrate the ability to act as the 'system prime' contractor managing the integration of the systems and their platform host – be it an aircraft, a ship, a submarine or a military satellite. This paradigm shift in the market was reflected in the company by a complete restructuring and re-alignment of its businesses and the re-definition of its name and corporate image.

2 After a major downturn in the global civil aerospace market post the events of 11 September, 2001 BAE SYSTEMS announced its decision to cease regional jet manufacture.

3 Recent events have caused the number to increase but the robustness of the processes in

place have meant that the organisation continues to manage its business to drive the maximum value whilst minimising the risks.

4   Source: **Airline Business**, 2002, "The Game Changes", February, pp. 46–52.
5   RISConsulting have contributed a chapter to this book in which they write about economic modelling for lease aircraft fleets.
6   At the commencement of the FRIP there were in fact a very small number of non-British Aerospace-manufactured aircraft. These aircraft were financed using US leveraged lease structures. They had originally entered the portfolio when British Aerospace assumed the position of head lessee/sub lessor as part of transactions in which British Aerospace placed its own manufactured aircraft on lease. The aircraft have now been returned to the owner at the end of the US leveraged lease term and as a result they have exited the portfolio.
7   "Note 20 Commercial Aircraft Financing.

Commercial aircraft are frequently sold for cash with the manufacturer retaining some financial exposure. Aircraft financing commitments of the BAE SYSTEMS Group can be categorised as either direct or indirect. Direct commitments arise where the Group has sold the aircraft to a third-party lessor and then leased it back under an operating lease (or occasionally a finance lease) prior to an onward lease to an operator. Indirect commitments (contingent liabilities) may arise where the Group has sold aircraft to third parties who either operate the aircraft themselves or lease the aircraft on to operators. In these cases the Group may give guarantees in respect of the residual values of the related aircraft or certain head lease and finance payments to be made by either the third parties or the operators. The Group's exposure to these commitments is offset by future lease rentals and the residual value of the related aircraft.

During 1998, an external review was commissioned of the likely income to be generated from the portfolio of aircraft to which the Group has either direct or indirect financing exposures. This review identified a most likely level of income of some £2.4 billion. Following this analysis, in September 1998, the Group entered into arrangements which have reduced its exposure from commercial aircraft financing by obtaining insurance cover from a syndicate of leading insurance companies over a significant proportion of the contracted and expected income stream from the aircraft portfolio including those aircraft where the Group has provided residual value guarantees. At the start of the insurance arrangements a minimum level of income of £2.2 billion was underwritten.

As a consequence the net exposure of the Group to aircraft financing has been reduced by the insured amount and as at 31 December, 1998 was:

	1998 £m	1997 £m
Direct operating lease commitments	854	1,012
Direct finance lease commitments	6	8
Indirect exposure through aircraft contingent liabilities	1,481	1,530
Exposure to residual value guarantees	504	420
Income guaranteed through insurance arrangements	(2,053)	–
Net exposure	792	2970
Expected income not covered by insurance arrangements	(43)	(2,253)
Expected income on aircraft delivered post insurance arrangements	(99)	–
Adjustment to net present value	(160)	(181)
Recourse provisions	490	536

Income guaranteed through insurance arrangements represents the future income stream from the aircraft assets guaranteed under the insurance arrangements after deducting the policy excess.

The external review identified likely income of £250 million above the level guaranteed under the insurance arrangements. *Expected income not covered by insurance arrangements and on aircraft delivered post insurance arrangements* represents the amount of this income assumed by management for the purpose of provisioning.

Given the long-term nature of the liabilities, the directors believe it is appropriate to state the recourse provision at its net present value. The provision covers costs to be incurred over a forecast period of 14 years from the balance sheet date. The *adjustment to net present value* reduces the expected liabilities from their outturn amounts to their anticipated net present value."

8   SKr = Swedish Kroner.

9   This would not be possible for aircraft financed on US leveraged leases for reasons explained earlier.

21

Private Equity Capital Guarantee Structures

Gabriele Zeindler*

Swiss Re Credit Solutions & Asset Re

This chapter examines the principal protection of alternative assets, and in particular of private equity. We begin by looking at how these assets can be principal protected, be it in the form of insurance (risk transfer) or in other capital guarantee forms. We then discuss the obstacles for an investor to enter private equity and how they can be addressed by structured products. We then give an overview of the developments and publicly announced transactions so far, and of other possible new products. Finally, we conclude by explaining the different forms of principal protections or capital guarantees and then compare the risk behaviour of the insurance of, or investment in, private equity.

SECURITISATION AND INSURITISATION

The financial and insurance industries are in the process of convergence. Whilst for the retail segment this has happened by combining the distribution channels of banking and insurance products (especially life insurance), the convergence in the industrial area has taken the route of transferring insurance risks into the capital markets using financial markets techniques (securitisation). Securitisation has created a product-based linkup between the insurance and the capital markets, and has gained recognition largely in the form of catastrophe (cat) bonds. These are used to transfer insurance risks such as Californian earthquakes, US windstorm or weather risks to the capital market, in exchange for a comparatively high return for the investor, and a low correlation to its existing investment portfolio. (See Murray, 1998; Croson and Kunreuther, 1999; DeFontaine, 2001.)

It is also possible to make use of insurance techniques for capital market risks (insuritisation). The core competence of insurance is the

---

* The opinions expressed herein are solely the ones of the author and do not represent the opinion of Swiss Re.

diversification of non-systematic risk. Therefore, the main prerequisites for this technique are alternative assets as insurable objects. These are assets which have special characteristics such as illiquidity, a high degree of diversifiability, limited systematic risk and a high level of individual volatility. These requirements are met by, amongst others, private equity/venture capital as well as hedge funds, real estate, intellectual property, brands, etc.

Alternative assets typically show significant financial inefficiencies, and in addition have a number of characteristics which render financial market risk management techniques unreliable. The introduction of insurance strategies in the form of "insuritisation" provides a competitive alternative. Insuritisation consists of the construction of equilibrated portfolios, of diversification of the basis risk of such portfolios against other risk classes, and of smoothing the remaining risk.

ALTERNATIVE ASSETS
Definition and classes

Alternative assets are considered to be alternative (in comparison to traditional stock and bond investments) because they strive for absolute rather than relative rates of return. (See Alford, 2001; Grunbilcher, Graf and Gruber, 2001.) In addition, such investments are not normally listed and, therefore, are not liquid. They often include a premium for such illiquidity.

Besides the sometimes exciting returns that can be expected from such investments, these asset classes involve a good deal of specialised expertise, and sometimes even a closeness to the investment object (in the case of real estate and private equity investments) which are appreciated by many investors. Such alternative assets show a different risk/return pattern from traditional investments, and help to diversify existing asset portfolios by adding lowly correlated assets over longer time periods (see Figure 1).

Demand for structured products

Concurrent to the industry convergence, both the interest in alternative asset investing and the demand for protected investments is increasing rapidly (see Goldman Sachs, 2001; Standard & Poor's Structured Finance, 2002) due to a broad market, driven by investors such as pension funds, life insurance companies, corporations, etc, as well as the everyday private investor. Obviously, the interest in alternative assets and the demand for guarantees are tightly linked. Therefore, the potential to structure and deliver solutions in this market segment is significant.

In addition, the regulatory environment plays an important role in determining the portfolio allocation of alternative assets within each country.[1] In some instances, principal protection allows investors to change the asset allocation towards high performance asset classes within the given investment criteria (with a structured product he receives a highly rated

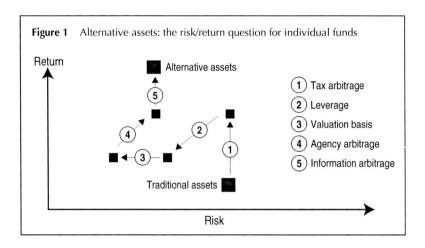

Figure 1 Alternative assets: the risk/return question for individual funds

Return

Alternative assets

5

2

4

1

3

Traditional assets

Risk

1. Tax arbitrage
2. Leverage
3. Valuation basis
4. Agency arbitrage
5. Information arbitrage

security instead of having to show "risky" private equity investments), or alternatively allows the creation of higher leverage on an investment portfolio than otherwise possible (if, for example, a portfolio is sold and wrapped with a highly rated insurer which results in a direct risk capital relief of the seller, while income streams such as asset management fee remain with him). In other situations, structured transactions can lead to an alternative accounting, and thereby alternative treatment, of existing portfolios, with the respective capital arbitrage or tax optimisation.

In the area of asset management, the addition of alternative assets in the form of structured products allows a broadening of the client base by including investors that are otherwise regulated or restricted in their investments in alternative assets.

PRIVATE EQUITY
The investor
In the past, private equity constantly outperformed public equity and showed rather moderate correlations with traditional investments (see Axa, 2001; EIMS, 2002). This makes it an interesting asset class, however it has a number of disadvantages that make it difficult for a "normal" investor to enter private equity. Some of the specific aspects include (see *Structured Finance International*, 2001):

❑ high upfront investments needed (usually between US$1 to 5 million requested);
❑ this leads to a low diversification unless an investor has the capital to invest in many different partnerships or single investments; the investor has to commit himself; subsequently, it takes one to four years before such "commitments" are drawn and actually invested in private equity;

❑ this time lag leads to a low investment level – to increase this, the investor will have to drive a special "overcommitment strategy": more commitments are made than actual funds are available; a special steering process is needed;

❑ the capital is bound for several years until returns ("distributions") flow back;

❑ very limited liquidity (secondary market);

❑ private equity needs a high degree of specialised expertise about players, markets, new developments and expected future developments: for an investor, it is almost impossible to follow more than a few industry segments, therefore, he may concentrate on some specific industries which again has a negative impact on the diversification;

❑ administration: the tracking of private equity investments with regard to commitments, draw downs, distributions, and the valuation of the investments require significant administrational effort; and

❑ new investors may have difficulty in entering worthwhile partnerships as they are sometimes locked (see Lerner, 2000).

The asset manager

For structuring alternative asset transactions, the (re)insurer works very closely with the private equity specialists that want to set-up such insuritised transactions, for example, investment banks with proprietary private equity books and (usually smaller) asset managers specialising in this asset class. Both need to have clear investment processes, a good track record and an efficient operational set up, that, depending whether it is a fund or a fund of funds, specialises at partnership level or at single investment level, all of which is verified in a detailed due diligence process.

It is on this level that the information asymmetry that is inherent in the whole private equity world is of highest importance. For every new investment, the possible investees (partnerships or single investments) are under scrutiny, due diligence processes are exercised, exit strategies are discussed, and the administration, which is considerable in private equity, is organised.

During the lifetime of the insuritised product, the asset manager, be it exclusively or together with a co-manager, is responsible for picking the best investments and making the product a success. Whereas a traditional asset manager with superior skills does not beat the index, alternative asset managers can create considerable economic value by exploiting the asymmetric information. Due to the crucial role of the asset manager in the whole set-up, the (re)insurer usually performs a due diligence process on the set-up, legal framework, and operation and risk management, in addition to the structural elements that are built into the transaction itself (eg, alignment of interest or key person clauses, etc).

The (re)insurer

The (re)insurer's goal is to build diversified portfolios of the alternative asset class: better diversification lowers the downside risk as well as the risk capital that has to be underpinned on every risk class (see Figure 2).

Considering the overall diversification of big (re)insurance companies, such portfolios include, in the non-life area, insurance lines such as accident, aviation, business interruption, credit insurance, engineering, fire, liability, hail crop, marine, motor and property insurance. In addition, life and health business and natural catastrophe business add to the diversification.

On the other side of the balance sheet, the (re)insurer has additional exposure from his own investments. Private equity, with its moderate correlation to the existing investment portfolio, adds to the diversification of the (re)insurer. Additionally, structured products in this area add to the convergence of the two industries, banking and insurance. Due to the (as yet) limited availability of insurance capacity and the novelty of the structured solutions, the (re)insurer's remuneration is interesting.

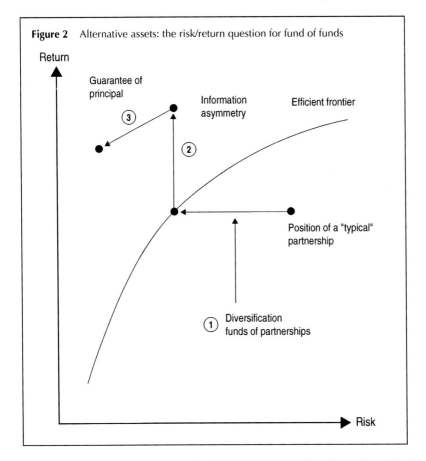

Figure 2   Alternative assets: the risk/return question for fund of funds

STRUCTURING AND INSURITISATION OF PRIVATE EQUITY TRANSACTIONS

The term "structuring" includes a wide variety of expertise, details and negotiation that are built into new products. Normally, a clarification of the needs and goals of partner/client and desired product is the first step in starting a transaction. For example, it makes a major difference to the structure whether it will be addressing German retail investors or US life insurers and pension funds. The addressee and the relevant legal, tax and accounting environment have a direct influence on the structure, including the duration. These factors also determine whether the capital all has to be paid in at the beginning, or whether a security needs to be listed, or rated, or whether a coupon is required, where and how special purpose vehicles (SPVs) have to be set up, who the equity holders will be, whether it is an open ended (evergreen) or closed-end product, etc. Additional features such as the placement need and power, a possible overcommitment structure, or possible combinations of asset classes etc, need to be considered. These concepts lead into the first and theoretical calculation of risk and return for all involved parties. Subsequently, the structure is changed until the risk/return patterns look as favourable as possible to all involved parties.

The specialities of private equity have to be known in depth in order to make optimal use of its diversification possibilities and effects. Therefore, analyses and observations are made about different investment stages (such as *early stage* (venture capital), *later stage/growth, middle market* (including buy-outs), *mature and distressed* (including *special situations, turnarounds, mezzanine, distressed debt*)), different geographies, different industries (information technology, life sciences, biotechnology, energy, transportation etc) based on data from the past. The behaviour is measured with regard to expected return, volatility, dispersion, correlation and shortfall.

In a further step, specific issues like the commitments that are made to a partnership and the respective drawdowns, usually with a time lag of one to four years, and the impact on the forecasted liquidity of the vehicle are considered. In addition, the expected returns and distributions of each different sub-class in private equity, which differ in expected amounts and time, are modelled.

All this data provides the (re)insurer with the background to model the asset class, to come up with the appropriate insurance premium, to provide investment guidelines for the vehicle ("top-down approach") and to give investment advice with regard to such a top-down approach, also with regard to the overcommitment strategy, to asset managers.

The investment guidelines have to be adhered to for the lifetime of the insured product. They not only provide the (re)insurer with the comfort that the loss expectation decreases due to the diversification, they are also essential for any investor that counts on the diversification effect of such a product in comparison to its existing investment book.

The investment guidelines include:

❏ an upper limitation per partnership investment;
❏ a minimum number of partnerships;
❏ allocation minimum and maximum in terms of geography, industry, investment stage (style in hedge funds); and
❏ provisions in regards to listed/exchange traded companies, vintage years, etc.

A second pillar in the structuring is the reporting which is crucial due to the fact that such structured transactions have usually quite a long lifetime. The reporting requirements are as follows (for private equity reporting requirements see EVCA, 2002):

❏ on the investments: at least quarterly, providing a thorough analysis of the portfolio and the investments, particularly their performance, along with decisions to add or liquidate investments;
❏ on the risk: at least quarterly, providing a statistical analysis on the portfolio with specific emphasis on volatility, correlation and draw downs; and
❏ on the portfolio development: at least quarterly, reporting any shift in strategy, monitoring market and industry events that might have an adverse impact on the portfolio. For example, a readjustment of the mix of style, in the case of hedge funds, at least once a year. Also, style drift control reports (private equity and hedge funds).

There are other structural elements to consider, for example, the (re)insurer might want to achieve an alignment of interest: all parties would be interested in having a product that is doing well, but also all parties have to be aligned in case things go wrong. This alignment can be achieved by a variety of structural elements, such as retentions that have to be carried by the partners, setting part of the management fee aside (in a trust account as a first-loss cushion), building finite (re)insurance layers, or linking other forms of remuneration to the development of the product, for example the upside participation of asset manager and insurer. Another element is the mitigation right of the (re)insurer in case certain thresholds are not met.

ACHIEVEMENTS THROUGH INSURITISED TRANSACTIONS
Investor's side
Guaranteed bond
The investor in an insuritised private equity product benefits in a variety of ways. In the case of private equity, the investor receives an insured product in the form of a bond (the rating being based on the rating of the (re)insurer) which has a low correlation with his remaining investment

portfolio. Even smaller investors benefit from the wide diversification of the underlying private equity investment portfolio to which they have access. Nevertheless, the investor can expect to earn the customary returns on private equity investments, since the risk is transferred by a genuine risk transfer arrangement. He therefore, has no downside risk, but still almost all of the upside.

In addition to a relatively low correlation with his other investment portfolio, the investor reaps further benefits from the insured private equity bonds. Generally, high minimum investments are required from private equity investors before they can participate as limited partners in a private equity partnership. In the case of a bond, however, small denominations are quite common. This provides small investors with access to (insured) private equity investments.

Another characteristic of private equity is its lack of liquidity. Once the commitments are made, the investor might find it difficult to sell his participation prior to the occurrence of a natural exit. Depending on the particular stage of financing, the natural exit, which covers in particular Initial Public Offerings (IPOs), management buyouts and trade sales, could actually occur several years down the road. This problem can be best addressed by private equity securities being listed on a stock exchange, and by the corresponding market making, although reality shows that some of the exchange listed fund of funds vehicles trade at a discount and have limited liquidity.

Another advantage is the applicable tax exemption for capital gains for some forms of investments in various countries.

All these advantages (which are not all purely based on the existence of an insurance protection, but can also be achieved by "normal" structures) are of course counterbalanced by the price of the insurance protection as well as the cost of the professional private equity management in fund of funds structures.

Fund investments
Most investors consider carefully the advantages/disadvantages of direct fund investments against fund of funds vehicles. For example, direct fund investments result in a series of expenses. These include the cost of a careful selection of the best partnerships with background checks of all involved parties; investments and their interim valuations must be dealt with administratively – which generally involves considerable expense in the case of private equity. In addition, the investor usually needs to consider further portfolio issues, including not only the various forms of diversification (geographic, market segment, etc) but also the various financing stages, business segments, and effective cashflow positions (draw downs vs distributions). Moreover, a possible credit line will have to be made available if an overcommitment strategy is directly pursued. Even if

an individual investor can fulfil these requirements in his areas of speciali-sation and with his specific expertise, this may become difficult in other geographic areas or business segments.

Asset manager's side

The demand is mostly driven by getting additional assets under manage-ment and by the respective remuneration as asset manager, which, in the case of principal protected products, normally is predefined for the period of the underlying transaction (which is between 7 and 15 years). In addi-tion, guaranteed products include a certain reputation protection for the asset manager; if everything goes wrong his investors get back at least their principal.

Other transactions cover special needs like capital relief on the balance sheet, or other aspects, as discussed further below. In addition, the reputa-tional side of issuing highly structured and innovative products may be interesting as well.

(Re)insurer's side

The innovative approach of creating a convergence between the insurance and the banking world, together with an attractive risk/return pattern, makes this kind of transaction strategically important. More importantly, however, is the exploitation of the insurer's diversification capability, and the better use of its risk capital which leads to a nearly infinite demand for guaranteed products in the area of alternative asset classes.

In addition, the complexity, the broad expertise base needed, the required pioneering spirit and endurance, but also the reward and public-ity received from in and outside the company, makes this area of business a welcome challenge for talented professionals.

PUBLICLY ANNOUNCED TRANSACTIONS
Princess Private Equity Holding Ltd

In June, 1999, Swiss Re announced the formation of a joint venture, Princess Private Equity Holding Ltd, between Swiss Reinsurance Company and Partners Group, a Zug-based investment management company. The Partners Group and Swiss Re hold 80.1% and 19.9% interest in the joint venture company, respectively (see Deutsche Bank, 1999; *Financial Times*, 1999; Schneider, 1999; Partners Group, 2002).

The Guernsey-based Princess Private Equity Holding Ltd issued US$700 million of convertible zero-coupon bonds with conversion rights into shares in the joint venture company as of January 1, 2007 until maturity at December 31, 2010.

The bonds were aimed at institutional investors, pension funds, other institutions and wealthy private persons predominantly in Switzerland and Germany. The small denomination of US$1000 also made the bond accessible for smaller investors. Through its listing on the Luxembourg and the Frankfurt Stock Exchange, a certain moderate liquidity is provided.

The proceeds of the bonds were invested in private equity funds with a particular focus on industry sectors such as high-tech, information technologies, life sciences, media, retail and financial services (excluding insurance and reinsurance) on a worldwide basis.

The fund is managed by a second joint venture, Princess Management & Insurance Ltd, where Swiss Re owns 49. 9% and Partners Group owns 50.1%. The management company is based in Guernsey and acts at the same time as insurance provider for Princess Holding. The insurance premium is 1. 5% pa on the net asset value (NAV).

During the conversion period from 2007 to 2010, the conversion prices start at US$100 in 2007 and are increased by 1.5% per year. Like this, the insurance premium of 1.5% pa on the NAV is paid indirectly by the investors that remain bondholders (and thus are protected by the insurance cover), in comparison to the bondholders that already have converted and, as shareholders of Princess Private Equity Holding Ltd, are not protected any longer.

Figure 3 shows the structure of the Princess transaction.

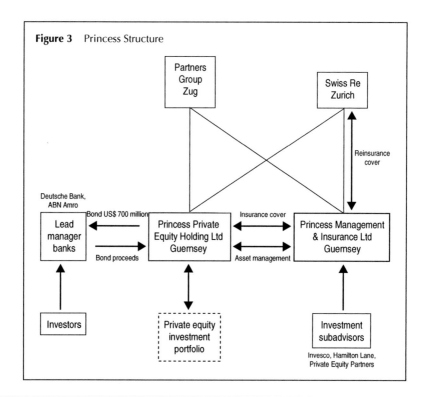

Figure 3   Princess Structure

Investments reflect advice given by investment subadvisors (Hamilton Lane, Invesco and the Partners Group). The overall diversification of the fund investments is maintained and ensured by investment guidelines that have to be adhered to by Princess.

ABN Amro Bank and Deutsche Bank were the lead banks in the placement and market making.

Investors in the bond are offered the security of an AAA-rated protection of the principal sum at maturity through reinsurance provided by Swiss Re.

The transaction was the first of its kind in relation to private equity/ venture capital and insurance, where the protection of the principal amount was secured by reinsurance and not by zero-coupon bonds structures nor a dynamic hedging approach as typically has been the case through the traditional financial markets.

In addition to the principal protection, Swiss Re, together with the Partners Group, developed an innovative top-down approach that involves the use of cashflow, risk-return and portfolio optimisation models. The goal of this approach was to create a regularly updated, forward-looking investment strategy that maximises return while minimising short-term and long-term volatility and reducing the correlation to the market.

Pearl Private Equity Holding Ltd

Pearl was the second transaction in the area of alternative asset reinsurance, with a first closing in September, 2000 (see Primack, 2001; Partners Group, 2002). Issuing €660 million in principal protected, 2% Coupon Convertible Bonds due 2010, the structure was quite similar to Princess, with the main exception that the 2% Coupon was guaranteed as well. The offering was made by DGZ Deka Bank, together with the Partners Group and others, and was insured by European International Reinsurance Ltd, Barbados, a Swiss Re subsidiary.

The main differences were, besides the currency and the coupon, the clients that were approached and the different ownership structure of the issuer.

Prime Edge Capital plc

Prime Edge, a €150 million private equity fund of funds collateralised debt obligation (CDO), was structured by Deutsche Bank, Allianz Risk Transfer and Capital Dynamics and closed in June, 2001. It is a twelve-year transaction with three tranches of notes and pays running coupons. (See Deutsche Bank, 2001; Primack, 2001; Standard & Poor's, 2001.)

While Princess was rated AAA(r) (the "r" standing for "principal only") and Pearl was rated AAA, both ratings were based on the unconditional insurance cover of Swiss Re and its affiliates.

The big achievement of Prime Edge however was to get a stand-alone rating from Standard & Poor's for each of the notes layers (obtaining BBB and A ratings). Allianz Risk Transfer facilitated the notes issuance through a financial guarantee of the senior notes and by providing a liquidity facility.

As can be seen by one of the following structures, the stand-alone rating of this transaction opened up the direct access to the financial market, independently of the availability of insurance capacity.

GFG Next Generation Fund

The next announcement was made in August, 2001 by Global Financial Group regarding a fund of funds structure that would purchase bonds with guaranteed investment principal if heid until maturity in thirty years. Guaranteed by AIG Financial Products, it was targeted to place up to US$1 billion of Zero Coupon Bonds (*Private Equity Analyst*, 2001).

Private Equity Partnership Structures I, LLC

The stand-alone credit ratings of Standard & Poor's opened up the market for securitisations of private equity structures. The first came in January, 2002, when AON Corporation announced a US$450 million securitisation of limited partnership investments and its associated limited partnership commitments. A main feature of this transaction is a relatively high equity tranche of the issuer. (See AON Corporation, 2001; *International Financing Review*, 2002; Kreutzer, 2002.)

According to Standard & Poor's, further transactions can be expected in the near future (Standard & Poor's Structured Finance, 2002). On the hedge fund side, however, CDO structures have already appeared in the US while in Europe, many major banks are structuring hedge fund collateralised debt obligations (Wolcott, 2002).

OTHER PRODUCTS

Besides the pure risk transfer structures of big fund of funds securitisations and insuritisations, there are other possible structures that more specifically address special features of the asset class, or solve specific issues of asset managers or investors. Outlined below are some possible structures; some of them are already in place, others are discussed in the market and within the company or are simply untested ideas, and are not yet in place.

Overcommitment insurance

Private equity commitments (promises to invest and provide capital by the investor) are normally drawn-down by fund managers over a term of four to five years. Simultaneously (under normal circumstances), during the same period, investors already receive some first distributions from their investments. Additionally, a certain fraction of the commitments are never drawn down and expire contractually after a certain period. This leaves private equity investors with the potential problem of significant underinvestment and consequential dilution issues.

In order to receive a high investment degree, many private equity investment vehicles commit more investments than they have available in cash. As commitments are drawn-down, cash distributions by the partnerships in the first vintage years serve to fund the commitments, which exceed the initial cash level (ie, the overcommitment). If take downs accelerate or distributions slow down, there is the inherent risk in such a strategy that there will not be sufficient cash available to respond to take down calls from the partnership.

In such circumstances, the fund manager might find it difficult to contract a credit line to finance such calls, as:

❏ investment vehicles do not present an interesting relationship for most commercial banks; and
❏ the quality of the collateral (ie, private equity limited partnership interest) is viewed critically at the same time.

Alternatively, sales in the secondary market will occur at distressed prices, will be only possible for quality partnerships and will seriously damage the vintage year diversification of the fund of funds. Contingent capital in the form of the overcommitment credit facility enhancement may be the right product for helping funds to conduct a risk-optimised commitment strategy. In addition, specialised consulting on the overcommitment strategy, that takes into account the expected draw down and payoff patterns, helps to optimise the capital allocation and risk and return on an overcommitted investment strategy.

Stable income instead of J-curve effect
Due to the lengthy development of private equity investments and the time delay until distributions flow back, the high upfront set-up cost lead to the so-called "J-curve effect". During the first one or two years there are no, or even negative, returns, but all the costs have to be written down. Therefore, the NAV usually drops below the initial capital amount. There are investors that would like to invest in the asset class, but who need to be able to show even, low but constant, positive returns. One way to address this issue is to create a product that exchanges volatile or insufficient returns against stable cashflows. The structure could be made in the form of a combination of long-term zero coupon bonds, risk transfer, finite risk and a swap.

CDO insurance wraps / CFO "Collateralised Fund Obligations"
Other structures focus on achieving more favourable regulatory treatment as opposed to gaining additional assets under management. In particular, the capital underpinning rules for private equity investments for US investment banks make such investments costly in terms of the risk capital

they require (see Securitization.net, 2002; Bank for International Settlements, 2001). With CDO structures, an existing private equity portfolio of an investment bank, for example, can be sold into an SPV that refinances itself with investors with a different risk appetite (ie, predefined interest rates on bonds financing the senior layers, from the first year on, instead of future uncertain private equity returns). Therefore, the portfolio is off-balance sheet of the seller. Because of the leverage, some of the returns on such portfolios are re-directed back to the original holder of the assets. Together with the respective capital relief, this leads to an enhanced return on equity.

Additional leverage can be created through the use of a highly rated insurance coverage provider. Insurance cover is provided to the SPV in the form of a protection of the senior layers. This leads to an enhanced credit quality of the securitisation, and therefore to lower refinancing costs, which again enhances the return on equity of the original seller. The special value of insurance lies in the BBB to B-rated layers as they are sometimes difficult to place with investors. A problem however is the leverage-dilution over time that needs refined structuring. The overall result achieved with such a CDO structure is an extremely powerful product for the seller of the assets.

Alternative asset reinsurers

An extremely interesting and lively development is going on, mainly in Bermuda (see Fitch IBCA, Duff & Phelps, 2001; Lux, 2001; Sulima 2001). This development involves so-called hedge fund reinsurers that leverage their shareholders' capital in three different ways. Firstly, they invest it in alternative (and some traditional) asset classes. At the same time, the capital is used as risk capital creating underwriting capacity for stable and premium intensive insurance business. In addition, some of the companies prepare themselves for a possible IPO (some already had their IPOs, with interesting price/earnings ratios). All of this is done in a tax efficient manner.

US taxpayers that invest directly into hedge funds have to pay income tax on realised profits every year. However, in the case of (re)insurance companies, insurers are exempt from registering as investment companies, which means that no annual distribution of profits has to be made. They are also not taxed as investment vehicles under the Internal Revenue Service code, and in addition, Bermuda has no taxes at the corporate level, therefore the investment returns can be accumulated tax-free. The investment portfolio of the (re)insurer and the return on it is considered to be a by-product of the core insurance business. The investment returns and the returns from the insurance business can be steered back to the shareholders in the form of dividend payments (see Figure 4). The legal qualification will presumably be an investment in an insurance company (instead of alterna-

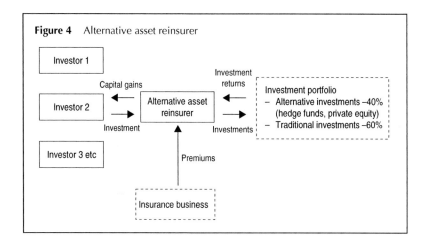

Figure 4 Alternative asset reinsurer

tive assets). This has the effect that taxes only have to be paid when an investor sells his shares. The positive add on is that the applicable tax rate is the lower capital gains rate instead of the income tax rate.

The most famous representatives of this set-up are Grand Central Re, Hampton Re, Imagine Re, Max Re, Select Re, Stockton Re, and others that are as yet in a start-up phase. While the structural set-up, the insurance business, the investors and the investment portfolio differ, they all combine alternative investments and insurance in one way or another.

A further interesting combination would be to make use of the credit rating of these companies, and combine it with a securitisation/leverage on alternative assets, or to create a principal protected issue of alternative asset securities.

Given the political pressure from other countries to get Bermuda to set up a similar tax system to the ones that they have, other countries may participate in the follow-up demand for such structures.

Life insurers and pension plans

In life insurance policies, as well as in pension plan contracts, the entities have to guarantee certain minimum performances, and at the same time are restricted in the investments they make. A product that would address such difficulties could be in the form of a private equity or hedge fund product. The asset class would bring the necessary returns, and a principal protection would ensure the asset classification for "eligible assets" and would also avoid the downsize risk. A combination with a swap converts uncertain (possibly insufficient) returns into stable returns. Naturally, the different payoff patterns have to be steered very carefully when setting up the structure.

Liquidity products

One of the most difficult aspects of private equity investing is the measurement of the NAV. Due to the reporting lines of the partnerships, the fund of funds and the investors have to wait up to several months until the NAV of a product is known. Additionally, the valuation methodology leaves a certain degree of judgemental freedom. This sometimes results in a discount of exchange-traded vehicles, due to the lack of liquidity and incorporated expectations of further developments. To address these issues, the (re)insurer may create products that on the one hand eliminate the discount by opening up the vehicle for direct trading (similar to mutual funds), and on the other hand providing a reporting system that is much faster and more accurate than figures that are months old.

Single partnerships

Due to the fact that only the publicly placed products are widely announced, smaller business like insurance covers for single partnerships is rarely seen or known about. While well diversified private equity portfolios can be insured due to the broad investment base and the low insurance premium, the (re)insurer will have more difficulty in insuring small single partnerships, mainly because:

❑ the premium would be too high to be attractive; and
❑ of the structural work that needs to be done nevertheless.

A possible way out is to use features of (long-term) finite reinsurance, where part of the risk has to be funded by the single partnerships themselves (or the general partner). This could dramatically reduce the insurance premium. As soon as a portfolio of several partnerships has been built up by the (re)insurer, the (re)insurer may want to distribute the overall portfolio risk by one of the standard methods, namely retrocession or securitisation.

As can be seen, there are a wide variety of structures that, on a stand-alone basis or in combination, directly address the needs and goals of investors, asset managers, as well as (re)insurers. Although the above only covers private equity specific issues, the field of alternative assets and inefficiencies in the capital markets is much broader.

INSURANCE COVER AND OTHER GUARANTEE FORMS
Insurance capacity
Risk transfer

The (re)insurer as risk taker plays a key role in such structures, mainly because of the risk transfer that eliminates the downside risk, but also because of other achievements such as a credit enhancement or the reclassification of an alternative (and sometimes restricted) asset class into an eligible asset.

As a new class of business to the insurance industry, the insurance capacity for private equity and hedge funds is restricted. This is mainly due to the relatively small risk capital base of the insurance world, but also due to the limitation arising from the overall diversification (risk accumulation control). In addition, the restriction arises from the time the build-up phase of a portfolio of similar risks takes and from the new experience and expertise that has to be collected and built up over a certain period of time. In addition, recent developments on the financial markets and their impacts on the insured private equity portfolios have now to be compared with the collected underwriting information from the past. The respective conclusions may have an impact on the insurance capacity available.

The insurer will not only consider exposure assumed from insuring alternative asset classes, but will use a consolidated view of insurance risk and investment risk in the same underlying alternative asset class, which may lead to further restrictions of capacity.

In addition to the previous capacity restrictions, due to the events of September 11, 2001, a huge amount of insurance capacity has been destroyed, and the price for capacity has increased dramatically (see Sender and Oster 2001; Crombie, 2002). This again has an impact on the attractiveness of insuritised solutions. The premium that the insurer can ask for the risk he assumes is somewhat limited by the investor's targeted return. The solutions become unattractive as soon as the expected returns for such a private equity product (including other features such as the gains from a possible capital relief) are lower compared to the premium (and costs) that are deducted.

The challenge for the structurer is therefore to optimise the use of any available insurance capacity (be it in-house capacity or from other markets via coinsurance or retrocession) and to use substitutes wherever possible. Such substitutes contain different combinations of insurance techniques (layering, retrocession, finite reinsurance, combination of risks or of asset classes, decomposition of the risk into systematic and non-systematic risks and the respective dynamic hedging of the systematic part of it).

The situation regarding the capacity restrictions changed dramatically last year, when Standard & Poor's came up with the techniques and models to provide a stand-alone rating on the risk of different (more senior) layers of a private equity backed securitisation (Standard & Poor's, 2001).

The possibility to have such risk layers rated broadens the variety of additional capacity providers, including, but not limited to, companies whose restrictions require superior Standard & Poor's product ratings (such as the credit monoliner market in the US) and the financial markets with techniques such as securitisation, equity and debt placement and zero bonds.

Capital underpinning requirements for insurance risks

Each and every risk that an insurance company assumes, needs to be underpinned by the insurer's capital on which the insurer needs to achieve a certain return. The risk capital needed is measured, for example, by the shortfall risk of the underlying portfolio, but it also depends on the structure of the overall risk basket. The broader a diversification an insurer has, the less risk capital (and therefore return on risk capital) per risk unit he needs.

The premium an insurer requests is not only determined by the investment's original return, implied volatility or loss expectation, but also by the return on the underlying risk capital and thus the shortfall risk of the portfolio and the risk landscape of the (re)insurer.

In order to save the premium, the investor could also consider diversifying on his own, thereby putting up the corresponding risk capital directly. However, his weaker risk diversification would require him to put up much more risk capital than a widely diversified (re)insurer. He would need his return on a relatively higher risk capital, which results in a more expensive solution than the (re)insurance solution.

This is also the case for an investor with a larger balance sheet than the insurer, since the required capital is only minimised by the diversification of risk, and not by the size of the balance sheet as such. The investor's requirement for risk capital could be drastically reduced if an AAA-rated bond appears on the books in place of an unsecured independent private equity portfolio. This consideration only becomes apparent if risk measurement systems such as "value-at-risk", "shortfall" or "risk adjusted capital" are applied, where the safed risk capital of the investor is measured against the smaller additional risk capital of the insurer. In the area of measurement systems, institutional investors naturally have an edge over private investors.

Finite structures

A powerful tool is created by having the investors or the asset managers take a part of the most risky layers for themselves, while the senior parts are insured. This has the impact that the (re)insurer is not the only risk taker, but also that the investor or asset manager participates in the downside risk. On the other hand, the insurance premium is reduced, while the investor or asset manager still can participate on the upside, and additionally can receive a no-loss bonus should the product run well. Further considerations include possible tax advantages. The main economic implication of this solution is the leverage of return.

Zero coupon bond structures

In zero coupon bond structures, the principal guarantee is created by way of the principal itself, of which a good part is set aside and invested in a zero coupon bond that grows to the principal amount until maturity. The main disadvantage for the investor is that with such a product, his exposure to the preferred asset class is rather limited, as most of the principal is used for the zero bond. As an example, for a five year principal protection and with a discounting factor of 5% and an assumed performance of the asset class of 15%, about 78% of the initial principal needs to be invested in zero bonds. That leaves only 12% to be invested in the desired asset class. Of course, depending on the level of the risk free interest rate and the time available until maturity, this solution can be more or less attractive.

Another difficult feature is the so called stop-out risk: if the whole amount that was invested in the desired asset class is lost during the running period of the transaction, the investor sits on a dead zero coupon investment until the end (path dependency).

Table 1 shows the different return scenarios for the investor.

Table 1

Investment: US$100/Time Period: 5 years/Performance of asset class: 15% pa/ Risk-free rate: 5%

	Without insurance	With insurance (2% fee*)	Zero-bond solution
End of period	US$201	US$188	US$144

* on the Initial Investment Amount pa

Dynamic hedging ("portfolio insurance")

As in the zero coupon bond solution, the dynamic hedging solution consists of two investments: zero coupon investments and an investment in the underlying asset class.

The main difference is that at inception no zero coupon bond is actually purchased, but a guarantor issues a letter of credit (LOC) on behalf of the issuing SPV to assure the repayment of the principal investment at maturity.

During the lifetime of the product, the guarantor monitors a "reference curve", which shows the amount of capital that would have to be invested in zero coupon bonds at each point in time in order to achieve a payoff of 100% at maturity. As long as the NAV of the investment portfolio is far enough above the reference curve, 100% of the capital remains invested in the desired asset class.

If the NAV drops towards the reference curve, the guarantor will divest part of the investment portfolio to allocate more capital to zero coupon bonds. Of course, such divestment must be in line with the liquidity that the asset class has. In private equity, the liquidity is limited to any distributions that are flowing back, therefore, private equity is not really adopted for dynamic hedging; instead of reinvestment commitments, zero coupon bonds are bought. This feature is easier in hedge funds where liquidity is given (although often overestimated).

If the NAV falls down to the reference curve, the guarantor will divest the whole investment portfolio. In this case, the investor is stuck with a "dead" zero coupon bond until maturity ("stop-out risk").

Initially, all the investors' money is invested in alternative assets, so the initial upside participation is 100%. However, as soon as zero coupon bonds have to be bought, the upside participation is reduced. This can end in a zero upside participation in the case of a stop-out situation, where the whole alternatively invested amount is used for buying zero coupon bonds. Therefore, the risk remains with the investor: if things are going wrong, he has bonds instead of having the chance to make reinvestments. The guarantor however only takes the timing risk and the interest rate risk. A difficult situation can arise in the case that the risk free interest rates decrease. If the alternative asset class is working close to the reference curve and the interest rates fall, suddenly the point is reached that the zero coupon bonds need to be bought.

Dynamic hedging solutions are popular because they offer (in contrast to the zero coupon solution) almost 100% participation if the alternative asset class performs well, but they are viewed negatively because of their path dependency.

The cost of the protection is the difference in the returns between the alternative asset portfolio and the replicating portfolio. Unfortunately, they are not known in advance and can get out of control in the case of large market movements. The strategy of dynamic hedging requires high liquidity of the underlying asset class, which in private equity normally is not given. In case of liquidity shortenings, the strategy fails. Therefore, dynamic hedging can be questionable precisely in downside situations.

Profit lock-in
A "profit lock-in" feature can be used in the zero coupon bond solution as well as in the dynamic hedging solution, to guarantee more than 100% at maturity if the alternative asset portfolio performs well during the lifetime of the product.

The profit can be locked in after a certain period of time, if part of the profit is used to buy additional zero coupon bonds, which results in a guarantee of more than 100% payoff at maturity. However, every time more zero bonds are bought, the future upside participation on the desired asset class decreases.

In the example of the dynamic hedging solution, the guarantor shifts the "reference curve" upwards. If part of the money in the portfolio is lost, the guarantor will begin to buy zero coupon bonds earlier, which again results in a guarantee of more than 100% payoff at maturity. Again, any locked-in profit results in a decreased upside participation.

Cross-hedging

Private Equity and other alternative asset classes have a risk profile that can be split into two different risk dimensions. While the so called "non-systematic" or "residual" risk (the risk that is not correlated with the financial markets) helps the insurer to diversify its existing overall book of business, the "systematic" risk (the risk that fully correlates with the financial markets) accumulates and adds to its market exposure which usually is the biggest part of its book. Therefore, it is appropriate to split the welcome non-systematic risk from the less welcome systematic risk, and to hedge the systematic risk. Of course, during the lifetime of a transaction the hedging portfolio has to be adequately monitored and adjusted. The cross-hedging based on a risk decomposition model applied by Swiss Re is a way of dealing with these risks (see Winkelmann, 2000). The most challenging parts are the decomposition of the risk, to define the proper, most similar basket of financial markets index (for example Stoxx 50 or S&P 500) and to constantly readjust the hedge depending on the index basket and the private equity portfolio.

Securitisation/CDO structures

First, the issuer raises money for the CDO tranches/classes of different seniority according to the stand-alone credit rating they have received. The investor has the choice in which of the tranches he wants to invest. The whole proceeds are invested by the issuer into the desired alternative asset class.

In case of a loss, the most subordinated (lowest rated) tranches are wiped out first. They build a cushion for the more senior tranches. Such junior tranche is frequently not paid a coupon, but receives a distribution of the surplus NAV at maturity. Therefore, the junior tranche has features of leveraged equity and receives an upside participation of up to 100%, minus the interests for the senior layers. The senior (highest rated) tranches usually receive coupons and normally do not participate on the performance of the underlying investments by ways of any upside. Losses have to be carried only after the complete loss to any junior noteholder.

Due to the constant returns of the senior layers, senior tranches have a leveraging impact on the junior tranche. Due to accounting reasons, such structures normally require a significant equity tranche (of up to 30%) which is generally rather difficult to place.

Warehousing

Very similar to the CDO is the warehousing approach, in which the (re)insurance company first takes the whole risk and secondly offers certain tranches to the financial markets. This results in a highly rated securitisation offering (based on the rating of the (re)insurer).

For the issuer, the warehousing approach has the advantage that the (re)insurer can accept the whole risk at once, so that the issue is placed as a bond, rated according to the (re)insurer's rating. However, for the (re)insurer the risk of a successful securitisation remains.

Table 2 shows a comparison of the various types of guarantee forms.

DIFFERENCES BETWEEN INSURITISATION AND SECURITISATION

While in insuritisation the downside of an investment portfolio is being taken by the insurer, in the securitisation the hazard risk of the insurance is being taken by the financial markets. Previously, cat bonds for natural disasters (earthquake, windstorm) were structured, the new field of insuritisation of alternative assets now brings the two developments together. While the (re)insurer might take up the risk initially (*insuritisation*), it will want to redistribute some considerable risk amounts with:

Table 2 Comparison of guarantee forms

	Insurance risk transfer	Finite reinsurance	Zero-bond solution	Dynamic hedging	Cross- hedging	Securitisation & warehousing (CDOs)
Risk assumed by:	insurer	insured for the funded layer; insurer for the unfunded layers	no risk transfer	insurer or bank until hedge is bought	systematic risk: hedged ("no risk") unsystematic risk: insurer	investor in the CDO
Upside participation of investor:	nearly 100%	nearly 100%	very limited	100% until hedge is bought	limited	100% (even leverage possible)
Exposure to asset class:	nearly 100%	nearly 100%	10% – 60%	100% until hedge is bought	variable, depending on split	100%
Correlation with bond markets:	no	no	no (defined at beginning)	yes for hedged part	yes for hedged part	yes
Pricing based on:	expected loss	funding of layer and expected loss of underlying risk transfer layer	duration, discounting factor (risk -free rates)	option pricing	systematic risk: option pricing; unsystematic risk: expected loss	stand-alone credit rating of each tranche; includes credit risk, risk - free rate and expected loss

a) other (re)insurers (retrocession/syndication); or
b) investors (securitisation if made directly and warehousing if a (re)insurer first takes all the risks and spreads them afterwards).

The investors buying layers of the risk might have the advantage that they know about the asset class and can participate with limited amounts on a securitised product.

The appealing features of a natural catastrophe securitisation via cat bonds are the following. The investor provides capital on call via an SPV. Although the risk usually is priced at LIBOR plus 4.5% to 6% for a BBB to B rated underlying cat risk, the credit quality of the insurer as seller of the bond is normally excellent. The probabilities of a loss of these layers are calculated to be "one event in between 50 and 200 years", and the risk behaves mostly independently of the stock markets. Due to the very limited volatility of the bond price, this is a stable asset in every bond portfolio. Changes should normally only be based on:

a) an actual event like an earthquake or a windstorm that leads to a loss, or
b) new developments in science that lead to a changed view of the risk.

The most difficult task might be to properly define the loss event and amount.

Securitisation of alternative assets can be made by a variety of market players such as asset managers, investment banks, or by broker companies. As with cat bonds, the portfolio management is reduced to monitor any loss, and the investor in a securitised alternative asset product will have to keep track of the constant development. The price will be based less on the interest rates, the credit quality of the issuer and the probability of a loss as with cat bonds, but more on the expected performance of the underlying alternative asset portfolio.

INVESTING IN OR INSURING PRIVATE EQUITY

By investing in alternative assets through a securitised bond, the investor assumes risk in the underlying asset class. The same is true if he invests directly into the same asset class. Therefore, the different risk/return pattern and the specific risk appetite of the investor will be crucial in defining his willingness to either invest directly or indirectly, via insuritisation and securitisation, into the asset class.

Besides the issuer who may make a difference (be it an SPV on the one hand, or a reputable (re)insurance company on the other), further features like the liquidity of the specific product, trading restrictions, denomination or classification of the product as an 'eligible asset' might be decisive in the choice of one product over the other. However, most important are the different payoff patterns in terms of risk and return. If the investor invests in a securitised product, he assumes a risk/return pattern similar to the one of the (re)insurer: when the performance is positive, he earns the premium as an insurer does, and in the event of a loss, he loses his principal (whole downside, limited upside). The investor in the underlying asset class however, has the whole downside and the whole upside. As a last comparison, the investor in an insuritised product has no downside, and the upside is somewhat reduced due to the costs of the insurance.

Therefore, depending on the risk appetite, but also on the expectations the investor has towards the asset class, he might prefer one product to the other.

Figure 5 shows the payoff patterns for investing in or insuring private equity.

ROLES OF THE (RE)INSURER

In setting up transactions in combinations of insuritisation and securitisation based on equilibrated portfolios of alternative asset classes, the (re)insurer has many roles. One of his roles is to be the risk taker who must know about risk and the modelling of it. Further roles involve being a joint venture partner in the event that SPVs are set up, attending board meetings, servicing the investments or participating in an advisory committee. The (re)insurer may also help with marketing, credit enhancements of line of credits, or modelling overcommitment strategies and the respective cash levels that are needed.

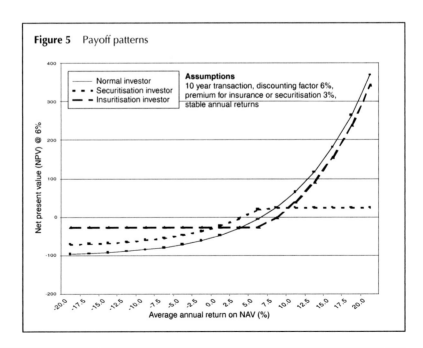

Figure 5 Payoff patterns

INSURITISATION AND SECURITISATION OF ALTERNATIVE INVESTMENTS – A MARKET OF THE FUTURE

The first transactions in which illiquid assets were insured (Princess Private Equity Holding and Pearl Private Equity Holding) show that this is an open field for the (re)insurer. It is also one that can be further developed, not only for private equity and hedge funds, but also for other alternative asset classes such as intellectual property, natural resources (including farmland, timberland and oil & gas investment programmes), real estate (including hotel and shopping centre real estate investment programmes), high yield ("junk") bonds and distressed ("vulture") investment programmes.

While the first insuritisations consisted of a pure risk transfer from the capital markets to the insurance markets, further developments tend to address special needs within the private equity world. For example, structures that help with the capital underpinning, or create stable returns instead of low returns at the beginning and high returns at the end (the J-curve effect in private equity), or the insurance of overcommitment strategies which help to get access to more favourable line-of-credits, or structures that avoid the feared discount on publicly traded private equity fund of funds, insurance covers for single partnerships or specialised alternative asset reinsurance vehicles.

The future will show how quickly the market will adopt the new techniques to securitise insurance-wrapped transactions, and to create additional insurance capacity for the insurer on the one hand, and new investment opportunities for investors on the other. As outlined before, to date, there are very few products in the area of private equity. More insurance-wrapped private equity transactions will be seen in the near future. On the hedge fund side, there are many more secured transactions, most of them issued by banks (see Ritzi, 2000; Ferro, 2001; Fitch IBCA, Duff & Phelps, 2001).

Due to the complexity and the lengthy development process of these types of transactions, as well as the broad know-how base needed from the underwriters/structurers on both insurance, corporate finance and investment banking, a dedicated team effort to move things forward, and a clear understanding of the investors to be addressed by such products are key factors to success in this area.

For the future, streamlined and standardised processes are expected on several structural and legal issues. In addition, growing sophistication of the investors who directly invest in such products, but also of investors who indirectly provide capacity through insuritisation and securitisation, will lead to a more efficient market from the competitor's and the co-insurer's side. Overall, this is the edge of some very exciting developments of new products.

1   For example, Switzerland for technical reserves of insurance companies: Art. 23ff. der Lebensversicherungsverordnung vom 29. 11. 1993 (LeVV; SR 961. 611), Art. 15ff. der Schadenversicherungsverordnung vom 8. 9. 1993 (SchVV; SR 961. 711) and Art. 30 der Aufsichtsverordnung vom 11. 8. 1931 (AVO; SR 961. 05), URL: http://www. bpv. admin. ch/de/pages/sicherer/bewillig. asp, and for pension funds: BVV 2: URL: *http://www. zug. ch/abvsa/50_01_i. htm#bvv*

Another example is Germany: Riester Reform: "Gesetz zur Reform der gesetzlichen Rentenversicherung und zur Förderung eines kapitalgedeckten Altersvorsorgevermögens (Altersvermögensgesetz)" v. 26. 06. 2001, BGBl I, S. 1310, insurance authorities: Versicherungsaufsichtsgesetz, Art. 54 VAG and Lazard Asset Management GmbH, 2001: "Standpunkt: Das Dilemma der Versicherungen in einer Nidrigzinsphase", December 2001, www. lazardnet. com/lam/de/pdfs/Standpunkt_Versicherungen_1201. pdf.

BIBLIOGRAPHY

Alford, B.H., 2001, "Understanding Alternative Assets", *Wealth Perspectives,* URL: http://www.mycfo.com/our_perspectives/opr_alt_assets.html (March 29 2001).

AON Corporation, "Aon Securitizes Limited Partnership Interests; Provides Update on Non-Operating Segment Revenue for Fourth Quarter 2001 First-of-its-Kind Transaction To Reduce Earnings Variability", URL:http://www.aon.com/abo.../PressRelease.asp ?ID=79B746492EB8F 32C 86256B43005359B.html (16 January 2002).

AXA Investment Managers, 2001, "Private Equity _ Eine Anlageklasse von wachsender Bedeutung für deutsche institutionelle Investoren", URL: http://www.axa-im.de/PDF/ Oetker_Water.pdf+outperformance+private+equity+evca&hl=de&ie=ISO-8859-1

Bank for International Settlements, "The New Basel Capital Accord: Comments received on the Second Consultative Package", URL: http://www.bis.org/bcbs/cacomments.htm (21 August 2001)

Crombie, R., 2002, "Bermuda Startup Reinsurers Pursue Niches", *National Underwriter,* 12 February, 2002.

Croson, D.C. and Kunreuther, H.C., 1999, "Customizing Reinsurance and Cat Bonds for Natural Hazard Risks", *The Warton Financial Institutions Center and The Wharton Risk Management and Decision Processes Center,* URL: http://fic.wharton.upenn.edu/fic/ papers/99/pcat09.html (June 1999).

DeFontaine, P., 2001, "Vanishing Cat Bonds", *Best's Review,* January 2001, URL: http://www.bestreview.com/2001-01/pc_vanishing_cat_bonds.html

Deter, Dr., 2001, "Betriebliche Altersversorgung", *Wissenschaftlicher Dienst des Deutschen Bundestages: Der aktuelle Begriff,* URL: www.bundestag.de/aktuell/begriff/2001/ 15_2001.pdf

Deutsche Bank, "Erste Private Equity Wandelanleihe mit Kapitalschutz", URL:http:// public.deutsche-bank.de/deuba/db/aktuell.nsf/doc/JBOS-48PP2H?OpenDocument (9 June 1999).

Deutsche Bank, "Prime Edge Capital plc Successfully Issued €150 Million Private Equity CDO", URL: http://www.db.com/central/ver40/news/2001_q2/01062001b.html (1 June 2001).

EIMS, Graham Bannock & Partners Ltd (UK) EIMS Publication No (Contractor's Edition) "Pan-European study of the performance of venture capital, Summary of Results", URL: http://www.cordis.lu/eims/src/eims-r43.htm (last updated January 30, 2002).

European Venture Capital Association (EVCA), for Private Equity Reporting Requirements: 2002 Reporting Guidelines, URL: www.evca.com

Ferro, K., 2001, "The start of something big", *Risk & Reward,* April 2001.

Financial Times, 1999, "Swiss Re set for high risk AAA-rated issue" (8 June).

Fitch IBCA, Duff & Phelps, 2001, "Hedge Funds, A New Asset Class in Structured Finance", analysts: Eileen A.Fahey, Chicago, Richard V.Hrvatin, New York, Steve N.Lee, New York, Mitchell Lench, London, Roger W.Merritt, CPA, New York, John L.Schiavetta, CFA, New York, URL: http://www.fitchibca.com/corporate/search/ (search for hedge funds) (6 September 2001).

Goldman Sachs and Frank Russell Company, "Goldman Sachs and Russell Publish Fifth Global Report On Institutional Alternative Investing", URL:http://biz.yahoo.com/ bw/011219/ 192023_1.html (19 December 2001).

Grünbichler, A., S. Graf and A. Gruber, 2001, *Private Equity und Hedge Funds: Alternative Anlagekategorien im Überblick,* (Zürich: Verlag Neue Zürcher Zeitung).

International Financing Review, Issue 1418, "Securitization to play role in private equity sales", URL: http://www.ifrmagazine.com/ifr/protected/ZZZPV8P4IWC.html (26 January 2002).

Kreutzer, L., 2002, "AON is first: Big Hurdles Still Confront Efforts At Securitization", *The Private Equity Analyst,* Vol.XII, Issue 2, February.

Lerner, J., 2000, *Venture Capital and Private Equity – A Casebook,* (New York: John Wiley & Sons).

Lux, H., 2001, "The Great hedge fund reinsurance tax game", Institutional Investor Magazine (Americas Edition), April, pp 52–8.

Murray, A., 1998, "Securitization Beyond Cat Bonds", *National Underwriter Property & Casualty/Risk & Benefits Management Edition,* July 27, 1998, URL: http://www.nunews.com/ archives/pc_archive/1998/p07-27/30moody.asp

Partners Group Homepage, "Pearl Holding Limited", URL: http://www.partners group.ch/ en/produkte/index.shtml and www.partnersgroup.net

Primack, D., 2001, "Prime Edge and J.P.Morgan Partners Put Private Equity Into Debt", Venture Capital Journal, URL: http://www.ventureeconomics.com/vcj/ protected/ ZZZE8WZ2 XNC.html (1 July 2001).

Princess Webpage, URL: http://www.princess.combo.net/intro/index2.shtml.

Private Equity Analyst, 2001, "Global Financial Forms Bond Vehicle For Fund of Funds", August, p.9.

Ritzi, A., 2000, "The safe way to play hedge funds", *Hedge Fund Intelligence,* Institutional Guide to Hedge Funds, URL: http://www.hedgefundintelligence.com/eh/reports/ 2000_08/safeway.htm

Schneider F., 1999, "Partners Group und Swiss Re lancieren Privat- Equity-Dollar-Wandelanleihe", *Finanz und Wirtschaft,* (2 June).

Securitization.net, Mayer, Brown & Platt, "European Securitization: The new Basel Capital Accord and Asset Securitization", URL: www.securitization.net/pdf/mbpsecnews_0801.pdf

Sender, H., and C. Oster., "Insurers Are Raising Money With Ease As Other Sectors Face Credit Crunch", *The Wall Street Journal*, URL: http://www2.rmi.gsu.edu/faculty/klein/RMI_3500/Readings/Other/WTC_Capital_Raising.htm (24 October 2001).

Standard & Poor's Structured Finance, 2001 (Reprinted from RatingsDirect), "S&P Correct: First Structured Notes Backed by Private Equity Investments Rated", analysts: Erkan Erturk, PhD, New York and Soody Nelson, New York, URL: http://www.standardandpoors.com/PressRoom/Ratings/Articles/060401_fundoffunds.html (June 2001).

Standard & Poor's, "Private Equity Fund of Funds: Overview and Rating Criteria" analysts: Lily Cheung, New York, Erkan Erturk, PhD, New York and Winnie Fong, New York, URL: http://www.standardandpoors.com/emarketing/structuredfinance/copyof110701_fund.html (7 November 2001).

Standard & Poor's Structured Finance (Reprinted from RatingsDirect), "Innovative Structures Key to Growth in Market Value Sector for 2002", analyst: Soody Nelson, New York, URL: http://www.standardandpoors.com/emarketing/structuredfinance/copyof010702_innovative.html (7 January 2002).

Structured Finance International, 2001, "Deutsche's Prime Edge sparks private equity CDO boom", Issue 55, June.

Sulima, C.L., "Another Financial Bubble? Recent Trends in the Hedge Fund Industry and important implications for financial institutions", *Federal Reserve Bank of Chicago Capital Markets News*, CFA, URL: www.chicagofed.org/publications/capitalmarketnews/2001/cmn200109.pdf (September 2001).

Winkelmann, K., 2000, "Risk capital allocation: Applying risk to the portfolio", *Risk Magazine*, December 2000, URL: http://www.financewise.com/public/edit/riskm/rmforinvestors/rmforinvestors-riskcapital.htm

Wolcott, R., 2002, "Here Come European Hedge Fund CDO's", *Institutional Investor Newsletter*, 20 January, 2002, URL: http://www.bondweek.com/mbs+abs+and+cmbs/here+come+european+hedge+fund+cdos.asp

22

Applying Insurance Techniques and Structures to Manage Merger Risk

David Govrin and Andrew Kaiser

Goldman Sachs & Co

Potential and contingent liabilities can complicate mergers, acquisitions and other strategic transactions such as spin-offs and initial public offerings. Contingent liabilities arise where the occurrence or realisation of the liability is subject to an event or set of circumstances materialising, the likelihood of which may be difficult to predict. For example, the likelihood of an earthquake striking a building, the outcome associated with a recently filed lawsuit or the chance of a company filing for bankruptcy and defaulting on its unsecured debt. The existence of large contingent liabilities can result in inefficient transaction execution and, in extreme situations, can derail a transaction. In a merger context, buyers might be deterred by uncertain business or transaction risks and sellers might find that the presence of these risks limits the value they can obtain, prevents finality, or prevents a sale altogether.

Contingent liabilities in mergers and acquisitions have traditionally been managed in one of two ways – each almost always involving some erosion of value: either sellers agree to retain the risk or the universe of buyers is limited to those willing and able to take a view on the risk. If sellers retain the risk, they do so by either providing indemnities, in which case finality is not achieved, or with escrowed funds, allowing the sale of the asset with finality but with a potentially reduced valuation.

Quantifying contingent liabilities can be extremely difficult, and corporate management often lacks the time and expertise to do this. A negotiation setting gives the two sides strong incentives to take starkly opposing views on the value of contingent liabilities. Thus, when faced with a hard-to-quantify risk, strategic buyers may choose to forgo the acquisition in favour of a less risky target. Financial buyers may be uncomfortable with the liability and its potential volatility and will bid conservatively – if at all.

Insurance can provide a strategic alternative for managing, controlling, transferring or financing these risks in situations where there can be large differences in valuation by the parties contemplating transactions. The purchase of insurance can enable a seller to avoid retaining the risk or capitalising a large inefficient escrow without limiting the universe of potential buyers.

INTRODUCTION

This chapter focuses on the structuring and application of insurance products designed to enable or facilitate the execution of mergers and acquisitions. The chapter addresses the types of liabilities causing valuation differences between buyer and seller, insurance solutions designed to bridge the uncertainty giving rise to the valuation gap, the insurance underwriting process for these new types of transaction specific risks, the benefits of applying insurance to these situations, and finally some practical case studies.

TYPES OF RISKS THAT CAN AFFECT MERGER EXECUTION

A wide range of contingent liabilities can affect merger execution and or valuation. These can be categorised as risks resulting from or embedded in the business or risks inherent in the transaction structure and documentation.

Business risks

Various business-specific risks or liabilities exist but those most typically encountered include:

Pending litigation

In the current litigious environment, especially in the US, most companies being sold have outstanding and unsettled litigation of some sort – typically third-party or shareholder litigation – but litigation can also involve governments or other constituencies claiming damages. Litigation can cover a broad range of suits including shareholder class-action allegations of management malfeasance leading to a reduction in shareholder value or third-party allegations of damage resulting from acts such as copyright infringement, patent infringement or product liability.

In many instances the outstanding litigation is not material or is developed to the point where valuation can be reasonably assessed. However, in some instances there can be material litigation with significant volatility in potential outcome where the seller of the business and potential buyers have substantial valuation differences with respect to the likely ultimate financial outcome of the litigation.

Environmental liabilities

Many companies, but particularly those engaged in product manufacture, face liabilities for cleaning up environmental contamination and for associated third-party and other related damages. These liabilities can arise from contamination of specific known sites where pollution has occurred or can be associated with future discovery of contamination at locations that have yet to be identified.

Insurance reserves

Insurance companies establish reserves for liabilities pertaining to policies written prior to the date of a merger transaction. There can often be material valuation differences between buyer and seller in terms of the adequacy of these reserves, given that the reserves are actuarially based and are for loss occurrences that will happen in the future, or that have happened in the past but where the loss amount is not certain.

Warranties

Many companies offer warranties on end-user products, typically retail products or services. Reserves are normally established for future warranty liabilities. As with insurance reserves, there can be valuation differences between the buyer and seller with respect to the adequacy of these financial reserves.

Asset residual value

In situations where companies are involved in the lease or rental of assets, there can be material financial implications associated with the residual value established for the assets being leased or rented. These assets can range from real estate to automobiles.

Tax

Tax liabilities can be both a business risk and a transaction risk. We will elaborate below on tax liabilities as a transaction risk. With respect to business risk, a target company may have taken a position on a transaction that, although supported by tax analysis, is not free from future challenge by the Internal Revenue Service (IRS) or applicable tax authority. Challenge may be unlikely but, if successful, the subsequent tax liability may be financially material.

Transaction risks

Legal and other transaction-related opinions

There are numerous legal and other opinions that are obtained in the context of a transaction. Most of these opinions do not create execution issues or material differences in valuation if challenged. However, transactions that require support by certain legal or accounting opinions, if successfully

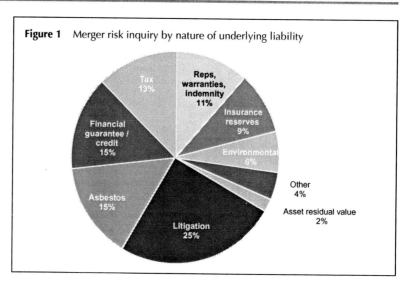

Figure 1 Merger risk inquiry by nature of underlying liability

challenged, could present material valuation issues. For example, a merger of a company that has recently undertaken a tax-free spin-off might be supported by a strong legal tax opinion, but if successfully challenged this could result in a substantial tax liability.

Indemnities

As discussed above, in many instances sellers are forced to indemnify buyers for a wide variety of issues. In some instances, sellers such as private equity funds, single shareholders, or closely held companies are unable or unwilling to provide the indemnities required. In other instances, the indemnities simply create a lack of finality.

Representations and warranties

In most transactions, both buyers and sellers provide specific contractual representations and warranties with respect to the transaction. A breach of a representation or warranty creates a liability for the party that breaches. However, in a public company context, or where the sale of an entire business occurs – in contrast with the case of an operating company – there is limited or no remedy for future discovery of a breach of a representation or warranty.

Figure 1 illustrates the approximate distribution of issues that have emerged in transactions with Goldman Sachs' client base since the beginning of 2001. In most instances the issues were addressed structurally or the transaction did not proceed for reasons other than the issue raised. In some situations, insurance played an important and strategic role, mostly in the areas of litigation; representations, warranties and indemnities; and insurance reserves.

TYPES OF INSURANCE STRUCTURES AND SOLUTIONS THAT CAN BE APPLIED

The liabilities that arise in the context of a merger or other strategic transaction are often traditional insurance liabilities that have developed in a non-traditional context (in the course of a corporate transaction as opposed to an insurance policy renewal). Another characteristic that distinguishes these liabilities is that they tend to be more retrospective than prospective in terms of the occurrence of the event that triggered the liability, although the uncertainty of loss associated with the ultimate outcome is entirely prospective. Buyers are frequently unwilling to accept the volatility associated with an uncertain outcome, regardless of whether the event has already occurred or may occur in the future.

Insurance solutions to these issues can take the form of traditional insurance structures, such as excess of loss or quota share agreements, or alternative risk transfer techniques such as finite risk or loss portfolio transfers, which is the transfer of loss or liability reserves and the associated cash (premium) to an insurer in exchange for the insurer's payment of all future liability (claims) associated with the transferred reserves. The policies are highly customised due to the unique nature of each situation and can provide coverage for prospective or retrospective liabilities. Regardless of the structure of the insurance policy, there are significant due diligence requirements with respect to the risk at hand and numerous questions and issues that must be addressed prior to determining the feasibility of an insurance solution and the optimal structure. Some of the key issues and questions that determine the most appropriate structure for a given situation are:

❏ Is the potential loss occurrence retrospective or prospective?
❏ Can the risk be reasonably assessed or estimated?
❏ What level of information exists with respect to the risk?
❏ Does the seller have financial and/or cash reserves established for the liability?
❏ Does insurance already exist for the liability?
❏ Is the seller willing to share the risk?
❏ Is the liability discrete or definable enough to allow for finality (capped/uncapped)?
❏ What are the seller's objectives, including the level of risk transfer desired, and is cash available to fund an insurance policy?

The structure of insurance solutions depends on the specific situation and the objectives of the parties concerned. Each policy is carefully crafted and negotiated, but the key elements that typically define the insurance structure are:

❏ Level of retention/deductibility.

❏ Form, timing and amount of premium.

❏ Desired insurance limit (the relationship of premium to limit is the key determinant to the level of risk transfer).

❏ Policy term.

❏ Form of indemnity.

❏ Event definition.

❏ Trigger mechanism.

❏ Loss calculation mechanism.

❏ Structural considerations, such as co-insurance, to address risk sharing and alignment of interests.

❏ Process for loss settlements, including defence strategy with respect to outstanding litigation.

❏ Treatment of current and future insurance recoveries.

❏ Exclusions, representations and warranties.

In cases where there is both a financial and cash reserve established for an existing liability but uncertainty in respect to the adequacy of the reserve and the timing of the payoff, the solution would typically be structured as a capped or uncapped loss portfolio transfer or an excess of loss insurance policy above the existing reserves. These transactions are also sometimes described as "liability buyouts". Loss portfolio transfers usually reference a portfolio of liabilities and associated reserves, which would typically be encountered where there is an aggregation of risk, as in an insurance company. Litigation buyout typically refers to insurance against an adverse result in specific litigation.

HOW DO INSURERS ASSESS THE RISK?

Each situation is unique, and the process of risk assessment differs depending on the facts and circumstances associated with the risk in question.

In some merger insurance instances, actuarial methodologies applied in more traditional insurance contexts can be used. These are characterised by the presence of significant historical or other data that can be used in the application of actuarial techniques to determine a range of future outcomes and an associated probability distribution. An actuarial approach to underwriting is favoured when the underlying loss events occur frequently enough to provide sufficient historical experience to apply these analytical techniques.

In situations where insurers cannot rely on traditional actuarial or loss simulation techniques it is necessary to employ expert analysis and to develop an understanding of the magnitude of events that need to occur in order for a loss to take place. The underwriting can then be accomplished by scenario analysis, various scenarios consisting of different outcomes and associated losses can be constructed, and probabilities of occurrence assigned to each. This technique relies heavily on the underwriter's judgement and experience.

For example, a company may be involved in litigation for liability associated with a specific product or action. Using historical experience with similar litigation, and engaging legal experts who will understand precedents and likelihood of outcomes, an insurer may be able to develop a view on the likelihood of settlement, the amount of settlement, and the likely outcome if the case were to go to trial, including the potential outcomes associated with appeals. An insurance policy can be structured in accordance with these views to remove uncertainty from a buyer who is less capable of coming to a view, and a seller who cannot achieve finality if the risk is retained.

BENEFITS AND ISSUES TO CONSIDER
Benefits of transaction-related insurance
Facilitation of the sale process
The implications of some risks for the transaction process depend on the number of bidders and their appetite for the asset. However, regardless of the bidder environment, contingent liabilities can create a large fluctuation in bids, and in any environment they can cause some, if not all, of the bidders to withdraw from the process. Insurance can facilitate the sale process in two distinct ways:

1. It allows the seller to offer the asset to the universe of bidders with or without the associated liability. This use of insurance helps to ensure that all potential buyers participate in the process, as long as they can be convinced of the adequacy of the insurance.
2. The ability to structure and price an insurance policy adds third-party comfort and validation of the price of the risk. The buyer may be more willing to accept the risk knowing that a third party has priced the risk, or the buyer may be more accepting of the seller's valuation of the risk given third-party validation.

Insurers are not usually in the business of performing due diligence and structuring and pricing an insurance policy so that others can properly value the risk. Thus, in structuring insurance solutions for these situations, purchasers of insurance should be aware that there might be a break-up fee associated with the non-purchase of insurance once terms have been proposed. These fee structures are individually negotiated based on the facts and circumstances of the situation, and should be viewed in comparison to the value that independent risk assessment adds to the overall transaction.

Facilitation of finality

For some risks, the seller is forced to retain all or a portion of the risk, typically by providing the buyer with an indemnity. This occurs if the buyer and seller cannot agree on value or to the adequacy of structural solutions such as an escrow or capped insurance. In situations where the seller is forced to retain the risk but wants to achieve finality in the sale, the seller can purchase an insurance policy for its own benefit, thus mitigating or removing the future financial impact of adverse loss development associated with the risk in question.

An insurance policy may be capped in the amount of protection it provides, but the seller can achieve finality so long as the cap is not breached. The seller is probably more familiar with the liability and better able to assess whether the capped insurance sufficiently protects the economics of the sale. The cost of the insurance policy is simply an up-front reduction of the sale proceeds in terms of valuing the sale itself.

Facilitation of bidding

If an asset is offered with a risk that bidders are likely to view in different ways, or if it is offered without an escrow or an insurance policy, a bidder may be able to enhance its bid for the asset by securing insurance and essentially bidding full value less the cost of the insurance.

Facilitation of tax-free spin-offs

Tax-free spin-offs can be complex, multi-stage processes that can take a year or longer to execute. Much of the execution time is associated with requesting and obtaining a ruling from the IRS on the tax-free nature of the spin-off. Moreover, there is no guarantee that a ruling will be provided or that it will contain a clear indication of the IRS's view of the proposed transaction.

The purchase of an insurance policy to cover the tax liability should the transaction ultimately be deemed taxable can offer comfort to the sponsor of the spin-off and expedite the execution time by substituting an insurance policy for an IRS ruling request. It takes substantially less time to obtain tax liability insurance than it does to obtain an IRS ruling. A client may still choose to request a ruling after purchasing an insurance policy, but the receipt of the ruling will be less critical to the execution of the proposed transaction.

Facilitation of acquisition financing

A target company may have trapped capital or cashflows associated with a business that can be monetised. The proceeds from the monetisation can be used as financing for the acquisition. Insurance can facilitate the monetisation by removing risk associated with the cashflows or trapped capital, thus providing the ability to add greater leverage or obtain more attractive terms.

Reduction of reliance on escrows

Buyer and seller disagreements over risk are often settled via the establishment of an escrow account, which earns minimal interest rates and cannot be leveraged in any way. The cash deposited into the escrow, and its associated interest, represent the funds available to pay for the liability. If the risk is quantifiable it may be possible to purchase an insurance policy instead of putting cash into escrow. Using insurance in this manner, the seller gives up most, if not all, of the upside associated with return of the escrow if the liability does not materialise in exchange for potential lower up-front funding and leverage of the funds that would have otherwise been escrowed.

Support for buyer due diligence and provision of breach protection

Through the purchase of insurance on the representations and warranties made by a seller, the buyer of an asset can purchase protection against damage associated with a breach of the representations and warranties while having a third-party expert validate the due diligence that was conducted.

Issues to consider when contemplating transaction-related insurance

Confidentiality

Mergers and acquisitions are highly confidential situations and there may be material implications if there is a breach of confidentiality. Bringing an insurance company or syndicate of insurance companies into a highly confidential transaction creates a risk of breach of confidentiality. Those involved with any insurance process must sign and honour confidentiality agreements. This means limiting knowledge of the transaction within the insurance company to a limited number of individuals who will be involved specifically in the insurance process.

Conflicts of interest

Insurance companies and other agents or principals that could become involved in an insurance process may have relationships with, or financial interests in, any number of the parties involved. It is critical that anyone involved in any insurance process ensures that conflicts of interest have been cleared and that it is acceptable and appropriate to become involved in the process.

Attorney-client privilege

In the course of risk assessment, insurers will require all relevant information in order to determine the feasibility and cost associated with insuring the risk. In some cases, especially those involving litigation, the insurers might require information that is subject to attorney-client privilege and where counsel is concerned that making this information available to insurers may jeopardise the privilege. In these instances, those involved in any insurance process must be thoughtful and careful to respect this issue and not jeopardise the treatment of such material.

Cost

In addition to the actual cost of any insurance policy, there will typically be two additional costs if insurance is ultimately not pursued: those of expense reimbursement and break-up fees.

Expense reimbursement serves to reimburse the insurers for the out-of-pocket expenses that they incurred when structuring an insurance policy and performing due diligence on the risk. Most of this cost is for due diligence, where insurers need to retain special outside legal or accounting expertise. The expense reimbursement is offset against the insurance premium so that it only serves as an incremental cost if the insurance policy is ultimately not purchased. This cost is incurred from the time the insurance company commits to conduct due diligence.

The break-up fee is an additional fee that is incurred when the insurance company provides an indication of insurance terms. This fee is to ensure that the insurers are not used as an information source to facilitate risk retention or risk sharing among the parties involved. The break-up fee is only incurred if terms are offered and an insurance policy is not purchased.

Insurance market capacity

The market for merger-related insurance products is growing but is limited to a small subset of the overall insurance market. For any given transaction there is a finite amount of capacity, which is typically less than the capacity for more traditional insurance risks. For most risks, the maximum risk transfer capacity that is achievable is in the range of US$300 million–US$400 million. In limited circumstances it might be possible to achieve up to, or in excess of, US$1 billion of risk transfer insurance. For finite insurance structures, the risk transferred to the insurer is materially less, as the premium is typically a much larger percentage of the limit and is returned via an experience account sharing. Thus capacity is more limited by the client's ability to fund the premium and the client's capacity for the credit risk of the insurance providers associated with loss recovery.

Insurance process

The principal steps in a process to procure insurance include:

❏ Selection of insurance process advisors.
❏ Selection of insurers to approach.

❑ Execution of confidentiality agreements.
❑ Development of insurance structure.
❑ Preparation of information materials.
❑ Solicitation of insurer feedback.
❑ Due diligence.
❑ Negotiation.
❑ Execution.

The advisor and insurers should conduct an efficient and organised process, bearing in mind that they are dealing with a strategic transaction for which the insurance is typically a small but important part. It is the responsibility of those involved with the insurance process to be thoughtful and efficient and it is the responsibility of the client to understand that insurance requires its own process and information and that it takes time to properly structure, to conduct due diligence, and to execute an insurance policy. Efforts to approach the insurance market "at the eleventh hour" may not achieve a satisfactory result. At the same time, insurers must realise that these situations are often critical and extremely time sensitive and may require extraordinary effort and long hours to execute a policy in a timeframe that is consistent with the status of the overall transaction.

Accounting, tax and legal considerations
These considerations depend upon each specific situation, so clients should consult with their relevant accounting, tax, and legal advisors to understand the implications of the pursuit and purchase of an insurance policy. The issues that should be addressed include, but are not limited to, treatment of the premium, treatment of any insurance recovery, disclosure of the insurance policy, and premium or other special taxes incurred, and treatment and disclosure of information.

WHEN INSURANCE MAKES SENSE: CASE STUDIES
Case 1: insurance company disposition
A large global insurance company was selling a core asset – a US-licensed property and casualty insurance company. The asset had potential appeal to both strategic and financial buyers. However, a large percentage of the balance sheet consisted of reserves for discontinued operations. These reserves were mostly for asbestos and other mass tort liabilities. These discontinued operations presented a problem for strategic buyers because of the potential volatility of the liability. For financial buyers, the asset was too large and difficult to finance because of the sizeable and volatile reserves. The global insurance company disposing of the asset hoped to achieve finality in the sale.

In order to facilitate the sale, an option on a loss portfolio transfer was structured and executed. This allowed the seller to offer the asset with and without the reserves. In the event that the buyer of the business did not want the insurance policy or the associated reserves, the option facilitated finality by allowing the seller of the asset to exercise the option and thus the only risk that the seller would retain was the adequacy of the insurance limit, which was well in excess of existing reserves.

This unique use of an insurance policy facilitated the sale by broadening the market of potential bidders for the asset. It ultimately allowed a financial buyer to purchase the asset and exercise the option for the insurance policy, using the insurance to finance the portion of the balance sheet associated with the reserves.

Case 2: insurance company acquisition

A US licensed property and casualty insurance company was contemplating a bid for the insurance operations of a corporate entity that owned an insurance operating company. There were a number of companies potentially competing for this asset. In preparing its bid, the US property and casualty company was concerned about overall reserve adequacy and was prepared to either not proceed with a bid for the asset or to be extremely conservative in its bid due to this uncertainty.

As it wished to proceed with an attractive bid, the US property and casualty company decided to purchase adverse reserve development reinsurance. Having secured the insurance protection for its bid, the buyer then made an offer to the seller, which included a reduction in its bid for the premium associated with the adverse reserve development policy. The policy was structured on a risk-transfer basis and initial indications were received prior to the bid being submitted. This allowed the US property and casualty company to bid with confidence, assuming that the policy could be executed after formal due diligence.

The bid was the winning bid and the insurance policy was instrumental in providing comfort with respect to the liabilities of concern and the valuation of those liabilities.

Case 3: corporate merger

A corporate client was contemplating an important strategic purchase of a public company. The target was viewed by the buyer as important to the growth of a particular business line and was to serve as a platform for the development of a new product area. The negotiation of key terms of the transaction was completed, but in the course of due diligence the buyer became concerned about the potential future financial implications of outstanding litigation at the target company. There had been prior settlement of some lawsuits and outstanding reserves for pending and future litigation but the buyer and seller held different views of the ultimate financial cost of the litigation.

To facilitate the purchase of the target, and to ensure that the buyer was comfortable with the valuation, including the potential for financial deterioration associated with the litigation, the buyer secured a catastrophic excess of loss insurance policy, protecting itself against the future financial effects of pending and future lawsuits.

Case 4: asset disposition

In conjunction with a merger, regulatory authorities required the combined entity to dispose of certain assets. A transaction was agreed with a third party for the disposal of these assets. Just prior to announcing the sale it was discovered that there was a technical breach in a license for one of the inputs required to produce the product that was manufactured by the company being purchased. This breach, although highly unlikely to have any future impact on the business or its operations, had the potential to result in increased production cost if an alternative source had to be used. The seller was forced to provide an indemnity for the potential increased cost to the buyer.

The seller had finality as a key objective and, although the probability of the indemnity being triggered was extremely low, the seller wanted to eliminate any potential future financial liabilities associated with this indemnity. An insurance solution was pursued whereby insurers agreed to assume the indemnity obligation. This insurance policy allowed the seller to achieve finality. Ultimately the license issue was resolved more quickly than originally anticipated and thus the insurance was not required. The ability to structure an insurance solution provided sufficient comfort to the seller and its board of directors to allow it to proceed with the transaction.

CONCLUSION

Historically, when disagreements between buyers and sellers in mergers and acquisitions have arisen, structural solutions have been found (escrow accounts, MAC clauses, etc) or the transaction value renegotiated or the transaction not executed. In this chapter we have discussed the most common risks that Goldman Sachs' clients have encountered in the course of merger and acquisition execution. We have addressed the ways in which insurance can be applied to facilitate execution where risks give rise to valuation differences or inability for one party to proceed with a transaction. We have also discussed issues related to the structuring and underwriting of the mergers and acquisitions insurance product. Finally, we have provided some practical case studies highlighting the value and strategic use of these new insurance tools.

The insurance market applying solutions to mergers and acquisitions is in its infancy. As advisors in merger transactions, including bankers, lawyers, and accountants, become aware of the ability to structure and execute insurance solutions for complicated and financially volatile risks, the demand for insurance products and capacity will increase.

Unlike traditional insurance, the flow of potential transactions is uncertain in number and timing and the process for executing insurance is typically different from a renewal process in a traditional insurance programme. The market needs to be ready and dedicated to serving flow, whenever it occurs. The market also needs to be flexible in its ability to underwrite unique risks and appreciate the strategic importance of the insurance to the overall merger.

The next stage of market development requires a number of interrelated efforts:

1. Advisors and their clients need to continue to be familiar with the applications and benefits of structuring and executing insurance in the context of a critical strategic transaction. These constituencies need to understand the products, market, costs, process and likelihood of successful execution. It is the responsibility of all parties involved in this market to focus on this education.
2. The insurers involved in underwriting these products need to continue to develop internal expertise to respond to the diversity of risks that emerge in merger transactions. This will require human assets with new and different expertise and backgrounds. Insurers need to combine their expertise in traditional insurance underwriting disciplines with knowledge of banking, legal, tax, and accounting practice. The underwriters of this product need to appreciate the confidentiality issues as well as the typical urgency of a transaction.
3. Perhaps most importantly, the market needs to expand beyond the handful of insurers committed to this product at the current time. Price is always an issue for the client but, due to the strategic value of the product, capacity and certainty of execution typically weigh more heavily than price in the execution decision. Capacity is severely constrained by the limited number of market participants and certainty of execution is reduced by reliance on a small segment of the overall insurance market.

There is enormous potential for the insurance market to generate significant incremental premiums by responding to situations that develop in the course of executing mergers and acquisitions. There may not be a more motivated buyer of insurance than the chief executive officer who, in the heat of a merger battle, wants to complete an important strategic transaction. If it is to capitalise on this opportunity, the insurance market needs to grow so that this particular product can become more responsive to the needs of the clients.

It is pleasing to develop a solution for a merger that is worth a few hundred million dollars, but there is a significant opportunity for the insurance market to craft solutions to multi-billion dollar transactions. Imagine the value and premium opportunity associated with facilitating a spin-off of an entity with a potential US$5 billion dollar taxable gain if the transaction were ultimately deemed taxable, requiring US$1.5 billion or more of insurance. The market must develop the capacity and breadth to respond to these opportunities.

23

The Role of Hedge Funds as Asset Managers in Pension, Life and Annuity Portfolios, and Property-Casualty Reinsurance Covers

David K. A. Mordecai

Clinton Group, Inc[1]

Hedge funds are privately organised, professionally managed investment vehicles that invest primarily in publicly traded securities and in derivatives on publicly traded securities.[2] In contrast to the buy-and-hold investment strategies of traditional asset managers, hedge fund strategies are primarily distinguished by their use of the short-selling of securities, derivatives, active trading and leverage to achieve high absolute returns (returns uncorrelated, on average, with the broad market return).

Hedge funds are uniquely positioned to bridge the asset-liability gap (the mismatch between asset portfolio returns and liabilities incurred under certain states of the world) within insurance and pension-fund portfolios. In particular, established fixed-income arbitrage hedge funds have specialised technical skills, sophisticated analytics, proprietary models and a trading-based infrastructure to manage the securitised and structured instruments that are becoming more prominent as insurance and pension investments. Furthermore, hedge fund-related structured products have demonstrated potential as customised solutions that enhance the risk-bearing capacity of alternative risk transfer (ART) and risk-financing vehicles, eg, captives, finite insurance covers, loss portfolio transfers, and spread loss treaties.

Hedge funds are highly specialised financial intermediaries that produce unique return distributions not directly achievable by other financial intermediaries. Synergies may be realised between hedge funds and other financial intermediaries (pensions, life and property-casualty insurers/reinsurers) in supplying risk-bearing and risk-distribution capacity to the market. For several years, banks and derivative product companies have been allocating capital to hedge funds in the form of structured products that bundle hedge fund payoffs with more generic financial instruments.

This trend of bundling the asset-liability management (ALM) services of hedge funds with those of less specialised financial intermediaries is far less developed among pensions and insurers.

Hedge funds play a unique role in providing ALM services to less specialised and more regulated financial intermediaries. The infrastructure (in economic terms the "cost-structure" and "production function") of more developed and better managed hedge funds allows them prudently and reliably to engage in dynamic investment strategies. These strategies allow hedge funds to replicate a diverse set of complex, state payoffs through the prudent use of leverage, active trading and long/short exposures. These dynamic investment strategies are not achievable for more regulated or less specialised financial intermediaries.

Insurers and reinsurers (as well as pension fund managers) considering hedge fund allocations as a customised ALM solution must consider the following questions:

❏ Which hedge fund strategies are best suited to bridge the asset-liability gap faced within the insurance industry?
❏ Within a suitable set of strategies, what hedge fund platform is best equipped to provide ALM services to large-scale institutions such as insurance companies or pensions?
❏ What characterises a prudent hedge fund management company?
❏ What are the historical return characteristics of a well-managed hedge fund?

INTRODUCTION

This chapter will provide an introduction to hedge funds as financial intermediaries and will explain their emerging role in ALM for insurers and pensions. It will also describe the particular relevance of their role within the context of new insurance financing techniques being developed to supplement existing risk-bearing capacity, while maximising after-tax returns.

The chapter is organised as follows:

❏ A general theory of financial intermediation provides a context for discussing the role and function of insurers and hedge funds.
❏ Some fundamental similarities and differences between insurers and hedge funds are highlighted.
❏ The emergence of ART and hedge fund investing by insurers is discussed in the context of a response to market demand for additional risk-bearing capacity and ALM solutions, respectively.
❏ The structure of the hedge fund industry is described within the context of specialised suppliers (and sophisticated consumers) of "insurance" related to adverse market events.

❏ Allocations to hedge funds (and hedge fund structured products) within insurance portfolios as ALM solutions are introduced and explored.
❏ Finally, a broad overview of hedge fund structured products is presented.

INSURANCE, HEDGE FUNDS AND THE THEORY OF FINANCIAL INTERMEDIATION

Financial intermediaries (such as banks, broker–dealers, insurers/reinsurers, pension funds, hedge funds, derivative product companies) perform a unique function within capital markets. Although they act primarily as principals that supply financial claims with payoff distributions that are difficult for investors in general to efficiently price and hedge – and therefore do not efficiently trade in organised secondary markets – they perform this function as agents for equity investors and other claimants.[3]

Examples of these non-redundant liabilities (ie, financial claims with payoff distributions that are difficult to replicate/hedge with exchange traded instruments) include over-the-counter (OTC) derivative contracts, insurance policies (life, annuity and property-casualty), reinsurance treaties, bank loans/deposits, and other illiquid financial instruments.

For the financial products produced by financial intermediaries to be non-redundant to those already traded in a competitive capital market, either the payoff distributions of these instruments should be difficult to replicate, or other market participants, although able to replicate the payoff distributions, are unable to achieve the low production cost of those institutions that specialise in supplying these claims. The financial intermediary bears the residual risk resulting from replicating these claims (ie, the basis risk between the incurred liability and an incomplete hedge), and is compensated accordingly for retaining this residual risk.

By reserving capital against extreme loss events, financial intermediaries act as warehouses for risk by producing payoffs that offset adverse events, reserving to finance risks that cannot be completely hedged (ie, perfectly replicated). Hence all financial intermediaries, including insurers and hedge funds, by functioning as asset-liability managers, contribute to "completing markets" by redistributing risk between consumers and suppliers of risk capital.

The theory of financial intermediation describes the production and distribution of risk-pooling and risk-sharing products by financial intermediaries. As firms that specialise in warehousing risk (optimally allocating capital for risks ceded by other firms), the primary function of financial intermediaries is to recharacterise and redistribute risks that do not efficiently trade in organised exchange markets. These intermediaries finance their activities by assuming less tradeable exposures and producing more tradeable financial instruments for consumption by other market participants in the organised capital markets.

By supplying non-redundant liabilities and reserving capital against extreme loss events, financial intermediaries effectively "warehouse" risks; they employ their capital structure to finance risks that cannot be directly priced and redistributed in the market by combining dynamic trading (hedging) and reserving. This is also the essence of ART.

The non-redundant contingent liabilities produced by a financial intermediary increase social welfare by spanning (ie, completing) markets. In other words, the market (and social) value of non-redundant contingent claims is derived from the unique payoffs of those claims as an offset against social risk, by paying claims in states of the market when other assets or liabilities do not do this (Föllmer and Sondermann, 1986).

Social risk – residual risk resulting from highly correlated claims against aggregate social income (Hirshleifer and Riley, 1994) – exists in risk-sharing arrangements where idiosyncratic risks do not perfectly offset each other (and are thus only partially mitigated by diversification), and hence where efficient trade cannot lead to the socially optimal allocation of these idiosyncratic risks. In the presence of social risk (those correlated loss events not fully mitigated by diversification), even with proportional risk-sharing arrangements, during bad states of the world (relative to more favourable states of the world), financial payoffs that (even partially) offset social risk command a higher price in the marketplace than payoffs that do not.

This provides the incentive for the activity of financial intermediaries such as reinsurers and hedge funds to supply payoffs that are uncorrelated with bad states of the world. The non-redundant liabilities produced by these financial intermediaries, being uncorrelated with the claims on total social income, should trade at a premium relative to other more generic market-traded instruments.

The comparative advantage of large, highly regulated institutions is capital accumulation and risk-pooling. However, the feasibility of investing to match assets and liabilities may be constrained by the increasing costs to scale inherent in high degrees of active trading, further compounded by the regulatory constraints imposed on the largest institutions.

Similarities and differences between insurers and hedge funds

Risk taking to produce non-redundant liabilities that span markets via non-linear, state-dependent payoffs is a highly specialised and capital-intensive activity. The asset-liability mismatch that results from reserving to issue complex liabilities can only be bridged via dynamic investment strategies, which require specialised skills and infrastructure. Buy-and-hold investing combined with excess reserves allocated in low-risk (and hence low-yielding) assets results in a negative carrying cost. This "negative carry" can only be mitigated by dynamically reallocating between reserve assets and higher yielding assets to maximise risk-adjusted return, conditioned on changing market conditions.

Dynamic investment strategies involve ongoing investment in proprietary risk estimation, portfolio optimisation, capital allocation and asset-liability management, as well as efficient governance and coordination mechanisms to manage asset selection, financing, hedging, and clearing/settling trading.

All active investment management is a form of financial intermediation. The more dynamic the investment strategy and the more complex the ALM role (ie, the more complex the payoff distributions, risk exposures, or financial instruments involved), the more critical the governance, coordination and infrastructure of the manager becomes.

As financial intermediaries, both insurers (including reinsurers and pensions) and hedge funds act primarily as principals to produce, for purchase by other parties, financial instruments and products that do not generally trade in organised secondary markets. This activity of explicitly producing liabilities by transacting exclusively in financial markets (as opposed to markets for non-financial goods and services) results in managerial and regulatory behaviour by the financial intermediary that is distinct from that of other types of firms. In the case of investment allocations to hedge funds, the managerial skill and discretion of the hedge fund manager is crucial to producing excess returns (returns that exceed and are not correlated with systematic market returns).

As stated previously, although both financial and non-financial firms use capital markets to fund their activities, financial intermediaries specialise in transforming and redistributing liabilities by assuming risks ceded by other firms. By warehousing risk and reserving (excess) capital against losses in order to transform and redistribute risk, in general, financial intermediaries provide a form of "insurance" to other participants in the capital markets.

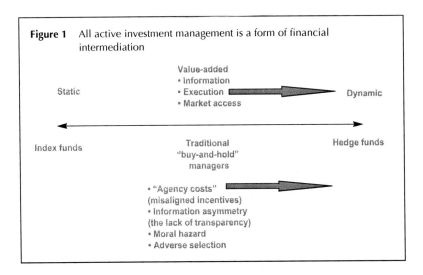

Figure 1 All active investment management is a form of financial intermediation

This characteristic shared by all financial intermediaries equates the risk allocation decision of a financial intermediary to a "supply decision". This supply decision is analogous to the capacity choice and location decisions studied in the theory of industrial organisation, and is synonymous with the leverage (ie, capital structure) and capital allocation decisions studied in the theory of corporate finance, as well as the asset-pricing and portfolio optimisation decisions studied in modern portfolio theory.

Financial theory (Merton, 1990) considers financial intermediaries to be specialist firms whose primary function is to aggregate and manage risk exposures, to have a distinct competitive advantage over other firms in estimating and monitoring illiquid risks. This transaction-cost advantage is derived from a dedicated production technology designed to support the estimation and monitoring of payoff distributions against which the activities of measuring, hedging and allocating capital are informationally intensive. Merton asserts that, in a competitive capital market, it is the production function of financial intermediaries as lowest cost transactors that makes them non-redundant to the market.

Pensions specialise in supplying risk-bearing capacity for smoothing long-tailed risks related to personal wealth and consumption. Insurance companies specialise in supplying risk-bearing capacity for mortality risk, personal injury, political risk, litigation risk, personal and product liability, residual property value, casualty and condemnation, as well as natural hazards to individual consumers and corporations. Reinsurers specialise in supplying risk-bearing capacity to primary insurers and often directly to corporations involved in self-insurance or ART. As specialists in supplying risk-bearing capacity and liquidity to other financial institutions (such as banks and organised exchanges), certain hedge funds are well suited to bridge the asset-liability gap in the portfolios of insurers, reinsurers and pensions.

Hedge funds are organised around functions that support proprietary trading. In contrast, insurers and pensions are organised around distribution, accounting and claims-processing functions. Like banks in the short- to medium-term markets, insurers and pensions are organised to be efficient storehouses and distributors of medium- to long-term capital. As such, they are granted broad regulatory discretion with regard to designing and issuing liabilities, and the ability to finance at relatively low cost (similar to the deposit-taking functions of banks).

However, as distributors of capital, insurers are not efficiently organised to actively trade or invest capital. The regulations imposed on these institutions, which in fact are highly levered, strictly limit their trading and investment activity in order to mitigate moral hazard and adverse selection problems.

The scale and scope of these institutions, combined with the ever-increasing regulatory constraints to which they are subjected, create diseconomies that impair their ability to earn adequate returns under varying market conditions to match their growing base of liabilities. Diverse hedge fund strategies delivered through appropriately structured financial products provide viable solutions to this asset-liability mismatch, by providing efficient access to the required trading expertise and flexibility.

Insurers as hedge fund investors

An increased demand by insurers and pension funds for outsourcing specialised investment services to hedge funds has resulted from increasing insurance industry competition, the proliferation of more complex investments, and pervasive underfunding and risk-adjusted investment performance concerns by insurers and pension managers.

As offshore reinsurance and ART (eg, finite risk insurance, or financial reinsurance) has grown since the early 1990s, some more innovative reinsurers and insurers have become more active hedge fund investors (eg, AIG, ACE, XL).[4] Moreover, at least one Bermuda reinsurer (Max Re) is 40% invested in hedge funds at the time of writing, with the remaining 60% of its investment portfolio being invested in investment-grade fixed-income.[5] Increasingly, large pension funds (such as CalPers, ABP) have been announcing multi-billion dollar target allocations to hedge fund investments.[6]

These instances serve as tangible evidence of the growing demand for unique return distributions produced by certain hedge funds, due to the ALM problem that insurers and pensions face. Exclusively relying on passive equity and bond investments makes it difficult to span different states of the market, and regulatory and infrastructure constraints (diseconomies of scope and scale) result in costs that limit the ability of insurers to act as specialists.

In addition to direct investment in hedge funds or indirect investments through funds of funds, insurers are beginning to invest in senior subordinated notes, principal-protected products, collateralised investment obligations (CIOs) and collateralised fund obligations (CFOs). Insurers are also beginning to sell insured products linked to hedge fund returns with a guaranteed return of principal, a payoff on the occurrence of an insurable event, or a minimum annuity stream to the beneficiary. As this practice grows, there will be a need for providers and purchasers of these products to tier hedge fund managers according to their suitability as asset-liability managers for insurance portfolios.

Hedge funds as insurers: the structure of the industry

As specialised financial intermediaries, the reinsurance and hedge fund industries share similar market dynamics. These common industry dynamics result in both the reinsurance and hedge fund industry being fragmented with relatively few dominant players.

The segmentation and specialisation of the hedge fund market is evident from the large number of relatively small hedge funds, as compared to the typical size of a single mutual-fund company. The fragmentation of the hedge fund industry is also evidence of the decreasing returns to scale exhibited by specialised firms in segmented markets.

In contrast to traditional managed portfolios (such as mutual funds), on average, some hedge funds appear to consistently earn higher average (annual) returns with lower volatility than most broad market indices (Ackerman, McEnally and Ravenscraft, 1999). Many hedge funds employ borrowed funds to increase trading size (or the number of positions), or to finance short selling and hedging in order to profit from idiosyncratic bets that other financial intermediaries cannot.

By financing trading activity with higher degrees of borrowed capital, the increase in hedge fund returns to equity is sometimes accompanied by a commensurate increase in risk. However, higher leverage does not necessarily result in higher risk; with prudent hedging and adequate reserving, in certain strategies the appropriate amount of leverage (dynamically adjusted) can result in lower risk (ie, standard deviation of returns) than a less levered, unhedged exposure to the same investment.

Those insurers seeking to allocate capital to hedge fund strategies should choose carefully. Hedge fund managers and strategies that are best suited to most insurance portfolios are those that employ moderate leverage with substantial hedging, and therefore exhibit stable returns (Libor plus 3%–12%, ie, 8%–15%, per annum) under all market conditions, with low volatility (3%–7% annualised).

Sustainable hedge fund management involves positioning, organising and managing funds to implement strategies within their capacity constraints, while minimising transaction costs. The most appropriate hedge fund strategies and the best-equipped hedge funds to achieve the investment objectives of large-scale institutions are internally diversified, and comprise highly coordinated teams within each strategy operating within a balanced organisational framework. This requires substantial investment by the hedge fund management company to establish infrastructure of sufficient scale and to develop an adequate risk-aggregation and capital-allocation model to manage diversified strategies. It also often demands more coordination across strategies than most funds of funds can achieve.

Specialisation and market segmentation within hedge fund trading strategies

Adaptation to changes in market conditions and responses to the evolving regulatory landscape results in the proliferation of new types of securities. Although the insurance and capital markets are converging, the economies of scope and scale associated with the growing complexity of financial markets also contribute to increased specialisation and market segmentation. This increased complexity, resulting from the introduction of new financial instruments, tends to present new arbitrage opportunities, corresponding to information asymmetries and liquidity (supply/demand) mismatches.

Hedge funds exploit price discrepancies between instruments and across markets according to a diverse array of complex strategies. As stated previously, this requires hedge fund managers to possess highly specialised knowledge regarding:

❏ the specific assets traded, including access to those markets and the flow of information regarding those assets;
❏ the execution of the trades that comprise particular arbitrage strategies; and
❏ position-level and portfolio-level risk management, the hedging and financing of assets within the context of a particular strategy, including managing the idiosyncratic risk of a portfolio of these positions and mitigating the effect of systematic risk on a portfolio of concentrated (idiosyncratic) investments.

There are certain notable trends regarding long-run entry (in contrast to patterns in the short-run trading activity) of hedge funds. The first trend is increased entry by managers from banks, investment banks and mutual funds with varying degrees of skill. This is due, at least in part, to regulatory and market pressure on banks to reduce balance-sheet volatility. Hence, banks are replacing proprietary trading functions with the activity of extending credit to hedge funds.

In general, proprietary traders tend to be better equipped than most other investment professionals to function in the more highly levered and active trading environment of the typical hedge fund, if they can adjust to the balance sheet constraints of a non-bank institution, and either duplicate or "rent" the necessary infrastructure. Furthermore, many mutual fund portfolio managers, attracted by fee income and flexible investment mandates of hedge funds, are leaving traditional fund managers for hedge fund startups. Although mutual fund managers are more accustomed than proprietary traders to meeting targeted investment objectives (sometimes with more limited resources), whether these no-leverage, long-only mutual fund managers can adapt to the more levered, long–short, derivatives-intensive world of hedge funds remains to be seen.

The second trend is the growing supply of long-term equity capital, both institutional and retail. The management fees commanded by hedge funds are also prompting many institutions to sponsor proprietary hedge funds, although it is questionable whether these large-scale institutions are organised to manage these functions effectively in house. Increasingly, endowments are both providing equity capital and engaging in direct arbitrage activity through in-house proprietary trading desks. In this manner endowments are combining allocations to third-party portfolio insurance with "self-insurance".

Hedge funds and alternative assets as "insurance" for the terminal wealth of an investment portfolio

As explained in the previous section, the risk-return profiles of hedge funds, although unique to the investment and financing practices of hedge funds (vs other managed funds) share common characteristics with various dynamic investment strategies, as discussed in various empirical studies (see bibliography). These studies also imply that variation in hedge fund leverage is correlated with extreme market rallies and declines, within and sometimes across markets (Richards, 1999), as hedge fund managers seek to manage their exposure to market volatility.

The statistical properties, ie, the skewness (asymmetry) and kurtosis (fat-tailed) of hedge fund returns relative to both a normal distribution and the distribution of returns for the S&P500 exhibit the property of "state-dependency" (returns that are not linear in risk under certain market conditions). To the extent that hedge fund trading strategies replicate state-dependent, non-linear absolute returns (uncorrelated on average with long-only, buy-and-hold investments), hedge fund allocations are a source of "time diversification". The notion of time diversification refers to the smoothing of the volatility of a joint-return process over time (when individual return processes comprising the joint-return process are uncorrelated), hence increasing the likelihood that a given portfolio achieves a given wealth target.

To some degree, hedge fund strategies generally employ leverage in order to profit from short-term price disparities, comparable to a liquidity premium (Liu and Longstaff, 2000). Actively trading with leverage to exploit these pricing errors produces complex payoff distributions that span states of the market not spanned by passive investing. Allocating capital to active investment strategies that prudently lever and hedge trading exposures can effectively smooth the volatility of a static investment portfolio. Such strategies and their uses are listed below:

❏ Event-driven strategies (distressed security, merger and risk arbitrage) predominantly trade listed warrants and options as well as stocks and bonds to exploit idiosyncratic discrepancies in market prices relative to fundamental value. These discrepancies develop in conjunction with public announcements related to certain corporate events, such as mergers, acquisitions, bankruptcies and reorganisations.
❏ Convertible bond arbitrage and capital structure arbitrage strategies attempt to exploit the relative mispricing of securities that constitute the capital structure of a particular firm.

❏ Long/short strategies and equity hedge strategies attempt to capture excess returns from changing market betas at industry and firm levels.
❏ Index arbitrage strategies attempt to profit from the mispricing between an index and the assets that comprise that index (eg, the S&P500 index and stocks that comprise the S&P500).
❏ Market-timing strategies seek to exploit intertemporal pricing changes with regard to possible time-varying returns of various asset classes.
❏ Market-timing funds increase market exposure when expected returns are high.
❏ Managed futures strategies engaged in by commodity trading advisors (CTAs) primarily trade futures contracts to profit from (a) price trends, and/or (b) mean reversion across markets.
❏ Relative-value strategies (eg, fixed-income arbitrage and statistical arbitrage) involve trading based on the convergence between spreads – temporary differences in prices or yields between securities that tend to behave as close but imperfect substitutes. These strategies involve adequate proficiency and infrastructure to manage the substantial volume of specialised trading positions, including short sales, repo, swaps and options.
❏ Multi-strategy overlays attempt to coordinate investment activity across strategies in order to maximise risk-adjusted and/or absolute returns by dynamically reallocating capital between various strategies.

Several academic empirical studies (eg, Fung and Hsieh, 2001) report correlation exhibited between returns to certain hedge fund strategies and various passive option portfolios.

FIXED-INCOME ARBITRAGE STRATEGIES' ROLE WITHIN ALM FOR INSURERS, REINSURERS AND PENSIONS

Most liabilities issued by life and annuity insurers, as well as property-casualty insurers, are more similar to bonds with embedded options than to other liabilities (such as equities). Moreover, in order to maintain the high credit ratings necessary to finance their activities, insurers' portfolios primarily consist of investment-grade fixed-income instruments, such as government bonds, agencies, and high-grade mortgage-backed and asset-backed securities. Therefore, the asset-liability mismatch implicit in these liabilities may be most effectively bridged by hedge funds involved in fixed-income arbitrage and volatility arbitrage strategies. Fixed-income and volatility relative-value hedge funds are highly skilled at the option-adjusted spread (OAS) and duration/convexity management techniques employed to price, hedge and trade options implicit in various financial instruments, in order to recharacterise the timing and severity of events underlying a variable stream of cashflows.

Relative-value analysis within fixed-income arbitrage (such as credit spread arbitrage, mortgage arbitrage) also maps gains/losses to a statistical process (such as default and recovery rates, prepayment speeds), analogous to actuarial risk analysis in insurance. Changes in the market value (ie, price, yield) of fixed-income securities are correlated with the timing and magnitude of cashflows corresponding to the underlying statistical process. Relative-value trading strategies within the fixed-income market, commonly referred to as "fixed-income arbitrage" include:

❏ mortgage arbitrage trading (difference in relative pricing of implied options inherent to mortgage pools);
❏ basis trading (synthetic options replication at lower cost using futures);
❏ intermarket spread trading (exploiting temporary price disparities substitutes traded in separate markets);
❏ yield- and spread-curve trading (exploiting temporary disparities in the slope and curvature of the term structure);
❏ relative-value options strategies (volatility arbitrage; exploiting disparities between implied and realised volatility);
❏ financing strategies (synthetic borrowing/lending to exploit disparities between forward and spot markets, eg, repo, swaps);
❏ credit arbitrage (exploiting temporary disparities between credit spreads and credit events such as default and migration in credit quality).

Hedge funds as suppliers of liquidity and market catastrophe insurance

As suggested by the empirical research and the general descriptions of hedge fund strategies summarised above, many hedge funds exhibit returns correlated with option strategies that provide downside protection to investors. Much like reinsurers, hedge funds are both suppliers and consumers of market catastrophe insurance. For example, when assuming long (short) exposure to market volatility, a hedge fund may limit its loss by buying (selling) protection against the occurrence of high severity market events, the "tails" (middle) vs the occurrence of lower severity market events, the "middle" (tails).

Anecdotal evidence and conventional wisdom suggest that hedge funds actively trade in order to profit from the difference between implied and realised volatility. Academic research suggests that this difference is due to either a volatility risk premium or a "peso effect" (in which the market incorporates a low probability but high severity shock into prices).

Merton, Scholes and Gladstein (1982) examine portfolios of options that, analogous to both portfolio insurance and hedge fund investing, when bought/sold by investment funds, produce positive excess returns by providing catastrophe insurance to the market when volatility premiums are high, but provide low-cost protection when volatility premiums are low. These authors conjectured that fund managers may dynamically replicate or explicitly trade such compound option positions.

As described by Baz, *et al.* (2000), the analogy between selling options and providing market catastrophe insurance is valid for two reasons. First, on average, these positions profit from the tendency for implied volatility to be higher than realised volatility. Second, hedge fund managers must prudently hedge, adequately reserve and intensely monitor portfolio leverage to avoid losses when extreme market conditions occur.

Furthermore, some of the hedge fund strategies described in the previous section may require a contingent supply of short-term liquidity under certain extreme market conditions, which can be bundled within a structured financial product or investment contract linked to the returns of the hedge fund. These structured products can be employed to enhance the investment returns of an insurer's asset portfolio, reduce the loss ratio of an insurer's liability cover, or to provide enhanced, tax-advantaged risk-bearing capacity for the investors via ART structures.

THE CONVERGENCE BETWEEN INSURANCE AND CAPITAL MARKETS
ART, the main theme of this book, is both an emergent risk management paradigm and a systematic framework in which the insurance and capital markets converge. Risk finance applies contingent claims analysis, derivatives strategies, and insurance coverage to the pricing, allocation, and distribution of risk.

The objective is to manage capital reserves in order to optimally defease unhedgeable risks (risks historically difficult to price or trade in liquid markets) over time. By acknowledging the concept of insurance as derivatives and derivatives as insurance, risk finance (ART) applies structured finance and derivatives techniques to insurance risks.

Bridging the asset-liability gap in insurance products with hedge fund payoffs increases the risk-bearing capacity of insurance providers.

However, credit risk is a relevant and fundamental factor in the transactions both of hedge funds and insurers. The mechanisms evolving for managing credit as a source of risk and return also provide a means of transferring hedge fund returns to insurance portfolios.

Financing risks and time diversification: the role of hedge funds in insurance liability portfolios
As mentioned in the previous section, ART involves the smoothing over time or time diversification (defeasance) of insurance losses. The objective is to increase the risk-bearing capacity of a unit of insurance premium by matching the insurance coverage with an investment portfolio that generates returns in excess of the insured losses incurred.

The rationale behind hedge fund investment as a form of portfolio insurance is also the smoothing of investment losses over time. As hedge fund returns increase marginal portfolio returns, risk-bearing capacity increases. The endusers of these products include banks, corporations and private citizens who face risks prohibitively costly to insure with third parties and hence "self-insure". Numerous financial instruments (such as asset and liability swaps) have property-casualty reinsurance analogues (such as catastrophe swaps, industry loss warranties (ILWs), spread loss treaties (SLTs), loss portfolio transfers (LPTs), etc) and vice versa. Hedge funds can play a role in employing these to provide customised ALM solutions to the insurance industry.

Hedge fund-linked life and estate management products

Similar structuring concepts can be applied to variable annuity and variable life products. These can be combined with other forms of liability insurance to create tax-advantaged ownership succession and asset-diversification programmes. Derivatives can be combined with hedge fund investments and insurance programmes to tailor the timing of taxable gains and tax-deductible insurance losses.

The objective is to maximise the after-tax benefits of insurance payments and investment income to private individual and estates. The costs of setting up these programmes make them best suited to high net-worth individuals and large estates. However, insurers can provide distribution to aggregated pools of smaller retail investors, much as pensions aggregate retirement claims and hence bundle investment services to reduce costs to the marginal investor.

The roles of insurers and hedge funds in the credit markets

As the markets for trading credit risk on an unfunded basis eclipse traditional credit markets, reinsurance companies and hedge funds have become two of the most active suppliers of liquidity to these markets.

Credit events are by their very nature *extremal* events (rare probabilistic events). Credit risk represents the losses in the market value of an asset – a financial claim (or portfolio of financial claims) correlated with changes in default expectations related to a particular asset or portfolio. The market value of an asset or portfolio is sensitive to expected losses in credit quality or the asset's migration toward default, much as duration loosely represents the yield sensitivity of a debt instrument to risk-free interest-rate volatility.

Hence, credit risk could be loosely interpreted as the market sensitivity of an asset or a bundle of assets to default expectations. Extreme downward market movements often correlate with trading gaps and illiquidity related to defaults. As markets become more volatile, they also become more correlated. This is especially evident when markets exhibit severe negative shocks.

Credit risk is idiosyncratic heterogeneous and sensitive to the contagion of extreme (downward) movements in prices, and thus is not readily diversified away. Moreover, credit risk has its own term structure, distinct from the term structure of interest rates.

Credit derivatives have traditionally existed since at least the early 1980s in the form of bond insurance and in other forms of credit protection constructed from more conventional credit facilities, for example, special-purpose or standby letters of credit. However, current credit derivative instruments are specifically designed to strip out and trade credit risk, to have a well-defined payoff and hence to be priced more efficiently, based on the perceived risk of a specific credit event, such as a default.

Credit derivatives, in one form or another, have enjoyed a long history in off-balance-sheet and non-recourse structured financing as traditional contingent products. For example:

❏ back-to-back loans have facilitated cross-border corporate borrowing;
❏ backup lines of credit have contributed to securitisation of corporate credit by supporting commercial paper issuance;
❏ other contingent credit issuances have served to guarantee project, equipment and trade financing;
❏ forward contracts;
❏ limited guarantees or third-party financial insurance;
❏ defeasance, escrow, reserve and collateral accounts; and
❏ backup and liquidity facilities.

Increasingly, these traditional credit facilities are being replaced by special-purpose credit-enhanced structures, and by OTC, market-traded credit derivatives.

In their simplest form, credit derivatives involve an exchange of cash-flows between two counterparties, based on some underlying notional amount, typically related to a traditional credit facility. Like other derivative products, simple credit derivatives can be broadly classified as swaps, options or forwards. More complex structures combine simpler credit derivatives to incorporate the correlation of state-dependent payoffs. Closely related to credit derivatives are insurance derivatives, which are tied to discrete events within an insurance portfolio, an index of losses or damage, or some event-intensity parameter.

The key point is that insurance derivatives and credit derivatives are interchangeable and as such can be employed to transform credit or asset risk into insurance risk and vice versa. As such these instruments can be used to intermediate in the transfer of risk and return between insurers and hedge funds.

The role of hedge funds in insurance asset-liability portfolios

The application of hedge fund ALM services to insurance portfolios and products promises to become more prolific over time. Areas of particular interest include stable-value products and insurance-wrapped investments, as well as defeased self-insurance for property-casualty risk. These applications all involve alternative forms of financial intermediation.

Stable-value products and separate-account guaranteed investment contracts

Stable-value portfolios and separate-account guaranteed investment contracts (GICs) can be described as insurance-wrapped managed portfolios. Insurance liability products (death benefit or annuity) bundled with hedge fund investment services are a recent innovation with significant potential applications. This basic principle is also related to wealth-management products for high net-worth markets (such as private placement insurance products as well as variable life and annuity products).

Funds of funds

Fund of funds managers are delegated monitors who are compensated by investors to perform manager selection, due diligence and capital allocation across funds and other critical tasks. As such, the fund of funds serves as an intermediary between investors and hedge funds by reducing the monitoring, information, and transactions costs of investing in hedge funds. Funds of funds are commonly employed in principal protected/guaranteed products in which investors forego gains above an upper threshold to avoid losses below a lower threshold.

Credit-linked notes and principal protection

Credit-linked notes (CLNs) are debt securities issued by an entity with conventional coupon, maturity and redemption features, similar to traditional notes or bonds. A credit-linked note differs from a more conventional debt instrument in that, by design, its performance depends on the performance of a pre-specified reference asset. In this way, credit risk can be unbundled and traded separately from interest rate and price volatility.

CLNs achieve this redistribution of credit risk by incorporating a credit derivative into the structure of the note. Unlike traditional credit issuance, where credit risk remains irrevocably linked with the asset of original issuance, credit derivatives permit the segregation and restructuring of the credit risk of an underlying financial instrument.

As a special class of synthetic securities or structured notes, CLNs typically use the set of bankruptcy-remote mechanisms that are common to the asset-backed securities market. These structures were developed in the secondary-market for mortgages and trade claims (inventory and receivables), and in the non-recourse financing of stand-alone projects, sale-leasebacks, leveraged leases and recapitalisations, and LBOs.

As an asset class, credit-linked investment vehicles provide access, at lower transaction costs, to both investment and risk management opportunities, for investors and hedgers seeking to achieve specific risk-reward profiles. The result is a redefined relationship between supply and demand for credit.

As CLN structures enable entities to synthesise their own AAA-rated swap counterparties, issuers may capitalise on comparative borrowing advantages. The off-balance-sheet treatment of credit derivatives enables participants such as insurers and pensions, restricted to investment-grade investments, to gain access to higher returns, while buyers of non-investment grade assets exchange a fraction of their higher spreads for a lower cost of funds.

CLNs and CDO structures effectively arbitrage the default-risk, maturity, liquidity, tax and regulatory premiums existing in the market. One could view the continued trend toward securitisation of credit-risk and event-risk as "the evolution of intermediation". Various credit structures may be employed to bridge the gap between assets and insurance (or pension) liabilities with hedge fund allocations, while maintaining the credit quality of the asset portfolio.

CLNs are synthetic debt securities issued by an investment-grade entity with more conventional coupon, maturity and redemption features, similar to traditional notes or bonds. However, CLNs differ from a more conventional debt instrument in that, by design, the performance of the CLN depends on the performance of a pre-specified reference asset.

In this way, credit risk can be unbundled and traded separately from interest rate and price volatility. CLNs achieve this redistribution of credit risk by incorporating a credit derivative into the structure of the note. Unlike traditional credit issuance, where credit risk remains irrevocably linked with the asset of its original issuance, credit derivatives permit the segregation and restructuring of the credit risk of an underlying financial instrument.

CDOs are vehicles that issue tranched obligations (funded or unfunded) and thereby lever a portfolio of asset and redistribute the cashflows. The distribution of spread from the assets is based on the risk of the claim in the underlying obligation purchased by each particular investor. A CDO effectively imposes a capital structure of rated debt securities on a pool of assets. The ratings are based on the diversity characteristics, aggregate risk and average spread of the pooled assets.

The discounted present value of the future (estimated) net asset value of a hedge fund investment can be borrowed, and a portion of the proceeds pledged to purchase protection (a floor) against severe losses. This principal guarantee is financed from foregone participation (a cap) on gains.

As shown in Figures 2 to 5, forms of leverage in these structures include total return swaps, repo, options on fund returns, and senior-subordinated structures (eg, managed CDOs). The forms of leverage can be employed to finance the purchase of principal protection in the form of zero-cost collars or put-call spreads. Various insurance agreements provide similar payoffs to these but price the underlying risks somewhat differently or receive different legal, regulatory, and/or tax treatments. This adds both value and complexity to the product.

Figure 2   Repo-based structure

- **A means of financing the investment in the alternative asset**
- **A means of enhancing yield on high-grade fixed-income investment**
- **Levered exposure to the alternative investment collateralised by a pledge of a marginable fixed-income instrument (treasury security, investment grade debt)**
- **Faces all of the documentation, margin and credit risk of any other repo transaction**

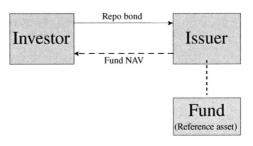

Figure 3   Total return swap structure

- **Unfunded investment in alternative asset (ie, contingent liability)**
- **Financing cost implicit in swap spread**
- **Similar pricing issue as zero cost collar: what is the implied volatility built into the financing rate?**
- **Analogous issue for repo-based structure: what is the implicit financing cost based on repo rate and collateral haircut?**

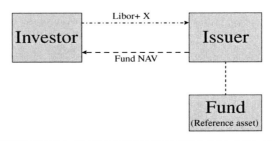

Figure 4   Option-based structure

- Investor faces similar counterparty credit risk from an issuer as with a repo-based and swap-based structure
- Issuer faces less counterparty risk from an investor than with swap-based structure (unless issuer finances option premium)
- Financing of premium results in risk similar to a margin loan
- Implicit financing cost can be hidden in implied volatility assumption

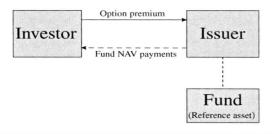

Figure 5   CDO structure

■Investor owns claim on cashflows of assets based on priority of payments

■Neither Issuer no counterparty unless it finances the investor purchase of note

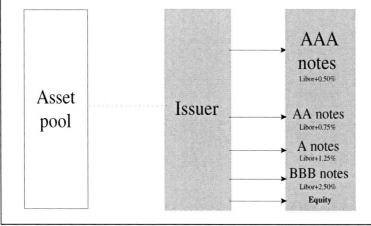

CONCLUSION

The convergence of structured financing techniques with hedge fund investment services in insurance and pension portfolios is only just beginning. The trend toward prudently and appropriately structured investment vehicles promises both long-term and more stable financing for hedge funds and more efficient capital investment for insurers and pensions.

This chapter has provided an introduction to the role of hedge funds as financial intermediaries and, more specifically, has made a case for hedge funds as asset-liability managers for insurers and pension funds. The chapter also discussed applications for insurers and described which hedge funds and strategies – fixed income and credit arbitrage funds with moderate returns (Libor plus 3%–12%) and low volatility (3%–7%) – are best suited to providing asset-liability and hedging services to insurance investment-grade asset portfolios and long-dated liabilities. Finally, the chapter has provided a brief overview of promising hedge fund-linked ART products.

1   This chapter is based on the independent research conducted by the author, in his former role as an academic. It does not necessarily represent the views of Clinton Group Inc. The author wishes to express his appreciation for the support of Clinton Group and George Hall, and for helpful discussions with Clinton Group colleagues Anthony Barkan, Richard Cohen, Greg Drennen, Seth Fischoff, Steven Moulding, Michael Pintar, Tom Schnepp, Vijay Sharma, Michael Vacca, Robert Wenzel and John Zhao. The author also thanks the Editor, Morton Lane, for helpful comments. Any errors are the author's.

2   The exception to this definition is private equity funds that invest in the equity of companies who are not publicly traded. The definition generally applies to managed futures funds, also referred to as commodity trading advisors (CTAs). CTAs share many similarities with hedge funds in general, but are registered with the Commodity Futures Trading Commission (CFTC). Although many US-based hedge funds are also registered as CTAs, CTAs primarily exploit trading opportunities in the exchange-traded futures and options markets. For the purpose of this preliminary discussion and analysis, the convention adopted by Fung and Hsieh (1997) has been used and references to "hedge funds" describe both hedge funds and CTAs, unless otherwise specified.

3   Merton (1990) refers to these difficult to replicate financial liabilities as "non-redundant claims".

4   See www.hedgeworld.com news releases.

5   See www.hedgeworld.com news releases.

6   See www.hedgeworld.com news releases.

BIBLIOGRAPHY

Ackerman, C., R. McEnally and D. Ravenscraft, 1999, "The Performance of Hedge Funds: Risk, Return and Incentives", *Journal of Finance*, 54, pp. 833–74.

Bansal, R., D. A. Hsieh and S. Viswanathan, 1993, "A New Approach to International Arbitrage Pricing", *Journal of Finance*, 48, pp. 1719–47.

Bansal, R., and S. Viswanathan, 1993, "No Arbitrage and Arbitrage Pricing: A New Approach", *Journal of Finance*, 48, pp. 1231–62.

Baz, J., V. Naik, D. Prieul, V. Putyatin and F. Yared, 2000, "Selling Risk at a Premium", *Risk*, pp. 135–8.

Black, F., and A. Perold, 1987, "Theory of Constant Proportion Portfolio Insurance", Unpublished Paper.

Bookstaber, R., and R. Clarke, 1984, "Option Portfolio Strategies: Measurement and Evaluation", *Journal of Business*, 57(4), pp. 469–92.

Brown S., W. Goetzmann and R. Ibbotson, 1999, "Offshore Hedge Funds: Survival and Performance, 1989–95", *Journal of Business*, 72, pp. 911–17.

Föllmer, H., and D. Sondermann, 1986, "Hedging of Non-Redundant Contingent Claims", in: W. Hildenbrand and A. Mas-Colell (eds), *Contributions to Mathematical Economics: In Honor of Gerard Debreu*, Elsevier, (New York: North-Holland).

Fung, W., and D. Hsieh, 1997, "Empirical Characteristics of Dynamic Trading Strategies: The Case of Hedge Funds", *Review of Financial Studies*, 10(2), pp. 275–302.

Fung, W., and D. Hsieh, 1998a, *Performance Attribution and Style Analysis: From Mutual Funds to Hedge Funds*, Working Paper, Fuqua School of Business, Duke University.

Fung, W., and D. Hsieh, 1998b, *A Risk-Neutral Approach to Valuing Trend-Following Trading Strategies*, Working Paper, Fuqua School of Business, Duke University.

Fung, W., and D. Hsieh, 1999, *A Primer on Hedge Funds*, Working Paper, Fuqua School of Business, Duke University.

Glosten, L., and R. Jagannathan, 1994, "A Contingent Claim Approach to Performance Evaluation", *Journal of Empirical Finance*, 1, pp. 133–60.

Hirshleifer, J., and J. G. Riley, 1994, *The Analytics of Uncertainty and Information*, (Cambridge University Press).

Leland, H., 1985, "Option Pricing and Replication with Transaction Costs", *Journal of Finance*, 40, pp. 1283–301.

Liu, J., and F. A. Longstaff, 2000, *Losing Money on Arbitrage: Optimal Dynamic Portfolio Choice in Markets with Arbitrage Opportunities*, UCLA Finance, Working Paper No. 9–00.

Merton, R. C., 1990, *Continuous Time Finance*, (Oxford: Blackwell Publishers).

Merton, R. C., M. S. Scholes and M. L. Gladstein, 1978, "The Returns and Risks of Alternative Call-Option Portfolio Investment Strategies", *Journal of Business*, 51(2), pp. 183–242.

Merton, R. C., M. S. Scholes and M. L. Gladstein, 1982, "The Returns and Risks of Alternative Put-Option Portfolio Strategies", *Journal of Business*, 55(1), p. 155.

Mordecai, D., 1998a, "Credit Arbitrage Using Event-Linked Synthetic Structures", in: S. Jaffer (ed), *Alternative Investment Strategies*, (London: Euromoney Books).

Mordecai, D., 1998b, "Event Risk Management and Arbitrage: Synthetic Credit Structures", in: *Credit Derivatives: Applications for Risk Management*, (London: Euromoney Books).

Mordecai, D., 1999a, "Alternative Risk Transfer: Investing Directly in Insurance Risk as an Alternative Investment Strategy", in: T. Schneeweis, and J. F. Pescatore (eds), The Handbook of Alternative Investment Strategies, Institutional Investor Books, New York.

Mordecai, D., 1999b, "Insurance Risk Securitization, Model Robustness, and the Convergence of Event and Credit Risk: A Rating Analyst's View", in: M. Himmick and S. Bouriaux (eds), Securitized Insurance Risk: Strategic Opportunities for Insurers and Investors, (Chicago: Glenlake Publishing Company).

Mordecai, D., 1999c, "The Use of Credit Derivatives in Credit Enhanced and Credit-Linked Structured Notes: A Former Rating Analyst's Perspective", in: J. Francis, J. Frost and G. Whitaker (eds), The Handbook of Credit Derivatives, (New York: McGraw-Hill).

Purcell, D., and P. Crowley, 1998, "The Reality of Hedge Funds", Warburg Dillon Read Research Report, October.

Richards, A., 1999, Idiosyncratic Risk: An Empirical Analysis with Implications for the Risk of Relative-Value Trading Strategies, IMF Working Paper.

Ross, S., 1977, "Return, Risk and Arbitrage", in: I. Friend and J. Bicksler (eds), Risk Return and Finance, (Cambridge MA: Ballinger).

Rubenstein, M., and H. Leland, 1981, "Replicating Options with Positions in Stock and Cash", Financial Analysts Journal, 43, pp. 63–72.

Schneeweis, T., and R. Spurgin, 1998, "Multifactor Analysis of Hedge Fund, Managed Futures and Mutual Fund Return and Risk Characteristics", Journal of Alternative Investments, 1, p. 124.

Schneeweis, T., and R. Spurgin, 2000, The Benefits of Index Option-Based Strategies for Institutional Portfolios: Summary Version, CISDM Working Paper.

Shleifer, A., and R. Vishny, 1992, "Liquidation Values and Debt Capacity: A Market Equilibrium Approach", Journal of Finance, 47, pp. 1343–66.

Shleifer, A. and R. Vishny, 1997, "The Limits of Arbitrage", Journal of Finance, 52, pp. 35–55.

Tomlinson, B., J. Taylor and M. Griffiths, 2000, Hedge Funds Revisited, Pension and Endowment Forum, Goldman Sachs & Co/Financial Risk Management Ltd Research Report, January.

Varian, H. R., 1987, "The Arbitrage Principle in Financial Economics", Economic Perspectives, 1, pp. 55–72.

Part 5

Portfolio considerations

24

The Cost of Risk and Cost of Capital in Capital-Budgeting and Risk Transfer Decisions[1]

Neil Doherty

The Wharton School, University of Pennsylvania

New investments projects will add value to a firm if their net present value (NPV) is positive. Risk must be taken into account when projects are evaluated; when discounting to calculate the NPV, the discount rate must be adjusted to reflect risk – this gives the risk-adjusted discount rate. The risk adjustment is made because investors typically do not like risk, especially if it cannot be diversified. The risk-adjusted rate can be calculated by asset pricing models such as the capital asset pricing model (CAPM).[2]

But this is not the only adjustment for risk that can be made. Risk imposes a set of frictional costs within the firm. For example, as the cashflows of a firm become more volatile, this tends to raise expected taxes, lowering the expected after-tax cashflows. Similarly, as cashflows become more volatile, the possibility of bankruptcy rises and, with it, the expected bankruptcy costs that are reflected in the cost of debt capital. The increased risk of financial distress triggers a set of further frictional costs of a principal agent nature (in that they cause a conflict of interest between creditors and shareholders), which further reduce the expected value of the firm.

The two ways in which risk can affect value are common, but rarely applied correctly, often seen as substitutes. The CAPM adjusts for the *systematic* risk. This is only a partial measure of risk – the correlation between the cashflow and a market index – but it is an adjustment for investor risk aversion. Other approaches, such as the risk-adjusted return on capital (RAROC) account for the total risk. Total risk includes the market risk but also project-specific risk factors uncorrelated with market risk. These two approaches, adjustments for systematic risk and total risk, are not substitutes for each other, they perform very different functions; if adjustment is made for the frictional costs, there is still a need to price the return delivered to investors by an appropriate risk adjusted rate. The expected rates of return required by investors do not reflect the frictional costs of risk. Rather, frictional costs typically reduce the *expected* earnings of the firm. However, these expected earnings still need discounting at an appropriate risk adjusted rate of return that reflects systematic risk.

INTRODUCTION

This chapter will begin by explaining the frictional costs of risk. We will review the CAPM in its simple and multi-factor forms and will look also at RAROC and show that both adjust for risk in different, but complementary, ways. The basic capital budgeting criteria will then be adapted to show how both types of risk costs are included. Finally we will discuss briefly some empirical issues in measuring the costs of risk.

THE COST OF RISK TO A FIRM[3]
Tax effects of risk

A firm's earnings are subject to taxation and typically the tax rate applicable increases as corporate earnings increase. There is a small amount of natural progressivity built into tax schedules but, more importantly, there are tax shields. For example, a firm is often able to make deductions for items such as carry backs (to offset negative earnings in previous years) or depreciation on purchases of durable assets. Thus, if the earnings are negative, or positive but small, the firm will incur no tax, but when earnings exceed a threshold, then incremental income is taxed. This describes a convex tax schedule.[4]

Convex tax profiles penalise volatile earnings. Think of volatility as earnings being either much lower or much higher than some mean point, X. If earnings are much lower, then we fall into the range of low or zero marginal tax rates and so the firm receives little or no reduction in taxes when earnings fall. When earnings rise, however, the firm falls into the high marginal tax bracket. There is an asymmetry. Tax falls only a little when earnings fall, but rises considerably when earnings rise. Thus volatility serves to increase the expected tax burden. Volatility in pre-tax income reduces the expected value of after-tax income.

On the other hand, stability reduces expected taxes. So hedging or insuring can benefit a firm by reducing its expected taxes.

Risk and post-loss investment

Firms create wealth by generating and implementing positive investment opportunities. By "investment" we refer not only to financial investments, such as stocks and bonds, but also real investment projects such as starting a new line of business, opening a branch in a new territory, or undertaking a marketing campaign.

A difference in the transaction costs of internal and external capital means that most firms prefer to use internal capital and set their dividend and cash-management strategies accordingly. Suppose some adverse event arises resulting in a serious reduction in the firm's earnings and there is now insufficient cash to finance upcoming investments. The firm now faces a dilemma. It can either pay the higher costs of external finance, or shelve the project. As a high rate of return is required to offset the high costs of external funding, many projects that otherwise would have had a positive NPV are indeed shelved. Prospectively, the greater the volatility of the firm's net cashflows, the greater the prospect that new investments will be lost and therefore the lower the long-run growth in value. This idea creates a rationale for hedging in order to protect internal funds from such shocks.

Costs of financial distress

Bankruptcy costs

When a firm becomes insolvent or goes bankrupt there are transaction costs. For example, bankruptcy involves a number of direct costs (the legal and administrative costs of the bankruptcy) and indirect costs (supervision by the bankruptcy court may interfere with the process of creating wealth). These costs are borne by the creditors. So if the firm is highly leveraged and its value is volatile, there is a significant probability of bankruptcy and the expected value of these costs will be discounted in the value of debt. In other words, this will raise the cost of debt capital.

For insurance firms, the risk of insolvency brings with it a set of regulatory costs. If the firm is liquidated, whatever franchise value it might have is lost. Even if it is not liquidated, regulatory supervision has its costs. For example, the firm may have to devote a lot of management attention to dealing with problems or the firm may be constrained from certain activities that, although risky, could have been profitable. These costs will raise the cost of both debt and equity capital.

Asset substitution

Limited liability means that the shareholders can walk away from the firm and cede it to creditors. Shareholders have the option to default and "put" the firm to creditors. This is like a put option in that when the equity falls below zero, shareholders can "sell" the firm to creditors for nothing. Thus, when the firm is risky, shareholders keep the upside risk and can walk away from part of the downside. Increased risk means more upside wealth for the shareholders to keep but it does not symmetrically increase the downside to the shareholders. So limited liability is a "heads-I-win-tails-you-lose" game. Playing by these rules, one might wish to increase risk. Another way of saying this is that, as with all put options, the value of the default put increases with risk, and because shareholders own this option, they have an incentive to select risky strategies. Thus there is always a tension between creditors and owners. Owners would like to take creditors' money and then switch to a more risky set of strategies.

Of course, creditors can anticipate this and, as they are the unfortunates who are left with this downside risk, will tend to discount the value of the debt accordingly. Then the cost of debt capital will tend to rise.

The default put option will distort the investment choices made by managers. The choices that increase the firm's overall value (those with the highest NPV) are not necessarily those that maximise equity price (these might be the ones with most risk). Managers will start to shift attention away from NPV in favour of sheer risk, when making investment choices and the firm will fail to maximise its potential value.

Underinvestment

A closely related distortion can arise when a firm becomes insolvent. Suppose this firm has an opportunity to invest in a safe, positive NPV project after the insolvency. If it does, some of the value of the project will shore up debt (including policyholder claims) and the full value of the investment is not captured by the shareholders. So the shareholders may simply decline to undertake positive NPV projects, preferring instead to walk away and pass the firm to creditors. This increases the costs of financial distress, increases the discount paid for the firm's debt and raises the cost of capital.

Risk and executive compensation

The design of executive compensation plans usually reflects a trade-off between two objectives. From a risk-sharing viewpoint, it makes sense to give executives a flat salary. If risky compensation is given to managers (profit-related bonuses, share ownership, stock options, etc) then managers will bear some of the risk. However, managers typically will not be so diversified as investors; a large portion of managers' wealth depends on the fortunes of their employer. Thus, if managers are risk averse, risky compensation imposes a cost. It therefore makes sense for the risk to be borne by shareholders and for managers to have a flat salary.

However, a competing idea is that of incentive compensation. To align the interests of managers and owners, managers should have a stake in the value of the firm, be it through bonuses, shares or options. As value is risky, however, this will put the managers' income at risk – but this is desirable because it will direct managers to work to protect and create value. However, because of risk aversion, the average level of compensation will have to increase and, indeed, most surveys show that compensation is usually higher on average when much of it comes from bonuses.

In practice, compensation plans compromise both these objectives. Compensation committees usually reject a pure incentive compensation plan that would make all compensation risky and provide maximum incentives for wealth creation. This would create too much risk for managers and would be unpopular. Rather, managers receive some fixed compensation and some risky, incentive, compensation. So incentives are not maximised. One would expect that, the more risky the firm, the more difficult and more costly it would be to load up the compensation package with incentive pay. On the other hand, if the firm's value is less risky (perhaps because it insures and hedges risk) then the firm can load up on incentive compensation without imposing too much cost on the executives. Thus, risk can interfere with efficient compensation design but, conversely, management of risk can enhance the efficiency of compensation design.

THE COST OF CAPITAL

The two main methods for calculating the cost of capital are variations on CAPM and RAROC. The second of these methods assumes that the cost of capital must be adjusted for risk and the first assumes that it should be adjusted only for risk that is not diversifiable. Firms usually choose one of these methods. We will look at each of these methods and outline their theoretical basis. It will be argued that they are not in competition with each other, and it will be shown that they can be combined into a composite cost-of-capital measure.

The CAPM

Consider first the CAPM and its derivatives. The basic idea is to see what rate of return is required by investors on an investment, given its risk characteristics. This model applies to all firms. An investor will be indifferent to the choice between getting return with certain risk characteristics from an insurance stock, a bank stock, a pharmaceutical stock or whatever else. The same asset-pricing model will apply to all stocks.

The important insight is that risk must be decomposed. If macroeconomic factors can cause widespread movement in stock prices, this does not mean that all stocks respond in exactly the same way, or to the same degree when economic conditions change. So, if one looks at the riskiness of returns on any individual stock, this can be attributed partly to a common movement between all stocks and partly by idiosyncratic price movements that are uncorrelated with the economic indices.

The common movement is called the market risk or systematic risk, and is measured by the stock's beta, β, which is the correlation between the return on the stock and the market return, divided by the market volatility.

The simple one-factor CAPM starts with this decomposition of risk and the assumption that investors are risk averse. As investors are risk averse, they will tend to form portfolios rather than put all their money in a single financial asset. Diversification reduces the riskiness of their portfolios; the standard deviation around the portfolio rate of return decreases the higher the number of stocks that are in the portfolio. Risk does not disappear, however, even if a very large number of different shares are purchased. There is correlation because stocks themselves are commonly correlated to wider economic factors. Although the idiosyncratic risk will, in the limit, disappear with diversification, this common movement cannot be diversified out. Thus, even if the investor is risk averse, diversifiable risk can be controlled through portfolio choice and is of little consequence. More specifically, it is not reflected in the stock price.

On the other hand, the risk attributed to common movements, market risk, cannot be diversified. One can think of the stock's β as indicating the amount by which the investor's portfolio risk will increase if that stock is included in the investor's portfolio. Thus, if investors were choosing between two securities to add to their portfolio that had the same expected return, they would always choose the one with the lower β. Of course, this choice would be made by all investors and the demand for this security would rise (whereas the demand for the higher market risk asset would fall). These demand shifts would change the prices of securities and the market would settle when the expected returns on the lower β were lower than for the higher β stock. Investors do not like high β's, so the security will be priced to offer a higher expected rate of return.

The CAPM can now be expressed as the following relationship

$$E(r_i) = r_f + \beta_i [E(r_M) - r_f] \tag{1}$$

which shows that the equilibrium expected rate of return on a stock i, $(E(r_i))$ depends on the risk-free rate of return, r_f, the β_I and the expected rate of return on the market portfolio, $E(r_M)$.

Equation (1) shows that the expected return is the risk-free rate plus a second component, which is the risk premium. The expression in brackets, $E(r_M) - r_f$, is the market risk premium, and the risk premium for the stock is the product of the beta and the market risk premium.

This simple, single-factor CAPM is not strongly supported by market evidence. Rather, evidence seems to indicate that there is not one but rather a number of factors (probably about three) that explain security return and that this multi-factor CAPM is the paradigm for explaining capital asset pricing.[5] We can now think of several market indices (each i) with an expected return of $E(r_{i,m})$, m = 1, 2, 3, etc, and the betas for each factor, m, are labelled $_{i,m}$

$$E(r_i) = r_f + \sum_m \beta_{i,m} [E(r_{i,m}) - r_f] \tag{2}$$

This equation presents the CAPM as a discount rate and the expected cash-flows will be discounted at this rate to give present value. Now we can present this relationship as an adjustment to the expected value in the following form. The present value of a cashflow, V_1 to be paid in one period is:

$$V_0 = E(V_1) - \sum_i \frac{E(r_M) - r_f}{\sigma^2(r_M)} COV(V_1; r_M) \qquad (3)$$

or, more compactly, $V_0 = E(V_1) - \lambda_i COV (V_1; r_M)$ where λ is the market risk premium

$$\lambda = E(r_M - r_f)/\sigma^2(r_M).$$

RAROC

Models, such as RAROC, that adjust for total risk, can represent the second set of approaches to the cost of capital. The motivation for these models typically is not theoretical. Sometimes it is used because the CAPM calculated cost of capital simply "does not feel right". For example, at a recent conference of actuaries several presentations used a total risk with the following explanation: much insurance risk is zero β, and use of CAPM would imply a risk-free discount rate. The answer was seen to be transparently wrong; others might use a total risk approach with more direct appeal to empirical tests of CAPM. As discussed above, the simple one-factor CAPM is not strongly supported and some studies have found that total risk seems to be important. However, the weight of evidence does now seem to favour the multi-factor CAPM as suggested above.

Another explanation for RAROC draws on the frictional costs of risk identified above. These frictional costs seem to be related to total risk, not to systematic risk. This needs careful handling. Firm value can be reduced by frictional costs and total risk proxies for these costs, but this adjustment has everything to do with the determination of cashflows within the firm and little to do with the way the capital market values returns with different risk characteristics.

Accounting both for frictional costs of risk and the cost of capital

The valuation process is presented schematically in Figure 1. There are several projects undertaken by the firm, and the expected cashflows are shown as $C1+C2+C3$. These values are taken at the end of the period and they are the values that would be expected before any deduction is made for the transaction costs of risk. However, the value of these combined cashflows after adjusting for risk, V_1, is less than the sum of $C1+C2+C3$. Indeed, the difference is the cost of risk within the firm. This is nothing to do with corporate risk aversion, but simply reflects that transaction costs are higher if the cashflows are volatile. Now, the value V_1 represents value created for investors and can be paid, for example, as dividends. The future

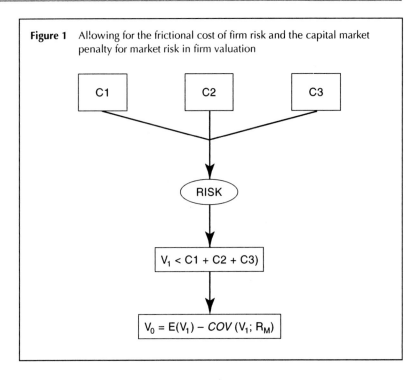

Figure 1 Allowing for the frictional cost of firm risk and the capital market penalty for market risk in firm valuation

value placed on V_1 in the capital market depends on its level of systematic risk and the risk aversion of investors.

CAPITAL BUDGETING AND THE COST OF RISK

Let us suppose that the firm has a set of m operations, each of which generates a net cashflow in one period's time (time 1) of C_i where i identifies each of the $i = 1, 2, \ldots m$, operations. These cashflows are determined as though none of the costs of risk (costs of distress, post-loss investment, tax costs, etc) were incurred. The total expected cashflows of the firm at the end of the period before risk costs are

$$E\left(\sum_{i=1}^{m} C_i\right)$$

And the risk of these cashflows is

$$\sigma^2\left(\sum_{i=1}^{m} C_i\right) = \sum_{i=1}^{m} \sigma_i^2 + \sum_i \sum_{j \neq i} \sigma_{i,j} = \sum_i \sum_j \sigma_{i,j} \tag{4}$$

The costs of risk depend on the level of risk and the notation

$$F\left(\sigma^2\left(\sum_{i=1}^{m} C_i\right)\right)$$

shows that the costs of risk are a function, F, of the variance (σ^2) of the cash-flows, ΣC_i. Thus the expected value, net of risk costs, at the end of the period is:

$$V_1 = E\left(\sum_{i=1}^{m} C_i\right) - F\left(\sigma^2\left(\sum_{i=1}^{m} C_i\right)\right) \qquad (5)$$

Now suppose the firm undertakes a new project, say adding a new product line, opening a branch, or buying or selling a hedge instrument. The cash-flow from that new project, before looking at the cost of risk, is C_n. We can now show the expected end-of-period value of the firm inclusive of the new project:

$$V_1' = E\left(\sum_{i=1}^{m} C_i + C_n\right) - F\left(\sigma^2\left(\sum_{i=1}^{m} C_i + C_n\right)\right) \qquad (6)$$

and the risk in this expression is:

$$\sigma^2\left(\sum_{i=1}^{m} C_i + C_n\right) = \sum_i \sum_j \sigma_{i,j} + \sigma_n^2 + 2\sum_{i=1}^{n} \sigma_{i,n} \qquad (7)$$

The gain in value from the new inclusion of the new project can now be represented as $\Delta V_1 = V_1' - V_1$ which is

$$\Delta V_1 = \left[E\left(\sum_{i=1}^{m} C_i + C_n\right) - F\left(\sigma^2\left(\sum_{i=1}^{m} C_i + C_n\right)\right)\right]$$
$$- \left[E\left(\sum_{i=1}^{n} C_i\right) - F\left(\sigma^2\left(\sum_{i=1}^{n} C_i\right)\right)\right] \qquad (8)$$

In order to understand this clearly, it is useful to make a simplification. Consider a special case where the risk bearing cost (shown by the function (F(.)) is linear. Equation (8) would simplify to:

$$\Delta V_1 = E(C_n) - F\left(\sigma_n^2 - 2\sum_{i=1}^{n} \sigma_{i,n}\right) \qquad (9)$$

Equation (9) can now be summarised. The value added at the end of the period is the expected value of the project (before deduction for frictional costs of risk) minus an adjustment for risk, which is the difference between the frictional costs of risk when the project is, and is not, included. This risk adjustment depends on:

❏ How much the project changes the firm's risk. Notice that this change in risk depends partly on the risk from the new project but more importantly on the correlations between the projects and the firm's existing operations.
❏ The magnitude of the frictions introduced by this risk (ie, the function F(.)). This function will be discussed below.

The final step in evaluating the NPV is to apply the CAPM to discount the time 1, V_1, value to give a present value, V_0.

$$\Delta V_0 = \Delta V_1 - \frac{E(r_M) - r_f}{\sigma^2(r_M)} COV(C_n; r_{i, M}) \tag{10}$$

The appendix shows that the same result can be achieved by discounting the expected cashflows, C, by a complex discount rate that accounts for both the β risk and the frictional costs of risk.

RISK TRANSFER

The capital budgeting approach can be used to assess the value created from transferring risk from one entity to another. Consider Equations (8–10), which (together with the equations for risk) give the criteria for capital budgeting. There is no reason why the project undertaken cannot be the purchase or sale of a hedge or insurance instrument. This type of decision involves a set of incremental cashflows that can be valued in the normal way. However, there are some points of interest.

When a hedge is purchased, interest centres on how the risk of the firm changes. Equation 9 shows that the risk adjustment depends largely on the correlation between the firm's existing operations and the cashflows from the hedge – $\sigma_{i, n}$. The point of the hedge is that this correlation is negative. Thus, the hedge should reduce risk, $\sigma(.)$, reduce the costs of risk, $F(\sigma(.))$, and thereby create value.

The second point of interest lies in considering the joint effect of the hedge on the parties taking the long and short positions; we will call them the policyholder and insurer but they could be other types of firms. Now, if we look at Equation 10, the risk adjustment for undiversifiable risk is, $COV(C_n; r_M) E(r_M - r_f)/\sigma^2(r_M)$. However C_n denotes the cashflows from the hedge, which are payments from one party to the other. This risk adjustment must be identical for both parties if the instrument is properly priced. No value can be created overall simply from transferring the systematic risk if the market is in equilibrium. If value is to be created from risk transfer, it must come from differences between the frictional costs of risk between the policyholder and insurer. This can happen in two ways: first, if the incremental increase in risk to the insurer is less than the incremental reduction in risk for the policyholder. This can happen either if the insurer is more diversified or if the risk has a lower correlation with the insurer's existing cashflows than with the policyholder's. Second, if the costs of bearing risk are lower for the insurer than for the policyholder. For example,

❏ the insurer has lower leverage;
❏ the insurer has more linear marginal taxes;

❏ the insurer has fewer investment opportunities and lower growth potential so is not worried about the distortions in future investment decisions;

❏ the insurer has more effective compensation design and corporate governance and can control the principal-agent problems that give risk to the costs of risk more effectively.

We can call these advantages that lead to trade in hedge instruments the "comparative advantage in risk bearing". The important point is that they have nothing to do with systematic risk, but all lead to differences in the F(.) functions between the parties.

MEASURING THE FUNCTION F(.); COST OF RISK BEARING

The tax distortions caused by risk are the easiest to measure in principle. If the firm forecasts its expected earnings and volatility by tax jurisdiction, it is easy to estimate taxes for each earnings scenario. Some firms use simulation models to assess their corporate risk and these models generate many possible earnings profiles, each depending on the chance realisation of interest rates, economic conditions, foreign exchange, liability losses, etc. It is straightforward to use these models to show how volatility affects tax. There may be cruder methods by which taxes can be estimated from simple mean and variance income projections for each tax jurisdiction.

Bankruptcy costs are a different matter. First, the expected costs of bankruptcy fall mostly on creditors (under absolute priority and insolvency, they fall entirely on creditors). Rationally, debt will be priced to reflect these costs. Thus, the yield for creditors will reflect these costs. However, the indirect costs of bankruptcy can fall largely on shareholders. The asset substitution, underinvestment, post-loss investment problems and the problems of managerial compensation and risk all address distortions in the selection of future investment projects that are related to risk. The higher the risk and leverage of the firm, the less likely it is that the firm will select the highest NPV project. Rather, the management will tend to distort its selection towards projects where the default put value is high. This will reduce the future returns to shareholders and it is this reduced in the estimated cashflow that needs to be valued. So the measurement of the F(.) function largely boils down to estimating this distortion.

We do know what drives the frictional cost of risk, we know something about modelling it and we have some empirical information about the size of this effect. The frictional costs of risk are related both to the leverage of the firm and to the expected growth rate. The higher the leverage, the greater the distorting influence of risk. Moreover, because risk and leverage lead to the loss of possible future investment, this effect will be greatest for firms with the higher growth potential. Perhaps the most direct evidence is from Minton and Schrand (1999) who show that capital expenditure for firms with high volatility is about 19% below the mean whereas capital expenditure for low-volatility firms is about 11% above the mean. This is only scratching the surface of this problem. To be of practical value we need to go beyond estimating the amount of capital expenditure that is displaced through earnings volatility, to estimating the value that is lost from the foregone investments. Hopefully future research will focus more directly on measuring the value that is lost through risk and the value that can be created through the management of risk. (See also Tufano, 1996, and Dionne, 2002).

CONCLUSION

This chapter has looked at an important relationship between risk management and capital budgeting. We have considered how to measure the cost of risk when making capital investment decisions. The problem is that risk plays two roles: an up-stream one and a down-stream one. First, if a firm's operating cashflows are volatile, then it will encounter a set of frictional costs. Expected taxes may increase with volatility, bankruptcy costs and principal agent costs increase with volatility, and the firm may experience difficulty in funding new positive-net-present-value investment if its earnings are volatile. These frictional costs are related to the total volatility of the firm's cashflows. To allow for the impact of these frictional costs, costs of capital methods, such RAROC, adjust the discount rate to reflect total volatility. But risk rears its head further down-steam when the firm "delivers" returns to its investors in the form of dividends and capital gains. If investors are risk averse, then any risk in their investment returns is costly if it is not diversifiable. Therefore, asset returns are priced relative to their degree of undiversifiable risk. CAPM and its derivatives price capital asset in this way.

In making capital investment decisions, both the up-stream and down-stream costs of risk need to be considered. Choosing a risky investment project can increase frictional costs and it will have to compensate investors for any undiversifiable risk. In this chapter we have shown how these two approaches to risk can be combined in a single capital budgeting structure.

APPENDIX: PUTTING THE "DOUBLE RISK" PREMIUM IN THE DISCOUNT RATE

The value the capital market places on an risky income stream C, is:

$$V(C) = E(C) - \frac{E(r_M) - r_f}{\sigma^2(r_M)} COV(C, r_M)$$

However, an income stream presented to investors (eg, dividends), will already have been depleted by the internal frictional costs of risk we have looked at in the text. We will show this depletion as follows. Consider that, in the absence of these frictional costs, an investment, I, would generate a risky value C^*. We can now think of the risk adjustment as a shift in the mean of the distribution of C^* by a factor of $1/(1+f)$ as follows:

$$E(C) = E\left[\frac{C^*}{1 + f\left(\sigma^2(C^*)\right)}\right]$$

where $f(.)$ can be thought of as the "discount" to reflect the various costs of risk (costs of distress, incentive conflicts, jeopardy of new projects) etc. In the body of the chapter slightly different terminology has been used for the higher case expression $F(.)$ to describe an additive risk adjustment. In contrast, the risk adjustment here, $f(.)$ is multiplicative.

Now the expected return on investment is.

$$\frac{E(C) - I}{I} = r_i$$

Therefore:

$$COV(r_i, r_m) = COV\left(\frac{C-I}{I}; r_M\right) = \frac{1}{I}\,COV(C; r_M)$$

So, appealing to the CAPM:

$$r_i = r_f + \beta\,(E(r_M) - r_f) = r_f + \frac{COV\left(\frac{C-I}{I}; r_M\right)}{\sigma^2(r_M)}\,(E(r_M) - r_f)$$

and

$$V_0 = \frac{E(C)\left[\dfrac{1}{1 + f((\sigma^2(C))}\right]}{1 + r_i} = \frac{E(C)}{[1 + r_f + \beta(E(r_M) - r_f)][1 + f(\sigma^2(C))]}$$

1 This paper is based on a set of ideas first explored in Doherty (1991) and in Froot and Stein, (1998).
2 See Brealey and Myers (2000) for an explanation of the CAPM.
3 The ideas in this section were developed by many authors over the 1980s and 1990s. A summary is given in Chapters 7 and 8 of Doherty (2000). This reports both on the underlying theories and the empirical support for these ideas.
4 This pattern is affected by tax carry forwards, which tend to reduce the convexity. However, because carry forwards do not accrue interest, and they are not certain to be used, then the convexity does not disappear although the tax schedule is straightened a little.
5 For a survey see Cochrane (2000).

BIBLIOGRAPHY

Brealey, R. A., and S. C. Myers, 2000, *Principles of Corporate Finance*, (Boston: McGraw-Hill).

Cochrane, J. H., 2001, "New Facts in Finance", in: *Economic Perspectives*, Federal Reserve Bank of Chicago.

Dionne, G., and M. Garand, 2002, "Risk Management Determinants Affecting Firm's Values in the Gold Mining Industry: New Empirical Results", Working Paper, HEC, Montreal.

Doherty, N. A., 1991, "The Design of Insurance Contracts when Liability Rules are Unstable", *Journal of Risk and Insurance*, LVIII, p. 227.

Doherty, N. A., 2000, *Integrated Risk Management*, (New York: McGraw Hill).

Froot, K., and J. Stein, 1998, "Risk Management, Capital Budgeting, and the Capital Structure Policy for Financial Institutions: an Integrated Approach", *Journal of Financial Economics*, 47, p. 55.

Minton, B., and C. Schrand, 1999, "The Impact of Cash Flow Volatility on Discretionary Investment and the Costs of Debt and Equity Financing", Working Paper, Wharton School, University of Pennsylvania.

25

Correlation in Risk Portfolio Management

Bill Riker

Renaissance Re

A portfolio of insurance or reinsurance contains correlated risk if policies within the portfolio are not independent of each other. For example, two homes located in Miami are correlated with each other in the event that a hurricane strikes Miami and both homes would experience losses in the same event.

In the past, many insurers and reinsurers have been lulled into thinking that they are not assuming correlated risk and have experienced some unpleasant surprises as correlations became evident in large catastrophes. Reinsurers who do not see their main function as managing correlation are doomed to be surprised as their portfolio does not perform as expected.

INTRODUCTION

This chapter will discuss how this problem has arisen and how it might be addressed. It will identify some historic examples of how correlation was misunderstood in insurance risk management and attempt to suggest some simple ways to address the issues in the future.

THE ASSUMPTION OF INDEPENDENCE

Many risk management and insurance professionals were first exposed to the principles of risk management by reading the following extract from the Chartered Property Casualty Underwriter 1 coursebook, *Principles of Risk Management and Insurance Vol. 1*.

> According to the Law of Large Numbers, as it is applied to exposures to acci-
> dental loss, as the number of units independently exposed to loss increases, it
> becomes more and more likely that the actual proportion of units that suffer
> losses will not differ by more than a specified amount from the estimated
> probability that each unit will suffer a loss.
>
> Increasing the number of homogeneous exposure units allows an insurance
> company to have a greater confidence that its experience will not differ

greatly from what is anticipated according to the loss distribution. Understanding the interactions between the number of exposure units, the probability of loss, the maximum difference criterion, and the desired confidence level is essential in reaching sound risk management decisions.

Many of the risk-management practices used today in the insurance industry have been derived from these two basic interrelated concepts.

In looking more closely at the above citation, there is one element that is not emphasised, although it is critical in making the insurance process work correctly. In the first part of the quotation, the requirement that units be *independently* exposed to loss is clear enough in its presentation, but the second part, which implores the reader to focus on the keys to risk management, unfortunately omits reference to this independence requirement.

If all insurance risks were independent of each other, effectively managing most insurance companies would simply depend on:

❑ properly estimating the expected loss value for pricing;
❑ amassing a sufficiently large number of risks to ensure that the annual outcome is close to the expected value; and
❑ being the lowest cost producer of these risks.

Many insurance problems have their roots in the mismanagement or ignorance of the issue of the correlation between risks. In reinsurance, the management of risk correlation is even more important than in insurance as policies that protect against large events or catastrophes are likely to exhibit more positive correlation in many instances. Unfortunately, many practices historically used in reinsurance are derivatives of concepts used to manage basic insurance risk and do not properly handle risk correlation. This management of correlation between risks is the key in managing an overall portfolio of insurance and especially reinsurance risk.

In considering a short history of events that have caused the insurance and reinsurance industries to experience financial problems or unexpected outcomes, it is the correlation or lack of independence between risks which has caused many of the problems in managing insurance risk. For an example of correlation mismanagement one only has to look at the experiences of the Lloyds market. Lloyds was the original reinsurance market and the pioneer in risk syndication. In its early days, each underwriter or syndicate would take a piece of each risk and, in the event that losses were to occur, each would pay its proportion of the loss. Most early polices were marine polices covering the loss of trade ships. The potential risk of each trade ship sinking was independent of the other ships in the underwriter's portfolio and thus the syndication process enabled each syndicate to create a portfolio of insurable risk. This system worked very well for many decades and the concept of risk syndication prospered.

Over time, the syndicates with the greatest access to desirable business began to look at other syndicates as a place for them to purchase protection for their own accumulated risks. Lloyds syndicates began to reinsure each other, even if the composition of their portfolios contained similar risks. Their understanding of the lack of independence or positive correlation of their risks was disregarded.

Hurricane Alicia and later Hurricane Hugo clearly demonstrated to the market participants that their business was indeed positively correlated. Most of the property reinsurance polices written by syndicates insuring other syndicates experienced losses in these events. The realisation of the positive correlation between their own reinsurances became known as the "LMX Spiral".

To the credit of the participants in Lloyds, appreciation of this phenomenon created a series of changes in the way in which business was conducted to avoid syndicates obtaining capital credit by passing correlated risks among themselves. Many of the changes were based upon the realisation that a single line of business, such as property reinsurance, can be highly correlated in the event of very large industry events.

The terrorist attack on the World Trade Center of September 2001 was another example of an unforeseen positive correlation between insurance products. The incident caused new correlations to become evident between lines of business that had previously been considered independent. In this event there were extreme losses experience by:

❏ property coverages;
❏ airline property and liability insurance;
❏ workers compensation;
❏ liability insurance;
❏ accidental death and dismemberment insurance; and
❏ life insurance.

Losses to these varied lines of business in a single event had never been experienced. If an actuary were to take the last 20 years of historical data and attempt to derive the correlation between these lines of business, it is not surprising the conclusion would be that these different lines of business show no statistical correlation and could be deemed independent for risk management purposes. The events of 11 September, 2001 have shown the fallacy and danger in this type of approach to risk management.

ESTIMATING CORRELATION
To date, much of the practical work in determination of correlation has involved trying to identify the existence of linear correlation between risks. Relatively limited amounts of data from a time-frame perspective (ie, there is lots of data, but the time frame of about 20 years is far too short to properly assess correlation in catastrophic events) have been analysed to

determine the independence of different lines of insurance risk, as well as independence of insurance risk from the other types of financial risk such as the risk in the equity and debt markets. If the management of an insurance entity reaches the conclusion that these risks are truly independent it increases the attractiveness of adding these risks together in a portfolio. Adding them together and diversifying away risk reduces the amount of capital required to support the risk of the portfolio. The assumption of correlation between risks can have huge differences in the required capital for a portfolio.

To demonstrate the problems with this type of analysis the author took the output of the simulation for two separate property reinsurance contracts. For each contract the profit position of the individual contracts was calculated for each simulated annual period. To look at the portfolio profit position the individual annual contract, profit and loss positions were combined for each year, then the results were sorted by the combined profit position.

To illuminate the issue of what the correlation between the two contracts was, the author calculated the linear correlation multiple times for different portions of the distribution, using some familiar points on the exceedence probability distribution. For example, the correlation for the worst 0.1% of the distribution, the worst 0.2% and so on were analysed down to the worst 5%, where the combined profitability of the two contracts become positive. The results of this calculation are demonstrated in Figure 1.

It is clear from Figure 1 that the linear correlation between the contracts increases as you move closer to the tail of the combined outcome. In other words, as you move further and further along the tail, the profit position of the portfolio becomes worse and the correlation between the contracts increases.

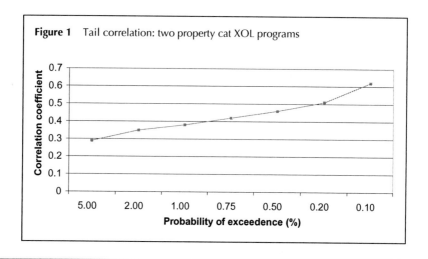

Figure 1   Tail correlation: two property cat XOL programs

If we were to look at the last 20 years of actual experience of these two contracts, we would see no instances where both contracts experienced losses in the same year. Thus if we had used traditional methods of looking at sparse historical data, we could have easily deemed these two contracts independent.

In this example we are fortunate to have catastrophe models that can capture the correlation between these contracts using the physical models of the events and running the simulation many times. Where there are different lines of insurance business, we are not as lucky and we have very little empirical data to enable us to measure what these correlations may be in the tail.

Understanding the correlation between policies is very difficult as there are very few historical data available. For this reason it is up to managements to select appropriate correlation coefficients when they are using dynamic financial analysis (DFA) techniques to determine the risk in their portfolios. Understandably, due to limited data, there is a tendency to select linear correlation coefficients that are calibrated to the more frequent parts of the outcome distribution but, as was noted earlier, the correlations can be most severe in the tails.

Underestimating these coefficients in the DFA models will underestimate overall risk and the capital required to support the individual risks. The incorrect selection of correlation coefficients will not change the expected values for each portfolio component, and thus the expected profit of the overall portfolio, but will overestimate the return on required capital, which will then translate into insufficient pricing on products. The use of DFA models to estimate required capital and return on equity for different segments of an insurer's portfolio is a powerful but dangerous new tool in management's toolbox. It is critical to understand the potential shortfalls in each analysis when using these tools to manage risk. The author believes that failure to do this is one of the major reasons for rampant underpricing during the late 1990s as managements underestimated tail correlations (with the help of their consultants and mathematicians) and thus underestimated capital requirements in the quest for diversification.

The insurance business is not alone in this problem. In the world of asset management, there are many different measures of risk used to manage portfolios of assets. Interestingly, most of the techniques are based on a "value-at-risk" (VAR) measure using historic pricing data for the associated asset classes. In calculating VAR for an asset portfolio, statistical distributions for individual and/or multiple asset classes are combined to determine points on an exceedence curve equivalent. A typical VAR measure is the potential loss of a portfolio at the 99% confidence interval or the amount of capital required to support the risk assuming all capital can be lost with a 1% probability. Often the bulk of the historic data used in the analysis is from the last three to five years of price movements of the particular asset class. Depending on the number of shock events in recent years, using this type of data to understand what could happen to the portfolio with a 1% probability is likely to be woefully inadequate. Examples of this problem include the following:

❏ Long Term Capital Management (LTCM) measured the correlation of different asset classes using traditional VAR-type analysis. They were extremely successful as long as the asset classes in which they were investing behaved in a way consistent with recent history. They underestimated the extreme correlation in liquidity that ensued in the credit markets in fall of 1998. Though many of their positions were theoretically hedged, they could not liquidate their positions in an orderly manner and many of their hedges became ineffective.

❏ Traditional VAR measures estimate the drop in equity values in 1987 as a 25-sigma event. This equates to greater than a one in 1,000,000 return time event. Most people versed in risk would not consider this event in the equity markets to be of this rarity.

MANAGING TAIL RISK

Experts in managing asset risk have made surprisingly little progress in managing the true tail risk in their business. In discussions with experts in the asset management field, the surprisingly naive response to questions about tail risk tend to be that it is "too hard to fathom" or that "the capital markets are huge and the risk is diversified away" and are delivered without much conviction. It is very likely that we will experience some significant tail events in the capital markets over the next few years, which will change the way these markets look at risk in the tails.

In the reinsurance market new products have been designed that have double triggers, which need both an insurance and asset event to occur in the same time period in order to create a loss payment. Most of these products are priced with the assumption of zero correlation between the separate events. Analysing 10–20 years of data, it is easy to reach this conclusion, but if these events have a certain amount of correlation in the tails, the pricing of these products is likely to be optimistic.

Modern DFA models require assumptions about the correlations of different lines of business that a company may write, as well as assumptions between the companies' liabilities and their different asset classes. Many models assumed that there was little or no correlation between lines. The better of these models will use scenario analysis or will create theoretical deterministic events to help examine the effect of a rare tail event on a portfolio of risk. Many insurance managements and rating agencies are beginning to use the DFA models as a major input into their risk management decisions. By incorporating these models into their everyday decisions they have raised the stakes on the proper consideration of tail correlation.

So how should the management of a risk-bearing company act in such an uncertain field? It can hire consultants to provide the framework for combining the different assets and liabilities on its balance sheet. It can conduct exhaustive statistical analysis on the correlation between the different segments of its portfolio though it is very likely that the statistical analysis performed will be inadequate to assess the actual risks to its business, due to the inadequacy of the time period being analysed. It can task its best actuaries to use the latest statistical techniques to better determine the joint probability distributions of its different risks. They can use thick-tailed distributions, combined with copulas to obtain a better assessment of the company's tail risk. Unfortunately the problem will remain that there are not enough observations to create statistically credible assessments of the risks of the tail correlations in insurance (or financial) organisations.

The only feasible course of action is for the senior management to work with its actuaries and statistical professionals to "take a view" on these issues and the parameters utilised in any DFA-type simulations. The process of selecting these parameters is not easy and requires an understanding of statistical processes that may be foreign to many senior managers in the insurance industry. The coupling of both probabilistic and scenario testing is often the most practical approach to understanding the reasonableness of parameter selection.

It is very likely that the rating agencies that are now focusing on DFA analysis and incorporating tail correlations in their analysis will start setting standards for how different assets and liabilities will be correlated for their rating analysis. This framework is still probably a few years away and it will be up to managements to do the preliminary legwork on appropriate selection of the parameters.

CONCLUSION

In managing correlation in a risk portfolio, managers should consider the following:

❏ correlations in tail events are likely to be higher than expected and the sparseness of recent data is unlikely to support rigorous statistical conclusions;

❏ the best way to manage correlation is on a scenario or event-by-event basis, but models that can create and quantify the effect of events on different lines of business are still in their infancy;

❏ stress test assumptions to see where risk might occur if correlations are underestimated; and

❏ examine explicit deterministic scenarios to better understand the composition of the simulated extreme events.

Primary insurance companies should be purchasing reinsurance to help them manage the correlations in their portfolios, particularly where their risks demonstrate tail correlation as this is where their financials can be the most stressed. Reinsurers who are accepting risk from their clients need to recognise they are acquiring correlated risk and that the management of this risk is the most important issue they face.

CONCLUSION

A management of tail correlation in insurance organisations is probably the most important and most difficult issue faced by insurance organisations. There have been few events that have showcased the issue, but, due to their rarity, when they do occur, these catastrophes often threaten the solvency of many players. The insurance industry has looked to developments in the so-called "state of the art" management of asset portfolios as a place to glean new ideas about how to manage risk. In this case it appears that the "state of the art" in the asset management field has yet to address the difficult questions of how to manage catastrophic events.

Insurance management will have to rely on a combination of judgement and statistical analysis to produce practical solutions that are useful in assessing risk. Reinsurers who assume this correlated risk will only be successful if they address the problem head on and do not fool themselves about the characteristics of the risks they assume.

BIBLIOGRAPHY

Reyda, G., 2001, Principles of Risk Management and Insurance, Seventh Edition, (Boston: Addison Wesley).

26

Integrated Simulation Techniques

Michael Steel

Benfield Group

Possibly the fastest and simplest way for (re)insurance entities to model the assumption of risk into their portfolios, particularly where complex (re)insurance contracts are underwritten, is through the use of simulation models. These enable risk assumers to simulate the interaction of different risks, their effect on capital/profitability and also any risk-mitigation strategies that they wish to pursue.

Some simple insurance problems may be solved algebraically but simulation is more appropriate for the more complex ones. Simulation techniques have been used in an insurance context for many years and the theories supporting the modelling undertaken today are quite old (see, for example, Pentikainen *et al.*, 1989). The advent of fast, cheap computer power has brought these techniques into everyday use.

Simulation is applied to insurance situations in many ways in the course of the risk assuming business, including underwriting, portfolio management and dynamic financial analysis (DFA) (modelling all of the risks of an insurance entity).

INTRODUCTION

This chapter addresses the practical application of portfolio management theories and modelling techniques. It discusses the key issues surrounding underwriting a portfolio such as correlations with existing business and management of the resulting aggregate exposures. The breadth of knowledge in this area is continuously evolving, as is the computing power and the intellectual capital to allow (re)insurers and other risk takers to gain a better understanding of their risks than ever before.

THE INSURANCE PROCESS

In order to understand how simulation techniques are used in portfolio management, we must first understand how a portfolio is created. The insurance company pools the risk from many individuals into a risk portfolio for which it receives premium income. As discussed elsewhere in this book, the pricing on such risk is determined to give the insurer an adequate return on its capital. The insurer is able to bear the cost of most types of events that affect its portfolio. However, the insurer must insure itself against the financial effect of risk aggregations from large events (eg, Florida Hurricane, California Quake) and the correlations within the portfolio. The aggregation risk is the risk that the insurer will suffer losses from more than one risk within the portfolio at the same time – for example, two properties in the same postal code in an area prone to earthquakes. The insurance companies insure with reinsurers, which may in turn lay off some portion of the risk to retrocessionaires (entities that reinsure reinsurance companies). This chapter will consider portfolio management in terms of this latter insurer-reinsurer-retrocessionaire step of the process.

INSURANCE RISK

To understand the process, we first consider the types of risk underwritten. These fall broadly into two classifications, short-tailed and long-tailed, which depend largely on the time between the event causing loss and the claim being paid by the reinsurer. There are, however, numerous classes of insurance risk within these broad classifications, such as marine, property, workers compensation and general liability and various sub-classes can exist within each of these classes, such as onshore and offshore within marine, or catastrophe and per risk, by location in property. (Re)insurance cover offered within each of these classes holds different risk/reward profiles and, importantly, different levels of correlation both with other risks and with an amassed portfolio.

As an example of how to analyse insurance losses, we consider a typical loss data set presented for a particular class of business and, using experience and rating analysis techniques, build up a statistical representation of the loss-generation process. We have been presented with 12 years of information (back to 1990) and use a basic inflation rate of 5% to bring the losses up to 2002 on-level dollars.

We split the loss generation process into two components: frequency of loss and severity of loss. Figure 1 shows the frequency of these events from 1990 to 2001, whereas Figure 2 shows their severity.

During the course of our analysis, we would adjust these two elements further for effects such as excess inflation, exposure changes, and continuing development of the loss.

Essentially, observation of these historical events can provide insights into the frequency with which events occur and the severity of those events when they do occur. These estimates then provide inputs to the simulation.

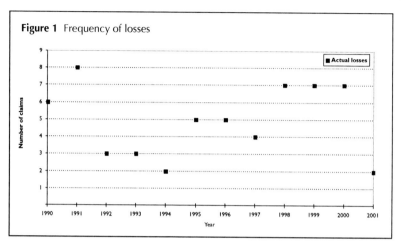

Figure 1 Frequency of losses

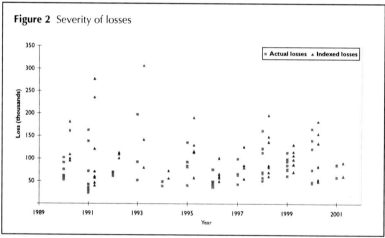

Figure 2 Severity of losses

UNDERWRITING

The majority of (re)insurance products are of a standard format, with standard language to assist in the wide placement of the risk. This homogeneity assists underwriters to focus on the nature of the risk rather the nuances of the contract's language or the subtle workings of various features in the contract. Different combinations of these off-the-shelf products may be used to allow cedents to protect themselves.

Since the early 1990s, bespoke solutions have been developed that catered almost exclusively for the needs of specific clients. These products tend to be unique. As a result, they have the added complication for underwriters that the transaction mechanics need to be well understood in addition to the risk and the sometimes-unique legal considerations.

Simulation modelling techniques are of great benefit to underwrite the first category of products, but are an absolute necessity to understand and underwrite the latter.

To illustrate the methodologies used, we will first construct our model of risk from our class of business. Using standard statistical techniques, we analyse the risks and determine that a Poisson distribution with a mean of five is the appropriate frequency generator (Figure 3) and a lognormal distribution with a mean of 100 and a standard deviation of 50 is the appropriate severity generator (Figure 4).

In a typical simulated year of loss activity we will select (at random) from the frequency distribution a number of events for that year. In turn, for each of these events, we will also select a quantum of loss from the severity distribution. In the simulation, we may go through this process 50,000 times to give an overall distribution of total loss activity.

From a reinsurers' point of view, we would apply each of these losses in each of the years to the reinsurance contract to see if any of the underlying losses resulted in a reinsurance loss. For example, suppose we (as a reinsurer) have been offered an annual reinsurance contract of US$100 xs US$200 with no reinstated limit.[1] Figure 5 shows a picture of how the risk definition and cashflows from this risk are modelled by the reinsurer and then assumed into its overall portfolio.

Obviously, more risks (and reinsurance contracts) can easily be added to this model as the reinsurer builds up its overall portfolio. Figure 6

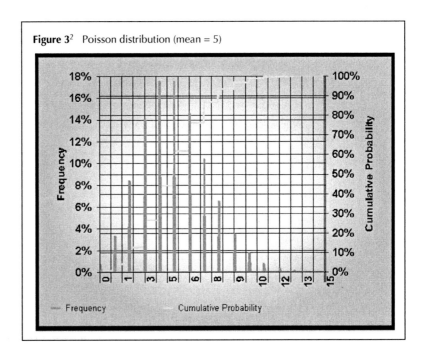

Figure 3[2]   Poisson distribution (mean = 5)

Figure 4   Lognormal distribution (mean = 100, standard deviation = 50)

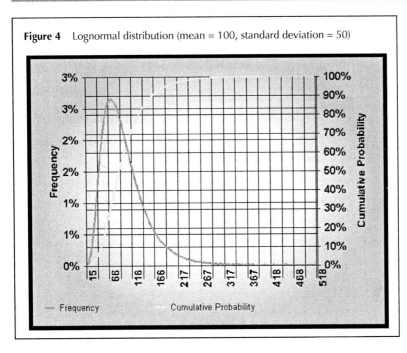

Figure 5   Reinsurer writing a single contract

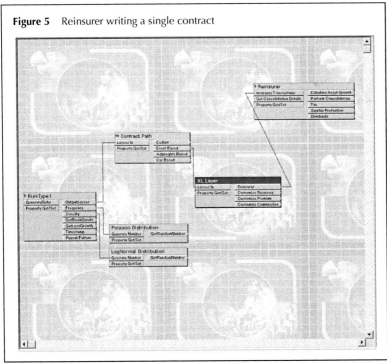

Figure 6   Reinsurer writing 5 contracts

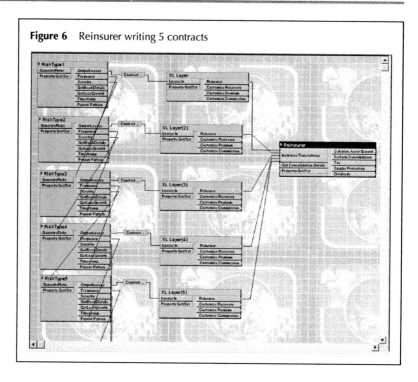

illustrates how a five-contract portfolio can be modelled in a similar fashion using simulation models.

PRICE TAKER/PRICE MAKER

If the reinsurer is merely a following market (a "price taker") then its sole decision is whether the pricing is sufficient to support the additional loss and overall volatility in his portfolio after that risk has been assumed. If the reinsurer is a "price maker", then it must decide the appropriate pricing. The setting of pricing is discussed elsewhere in this book and in Kreps (1990), so this chapter will focus on the "price taking" scenario.

To view the risk/reward ratio of the overall portfolio, consider a portfolio made up of five contracts as shown in Figure 6. To this we will add another (sixth) contract. The key characteristic for a reinsurer looking at this overall risk, in simple terms, is the probability distribution of premium less nominal losses (or underwriting result). This five-contract ("current") is illustrated in Figure 7. In practice, this metric would normally be extended to view the probability distribution of reinsurers' net present value, taking into account such factors as time-to-payoff losses, and overall investment return.

Key information to note from Figure 7 is an expected profit on the portfolio of US$36.5 million and a 1 in 10 downside probability of a loss of US$30.8

Figure 7 CDF of a reinsurers profit (current portfolio)

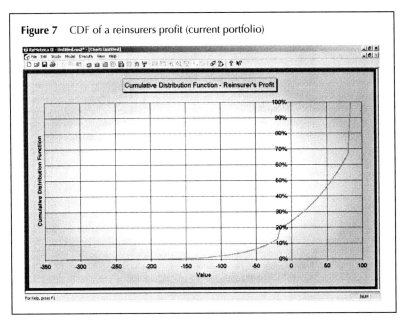

Figure 8 Comparison of CDFs of a reinsurers profit (current and new portfolios)

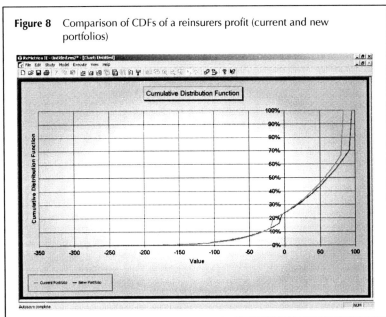

million, with a 1 in 100 chance of the reinsurer losing US$120 million. The probability of the reinsurer losing money from the portfolio is 24%.

Keeping things simple, consider the effect that the new contract has on the overall portfolio. Firstly we look at a situation where the new contract is uncorrelated with all of the previous contracts (Figure 8).

The contract had a premium of US$16 million for the assumption of up to US$100 million of losses. The overall expected (mean) profit has increased to US$43.8 million, whereas the reinsurer has a 10% chance of a loss of US$31.8 million, with a 1% chance of a loss of US$126.3 million, and the probability of the reinsurer losing money is 24%. This is shown by the darker line in Figure 8, with the lighter line being the reinsurer's profit on the portfolio prior to the addition of the new contract.

If we were to assume various positive correlations with the existing book of business of up to 60%, depending on class of business, then these numbers change. The overall expected (mean) profit remains at US$43.8 million, the 10% downside probability increases to a loss of US$38.1 million and the 1% downside probability increases to US$143 million.

PORTFOLIO NET PRESENT VALUE (NPV)

We can now broaden the scope of our analysis to look at imputed investment income. For example, if we assume that our aggregate distribution presented in Figure 8 was the NPV of the reinsurer's overall portfolio, then we can see the effect of adding the payoff risk (the risk of the losses paying earlier/later than expected). Such risk could arise for a multitude of reasons, such as early settlement of a court case, or an increase in the speed of processing claims.

Let us assume our base case of five contracts with no correlation. For simplicity we will assume bullet loss payments by the reinsurer at N years and assume that the reinsurer earns 5% on monies held. The effects of this may be seen in Table 1. As is shown, a payment lag has a significant effect on the reinsurer's overall level of profits, expected profits rise from US$36.5 million to US$45.9 million when a five-year payment lag is introduced.

Table 1 Portfolio – reinsurer's profit with differing payment lags

Delay	0	1	2	3	4	5
Mean (US$)	36.5	38.6	40.5	42.4	44.2	45.9
1 in 10 (US$)	−30.8	−25.6	−20.5	−15.8	−11.2	−6.9
1 in 100 (US$)	−120.0	−110.5	−101.4	−92.8	−84.5	−76.7
P(Loss) (%)	24	23	22	21	19	12

RETROCESSIONAL REINSURANCE

There are a number of ways to modify the overall risk characteristics of the portfolio. One way is to modify the business that is actually written, another could be to purchase retrocessional protection. Again simulation techniques are useful in evaluating the efficiency of any retrocession purchase both in terms of cost and the way in which the retrocession modifies the downside of the portfolio.

For example, suppose the reinsurer were to purchase an aggregate stop-loss on his overall result for his five-contract "current" portfolio. The attachment point for this could be at US$120 million of total aggregate losses (given a total premium income of US$80 million this would equate to a 150% loss ratio) and the limit of the contract is US$60 million.

The first issue for any retrocessionaire would be how to price such a contract. This is a simple process using simulation techniques, with the pricing of such contracts following various methodologies, such as Kreps (1990). The overall loss distribution for the retrocessionaire on our portfolio could be as shown in Figure 9.

For this contract, there is a 91.7% chance of no losses at all, but a 2% chance of a total loss of exceeding the limit of US$60 million. The expected losses to the contract are US$2.7 million.

Let us assume that the retrocessionaire requires a premium of US$6.6 million. This modifies the reinsurers' overall portfolio distribution as follows (compare Figures 10 and 7):

The lighter line in Figure 10 replicates the line in Figure 7. The dark line shows the same reinsurer's profit, but this time the reinsurer has purchased the retrocessional protection. The expected (mean) profit to the reinsurer is now US$32.58 million, with the 10% chance of a US$37.4 million loss, a 1%

Figure 9   CDF of total losses to an aggregate stop-loss contract

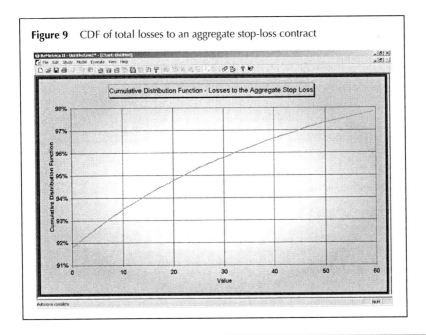

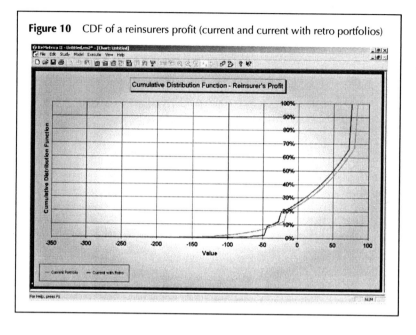

Figure 10 CDF of a reinsurers profit (current and current with retro portfolios)

chance of a loss of US$66.6 million and the probability of a loss of 26%. As can be seen, this lowers the reinsurers' overall expected profit from US$36.5 million to US$32.6 million (the retrocessionaire expects to make a profit on average out of the transaction) but also reduces the reinsurer's potential loss dramatically, this is shown as a reduction in loss at the one in 100 (1%) level from a loss of US$120 million to a loss of just US$66.6 million. Management can judge whether this new portfolio risk profile is in line with expectations, or whether they prefer the non-retrocession alternative. Other reinsurance structures could also be put in place to mitigate this risk further.

BESPOKE PRODUCTS

We can extend this approach to look at a variety of different types of trans-actions. We can examine the economics of the transactions from both buyers' and sellers' viewpoints and therefore construct transactions that fit each party's risk/reward requirements.

These products can take a multitude of forms, from simple multi-year transactions to contracts with any number of features. When sold or pur-chased, the products need to be considered from both an economic view and an accounting/regulatory view, with full account taken of such factors as risk transfer and accruals.

Using simulation techniques it is easy to view the cost/benefit of these types of transactions and to compare them with their simpler counterparts. A more interesting issue concerns the type of decision variables that a company employs to determine the effectiveness of any of the transactions. As discussed previously, in a DFA context, these can include return on capital measures (internal rate of return (IRR) or similar), solvency and other profitability measures.

CONCLUSION

Simulation techniques provide a valuable tool to assist in portfolio management. Their ability to quantitatively assess the effect of different types of risks and their interaction with each other is a key element in this process. Examining different risk mitigation strategies and assessing the impact of various strategies on key decision variables provides management with a very powerful toolkit.

In this brief overview of the subject, we have shown the effects of taking into account payoff patterns and retrocession strategies to affect the overall risk/reward dynamic facing every underwriter. These models can easily be extended to assess total risk within a risk bearing entity but, as with any model, the reader should be cautious as to the validity of the underlying assumptions.

1   US$100 xs US$200 is reinsurance shorthand for a contract where the reinsurer is responsible for losses of the first US$100 over and above US$200 worth of losses retained by the reinsured.
2   The graphical output and screen shots in this paper are from ReMetrica II, Benfield's proprietary risk modelling framework.

BIBLIOGRAPHY

Kreps, R., 1990, "Reinsurer Risk Loads and Marginal Surplus Requirements", *Proceedings of Casualty Actuarial Society*, LXXVII.

Pentikainen, T., H. Bonsdorff, M. Pesonon, J. Rantala and M. Ruohonen, 1989, *Insurance Solvency and Financial Strength* (Helsinki: Finnish Insurance Training and Publishing Co).

27

Improving Portfolio Performance with Catastrophe Bonds

David Heike and John Kiernan

Lehman Brothers

Catastrophe (cat) bonds provide a vehicle for investors to diversify their fixed-income portfolio. These insurance-linked securities are subject to credit losses that are not correlated with defaults of other bonds, which makes them unique among fixed-income asset classes. Defaults of cat bonds are solely driven by natural events such as hurricanes or earthquakes. This differs from defaults of other fixed-income assets, which are driven by economic, legal/regulatory, geopolitical, and other factors that affect corporate profitability. Due to their non-correlation, a small allocation of cat bonds will improve the risk-return profile of most fixed-income portfolios.

INTRODUCTION

This chapter examines the diversification benefits of catastrophe bonds in a fixed-income portfolio. Our analysis shows that the addition of a small allocation of cat bonds to a BB high-yield portfolio, represented by the Lehman Brothers BB High Yield Index, reduces the portfolio's return volatility and boosts its expected return. From a security selection perspective, we discuss differences between a multi-peril cat bond, a single-peril cat bond, and a portfolio of single-peril cat bonds. While a multi-peril cat bond is generally preferable to a single-peril bond due to its higher inherent yield, other concerns, such as exposure to tracking error, often lead portfolio managers to choose a portfolio of single-peril bonds.

LIMITED DIVERSIFICATION AMONG TYPICAL FIXED-INCOME ASSETS

Returns of traditional fixed-income assets historically have been highly correlated across asset classes. Table 1 shows monthly excess returns vs Treasuries for various Lehman Brothers fixed-income indices during the period of January 1989–March 2002. Excess returns show a high correlation across all rating classes of the high-grade credit and high-yield indices.

While the highest correlations are observed between adjacent rating classes, even relatively disparate rating classes show high excess return correlation. For example, there was a 47% correlation between excess returns to the top-rated Aaa index and the much lower rated Caa index.

Strong linkages also exist across other sectors; moreover, these linkages tend to strengthen during periods of high market volatility. Over the past decade, the financial markets have been rocked by various geopolitical events (eg, the Gulf War, the terrorist attacks of 11 September, 2001), credit/liquidity events (eg, Russian Default, Asian contagion), and corporate credit events (eg, Enron, Global Crossing, WorldCom). Returns on most risky financial assets – including corporate bonds, high-yield debt, emerging markets debt, and equity – all produced significantly negative returns during these periods. The strong positive correlation between asset returns during credit downturns diminishes the power of portfolio diversification when it is most needed. On balance, this suggests that the benefits of diversification within a fixed-income portfolio are somewhat illusory.

Why are fixed-income excess returns so highly correlated? A partial explanation is the strong positive correlation in default rates, which can be observed in historical data. Figure 1 shows the variation in Moody's 12-month trailing default rates for various rating classes over the 1981–2001 period. The Ba default rate showed a 72% correlation with the B default rate over this 20-year period. The default rate of Baa bonds, which default at a relatively infrequent rate, still showed more than a 34% correlation with Ba defaults and a 33% correlation with B defaults. The high correlation in default rates is not surprising because fluctuations in business cycles generally affect corporations across various rating classes in a similar fashion.

Table 1 Excess return correlation across Lehman indices, January 1989–May 2002 (%)

	Corporates				High yield			Other		
	Aaa	Aa	A	Baa	Ba	B	Caa	Agency	MBS	ABS
Aa	90									
A	85	95								
Baa	78	87	94							
Ba	60	68	77	81						
B	57	67	75	77	89					
Caa	47	57	67	68	75	87				
Agency	61	59	46	40	21	25	15			
MBS	48	50	43	41	35	35	25	45		
ABS*	64	66	61	58	44	48	42	57	42	
CMBS*	78	73	60	51	36	38	22	76	74	77

* ABS index returns available since January 1992; CMBS index returns available since July 1999.

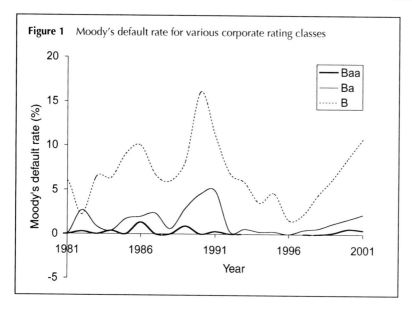

Figure 1 Moody's default rate for various corporate rating classes

During periods of elevated corporate defaults (both observed and anticipated), investors reflect the higher credit risk of corporate bonds by demanding wider credit spreads. This was observed during the 1998–2002 period, as rising high-yield defaults pushed credit spreads wider across all rating classes (Figure 2). For example, generic five-year Ba spreads widened by 500 basis points (bp) during this period, matching the weak-

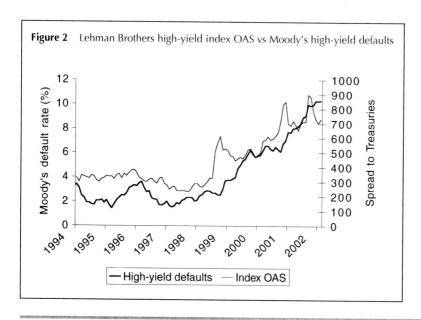

Figure 2 Lehman Brothers high-yield index OAS vs Moody's high-yield defaults

ening credit in the high-yield sector. The efficient repricing of changes in corporate credit risk has resulted in highly volatile excess returns for investment-grade and high-yield corporate bonds over the 1998–2002 period.

THE CASE FOR CAT BONDS

Cat bonds provide a vehicle for investors to diversify their fixed-income portfolio, since they are subject to credit losses that are not correlated with losses of other fixed-income assets. Defaults of cat bonds are solely driven by natural events such as hurricanes or earthquakes. This differs from defaults of other fixed-income assets, which are driven by economics (such as rising unemployment or slowing industrial activity), legal/regulatory issues (class action litigation, anti-trust suits), geopolitical changes (political instability, wars), and other factors that affect corporate profitability. The non-correlated nature of cat bonds makes them unique among fixed-income asset classes.

Since cat bond cashflows are not correlated with the cashflows of other fixed-income asset classes, it is not surprising that cat bond prices have little correlation with prices of bonds in other sectors. Primary and secondary market spreads for cat bonds have not tracked the spreads of other bonds. In the primary market, cat bonds have been priced at consistent spread levels since the market's inception, at roughly six or seven times expected losses. Indeed, historical pricing of USAA's residential reinsurance bonds, issued annually since 1997, shows that execution has actually improved on a spread/expected loss basis over the 1997–2001 period (Table 2). The relative stability in the cat bond new issue market is remarkable when compared with highly volatile prices in the corporate and high-yield markets.

In the secondary market, cat trading spreads have generally exhibited limited correlation with the movements in corporate/high-yield spreads. The events of 11 September, 2001 were a good test for the cat bond market; the experience initially affected cat bond valuations due to the impact on liquidity and increase in investor risk aversion. In the weeks following 11

Table 2   Residential reinsurance: securitisation of US hurricane risk

Issue	Issue date	Average life (yr)	Size (US$ million)	LIBOR spread	Expected loss (%)	Spread/ E(L)	Rating (S&P/Moody's)
Residential Re	Jun-97	1	400	576	0.59	9.8	BB/Ba2
Residential Re II	Jun-98	1	450	416	0.46	9.0	BB/Ba2
Residential Re III	May-99	1	200	366	0.44	8.3	BB/Ba2
Residential Re 2000	May-00	1	200	410	0.54	7.6	BB+/Ba2

September, BBB-rated cat bonds widened by 20bp, while mid-BB-rated cat bonds widened by 55–100bp. However, this spread widening was modest compared with similarly rated bonds in other sectors. For example, BB high-yield debt widened by as much as 300–400bp wider in some sectors by late September 2001. Moreover, cat bond spreads quickly returned to pre-crisis levels, while high-yield spreads remained elevated well into 2002.

PORTFOLIO DIVERSIFICATION WITH CAT BONDS

A small proportion of cat bonds will improve the risk-return profile of most fixed-income portfolios. The diversification benefits of cat bonds are clear. Due to the lack of correlation between cat bonds and other fixed-income assets, the risk associated with cat bonds does not contribute meaningfully to the overall volatility of returns to a well-diversified portfolio. Indeed, small amounts of catastrophic risk typically reduce the overall volatility of portfolio returns. Moreover, cat bonds typically offer a significant risk premium to investors despite their diversification benefit.

To illustrate the risk-return benefit of cat bonds, we used a Monte Carlo simulation to generate hypothetical excess returns to a portfolio that combines BB high-yield bonds and cat bonds. The returns for the high-yield portion of the portfolio were bootstrapped using excess returns to the Lehman Brothers BB High Yield Index over the period of January 1989–May 2001. This entire distribution was shifted to match its expected return with the prevailing spread of the BB index at the end of May 2001. We simulated returns for our representative cat bond – the Munich Re's Prime Capital CalQuake and EuroWind transaction issued in December 2000 – using the loss parameters of this security.

The results are shown graphically in Figures 3a and 3b. As is clear from Figure 3a, increasing the portfolio's allocation to cat bonds boosts the portfolio's expected return, due to higher spread of cat bonds (Libor + 750bp) vs the BB high-yield index (380bp over Treasuries). The volatility of excess returns also declines when small proportions of cat bonds are added, due to the diversification benefits arising from the non-correlated nature of cat bonds. There are limits to these diversification benefits: the portfolio reaches its minimum variance at 12% cat bonds, 88% high-yield bonds. As shown in Figure 3b, the risk-return profile of the portfolio increases for small proportions of cat bonds. The addition of a small allocation of cat bonds increases the portfolio's Sharpe Ratio, which is the ratio of expected excess returns over volatility of excess returns. The combined portfolio reaches its maximum Sharpe Ratio at 19% cat bonds, 81% high-yield bonds, although investors will probably choose much smaller cat bond allocations for other reasons, which will be discussed later.

To further illustrate the benefits of cat bonds, we examine the entire distribution of excess returns in Figures 4a and 4b. The first graph shows the distribution of the BB high-yield portfolio without any cat exposure. Due to

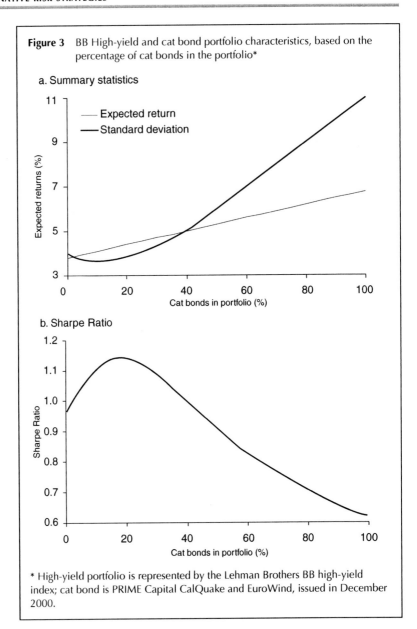

Figure 3   BB High-yield and cat bond portfolio characteristics, based on the percentage of cat bonds in the portfolio*

a. Summary statistics

b. Sharpe Ratio

* High-yield portfolio is represented by the Lehman Brothers BB high-yield index; cat bond is PRIME Capital CalQuake and EuroWind, issued in December 2000.

the high spread volatility of the corporate sector, the BB portfolio under-performs Treasuries almost 16% of the time in a given year in the Monte Carlo simulation. (The true historical averages are even worse – the BB index underperformed Treasuries four times during the 1989–2001 period.

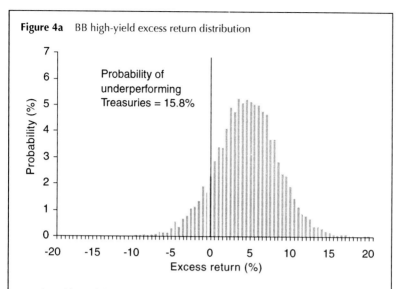

Figure 4a   BB high-yield excess return distribution

* High-yield portfolio is represented by the Lehman Brothers BB High Yield Index; cat bond is PRIME Capital CalQuake and EuroWind, issued in December 2000.

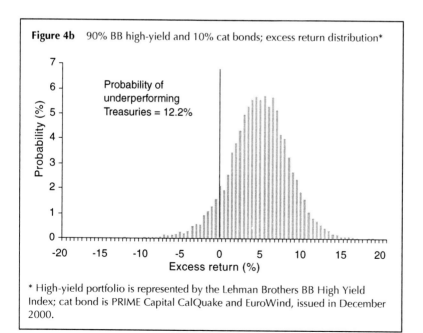

Figure 4b   90% BB high-yield and 10% cat bonds; excess return distribution*

* High-yield portfolio is represented by the Lehman Brothers BB High Yield Index; cat bond is PRIME Capital CalQuake and EuroWind, issued in December 2000.

In our analysis, we simulate the portfolio returns using the prevailing yield of the BB index of 380bp over Treasuries, which is much higher than the historical average realised return.) Adding cat bond exposure measurably improves the return performance of the BB high-yield portfolio. For example, a combined portfolio of 90% BB high-yield bonds and 10% cat bonds underperforms Treasuries only 12.2% of the time, reducing the probability of Treasury underperformance by almost 4%.

SECURITY SELECTION WITHIN THE CAT BOND SECTOR

Over the period 2001–2, there has been an increasing focus on multi-peril cat bonds – bonds where the principal may incur losses due to more than one catastrophic event. Multi-peril bonds typically have higher expected losses than single-peril bonds due to their exposure to multiple events. Moreover, they tend to price at wider spreads because they limit an investor's ability to diversify across perils within the cat sector. For example, in 2001 the SR Wind transaction (exposed to French Wind risk with a 68bp expected loss) priced at a spread of Libor + 525bp, and the March 2000 Seismic transaction (California Earthquake risk, 73bp expected loss) priced at a spread of Libor + 450bp. By comparison, the aptly named Prime CalQuake and EuroWind transaction, which priced in December 2000, was a multi-peril bond exposed to the same types of risk. The Prime security has a higher expected loss than the single-peril bonds (133bp), and priced at a much wider spread of Libor + 750bp.

Should cat investors choose single-peril or multi-peril securities? What about a portfolio of single-peril bonds? We extended the Monte Carlo analysis discussed above to determine what kind of cat exposure investors should add to their BB high-yield portfolio. In particular, we compared summary portfolio statistics for single-peril exposure (Seismic or SR wind), an equally weighted portfolio of single-peril bonds (50% Seismic plus 50% SR wind), or one multi-peril bond (Prime CalQuake and EuroWind). The results of our analysis are tabulated in Tables 3a, 3b, and 3c. In Table 3a, we examine the four scenarios based on expected return. The expected return, not surprisingly, increases most rapidly when Prime exposure is added to the portfolio, owing to the much wider spread of the Prime security.

In Table 3b, we examine the four scenarios based on volatility. These results are somewhat less intuitive. In isolation, the higher expected loss of the Prime bond makes its returns more variable than those of single-peril bonds, and much more volatile than the portfolio of two single-peril bonds that benefit from within-sector diversifications. Viewed in a portfolio context, however, the portfolio volatility differences between the four scenarios are small for low percentages of cat exposure (<5%). This is because the cat return variance makes very little contribution to the overall portfolio variance for small allocations of cat bonds. The more important contribution is the zero correlation between cat bonds and other securities

Table 3 High-yield BB portfolio plus cat bonds

a. Expected excess return vs treasuries

Cat bond	Peril	Portfolio in cat bonds (%)						
		0%	1%	2%	3%	4%	5%	10%
Seismic	CalQuake	3.80	3.81	3.82	3.83	3.84	3.85	3.90
SR Wind	French Wind	3.80	3.81	3.83	3.84	3.86	3.87	3.94
Seismic + SR Wind	CalQuake + French Wind	3.80	3.81	3.82	3.84	3.85	3.86	3.92
PRIME	CalQuake + EuroWind	3.80	3.83	3.86	3.89	3.92	3.95	4.10

b. Standard deviation of excess return vs treasuries

Cat bond	Peril	Portfolio in cat bonds (%)						
		0%	1%	2%	3%	4%	5%	10%
Seismic	CalQuake	3.94	3.90	3.86	3.82	3.79	3.76	3.62
SR Wind	French Wind	3.94	3.90	3.86	3.82	3.79	3.76	3.62
Seismic + SR Wind	CalQuake + French Wind	3.94	3.90	3.86	3.82	3.78	3.75	3.58
PRIME	CalQuake + EuroWind	3.94	3.90	3.86	3.83	3.81	3.78	3.71

c. Sharpe Ratio

Cat bond	Peril	Portfolio in cat bonds (%)						
		0%	1%	2%	3%	4%	5%	10%
Seismic	CalQuake	0.97	0.98	0.99	1.00	1.01	1.02	1.08
SR Wind	French Wind	0.97	0.98	0.99	1.00	1.02	1.03	1.09
Seismic + SR Wind	CalQuake + French Wind	0.97	0.98	0.99	1.00	1.02	1.03	1.09
PRIME	CalQuake + EuroWind	0.97	0.98	1.00	1.01	1.03	1.04	1.10

in the portfolio, which helps to reduce overall portfolio return volatility in all four scenarios. The differences in cat return volatility only become important when a significant percentage of the portfolio is dedicated to cat bonds (for example, 10% or more).

In Table 3c, we examine the four scenarios based on Sharpe Ratios. The multi-peril Prime bond dominates the other three scenarios based on this metric, due to significant differences in expected returns and relatively modest differences in volatility, especially for small allocations to cat risk. The portfolio implications from this analysis are fairly straightforward: investors who add a small percentages of cat bonds to their portfolio should choose the securities with the widest spread, which are typically multi-peril bonds.

Finally, we examine how cat bonds can help minimise downside exposure in a well-diversified portfolio. We use a value-at-risk (VAR) framework, which is a common way of looking at downside risk. It measures the monetary exposure of a portfolio over a given time horizon within a specified probability tolerance. In Table 4, we calculate 1% VAR of various cat-plus-BB portfolio combinations for a hypothetical US$1 billion total investment. The top left cell of the table reports the monetary exposure of a portfolio of BB high-yield bonds with no cat exposure. This portfolio has a 1% VAR of US$56.71 million over a one-year horizon. This means that there is a 1% chance that this portfolio will lose more than US$56.71 million in a given year. Compare this cell with the cell to its right in the table, which reports the 1% VAR of a portfolio of 99% BB bonds plus 1% Seismic cat bonds. The VAR of this portfolio is smaller than the BB-only portfolio at US$55.59 million. This implies that a 1% Seismic cat exposure reduces the downside risk of this portfolio by US$1.12 million.

This VAR analysis shows that a small addition of cat exposure (<5%) reduces the downside risk of the portfolio, independent of the choice of cat bonds. In addition, for small allocations of cat exposure, the multi-peril Prime bond is the most attractive from a VAR perspective due to its higher yield. For larger cat allocations, however, the volatility of the cat portion of the portfolio becomes more important. With a 10% allocation to cat bonds, for example, the portfolio of single-peril bonds has the least downside risk from a VAR perspective, and the multi-peril bond has the highest VAR.

A PORTFOLIO OF CAT BONDS PROVIDES ADDITIONAL DIVERSIFICATION

The above analysis makes a compelling case for cat bonds, particularly multi-peril securities, for managers of portfolios which do not closely track an index, such as collateralised bond obligations (CBOs), hedge funds, insurance companies, Yankee banks and active money managers. However, portfolio managers who hue closely to their index benchmarks face a different optimisation problem; these managers will examine the overall return performance of their portfolio but they will also be concerned about tracking error vs their benchmark. For these managers, the uncorrelated nature of cat bond returns is something of a double-edged

Table 4   VAR analysis for hypothetical US$1 billion portfolio, 1% VAR (US$ million)

Cat bond	Peril	Portfolio in cat bonds (%)						
		0%	1%	2%	3%	4%	5%	6%
Seismic	CalQuake	56.71	55.59	54.64	53.59	52.74	51.72	50.29
SR Wind	EuroWind	56.71	55.56	54.40	53.41	52.60	51.49	51.02
Seismic + SR Wind	CalQuake + EuroWind	56.71	55.57	54.44	53.47	52.33	51.27	46.99
PRIME	CalQuake + EuroWind	56.71	55.34	54.41	53.13	51.80	51.49	56.92

sword. On one hand, it helps to reduce the overall portfolio variance. On the other hand, cat bonds introduce tracking error into portfolio return performance, which results in an element of reputation risk.

A portfolio of cat bonds makes sense for these indexed portfolio managers. Since the occurrence of more than one independent catastrophic event is extremely unlikely, an investor can minimise the likelihood of a total principal loss by holding multiple independent single-peril bonds. From a statistical point of view, diversification within the cat bond sector effectively smoothes out the fat lower tail of the cat return distribution, reducing the portfolio's variance, skewness and kurtosis. From a more practical standpoint, a portfolio of cat bonds has a relatively low likelihood of realising a large loss of principal.

The recent securitisation of a broader range of perils has made it possible to create a diversified portfolio of cat bonds. Issuers initially focused on securitising the most common risks, notably hurricanes on the eastern seaboard of the United States and earthquakes in California. While these two perils still are predominant risks, the list of securitised perils has lengthened considerably to over a dozen independent perils. The newer securitised perils include exposure to earthquakes in Monaco and well as along the New Madrid fault, the most significant US fault zone east of the Rockies. In addition, the combined impact of Lothar and Martin in 1999 has increased securitisation of European windstorms, notably in France and Germany.

A diversified portfolio of single-peril cat bonds helps to manage tracking error for indexed managers. Consider the tracking error of a 1% allocation to cat bonds. A 1% cat allocation to the Prime CalQuake and EuroWind bond will experience a complete writedown 1.07% of the time, which would result in a 100bp underperformance versus the index. On the other hand, a typical portfolio of five cat bonds will almost never lose its entire principal because it would require the coincidence of five major catastrophes occurring simultaneously. In fact, a portfolio of five cat bonds will lose more than 20% of their principal less than 0.4% of the time, meaning that the probability of underperforming the index by more than 20bp is very low.

Finally, some portfolio managers who choose to hold a higher weighting of a given sector vs the benchmark weighting can use cat bonds to manage their tracking error. This is a reinterpretation of our analysis of excess return distributions. Portfolio managers who overweight a spread sector and underweight Treasuries (and thereby maintain a constant duration) can assess their tracking error by examining the distribution of the spread sector's excess returns versus Treasuries. In our earlier analysis, we showed that the risk-return profile of BB excess returns improves with the addition of cat bonds. This implies that cat bonds can reduce the tracking error of a portfolio indexed to an index such as the Lehman Aggregate index with a BB bond overweight (and a Treasury underweight).

CONCLUSION

The above analysis provides justification for the addition of catastrophic risk exposure to a well-diversified portfolio. Our Monte Carlo simulation and VAR analysis demonstrates that the wider spread of multi-peril bonds makes them preferable to single-peril bonds (or a portfolio of single-peril bonds) for small allocations of catastrophe risk. Concerns about tracking error, on the other hand, may lead some portfolio managers to prefer a portfolio of single-peril bonds.

28

Amending Lloyd's Risk-Based Capital Model for Financial Guarantee and Credit Insurance

Peter Allen, Derek Bain, Tony Jones and Samit Shah

Ernst & Young[1]

Alternative risk transfer (ART) gained prominence in the early 1990s as a result of catastrophe (cat) bonds, but a significant growth in the reverse phenomenon, namely property/casualty insurers assuming business, credit and banking risk, was observed in the late 1990s.

One reason for this growth was that the softest market for a generation led underwriters to investigate more innovative ways to risk their money. Bankers noticed regulatory arbitrage between the Bank for International Settlements (BIS) banking capital adequacy provisions and the capital demands made on insurers. The South East Asian crisis of 1998 convinced banks that the levels of exposure in their credit books were high.

Other reasons for the growth reflected more secular trends. The insurance market habitually seeks to expand the universe of insurable risk to cover the previously uninsurable, so if one expands the boundaries of operational risk, insurers will assume more business and credit risk. These trends resulted in a dramatic drive by major reinsurers and investment banks to transfer credit and business risk from the banking and capital markets into the insurance markets.

A number of market participants at Lloyd's had expressed interest in underwriting bespoke credit and business risk and a project was undertaken to amend Lloyd's already-established risk-based capital model to cope with financial guarantee and credit underwriting.

INTRODUCTION

This chapter describes some of the features of credit insurance that make it potentially riskier than other business underwritten through Lloyd's and the bespoke capitalisation structure that Lloyd's proposed to deal with this. It then goes on to describe the model built by Ernst & Young to evaluate the adequacy of this proposed capitalisation structure and the results of this evaluation. The chapter also suggests any possible improvements that could be made to the capitalisation structure.

CREDIT INSURANCE AT LLOYD'S

The underwriting of credit and financial guarantee business had been variously prohibited or restricted at Lloyd's since 1924 following a scandal in which Stanley Harrison, the underwriter of a five-Name syndicate, lost £367,787 by guaranteeing the value of used cars in dealers' lots.

Three aspects of the financial guarantee insurance business make it potentially riskier than the business traditionally underwritten at Lloyd's:

1. *Lack of familiarity.* Lloyd's underwriters are relatively unfamiliar with this business. Lloyd's has not traded in many areas of financial guarantee for 80 years; those classes currently exempted from the prohibition tend to be evolutionary developments from existing business – such as the development of trade credit written off a book of cargo business, or mortgage indemnity written off a book of term life.
2. *Moral hazard.* Such business is more vulnerable to moral hazard – the risk that a party to a transaction has not entered into a contract in good faith where an insured seizes on an aspect of a contract that allows them to take an unfair advantage of the insurer. Some forms of financial guarantee create an asset that can be used to support further transactions. Most are, in some respects, commercial alternatives to other financial instruments, which make use of different capital and pricing methods. Buyers can therefore weigh insurance against other forms of finance (whereas in conventional insurance they usually just weigh up insurance against no insurance) and underwriters may find assureds betting against them.
3. *Exposure to macroeconomic crises.* Credit insurance business tends to correlate with such crises. For example, a mixed book of residual value, credit, contract frustration and mortgage indemnity business in a number of countries responds adversely and simultaneously to one macroeconomic crisis.

A BESPOKE CAPITALISATION STRUCTURE FOR FINANCIAL GUARANTEE AND CREDIT INSURANCE

During 2000 Lloyd's developed and agreed a bespoke capitalisation structure for financial guarantee insurance trade excluding credit insurance, which will continue to be capitalised under Lloyd's normal method. The principal motivation for devising a structure different from Lloyd's conventional risk-based capital system was that the higher levels of correlation found in these classes, combined with the possibility that syndicates will write relatively few and relatively large risks, meant that premium (as used by the mainstream risk-based capital system) was not the only or the best proxy for risk.

Lloyd's proposed capital requirements were based upon a syndicate being required to set aside as Funds at Lloyd's (FAL) an amount equal to the maximum of the sums arrived at by:

❑ the "exposure" method, whereby

$$\text{capital required} = \sqrt{\sum_{i=1}^{n} k_i^2} + C$$

where n is the total number of risks, k_i is the net nominal value of the ith risk and C is a reinsurance credit risk factor.
❑ the "premium" method, defined as 230% of gross premium written on the portfolio of risks;
❑ the "realistic disaster scenario" (RDS) method, requiring syndicates to assess the impact of a number of realistic disaster scenarios.

This three-pronged method was chosen to account for the effect of correlation and for the inaccuracy of premium alone as a proxy for risk.

The structure allowed for credit facultative and financial guarantee-specific reinsurances placed with markets rated A+ and above (see explanation of credit ratings later), up to a maximum of £25m or 5% of syndicate stamp for each exposure. The credit factor was reached by applying Standard & Poor's charge factors to the relevant tranches of the potential reinsurance recoveries used in the above calculation. The premium multiple of 230% was initially derived from comparable figures displayed in the US financial guarantee industry. Syndicates were required to recalculate the additional FAL for all valid policies in every year to allow for the effect of multi-year policies.

EVALUATING THE STRUCTURE: MODELLING A BOND PORTFOLIO AND ITS CAPITAL REQUIREMENTS

Many financial guarantee risks have at their heart some form of credit enhancement or credit default risk. The banking and capital market industries have developed models for pricing and managing this. Ernst &Young applied these techniques to model the loss experience of a syndicate writing a portfolio of credit enhancement business in order to investigate the resilience of the financial guarantee capitalisation requirements.

In order to assess the adequacy of any proposed capitalisation regime it is necessary to define a measure by which the adequacy will be judged. The measure adopted is the "expected syndicate loss" (ESL) (where a syndicate loss is defined as the excess of portfolio losses over the capital plus premium) over the lifetime of a portfolio of credit enhancement business. The steps below summarise how this expected loss was calculated within the model – the approach follows that of CreditMetrics', full details of which can be found in Gupton, Finger and Bhatia (1987).

Step 1 – generate a portfolio of loans and its associated capital

Step 1A – generate a portfolio of loans

A portfolio of loans with an average nominal value of £35 million was generated. The nominal value of each loan was reached by randomly sampling from a loan size distribution with a mean of £500,000 (the distribution chosen was a beta(10, 10) defined over the range [250,000: 750,000]). In practice an individual syndicate's portfolio will depend on its specific circumstances. These assumptions were based on available information about what might be written by a syndicate starting to write financial guarantee business.

Step 1 B – calculate the associated capital requirements

The "exposure" capital requirement was calculated directly from the gross policy exposures (the loan nominal values). No reinsurance was assumed.

The "premium" capital requirement is estimated from the expected portfolio loss cost produced by the simulation model. This is based on the assumption that the actual premium would be based on accurate modelling work. In practice this would be a source of additional uncertainty.

The RDS capital requirement was ignored in this model. Thus the capital available to syndicates could be more than that included in this analysis.

Step 2 – generate a correlated list of defaulting loans

Central to any estimate of the aggregate portfolio loss distribution is a treatment of the correlations between bonds within the portfolio because ignoring such correlations would understate the potential syndicate loss. However, before tackling this, the simpler issue of calculating independent default rates was first addressed.

Step 2A – independent default rates

Independent default probabilities can be assigned to individual loans via a credit rating system. Credit rating systems are generally qualitative systems whereby an alphabetic label is assigned to a loan. These labels define an ordinal ranking of the probability of default. To develop a quantitative model it is necessary to associate a default probability with each rating category. Mappings between rating category and default probability have been developed by credit rating houses such as Moody's and Standard & Poor's by observing the historic default experience of loans within each rating category.

The methodology used relied on assigning a credit rating to each loan and using these ratings to determine the loan default probability.

Step 2B – correlating the default rates

The CreditMetrics approach was followed when modelling correlations. This approach can be described as an asset value approach and follows Merton's option theoretic approach to pricing corporate debt – see Merton (1990).

Essentially, the method is built on the observation that the correlation between the asset returns of obligators can be used to estimate their default correlation.

Merton's option theoretic model implies that the (log) normalised assets returns, R, are normally distributed. Using this model for asset returns, a connection between asset value default thresholds (the level of assets below which a firm will no longer be able to meet its debts) and loan default probabilities was established.

In order for the asset value to fall below the default threshold, the asset returns must be below their own asset return default threshold. The probability of this occurring can be expressed as:

$$Pr\{Default\} = P_{def} = Pr\{R < Z_{def}\} = \Phi - Z_{def})$$

where Z_{def} is the asset return default threshold and Φ denotes the distribution function for the standard normal distribution. As the probability of default is known (assuming that a credit rating has been assigned to the loan) the default threshold may be calculated by inverting the standard normal cumulative distribution function.

$$Z_{def} = \Phi^{-1}(P_{def})$$

In order to demonstrate how the introduction of correlations is achieved, the case of a portfolio comprising only two loans was considered. Firstly, the correlation between the asset returns of our obligators was estimated. Then, given this correlation, e, the joint probability of default can be expressed as

Pr{obligator 1 defaults and obligator 2 defaults} = $P(R_1 < Z_{def1}, R_2 < Z_{def2})$

$$P(R_1 < Z_{def1}, R_2 < Z_{def2}) = \Phi - Z_{def1}, Z_{def2}, e)$$

where $R_{1,2}$ are the normalised asset returns of obligators 1 and 2 respectively, $Z_{def1,2}$ are the asset return default thresholds and $\Phi - Z_{def1}, Z_{def2}, e)$ is the cumulative distribution function of the bivariate normal distribution with correlation e (see Figure 1).

Therefore, in order to determine which of the loans has defaulted only two correlated normal random variables need to be generated. Each of the correlated normal random variables is then attributed to a loan and compared to a default threshold to determine if the loan has defaulted.

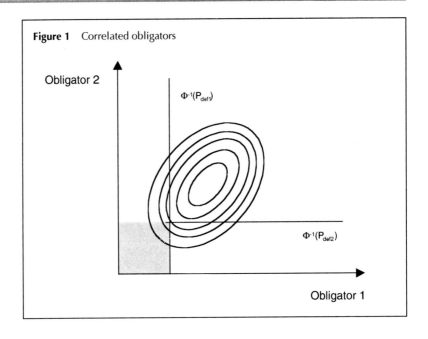

Figure 1 Correlated obligators

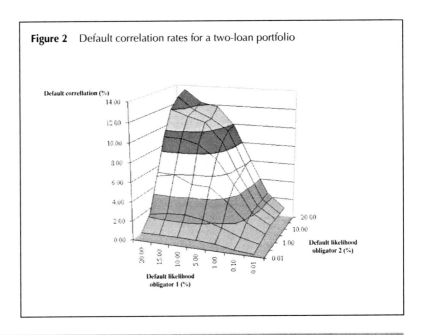

Figure 2 Default correlation rates for a two-loan portfolio

This method of generating correlated defaults is easily extended to arbitrarily large portfolios by replacing the bivariate normal density with correlation e, with the multivariate normal density with covariance matrix Σ.

Before examining the estimation of recovery rate it is worth considering the implication of the above approach. The use of the multivariate normal distribution imposes a correlation structure on the bond default rates with the effect that lower rated debt becomes more heavily correlated than higher rated debt (Figure 2), an effect that has been observed in practice in texts such as Pawlowski, Malhotra and Manning (2000) and Gupton, Finger and Bhatia (1987).

Step 3 – for each defaulted loan, generate the size of the loss
The main determinant of the size of the loss is the level of seniority of the debt. Average loss rates can range from 50% of the nominal value for senior secured debt up to 85% for junior subordinated debt. Moreover, as pointed out in Gupton, Finger and Bhatia (1997), loss rates generally exhibit high levels of volatility.[3]

Estimating syndicate losses
Steps one to three above summarise the approach to calculating the portfolio loss for one simulation. It is then possible, using Monte Carlo simulation, to estimate a portfolio loss distribution from which an average portfolio loss can be calculated.

In order to determine the ESL it is first necessary to calculate the syndi-

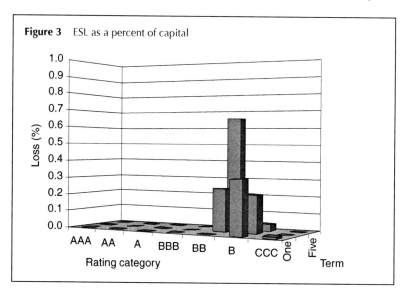

Figure 3 ESL as a percent of capital

cate loss arising during each simulation. To do this, the capital (as calculated in Step 1B) plus premium is compared with the estimated portfolio loss. These syndicate losses are then averaged over all simulations to estimate the ESL. Figure 3 shows a graph of the ESL as a percentage of the capital required to commence underwriting for a number of portfolios ranging from 100% AAA one-year term to 100% CCC five-year term.

Whether the "exposure" or "premium" method is triggered depended primarily on the probability of default. When this was low (high-rated debt or very short-term loans) the exposure method dominated. As the probability of default increased (low-grade debt and longer loan terms) the premium method became progressively more important. The highest ESL tends to occur around the crossover points between the two methods. However, even at these points the ESL remained very low.

AN ALTERNATIVE MEASURE TO ASSESS THE ADEQUACY OF THE CAPITALISATION STRUCTURE

An alternative measure of considering whether the proposed regime is adequate is to look at how likely it is that the capital set aside as FAL would prove insufficient. One possible requirement is that the capital set aside should be able to cover all events that are likely to occur more than once every 200 years – ie, the capital should be inadequate on average less than once every 200 years.

A portfolio loss distribution can be created employing the methodology used to obtain the ESL using Monte Carlo simulation. The 99.5th percentile

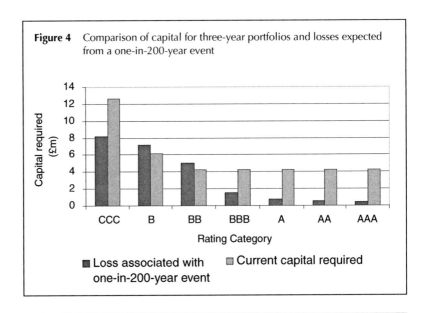

Figure 4 Comparison of capital for three-year portfolios and losses expected from a one-in-200-year event

of this loss distribution can easily be estimated by, for instance, looking at the fiftieth largest loss from a run of 10,000 simulations.

For most of the bond portfolios analysed the proposed capital required comfortably covers that required to meet a one-in-200-year loss (see Figure 4). For CCC-grade debt and high-grade debt, in fact, the capital required could potentially be viewed as excessive and unnecessary. For B and BB bonds the capital would not quite be sufficient to cover the potential losses from a one-in-200-year event. This is consistent with the results obtained when looking at ESL as a measure where the ESL is highest around the crossover point between the "premium" and "exposure" methods.

ANALYSING THE EFFECT OF ALTERNATIVE PORTFOLIOS OF LOANS

The results above all relate to a portfolio of 70 bonds with a nominal value generated by randomly sampling from a loan size beta(10,10) distribution defined over [250,000:750,000] with a mean of £500,000. This produces a portfolio of bonds whose nominal values are unskewed and that do not vary significantly in value (as Figure 5 shows).

In practice, an individual syndicate's portfolio would depend on its specific circumstances and hence the above assumptions may be inappropriate. To understand the effect of this on both the distribution of losses and the capital requirement, a highly skewed portfolio was used in place of the beta distribution created in Step 1A.

As one would expect, a one-in-200-year event would cause a much larger loss for a highly skewed distribution than for the unskewed beta distribution. However, the proposed capital requirement compensates to allow for this (see Figure 6). This is because although the value of the "premium" method does not change for a skewed distribution, as the expected value of

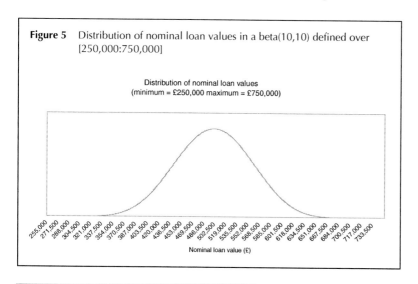

Figure 5   Distribution of nominal loan values in a beta(10,10) defined over [250,000:750,000]

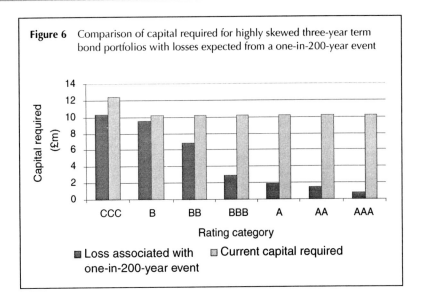

Figure 6 Comparison of capital required for highly skewed three-year term bond portfolios with losses expected from a one-in-200-year event

claims is unchanged, the "exposure" method increases to compensate for the extra risk involved.

AN ALTERNATIVE CAPITAL REQUIREMENT

In order to cope with the challenge that the capital required could be viewed as excessive and unnecessary, alternative capital requirements were explored, including using a different "premium" method (changing the percentage used from 230%), using a different "exposure" method (using a cube root of the sum of the cubes of exposure) and using some sort of weighted average of these methods instead of taking the maximum. It should be borne in mind that it is not possible to produce a simple formula that exactly replicates something as precise as the 99.5th percentile of the loss distribution. The best we could hope for was to find a formula that reasonably matched the distribution and that never falls significantly below it.

For example we looked at the following possible capital requirement:

$$\text{capital required} = \frac{\left(\sqrt{\sum_{i=1}^{n} k_i^2} + C + 170\%GWP \right)}{2} \times 1.5$$

where n is the total number of risks, k_i is the net nominal value of the ith risk, C is a reinsurance credit risk factor and GWP is the gross written premium.

As with the previous capital requirement, this is usually comfortably

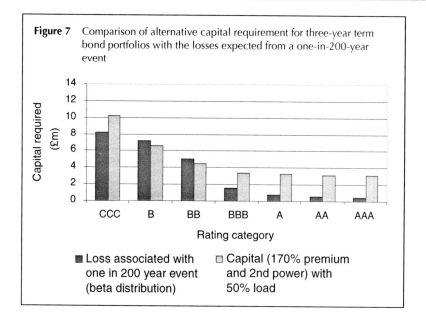

Figure 7 Comparison of alternative capital requirement for three-year term bond portfolios with the losses expected from a one-in-200-year event

larger than that required to cover a one-in-200-year loss (see Figure 7). However the amount of excess capital required for very low-grade or high-grade portfolios have now been reduced. The capital required for BB and B grade portfolios still does not cover a 99.5th percentile loss, although the amount of this deficiency has not increased and can be considered small. These results are duplicated when looking at bonds with terms of one or five years.

How does this capital requirement perform when using ESL as a measure? We can see from Figure 8 that the ESL is highest again for bond portfolios that are BB and B graded. However even here the ESL is very low and much lower than that for the original Lloyd's capital requirement. The mixed portfolio in Figure 8 corresponds to a portfolio made up of 10% BBB-, 15% BB-, 25% B- and 50% CCC-grade bonds. It is also worth noting that, because the exposure method term allows for the degree of diversification of a portfolio in terms of nominal loan size, the capital required does increase for "skewed" portfolios.

SUMMARY
❏ Lloyd's and Ernst & Young undertook a project to amend Lloyd's already-established risk-based capital system to cope with credit and financial guarantee insurance.
❏ Lloyd's had developed and agreed a bespoke capitalisation structure for these classes, based upon a syndicate being required to set aside, as FAL,

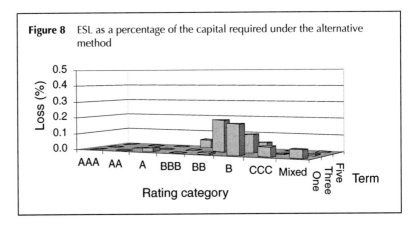

Figure 8 ESL as a percentage of the capital required under the alternative method

the maximum of an amount derived from the exposure to be insured, an amount derived from the premium to be written, and an amount derived from subjecting the book of business to a simulated disaster scenario.

❑ To evaluate the regime, we adopted a measure of expected syndicate loss, defined as the excess of portfolio losses over the capital plus premium.

❑ This evaluation showed that when the probability of default in the book was low, the exposure method of capitalisation dominated, and as the probability of default increased, the premium method became more important. The expected syndicate loss was at its highest where the two methods intersected.

❑ An alternative evaluation questioned whether the capital provided by the method would be adequate to cover a one-in-200-year loss. This confirmed that it would not quite be sufficient for portfolios of B and BB bonds – but that it might be excessive for portfolios of more and less risky securities.

❑ We therefore explored amendments to the capitalisation structure that changed the premium multiple used and applied an averaging mechanism. This resulted in less extreme overcapitalisation of A-rated and C-rated securities.

CONCLUSION

Under Lloyd's proposed capitalisation structure the estimated syndicate losses are relatively very low and for most bond portfolios the capital is sufficient to cover a one-in-200-year event. The cases where it is not quite sufficient were generally for portfolios of B and BB bonds. However, for other bond portfolios there was often a significant overcapitalisation.

It is possible to come up with alternative capitalisation structures which reduce the amount of overcapitalisation whilst still not significantly increasing estimated syndicate losses.

1   This chapter uses some material previously appearing in two articles in *Artwork*, Lloyd's journal of alternative risk transfer: *Financial Guarantee at Lloyd's* by Simon Johnson and *Unwrapping Credit Enhancement Modelling* by Derek Bain and Tony Jones. We are grateful to Lloyd's for allowing us to make use of the relevant material. Derek Bain, who was with Ernst & Young, is now Chief Actuary for AXA in Dublin.

2   See Pawlowski, Malhatra and Manning (2000).

3   The loss rates here are randomly generated from a beta distribution – see Gupton, Finger and Bhatia (1997) for a more detailed discussion.

BIBLIOGRAPHY

Gupton, G., Finger, C., and Bhatia, M., 1997, *CreditMetrics – Technical Document*, J. P. Morgan, URL: www.creditmetrics.com/pdf/CMTD1.pdf.

Merton, R. C., 1990, *Continuous-Time Finance*, (Oxford: Blackwell).

Pawlowski, J., Malhotra, N., and Manning, J., 2000, "Credit Models: the Next Generation", *Credit Magazine*, 1(4), (May 2000).

Part 6

Other perspectives

29

Accounting Issues in Finite Reinsurance and Alternative Risk Transfer Products

Mike Brosnan

Ernst and Young

The insurance and reinsurance industry has experienced significant change in recent times and new insurance products and other risk-management tools continue to emerge in response to the specific needs and expectations of the market place. As companies seek more effective ways to manage an increasingly diverse array of risks and exposures, the insurance products created to respond to such risks become necessarily more complex. Insurance and financial products continue to converge. This is particularly the case with respect to alternative risk transfer (ART) products and finite or financial reinsurance.

INTRODUCTION

This chapter addresses some of the issues involved in determining the appropriate accounting for a small sample of finite reinsurance and other products and transactions, focusing principally on financial reporting under accounting principles generally accepted in the US.

To assist the reader to better understand product differences, accounting requirements and potential financial statement reporting implications, this chapter addresses certain product convergence issues, the related authoritative guidance, methods of developing the appropriate accounting model, evaluating risk transfer and the differing perspectives of buyers and sellers.

PRODUCT CONVERGENCE

Convergence of insurance and financial products has expanded the quantity of risk-management tools available to companies. As a result, the number of companies that may be willing to assume particular risks to hedge against their own risk positions has increased and, similarly, counterparties other than insurance enterprises are now willing to accept a diverse portfolio of risks to diversify their own risks.

However, the convergence of products that may otherwise satisfy the economic objectives of two parties may bring about accounting results that are not consistent with their objectives. In the following example, assume that a reasonable assessment of the correlation and effectiveness of a particular transaction has been determined.

This example is of a trading company with exposure to the value of building materials, in an area subject to tropical storms, that is willing to accept exposure to a named weather event through an exchange-traded weather derivative. In this example, the trading company would receive a fee in return for an obligation to pay a notional amount solely if a named weather event occurs. The trading company's risk analysis might be based on the expectation that, following the named weather event, the value of building materials would increase, whereas in the absence of the named event the fee received for writing the weather derivative could provide an additional revenue opportunity. On the other hand, an insurance enterprise would purchase the weather derivative to reduce its financial statement exposure to insurance losses from a named event in the subject area.

In the case of the trading company, the company's economic and accounting objectives could be aligned to the extent that the weather derivative as well as its other portfolio risks (ie, the building materials) are marked-to-market at each balance sheet date with the change in those values recognised in the income statement. Therefore, the only effect on the income statement of the weather derivative is the recognition of the fee received and any ineffectiveness in the correlation between changes in the fair value of the weather derivative and the fair value of the building materials.

On the other hand, the insurance enterprise that purchased the weather derivative (seeking to reduce its financial statement exposure to insurance losses from a named event) would also be required to mark-to-market the weather derivative. As a result, the mark-to-market may increase the volatility of its accounting results even though the transaction reduces its overall economic exposure. For example, assume for a moment that, at the balance sheet date, a category-five hurricane was approaching the principal location of the insurance company's insured risks (ie, the subject area of the weather derivative). Although no insurance event had yet occurred, it is likely that the fair value of the weather derivative would increase significantly. In that situation, the insurer, in marking the derivative to market, would record a benefit in the period even though no insurance losses were incurred at the balance sheet date. In the subsequent period, if the hurricane caused insurance losses equal to the notional amount of the weather derivative (ie, perfect correlation), even though the insurer was economically indemnified, the insurer would still recognise a loss in that period because the majority of the benefit from the weather derivative would probably have been recognised in the prior period as part of the mark-to-market adjustment.

Similarly, if the hurricane changed course in the subsequent period and the insurance enterprise avoided a loss event, the insurer would still report a loss from the reduction in the mark-to-market adjustment from the prior period, as the fair value of the weather derivative would probably decline in the absence of an event.

Ignoring the issue of practicality and the efficiency of the derivative markets, the insurer could avoid undesired accounting by requiring a double trigger in the derivative instrument whereby the counterparty would only pay (up to the notional amount) if the insurer actually incurred losses from the named event (ie, if the contract is effectively a reinsurance contract).

However, the trading company, assuming it could write such a reinsurance contract, would be required to account for the contract as reinsurance as opposed to following mark-to-market accounting – and that would probably result in undesired results in the company's financial statements.

AUTHORITATIVE GUIDANCE

In order to illustrate the diverse array of accounting literature that needs to be considered in determining the appropriate accounting for any transaction, this section gives a brief overview of some of the specific literature and related interpretations that support the various accounting models that could apply to finite reinsurance and other risk mitigation products relevant to finite reinsurance and alternative risk transfer products.

❏ Financial Accounting Standards Board Statement of Financial Accounting Standards (SFAS) 5 states: "To the extent that an insurance contract or reinsurance contract does not, despite its form, provide for indemnification of the insured or the ceding company by the insurer or reinsurer against loss or liability, the premium paid less the amount of the premium to be retained by the insurer or reinsurer shall be accounted for as a deposit by the insured or the ceding company. Those contracts may be structured in various ways, but if, regardless of form, their substance is that all or part of the premium paid by the insured or the ceding company is a deposit, it shall be accounted for as such."
❏ SFAS 60 establishes accounting and reporting standards for the general-purpose financial statements of stock life insurance enterprises, property and liability insurance enterprises and title insurance enterprises.
❏ SFAS 113 applies to all insurance enterprises to which SFAS 60 applies. Insurers may enter into various types of contracts described as reinsurance, including those commonly known as "fronting arrangements". Statement 113 provides guidance on determining whether those contracts indemnify the ceding enterprise against loss or liability and therefore meet the conditions for reinsurance accounting. Contracts that meet those conditions must be accounted for as reinsurance; other

contracts with reinsurers are accounted for as deposits. The accounting provisions for reinsurance depend on whether the contract is long duration or short duration and, if short duration, on whether the contract is considered prospective reinsurance or retroactive reinsurance. Regardless of its form, any transaction that indemnifies an insurer against loss or liability relating to insurance risk must be accounted for according to the provisions of SFAS 113.

❑ SFAS 133 addresses accounting for derivative instruments, including certain derivative instruments embedded in other contracts, and hedging activities. In particular:

  ❑ "Derivative instruments represent rights or obligations that meet the definitions of assets or liabilities and should be reported in financial statements."

  ❑ "Fair value is the most relevant measure for financial instruments and the only relevant measure for derivative instruments. Derivative instruments should be measured at fair value, and adjustments to the carrying amount of hedged items should reflect changes in their fair value (that is, gains or losses) that are attributable to the risk being hedged and that arise while the hedge is in effect."

  ❑ "Only items that are assets or liabilities should be reported as such in financial statements."

  ❑ "Special accounting for items designated, as being hedged should be provided only for qualifying items. One aspect of qualification should be an assessment of the expectation of effective offsetting changes in fair values or cash flows during the term of the hedge for the risk being hedged."

❑ SFAS 140 states "an objective in accounting for transfers of financial assets is for each entity that is a party to the transaction to recognize only assets it controls and liabilities it has incurred, to derecognize assets only when control has been surrendered, and to derecognize liabilities only when they have been extinguished. Sales and other transfers frequently result in a desegregation of financial assets and liabilities into components, which become separate assets and liabilities. For example, if an entity sells a portion of a financial asset it owns, the portion retained becomes an asset separate from the portion sold and separate from the assets obtained in exchange."

❑ Emerging Issues Task Force (EITF) No. 86–12 affirms that SFAS 5 requires an enterprise to record a liability for the probable losses from incurred but not reported (IBNR) claims and incidents if the loss is probable and reasonably estimable. "The estimated cost of purchasing tail coverage is not relevant in determining the loss to be accrued if the enterprise has not purchased such coverage. However,...if the insured had the unilateral option to purchase tail coverage at a premium not to exceed a specified fixed maximum, then the maximum premium for tail coverage under such an option (after considering deductibles) could effectively impose a ceiling on the estimated IBNR liability, provided the IBNR does not exceed the limits in the tail coverage policy and the enterprise intends to purchase the coverage ... purchase of tail coverage does not eliminate the need to determine if an additional liability should be accrued because of policy limits or other factors."

❏ EITF No. 93–6 consensus states that "in order to be accounted for as reinsurance, a contract that reinsures risks arising from short-duration insurance contracts must meet all of the following conditions":

   ❏ "the contract must qualify as a short-duration contract" under paragraph 7(a) of SFAS 60;

   ❏ "the contract must not contain features that prevent the risk transfer criteria in paragraphs 8–13 of SFAS 113 from being reasonably applied (and those criteria must be met)"; and

   ❏ "the ultimate premium expected to be paid or received under the contract must be reasonably estimable and allocable in proportion to the reinsurance protection provided" as required by paragraphs 14(a) and 14(b) of SFAS 60 and paragraph 21 of SFAS 113. "If any of these conditions are not met, a deposit method of accounting should be applied by the ceding and assuming enterprises."

The EITF also states that "determining the substance of a contract is a judgmental matter. If an agreement with a reinsurer consists of both risk transfer and nonrisk transfer coverages that have been combined into a single legal document, those coverages must be considered separately for accounting purposes."

❏ EITF No. 93–14 consensus states that "in order to be accounted for as insurance, an insurance contract must indemnify the insured" as denoted by paragraph 44 of SFAS 5. "For those contracts that do not provide indemnification, the premium paid, less the amount of the premium to be retained by the insurer, should be accounted for as a deposit by the insured. For a multiple-year retrospectively rated insurance contract accounted for as insurance, the ... insured should recognize a liability and the insurer should recognize an asset to the extent that the insured has an obligation to pay cash (or other consideration) to the insurer that would not have been required absent experience under the contract. The amount recognized in the current period should be computed, using a with-and-without method, as the difference between the insured's total contract costs before and after the experience under the contract as of the reporting date, including costs such as premium adjustments, settlement adjustments, and impairments of coverage. The amount of premium expense related to impairments of coverage should be measured in relation to the original contract terms. Future experience under the contract (that is, future losses and future premiums that would be paid regardless of past experience) should not be considered in measuring the amount to be recognized."

❑ The EITF No. 99–2 consensus deals with accounting for weather derivatives, the EITF recognises that, in accordance with SFAS 133, "contracts that are not exchange traded are not subject to the requirements of that Statement if settlement is based on a climatic or geological variable or on some other physical variable. Any derivative based on a physical variable that eventually becomes exchange traded will automatically become subject to the requirements of Statement 133". The EITF also states that "This Issue does not apply to contracts written by insurance companies, which entitle the holder to be compensated only if, as a result of an insurable event, the holder incurs a liability or there is an adverse change in the value of a specific asset or liability for which the holder is at risk." The EITF concludes that "an entity that purchases a non-exchange-traded option-based weather derivative in connection with nontrading activities should amortize to expense the premium paid (or due) and apply the intrinsic value method" at each interim balance sheet date. The intrinsic value method computes an amount based on the difference between the expected results from an upfront allocation of the cumulative strike and the actual results during a period, multiplied by the contract price (for example, dollars per heating degree-day). The intrinsic value method first requires that the reporting entity allocate the cumulative strike amount to individual periods within the contract term. Also, "allocation should reflect reasonable expectations at the beginning of the contract term of normal or expected experience under the contract … allocation should be based on data from external statistical sources, such as the National Weather Service. The "intrinsic value" (or "intrinsic value measure") of the contract at interim dates would then be calculated based on cumulative differences between actual experience and the allocation through that date". "All entities that sell or write a non-exchange-traded option-based weather derivative should initially recognize the premium as a liability and recognize any subsequent changes in fair value currently in earnings (the premium would not be amortized)."

❑ EITF Topic D34 addresses accounting for reinsurance and contains questions and answers about SFAS 113, "a principal objective of Statement 113 is to account for an agreement with a reinsurer according to its substance. Many of the implementation questions addressed in EITF Topic D34 involve potential differences between a contract's form and its substance. Difficulty in evaluating a contract under Statement 113 is an indication that the contract's form and substance may differ. For example, EITF Topic D34 states that when complicated adjustable features or options are present in a contract, close analysis may be required to determine the effect of those contractual provisions on risk transfer."

❏ In EITF Topic D79, the FASB concluded that "purchased retroactive insurance contracts that indemnify the insured should be accounted for in a manner similar to the manner in which reinsurance contracts are accounted for under Statement 113. That is, amounts paid for retroactive insurance should be reported as a receivable to the extent that those amounts do not exceed the recorded liabilities relating to the underlying insured event. If the recorded liabilities exceed the amounts paid for the insurance, insurance receivables should be increased to reflect the difference and the resulting gain deferred. If the amounts and timing of the insurance recoveries can be reasonably estimated, the deferred gain should be amortized using the interest method over the estimated period over which the entity expects to recover substantially all amounts due under the terms of the insurance contract. If the amounts and timing of the insurance recoveries cannot be reasonably estimated then the proportion of actual recoveries to total estimated recoveries should be used to determine the amount of the amortization."

❏ The American Institute of Certified Public Accountants (AICPA) Statement of Position SOP 98–7, "Deposit Accounting – Accounting for Insurance and Reinsurance Contracts that do not Transfer Insurance Risk" provides guidance on how to account for insurance and reinsurance contracts that do not transfer insurance risk, using "deposit accounting". It applies to all entities, including non-insurance companies, which have insurance contracts and reinsurance contracts that do not transfer insurance risk, except for long-duration life and health insurance contracts.

DETERMINING THE APPROPRIATE ACCOUNTING MODEL

A complete understanding of all contract terms and conditions must be obtained in order to determine whether insurance and reinsurance accounting, deposit accounting or a fair value model is most appropriate for a particular transaction. The threshold issues are:

❏ Regardless of its form, any transaction that indemnifies an insurer against loss or liability relating to insurance risk shall be accounted for according to the provisions of SFAS 113; other contracts are accounted for as deposits (SFAS 113, paragraph 6).

❏ Indemnification against loss or liability relating to insurance risk requires both of the following criteria to be met (SFAS 113, paragraphs 9a and 9b):
1. "The reinsurer assumes significant insurance risk under the reinsured portions of the underlying insurance contracts."
2. "It is reasonably possible that the reinsurer may realize a significant loss from the transaction."

❏ "An entity shall recognize all of its derivative instruments in its statement of financial position as either assets or liabilities depending on the rights or obligations under the contracts. All derivative instruments shall be measured at fair value" (SFAS 133, paragraph 17).

❏ Certain insurance contracts are not subject to the requirements of SFAS 133, whether or not they are written by insurance enterprises, if they "entitle the holder to be compensated only if, as a result of an identifiable insurable event (other than a change in price), the holder incurs a liability or there is an adverse change in the value of a specific asset or liability for which the holder is at risk" (ie, the payment of benefits is the result of an identifiable insurable event – for example theft or fire – instead of changes in a variable) (SFAS 133, paragraph 10).

Evaluating risk transfer

A subjective yet significant area associated with determining the appropriate accounting for an insurance or reinsurance contract is the determination of whether or not the contract transfers insurance risk. Both SFAS 5 and 60 require that contracts transfer risk in order to be accounted for as insurance, otherwise deposit accounting is required. However, as discussed above, SFAS 113 paragraphs 9a and 9b increased the focus on this requirement and provided both quantitative and qualitative considerations that must be addressed in evaluating risk transfer.

First, paragraph 9a specifically addresses the requirement that a contract must transfer insurance risk and that insurance risk incorporates both underwriting and timing (regardless of how catastrophic either the underwriting or timing exposure is, if both elements are not present the contract must be accounted for as a deposit).

Second, paragraph 9b requires that the reinsurer be exposed to a significant risk of loss (there must be a reasonable possibility that the net present value of all contractual cashflows could result in a significant loss to the reinsurer as measured against the gross contract premiums).

There is no specific threshold for measurement specified in SFAS 113 regarding the assessment of significant loss to the reinsurer. Accordingly, practice and the resulting assessments vary. For example, some have promulgated a concept that a 10% chance of a 10% loss to the reinsurer satisfies the significance criteria. However, whereas many desire a numerical threshold against which to measure the expected cashflow to determine whether the significant loss criteria has been met, such an approach could potentially allow a contract to meet the significance criteria even if only a limited number of scenarios resulted in a loss to the reinsurer (for example, if in 90% of scenarios the reinsurer retained a specified margin). In such situations one could challenge whether the absence of significant variability was consistent with the concept of significant insurance risk.

A more pragmatic view, based on a complete understanding of the reinsurance contract, would consider the potential variability of expected results. Such consideration should take into account the nature of the underlying risks (eg, property or casualty), the limits profile of the underlying contracts reinsured, the coverage limits provided and all retrospective rating features. There should be some consideration of the correlation between the potential gain to the reinsurer and the potential loss.

To date, SFAS 113 has been applied for almost 10 years and many diverse approaches to risk assessments are used by assuming and ceding companies. It appears that this diversity is likely to continue for the foreseeable future. However, to the extent that such practices continue to create a movement towards more aggressive acceptance of limited risk-transfer transactions, regulatory scrutiny and increased interpretative guidance is likely.

Ceding and assuming company viewpoints

The divergent objectives of the ceding and assuming companies form one of the difficulties in dealing with more complex products. The ceding company, among other things, tends to look for ways to provide additional capacity, limit risk exposure from its most volatile risks, or enhance its regulatory financial position. The assuming company, on the other hand, is more focused on – among other things – obtaining a fair return for assuming the more volatile product risks with which the reinsurer is presumably more experienced, entering new markets and/or lending its capital base to assist clients. In the end, it is the differences between the reinsurer's and the ceding company's view of the correct price to completely transfer a risk to the reinsurer, and the ceding company's business objectives, that result in many contract features that have become common in structured reinsurance products.

A complete understanding of the contract and the nature of the underlying risks is therefore a prerequisite for the determination of the appropriate accounting. Accordingly, although an infinite number of circumstances and examples could be enumerated (such as discounting and the time value of money) unless one takes the view that the counterparty is incompetent, which, of course introduces many other business issues, or unless there is a total arbitrage of accounting differences between jurisdictions, it would be reasonable to assume that a contract that transfers a finite amount of risk to the reinsurer should generally preclude recognition of more than a finite benefit by the ceding company.

Special purpose entities

Special purpose entities (SPEs), which have been used for some time in a number of different types of transactions (such as cat bonds, securitisations and trust preferred securities), have been the subject of specific accounting standards and numerous EITF interpretations. As a result, there are too many complex issues to address in detail here. For example, SFAS 140 addresses qualifying special purpose entities (QSPEs), which are generally not applicable to insurance transactions. Accordingly, the remainder of the section addresses the general nature of SPEs.

The principal issues surrounding SPEs relate to whether or not a SPE should be consolidated and how to determine the amount of revenue/expense that should be recognised in transactions between the reinsurance company and the SPE.

The criteria that need to be addressed to evaluate whether or not to consolidate a SPE generally include:

❏ the amount of outside equity investment in the SPE;
❏ the extent of the reinsurance company's influence on the operations of the SPE (controlled by management contract, Board representation or vote);
❏ the identity of the trust beneficiary;
❏ the size of any residual interest in the SPE; and
❏ the extent to which related risks and rewards have been transferred to outside interests.

Each of these considerations must be considered in the context of the overall transaction and none is necessarily more important than the others. Nevertheless, one area of focus has always been the amount of third-party equity investment in the SPE. Practice has generally been that SPEs with no third-party residual equity (where the equity is subject to first dollar of loss) are merely conduits for the sponsor and are consolidated by the sponsor.

Similarly, even if the SPE is 100% owned by a third party, practice has evolved that, if the amount of the third-party residual equity interest is not at least equal to 3% of the notional amount at risk for the transactions included in the SPE, consolidation by the sponsor company would also probably be required. The 3% threshold originated in EITF Topic D14 and EITF No. 90–15 and was originally applicable to leasing transactions.

EITF No. 90–15 states that:

❏ 3% is the minimum acceptable investment; and
❏ a greater investment may be necessary depending on the facts and circumstances, including the credit risk and market risk factors associated with the transaction.

The second part of the above criteria has not always been rigorously applied in practice. However, this could change given the focus on SPE's by congress and regulators in recent times. Recently, EITF discussions to consider raising the 3% threshold to 10% resulted in the tentative conclusion that the minimum amount of substantative equity at risk should be the amount of equity that would allow the SPE to fund or finance its operations without assistance or reliance on the primary beneficiary. This amount was presumed to be at least 10% of the SPE's total capital and would be expected to be overcome only in very limited situations. Additional interpretative guidance from the EITF is also likely. Consequently, analysts, regulators and others will probably scrutinise even more closely even legitimate SPE transactions for the foreseeable future.

Transformers

Legal and other requirements in many jurisdictions may limit the type of business activity in which an entity is permitted to engage. As a result, the concept of a "transformer" has emerged, whereby the legal form of the vehicle typically used to transfer a particular risk is changed (eg, from an insurance contract to a derivative or vice versa) through a number of back-to-back transactions with different entities. This emerging market has complicated many accounting analyses with respect to determining the appropriate accounting model. In fact, many have asserted the position, and perhaps believe, that the financial "books" of the world are not required to be in balance (ie, two counterparties could have different views of the same facts and that two institutions could follow different accounting models for the same transaction). As a result, many have developed theories to arbitrage accounting models and in recent times transformers have also been used to attempt to alter the character of risks.

The contract designers have sometimes convinced themselves that one should accept a transaction based on the form in which it is executed, irrespective of its prior heritage. For example, if company A entered into a stand-alone ISDA credit default swap with company B, all would agree that such a transaction would be a derivative contract subject to SFAS 133 and probably require mark-to-market accounting by both parties.

However, if company A entered the same standard ISDA credit default swap with company C and company C purchased an insurance contract from company D, with respect to any loss on the referenced swap contract with company A and company D, in turn, obtained a 100% quota share reinsurance agreement from company B with respect to the referenced risk under its insurance contract, would it be appropriate for company B to follow an insurance accounting model? Presumably not, because the underlying contracts are derivatives (ie, because the underlying contract risk – the ISDA credit default swap – is a derivative, any loss therefrom is a trading loss, not an insurable event, and is therefore excluded under the SFAS insurance exemption).

Furthermore, if the example is extended to include reinsurance of company D's risks through any number of quota share reinsurance transactions with different counterparties before company B assumed the risk, it would still be inappropriate for company B to follow an insurance accounting model because the underlying contracts' risk is still a derivative (ie, any loss to company B would result from the ISDA credit default swap therefore making it a trading loss and still exempt from insurance).

However, some might argue that it is too difficult to ascertain the nature of the original risk assumed and that the only appropriate accounting model is to follow the form of the contract underwritten by the risk assumer itself. However, the appropriate accounting model is based on a question of fact and all the relevant facts need to be compared with the requirements of the relevant literature regardless of how difficult that may be (ie, the correct accounting is not superseded if it is too difficult to apply).

US statutory accounting

One fact that must be understood when considering the statutory financial statements of any US insurance enterprise is that their regulatory financial reports are based on their domiciliary states' requirements, and there may be significant differences from state to state. Nevertheless, in 2001 a single framework of Statements of Statutory Accounting Principles (SSAP) was established. These SSAPs, which can be adjusted by regulators on a state-by-state basis, are expected to provide a consistent framework for regulatory reporting.

Generally, statutory accounting would not differ significantly from any comments provided elsewhere in this chapter. In addressing US statutory accounting, with respect to matters discussed in this chapter and in general, there would be two major differences with respect to US generally accepted accounting principles (GAAP).

First, SFAS 113 states that, "for all reinsurance transactions, immediate recognition of gains is precluded unless the ceding enterprise's liability to its policyholder is extinguished". SSAP 62 permits immediate gain recognition from a retroactive reinsurance contract provided the gain is reported in other income, and the recoverable amounts separately reported in the statutory annual statement and the gain is also tracked separately as a segregated surplus amount (ie, segregated surplus amounts are not available for dividends and certain other transactions). The other significant difference would relate to the fact that many states prohibit any transactions in derivatives other than for risk mitigating activities.

A few key items are highlighted here, but there are many differences between statutory financial reporting for regulatory purposes and under US GAAP, and in fact such differences are a principle reason for the need for financial reinsurance and alternative risk transfer products.

CONCLUSION

It would be impossible to capture all the nuances of the accounting requirements and practices related to finite insurance and alternative risk products in this chapter. However, this discussion provides some fundamental information and indicated the complexity of many of the issues that need to be addressed.

BIBLIOGRAPHY

American Institute of Certified Public Accountants, 1998, "Statement of Position 98–7 Deposit Accounting: Accounting for Insurance and Reinsurance Contracts That Do Not Transfer Insurance Risk" October.

Financial Accounting Standards Board, 1975, "Accounting for Contingencies", Statement of Financial Accounting Standards 5, March.

Financial Accounting Standards Board, 1982, "Accounting and Reporting by Insurance Enterprises", Statement of Financial Accounting Standards 60, June.

Financial Accounting Standards Board, 1986 "Accounting by Insureds for Claims-Made Insurance Policies", Emerging Issues Task Force, 86-12.

Financial Accounting Standards Board, 1989–90, "Transactions involving Special-Purpose Entities", Emerging Issues Task Force Topic, D-14.

Financial Accounting Standards Board, 1990, "Impact of Nonsubstantive Lessors, Residual Value Guarantees, and Other Provisions in Leasing Transactions", Emerging Issues Task Force, 90-15.

Financial Accounting Standards Board, 1992, "Accounting and Reporting for Reinsurance of Short-Duration and Long-Duration Contracts", Statement of Financial Accounting Standards 113, December.

Financial Accounting Standards Board, 1993a, "Accounting for Multiple-Year Retrospectively Rated Contracts by Ceding and Assuming Enterprises", Emerging Issues Task Force, 93-6.

Financial Accounting Standards Board, 1993b, "Accounting for Multiple-Year Retrospectively Rated Insurance Contracts by Insurance Enterprises and Other Enterprises", Emerging Issues Task Force, 93-14, November.

Financial Accounting Standards Board, 1993c, "Accounting for Reinsurance: Questions and Answers about FASB Statement No. 113", Emerging Issues Task Force Topic, D-34, July.

Financial Accounting Standards Board, 1993d, "FASB Staff Views on Issue No. 93-6, "Accounting for Multiple-Year Retrospectively Rated Contracts by Ceding and Assuming Enterprises"", Emerging Issues Task Force Topic, D-35, July.

Financial Accounting Standards Board, 1998, "Accounting for Derivative Instruments and Hedging Activities", Statement of Financial Accounting Standards 133, June.

Financial Accounting Standards Board, 1999a, "Accounting for Retroactive Insurance Contracts Purchased by Entities Other Than Insurance Enterprises", Emerging Issues Task Force Topic, D-79, May.

Financial Accounting Standards Board, 1999b, "Accounting for Weather Derivatives", Emerging Issues Task Force, 99-2.

Financial Accounting Standards Board, 2000, "Accounting for Transfers and Servicing of Financial Assets and Extinguishments of Liabilities", Statement of Financial Accounting Standards 140, September.

30

Legal Risks Mitigating Document Risk – Some Hard Lessons Learned

Clive O'Connell

Barlow, Lyde & Gilbert

Alternative Risk Transfer (ART) products are, by their very essence, non-standard; they are alternatives to standard products. They are also diverse, both in the nature of the product and in geographical and jurisdictional scope. ART products are a global solution to global challenges and, accordingly, are not restricted to one set of laws, one judicial system, one regulatory environment or one fiscal system.

This diversity renders impossible a simple exploration of the legal issues faced by those who would develop, sell and purchase an ever-increasing array of financial products that cross the boundaries between insurance and banking.

INTRODUCTION

Instead of attempting such a feat as to give a brief explanation of all the legal issues involved, this chapter will focus on a number of significant issues that exist in practice with the development of ART products and will do so from the perspective of English law. While the choice of English law may seem parochial, English law has the benefit of sharing many of its principles with other legal systems and, being part of the EU, sharing much of its regulation with other EU countries.

REGULATORY DEFINITIONS AND DISTINCTIONS BETWEEN BANKS AND INSURERS

ART exists in the grey area between banking and insurance and while its practitioners recognise ART products as such, regulators and courts require products, or parts of transactions, to be recognisable as either a banking product or an insurance one. They will, oftentimes, also require the banking product to be provided by a bank and the insurance product by an insurer. It therefore becomes important to distinguish banking products from insurance products. Table 1 shows the distinctions between

Table 1 Elements of insurance and banking contracts

Insurance contracts	Banking contracts
Fortuity	Security
Insurable interest	Ability to hedge
Uberimmae fides	*Caveat emptor*
Disclosure	Due diligence
Claim adjustment	Automatic payment

insurance and banking that this chapter will cover. In English regulation, the easiest means of establishing the distinction is to focus on what constitutes an insurance product. This is because insurers may only conduct insurance business whereas banks have somewhat more freedom.

Insurance companies are regulated under the Insurance Companies Act 1982.[1] Section 16 of that Act provides that an insurance company so regulated "shall not carry on any activities, in the United Kingdom or elsewhere, otherwise than in connection with or for the purposes of its insurance business." The same Act provides, under Section 2, that only insurers authorised under the Act may carry on insurance business within the United Kingdom. Additionally, Rule 3.1 of the Financial Services Authority's Insurance Interim Prudential Sourcebook provides:[2]

> "An insurer must not carry on any commercial business in the United Kingdom or elsewhere other than insurance business and activities directly arising from that business"

The addition of the words "or elsewhere" precludes a UK authorised insurer who wishes to retain that authorisation from operating more flexibly in more liberal regulatory environments. While speculation and expectation points to a liberalisation of the regulation in the UK that would allow insurers to compete more freely with banks, the position at present remains that insurers are restricted to insurance. On the other hand, banks have more flexibility to devise new products and develop novel ways of transferring risk. They may not, however, under Section 2 of the Insurance Companies Act 1982, carry on the business of insurance.

Thus it may be fair to say that if a product or part of a transaction is an insurance product, it must be accepted by an insurer and if an insurer is accepting risk, it must be accepting that risk by way of an insurance contract. The determination of what is an insurance product is, accordingly, a key one. There are two key elements to an insurance contract that assist in distinguishing it from banking agreements: an insurance contract must, in English law, protect against a fortuity and the insured must have an insurable interest.

A contract of insurance is one under which a person secures (usually by the payment of money) a benefit (usually the payment of some larger sum of money) on the happening of an event which is uncertain (perhaps as to whether it will happen at all or merely as to when it will happen) (Prudential Insurance v IRC, 1904).[3] Very simply, a contract that requires the payment of a sum of money on a particular date is not an insurance contract; a contract that provides that party A pays a smaller sum to party B in return for party B paying a greater sum on an appointed day is a loan agreement. The coming of the appointed day is not, other than in philosophical terms, fortuitous. The day will come and payment will be due.

The mere introduction of fortuity itself is not enough to create an insurance contract. A contract that provides that party A pays a smaller sum to party B in return for party B paying a greater sum on an appointed day if it is raining on the appointed day is not, without further elements, an insurance contract. It is a wagering agreement, as are contracts that require payment should it snow more than a certain amount, an earthquake strike a particular area or hurricane damage exceed certain levels.

The benefit which is to be received under the contract must be intended to meet some loss or detriment that the person will suffer on the happening of the uncertain event, which is to say that the person must have an insurable interest in the subject matter of the contract (Lucena v Craufurd, 1806).[4] The person has an insurable interest in relation to the uncertain event if he will suffer a loss if it occurs and/or gain an advantage if it does not (Wilson v Jones, 1867).[5] The loss or advantage, however, must depend upon a right that the law recognises as enforceable. In practice this normally means that the person must own or have some right in respect of the subject matter of the insurance.

The area of insurable interests is one that has vexed the insurance industry in a variety of ways for many years. The importance of determining whether there is an insurable interest is considerable. If there is no insurable interest, at best, the contract is unenforceable as a wagering agreement under Section 18 of the Gaming Act 1845.[6] At worst it may also constitute a criminal offence.

The development of an excess of loss reinsurance in the marine market in London in the 19th century was the result of a number of attempts to simplify the basis on which insurers protected themselves. The matter of ensuring that vessels or voyages were declared to reinsurers and then proving losses thereafter could, in pre-electronic days, lead to unforeseen gaps in cover. Eventually, treaty reinsurance with automatic cessions or cover became the norm. However, a number of methods were devised to avoid such problems. In earlier days, one method of achieving this result to be attempted was "tonners". An insurer would purchase a pessimistic tonner from a reinsurer. In this context the terms "insurer" and "reinsurer" are used loosely as the first did not have to be an insurer and the latter was almost certainly not a reinsurer. The slip cover would be marked "Policy Proof of Interest" or "PPI" and would provide that for a premium of, say, £100, the reinsurer would pay £50 for each vessel in excess of ten vessels which sank in a particular area or under a certain flag during the period of cover, up to a limit of five vessels. Thus if eleven ships sank in the North Atlantic that winter, the reinsurer would receive premium of £100 and pay £50 in claims, a profit of £50. If thirteen ships sank, the reinsurer would have a net loss of £50 and the insurer would make a profit of the same amount. This would, or at least could, be pure profit, as the insurer need not actually insure any vessels at all, let alone those that actually sank. A tonner was nothing more than a wager on whether or not ships would sink.

The story of tonners is an interesting one and not divorced from a consideration of ART. Marine tonners were able to operate – despite the fact that they were written in contravention of Section 18 of the Gaming Act 1845 – because they were traded within a small and confined market place where good faith and honour were enforced by peer pressure and the certain knowledge of ostracism should one party welch on a deal. They continued until the passing of the Marine Insurance (Gambling Policies) Act 1909 which, in its one substantive section, prohibited the effecting of policies of marine insurance other than by those with a "bona fide interest, direct or indirect, either in the safe arrival of the ship in relation to which the contract is made or in the safety or preservation of the subject-matter insured, or a bona fide expectation of acquiring such an interest".[7] Brokers and insurers participating in such contracts were also liable to prosecution. The present penalty for breach of this statute is a fine or six months imprisonment together with forfeiture of any money received from the wager. The purpose of the Act was clear: it was directed at the public policy of preventing the deliberate wrecking of ships by or on behalf of those who had no interest in their safety but much to gain by their loss.

The statute prevented gambling policies on marine risks. It did not cover the non-marine market nor the then unknown (or at best "fledgling") aviation market. A consequence of this was that 60 years later a market had developed in London, particularly at Lloyd's, for aviation tonners. Deals were being struck, without any necessary insurable interest, based upon the numbers of planes that would crash, the cost of such losses to the market or, macabrely, the numbers killed in plane crashes. Lloyd's outlawed this practice in the early 1980s. Outside Lloyd's the legal unenforceability of wager policies appears to have determined their fate and, apart from a small amount of anecdotal evidence, it would appear that tonners have been consigned to history as a curiosity.

Or so it seemed until the early 1990s when, as a result of the capacity crisis engendered by Hurricane Andrew, Piper Alpha and other disasters, some in the market looked to find ways in which protection could be provided in an alternative way. One product that emerged was the "double trigger" catastrophe cover that required not only a loss to the reinsured but also a market-wide loss of a certain severity to enable recovery. The actual loss trigger provided the necessary insurable interest, whereas the market-wide loss trigger introduced a more speculative element. Although brokers had some success in marketing these covers, many found the second trigger, with the possibility of a substantial actual loss with no recovery, unattractive. The covers made it difficult to plan for the individual nature of one's own exposure and left potentially unpredictable gaps in cover. Any attempt to fill these gaps could have led to double indemnity and a consequential reduction in cover for no reduction in premium.

Another solution that was offered to the market at the time was the idea of purchasing weather or other derivatives. A derivative purchased against an eventuality would pay should that eventuality occur. A weather derivative that requires a certain amount of snowfall in a particular area in a given month clearly has an element of fortuity. Derivatives against hurricane damage based upon objective indices presented the market with an interesting alternative to catastrophe reinsurance. Some were bought. One difficulty in selling derivatives to insurers was that derivatives were products sold by banks or financial institutions. They constituted "banking risk" and therefore attracted banking rates. They were, quite simply, too expensive for the insurance industry which, by the time that the products had been fully developed, was away from the capacity crisis of the early 1990s and into the soft market of the late 1990s.

Today, derivatives have found a market place; weather derivatives are very attractive to certain industries (cold drinks, ice cream and tourism to name but a few) which suffer loss as a result of the vagaries of the weather but might have difficulty in defining the extent and nature of their loss and proving that loss in the manner necessary in an insurance policy.

The proffering of these products by banks led some insurers to question whether they could offer such products themselves in a manner that competed with the high rates being quoted by the banks. The risks entailed were likely to be diverse and different from the rest of the insurer's book and, at a time when insurance rates were depressed, an attractive source of profitable business.

While fortuity exists in derivatives, the lack of any insurable interest renders them incapable of being insurance contracts and, instead, in the hands of insurers, renders them wagering agreements, which are unenforceable under Section 18 of the Gaming Act 1845. Banks can, however, enter into derivative contracts, by virtue of a saving under Section 63 of the Financial Services Act 1986 which provides:[8]

"(1) No contract to which this section applies shall be void or unenforceable by reason of (a) section18 of the Gaming Act 1845 …

(2) this section applies to any contract entered into by either or each party by way of business".

The section applies to banks, regulated pursuant to the statute, which are clearly entering into derivative contracts by way of their business.

A bank can therefore sell a derivative based upon a fortuity in which the purchaser has no interest or no means of proving any interest. Banks can, and do, often hedge positions by buying and selling derivatives and making money on the margins between moving sale and purchase prices. While others engaged in such activity could be seen to be gambling and thus risk a lack of enforceability, banks can enforce their contracts and, importantly, can have contracts enforced against them.

It is this enforceability that led to the next stage in the development of an insurance-based derivative product through which an insurer could participate in the expected riches of the derivatives market alongside the banks. As banks have an obligation, enforceable at law, to pay under a derivative contract should the fortuity occur, the banks have an insurable interest despite the person who buys the derivative from the bank having no need to have any interest whatsoever. Thus a speculator in Rhode Island can purchase a derivative from a bank in London which provides for a payment should a particular event occur in Taiwan, a place where the speculator has never been and in which he has no interest whatsoever. The bank, in selling the derivative, accepts a legally enforceable obligation to pay should the event occur and therefore may in turn insure against that event with a UK authorised insurer. Should the bank hedge its position by purchasing a derivative from another bank, it does not diminish its legal obligation to pay to the original speculator as the second derivative need not have any relationship to the first and does not diminish the legal obligation that is insured. It does, however, limit the financial exposure of the bank, which becomes a risk management issue for the insurer.

Therefore, for a product to be accepted by an insurer, it must be an insurance product. If it is not, it is either a wagering agreement and unenforceable or contrary to Section 16 of the Insurance Companies Act 1982 and therefore beyond the company's authority and, again, possibly unenforceable, if not void, due to illegality; if an insurance product is provided by an entity that is not an insurer, it is certainly contrary to Section 2 of the Insurance Companies Act and may therefore be void for illegality.

It should be noted here that the fact that someone has an interest that is insurable does not prevent that person from entering into a contract that would, if it required an insurable interest, be an insurance contract. A football club can insure against failing to qualify for European competition and the monetary loss that will be suffered as a consequence. The team's chairman and owner can also place a bet upon its rival gaining the last remaining European slot. Winning the bet may in some way compensate for the loss of revenue but is itself not insurance. Similarly an ice cream manufacturer can buy a derivative protecting against a poor summer and could also, probably, devise a contingency insurance product that would compensate for losses in sales. The derivative contract is not an insurance contract and will survive even if the company withdraws from the ice cream market and sells hot chestnuts instead.

In addition to regulatory differences and distinctions with respect to essential ingredients, there are further differences between insurance contracts and banking instruments that play a great part in ART transactions. These distinctions arise, mainly from differences in the legal framework under which insurance and banking contracts have developed and play a crucial role in the differences in pricing and structuring of the insurance and banking elements of ART transactions.

UTMOST GOOD FAITH AND WARRANTIES
Insurers

Insurance contracts are contracts of utmost good faith or *uberrimae fides*. In this context, utmost good faith means that there is a duty not merely to tell the truth when negotiating a contract but also a duty to tell the whole truth; a duty of full disclosure of all material facts. Failure to abide by this duty will result in an avoidance of the contract from inception or *ab initio*. This will occur whether the non-disclosure (or misrepresentation) is innocent, negligent, reckless or fraudulent. Avoidance from inception requires a return of premium (save in cases of fraud where the premium can be retained as a windfall) and a return of all claims paid. The parties are put back into the position in which they would have been had the contract never come into being. The theory is that the contract would not have come into being if the facts had been correctly stated and that, accordingly, the remedy is appropriate. The remedy is, undoubtedly, draconian. There is no middle ground. There is no room to argue that had information been disclosed the insurer would have simply charged more premium or taken a smaller line and that, accordingly, the contract should be amended to reflect this. It is avoidance or performance.

The principle of utmost good faith is not a new one, having developed over centuries of legal interpretation. The common law principles are codified in the Marine Insurance Act 1906 Section 18, which provides:[9]

"(1) ... the assured must disclose to the insurer, before the contract is concluded, every material circumstance which is known to the assured, and the assured is deemed to know every circumstance which, in the ordinary course of business, ought to be known by him. If the assured fails to make such disclosure, the insurer may avoid the contract.

(2) Every circumstance is material which would influence the judgment of a prudent insurer in fixing the premium, or determining whether he will take the risk"

The Act has been held to be of equal application to marine and non-marine risks, both insurance and reinsurance.

The rationale for the extreme remedy available to insurers is that the insured is in possession of the facts surrounding the risk to be insured. If the insurer were to be obliged to investigate the facts that are material to the risk that the insurer is to assume, insurance premiums would rise to an unsustainable level; an applicant for life insurance knows whether or not he smokes and how much he drinks; a motorist knows what his accident record is and how many speeding fines he has paid; a factory owner knows whether or not his factory has a sprinkler system. An insurer could ascertain these facts but it would take time and increase the cost of doing business. Insureds are willing, in commercial terms, to accept the consequences of cheaper insurance rates.

Similar considerations apply to warranties in insurance contracts. The courts have held that terms in insurance contracts are warranties, conditions or innominate terms. Innominate terms are those whose breach does not necessarily lead to repudiation or damages. The remedy will be determined by the nature of the breach. Conditions will lead to damages or, for example in the case of conditions precedent, to the avoidance of particular liabilities. Breaches of warranties will result in the contract becoming void from the time of breach.

The essence of warranties is very similar to that of utmost good faith. The insured has control of the subject matter of the risk and, accordingly, must operate in accordance with the terms laid down by and agreed with the insurer. Thus a warranty that there would be a 24-hour watch on an insured fish farm will reduce the risk and have a consequential reduction in premium. To police it, the insurer is able to treat the contract as void from the moment of breach. Whether or not the warranty is breached, is in the hands of the insured. The breach need not be causative of any loss.

There are two types of warranty. One type deals with the performance of the contract. Examples of this type are a premium warranty, which promises payment of premium within a certain number of days of inception or the 24-hour watch warranty referred to above. If there is a breach of the warranty the contract comes to an end. The other type of warranty is a promissory warranty, which provides for the veracity of certain facts or circumstances disclosed or existing at inception. These can range from simply stating "warranted no known losses" in a contract accepted after inception, to ones which provide a warranty as to the veracity of information provided during negotiation. The latter warranty can be used to ensure that arguments do not arise as to whether there was inducement of the actual underwriter. Breaches of promissory warranties also operate to void the contract from the time of breach. The breach is, in such cases, from inception.

Relying upon utmost good faith and using warranties, insurers are therefore able to assess risk swiftly and cheaply, knowing that if there has not been a fair presentation of all material facts, avoidance will be possible and if there is a breach of warranty, the contract will be voided. Obviously questions arise as to whether or not full disclosure has been made, whether the facts or circumstances are material and whether they did induce or would have induced the underwriter to accept the risk. Once accepted, the insurer is able to provide cheap coverage policed by effective warranties. From a prospective insured's position, however, the issue is simple; if there is a question as to whether or not something should be disclosed, disclose it; comply with warranties.

Banks

Banking operates very differently, however. Where insurers rely upon the concept of *uberrimae fides*, banks use the opposing maxim of *caveat emptor* – "buyer beware"; the business of insurance is the business of the assessment and acceptance of risk, whereas banks seek to minimise and avoid risk where possible; banks do not require fortuity. Thus they will seek security for loans and when providing guarantees or letters of credit will always seek to collateralise those deals to ensure that they can recover all that they expend. Banks are able to charge higher amounts for lending or accepting credit risk as they provide customers with the money or facilities required. Insurers only provide protection in the event of misfortune – misfortune that their customers hope to avoid.

Before lending money, banks make sure that the money can be recovered: they obtain security and guarantees and their lawyers scrutinise the documentation to ensure that recovery can easily be made. Frequently, in commercial transaction, the lawyers acting for banks are paid for by the borrowers, ensuring that the cost of achieving the minimum of risk is an integral part of the borrowing. For this reason, banks have no need of the protection of utmost good faith when accepting risk. Instead, banks look to mechanisms that allow swift enforcement of transactions. It is also to be remembered that in most banking transactions, the bank will advance money in return for future performance by its customer. Insurers receive money at inception against their own future performance. These differences have caused a very significant conflict in the establishment and operation of ART transactions involving banks and insurers and may lie at the heart of future problems.

Whereas insurers sell their assumption of risk cheaply but rely upon full disclosure and effective warranties, banks assume risk more expensively and rely on their own due diligence. Insurance contracts can be complicated in enforcement and issues may be raised by insurers to frustrate performance; banks have a real interest in ensuring the ease and speed of enforcement of banking instruments.

Interaction between banks and insurers

When insurers assume banking risks from banks, they do so in order to enter a market which they see as premium-rich and away from accumulations of their traditional exposures. When banks pass risks to insurers, they do so because insurers sell their capital more cheaply than banks do. Banks will not pass on such risk, however, without safeguards; they cannot allow themselves to be caught having to perform on a deal at the front end yet not being able to recover at the other. Furthermore, banks conduct what due diligence they do upon the basis of the risk as they see it and do not always look to issues that may be material to an insurer. The result is a conflict that has its resolution (generally) in the comparative economic might of the two protagonists. Banks will only cede risk to insurers in a way that is acceptable to them. Insurers can generally only obtain risk from banks, and with it significant premiums, if they accept the terms laid down by banks.

WAIVERS DUE TO NON-DISCLOSURE AND MISREPRESENTATION

Banks are averse to the risks inherent in contracts of utmost good faith. They cannot determine, necessarily, if full disclosure has or can be made of all material circumstances. They are also wary of warranties or anything else that could frustrate the enforcement of a contract and render it void. They therefore seek to avoid the issue by inserting waivers of the duty of disclosure.

The right to disclosure is not an essential ingredient of an insurance contract as insurable interest and fortuity are. It is a duty that exists in the creation of every insurance contract unless it is waived. The Marine Insurance Act 1906 provides for the possibility of waiver. In Section 18 (3) it is enacted that:

> "In the absence of inquiry the following circumstances need not be disclosed, namely:-
> … (c) Any circumstance as to which information is waived by the insurer."

Banks regularly require clauses to be inserted into ART contracts by which insurers waive the right to full disclosure.

The effectiveness of these waivers has been tested recently in a series of cases primarily emerging from film finance insurance agreements whereby insurers provided cover that protected the financing of films and the possibility of the film failing at the box office. HIH Casualty and General Insurance Limited v New Hampshire Insurance Company (2001), the so-called "Rojak decision", for example, dealt with the issue of notes constituted by a trust deed with Law Debenture Trust (Channel Islands) Limited ("LDT") as the named trustee.[10] A pecuniary loss indemnity policy protected the transaction. LDT was the named assured on behalf of the bondholders. The policy was designed to protect the bondholder in the event that the film did not generate sufficient funds to pay the interest and the principal borrowed. From the perspective of the bondholder, the policy was a credit enhancement product similar to an unconditional guarantee that one might purchase from a bank. A significant difference was that insurers provided the cover for a considerably smaller risk premium than banks would have contemplated.

The insurance contract contained a waiver clause that provided:

> "To the fullest extent permissible by applicable law, the insurer hereby agrees that it will not seek to or be entitled to avoid or rescind this policy or reject any claim hereunder or be entitled to seek any remedy or redress on the grounds of invalidity or unenforceability of any of its arrangements with Flashpoint Limited or any other person (or of any arrangements between Flashpoint Limited and the Purchaser) or non-disclosure or misrepresentation by any person or any other similar grounds. The Insurer irrevocably agrees not to assert and waives any and all defences and rights of set-off and/or counter-claim (including without limitation any such rights acquired by assignment or otherwise) which it may have against the Assured or which may be available so as to deny payment of any amount hereunder in accordance with the express terms hereof."

A second Court of Appeal decision relating to film finance covers that involved gap insurance policies was HIH Casualty & General Insurance Limited v TV Chase Manhattan Bank (2001), (dubbed the "Phoenix" case).[11] In the Phoenix case, the policies protected Chase Manhattan Bank who sought to guarantee reimbursement of capital and interest loaned to various film production companies in respect of a number of films in case those films did not achieve an anticipated level of revenue. The question for the Court of Appeal in the Phoenix case went further than that in the Rojak decision; the Court was asked to consider whether a waiver clause in the Phoenix policy excluded the consequences of both negligent and fraudulent misstatement. The waiver clause in the Phoenix case provided:

> "the insured will not have any duty or obligation to make any representation, warranty or disclosure of any nature, express or implied (such duty and obligation being expressly waived by the insurers) and shall have no liability of any nature to the insurers for any information provided by any other parties and any such information provided by or non-disclosure by other parties, including but not limited to [the brokers] shall not be a ground or grounds for avoidance of the insurer's obligations under the Policy or the cancellation thereof."

It was held in the Rojak case that the duty of utmost good faith is a "unitary" duty. The duty existed in one form and there was no distinction between negligent or innocent misrepresentation or non-disclosure. As a consequence, clauses in insurance or reinsurance contracts need not distinguish between different types of misrepresentation or non-disclosure in order to exclude their consequences. Thus the clause waived the remedy for non-disclosure and misrepresentation as a whole and it was not possible to argue that it only operated to waive a particular remedy or right. There was no other remedy for non-disclosure and misrepresentation except for avoidance. Once that remedy was waived, there was no other remedy open to the insurer.

In the Phoenix case, the Court of Appeal followed the same reasoning as in Rojak and confirmed that the only remedy for breach of the duty of utmost good faith is avoidance, and there is therefore no entitlement to damages for non-disclosure or misrepresentation in an insurance contract. The Court did recognise, however, a possible ground for damages based on negligent misstatement and under the Misrepresentation Act 1967.[12]

The Court held that the waiver clause in Phoenix, in a similar way to the waiver clause in Rojak, successfully excluded the available remedies for negligent misrepresentation and non-disclosure. It went further, holding that while there might be a remedy in some cases for damages for negligent misstatement under the Misrepresentation Act 1967, this remedy was also validly excluded by the waiver clause. Further, it validly excluded claims for damages for negligent misstatement and misrepresentation under the Act.

There are three types of non-disclosure and misrepresentation in law; innocent, negligent and fraudulent. In the Phoenix and Rojak cases, the Court of Appeal rejected any distinction, in the context of insurance, between innocent and negligent misrepresentation. The Court did, however, acknowledge, that fraudulent misrepresentation could give rise to a claim for damages under the tort of deceit. Whether this remedy would have been open to the insurers operating under the Phoenix and Rojak waivers was left open. The Court of Appeal in the Phoenix case did, however, find that, based on public policy, a clause could never protect the insured from the consequences of his own fraud in inducing the contract.

In the Phoenix case, there was an allegation that there had been fraud on the part of the broker acting for the bank. The Court of Appeal held that while it was possible for an insured to exclude the consequences of his agent's fraud in inducing the insurer into the contract, this would have to be done with very clear words and almost certainly an express reference to "fraud" would be necessary in the waiver clause to achieve this result. The Court of Appeal found that the waiver clause in the Phoenix policy did not exclude the agent's fraud because there was no express reference.

In the Rojak policy there was a warranty that provided that "slates" of six and 10 films would be made. The Court had to consider whether the waiver clause prevented reinsurers from relying on a breach of warranty and claiming the contract void from the time of breach. It was held that the waiver clause in question did not exclude the consequences of a breach of the warranty. The waiver clause, in dealing with misrepresentation and non-disclosure, was concerned with pre-contractual negotiations, whereas a breach of a warranty is a breach of the contract of insurance itself. Furthermore, with non-disclosure or misrepresentation, nothing happens to the contract unless the (re)insurer elects to avoid it. A breach of warranty on the other hand automatically discharges (re)insurers from liability under the contract. As a consequence, it is evident from this decision that if the consequences of a breach of warranty are to be excluded, the waiver clause must make specific reference to "warranties". A summary of the two cases can be seen in Table 2.

These two cases show that the Courts will allow waiver of remedies and that, if the remedy of avoidance is waived, insurers may be left with no other remedy to protect itself from the wrongful actions or inactions of its insureds. On the other hand, the Courts will scrutinise waivers carefully and will require clear and express language to be used in those waivers. Most particularly, the Courts will not allow a party to waive its own fraud. Banks can therefore insist upon insurers waiving many of the rights that exist in most insurance contracts if they wish. With the benefit of the Rojak and Phoenix cases, the banks and their lawyers are able to draft contracts carefully to remove any remaining remedies open to insurers (other than those for the banks' own fraud). Insurers accepting banking risk may be obliged to do so on banking terms, that is upon terms that are consistent with a readily enforceable guarantee. Insurers do this frequently at rates that reflect insurance rather than banking risk. Insurers also enter into such contracts often without legal advice or, if they take legal advice, they are restricted to advice that can be paid for out of the restricted premiums that they charge.

When creating an ART contract, it is clearly essential to ensure that the contract reflects a transaction that is permissible in regulatory terms; the ART contract must contain the essential ingredients of an insurance contract: fortuity and an insurable interest. Implications of reinsurance on ART transactions will follow from any regulatory questioning of insurable interest and fortuity. Banks are unlikely to throw up such arguments to defeat their own recoveries. Regulators are unlikely to become aware of specific details of transactions unless a problem arises. Reinsurers may well, when faced with sizeable losses (and ART contracts protect large sums of money) raise all arguments available to them, including the illegality or unenforceability of a transaction. Again, a risk exists of the insurer being left with liability for the whole loss.

It is also essential that there is an insured and the insured is the person with the insurable interest. Often, in the complexity of negotiations, draft wordings emerge which either fail to name an insured at all or name a party as the insured who has no insurable interest. These issues can be avoided but remain commonplace in circumstances where the parties are

Table 2 Comparison of the "Rojak" and "Phoenix" cases

HIH Casualty and General Insurance Ltd & Ors v New Hampshire Insurance Co & Ors (Court of Appeal, 2 May 2001) – The "Rojak" case	HIH Casualty and General Insurance Ltd & Ors v Chase Manhattan Bank & Ors (Court of Appeal, 31 July 2001) – The "Phoenix case
Policy/clause involved: ❑ A pecuniary loss indemnity policy that contained a waiver clause purporting to prevent the policy from being avoided on grounds of non-disclosure or misrepresentation.	*Policy/clause involved:* ❑ A gap insurance policy that contained a waiver clause purporting to exclude the consequences of both negligent and fraudulent statements.
Negligent & innocent misrepresentation/ non-disclosure: ❑ The duty of good faith was a "unitary" duty. There was no distinction between negligent or innocent misrepresentation or non-disclosure.	*Negligent & innocent misrepresentation/ non-disclosure:* ❑ There was no distinction between negligent or innocent misrepresentation or non-disclosure.
The effect of the waiver clause: ❑ The waiver clause in question operated successfully to exclude the remedy for misrepresentation and non-disclosure.	*The effect of the waiver clause:* ❑ The waiver clause in question operated successfully to exclude the remedy for misrepresentation and non-disclosure. ❑ The waiver clause's application was extended so that it excluded the possibility of damages being awarded under the Misrepresentation Act 1967 for negligent misstatements and misrepresentation under the Act.
Remedies available: ❑ The only remedy available for non-disclosure and misrepresentation is avoidance.	*Remedies available:* ❑ The only remedy available for breach of the duty of utmost good faith is avoidance.
Warranties: ❑ The waiver clause in question did not exclude the consequences of a breach of warranty. It was noted that unlike misrepresentation and non-disclosure a breach of warranty automatically discharges (re)insurers from liability under the contract. ❑ To exclude the consequences of a breach of warranty, the waiver clause must make specific reference to "warranties".	*Fraud:* ❑ Based on public policy, a clause could never protect the insured from the consequences of his own fraud in inducing a contract. ❑ It was possible to exclude the fraud of an insured's agent in inducing the insurer into the contract. The waiver clause would have to refer expressly to "fraud" and use very clear words in order to achieve this result. ❑ The waiver clause in this case was held not to exclude the agent's fraud because there was no express reference to "fraud" being excluded.

seeking to express what is more commonly a banking concept in terms of an insurance policy. It is, however, essential, that care is taken to reflect the correct form. If the document that is drafted does not reflect an insurance policy but a banking instrument, significant consequences can flow, from illegality and unenforceability to a failure of reinsurance protections.

This latter issue, the potential failure of reinsurance protection, is a very important point to consider when negotiating and documenting an ART transaction. The participation of insurers in such deals is often leveraged through reinsurance. The commercial position between insurers and reinsurers is not the same as that between banks and insurers; the deals struck with reinsurers are more likely to reflect the usual practices of the insurance and reinsurance market place. Consequently, a waiver of remedies expressed in an underlying insurance policy is not necessarily effective against reinsurers. The Courts have held that the duty of disclosure is absolute; it does not require knowledge of the circumstances by the reinsured. Innocent non-disclosure is as actionable as negligent non-disclosure. Thus if a bank fails to disclose information to an insurer, that insurer will face the prospect of having waived its remedies against the bank while still having to face the consequences of its own reinsurer's avoidance. While this can be remedied by carefully expressing a waiver in identical terms in the reinsurance cover, care must be taken. It is unclear whether "as original" language will incorporate a waiver. It is clear that such language will not expressly waive an agent's fraud. Furthermore, as more deals are struck, the use of treaty reinsurance becomes more prevalent. Treaties must be drafted with care to ensure that the reinsurer is given no greater remedies against the insurer than the insurer has against its insured.

CLAIMS HANDLING

It is not just in the areas of non-disclosure, misrepresentation and breach of warranty that conflicts arise between the economics and practices of banking and insurance. Claims handling is also conducted very differently. Banking agreements require swift enforcement. If there is to be dispute, it is postponed until after the contract has been performed. Insurance contracts are only performed after careful scrutiny of the claim. It may be said that, generally speaking, insurers do their due diligence at the time of loss rather than at the time of acceptance. When banks purchase insurance contracts that cover traditional banking risk, the banks look for immediate performance in the event of a loss trigger occurring. This is a matter of negotiation between the bank and the insurer. It must, however, be borne in mind that the insurer's reinsurers may well expect that claims are handled in a "business-like manner" and will decline to pay them unless the usual conditions of "follow the fortunes" or "follow the settlements" clauses are adhered to.

Under reinsurance contracts, the reinsured must prove its loss in order to be able to recover. Very frequently this obligation is expressed in terms of a follow fortunes/settlements clause (clauses that regulate the manner in which a reinsurer must abide by the claims settlements of the reinsured). Under such a clause, and depending upon the particular words used, a reinsurer is entitled to determine that the claim falls within the terms of the contract and, in some cases the underlying contract, that there is an absence of fraud and that the claim has been adjusted in a proper and business-like manner. In a case where claims must be paid first and disputed later, this will not be possible and, in the absence of saving language, the insurer may, at very least, be subject to a cashflow penalty as a consequence.

RETENTION OF RISK

Additional issues to consider when negotiating and documenting ART transactions include the retention of risk. Insurers and reinsurers frequently see the retention of an element of risk by their insureds or reinsureds as an essential tool of risk management. If the insured or reinsured has an interest in the subject matter of the risk, there is a greater chance that that insured or reinsured will act in a way to avoid or mitigate loss. This does not apply to banks who can hedge risk without retention because the risk that they are ceding does not require an insurable interest and is, therefore, not finite in nature. A bank insuring its participation in a derivative, while it cannot doubly insure a particular liability, can buy other derivatives as hedges without reducing its insurable interest in the protected derivative.

JURISDICTION AND ARBITRATION

Choices of law and jurisdiction as well as questions of whether to use an arbitration clause are very important in drafting an ART contract. One element of the choice has to be how one can most effectively attain certainty and how swiftly a result can be achieved. Banks, who prefer to operate on the basis of paying first and disputing later, frequently prefer the jurisdiction of courts where summary judgment can be obtained. Insurers (and particularly reinsurers) have good reason to prefer the flexibility of arbitration. Much is to be said for the same system operating for both the insurance and reinsurance contract, provided that the system chosen is one that is capable of dealing with the issues and determining them in a predictable manner.

CONCLUSION

The development of ART has come about because of imbalances in the positions of banks and insurers. Such imbalances have given scope to both insurers and banks to profit from novel and often ground-breaking transactions. As profit comes from assuming risk, it is essential that the precise nature of that risk is determined and understood by both parties before embarking on a transaction. A failure by either party to comprehend fully the nature of the bargain will undoubtedly lead to dispute and, in that dispute, an erosion of any remaining profit margin. The risk of dispute is as much a transactional risk that requires assessment as any other. In novel and ground-breaking areas, that risk can be high, particularly where the sums involved are significant. In buying and selling risk, both parties must consider the nature of the transaction and ensure that it is properly priced. To sell banking risk on banking terms at insurance rates is a high-risk business.

1   Insurance Companies Act 1982 (1982 c. 50), ss. 2, 16, see Brown, M. (2000), pp. 109, 123.
2   (IPRU (INS)), R.1.3(1), p. 11.
3   Prudential Insurance Company v Inland Revenue Commissioners [1904] 2 K.B. 658.
4   Lucena v Craufurd (1806) 2 B. & P. 269.
5   Wilson v Jones (1866–67) L.R. 2 Ex. 139.
6   Gaming Act 1845 (1845 c. 109), s.18, see *Halsbury's Statutes* (1998), p. 17.
7   Marine Insurance (Gambling Policies) Act 1909 (1909 c. 12), see *Halsbury's Statutes* (2000), p. 70.
8   Financial Services Act 1986 (1986 c. 60), s. 63, see *Halsbury's Statutes* (1991), p. 237.
9   Marine Insurance Act 1906 (1906 c. 41), s. 18, see Brown, M. (2000), p. 16.
10 HIH Casualty & General Insurance Ltd v New Hampshire Insurance Company [2001] 2 All E.R. (Comm) 39.
11 HIH Casualty & General Insurance Ltd v Chase Manhattan Bank [2001] Lloyd's Rep. I.R. 703 (CA).
12 Misrepresentation Act 1967 (1967 c. 7), see Brown, M. (2000), p. 1034.

BIBLIOGRAPHY

Brown, M., 2000, *Butterworths Insurance Law Handbook,* Sixth Edition, (London: Butterworths Tolley).

Financial Services Authority, 2001, *Interim Prudential Sourcebook for Insurers,* 1, (London: FSA) p. 11.

Halsbury, 1991, *Halsbury's Statutes,* 30, Fourth Edition, (re-issue), (London: Butterworths Tolley).

Halsbury, 1998, *Halsbury's Statutes,* 5, Fourth Edition (re-issue), (London: Butterworths Tolley).

Halsbury, 2000, *Halsbury's Statutes,* 22, Fourth Edition, (re-issue), (London: Butterworths Tolley).

31

Alternative Risk Strategies – Regulation

Nigel Davies*

Financial Services Authority

In the financial services industry, regulators and other lawmakers are giving consideration to producing guidelines and/or regulation to remove legal uncertainty relating to the products and participants in this area. Their prime function however is usually to protect the interests of the consumer and not the practitioners.

REGULATORY CONTEXT
The pace of change and an overview of what needs to be done

One area in which practitioners are subject to legal and regulatory risk is in the alternative risk transfer (ART) market. The ART market is characterised by innovative thinking and the combination of techniques from what has been assumed, until recently, to be separate, discrete and distinct fields within the financial services industry. Market practitioners and regulators alike have to learn the concepts, risks and techniques that are common to areas of financial services other than their own. This brings, in its train, a number of difficulties. Insurance, banking and securities legislation have evolved in their own distinct spheres and, consequently, impose different capital and disclosure requirements. In addition to this sectoral diversity, there is a wide geographical or jurisdictional diversity. This exposes practitioners in the ART market to legal and regulatory risk.

Practitioners in the ART market not only have to deal with legal and regulatory risk, but are also faced with a bewildering variety of legal, regulatory and fiscal regimes. They must deal with what may be described as a range of different attitudes from those who are charged with enforcing a particular regime in their jurisdiction. The variety of attitudes may be due, in part, to the fact that there appears to be little consensus on whether ART will be an important feature in the spectrum of financial services products.

---

* This chapter expresses the views of the author and not necessarily those of the FSA.

The degree of awareness of ART products amongst regulators is, therefore, variable. Likewise, the degree to which regulators keep apprised of (or even wish to be apprised of) developments is also variable. From the author's perspective many market practitioners are reluctant to speak to the regulator or any other lawmaker, perhaps because an early regulatory rebuff would be a deal breaker. To overcome this, they are obviously more comfortable with taking legal advice to ensure that, as far as possible, their deals fit in with existing law. This serves to further distance a regulator from the ART evolutionary process, resulting in increased frictional costs; decreased speed to market and persistence of legal or regulatory risk. To the author's knowledge no court has yet handed down a decision on this issue. This is a paradox and a vicious circle. Regulators and other lawmakers can change the law to reduce or eliminate legal or regulatory risk, but they are not in a position to actually reduce or eliminate legal or regulatory risk. Against this background, it is difficult to expect that a coherent international framework of regulation will ever emerge. Yet this is what is required, is often called for in public conferences, and the international dimension must be emphasised due to the international nature of the business. Is this too tall an order, given that practitioners are usually reluctant to talk to regulators about novel types of deals?

There are a number of regulators in the world with an active interest in this subject. For example, the Financial Services Authority in the UK, has four fundamental tenets: market confidence, promoting public awareness, consumer protection, and the reduction of financial crime. One of its principles of good regulation is to facilitate innovation. This particular principle of good regulation is germane to the ART market. Moreover, the International Association of Insurance Supervisors (IAIS) now has a sub-group that is looking at the areas of securitisation of risk and other ART products in general.[1] This sub-group has an active liaison with the International Organization of Securities Commissions (IOSCO) (the Securities equivalent of the IAIS) and is fostering an open dialogue with market participants. The aim of the IAIS is to produce global standards on insurance supervision. The aims of its Securitisation sub-group are to achieve this in the ART field, together with ensuring, as far as possible, compatibility between insurance, banking and securities regulators. A consistent and certain framework of regulation is often called for in public conferences; one within which business may be conducted on an international basis, to agreed standards in a manner which is safe for the practitioners and (ultimately) consumers alike.

Conflicts and uncertainties
Market commentators, practitioners and regulators are a mixed bag. As yet there appears to be little consensus on whether there is actually a promising future for the more novel forms of risk transfer. Some would argue that

in a soft reinsurance market there is insufficient demand for ART products to make them a viable and separate discipline in themselves. Others would argue that the soft reinsurance market is persistent, with only transient periods of scarce capacity and high prices, for example the reinsurance renewal season of January 2002. No doubt, there is some form of unstable equilibrium between a hard and a soft reinsurance market, and recent history does indicate that, on balance, the market is predominantly soft. Nevertheless, there is a persistent, if not a large, demand for these products in spite of their high frictional costs, slow speed to market and inherent legal risk. As the number and type of in-force ART products continues to rise, no regulator can afford to ignore them for much longer.

The market dynamics and supply and demand are complicated areas to understand. Supply and demand are factors that primarily affect price, but this may not be the prime concern of regulators. Our prime concerns are whether the market participants actually understand each other; whether the products actually perform in the ways intended, if, or to what extent, the consumer will suffer in the event of a default and whether such contracts facilitate or conceal financial crime. There may be a great deal of innovation in this area, and there is certainly a great deal of publicity. Arguably, in the predominance of a soft reinsurance market, the principle benefit to be derived from protection by an ART product is the positive effect on corporate image. Comments such as these do not serve to send ART regulation further up the list of priorities in what may otherwise be overcrowded legislative timetables. Nevertheless, the outlook for ART is thought by many to be far less pessimistic than this. The disruption caused by large scale terrorist activities, the failure of large corporations or even emerging, localised systemic weaknesses in the financial system may serve to increase demand for a more diversified range of risk transfer methods and a more diversified range of risk carriers.

International issues and inconsistencies

The ART market presents regulators with mixed signals as to its importance, and a technical challenge in understanding the implications for the numerous counterparties in numerous jurisdictions. This is set against a background where regulatory, accounting and fiscal regimes are inconsistent between jurisdictions and where the level of communication and co-operation between jurisdictions varies, sometimes quite significantly. This must also be set in the context of the revision to capital standards required of insurers, banks and securities houses.[2]

Current position and way forward

The interests of the regulator may vary from jurisdiction to jurisdiction. In general, the job of the regulator is to secure, as far as possible, the interests of the consumer while facilitating innovation and enhancing market confidence. Some regulators, however, serve to promote activity in their territory, encouraging businesses to set up there, while perhaps not asking enough questions about the nature or legality of those businesses. The innovative nature of ART, and the associated legal risk in the more highly regulated environments serve to encourage innovative activity to be domiciled in those areas with permissive laws and unintrusive or unobstructive disclosure regimes. Such domiciles may also offer the benefit of relatively light taxation. There are, nevertheless, a great many international organisations that are currently active in the area of levelling the legal, regulatory and fiscal playing fields.

❑ The IAIS is concerned with harmonising supervisory standards amongst its members on a whole range of issues from ART to exchange of information between supervisors.
❑ The European Union (Commission Services) is currently considering a directive on reinsurance supervision and the capital regime for companies.
❑ The National Association of Insurance Commissioners (NAIC) have adopted a model law on special purpose vehicles (SPVs)
❑ The National Conference of Insurance Legislators (NCOIL) is taking an increasing interest in international issues.
❑ The Organisation for Economic Co-operation and Development (OECD) looks at insurance solvency, exchange of information and, importantly, has recently issued pronouncement on what it calls harmful tax practices in certain jurisdictions.
❑ The Association of Latin American Insurance Supervisors (ASSAL) covering Central and South America, is an active member of IAIS and is keen to ensure the standards of its members are compatible with those in the so-called developed economies.

It has been announced in the UK that an overhaul to the capital regime that applies to insurance companies would be desirable. This implies a Basel-style approach to capital requirements. Thus, current developments in the overhaul of the Basel Accord are directly relevant to this strand of work. The detailed study is currently being conducted by a working group of EU insurance regulators – and as yet is unpublished – through the medium of solvency margin review, the aim of which is to introduce new directives that would affect the EU area in total. Banking, securities and insurance capital regimes should ultimately look and feel very similar. This would be good news for practitioners in the ART market because it should mean that a great many of the inconsistencies or uncertainties that currently exist would disappear. Nevertheless, this work is not fully developed and a source of great interest in the work to come will be that relating to those instruments that will qualify a company for a capital credit in the new regime. This will be of prime importance to ART practitioners.

INTERNATIONAL RELATIONS

A spirit of co-operation between regulators and lawmakers will facilitate progress towards common standards. Whereas we can be optimistic about common supervisory standards amongst IAIS members, of which there are now some 150 member states, and certain of consistency in Europe because of the need to comply with directives, we are less certain about global consistency in everything. The US has had a credible risk-based method of insurance supervision for quite some time and it would be unrealistic to expect change. Nevertheless, it is not unrealistic to expect that, in due course, equivalent systems of supervision and monitoring, enhanced by greater exchange of information between supervisors, will obviate the need for duplicate reporting or any other type of cross-border barrier to doing business. The barriers to achieving these goals are rooted in unwillingness to change and, in some places, the need to preserve a local lucrative business centre.

Overcoming the barriers to change, drafting and agreeing the required standards and transposing them into national law will take a number of years to achieve. The process of negotiation should include interested members of the financial services industry – and only this would ensure the correct balance between capital adequacy and capital efficiency. This would also ensure the continued supply of competitively priced products to the consumer whose demands are becoming ever more sophisticated. If it is ever possible to define the end point of this process, it would be one where consistent or equivalent regimes are enforced in a wide range of jurisdictions, are applicable to a wide range of products, including ART, and are stable but flexible. This would mitigate legal and regulatory risk, but we have a great deal of work to do between then and now.

PRODUCTS AND PARTICIPANTS

The ART market is the meeting place of all participants in the financial services sector, together with the consumers of those services. The prime concern of the regulator is for the consumer and so he is charged with understanding and dealing with the risks and financial resources of the market participants. Regulators are traditionally mono-sectoral be that insurance, banking or securities. If the market barriers between these areas are breaking down, then so should the traditional mono-sectoral nature of regulation.

It is, therefore, necessary to give a very broad overview of what is happening in the ART market. There is a bewildering morass of detail, including types of deal, legal complexities and mathematical models, which is exacerbated by the fact that this area is both evolving and being used as a publicity vehicle by clever service providers. Nevertheless, the underlying processes are very simple: a consumer buys a financial service, the financial service provider funds the risk, either through their own funds, or lays off all or part of the risk to another party, maybe from a different financial service sector, with the payment of a fee. This may appear to be an oversimplification, but it is not. The complexities arise from only two conditions. Firstly, the mechanisms and media by which, and through which, cross-sectoral risk transfers take place. Secondly, from the fact that different laws and regulations apply to different financial services sectors and in different jurisdictions. The mechanisms and media can be best illustrated by the transactions that occur through SPVs; protected cell companies (PCCs), transformer companies, and by standard International Swaps and Derivatives Association (ISDA) documentation through any of the foregoing or through conventional companies.

The regulatory position is, therefore, best illustrated by taking an example of an outward cross-sectoral risk transfer from the insurance sector, eg securitisation, and a credit or weather insurance deal as an example of an inward cross-sectoral risk transfer which is sometimes referred to as "insuratisation". Whereas it is relatively straightforward to survey the current ART landscape, there remains one obvious question: what will the regulators do about it?

Risk transfer from the insurance sector via SPVs, PCCs or transformer companies

The securitisation of insurance risk has been an accepted feature of the insurance and reinsurance market for a number of years. The principal reason for this acceptance is the fact that they provide full funding for the subject risk. For this reason, they are sometimes regarded by some as a powerful statement of financial security and this might be why activity continued through the soft reinsurance market of the late 1990s. In more technical terms, they serve to minimise credit and timing risk in the settlement of claims. They are not, however, risk free but the areas of uncertainty have not been tested by the market or by the courts.

The migration of risk between jurisdictions and financial services sectors will incur a certain amount of operational risk. The major element of operational risk arises from the fact that the originator of the insurance business, the entity that cedes risk to the SPV, retains the obligation to pay claims to its customers. If, therefore, the securitisation structure failed to operate for any reason, the originator may either find itself in a parlous financial condition, or lose the confidence of the market in general or both. The inability of the originator to divest itself of its primary obligations is in contrast to securitisations that occur in the banking sector, where legal separation from the underlying subject business is one of the prime considerations when setting up a deal.

The issue of legal separation raises the interesting question of the comparison of triggers between the banking and insurance sectors. In the banking sector there are basically four methods of transferring business to the SPV. In decreasing order of certainty of legal separation they are; nova-tion, assignment, declaration of trust and sub-participation. In the insurance sector, there are basically three methods of transferring risk to the SPV. These are defined by the trigger mechanism and, in approxi-mately decreasing order of certainty or quality (depending on the ability of the trigger to mitigate basis risk) of transfer, are; indemnity trigger, index-based trigger and parametric trigger. It could be argued that the sub-participation method from the banking sector and the indemnity trig-ger from the insurance sector have many features in common and may be regarded as analogous. If this argument is accepted, then it is possible to view this list as a single continuum of seven methods of business transfer.

This type of cross-sectoral connection inevitably leads to the issue of joined-up cross-sectoral regulation; as can be seen by the trend for national financial service regulators to be amalgamated into a single body, as in the UK, Germany, Ireland and Mexico who are currently going through the process. No doubt, there is much that the banking and insurance regulators could learn from each other, but there are fundamental differences between banking and insurance securitisations. The former is the re-packaging of assets and the latter is the re-packaging of liabilities. The differences lead to a different set of market dynamics, but moreover, for regulatory purposes, the different sectors are subject to different laws. For example, there are questions about whether the issuance of a bond by an SPV is a contract of insurance, or whether the bondholder is carrying on insurance business and, as such, would need to be licensed. There are also issues surrounding the opacity of the secondary market in these bonds, and the opportunities that it affords for financial crime.

The legal issues have been dealt with by a number of jurisdictions in a variety of different ways. In Bermuda, a law has been passed to empower the regulator to deem whether a transaction is one of insurance or not.[3] This must be a useful method of overcoming legal uncertainty on an indi-vidual deal basis. In such a case, the SPV may act as a transformer company, translating a package of business from one set of laws into another. This type of regime may not, however, be practical or even acceptable in some jurisdictions that have a need for a completely trans-parent regime with minimal requirement for regulatory discretion. To date, the UK has no written law in the area of insurance risk securitisation. Indeed, the UK law relating to the identification of an insurance contract is based in case law – the effect of which is to avoid a precise definition of such a contract. The reason for this is to ensure, as far as possible, that no condition is inadvertently excluded from insurance that may subsequently prove to be detrimental to the interests of consumers. Nevertheless, the position in the UK is that a bondholder (*qua* bondholder) is not deemed to be carrying on insurance business, and does not need to be licensed as such. The rationale for this is that a shareholder (*qua* shareholder) of an insurance company is not deemed to be carrying on insurance business. For these purposes the position of the bondholder and the shareholder are analogous. This has not, however, been tested in the courts.

The conventional medium for the transfer of risk from the insurance sector to the capital markets is the SPV. The costs associated with such a structure are high, and the PCC has evolved in an attempt to reduce these costs.[4] A PCC is a single legal entity that is comprised of, or contains, discrete cells, the contents of which are financially independent from those outside the cell. This type of structure could streamline the business of rent-a-captives, but there is also the possibility of the issuance of, for example, cat bonds from a cell into which the original business has been transferred. The aim is to preserve bankruptcy remoteness but, as with many areas of ART, the effectiveness has not been tested by the courts. Furthermore, the PCC structure would be more cost effective than the SPV structure, but the effect on the cost of the entire deal would be marginal because of the continued need for lawyers.

Risk transfer into the insurance sector via SPV

Insurance companies accept risk from other financial services sectors through traditional insurance contracts, but also through an increasing volume of novel transactions involving SPVs (or PCCs) which act as transformers. A relatively new form of risk involves the insurance of a transformer (whether a conventional company, SPV or PCC) that has assumed a credit risk by the assumption of, for example, a credit default swap. The difference here is that there is no attempt to transfer the underlying assets (or liabilities) and these are called synthetic securitisations.

This leads to another direct comparison between insurance and banking regulation. It could be argued that this type of transaction would not occur if it were not for the fact that the deal counterparties benefit from the opportunity of regulatory arbitrage. Clearly, there are a number of drivers for such a transaction, as listed below.

❏ Banks originate large credit portfolios – capital constraints are main drivers for credit risk mitigation tools.
❏ Insurers generate large "indemnity" portfolios and in a soft competitive market actively seek opportunities for further diversification.
❏ Counterparties seek to undertake business with the minimum cost of capital and this leads to regulatory or capital arbitrage and careful tax planning.
❏ Banks use credit derivatives as a medium for market making and trading.
❏ Intermediaries may drive these transactions to generate high levels of fees.
❏ Insurers from continental Europe have been known to buy credit bonds to increase the diversity of their investment portfolios and to achieve

higher rates of return. The motivation is to overcome what they perceive as restrictive regulations governing the nature of the assets in which they are allowed to invest.

The credit derivative market is growing, but is still very small compared to currency and interest rate derivative markets. Nevertheless, the assumption of an increasing amount of credit risk by the insurance industry, at the time of an approaching economic recession gives cause for prudential regulatory concern.

The transfer of credit risk into the insurance sector raises a number of cross-sectoral legal issues. In the UK, the business of an insurance company is restricted to the assumption of insurance risk.[5] The rationale is that it should not undertake speculative ventures that may cause its assets to dissipate; the assets should be preserved in order to pay the claims of the insured. This is also the rationale for the conservative investment rules to which they must adhere. Credit default swaps may have features in common with insurance contracts; both instruments mitigate or transfer defined risks. Credit derivatives, however, are not regarded as contracts of insurance because they do not provide indemnity for a credit loss (the authority for this comes from Potts QC in his opinion to ISDA in 1997.[6] Credit derivatives cannot, therefore, be purchased by an insurance company as a form of quasi-underwriting, they can only be purchased directly to mitigate other forms of risk in the asset portfolio.

It is evident, therefore, that if an insurer is to assume risk via a credit derivative, it must be achieved through some kind of transformer mechanism. This mechanism is one that is also commonly used to assume weather-related risk.

Risk transfer into the insurance sector via a transformer – using the example of weather derivatives

This mechanism involves an offshore transformer that assumes the obligation to pay stipulated amounts depending on the weather-related factors, such as a defined change in temperature or a defined amount of rainfall – a parametric trigger. Such a contract is not regarded as a contract of insurance. It is analogous to the credit derivative position on which Potts QC opined. Nevertheless, the transformer assuming this obligation, being an offshore insurance company, can reinsure itself in an onshore market. This begs the question that if the primary "insurance contract" in the offshore transformer would not constitute a valid onshore contract, then why is its reinsurance treated as valid? The difference revolves around the insurable interest in a reinsurance transaction. The protection of an insurance company against payment claims is a valid insurable interest in a reinsurance transaction. Again, this principle has not been tested in the courts.

Participants in the credit insurance market do not overlap significantly with those in the weather insurance market. There are many similarities in the mechanisms used, with one major exception. Those active in the credit derivative market have the benefit of standard documentation.

The use of standard documentation

Credit risk transfers are generally carried out by means of standard ISDA documentation.[7] Industry standard contract wordings are cost effective and serve to reduce the attendant legal and operational risk. Moreover, such standards substantially obviate the need for transformer companies and the expense of hiring lawyers.

The insurance industry has standard contract wordings as does the banking/credit industry. When these two sectors deal with each other, it seems very difficult to devise standard contract wordings that are acceptable, or even understandable, to both sides. This is perhaps one of the greatest shortcomings of the ART market, because a greater cross-sectoral understanding would facilitate the evolution of standard wordings. Furthermore, it is sometimes difficult, if not impossible, to use standard wordings for complex transactions. Nevertheless, on a more optimistic note, the use of standard wordings would decrease frictional costs, increase the speed to market and decrease legal and operational risk. In short, standard documentation would greatly increase the liquidity of the market. The imposition of standard contract terms is not, however, a function of European insurance regulators. This is laid down in Article 29 of the third non-life Directive.[8]

Standardisation, or the lack of it, is therefore a problem. Rating agencies play a significant role in imposing a degree of standardisation on the understanding of the risks.

THE PLACE OF RATING AGENCIES

Rating agencies play an essential, if not central, role in the issuance of bonds to investors. They communicate the estimated level of risk by means of a simple index that informs the level of return required by the subject instrument. This is central to the marketability of instruments in all sectors of the financial services industry, and agencies attempt to ensure that ratings are assigned in a manner that is consistent across all sectors. In theory, the riskiness of a US earthquake cat bond could be directly compared to the riskiness of a UK credit portfolio. This may sound impossible and, no doubt, the agencies exercise a great deal of judgement. Before assigning a rating, they will examine the principal features of a deal including, say, the catastrophe model, bankruptcy remoteness and other structural issues. They fulfil the role of an independent third party and often suggest changes to models in order that certain published ratings are achievable. Business models are an essential feature in modern risk analysis. There are, however, general reservations about their ability to identify and deal with aggregations of correlated risk.

The need for the assignment of a rating has increased the transaction lead time because the agency must perform its due diligence checks. This lead time appears to be decreasing as their experience in this area grows. It may be concluded, therefore, that the quality of the ratings are improving in respect of cat bonds, and that they play an important role in the mitigation or clarification of risk.

It is, nevertheless, impossible to be unequivocal about the veracity of a rating. It is impossible to predict the level of insurance claims or to foresee how the various forms of legal, operational or even regulatory risk will crystallise. Indeed, many market participants, specifically investors, appear to undertake their own due diligence examinations to verify the public rating. This appears to be particularly marked in the insurance of credit risk, where the rate of business declinatures are relatively high. In this sector, a rating assessment may be devalued because the agency may have insufficient comparative information on which to base its opinion due to, for example, the relative obscurity of the subject business. Reliance on a rating is, therefore, not without its own element of risk.

HARMONISATION OF REGULATION

ART is a relatively new area and there are still barriers and inconsistencies between the financial services sectors. This is illustrated by the fact that the definition of insurance risk is perhaps more elusive than that of credit risk, and the rate of its crystallisation more difficult to estimate. Nevertheless, there are remarkable similarities. For example, the overall risk profile of a specialist monoline credit insurer will be similar to that of a bank.

A combined, consistent approach to cross-sectoral harmonisation should have regard to the following issues.

❑ Capital charge and arbitrage
❑ Analogous capital relief instruments treated consistently
❑ Prudent, effective rules for asset side
❑ Cross-sectoral, multi-jurisdictional supervision
❑ Proper risk definition and risk-sensitive supervision
❑ Converging business mechanisms
❑ Shortcomings of ratings and internal models

There are a great many similarities and a great many differences between the methods of risk transfer across financial services boundaries. The difficulties and costs arise from the fact that there are a variety of attitudes, approaches, laws and regulations in a variety of jurisdictions. Yet it is possible to conceive of relatively harmonised capital regimes and supervisory standards across the financial services sectors, although it will take years to achieve. Such a system should be:

❑ effective and efficient;
❑ transparent;
❑ stable, durable yet flexible;
❑ indiscriminate between large and small companies; and
❑ no artificial barrier to trade.

It has already been mentioned that there is a large flow of new law, regulation and standards from a number of international bodies. The UK has announced that it intends to adopt a Basel II-style approach to insurance supervision, the features of which are as follows.

❑ Pillar 1 – minimum capital requirements.
❑ Pillar 2 – supervisory review.
❑ Pillar 3 – market discipline (via disclosure).[9]

The Basel II style can be applied on a consolidated basis and this is already reflected in European insurance regulation through the Insurance Groups Directive.[10] Group supervision will be augmented, in due course, by the implementation of the Financial Conglomerates Directive.[11]

The intention is for regulation to become more risk sensitive and to be consistent and fair to all consumers and participants. This has a number of implications. Firstly, greater attention will need to be given to internal business models, having regard to their strengths and weaknesses. Secondly, greater attention will need to be given to instruments that provide relief from capital charges. Analogous instruments arising in different sectors will require similar treatment. In addition, a "prudent person" approach to investment regulation would allow flexibility to manage assets in a way that best fits the needs of the individual entity. This approach to the asset side of the balance sheet may not, however, be easily enforced and is not the preferred option of many regulators who argue for more prescriptive rules. Nevertheless, the debate continues in many fora and progress will be made.

REGULATION AND CORPORATE BEHAVIOUR
The uncertainties associated with ART have driven much of the business into jurisdictions with permissive, unobtrusive regulation. Yet regulation *per se* is not one of the major costs to the ART sector. A more important driver is the mitigation of tax liability, and between the so-called tax-friendly jurisdictions, those with passive, permissive regulations have emerged as the favoured locations.

Regulations exist primarily to protect the interests of the consumer. When regulations are non-existent or not enforced, the interests of the consumer are at risk. In such cases, a company may only service the interests of the shareholders and pay scant regard to the interests of consumers whose financial well-being may, in fact, be dependent on the performance of its financial services providers. Regulators are, however, attuned to the balance of interests that exist and are aware of the potential conflict between capital efficiency and capital adequacy.

CONCLUSION

Capital and supervisory regimes are undergoing a change, and regulators and lawmakers would appreciate an open candid dialogue with market participants, via market associations if necessary, in order that this balance of interests is fairly struck. Such a dialogue would, in itself, be progress. This is because the fear of regulatory rejection has inhibited the practitioner from coming forward very much to date. Such an attitude is ultimately counter-productive and will inhibit the evolution of law that facilitates innovation. It would be edifying and enlightening to experience a meeting of minds between market participants over the realisation that risks are basically generic regardless of deal structure, and likewise, to experience a meeting of minds between the world's regulators over the fact that similar risks might be covered by equivalent amounts of capital. Capital is essential; it must be efficient but it must also be adequate to cover the risks in the interests of the consumers. Global equivalence of capital and supervisory standards is a lofty aspiration, but it better serves the consumer and the industry.

1   See http://www. iaisweb. org
2   *FSA plans shake-up for prudential regulation of insurance*, 2001 [see http://www.fsa.gov.uk/pubs/press/2001/0.31.html and http://europa.eu.int and follow links to "The European Union Online", then "Official documents" and then "EUR-Lex, European Union law".
3   See http://www.bma.bm.
4   Legislation about captives (for insurance – also including rent-a-captives) and then PCCs has been passed in the following jurisdictions (however, this is not an exhaustive list):
   a) Guernsey
      i) 1997: The Protected Cell Companies Ordinance 1997 – promoting protected cell companies.
      ii) 2001: The Protected Cell Companies (Special Purpose Vehicle) Regulations 2001; Guernsey recognises an SPV as one that is "established principally for the purpose of issuing bonds or other debt securities where the repayment is to be funded from the proceeds of the company's investment". An example of such a company is the Zurich Re PCC Ltd, and there are now 23 such companies in Guernsey.
   b) Cayman Islands
      i) 1998: Segregated Portfolio legislation.
   c) Bermuda
      i) 2000: Segregated Accounts Act 1999; Bermudan legislation provides for both rent-a-captives and for PCCs.
   d) Mauritius
      i) 2000: Protected Cell Companies Act 1999; attributes assets of each cell to that cell alone and creditors of one cell have no recourse to assets of any other cell.
   e) US states: captive legislation

i)   Colorado (1972)
ii)   Tennessee (1978)
iii)   Virginia (1980)
iv)   Vermont (1981)
v)   South Carolina (2000)
vi)   Hawaii (2000)
vii)   Maine (1997)
viii) Illinois – INEX Regulation 27 (1998)

f) US states – NAIC Protected Cell Company Model Act 1999.

This law aims to provide a basis for the creation of protected cells by a domestic insurer as one means of assessing alternative sources of capital and achieving the benefits of insurance securitisation. It has been adopted by law in six US states:

i) Illinois 2001 – Protected Cell Company Law; allows establishment of SPVs to participate in securitisation of insurance risk.

ii) Vermont 1999 – Sponsored Captive Law; allows a captive to be owned by an insurer with legally protected cells.

iii) South Carolina 2000 – Protected Cell Legislation.

iv) Iowa 2000 – Protected Cell Legislation.

v) Kentucky 2000 – Protected cell and Captive Legislation.

g) Proposed US Legislation 2001: Special Purchase Reinsurance Vehicle Model Act.

Other captive domiciles include: Barbados, British Virgin Islands, Bahamas, Turks and Caicos, Ireland, Isle of Man, Jersey, Luxembourg.

5   FSA Rulebook, Restriction to Business of Insurance, IPRU (INS) 1.3(1), AUTH 3.12.3G.
6   FSA Discussion Paper, 2002, *Cross-sectoral Risk Transfer*, forthcoming.
7   See Gooch, A. and L. Klein., 1993, *Documentation for Derivatives* (London: Euromoney).
8   Third non-life Directive reference 92/49/EEC. See http://europa.eu.int/index-en.html.
9   See note 3 (FSA press release).
10 See http://www.fsc.gi/download/adobe/idgconsult.pdf.
11 See http://europe.en.int/comm/internal-market/en/finances/crosssector/conglomerates2.html.

32

Alternative Risk Transfer and Financial Stability[1]

David Rule*

Bank of England

Previous chapters have described a wide range of less conventional ways in which insurance companies are taking on and shedding risk, which can be grouped conveniently under the heading 'alternative risk transfer' (ART). This embraces new types of risk, such as credit portfolios or weather; different ways of organising insurance cover for large corporate customers, such as multi-year policies and the use of captives; alternative ways of shedding risk, such as catastrophe (cat) bonds, risk swaps and finite reinsurance; and the unbundling of capital market transactions into the parts which can be sold into (liquid) securities or derivatives markets and any remaining risks, for which the cost of insurance might be lower, such as an issuer's potential environmental liabilities or the residual value of an asset.

INTRODUCTION

Other authors have discussed the ways in which ART might benefit those involved directly in such transactions. This chapter asks some wider questions about whether ART matters for the international financial system as a whole. In particular, does ART have any consequences for financial stability and for authorities tasked with maintaining financial stability?

Rather like ART, financial stability is not easy to define. In its June 2000 *Financial Stability Review*, the Bank of England described it in these terms:[2]

"Stability is necessary for the financial system to perform its key functions effectively – including the provision of a secure means of holding monetary and other financial assets, the payment and settlement of financial and other claims, and the efficient allocation of savings amongst competing investments. This entails the financial sector as a whole being sound, with confidence in

---

* This chapter represents the views of the author and not necessarily those of the Bank of England.

its ability to meet its obligations; but it does not mean that no individual firm should ever fail. It also requires financial markets in which participants can transact at prices that reflect fundamental forces and that do not vary substantially over short periods in the absence of changes in fundamental factors.[3] At the opposite end of the spectrum is a systemic financial crisis, which has been defined as 'a disturbance that severely impairs the working of the financial system and, at the extreme, causes a complete breakdown in it'".[4]

The development of ART might potentially have some influence on both the soundness of the financial sector as a whole and the existence of financial markets in which participants can transact at prices that reflect fundamental forces. As regards financial sector soundness, a key question is the extent to which ART encourages better diversification of risk exposures, making the financial sector less vulnerable to particular shocks. Another question is how regulatory, accounting and other regimes for financial sector firms will need to adjust to ART and, in particular, greater convergence between banks and insurance companies. As regards the existence of financial markets, a question that might be posed is how far ART is leading to the development of new markets in which firms can trade and hedge risk, and how liquid are those markets. The remainder of this article addresses these questions in the following order:

1. ART: new, liquid markets?
2. ART, 'convergence' and regulatory regimes,
3. ART and risk diversification.

Reflecting my background as a central banker, the focus is on credit risk and the stability of the banking sector.[5] But the article touches on the range of ART markets, reflecting the increasing links between insurance and banking, not least as a result of ART.

ART: new, liquid markets?

Some elements of ART (credit derivatives, cat bonds, weather derivatives) can be seen as part of a wider development in financial markets towards more risks being tradable. Risks are traded in two main ways: by embedding them in securities which can be bought and sold in a secondary market; and by using standardised derivatives contracts, so that positions can be hedged by entering into equal and opposite trades, usually in over-the-counter markets. Tradability encourages disintermediation: for example, companies issuing bonds rather than borrowing from banks. It also enables financial institutions to transfer risks from their own balance sheets. This takes two main forms:

❏ *Unbundling risks in order to trade them*: derivatives contracts, in particular, are more likely to trade in liquid markets if they give exposure to single risks in a relatively 'clean' way. For example, some of the risks (interest rate, exchange rate, credit) associated with bank loans can be unbundled and traded using interest rate swaps, foreign exchange swaps and credit default swaps.

❑ *Bundling risks and tranching them*: the alternative route is to put risks together in order to create portfolios with characteristics that meet more closely the preferences of potential risk-takers, typically tranched in order to satisfy their different risk appetites. For example, asset-backed securities bundle together the risks on portfolios of consumer loans in order to create a number of tranches with leverage to suit different risk-takers.

So far, these developments have been more evident in banking than insurance markets: for example, notional principal outstanding on over-the-counter derivatives linked to interest rates amounts to US$65 trillion and outstanding US dollar-denominated asset-backed securities and commercial paper amount to around US$2 trillion.[6] Insurance companies have been most involved as risk-takers – for example, taking on the credit risk on tranches of credit portfolios. Life insurance companies – reflecting their intermediation of long-term household savings into investments – have taken on credit risk embedded into (funded) securities, such as collateralised debt obligations (CDOs) and asset-backed securities (ABS). While use of credit derivatives and credit insurance linked to portfolios has enabled property and casualty insurers, reinsurers and the monoline credit insurers, to take on credit risk in unfunded forms. The tranching of CDOs, in particular, has meant that relatively risk-averse institutions – such as reinsurers and the monolines – have been able to take on the most senior tranches of credit portfolios, even if the underlying credits are sub-investment grade. In effect, this has broadened the range of institutions prepared to take on credit risk, perhaps leading to a downward shift of the supply curve in credit risk markets.

Some have argued that the consequent potential for arbitrage between the price at which credit risk can be shed on a diversified, tranched portfolio of corporate exposures and the secondary market prices of bonds issued by the underlying companies has increased liquidity and reduced price volatility in the corporate bond market. For example, the fall in the yield spread of sub-investment over investment grade bonds in the first half of 2001 – at a time of deteriorating macro-economic prospects and rising default rates – may in part have reflected hedging by intermediaries left 'short' of credit risk after shedding it via CDOs and other portfolio credit transactions, see Figure 1.

In a similar way, growth in the CDO market – particularly so-called synthetic CDOs in which the risk-shedder transfers risk using credit derivatives rather than by selling underlying assets and/or the risk-taker

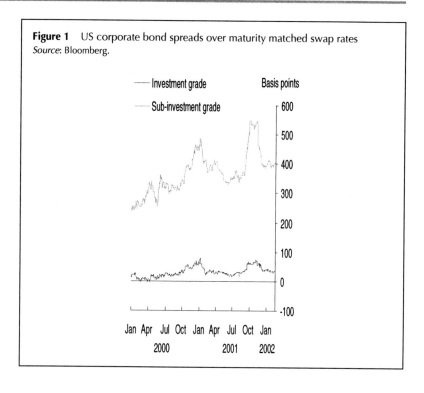

Figure 1 US corporate bond spreads over maturity matched swap rates
Source: Bloomberg.

takes on risk through credit derivatives rather than by investing in a security – has encouraged liquidity in the single name credit default swap (CDS) market. For example, intermediaries have issued CDOs referenced to companies to which they do not have existing exposures and have often chosen to hedge their positions by taking on credit risk via single name CDS. The credit risk on a few hundred or so large companies and sovereigns is now said to trade in a fairly liquid inter-dealer CDS market.

Transfer of insurance risk in tradable form – whether via insurance-linked derivatives or by embedding insurance risks in securities, such as cat bonds – has not yet taken off in the same way (see Figure 2). This might reflect inherent problems associated with the uniqueness of insurance risks, which makes standardisation and therefore trading in a liquid market impossible. After all, the nature of insurance is to aggregate idiosyncratic, and therefore diversifiable, risks. Another possibility is that some insurance risks could be tradable but gains from trade between potential risk shedders (insurance companies) and risk takers (pension and investment funds, banks) have not existed because insurers and reinsurers will bear the risks at lower cost. According to market participants, the relative cost of cat bond issuance has been higher than reinsurance, although this balance may change as the techniques become more established (reducing legal costs), as investors obtain any necessary authorisations from trustees and regulators to purchase the bonds and also if reinsurance rates continue to harden.

Whatever the reasons, issuance of insurance-linked securities – principally tied to cat risk associated with earthquakes and windstorms – has so far been quite low, as illustrated in Figure 2 . Insurance companies do not therefore have liquid, traded markets in which to transfer insurance risks and rely either on their own capacity to retain risk or on the availability of reinsurance. The development of other new markets for hedging or diversifying insurance risks, such as weather derivatives, has also so far been rather limited. For example, according to the Weather Risk Management Association, only five thousand contracts with a notional value of US$7.5 billion were traded between November 1997 and March 2001.[7]

ART, 'convergence' and regulatory regimes

Effective regulation can make an important contribution to maintaining the soundness of the financial sector as a whole. But regulation needs to adapt to developments in financial markets and financial techniques, such as ART. Two aspects of ART in particular raise potential challenges for financial regulators and designers of regulatory regimes:[8] first, the interchange of techniques between bankers and insurers as part of a broader process of convergence; and second the reduction in the cost of risk transfer

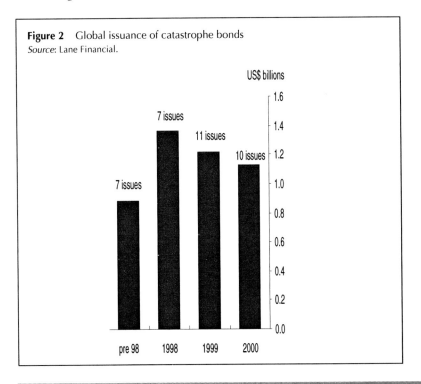

Figure 2   Global issuance of catastrophe bonds
Source: Lane Financial.

transactions, making it easier for banks and insurers to exchange risk expo-sures, often reflecting underlying economic motivations such as better diversification, but also to take advantage of differences in regulatory or accounting treatments.

Convergence has involved changes to the business of banks and insur-ance companies. Traditionally, insurers wrote policies covering specific risks, renewable (and so repriced) annually. Banks, by contrast, have tended to take on a bundle of risks attached to term lending. These might include interest rate, currency, credit, funding, prepayment and legal risks; and, within credit risk, the different risks that affect a borrower's willing-ness and ability to pay eg, business, operational, political, etc.

Over the past two decades, however, banks have increasingly been unbundling their lending risks. The use of interest rate and currency derivatives for that purpose is familiar. Some banks also buy, for example, political risk insurance cover against emerging market economy exposures. More generally, the techniques developed in recent years to split out credit risk into tranches have been broadly akin to the layering of insurance and reinsurance; and in pricing terms, the spread over risk-free interest rates on a corporate bond and the premium paid on a credit default swap can be compared to the credit reinsurance 'rate-on-line'.[9]

On the insurance side, packages are now available to cover all or most of a corporate customer's potential liabilities and losses, sometimes for terms beyond a year (so-called multi-trigger and multi-year policies). And finite risk reinsurance, with its origin in the 1970s Lloyd's 'time and distance' policies, combines a degree of risk transfer with what amounts to a form of revolving loan and/or investment facility for insurers.[10] In economic terms, the reinsurer provides liquidity insurance, a core commercial bank-ing activity.

The formation of so-called bancassurance groups via the merger of a retail bank and insurance company (typically a life company) is another manifestation of the banking and insurance links.[11] Many of these deals seem to have been motivated by the aim of securing efficiency gains in the distribution of short and long-term retail savings products. But they also produce combined portfolios carrying a mixture of banking and insurance exposures, which is likely to alter their diversification/concentration char-acteristics. Bank/insurance company mergers are not, however, essential to achieve this type of risk diversification.

Such examples of convergence might mean regulatory capital require-ments need to be re-examined in some areas, although the extent of change to the business of most banks and insurance companies probably remains limited at this stage. Perhaps a more significant development for regulators is the associated development of risk transfer techniques, which has reduced the barriers and frictions keeping insurance and banking risks in their separate boxes. Part of the explanation for both the direction and form of such transfers has lain in differences in the regulatory, accounting and tax treatment of banks and insurance companies across different jurisdictions. This chapter will not attempt a detailed analysis of these differences.[12] But a recent report by a joint committee of banking, insurance and securities regulators found that comparing the respective capital requirements applied to the same risks across the different sectors is not straightforward.[13] In particular, regulators require banks to hold capital according to a standardised framework of risk-based requirements applied to all international banks.[14] But insurers will hold both capital requirements to cover 'unexpected' losses and, perhaps, technical reserves based on an actuarial assessment of the 'expected' loss. So the relative overall capital cost to a bank or an insurance company might depend upon this actuarial risk assessment, which might differ from company to company. Regulatory capital requirements for insurance companies also vary to a greater degree than for banks according to the type of company, its jurisdiction and whether risks are taken onto the asset (investment) or liabilities (underwriting) side of the balance sheet. Some types of insurer have very specific regulatory regimes: for example, that applied to monoline credit insurers under New York insurance law and replicated by a number of other US states.[15]

It is not *necessarily* a sign of bad regulatory design that institutions have regulatory incentives for risk transfer: in other words, that they are not subject to identical capital and other regulatory requirements for every instrument and transaction type. Regulation of different types of financial institution may have different objectives – reflecting, for example, differences in asset and liability structures or varying social costs of failure etc – and a redistribution of risk may be entirely consistent with these. But it is clearly important to monitor risk transfers carefully as an indicator of possible regulatory differences. Where regulatory capital requirements exceed the economic risk, the development of ART and other risk transfer techniques has made it less costly to move the exposure to other institutions in a less onerous regulated or an unregulated environment. Such market forces should be a powerful discipline against the imposition of costly over-regulation. But there is also a risk that exposures might migrate to the most lightly regulated institutions, especially if they underestimate the economic risk or fail to take into account any social costs of their own failure (externalities), which should be incorporated in the requirements of a well-designed regulatory regime.

Henceforward, designers of regulatory regimes will perhaps have to give even greater thought to the incentives given to managers of institutions to adjust portfolios dynamically as well as to the static effect of changes to regulation on existing businesses. In principle, an alternative approach might be to try to prevent risk transfers in order to keep risks where they were originated and subject to the associated regulatory regime. But this would deny the benefits of risk transfer to both individual firms and the wider financial system. It would probably also prove difficult to achieve in a world of capital mobility. At the extreme, it might actually increase risk by forcing firms to use artificial devices rather than transacting in the most appropriate ways. An example is the restrictions that insurance companies face in a number of countries on taking on risk using derivatives. These do not appear to have prevented the companies from gaining exposure to the risks that would normally be transferred using derivatives, eg, interest rate and credit. But instead of entering into derivatives directly, they have either purchased securities with embedded derivatives[16] or, in some cases, provided insurance to offshore[17] vehicle companies ('transformers') that, in turn, enter into a corresponding derivatives contract.[18] The transformer structure is designed to add nothing to the economics of the transaction but may expose the underlying parties to some operational and, conceivably, even legal risks.

In general, it may become increasingly difficult for regulators to prevent firms from entering into particular types of transaction when management believes it would be profitable business. Indeed, a significant part of the business of modern investment banking appears to be the transformation of substantially the same economic risks from one form to another in order to meet the needs of market participants facing different legal, regulatory, accounting and tax constraints. This is a deadweight loss for society and often involves the use of structures so complex that the ability of investors, lenders and the authorities to assess risk and return is impaired significantly.

ART and risk diversification.
The greatest potential benefit of ART and risk transfer more generally for financial stability is that it might lead to a better distribution of risk throughout the financial sector, leaving firms and sectors less vulnerable to particular shocks. By making risks tradable, it might also lead to more transparent and efficient pricing. Other things being equal – including, crucially, that firms understand the extent of the true, economic transfer of risk and hold adequate capital to support risks that they have taken on – the international financial system should be more stable if exposures to credit, insurance and other risk events are more dispersed internationally and across different types of financial firm. ART markets open up new ways for insurance companies and banks to shed risk, adding to long-standing techniques such as reinsurance of insurance risks and syndication of bank loans. They also allow them to take on new risks in order to diversify exposures. This moves firms further away from a world in which exposure to risks is simply a passive consequence of the nature of the underlying business: so that, for example, a Japanese household insurer is very heavily exposed to the possibility of a Japanese earthquake.

Ultimately, it is possible to imagine a world in which risk transfer markets are sufficiently complete so that firms can optimise their risk exposure separately from their underlying businesses. In reality, however, there are good reasons why this extreme outcome is highly unlikely. For example, the originator of a risk exposure is often best placed to assess and monitor it; and this better access to information will make others less willing to take on the risk (and charge a higher price) for fear of opportunistic behaviour by the risk shedder/originator. Such asymmetric information problems are likely to limit the development of risk transfer markets unless ways can be found to ease them: such as more disclosure of reliable information needed to assess and monitor risks.

At present, it is unclear how far we have moved across the spectrum from no risk transfer markets at one extreme to complete markets at the other. Data on market size is patchy.[19] It appears that insurance companies have taken on a significant amount of credit risk through portfolio credit risk transfer markets in recent years – at a rough estimate, some US$100 to US$500 billion.[20] Transfers of insurance risk from the insurance sector have been tiny by comparison. With the exception of perhaps a score of investors in Europe and Asia, the main investors in cat bonds are said to have been US institutions, including a number of insurance and reinsurance companies – another indication that the extent of risk redistribution has been limited so far.

Another problem is that risk transfer transactions are not always all that they seem. The risk shedder might often retain a significant part of the economic exposure even if accounting and regulatory reporting might sometimes suggest otherwise. For example, finite reinsurance policies might leave the insurer (risk shedder) with an obligation to pay higher premiums (or a lower investment return on premiums already paid) following a claim; and risk shedders through securitisation will often retain the first loss tranche – in effect, purchasing protection against unexpected losses only. It is clearly important that neither market participants nor auditors (on which investors, creditors and regulators rely), nor regulators are misled as to the nature of such risk transfer transactions.

Risk management standards
Although further development of risk transfer markets is, on balance, highly desirable, this problem of sometimes distinguishing appearance from reality is one of a number of caveats. Another flows from the asymmetric information question referred to earlier. It is possible that this will limit the further development of the ART market. But if it does not, a question is whether poorer access to information will leave those taking on risks less able to manage them than those shedding them. Ultimately this might mean lower aggregate standards of risk assessment and monitoring. In the case of credit risk, a bank's relationship with a customer gives access to

information about its payment flows and underlying business, which might be an important advantage in assessing creditworthiness. Insurance, however, is often designed on the basis that the insurer is not in an informed position to assess and monitor risk, relying instead on contractual provisions to align the incentives of insurer and insured as well as on portfolio diversification. This might suggest that any potential decline in risk management standards resulting from more widespread risk transfer might be a lesser problem in insurance than credit markets. Put in this way, however, the difference is probably too stark. Some credit risk is originated based largely on a portfolio approach (eg, many loans to individuals) and, equally, expert underwriting should be key to the assessment of some insurance risks.

Overall, the scope for any deterioration in risk management standards must vary depending on:

(a) the size of any potential information asymmetries between the originator of a risk and others (whether arising from other business relationships or other sources of particular knowledge), and

(b) the effectiveness of any contractual steps taken to align the incentives of the risk shedder and risk taker, eg, the risk shedder retaining a 'first loss' exposure.

On the positive side, demand from risk takers for more information may actually stimulate greater public disclosure of information to assess risks. Broader participation in markets might also encourage a wider range of views and better debates about risk, including new approaches to risk measurement and modelling. The availability of market prices also gives risk-takers a clear benchmark against which to compare their own risk judgements.

Reliance on rating agencies

One approach to risk assessment might, in effect, be to outsource decision-making to an external specialist agency. Risk assessment requires expert staff and firms diversifying into new areas using risk transfer markets may believe it is not cost effective to build in-house teams. Relying on rating agency opinions is one obvious way of outsourcing. But rating agencies are not directly exposed to credit losses as a result of their credit judgements and so may have somewhat different incentives to lenders.

One particular area in which reliance on ratings has become common is as a solution to principal: agent-type problems, where a principal wants to ensure that an agent does not take excessive credit risk if the principal might be exposed. Examples include investment mandates given to fund managers, regimes setting minimum risk-based capital requirements for regulated firms and contracts designed to protect financial market participants against a decline in the creditworthiness of a counterparty. It may be a rational decision to use ratings as an independent and quasi-objective measure of credit risk in individual cases. But at an aggregate level, the consequences of a large number of market participants choosing to rely on ratings could be less desirable, especially if they are contractually bound to react to ratings decisions in a similar way. 'Hard wiring' decision-making to external ratings in this way may also make it more difficult for rating agencies to form objective risk opinions because their actions might have significant, unintended behavioural consequences.[21]

Counterparty risk

Another possible issue arising from the development of risk transfer markets is the higher counterparty exposures that might arise if risk is transferred using unfunded instruments, such as derivatives and reinsurance. From a wider financial stability perspective, such exposures, if uncontrolled and allowed to grow very large, raise the possibility of knock-on failures of financial institutions, including perhaps between banks and insurance companies if they become more inter-dependent. One way of limiting counterparty exposures is to introduce collateral management agreements, allowing for the mark-to-market value of exposures to be collateralised with securities or cash. Collateralisation, however, cannot easily eliminate counterparty risk on transactions linked to underlying prices or events that have the potential to jump suddenly, such as credit or insurance. Also some insurance companies are subject to regulatory restrictions on pledging assets as collateral; and the counterparty exposures that insurers take on reinsurers are rarely, if ever, collateralised nor are they subject to regulatory capital requirements to reflect counterparty risk. The scale of unfunded ART markets is probably not sufficient for counterparty exposures to be a systemic issue at present. But this is an area for market participants and financial stability authorities to watch in future.

Possible new concentrations of risk

Effectively functioning risk transfer markets should disperse exposures as firms are given greater scope to improve risk-adjusted returns through diversification. One safeguard against the development of any new unexpected risk concentrations should be effective counterparty risk management by other firms. However, it is still possible that a firm could take large aggregate risk exposures by trading with a wide range of counterparties and risk transfer markets may allow a more rapid build up of exposure than origination of new business. Effective disclosure by financial firms might become more important to ensure market discipline.

One area in which activity might concentrate is intermediation. If a few firms develop a competitive advantage in the distribution of risks, it is easy to see how better knowledge of flows might re-inforce dominant market positions. Intermediaries would normally seek to have a relatively matched book but, particularly where intermediation involves the repackaging or transformation of risks, they may be left with some mismatches (eg, of documentation) or 'rump' positions (eg, if they have repackaged single risks into a portfolio, they might be left with the 'first loss' exposure).

Another area in which market forces might lead to consolidation is the provision of protection against the most extreme credit events – for example, unfunded risk transfer using derivatives, insurance or guarantees on the most senior tranches of portfolio transactions. Only the most creditworthy institutions can provide a guarantee that has any value in such extreme credit conditions because of the potential impact on their own ability to pay. Such institutions must be either government-backed (eg, the German landesbanks are thought to have done such business), extremely large and well diversified, and/or highly risk averse overall. Especially with the withdrawal of government guarantees of financial institutions in most developed countries, they are in the future likely to be fewer in number.

A few large multiline insurers and reinsurers write such business. The monoline credit insurers are also able to sell protection against extreme credit events, partly because of their risk averse underwriting policies, which has helped them to preserve triple-A ratings. But equally the capital requirements applied to them by the rating agencies in order to maintain the triple-A rating seem to limit to investment grade the exposures they are able to take economically.

Buyers of unfunded protection against more extreme events make their own judgement about whether the protection seller will be able to perform in such circumstances, taking account of the other likely calls on their capital and liquidity from other business they have written. In the case of the monolines, the rating agencies address such questions through stress tests based either on the 1930s Depression or factor models and Monte Carlo-type simulations;[22] some of the monolines themselves also use portfolio credit risk models. Financial stability authorities have an interest in understanding those institutions that might be seriously exposed in circumstances of extremely high losses, and hence incipient if not actual financial instability, especially if a wide range of other market participants are expected to rely on them.

CONCLUSION
Risk transfer markets have the potential to enhance the stability and efficiency of the international financial system by giving banks, insurers, asset managers and others greater freedom to shed and take on credit, insurance and other risks in order to diversify their overall risk portfolios. This should make the international financial system as a whole more robust in the face of particular shocks. There are some actual or potential qualifica-

tions to this overall conclusion. These include: problems in some cases distinguishing the reality from the appearance of risk transfer; questions about how risk transfer will affect ability and incentives to manage risk across the financial system; whether it might encourage excessive reliance on rating agency opinions; the potential for an increase in counterparty exposures; and the possibility that new concentrations of risk might arise. The job of regulators, and designers of regulatory regimes, might also become more difficult, although it could be beneficial if greater market discipline draws attention to inappropriate regulation. On balance, the message is positive. But market participants and the authorities need to keep these possible pitfalls in mind as the market develops so that the potential benefits are fully realised.

1   This chapter draws heavily on my article 'Risk transfer between banks, insurance companies and capital markets: an overview' in the Bank of England, *Financial Stability Review*, December 2001, pp. 137–59. Available at www.bankofengland.co.uk/fsr.

2   Financial Stability Conjuncture and Outlook, Bank of England, *Financial Stability Review*, June 1999, page 5. Available at www.bankofengland.co.uk/fsr.

3   An analysis along these lines is set out by Andrew Crockett, General Manager of the BIS, 1997, 'Why is Financial Stability a Goal of Public Policy?' Federal Reserve Bank of Kansas City Symposium: 'Maintaining Financial Stability in a Global Economy'.

4   Euro-currency Standing Committee, now the Committee on the Global Financial System, which reports to the G10 central bank governors. ECSC (1992): 'Recent Developments in International Interbank Relations'.

5   Interest rate risk transfers are also of interest to central banks and discussed in my December 2001 *Financial Stability Review* article.

6   Sources: BIS triennial derivatives survey; Bond Market Association; Federal Reserve Bank of New York.

7   See the Gibbas and Lee chapter in this volume.

8   The Bank of England, together with the UK Financial Services Authority, is represented on the Basel Committee on Banking Supervision, which reports to the G10 central bank governors.

9   See, for example, Morton Lane, 'CDOs as self-contained reinsurance structures', December 10 2000, available at www.lanefinancialllc.com.

10 For further information on time and distance policies see Phifer, R., 1996, Reinsurance Fundamentals: Treaty and Facultative (Chichester: John Wiley & Sons).

11 For example, Citibank and Travellers; Dresdner Bank and Allianz; Lloyds Bank, Abbey Life and Scottish Widows.

12 The Davies chapter in this volume mentions some aspects of US and UK regulation of insurance companies.

13 'Risk Management Practices and Regulatory Capital: Cross Sectoral Comparisons', Joint Forum 2001, available at www.bis.org.

14 The proposed changes to the Basel Accord will introduce greater scope for differences between banks in the regulatory capital they hold against the same risks: for example, capital requirements for banks on the so-called standardised approach will be based on the external rating of a borrower whereas banks on the so-called internal ratings-based and advanced approaches will use their own internal ratings to assess a probability of default. Banks on the advanced approach will also make their own assessment of likely loss-given-default.

15 The relevant New York law is Article 69 of its insurance code (1989).

16 For example, rather than purchasing a fixed-rate bond issued by a bank and separately entering into a credit default swap with the bank, the bank might issue a credit-linked note on which the coupon payments and principal repayment mirror the combined cashflows on the credit default swap and the fixed rate bond.

17 In some offshore jurisdictions, insurance companies are permitted to enter into derivatives freely (eg Bermuda), allowing the transformer vehicles to convert risk between derivatives and insurance form.

18 See my article 'The Credit Derivative Market: Its Development and Possible Implications for Financial Stability', Bank of England, *Financial Stability Review*, June 2001, for more on transformers.

19 See my article 'Risk transfer between banks, insurance companies and capital markets: an overview' in the Bank of England, *Financial Stability Review*, December 2001, pages 137–59 for some estimates of the size of credit risk transfer markets.

20 The number will depend upon whether the monoline credit insurers are included and also whether structured credit securities (eg, CDOs) purchased for investment purposes, particularly by life insurers, are included.

21 Rating agencies themselves have recently drawn attention to similar concerns about 'hardwired' rating triggers. See, for example, 'The Unintended Consequences of Rating Triggers', Moody's Special Comment, December 2001.

22 See, for example, the rating agency publications available via the website of the Association of Financial Guaranty Insurers (www.agfi.org).

Whither Securitisation?

Morton Lane

Lane Financial LLC

The editor of a multi-contributor book is a midwife, and neither a parent nor a child of the union of the contributors. As such editors are usually allowed limited indulgence to reflect their own views other than those that are conveyed by their selection of authors. The opening chapter is usually the place for that indulgence, but I have chosen to put this last so as not to detract from the other views, and because the message in this chapter derives in part from having read all of the others.

INTRODUCTION

What follows is an attempt to suggest an avenue where solutions, or at least approaches might be found, that address some vexing questions that insurance securitisation has exposed. One particular question is: "How should risk be priced?". Section 2 of this book focuses on the price of risk transfer, and it blends together observations on how it has been priced historically as well as what the existing theories might suggest. Insightful as it is, even the authors in that section would agree that a recognised and well accepted price formulation for risky instruments has yet to be discovered. The title of a recent paper by Bantwal and Kunreuther (2000) *A Cat Bond Premium Puzzle* nicely captures the state of affairs.

There currently exist no equivalents to the Black–Scholes options pricing formula, no capital asset pricing model (CAPM), no theory of corporate debt nor a theory of the cost of capital to guide thought on insurance securitisation pricing. None has been necessary heretofore for the simple reason that insurance pricing previously sat within the insurance markets and was not transferred outside of them. Securitisation has changed that, forcing cedents and investors to compare prices with other instruments and to evaluate the potential position of insurance risk in an otherwise conventional investment portfolio. Insurance now meets finance, and its intellectual place must be found.

One feature of all the well-known theories of finance is that they all emanate from, or at least find their credentials in, some form of arbitrage theory. This thought was brought home to me recently when reading, at the suggestion of Paul Embrechts, Bernstein's *Capital Ideas*, a layman's history (the best kind of history when done right as here) of finance.[1] Modiglianni and Miller did not make their breakthrough on the theory of the cost of capital without the final step being an arbitrage argument.[2] Black and Scholes' options pricing rests on the equivalence of a series of "delta" transactions on the underlying to the option itself.[3] Puts are the arbitrage equivalent of a short forward plus a long call. This matters not just at the theoretical level. Try getting an option price from a trader where there is no way for him to construct some arbitrage equivalent! Theory is important because it gives confidence (and profit) to arbitrage practitioners. Insurance securitisation lacks that confidence. Intermediaries (arbitrageurs) do not slice and dice insurance risk redistributing the pieces to different parts of the capital market with the confidence that they can make a decent risk adjusted market return. And yet I expect that this will have to be the case and will be a necessary foundation for securitisations to flourish. What is required is the risk algebra and risk pricing for arbitrage. Furthermore, our sense of arbitrage should not be confined to finance analogues. There is no 'underlying' in most insurance covers, delta hedging is not applicable. However, two adjacent layers are the equivalent to the combined layer, a "first-event" cover plus an "all subsequent events" cover equals a "multiple occurrence" cover. In these identities lay the possibilities for insurance securitisation arbitrage theory. It is difficult and new, but potentially very exciting as well.

What follows is an attempt to explore this arbitrage idea further. It seems a fitting note to end a book on – where we go from here. I review the current state of securitisation by providing a personal perspective of historical developments. Thus an attempt is made to show how different types of catastrophe (cat) bonds have evolved, and to show their equivalents. Using these basic types of cat bonds, a forensic risk analysis is applied to Munich Re's PRIME securitisations. Not least of the reasons for choosing PRIME is the candour with which Manfred Seitz has addressed his appraisal of Munich Re's accomplishments with this securitisation. I am grateful for both his public remarks and his private conversation. However, neither the following conclusions nor suggestions should be taken as emanating exclusively from this particular deal. Many of these findings apply equally well to any number of the recent securitisations.

An historical review

Exactly ten years prior to this publication, in 1992, Merrill Lynch structured the first cat bond on behalf of American International Group (AIG). The bond was for US$100 million and covered three risks, Florida hurricane,

California earthquake and Japanese earthquake. Its term was three years. Loss under any of the three named perils would cause the investor to lose principal, although no one peril could exhaust the capital.

The bond represented the birth of an extremely original concept: transference of insurance risk to the capital markets in the form of a security – insurance securitisation.

Unfortunately it was also a stillbirth.

For reasons never articulated, the bond was withdrawn after documents and the other paraphernalia of securities issuance had been prepared, but before investor funds were solicited. That withdrawal decision was momentous.

Within months the industry suffered its worst loss ever from Hurricane Andrew.

Eighteen months after that it suffered its second worst loss from the Northridge Earthquake. Both events were eligible for recovery under the terms of the stillborn bond.

Investors had dodged a bullet.

The issuer, AIG, must have gnashed its teeth.

However, at the close of 1992 there was no time for regret. There was an industry scramble to raise capital to replace the Hurricane Andrew losses. Two well-known phenomena resulted from that scramble. First, was the growth of specialist property catastrophe reinsurers, located principally in Bermuda. Second, was the beginning of trading in catastrophe derivatives at the Chicago Board of Trade (CBOT) at the end of 1992. Both phenomena have had a limited life. The Bermuda specialist catastrophe company now lives in the personage of just two companies.[4] At its height around 1999 there were arguably nine such specialist companies.[5] Property catastrophe underwriting had been conducted as part of multiline property and casualty reinsurance prior to 1992. In the soft market conditions of the late 1990s it returned, with some notable exceptions (Renaissance Re and PXRE Re) to multiline roots by simple acquisition.

Catastrophe derivatives suffered a similar fate. Originally based on an Insurance Services Office (ISO) formula, they were upgraded to a Property Claims Service (PCS) index and began to prosper. The concept caught the mesmerised attention of the industry and competitor contracts were proposed to preserve a share of the business. Once again the aggressive AIG sponsored a rival exchange in Bermuda.[6]

Sadly the same soft market conditions that deprived most stand-alone cat companies of their independent existence, together with the inattention of the CBOT, drove a stake through the heart of originator and copier exchange alike. Catastrophe derivatives lived for five years.[7]

But what of insurance securitisation? Its experimentation continues and is the subject of several prior chapters of this book.

Three stages of securitisation

1 Pre-assembled packages of risk (Type 1 deals)

Securitisation of catastrophes did not appear again on the reinsurance scene officially until 1996, a gap of four years since the AIG unfortunate withdrawal decision. But again it was an AIG unit, AIG Combined Risks (AIGCR) headed by Diego Wauters that broke the new ground. AIGCR worked with the predecessor of today's Benfield Group and on April 30 1996 *Insurance Day* gushed 'Benfield/AIGCR issue may herald new era for industry'.[8] This time the bond was for five geographical regions (US, Caribbean, Japan, Australia and Western Europe) and the specified term was for little more than one year. Neither the size nor the cedent's name was disclosed, but the best guesses are US$10 million and PXRE respectively.

There followed a ferment of competitive activity. Goldman Sachs, Swiss Re, Winterthur, Sedgwick Lane, Guy Carpenter, ACE, Cat Ltd, Hanover Re, Merrill Lynch, Citibank and Morgan Stanley all sponsored deal proposals with various unique and original features. Some saw the market light of day but many failed the launch phase. If generalising about the successful transactions one could describe them as a) small and b) quite opaque. As the sponsors struggled to overcome a variety of newly confronted legal and regulatory issues they were, at the same time, attempting to maintain a competitive advantage. Few were rated, all were experimental.

As far as today's participants are concerned, this might be considered as pre-history, but there are some features which are still relevant today. The then prevailing theory was that, while the stock market diversification and superior return arguments ought to be enough motivation for adventurous investors, those same investors would probably not accept single insurance risks or perils. Accordingly, all the early deals were based on portfolios of insurance risk. In these early deals it was impossible to exhaust capital on a single event. The ultimate portfolio example – and the largest early deal – was Georgetown Re. Issued in January 1997, for an amount at US$68.5 million, it represented a quota share of St Paul Re's book.

Generally, investors were intrigued but not excited, arms were twisted, deals were done, but enthusiasm outside the fringes of reinsurance was limited. There existed a state of supply without demand. It is worth noting however, that Type 1 deals may now be making a comeback in the guise of "whole business securitisations". Millette et al discuss such a deal in this volume.

2 Self-assembly of single risks (Type 2 deals)

The existing theory that investors were not likely to accept single insurance risks changed in June of 1997 when Goldman Sachs brought a US$399.5 million deal to market on behalf of USAA, a domestic US insurance company. This transaction gave lie to the idea that investors needed a portfolio of risks. The USAA deal referred to as Residential Re, (after its Cayman Island special purpose reinsurance vehicle (SPRV)) was distinctive in that only a single peril was embedded in the bond. The investors could lose their entire principal if the wind blew hard enough along the East Coast of the US. The market had spoken – in size.

Evidently investors had begun to buy into the idea that they could control their exposure by the size of their purchase and they could also get diversification by purchasing a variety of such bonds. The sponsors took note. The flow of single peril bonds began to pick up. Deals covering Florida wind, California earthquake, Japanese typhoon, Japanese earthquake, US East Coast wind, credit, and weather appeared and were reissued progressively between 1997 and 2000.

Deals with portfolios of risk were still issued during this period but they were generally smaller than the single peril bonds and they began to change character, as we are about to discuss. Supply equalled demand but was not growing rapidly.

3 Accumulating multiple risks (Type 3 deals)

At the close of 2000 Munich Re issued its now famous PRIME securities. Two securities, PRIME Capital Hurricane Limited and PRIME Capital Calquake and Eurowind Limited were issued in amounts of US$165 million and US$135 million respectively. These are distinctive in several respects. Importantly, both bonds embedded more than one risk or risk zone. For example, PRIME Hurricane could lose principal from a hurricane striking a pre-defined New York geographic 'gate' (or zone), as well as two pre-defined Miami 'gates'. More significantly, the whole of the investor's capital could be exhausted from any one of these three zones. This differed from the early 'portfolio' deals where only a third of the investor's capital, say, could be exhausted from any of three defined risks. Or to put it another way, the limit of exposure to *each* of the defined risks was equal to the total limit of exposure from the bond as a whole. *Any* defined risk could blow the bond!

There are some important subtleties here. Single peril bonds can also be blown by a single risk. However, the investor confronted with a choice of single risk bonds can choose the amount of exposure to each risk as appropriate to his existing portfolio of such risks. This can be done on a one by one basis. However, confronted with a bundle of risks that can *each* exhaust the bond, the investor must add that potential loss amount to their existing portfolio exposures in *each* of their outstanding perils that overlap with the bond. Necessarily, their purchase size will be limited to the minimum peril room available.

This characteristic is defined here as self-accumulating multiple risks and it has been characteristic of several issues in the period 2001–2002. The Atlas and Tricom deals are part of the group that started with PRIME.[9]

While these deals appear to satisfy the needs of issuers, it is less clear that they serve investor desires. After all, investors would prefer to self accumulate Type 2 transactions The result has been a mis-match situation of demand and supply. In the end the market will only be advanced if terms can be found to match issuers to investors. Given the three classes of deal described above (admittedly a very personal characterisation) it is worth looking at their equivalents.

Equivalent structures

Consider three independent binary risks, similar to California earthquake, Florida hurricane and Japanese earthquake industry loss warranties (ILWs). Then three different securities can be constructed similar to the characteristics of the three phases of the market described above.[10] Assume that the amount of coverage required is US$100 million per risk. Then the three potential deal structures are:

1. one US$300 million security, sub-limited to US$100 million per risk;
2. three US$100 million securities each for a single risk of US$100 million;
3. a US$100 million security covering each of the three risks for US$100 million.

The important questions are, "Are these structures identical?" and if not, "In what respects are these deals the same and in what respects are they different?"

To start with the obvious, each of the above structures has exactly the same probability of making some recovery for the issuer. Each has the same corresponding probability of loss to the investor(s). However, Structures 1 and 2 have a very low probability of exhausting investor capital, because all three independent events have to occur within the same period to exhaust that capital. Accordingly, there is a corresponding (low) probability of the issuer making full recovery. To provide a concrete example: if the probability of each loss is one in a hundred, the probability of some loss is around 3% (exactly 2.97%), but the probability of full loss is one in a million.

It appears that 1 and 2 are identical from the issuers' point of view. But they may not be considered the same from the point of view of the investor. Investors in Structure 1 purchase the whole bundle of risks. Investors in Structure 2 may choose part of, or the whole bundle. Providing that the issuer pays the same price for 1 or 2, they would be indifferent between the two alternatives. On the other hand, if the issuer is able to acquire a rent for pre-assembling the diversified portfolio they may prefer to issue that way. A self assembling investor in single risk bonds will try to harvest that rent for themselves. The rent may be justified since they may not be able to acquire all three risks simultaneously and might therefore be left with a mis-balanced portfolio. Investors in Structure 1 securities may pay up to avoid bearing that risk.

However, Structure 3 is distinctly different from 1 and 2, not least of the reasons being that the total exposure is US$100 million vs US$300 million in Type 1 and 2. In the numerical example it has the same probability of some recovery from any of the risks, ie 2.97%. However, the chance of recovery from all three risks is zero. Only one risk is recoverable, although exactly which one is undetermined until an actual occurrence. In reality, Structure 3 is equivalent to only part of 1 or 2. It is the equivalent of the equity tranche, as is illustrated in Figure 1. Furthermore, there is no way for either the issuer or the investor to make a scaled equivalent of 1 or 2 by purchasing more or less of Structure 3. US$300 million invested in 3 is by no means identical to US$300 million invested in Structure 1.

Note that in this example, since the sublimit, or event limit, is equal to US$100 million and the Type 3 cover is US$100 million, this particular equity tranche is also identical to a "first event" cover. That is not generally the case. Equity tranches are equivalent to "first event" covers only if the event and the whole limits are the same, and/or the cover is for single rather than multiple occurrences.

The fact that a Type 3 cover is the equivalent of the equity tranche of a type 1 cover says something about their relative prices. In an arbitrage-free setting, the price of a Type 1 structure (with identical underlying risks) should equal the price of the equity tranche plus the price of the remaining subordinated tranche. Clearly the equity tranche involves lower cost outlay for the issuer and less reward for the buyer relative to a Type 1 alternative. This may explain why there has been a recent trend toward Type 3 deals and why they may be resisted by investors. Another possible explanation for issuers favouring Type 3 deals is that they tend to be smaller (US$ 100 million vs US$ 300 million in the example). Investment banking and other

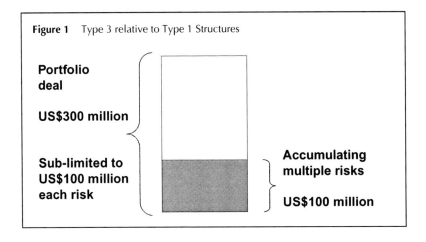

Figure 1 Type 3 relative to Type 1 Structures

Portfolio deal

US$300 million

Sub-limited to US$100 million each risk

Accumulating multiple risks

US$100 million

fees being what they are, issuers would prefer to minimise deal size to min-imise fees.

In the absence of transaction fees, the identification of equivalent struc-tures can still be used to make inferences about prices. The algebra of equivalents can also be used to design hedges and other risk mitigating strategies.

Suppose for example that an investor only wants to acquire one of the perils in the bundle? Presented with a Type 3 transaction, could the investor acquire the deal and sell off the risks that they might not want? In principal yes, in practice it would be difficult. It is also quite tricky. It is by no means as simple as trimming a Type 1 bundle of unwanted risks. That can be done by buying simple offsetting hedges, ie, issuing cat bonds, for each of the non-required perils. For Type 3 risks the investor would have to sell off a Type 3 deal for the two non-required perils. But that by itself would not be enough. Some form of joint event coverage would have to be bought back to leave the investor in an identical position. The original pur-chase and sale would offset in those cases where a non-required peril blew. The joint event cover would effectively maintain the investor's desired exposure. More generally, hedging with Type 3 covers follows something like the laws of probability:

$$P(A \cup B) = P(A) + P(B) - P(A \cap B)$$

Where $P(A \cup B)$ is the union of either A or B (analogous to Type 3 covers) and $P(A \cap B)$ is the joint occurrence of both A and B. (In our three risk example B would be the union of the two non-required risks.)

Thus to retain one risk, say A, from a deal of Type 3, the equivalent structure is the hedge combination:

$$P(A) = P(A \cup B) - P(B) + P(A \cap B)$$

In words: buy the offered deal, issue a similarly structured deal (leaving out the required risk) and buy a cover that pays only when both required and non-required risks blow. From an arbitrageur's point of view this is quite complicated. There is an execution risk. It will only work if transac-tion costs are low, a detail presently at odds with reality, and if the arbitrageur can be confident of assembling, ie, sourcing and distributing, the various pieces.

For the market as a whole, these problems arise if issuers want to use Type 3 structures and investors want to be in Type 1 portfolios. For the market to progress, a way must be found to bridge these different charac-teristics of supply and demand. And of course, such restructuring has to be done economically enough to leave the rewards commensurate with the desired retained risk.

Arbitrage algebra of risks and arbitrage algebra of prices need to be developed that allow such a bridge to be built. Further specific examination of the PRIME deal may serve to illustrate the direction in which other arbitrage might be found.

Tranching the PRIME structure.
In March 2001, at the inaugural Bond Market Association Risk-Linked Securities Conference at Turnberry Isle in Florida, Manfred Seitz, chief mover of the securitisations at Munich Re, reflected on his experience with the PRIME deal. He said that while he was pleased with the success of the placement it was not sizeable enough to get the coverage he wanted. Essentially he had six defined zones that he would have liked to have covered (Northern and Southern California, New York gate, two Miami gates and European wind). Ideally he wanted US$500 million coverage for each zone, but he was prepared to settle for US$300 million. Ideally he wanted to get coverage of Type 3, ie, a single US$300 million issue paying out in full if any of the defined risks were hit. He had been advised that the market was insufficiently big and so he was forced to make a series of accommodations in order to execute the transaction.

His first accommodation was a stepwise payoff function instead of a binary payoff-in-full structure. This did have the compensating advantage that recovery did not depend on a single number, with the attendant prospect of disputes about measurement error, but it was nevertheless a market compromise. Second, he was advised that inclusion of all the six zones in the same deal would lead to too high a probability of first dollar loss and could therefore not be rated satisfactorily. Instead he split the deal vertically into two – PRIME Capital Hurricane Limited and PRIME California Quake and EuroWind Limited – each containing three zones and each achieved a BB+ rating.[11] Third, of course, was a market compromise: US$165 million of the PRIME hurricane notes were issued and US$135 million of the PRIME California notes were issued.

In the fourth quarter of 2000 the PRIME securitisations represented the largest BB bond to successfully come to market! That particular quarter was a dismal one for the bond markets and the acceptance of PRIME says volumes about its success. It is also a useful reminder that notwithstanding the intrinsic merits of a transaction the timing of market issuance can be either a positive or negative influence. PRIME was a very successful transaction, what is examined here should not be construed to the contrary. It is only by examining transactions ex-post that lessons can be learned for the future.

Figure 2 illustrates the nature of the Munich transaction. Actually, it is only a representation, not an exact depiction of the PRIME deals. Only two dimensions are shown that correspond to the two deal definitions, as it is otherwise graphically impossible to represent six dimensions.

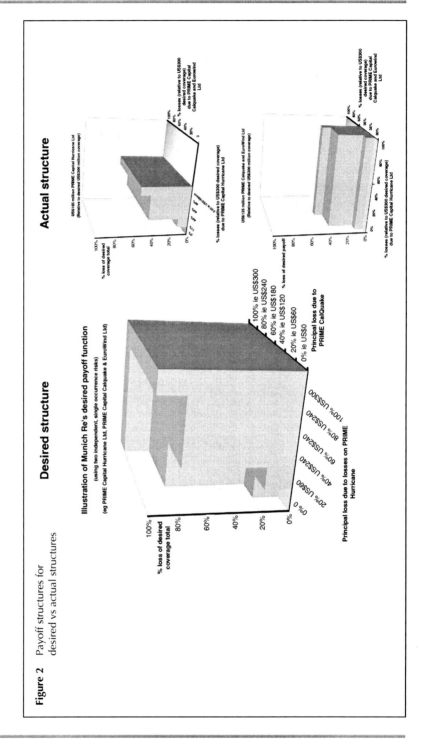

Figure 2 Payoff structures for desired vs actual structures

The other detail not captured in Figure 2 is that the actual deals were multiple occurrence structures, whereas what is shown is a single occurrence structure. This Figure otherwise captures the essence of the transactions. A desired single deal was split into two independent deals.

Is there another way to view the two deals? And could this have led to another way of structuring the bond for Munich Re? Hindsight is a fine thing of course. We are not suggesting that at the time of the transaction it could have been done as examined below. It is presumed that Munich Re and its advisors made the optimal contemporary decisions. However, given the luxury of hindsight, forensic analysis of the deal can be used to suggest alternate structures that may be useful in the future. Suppose that the deal was issued as a single bond with a full limit of US$300 million together with sub limits on each of the deal – part of US$165 million and US$135 million respectively? The loss recovery possibilities from Munich Re's point of view would be identical to what they actually achieved with their two issues. Instead of issuing two Type 3 bonds Munich Re would potentially issue a Type 1 bond. The payoffs from the 'combined structure', or the losses to the potential investor, are illustrated in Figure 3 (with the same caveats as before about two dimensions and single occurrences).

Now imagine that the single structure in Figure 3 is tranched up as shown in Figure 4. The three tranches would be 20% xs 0%, 50% xs 20% and 30% xs 70%.[12] In other words, investors in the first tranche would be responsible for the first 20% of Munich Re's structured losses. Investors in

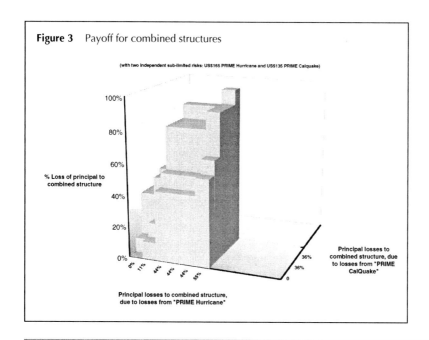

Figure 3   Payoff for combined structures

(with two independent sub-limited risks: US$165 PRIME Hurricane and US$135 PRIME Calquake)

% Loss of principal to combined structure

Principal losses to combined structure, due to losses from "PRIME CalQuake"

Principal losses to combined structure, due to losses from "PRIME Hurricane" the second tranche would be responsible for the next 50% and investors in the third tranche would be responsible for the last 30% of the structured loss.

The total deal size is US$300 million, so the first tranche size is US$60 million. Furthermore, the character of the first tranche is 'equity like' as in Type 3 deals. Like the original deal it is probably unrateable. However, the second and third tranches are eminently rateable. The third tranche is likely AAA rated. Recall that to exhaust the last (senior) 30% of the combined deal, both sub limits must exhaust in full and each has probabilities of 1.08% and 1.07% respectively. The probability of both occurring is .01155% (=1.08% x 1.07%) or one in 8,658 years. AAA securities typically have probabilities of around one in 5000 years. The middle tranche would likely be rated around B+ or higher.

Assuming that the tranched structure is executable, what might it have achieved? It has shown an alternative way of accessing the market. Instead of two Type 3 transactions it has provided three deals only one of which, the junior tranche, is purely Type 3. Furthermore, the junior or equity layer, which is typically harder to place, is smaller than either of the two actual issues. It remains to be seen if the middle layer will attract investors, but while it has some of the same problems as the existing issues, it has some nicer features as well. The senior piece with a high rating looks very attractive, and based on recent market reaction to the senior "Atlas 2 A" deal piece, there appears to be good market demand if the structures can be well rated. At issue in December 2001, the senior tranche (2A) of the Atlas deal was rated A-, the highest rating of a cat bond tranche in many a day. It was extremely well priced, and rapidly traded to a premium in the after market, endorsing the view that there is pent-up demand for highly rated cat bonds.

There is another potential benefit. Part of the equity tranche could be purchased by the issuer. The issuer starts with the risk – if they purchase some of the junior tranche then they retain what they started with. There are two reasons that this move would be justified. The first would be to reduce the size of the difficult to place tranche. The second reason would be to inoculate the deal from charges of moral hazard.

Essentially this tranching analysis borrows from the technology of the collateralised debt obligation (CDO) market. In that market, the average sub limit is 1–3% of full limit. In this example, the sub limits are 55% and 45% of full limit. However if more risks could be added, each with lower sub limits, the CDO like benefits could be even greater. Some past securitisations, notably Gold Eagle and Atlas have already pointed in the CDO direction, but in the future more such structures are likely to be issued as the bridge between investor desires and issuer needs is built.

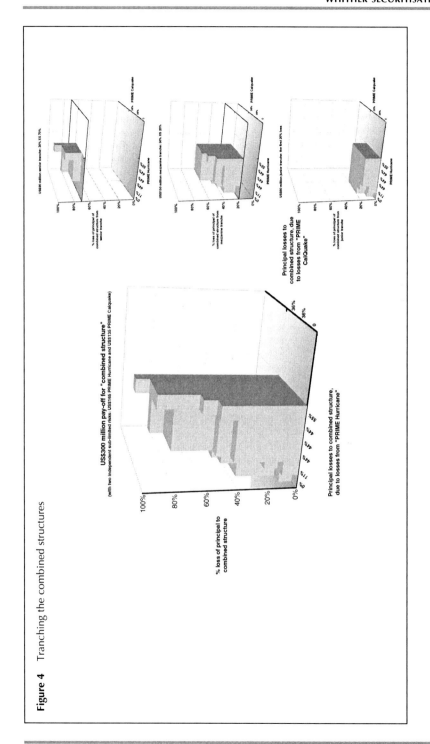

Figure 4 Tranching the combined structures

Pricing alternative structures.

In his discussions of the exigencies of issuing the PRIME deals, Manfred Seitz, was also concerned with price. Even if arbitrage structures can be found that match issuer coverage to investor acceptance – a condition necessary to a successful market – it will not be sufficient. Prices (costs) must also satisfy both parties. Here also the market needs development. Section 2 of this book has dwelled upon the issue of price. There is no single accepted price formula for insurance risk as there is, arguably, in the case of options prices and other instruments of finance. Elsewhere I have developed certain empirical approaches to characterising cat bonds prices.[13,14] As they describe earlier in this volume, Kreps and Major have also developed empirical approaches for the case of reinsurance. These are not the only approaches but they are representative of different attacks on pricing.

In *Analyzing the Pricing of the 2001 Risk-Linked Securities Transactions* the issue prices of the PRIME deals and 14 other deals or tranches issued during 2001 were fitted to a functional form shown below.[14] The resulting estimated parameters are also shown, they are:

$$premium = EL + .431*(PFL^{0.474})*(CEL^{0.326})$$

where EL is "expected loss", PFL is the "probability of first dollar loss" and CEL represents "conditional expected loss".

PFL and CEL can also be thought of as frequency and severity of loss. The same issue price data has been used to fit the forms of price formula preferred by Kreps and Major, as described in this volume. Those results were:

$$premium = 0.6883*(EL)^{0.5257}$$

And the more common mark-up based on standard deviation:

$$premium = EL + 0.5309*(standard\ deviation)$$

(Note that the parameters are not Kreps and Major's. They are Kreps and Major's equations with data estimated by myself from the 2001 securitisations. Also, these are intended as explanatory models, they are not being used for prediction of prices of securities contained in the data set.)

Table 1 shows the effect of using any of these formulas for pricing the various equivalent structures. The left hand columns show the actual issues. In each respective column the actual price and the theoretical price of each issue is shown. The third column shows the weighted average prices of the two deals. Clearly the first two models show prices quite similar to what was achieved. The models would have discriminated less between the two issues, but the net cost would have been quite similar (695 basis points (bp) vs 694, 693 or 714 for each of the models). Note that the least good model is the one most often cited, that prices ought to be EL plus a fraction of the standard deviation.

It is evident that these formulae provide quite a decent estimate for pricing the vertically equivalent structures. However, they do a less good job of pricing the horizontally equivalent structures. The right hand panel of Table 1 shows the theoretical prices of the three horizontal tranches described above. The prices from each model show the same order of magnitude in tranche prices, but the weighted average cost is much lower than the price of the untranched 'combined structure'. In fact they show that the combined price of the horizontal tranches is 45 to 96 bp less than the price paid by Munich Re (695 vs 629, 599 or 650 bp respectively).

An important implication of this is that Munich Re could have saved money by issuing as a tranched deal instead of the two bonds actually issued. Alternatively, market participants could have purchased all the bonds themselves and tranched up the deal and sold the separate pieces, for an arbitrage profit of around 60 bp, less transaction costs. Either way, if the formulas are correct, there are arbitrage opportunities. These opportunities would also exist with other deals for example in re-dividing the USAA transaction.

Of course another explanation might be that the pricing formulas are wrong! Either the price formulas are correct and profits are available, or they are in error and must be replaced. I suspect both statements have some truth. Another more academic way to describe the dilemma is to say that present pricing methods do not achieve 'layer independence'. Issuer costs should not depend on where the deal is tranched. That is why Shaun Wang's pricing endeavours described in Chapter 11 are important. He is trying to achieve pricing approaches that will at least be indifferent to tranching. As I have tried demonstrating here, tranching is an important but not the only form of structure equivalence – ultimately pricing must be robust enough to incorporate all possible restructurings. Layer independence is a merely a first step towards achieving full arbitrage free prices.

The discerning reader will have realised that the equivalents argument is not confined to cat bonds; it is merely exposed by them. Mocklow, DeCaro and McKenna discuss the idea that cat bonds should be evaluated on an EL – or expected profit – equivalent basis, but equally Takeda (in Chapter 5) talks about equivalents in the context risk swaps (Should the swaps have equal frequency, or equal severity?). Equivalence is implicit in all of the allocation discussions in Section Five. Pricing theories have ripple implications in all the contributions of this book.

CONCLUDING REMARKS
Securitisation is an important concept. It has yet to prove that it will be an important reality. Securitisation potentially benefits issuers (as an

Table 1 Actual vs theoretical equivalents

	Actual issuance			Theoretical equivalents				
Characteristics	PRIME CAPITAL HURRICANE Ltd	PRIME CAPITAL CAL-QUAKE AND EUROWIND Ltd	Weighted average cost of two separate issues	"PRIME COMBINED"	Weighted average cost of three separate tranches	"PRIME COMBINED" WITH LOSS % TRANCHING (JUNIOR-MEZZANINE-SENIOR STRUCTURE)		
						Junior tranche	Mezzanine tranche	Senior tranche
	Aggregate occurrence limit	Aggregate occurrence limit		Aggregate occurrence with sub-limits				
Actual financials								
Amount	US$165million	US$135million		US$300million	US$300million	US$60million	US$150million	US$90million
Actual coupon	L + 650 bp	L + 750 bp	695	L + 695 bp				
Equivalent coupon								
Theoretical pricing								
LFC 2001	L + 681	L + 710	694		L + 629	L + 1093	L + 779	L + 69
K & M	L + 685	L + 702	693		L + 599	L + 1047	L + 739	L + 66
SD Mark Up	L + 708	L + 721	714		L + 650	L + 1180	L + 789	L + 66
Statistics of theoretical equivalents								
Expected Loss	1.27	1.33		1.30		2.85	1.46	0.02
PFL	1.46	1.69		3.15		3.13	2.56	0.02
PLL	1.08	1.07		0.01		2.56	0.02	0.01
CEL	0.87	0.79		0.41		0.91	0.57	0.89
SD	10.95	11.07		–		16.87*	12.1*	1.22*
S & P Rating	BB+	BB+		B+/ BB		NR	B+	AAA
Moodys Rating	Ba3	Ba3		–				
Possible Rating								

* uses square root of expected loss as first approximation to SD

		Sub-Limit 1: New York, Miami A, Miami B; Sub-Limit 2: No Cal Quake, So Cal Quake, EuroWind	Sub-Limit 1: New York, Miami A, Miami B; Sub-Limit 2: No Cal Quake, So Cal Quake, EuroWind	Sub-Limit 1: New York, Miami A, Miami B; Sub-Limit 2: No Cal Quake, So Cal Quake, EuroWind	Sub-Limit 1: New York, Miami A, Miami B; Sub-Limit 2: No Cal Quake, So Cal Quake, EuroWind
Covered events of theoretical equivalents	Hurricanes in: New York, Miami A, Miami B — Earthquakes in: No Cal Quake, So Cal Quake and EuroWind				
Event payoffs	0%, 20%, 80% or 100% of principal from ANY of covered events — 100% of principal from ANY of covered events	0%, 11%, 44% or 55% of principal from ANY of covered event from Sub-Limit 1 PLUS 0%, 9%, 36%, 45% of principal from ANY of covered event from Sub-Limit 2	First 20% of payoffs arising from coverages as described under Prime Combined	50% XS 20% of payoffs arising from coverages as described under Prime Combined	30% XS 70% of payoffs arising from coverages as described under Prime Combined
Sub-limits	none	55% Sub-Limit 1, 45% Sub-Limit 2	As in Prime Combined	As in Prime Combined	As in Prime Combined

649

alternative source of secure capital), investors (as a diversifying investment) and regulators (as fully funded cover). Its future seems inevitable.
And yet the tumblers that can unlock that future have not quite fallen into
their exact places. This Afterword has sought to identify what needs to be
done to nudge the tumblers into their proper places. The asserted answer is
a theory of insurance arbitrage. By drawing up distinctions between certain
types of past securitisations and by forensically analysing a recent successful transaction (PRIME) I have illustrated how arbitrage can be interpreted
in the context of insurance securitisation.

Full development of an arbitrage theory will no doubt emerge in the
near future. Not that its absence need necessarily hold up practical developments. After all, options traded on and off for hundreds of years before
the contribution of Black and Scholes. However, after their contribution,
the use of options exploded. I would expect insurance securitisation to follow a similar path.

Arbitrageurs are fond of saying that they are in the slicing and dicing
business. They create market solutions to satisfy disparate needs by dividing and recombining risks for different players. Their reward for
performing this economically important task is their long run arbitrage
profit. Similarly, at the investor level portfolio managers have to understand positions and hedging so as to maximise their risk-adjusted rates of
return. Derivative market participants used to say 'Show me a trader who
does not know how to hedge his position and I'll show you one who does-
n't know the risk he has'. To date, those same market participants have not
risen to the challenge of slicing and dicing insurance risk. Neither they nor
insurance market players have had to prior to the last ten years.
Securitisation forces the question. However, arbitrage in insurance will not
fall easy prey to existing slicing and dicing techniques. New ones will have
to be found. The benefits of securitisation are clear enough, I expect that
they will be sufficient to motivate changes and it is likely we will find them
in directions suggested above.

There is opportunity here for both practitioners and theoreticians.

1 Bernstein, P. L., 1992, *Capital Ideas*, The Improbable Origins of Modern Wall Street (New
   York: The Free Press)
2 Modiglianni F. and M. H. Miller, 1958,The Cost of Capital, Corporate Finance and the Theory
   of Investment, *American Economic Review*, 48(3) pp. 655–69
3 Black F. and M. Scholes, 1973, The Pricing of Options and Corporate Liabilities, *Journal of
   Political Economy*, 81,pp. 637–54.
4 Rennaisance Re and PXRE .
5 Centre Cat Ltd, Global Capital Re, IPC Re, LaSalle Re, Mid-Ocean Re, Partner Re, PXRE,
   Rennaissance Re, and Tempest Re.
6 The Bermuda Commodity Exchange.
7 1992–7.
8 (Hanover Re's deals, called Kover, may have preceded AIGCR's but details were not
   forthcoming until after the publicity of AIG's transaction.)

9 Further details of the Atlas and Tricom deals can be found in the Mocklow, DeCaro and McKenna chapter of this volume.

10 It is assumed that a single occurrence of each risk is covered. Multiple occurrences of each risk could be allowed in Structure 1 which would make it significantly different from Structure 2. Multiple occurrence structures are not discussed in this chapter.

11 Theoretically the deal could have been split vertically six ways. This would have cost a) more premium and b) greater transaction costs, both of which would have been excessive.

12 The term "xs"is shorthand for "in excess of".

13 Lane, M. 2000, Pricing Risk Transfer Transactions, *ASTIN Bulletin*, 30, (2), pp. 259–93

14 M. Lane, 2001, *Analyzing the Pricing of the 2001 Risk-Linked Securities Transactions* (available from: http://www.lanefinancialllc.com/pub/sec1/Analyzing_the Pricing_of_the_ 2001_Risk-Linked_Securities_Transactions.pdf)

BIBLIOGRAPHY

Albrecht, P., 1992, Premium Calculation with Arbitrage? A note on a contribution by G. Venter, *ASTIN Bulletin*, 22, pp. 247–54.

Bantwal, V.J. and H.C. Kunreuther, 2000, A Cat Bond Premium Puzzle?, *The Journal of Psychology and Financial Markets*, 1, (1), pp. 76–91.

Canabarro, E., M. Finkemeier, R.R. Anderson and F. Bendimerad, 1998, Analyzing Insurance-Linked Securities, *The Journal of Risk Finance*, 1, (2), pp. 49–75.

Canter, M., J. Cole, and R. Sandor, 1996, Insurance Derivatives: A New Asset Class for the Capital Markets and a New Hedging Tool for the Insurance Industry, *Journal of Derivatives*, Winter [pp.?]

Doherty, N.A., and C. W. Smith, Jr., 1993, Corporate Insurance Strategy: The Case of British Petroleum, *Journal of Applied Corporate Finance*, 6, (3).

Froot, K.A. and S. Posner, 2000, *Issues in the Pricing of Catastrophe Risk.* Guy Carpenter, Marsh & McLennan Securities White Papers, May. [Available at: http:// www.guycarp.com/publications/white/whitep.htm.]

Froot, K.A. and S. Posner, 2001, The Pricing of Event Risk with Parameter Uncertainty, Working Paper 8106, *National Bureau of Economic Research.* [Available at: http:// www.nber.org/papers/w8106]

Kreps, R.E., 1990, *Reinsurer Risk Loads from Marginal Surplus Requirements*, PCAS LXXVII.

Kreps, R.E., 1998, *Investment-Equivalent Reinsurance Pricing*, PCAS Proceedings. [Also available from Guy Carpenter Instrat Publications, 14 February 2000, http:// www.guycarp.com/products/dorweil/kreps.html]

Lane, M.N., 1998, Price, Risk, and Ratings for Insurance-Linked Notes: Evaluating Their Position in Your Portfolio, *Derivatives Quarterly*, 4, (4).

Lane, M.N. and O.Y. Movchan, 1999, *Risk Cubes or Price, Risk and Ratings (Part II)*, Sedgwick Lane Financial L.L.C. Trade Notes, March 15 [Available at: http://www.lanefinancialllc.com]

Lane, M. N., 2000, Pricing Risk Transfer Transactions, *ASTIN Bulletin*, 30, (2), 2000, pp. 259–93 [This paper was awarded the 2000 CAS Hachemeister Prize]

Lane, M.N. and Beckwith, R.G., 2000, *Trends in the Insurance-Linked Securities Market*, Lane Financial L.L.C. Trade Notes, May 31, [Available at: http://www.lanefinancialllc.com]

Lane, M.N., 2000, *CDOs as Self-Contained Reinsurance Structures*, Trade Notes, December 10, Lane Financial L.L.C. [Available at: www.lanefinancialllc.com]

Mango, D., 1999, Risk Load and the Default Rate of Surplus, *Casualty Actuarial Society Discussion Papers on Securitization Risk*, http://www.casact.org/pubs/dpp/dpp99/index.htm

Venter, G.G., 1991, Premium Calculation Implications of Reinsurance without Arbitrage, *ASTIN Bulletin*, 21, pp. 223–30.

Wang, S., 1995, Insurance Pricing and Increased Limits Ratemaking by Proportional Hazards Transforms, *Insurance: Mathematics and Economics*, 17, pp. 43–54.

Wang, S., 1996, Premium Calculation by Transforming the Layer Premium Density, *ASTIN Bulletin*, 26, (1), pp. 71–92.

Bibliography

Ackerman, C., R. McEnally and D. Ravenscraft, 1999, "The Performance of Hedge Funds: Risk, Return and Incentives", *Journal of Finance*, 54, pp. 833–74.

Agostino, D. J., and W. J. Cosgrove, 1990, "The Securitization Solution", *Best's Review*, January, p. 44.

Ahn, D., J. Boudoukh, M. Richardson, R. and Whitelaw, 1999, "Optimal Risk Management Using Options", *Journal of Finance*, 54, pp. 359–75.

Akerlof, G., 1970, "The Market for 'Lemons': Qualitative Uncertainty and the Market Mechanism," *Quarterly Journal of Economics* 43, pp. 448–500.

Albrecht, P., 1992, Premium Calculation with Arbitrage? A note on a contribution by G. Venter, *ASTIN Bulletin*, 22, pp. 247–54.

Alford, B.H., 2001, "Understanding Alternative Assets", *Wealth Perspectives*, URL: http://www.mycfo.com/our_perspectives/opr_alt_assets.html (March 29 2001).

American Academy of Actuaries, 1999, "Evaluating the Effectiveness of Index-Based Insurance Derivatives in Hedging Property/Casualty Insurance Transactions", Report of the Index Securitization Task Force, Washington DC.

American Institute of Certified Public Accountants, 1998, "Statement of Position 98–7 Deposit Accounting: Accounting for Insurance and Reinsurance Contracts That Do Not Transfer Insurance Risk" October.

AON Corporation, "Aon Securitizes Limited Partnership Interests; Provides Update on Non-Operating Segment Revenue for Fourth Quarter 2001 First-of-its-Kind Transaction To Reduce Earnings Variability", URL: http://www.aon.com/abo.../PressRelease.asp ?ID=79B746492EB8F 32C 86256B43005359B.html (16 January 2002).

Applied Insurance Research, 1999, "AIR Tropical Cyclone Model: United States Region", Technical Document TCUS 9904, AIR, Boston.

Arabeyre, V., and S. Hardwick, 2001, "From Embedded Value to Share Price", URL: http://www.towers.com/towers/publications/emphasis/emp2001-1/embedded.htm.

Arquilla, J., D. Ronfeldt and M. Zanini, 2000, "Information-age terrorism", *Current History*, Vol. 99, pp. 179–185.

ATC-13, 1985, *Earthquake Damage Evaluation Data for California* (Redwood City, CA: Applied Technology Council).

AXA Investment Managers, 2001, "Private Equity _ Eine Anlageklasse von wachsender

Bedeutung für deutsche institutionelle Investoren", URL: http://www.axa-im.de/PDF/Oetker_Water.pdf+outperformance+private+equity+evca&hl=de&ie=ISO-8859-1

Banham, R., 2001, "Clocs Ticking to New Market," *Reactions* (April).

Bank for International Settlements, 2001, "The Global OTC Derivatives Market at End- June 2001", Press release, 20 December.

Bank for International Settlements, "The New Basel Capital Accord: Comments received on the Second Consultative Package", URL: http://www.bis.org/bcbs/cacomments.htm (21 August 2001).

Bansal, R., D. A. Hsieh and S. Viswanathan, 1993, "A New Approach to International Arbitrage Pricing", *Journal of Finance*, 48, pp. 1719–47.

Bansal, R., and S. Viswanathan, 1993, "No Arbitrage and Arbitrage Pricing: A New Approach", *Journal of Finance*, 48, pp. 1231–62.

Bantwal, V.J. and H.C. Kunreuther, 2000, A Cat Bond Premium Puzzle?, *The Journal of Psychology and Financial Markets*, 1, (1), pp. 76–91.

Barnston, A. G., 1994, "Linear statistical short-term climate predictive skill in the Northern Hemisphere", *Journal of Climate*, 7, pp. 1513–1564.

Barnston, A.G., H.M. van Dool, S.E. Zebiak, T.P. Barnett, M. Ji, D.R. Rodenhuis, M.A.Cane, A. Leetmaa, N.E. Graham, C.R. Ropelewski, V.E. Kousky, E.O. O'Lenic, and R.E.Livesey, 1994, "Long-lead seasonal forecasts-where do we stand?" *Bulletin American Meteorological Society*, 75, pp. 2097–2114.

Barry, M., J. C. Mezzanotte, and F. Phillip, 2001, "Use of Insurance Policies as Credit Enhancement in Structured Finance", Fitch Special Report on Structured Finance, June, Fitch Ibca, Duff & Phelps.

Bawcutt, P., 1997, *Captive Insurance Companies*, Fourth Edition, (London: Whiterby & Co Ltd).

Baz, J, V. Naik, D. Prieul, V. Putyatin and F. Yared, 2000, "Selling Risk at a Premium", *Risk*, pp. 135–8.

Bonabeau, E., M. Dorigo and G. Theraulaz, 1999, *Swarm Intelligence*, (Oxford University Press).

Bergen, P. L., 2001, *Holy War, Inc.* (London: Weidenfeld and Nicholson).

Bernstein, P. L., 1992, *Capital Ideas, The Improbable Origins of Modern Wall Street* (New York: The Free Press).

Bernstein, P. L., 1996, *Against the Gods, The Remarkable Story of Risk* (New York: John Wiley & Sons, Ltd).

Best, A. M., 2001, *Captive Directory*, 2001 Edition, (New Jersey: AM Best Company).

Black, F., and A. Perold, 1987, "Theory of Constant Proportion Portfolio Insurance", Unpublished Paper.

Bookstaber, R., and R. Clarke, 1984, "Option Portfolio Strategies: Measurement and Evaluation", *Journal of Business*, 57(4), pp. 469–92.

Booth, G., ed., 2000, *Modern ART Practice* (London: Reactions Publishing Group).

Borronow, G., and T. Mazzaferro, 1996, American Skandia Press Release, December 17.

Bowyer Bell, J., 2000, The IRA, 1968–2000 (London: Frank Cass & Co).

Brealy, R. A., and S. C. Myers, 2000, *Principles of Corporate Finance*, Sixth Edition, (New York: McGraw-Hill).

Briys, E., and F. deVarenne, 2000, *The Fisherman and the Rhinoceros, How International Finance Shapes Everyday Life* (Chichester: John Wiley & Sons, Ltd).

Brown, M., 2000, *Butterworths Insurance Law Handbook*, Sixth Edition, (London: Butterworths Tolley).

Brown S., W. Goetzmann and R. Ibbotson, 1999, "Offshore Hedge Funds: Survival and Performance, 1989-95", *Journal of Business*, 72, pp. 911–17.

Bühlmann, H., 1970, *Mathematical Methods in Risk Theory*, (Berlin: Springer-Verlag).

Canabarro, E., M. Finkemeier, R.R. Anderson and F. Bendimerad, 1998, Analyzing Insurance-Linked Securities, *The Journal of Risk Finance*, 1, (2), pp. 49–75.

Cane, M., and S.E. Zebiak, 1987, "Prediction of El Niño events using a physical model", in H. Cattle (ed), *Atmospheric and Oceanic Variability*, pp. 153–182 (London: Royal Meteorological Society Press).

Canter, M., J. Cole, and R. Sandor, 1996, Insurance Derivatives: A New Asset Class for the Capital Markets and a New Hedging Tool for the Insurance Industry, *Journal of Derivatives*, Winter.

Canter, M., J.B. Cole, and R. L. Sandor, 1997, "Insurance Derivatives: A New Asset Class for the Capital Markets and a New Hedging Tool for the Insurance Industry", *Journal of Applied Corporate Finance*, 10(3), pp. 69–83.

Carl, U., 2002, "Financial Guaranty and Credit Securitisation", ART Academy Presentation 2001, Swiss Re internal paper presented to ART Academy, p. 2.

Carter R., L. Lucas and N. Ralph, 2000, *Reinsurance*, Fourth Edition, (London: Reactions Publishing Group in association with Guy Carpenter & Company), pp. 98–101.

Cheng, V., 2001, "Credit Derivatives – A Good Thing if Done Right", US Financials Strategy Research 13/2001, Fox-Pitt, Kelton Group.

Chookaszian, J., and T. Ward, 1998, "Risk Securitization Products on the Rise", *National Underwriter (Property and Casualty/Risk and Benefits Management)*, 102(20), pp. 9, 23.

Clemmons, L., 2002, "Weather risk management: practical uses in industry", Presentation to the MIT Sloan Energy and Environmental Finance Club.

Coburn, A. and Spence, R., 1992, *Earthquake Protection*, (Chichester: John Wiley & Sons).

Cochrane, J. H., 2001, New Facts in Finance, in *Economic Perspectives*, Federal Reserve Bank of Chicago.

Coleman, E., 2002, "2001 Review and 2002 Outlook – Collateralized Debt Obligations in Europe: Bigger and Bigger it Grows", International Structured Finance, January.

Cooke, R. M., 1991, *Experts in Uncertainty* (Oxford University Press).

Corcoran, J. P., 1989, Securitization of Future Premiums – Statutory Accounting Treatment, New York State Department of Insurance Circular Letter (1989-7).

Crombie, R., 2002, "Bermuda Startup Reinsurers Pursue Niches", *National Underwriter*, 12 February, 2002.

Croson, D.C. and Kunreuther, H.C., 1999, "Customizing Reinsurance and Cat Bonds for Natural Hazard Risks", *The Wharton Financial Institutions Center and The Wharton Risk Management and Decision Processes Center*, URL: http://fic.wharton.upenn.edu/fic/papers/99/pcat09.html (June 1999).

Crouhy, M., D. Galai and R. Mark, 2000, *Risk Management*, (New York: McGraw-Hill).

Culp, C. L., 2001, *The Risk Management Process: Business Strategy and Tactics* (New York: John Wiley & Sons).

Culp, C. L., 2002a, *The ART of Risk Management: Alternative Risk Transfer, Capital Structure, and Convergence in Insurance and Capital Markets* (New York: John Wiley & Sons).

Culp, C. L., 2002b, "The Revolution in Corporate Risk Management: A Decade of Innovations in Process and Products," *Journal of Applied Corporate Finance* 14, 4, forthcoming.

Culp, C. L., 2002c, "Contingent Capital and the Theory of Risk Capital", *Journal of Applied Corporate Finance* 15, 1, forthcoming.

Culp, C. L., and M. H. Miller, 1995a, "Metallgesellschaft and the Economics of Synthetic Storage", *Journal of Applied Corporate Finance* 7, 4, pp. 62–76.

Culp, C. L., and M. H. Miller, 1995b, "Hedging in the Theory of Corporate Finance", *Journal of Applied Corporate Finance*, 8,1, pp. 121–7.

Cummins, J., and P. Danzon, 1997, "Price Shocks and Capital Flows in Liability Insurance," *Journal of Financial Intermediation*, 6 , pp. 3–38.

Cummins, J. D., D. Lalonde and R. D. Phillips, 2002, *The Basis Risk of Index-Linked CAT Loss Securities*, Working Paper, Wharton Financial Institutions Center, Philadelphia.

Cummins, J. D., C. M. Lewis, and R.D. Phillips, 1999, "Pricing Excess of Loss Reinsurance Against Catastrophic Loss", in: K. A. Froot (ed.) *The Financing of Catastrophe Risk*, (University of Chicago Press).

Cummins, J. D. and M. A. Weiss, 2000, "The Global Market for Reinsurance: Consolidation, Capacity, and Efficiency", Brookings-Wharton Papers on Financial Services.

DeCaro, J, 2001, *Risk-Linked Securities Market – 2001 Review*, Research Report, 4 February 2002, Cochran, Caronia Securities LLC.

DeFontaine, P., 2001, "Vanishing Cat Bonds", *Best's Review*, January 2001, URL: http://www.bestreview.com/2001-01/pc_vanishing_cat_bonds.html

Deter, Dr., 2001, "Betriebliche Altersversorgung", *Wissenschaftlicher Dienst des Deutschen Bundestages: Der aktuelle Begriff*, URL: www.bundestag.de/aktuell/begriff/2001/15_2001.pdf

Deutsche Bank, "Erste Private Equity Wandelanleihe mit Kapitalschutz", URL:http://public.deutsche-bank.de/deuba/db/aktuell.nsf/doc/JBOS-48PP2H?OpenDocument (9 June 1999).

Deutsche Bank, "Prime Edge Capital plc Successfully Issued €150 Million Private Equity CDO", URL: http://www.db.com/central/ver40/news/2001_q2/01062001b.html (1 June 2001).

Diamond, D., 1984, "Financial Intermediation and Delegated Monitoring", *Review of Economic Studies*, 51, pp. 393–414.

Diamond, D., 1991, "Monitoring and Reputation: The Choice Between Bank Loans and Directly Placed Debt", *Journal of Political Economy*, 99 pp. 689–721.

Dionne, G., and M. Garand, 2002, Risk Management Determinants Affecting Firm's Values in the Gold Mining Industry: New Empirical Results, Working Paper, HEC, Montreal.

Doherty, N., 1985, *Corporate Risk Management: A Financial Exposition*, (McGraw Hill).

Doherty, N. A., 1991, "The Design of Insurance Contracts when Liability Rules are Unstable", *Journal of Risk and Insurance*, LVIII, pp. 227-46.

Doherty, N. A., 1997, "Financial Innovation in the Management of Catastrophe Risk", *Journal of Applied Corporate Finance*, 10, pp. 84–95.

Doherty, N. A., 2000, *Integrated Risk Management* (New York: McGraw-Hill).

Doherty, N.A., and C. W. Smith, Jr., 1993, Corporate Insurance Strategy: The Case of British Petroleum, *Journal of Applied Corporate Finance*, 6, (3).

Doherty, N., Lamm-Tennant, J. and Starks, L, 2002, "Market Shocks and The Value of Transparency", Working Paper.

Dorer, J., S. Rouyer, and L. Levenstein, "Financial Guaranty Industry Outlook", Global Credit Research January 2002, Moody's Investor Service.

Eckbo, B. E, and R. W. Masulis, 1995, "Seasoned Equity Offerings: A Survey", *Handbooks in Operations Research & Management Science, Vol. 9, Finance* (Amsterdam: Elsevier).

EIMS, Graham Bannock & Partners Ltd (UK), EIMS Publication No (Contractor's Edition) "Pan-European study of the performance of venture capital, Summary of Results", URL:http://www.cordis.lu/eims/src/eims-r43.htm (last updated January 30, 2002).

Embrechts, P., ed., 2000, *Extremes and Integrated Risk Management* (London: Risk Books).

Embrechts, P., A. Hoeing and A. Juri, 2001, "Using Copulae to Bound the Value-at-Risk for Functions of Dependent Risks", Working Paper, ETH Zurich.

Embrechts, P., C. Klüppelberg and T. Mikosch, 1997, *Modelling Extremal Events for Insurance and Finance* (Berlin: Springer-Verlag).

Embrechts, P., F. Lindskog and A. J. McNeil, 2000, "Modelling Dependence with Copulas and Applications to Risk Management", forthcoming in: *Heavy-Tailed Distributions in Finance*, 2002, S.T. Rachev (ed), (Amsterdam: North Holland).

Embrechts, P., A. J. McNeil and D. Straumann, 1999, "Correlation: Pitfalls and Alternatives", *Risk Magazine*, 5, pp. 69–71.

Embrechts, P., A. J. McNeil and D. Straumann, 2002, "Correlation and Dependence in Risk Management: Properties and Pitfalls, in: *Risk Management: Value at Risk and Beyond*, M. Dempster (ed), (Cambridge University Press) pp. 176–223.

Erie Insurance Group, company website, URL: http://www.erieinsurance.com/reinsurance/reinsaboutus.html>.

European Venture Capital Association (EVCA), for Private Equity Reporting Requirements: 2002 Reporting Guidelines, URL: www.evca.com

Fallmer, H., and D. Sondermann, 1986, "Hedging of Non-Redundant Contingent Claims", in W. Hildenbrand and A. Mas-Colell (eds), *Contributions to Mathematical Economics: In Honor of Gerard Debreu*, Elsevier, (New York: North-Holland).

Fama, E. F., and K. R. French, 2000, "Testing Tradeoff and Pecking Order Predictions About Dividends and Debt", Graduate School of Business, The University of Chicago, Center for Research in Security Prices, *Working Paper No 506*.

Fama, E. F., and M. H. Miller, 1972, *The Theory of Finance* (New York: Holt, Rinehart, and Winston).

Federal Coordinator for Meteorological Services and Supporting Research, 1994, "Federal standard for siting meteorological sensors at airports", FCM-S4-1994, Washington DC.

FEMA 366, 2000, *HAZUS 99 Estimated Annualized Earthquake Losses for the United States* (Washington, DC: Federal Emergency Management Agency).

Ferro, K., 2001, "The start of something big", *Risk & Reward*, April 2001.

Financial Accounting Standards Board, 1975, "Accounting for Contingencies", Statement of Financial Accounting Standards 5, March.

Financial Accounting Standards Board, 1982, "Accounting and Reporting by Insurance Enterprises", Statement of Financial Accounting Standards 60, June.

Financial Accounting Standards Board, 1986 "Accounting by Insureds for Claims-Made Insurance Policies", Emerging Issues Task Force Statement, 12.

Financial Accounting Standards Board, 1989–90, "Transactions involving Special-Purpose Entities", Emerging Issues Task Force Statement, D-14.

Financial Accounting Standards Board, 1990, "Impact of Nonsubstantive Lessors, Residual Value Guarantees, and Other Provisions in Leasing Transactions", Emerging Issues Task Force Statement, 15.

Financial Accounting Standards Board, 1992, "Accounting and Reporting for Reinsurance of Short-Duration and Long-Duration Contracts", Statement of Financial Accounting Standards 113, December.

Financial Accounting Standards Board, 1993a, "Accounting for Multiple-Year Retrospectively Rated Contracts by Ceding and Assuming Enterprises", Emerging Issues Task Force Statement, 6.

Financial Accounting Standards Board, 1993b, "Accounting for Multiple-Year Retrospectively Rated Insurance Contracts by Insurance Enterprises and Other Enterprises", Emerging Issues Task Force Statement, 14, November.

Financial Accounting Standards Board, 1993c, "Accounting for Reinsurance: Questions and Answers about FASB Statement No. 113", Emerging Issues Task Force Statement, D-34, July.

Financial Accounting Standards Board, 1993d, "FASB Staff Views on Issue No. 93-6, "Accounting for Multiple-Year Retrospectively Rated Contracts by Ceding and Assuming Enterprises", Emerging Issues Task Force Statement, D-35, July.

Financial Accounting Standards Board, 1998, "Accounting for Derivative Instruments and Hedging Activities", Statement of Financial Accounting Standards 133, June.

Financial Accounting Standards Board, 1999a, "Accounting for Retroactive Insurance Contracts Purchased by Entities Other Than Insurance Enterprises", Emerging Issues Task Force Statement, D-79, May.

Financial Accounting Standards Board, 1999b, "Accounting for Weather Derivatives", Emerging Issues Task Force Statement, 2.

Financial Accounting Standards Board, 2000, "Accounting for Transfers and Servicing of Financial Assets and Extinguishments of Liabilities", Statement of Financial Accounting Standards 140, September.

Financial Services Authority, 2001, *Interim Prudential Sourcebook for Insurers,* 1, (London: FSA) p. 11.

Financial Times, 1999, "Swiss Re set for high risk AAA-rated issue" (8 June).

Fitch IBCA, Duff & Phelps, 2001, "Hedge Funds, A New Asset Class in Structured Finance", analysts: Eileen A. Fahey, Chicago, Richard V. Hrvatin, New York, Steve N. Lee, New York, Mitchell Lench, London, Roger W. Merritt, CPA, New York, John L. Schiavetta, CFA, New York, URL: http://www.fitchibca.com/corporate/search/ (search for hedge funds) (6 September 2001).

Florida Insurance Council, 1998, *Computer Modeling of Catastrophic Losses,* February, Fact Book URL: http://www.flains.org/newfic/mediapublic/).

Flynn, S. E., 2001, "The Unguarded Homeland", in: J. F. Hoge and G. Rose (eds), *How Did This Happen?* (Oxford:PublicAffairs Ltd).

Freeman, J. R, 1932, *Earthquake Damage and Earthquake Insurance* (New York: McGraw-Hill).

Froot, K., 1998a, *The Evolving Market for Catastrophic Event Risk* (New York: Marsh & McClennan Securities Corp and Guy Carpenter Special Report).

Froot, K. A., 1998b, "Mid Ocean Limited – Trading Catastrophe Index Options", Harvard Business School Case 9-278-073, (Boston: Harvard Business School Publishing).

Froot, K. A., 1999, *The Financing of Catastrophic Risk* (Chicago: The University of Chicago Press).

Froot, K. A., 2001, "The Market for Catastrophe Risk: A Clinical Examination", *Journal of Financial Economics*, 60, pp. 529–71.

Froot K. A. and P. J. G. O'Connell, 1999, "The Pricing of US Catastrophe Reinsurance", in: K. Froot (ed.) *The Financing of Catastrophe Risk*, (University of Chicago Press).

Froot, K.A. and S. Posner, 2000, Issues in the Pricing of Catastrophe Risk, Guy Carpenter, Marsh & McLennan Securities White Papers, May. [Available at: http://www.guycarp.com/ publications/white/whitep.htm.]

Froot, K.A. and S. Posner, 2001, The Pricing of Event Risk with Parameter Uncertainty, Working Paper 8106, National Bureau of Economic Research. [Available at: http://www.nber.org/ papers/w8106]

Froot, K. A., D. S. Scharfstein, and J. C. Stein, 1993, "Risk Management: Coordinating Investment and Financing Policies", *Journal of Finance*, 48, 5, pp. 1629–58.

Froot, K., and J. Stein, 1998, "Risk Management, Capital Budgeting, and the Capital Structure Policy for Financial Institutions: an Integrated Approach", *Journal of Financial Economics*, 47, pp. 55-82.

Fung, W., and D. Hsieh, 1997, "Empirical Characteristics of Dynamic Trading Strategies: The Case of Hedge Funds", *Review of Financial Studies*, 10(2), pp. 275–302.

Fung, W., and D. Hsieh, 1998a, *Performance Attribution and Style Analysis: From Mutual Funds to Hedge Funds*, Working Paper, Fuqua School of Business, Duke University.

Fung, W., and D. Hsieh, 1998b, *A Risk-Neutral Approach to Valuing Trend-Following Trading Strategies*, Working Paper, Fuqua School of Business, Duke University.

Fung, W., and D. Hsieh, 1999, *A Primer on Hedge Funds*, Working Paper, Fuqua School of Business, Duke University.

Galai, D., and M. I. Schneller, 1978, "Pricing of Warrants and the Value of the Firm", *Journal of Finance*, 33, 5, pp. 1333–42.

Garrison, R. W., 2001, *Time and Money: The Macroeconomics of Capital Structure* (London: Routledge).

Gehriger, P. O., 2001, "Besteuerung von Captives und Steuerplanung mit Captives", in: *SteuerRevue*, 10, pp. 642–59.

Genest, C., K. Ghoudi and L.-P. Rivest, 1995, "A Semiparametric Estimation Procedure of Dependence Parameters in Multivariate Families of Distributions", *Biometrika*, 82(3), pp. 543–52.

Genest, C., C. K. Ghoudi and L.-P. Rivest, 1998, "Commentaire sur l'article de E. W. Frees et E. A. Valdez intitulé "Understanding relationships using copulas", *North American Actuarial Journal*, 2, pp. 143–9.

Gibson, R. (ed), 2000, *Model Risk: Concepts, Calibration and Pricing*, (London: Risk Books).

Gisler, A. and P. Frost, 1999, "An Addendum and a Short Comment on the Paper from U.

Schmock, "Estimating the Value of the WinCAT Coupons of the Winterthur Insurance Convertible Bond: A Study of the Model Risk", *Astin Bulletin*, 29(1), pp.165–71.

Glosten, L., and R. Jagannathan, 1994, "A Contingent Claim Approach to Performance Evaluation", *Journal of Empirical Finance*, 1, pp. 133–60.

Goldberg, D. E., 1989, *Genetic Algorithms in Search, Optimization and Machine Learning*, (Reading: Addison-Wesley).

Goldman Sachs and Frank Russell Company, "Goldman Sachs and Russell Publish Fifth Global Report On Institutional Alternative Investing", URL:http://biz.yahoo.com/ bw/011219/ 192023_1.html (19 December 2001).

Graham, R.J., A.D.L. Evans, K.R. Mylne, M.S.J. Harrison, and K.B. Robertson, 2000, "An assessment of seasonal predictability using atmospheric general circulation models", *Quarterly Journal of the Royal Meteorological Society*, 126, pp. 2211–2240.

Gron, A., 1994, "Capacity Constraints and Cycles in Property-Casualty Insurance Markets," *Rand Journal of Economics* 25, pp. 110–27.

Gron, A., and A. Winton, 2001, "Risk Overhang and Market Behavior," *Journal of Business*, 74, pp. 591–612.

Grünbichler, A., S. Graf and A. Gruber, 2001, *Private Equity und Hedge Funds: Alternative Anlagekategorien im Überblick*, (Zürich: Verlag Neue Zürcher Zeitung).

Gupton, G., Finger, C., and Bhatia, M., 1997, *CreditMetrics – Technical Document*, J. P. Morgan, URL: www.creditmetrics.com/pdf/CMTD1.pdf.

Haller, M., and W. Ackermann, 1992, *Versicherungswirtschaft – kundenorientiert*, (Zürich: Verlag des Schweizerischen Kaufmännischen Verbandes).

Halsbury, 1991, *Halsbury's Statutes*, 30, Fourth Edition, (re-issue), (London: Butterworths Tolley).

Halsbury, 1998, *Halsbury's Statutes*, 5, Fourth Edition (re-issue), (London: Butterworths Tolley).

Halsbury, 2000, *Halsbury's Statutes*, 22, Fourth Edition, (re-issue), (London: Butterworths Tolley).

Hannover Re, 1998, "Hannover Re Completes First-Ever Life Reassurance Transaction with Capital Markets", *Hannover Re Newsletter* (April 15).

Harrington, S. E. and G. Niehaus, 1999, "Basis Risk with PCS Catastrophe Insurance Derivative Contracts", *Journal of Risk and Insurance*, 66, pp. 49–82.

Harris, M. and A. Raviv, 1991, "The Theory of Capital Structure", *Journal of Finance*, 46, 1, pp. 297–355.

Harris, S., 2002, Moody's Analysis of Life Insurance Embedded Values and Their Securitisation. Moody's Rating Report Publication, January.

HAZUS99, 1999, "Earthquake Loss Estimation Methodology HAZUS 99 Service Release 2 (SR2)", Federal Emergency Management Agency Washington, DC and National Institute of Building Sciences Washington, DC.

Himick, M., ed., 1998, *Securitized Insurance Risk, Strategic Opportunities for Insurers and Investors* (Chicago: Greenlake Publishing Company, Ltd).

Hicks, J., 1973, *Capital and Time* (Oxford: Clarendon Press).

Hirshliefer, J., and J. G. Riley, 1994, *The Analytics of Uncertainty and Information*, (Cambridge University Press).

Hottensen, R., G., M. S. Hodges, J. Lustbader, and J. Simon, 2001, "Specialty Finance: Financial Guarantors", Goldman Sachs Global Equity Research December 2001, Goldman Sachs.

Hull, J., 1993, *Options, Futures and other Derivative Securities,* Second Edition, (New Jersey: Prentice-Hall).

Hwang, H. H. M., H. Lin and J.-R. Huo, 1997, "Seismic Performance Evaluation of Fire Stations in Shelby County, Tennessee, *Earthquake Spectra,* 13(4), pp. 759–72.

Ingersoll, J. E. Jr., 1987, *Theory of Financial Decisionmaking* (Maryland, USA: Rowman & Littlefield).

International Financing Review, Issue 1418, "Securitization to play role in private equity sales", URL: http://www.ifrmagazine.com/ifr/protected/ZZZPV8P4IWC.html (26 January 2002).

Jaeger, L., *Managing Risk in Alternative Investment Strategies* (New Jersey: Prentice Hall), forthcoming.

Jaffee, D. M. and T. Russell, 1997, "Catastrophe Insurance, Capital Markets, and Uninsurable Risks", *Journal of Risk and Insurance,* 64, pp. 205–30.

Ji, M., A. Kumar, and A. Leetmaa, 1994b, "An experimental coupled forecast system at the national meteorological center: some early results", Tellus, 46A, pp. 398–419.

Ji, M., A. Kumar, A. Leetmaa, and M.P. Hoerling, 1993, "Coupled ocean-atmosphere climate forecast system for ENSO predictions", *Proceedings of the Workshop on Numberical Extended Range Weather Prediction,* Airlie, Virginia, pp. 141–144.

Joe, H., 1997, *Multivariate Models and Dependence Concepts,* (London: Chapman & Hall).

Johnson, S., 2001, *Emergence* (London: Allen Lane, the Penguin Press).

Jones, J. G., and J. S. Tuczak, 1996, ASLAC Funding Trust, Duff & Phelps Credit Rating Agency Company Report.

Juri, A. and M. Wüthrich, 2001, "Copula Convergence Theorems for Tail Events", Working paper, ETH Zurich.

Kennedy, J., and R. C. Eberhart, 2001, *Swarm Intelligence* (San Francisco: Morgan Kaufmann Publishers).

Kessler, M., and L. Levenstein, 2001, "Credit Default Swaps versus Financial Guaranties – Are the Risks the Same?", Global Credit Research June 2001, Moody's Investor Service.

Kiln, R., and S. Kiln, 1996, *Reinsurance Underwriting,* Second Edition (London: LLP Ltd).

Kircher, C. A. *et al,* 1997, "Estimation of Earthquake Losses in Buildings", *Earthquake Spectra,* 13(4), pp. 721–38.

Kirtman, B.P., J. Shukla, B. Huang, Z. Zhu, and E.K. Schneider, 1995, "Multiseasonal predictions with a coupled tropical ocean/global atmosphere system", *Monthly Weather Review,* 125, pp. 789–808.

Knepper, L., 2002, "Unwrapping the Wrappers", *Barclays Capital Securitisation Research.*

Kreps, R. E., 1990, "Reinsurer Risk Loads from Marginal Surplus Requirements", *Proceedings of the Casualty Actuarial Society,* Volume LXXX, pp. 196–203.

Kreps, R.E., 1998, Investment-Equivalent Reinsurance Pricing, PCAS Proceedings. [Also available from Guy Carpenter Instrat Publications, 14 February 2000, http://www.guycarp.com/products/dorweil/kreps.html]

Kreps, R. E., 1999, "Investment-Equivalent Reinsurance Pricing", in O. E. Van Slyke (ed), *Actuarial Considerations Regarding Risk and Return in Property-Casualty Insurance Pricing,* pp. 77–104, (Alexandria, VA: Casualty Actuarial Society).

Kreutzer, L., 2002, "AON is first: Big Hurdles Still Confront Efforts At Securitization", *The Private Equity Analyst*, Vol.XII, Issue 2, February.

Krishnamurti, T.N., C.M. Kishtawal, T. LaRow, D. Bachiochi, Z. Zhang, C.E. Williford, S. Gadgil and S. Surendran, 2000, "Multi-model super-ensemble forecasts for weather and seasonal climate", *Journal of Climate*, November.

Kunreuther, H. and R. J. Sr. Roth, eds., 1998, *Paying the Price* (Washington: Joseph Henry Press).

Lamm-Tennant, J., 1999, "Economic Value Added of the Property-Casualty Insurance Industry," Working Paper.

Lamm-Tennant, J. and Weiss, M., 1997, "International Insurance Cycles: Rational Expectations/Institutional Intervention," *Journal of Risk and Insurance*, 64 (3), pp. 414–39.

Lane, M.N., 1998, Price, Risk, and Ratings for Insurance-Linked Notes: Evaluating Their Position in Your Portfolio, *Derivatives Quarterly*, 4.

Lane, M. N., 1999, "An Optionable Note: The Reliance III Case Study", *Lane Financial LLC Trade Notes*.

Lane, M. N., 2000, CDOs as Self-Contained Reinsurance Structures, Trade Notes, December 10, Lane Financial LLC [Available at: www.lanefinancialllc.com].

Lane, M. N., 2000, Pricing Risk Transfer Transactions, *ASTIN Bulletin*, 30, (2), 2000, pp. 259–93 [This paper was awarded the 2000 CAS Hachemeister Prize].

Lane, M. N. and Beckwith, R.G., 2000, Trends in the Insurance-Linked Securities Market, Lane Financial LLC Trade Notes, May 31, [Available at: http://www.lanefinancialllc.com].

Lane, M. N. and O.Y. Movchan, 1999, Risk Cubes or Price, Risk and Ratings (Part II), Sedgwick Lane Financial LLC Trade Notes, March 15 [Available at: http://www.lanefinancialllc.com].

Lehmann, A., and M. Jutzi, 1991, "Risikofinanzierung – wachsende Bedeutung als Teilaspekt im Risikomanagement", in: *Zeitschrift für Versicherungswesen*, (Hamburg: Allgemeiner Fachverlag Dr Rolf Mathern GmbH), pp. 325–7.

Leland, H., 1985, "Option Pricing and Replication with Transaction Costs", *Journal of Finance*, 40, pp. 1283–301.

Lennon, T., 1990, "Securitization: A Regulatory View", *Bests Review*, January, pp. 45-6, MetLife Inc, URL: www.sec.gov. SEC Form 10-K. March 14, 2001.

Lerner, J., 2000, *Venture Capital and Private Equity – A Casebook*, (New York: John Wiley & Sons).

Lewin, P., 1999, *Capital in Disequilibrium: The Role of Capital in a Changing World* (London: Routledge).

Litzenberger, R. H., D. R. Beaglehole, and C. E. Reynolds, 1996, "Assessing Catastrophe Reinsurance-linked Securities as a New Asset Class", *Journal of Portfolio Management*, December, pp. 76–86.

Liu, J., and F. A. Longstaff, 2000, *Losing Money on Arbitrage: Optimal Dynamic Portfolio Choice in Markets with Arbitrage Opportunities*, UCLA Finance, Working Paper No. 9–00.

Lux, H., 2001, "The Great hedge fund reinsurance tax game", Institutional Investor Magazine (Americas Edition), April, pp 52–8.

Macy, S. C., 2002, "Approach to Rating Operating Company Securitizations", Moody's Rating Agency Report, February 8.

Major, J. A., 1999, "Index Hedge Performance: Insurer Market Penetration and Basis Risk", in: K. A. Froot (ed.) *The Financing of Catastrophe Risk*, (University of Chicago Press).

Mango, D., 1999, Risk Load and the Default Rate of Surplus, Casualty Actuarial Society Discussion Papers on Securitization Risk, http://www.casact.org/pubs/dpp/dpp99/index.htm

Mayers, D., and C. W. Smith, Jr., 1982, "On the Corporate Demand for Insurance", *Journal of Business*, 55, 2, pp. 281–96.

McNeil, A. J., 1997, "Estimating the Tails of Loss Severity Distributions Using Extreme Value Theory", *Astin Bulletin*, 27(1), pp. 117–37.

McNeil, A. J. and R. Frey, 2000, "Estimation of Tail-Related Risk Measures for Heterocedastic Financial Time Series: An Extreme Value Approach", *Journal of Empirical Finance*, 7, pp. 271–300.

Merton, R.C., 1977, "An Analytic Derivation of the Cost of Deposit Insurance and Loan Guarantees: An Application of Modern Option Pricing Theory", *Journal of Banking and Finance* 1 (June), pp. 3-11.

Merton, R. C., 1990, *Continuous-Time Finance*, (Oxford: Blackwell).

Merton, R. C., and A. F. Perold, 1993, "Management of Risk Capital in Financial Firms", in *Financial Services: Perspectives and Challenges* (Boston: Harvard Business School Press).

Merton, R. C., M. S. Scholes and M. L. Gladstein, 1978, "The Returns and Risks of Alternative Call-Option Portfolio Investment Strategies", *Journal of Business*, 51(2), pp. 183–242.

Merton, R. C., M. S. Scholes and M. L. Gladstein, 1982, "The Returns and Risks of Alternative Put-Option Portfolio Strategies", *Journal of Business*, 55(1): pp. 155.

Milgrom, P., and J. Roberts, 1986, "Price and Advertising Signals of Product Quality", *Journal of Political Economy,* 94, 4, pp. 796–821.

Miller, M. H., and K. Rock, 1985, "Dividend Policy Under Asymmetric Information", *Journal of Finance,* 40, 4, pp. 1031–51.

Minton, B., and C. Schrand, 1999, The Impact of Cash Flow Volatility on Discretionary Investment and the Costs of Debt and Equity Financing, Working Paper, Wharton School, University of Pennsylvania.

Modigliani, F., and Miller, M. H., 1958, "The Cost of Capital, Corporation Finance, and the Theory of Investment", *American Economic Review*, 47, pp. 261–97.

Modigliani, F., and Miller, M. H., 1963, "Corporate Income Taxes and the Cost of Capital: A Correction", *American Economic Review*, 53, 3, pp. 433–43.

Moody's Investor Service, 1997, Approach to the Rating of Catastrophe-Linked Notes, Special Report, September.

Mordecai, D., 1998a, "Credit Arbitrage Using Event-Linked Synthetic Structures", in: S. Jaffer (ed.) *Alternative Investment Strategies*, (London: Euromoney Books).

Mordecai, D., 1998b, "Event Risk Management and Arbitrage: Synthetic Credit Structures", in: *Credit Derivatives: Applications for Risk Management*, (London: Euromoney Books).

Mordecai, D., 1999a, "Alternative Risk Transfer: Investing Directly in Insurance Risk as an Alternative Investment Strategy", in: T. Schneeweis, and J. F. Pescatore (eds.) The Handbook of Alternative Investment Strategies, Institutional Investor Books, New York.

Mordecai, D., 1999b, "Insurance Risk Securitization, Model Robustness, and the Convergence of Event and Credit Risk: A Rating Analyst's View", in: M. Himmick and S. Bouriaux (eds), *Securitized Insurance Risk: Strategic Opportunities for Insurers and Investors*, (Chicago: Glenlake Publishing Company).

Mordecai, D., 1999c, "The Use of Credit Derivatives in Credit Enhanced and Credit- Linked

Structured Notes: A Former Rating Analyst's Perspective", in: J. Francis, J. Frost and G. Whitaker (eds), *The Handbook of Credit Derivatives*, (New York: McGraw-Hill).

Moussalli, A. S., 1993, *Radical Islamic Fundamentalism: The Ideological and Political Discourse of Sayyid Qutb* (NY: Syracuse University Press).

Murray, A., 1998, "Securitization Beyond Cat Bonds", *National Underwriter Property & Casualty/Risk&Benefits Management Edition*, July 27, 1998, URL: http://www.nunews.com/archives/pc_archive/1998/p07-27/30moody.asp

Murray, J. B., D. J. Bennett, P. Headly, A. D. Affleck, N. Bauer, A. Rayner, 2001, Use of Embedded Values at United States and European Insurance Companies, Milliman Global Research Report.

Myers, S. C., 1977, "The Determinants of Corporate Borrowing", *Journal of Financial Economics*, 5, pp. 147–76.

Myers, S. C., 1984, "The Capital Structure Puzzle", *Journal of Finance*, 39, 3, pp. 575–92.

Myers, S. and Majluf, N., 1984, Corporate Investment and Financing Decisions When Firms Have Information That Investors Do Not Have," *Journal of Financial Economics*, 13, pp. 187–222.

Nakada, P., H. Shah, H. U. Koyluogle and O. Collignon, 1999, "P&C RAROC: A Catalyst for Improved Capital Management in the Property and Casualty Insurance Industry", *The Journal of Risk Finance*, 1(1), Fall.

Nelsen, R. B., 1999, *An Introduction to Copulas* (New York: Springer-Verlag).

Nelson, P., 1970, "Information and Consumer Behavior", *Journal of Political Economy*, 78, 2, pp. 311–29.

Nelson, P., 1974, "Advertising as Information", *Journal of Political Economy*, 82, 4, pp. 729–54.

Ness, I., 1988, "Pru Cashes in on Policy Loans" *National Underwriter*, February 15.

Ness, I., 1989, "New York Insurance Department Opposes Securitizations", *National Underwriter*, March 27.

NOAA, 1972, "A study of Earthquake Losses in the San Francisco Bay Area", National Oceanographic and Atmospheric Administration of the Department of Commerce for the Office of Emergency Preparedness, Washington.

O'Kane, D., 2001, "Credit Derivatives Explained: Market, Products and Regulations", Lehman Brothers Structured Credit Research March 2001, Lehman Brothers.

Pais, A., 1983, "Subtle is the Lord: the Science and the Life of Albert Einstein", (Oxford University Press).

Partners Group Homepage, "Pearl Holding Limited", URL: http://www.partnersgroup.ch/en/produkte/index.shtml and www.partnersgroup.net

Pawlowski, J., Malhotra, N., and Manning, J., 2000, "Credit Models: the Next Generation", *Credit Magazine*, 1(4) (May 2000).

Pentikainen, T., H. Bonsdorff, M. Pesonon, J. Rantala and M. Ruohonen, 1989, *Insurance Solvency and Financial Strength* (Helsinki: Finnish Insurance Training and Publishing Co).

Petak, W. J., and A. A. Atkinson, 1982, *Natural hazard risk assessment and public policy: anticipating the unexpected* (New York: Springer).

Pfister, B., 2000, "Whole Business Securitisations: A Unique Opportunity for UK Assets", Moody's Rating Agency Report, October 19, Prudential Financial, Inc, 2001, SEC Form S-1, December 12.

Pinter, J. D., 1996, *Global Optimization in Action: Continuous and Lipschitz Optimization – Algorithms, Implementations and Applications*, (Norwell MA: Kluwer Academic Publishers).

Potts, J.M., C.K. Folland, I.T. Jolliffe, and D. Sexton, 1996, "Revised "LEPS" scores for assessing climate model simulations and long-range forecasts", *Journal of Climate*, 9, pp. 34–53.

PricewaterhouseCoopers, 2001, Report: "The weather risk management industry: survey findings for November 1997 to March 2001".

Primack, D., 2001, "Prime Edge and J.P.Morgan Partners Put Private Equity Into Debt", Venture Capital Journal, URL: http://www.ventureeconomics.com/vcj/ protected/ZZZE8WZ2 XNC.html (1 July 2001).

Princess Webpage, URL: http://www.partnersgroup.net/pdf_downloads/

Private Equity Analyst, 2001, "Global Financial Forms Bond Vehicle For Fund of Funds", August, p.9.

Puccia, M., 2001, "Reducing Risk Through the Creation of a Closed Block", *RatingsDirect Commentary*, September, URL: http://www.ratingsdirect.standardandpoors.com.

Punjabi, S., and J. F. Tierney, 1999, "Synthetic CLOs and their Role in Bank Balance Sheet Management", Fixed Income Research March 1999, Deutsche Bank Research.

Purcell, D., and P. Crowley, 1998, "The Reality of Hedge Funds", Warburg Dillon Read Research Report, October.

Qutb, S., 1991 "Milestones", (American Trust Publications).

Raturi, M., and B. Schmolck, 2000, "Trade Credit Insurance: Globalisation and E-business are the Key Opportunities", Sigma 7/2000, Swiss Reinsurance Company.

Reed, I., J. U. Dhru, J. Doona, J. Siberon and M. Puccia, 2001, "Interest in Life Insurance Securitization Heats Up", *RatingsDirect Commentary*, October 23, URL: http://www.ratingsdirect.standardandpoors.com.

Reeve, S., 1999, *The New Jackals*, (London: Andre Deutsch).

Reyda, G., 2001, Principles of Risk Management and Insurance, Seventh Edition, (Boston: Addison Wesley).

Richards, A., 1999, *Idiosyncratic Risk: An Empirical Analysis with Implications for the Risk of Relative-Value Trading Strategies*, IMF Working Paper.

Ritzi, A., 2000, "The safe way to play hedge funds", Hedge Fund Intelligence, Institutional Guide to Hedge Funds, URL: http://www.hedgefundintelligence.com/eh/reports/2000_08/safeway.htm

Ronfeldt, D., and J. Arquilla, 2001a, "Networks, Netwars, and the Fight of the Future", *First Monday*, 6(10).

Ronfeldt, D., and J. Arquilla, 2001b, "Networks and Netwars: The Future of Terror, Crime and Militancy", (Washington: RAND Corporation).

Ross, S., 1977, "Return, Risk and Arbitrage", in: I. Friend and J. Bicksler (eds.), *Risk Return and Finance*, (Cambridge MA: Ballinger).

Ross, S., 1977, "The Determination of Financial Structure: The Incentive Signaling Approach", *Bell Journal of Economics*, 8, 1, pp. 23–40.

Rubenstein, M., and H. Leland, 1981, "Replicating Options with Positions in Stock and Cash", *Financial Analysts Journal*, 43, pp. 63–72.

Rytgaard, M., 1996, "Simulation Experiments on the Mean Residual Life Function $m(x)$", in: *Proceedings of the XX VII ASTIN Colloquium*, Copenhagen, Denmark, 1, pp. 59–81.

Saunders, A. J., 2000, "Securitization and Other Financing Options Available to Life Companies", *Institute of Actuaries and Faculty of Actuaries*.

Scawthorn, C., M. Khater and C. Rojahn, 1993, "Seismic Vulnerability and Impact of Disruption of Lifelines in the Conterminous United States", National Earthquake Conference, Memphis TN.

Scawthorn, C., and M. Khater, 1992, "Fire Following Earthquake – Conflagration Potential in the Greater Los Angeles, San Francisco, Seattle and Memphis Areas", Natural Disaster Coalition, EQE International, San Francisco.

Schenk, C., 2000, "Michelin: Setting the Standard", *Alternative Risk Strategies: Special Supplement to Risk Magazine* (December).

Schmidt, W., and I. Ward, 2002, Pricing Default Baskets, *Risk Magazine*, 1, pp. 111–14.

Schmock, U., 1999, Estimating the Value of the WinCAT Coupons of the Winterthur Insurance Convertible Bond: A Study of the Model Risk. *Astin Bulletin*, 29(1), 101–63.

Schneeweis, T., and R. Spurgin, 1998, "Multifactor Analysis of Hedge Fund, Managed Futures and Mutual Fund Return and Risk Characteristics", *Journal of Alternative Investments*, 1, pp. 124.

Schneeweis, T., and R. Spurgin, 2000, *The Benefits of Index Option-Based Strategies for Institutional Portfolios: Summary Version*, CISDM Working Paper.

Schneider F., 1999, "Partners Group und Swiss Re lancieren Privat- Equity-Dollar-Wandelanleihe", *Finanz und Wirtschaft*, (2 June).

Schorin, C., 2000, "Monoline Bond Insurers: Are All AAAs Created Equal?", *Morgan Stanley Dean Witter Special Report* (January).

Securitization.net, Mayer, Brown & Platt, "European Securitization: The new Basel Capital Accord and Asset Securitization", URL: www.securitization.net/pdf/ mbpsecnews_0801.pdf

Sender, H., and C. Oster., "Insurers Are Raising Money With Ease As Other Sectors Face Credit Crunch", *The Wall Street Journal*, URL: http://www2.rmi.gsu.edu/faculty/klein/RMI_3500/ Readings/Other/WTC_Capital_Raising.htm (24 October 2001).

Shante, V. M., 1989, "Securitization and Sale of Future Revenue Streams", Prudential- Bache Capital Funding, Unpublished Paper.

Shih, J. H., and T. A. Louis, 1995, "Inferences on the Association Parameter in Copula Models for Bivariate Survival Data", *Biometrics*, 51, 1384–99.

Shimpi, P., 1999, *Integrating Corporate Risk Management*, (New York: Texere LLC).

Shimpi, P., 2001, *Integrating Corporate Risk Management* (New York: Texere LLC).

Shleifer, A., and R. Vishny, 1992, "Liquidation Values and Debt Capacity: A Market Equilibrium Approach", *Journal of Finance*, 47, pp.1343–66.

Shleifer, A. and R. Vishny, 1997, "The Limits of Arbitrage", *Journal of Finance*, 52, pp.35–55.

Shukla, J., 1981, "Dynamical predictability of monthly means", *Journal of Atmospheric Science*, 38, pp. 2547–2572.

Skaar, A. A., 1998, *Taxation Issues Relating To Captive Insurance Companies*, (Amsterdam: IBFD Publications BV).

Smith, C. W., Jr., and R. M. Stulz, 1985, "The Determinants of Firms' Hedging Policies", *Journal of Financial and Quantitative Analysis*, 20, 4, pp. 391–405.

Spence, M., 1973, "Job Market Signaling", *Quarterly Journal of Economics*, 87, pp. 355–74.

Standard & Poor's Structured Finance, 2001 (Reprinted from RatingsDirect), "S&P Correct: First Structured Notes Backed by Private Equity Investments Rated", analysts: Erkan Erturk, PhD, New York and Soody Nelson, New York, URL: http://www.standardandpoors.com/PressRoom/Ratings/Articles/060401_fundoffunds. html (June 2001).

Standard & Poor's, "Private Equity Fund of Funds: Overview and Rating Criteria" analysts: Lily Cheung, New York, Erkan Erturk, PhD, New York and Winnie Fong, New York, URL: http://www.standardandpoors.com/emarketing/structuredfinance/ copyof110701_fund.html (7 November 2001).

Standard & Poor's Structured Finance (Reprinted from RatingsDirect), "Innovative Structures Key to Growth in Market Value Sector for 2002", analyst: Soody Nelson, New York, URL: http://www.standardandpoors.com/emarketing/structuredfinance/ copyof010702_innovative.html (7 January 2002).

Steinbrugge, K.V, 1982, *Earthquakes, Volcanoes and Tsunamis, An Anatomy of Hazards* (New York: Skandia America).

Strain, R. W., ed., 1980, *Reinsurance* (New York: Strain Publishing Inc).

Structured Finance International, 2001, "Deutsche's Prime Edge sparks private equity CDO boom", Issue 55, June.

Stulz, R. M., 1996, "Rethinking Risk Management," *Journal of Applied Corporate Finance*, 9, 3, pp. 8–24.

Sulima, C.L., "Another Financial Bubble? Recent Trends in the Hedge Fund Industry and important implications for financial institutions", *Federal Reserve Bank of Chicago Capital Markets News*, CFA, URL: www.chicagofed.org/publications/capitalmarketnews/2001/cmn200109.pdf (September 2001).

SwissRe, 1997, "Too Little Reinsurance of Natural Disasters in Many Markets", *Sigma*, 7, pp. 3–22.

Swiss Re, 2001, "Capital Market Innovation in the Insurance Industry", *Sigma*, 3.

Swiss Re, 2002, "Natural Catastrophes and Man-Made Disasters in 2001: Man-Made Losses Take on a New Dimension" *Sigma*, 1.

Thompson, W., 1891, *Popular Lectures and Addresses* (London: Macmillan and Co).

Tomlinson, B., J. Taylor and M. Griffiths, 2000, *Hedge Funds Revisited*, Pension and Endowment Forum, Goldman Sachs & Co/Financial Risk Management Ltd Research Report, January.

Tufano, P., 1996, "Who Manages Risk? An Empirical Examination of Risk Management Practices in the Gold Mining Industry", *Journal of Finance* 51, 4, pp. 1097–137.

Varian, H. R., 1987, "The Arbitrage Principle in Financial Economics", *Economic Perspectives*, 1, pp. 55–72.

Venezian, E., 1988, "Ratemaking Methods and Profit Cycles in Property and Liability Insurance, *Journal of Risk and Insurance*, 52, pp. 477–500.

Veno, D., 2001, "Bond Insurance and Credit Default Swaps", *Standard & Poor's Bond Insurance Book 2001*, pp. 28–29 (New York: McGraw-Hill).

Venter, G.G., 1991, Premium Calculation Implications of Reinsurance without Arbitrage, *ASTIN Bulletin*, 21, pp. 223–30.

Waldrop, M. M., 1992, *Complexity* (London: Viking Press).

Wang, S., 1995, Insurance Pricing and Increased Limits Ratemaking by Proportional Hazards Transforms, Insurance: Mathematics and Economics, 17, pp. 43–54.

Wang, S., 1996, Premium Calculation by Transforming the Layer Premium Density, *ASTIN Bulletin,* 26, (1), pp. 71–92.

Whitman, R.V. *et al,* 1997, "Development of a National Earthquake Loss Estimation Methodology", *Earthquake Spectra,* 13(4), pp. 643–62.

Wiggins, J. H., 1979, "Estimated building losses from US earthquakes", Second US National Conference on Earthquake Engineering, Earthquake Engineering Research Inst, Berkeley pp. 253–62.

Wilkinson, P., 1995, "Terrorism, motivation and causes", (Canadian Security Intelligence Service, Commentary No. 53).

Wilson, E. O., 1975, *Sociobiology* (Cambridge, MA: Harvard University Press).

Winkelmann, K., 2000, "Risk capital allocation: Applying risk to the portfolio", *Risk Magazine,* December 2000, URL: http://www.financewise.com/public/edit/riskm/rmforinvestors/ rmforinvestors-riskcapital.htm

Winter, R., 1988, "The Liability Insurance Crisis and The Dynamics of Competitive Insurance Markets." *Yale Journal of Regulation,* 5, pp. 455–99.

Wöhrmann, P., and C. Bürer, 2000, "La Suisse Attire les Assurance Captives", in: *Banque Assurance,* 6, November/December, pp. 48–50.

Wöhrmann, P., and C. Bürer, 2001, "Instrument der alternativen Risikofinanzierung", in: *Schweizer Versicherung,* 7, July, pp. 14–17.

Wolcott, R., 2002, "Here Come European Hedge Fund CDO's", *Institutional Investor Newsletter,* 20 January, 2002, URL: http://www.bondweek.com/mbs+abs+and+cmbs/ here+come+ european+hedge+fund+cdos.asp

Woo, G., 1989, "Is the risk of human intrusion exaggerated?", in: Proceedings of NEA workshop on: *Risks With Human Intrusion at Radioactive Waste Disposal Sites,* (Paris: OECD).

Woo, G., 1999, *The Mathematics of Natural Catastrophes* (London: Imperial College Press).

Yamai, Y. and T. Yoshiba, 2001, "On the Validity of Value-at-Risk: Comparative Analyses with Expected Shortfall", Institute for Monetary and Economic Studies, Bank of Japan, Discussion Paper 2001-E-4.

Index